THE COLLECTED WORKS OF
ABRAHAM LINCOLN

THE COLLECTED WORKS OF
ABRAHAM LINCOLN

THE ABRAHAM LINCOLN ASSOCIATION
SPRINGFIELD, ILLINOIS

VII

ROY P. BASLER, *EDITOR*

MARION DOLORES PRATT AND LLOYD A. DUNLAP
ASSISTANT EDITORS

RUTGERS UNIVERSITY PRESS
NEW BRUNSWICK, NEW JERSEY

THE HISTORY BOOK CLUB EDITION

———

COMPOSED IN INTERTYPE WAVERLEY
BY H. WOLFF BOOK MANUFACTURING COMPANY, NEW YORK CITY,
PRINTED BY MURRAY PRINTING COMPANY, FORGE VILLAGE, MASSACHUSETTS,
AND BOUND BY THE HADDON CRAFTSMEN, SCRANTON, PENNSYLVANIA

———

TITLE PAGE WOOD ENGRAVING BY STANLEY RICE
DESIGN BY P. J. CONKWRIGHT

SOURCES
AND LOCATION SYMBOLS

DESCRIPTION OF SOURCES

THE following symbols provide a description of sources as cited at the beginning of the first footnote to each item. In addition to the customary symbols for describing manuscripts, the editors have employed symbols or single words to identify other sources which have been cited repeatedly in the first footnote.

AD	Autograph Document
ADS	Autograph Document Signed
ADf	Autograph Draft
ADfS	Autograph Draft Signed
AE	Autograph Endorsement
AES	Autograph Endorsement Signed
AL	Autograph Letter
ALS	Autograph Letter Signed
ALS copy	Autograph Letter Signed, copied by Lincoln and preserved in his papers
Copy	Copy not by Lincoln
D	Document
DS	Document Signed
Df	Draft
DfS	Draft Signed
ES	Endorsement Signed
F	Facsimile—following any of the preceding symbols
LS	Letter Signed
P	Photostat—following any of the preceding symbols

Angle	*New Letters and Papers of Lincoln.* Compiled by Paul M. Angle. Boston and New York: Houghton Mifflin Company, 1930.
Herndon	*Herndon's Lincoln: The True Story of a Great Life.* By William H. Herndon and Jesse W. Weik. 3 volumes. Chicago, New York, and San Francisco: Belford, Clarke & Company, [1889].
Hertz	*Abraham Lincoln: A New Portrait.* By Emanuel Hertz. 2 volumes. New York: Horace Liveright, Inc., 1931.
Lapsley	*The Writings of Abraham Lincoln.* Edited by Arthur Brooks Lapsley. 8 volumes. New York: P. F. Collier and Son, 1905.

NH   *Complete Works of Abraham Lincoln.* Edited by John G. Nicolay and John Hay. 12 volumes. New York: Francis D. Tandy Company, 1905.

OR   *The War of the Rebellion: A Compilation of the Official Records of the Union and Confederate Armies.* 4 series; 70 "volumes"; 128 books. Washington: Government Printing Office, 1880-1901. Roman numerals are used for Series, Volume, and Part (if any); pages are in arabic.

Tarbell *The Life of Abraham Lincoln.* . . . By Ida M. Tarbell. 2 volumes. New York: The Doubleday & McClure Company, 1900.

Tracy *Uncollected Letters of Abraham Lincoln.* Edited by Gilbert A. Tracy. Boston and New York: Houghton Mifflin Company, 1917.

Wilson *Uncollected Works of Abraham Lincoln.* Edited by Rufus Rockwell Wilson. 2 volumes. Elmira, New York: Primavera Press, 1947-1948.

LOCATION SYMBOLS

CCamStJ St. John's Seminary Library, Camarillo, Calif.

CLCM Los Angeles County Museum Library, Los Angeles, Calif.

CSmH Henry E. Huntington Library, San Marino, Calif.

CoHi   State Historical Society of Colorado, Denver, Colo.

CoU   University of Colorado Library, Boulder, Colo.

Ct   Connecticut State Library, Hartford, Conn.

CtHi   Connecticut Historical Society, Hartford, Conn.

CtLHi Litchfield Historical Society, Litchfield, Conn.

CtSoP Pequot Library, Southport, Conn.

CtWat Watertown Library Association, Watertown, Conn.

CtY   Yale University Library, New Haven, Conn.

DLC   Library of Congress, Washington, D. C.

DLC-HW Herndon-Weik Collection, Library of Congress

DLC-RTL The Robert Todd Lincoln Collection of the Papers of Abraham Lincoln, Library of Congress

DLM   Lincoln Museum, Ford's Theatre, National Park Service, Washington, D. C.

DNA   National Archives, Washington, D. C. All additional abbreviations and numbers given with this symbol are those employed by the National Archives at the time the manuscript was located.

DNM   National Museum Library, Washington, D. C.

DeHi	Historical Society of Delaware Library, Wilmington, Del.
DeWI	Wilmington Institute Free Library, Wilmington, Del.
I-Ar	Archives Division, Illinois State Library, Springfield, Ill.
IBloHi	McLean County Historical Society, Bloomington, Ill.
ICHi	Chicago Historical Society, Chicago, Ill.
ICU	University of Chicago Library, Chicago, Ill.
IDecJ	James Millikin University Library, Decatur, Ill.
IFre	Freeport Public Library, Freeport, Ill.
IHi	Illinois State Historical Library, Springfield, Ill.
IJI	Illinois College Library, Jacksonville, Ill.
ISLA	The Abraham Lincoln Association, Springfield, Ill.
IU	University of Illinois Library, Urbana, Ill.
IaCrM	Iowa Masonic Library, Cedar Rapids, Iowa
IaDaM	Davenport Public Museum, Davenport, Iowa
IaHA	Iowa State Department of History and Archives, Des Moines, Iowa
In	Indiana State Library, Indianapolis, Ind.
InFtwL	Lincoln National Life Foundation, Fort Wayne, Ind.
InHi	Indiana Historical Society, Indianapolis, Ind.
InLTHi	Tippecanoe County Historical Association, Lafayette, Ind.
InU	Indiana University Library, Bloomington, Ind.
KyBC	Berea College Library, Berea, Ky.
KyU	University of Kentucky Library, Lexington, Ky.
LU	Louisiana State University Library, Baton Rouge, La.
MB	Boston Public Library, Boston, Mass.
MCon	Free Public Library, Concord, Mass.
MFai	Millicent Library, Fairhaven, Mass.
MH	Harvard University Library, Cambridge, Mass.
MHi	Massachusetts Historical Society, Boston, Mass.
MS	Springfield Library Association, Springfield, Mass.
MSHi	Connecticut Valley Historical Society, Springfield, Mass.
MdAA	Hall of Records, State of Maryland, Annapolis, Md.
MdHi	Maryland Historical Society, Baltimore, Md.
MeHi	Maine Historical Society, Portland, Me.
MiD	Detroit Public Library, Detroit, Mich.
MiK-M	Kalamazoo Public Library Museum, Kalamazoo, Mich.
MiU-C	William L. Clements Library, University of Michigan, Ann Arbor, Mich.

MiU-Hi	Michigan Historical Collection, University of Michigan, Ann Arbor, Mich.
MnHi	Minnesota Historical Society, St. Paul, Minn.
MnSM	Macalester College Library, St. Paul, Minn.
MoHi	State Historical Society of Missouri, Columbia, Mo.
MoSHi	Missouri Historical Society, St. Louis, Mo.
N	New York State Library, Albany, N. Y.
NAuE	Fred L. Emerson Foundation, Auburn, N. Y.
NBLiHi	Long Island Historical Society, Brooklyn, N. Y.
NBuG	Grosvenor Library, Buffalo, New York
NBuHi	Buffalo Historical Society, Buffalo, N. Y.
NDry	Southworth Library, Dryden, N. Y.
NHi	New-York Historical Society, New York City
NIC	Cornell University Library, Ithaca, N. Y.
NN	New York Public Library, New York City
NNC	Columbia University Library, New York City
NNP	Pierpont Morgan Library, New York City
NRU	University of Rochester Library, Rochester, N. Y.
NSh	John Jermain Memorial Library, Sag Harbor, N. Y.
NSk	Skaneateles Library Association, Skaneateles, N. Y.
NWM	U. S. Military Academy Library, West Point, N. Y.
NbO	Omaha Public Library, Omaha, Nebr.
NcGu	Guilford College Library, Guilford, N. C.
NhExP	Phillips Exeter Academy, Exeter, N. H.
NjP	Princeton University Library, Princeton, N. J.
OCHP	Historical and Philosophical Society of Ohio, Cincinnati, Ohio
OClCS	Case Institute of Technology, Cleveland, Ohio
OClWHi	Western Reserve Historical Society, Cleveland, Ohio
OFH	Hayes Memorial Library, Fremont, Ohio
OMC	Marietta College Library, Marietta, Ohio
ORB	Oliver R. Barrett Collection, Chicago, Ill.*
OSHi	Clark County Historical Society, Springfield, Ohio
OrHi	Oregon Historical Society, Portland, Ore.
PHC	Haverford College Library, Haverford, Pa.
PHi	Historical Society of Pennsylvania, Philadelphia, Pa.

* After the *Collected Works* was in press, the collection of the late Oliver R. Barrett was sold at auction by Parke-Bernet Galleries (Catalog 1315) on February 19-20, 1952. It has been impossible to trace all new owners of the more than two hundred items, and impracticable to change the source citations for those which are known, but many of the more important items went to such well-known collections as those in the Library of Congress (Debates Scrapbook, purchased for the Alfred Whital Stern Collection) and Illinois State Historical Library (letters to Joshua F. Speed, etc.).

PMA	Allegheny College Library, Meadville, Pa.
PP	Free Library of Philadelphia, Philadelphia, Pa.
PPDrop	Dropsie College Library, Philadelphia, Pa.
PSt	Pennsylvania State College Library, State College, Pa.
PU	University of Pennsylvania Library, Philadelphia, Pa.
RPAB	Annmary Brown Memorial Library, Providence, R. I.
RPB	Brown University Library, Providence, R. I.
THaroL	Lincoln Memorial University, Harrogate, Tenn.
THi	Tennessee Historical Society, Nashville, Tenn.
ViU	University of Virginia Library, Charlottesville, Va.
VtU	University of Vermont Library, Burlington, Vt.
WBeloHi	Beloit Historical Society, Beloit, Wis.
WHi	State Historical Society of Wisconsin, Madison, Wis.
WvU	West Virginia University Library, Morgantown, W. Va.

Courtesy of Frederick Hill Meserve

NOVEMBER 15, 1863
By Alexander Gardner

THE COLLECTED WORKS OF
ABRAHAM LINCOLN

THE COLLECTED WORKS OF

ABRAHAM LINCOLN

———— ◆◀◉▶◆ ————

To Nathaniel P. Banks[1]

Executive Mansion,
Major General Banks   Washington, Nov. 5. 1863.

Three months ago to-day I wrote you about Louisiana affairs, stating, on the word of Gov. Shepley, as I understood him, that Mr. Durant was taking a registry of citizens, preparatory to the election of a constitutional convention for that State. I sent a copy of the letter to Mr. Durant; and I now have his letter, written two months after, acknowledging receipt, and saying he is not taking such registry; and he does not let me know that he personally is expecting to do so. Mr. Flanders, to whom I also sent a copy, is now here, and he says nothing has yet been done. This disappoints me bitterly; yet I do not throw blame on you or on them. I do however, urge both you and them, to lose no more time. Gov. Shepley has special instructions from the War Department. I wish him— these gentlemen and others co-operating—without waiting for more territory, to go to work and give me a tangible nucleus which the remainder of the State may rally around as fast as it can, and which I can at once recognize and sustain as the true State government. And in that work I wish you, and all under your command, to give them a hearty sympathy and support. The instruction to Gov. Shepley bases the movement (and rightfully too) upon the loyal element. Time is important. There is danger, even now, that the adverse element seeks insidiously to pre-occupy the ground. If a few professedly loyal men shall draw the disloyal about them, and colorably set up a State government, repudiating the emancipation proclamation, and re-establishing slavery, I can not recognize or sustain their work. I should fall powerless in the attempt. This government, in such an attitude, would be a house divided against itself. I have said, and say again, that if a new State government, acting in harmony with this government, and consistently with general freedom, shall think best to adopt a reasonable temporary arrangement, in relation to the landless and homeless freed people, I do not object; but my word is out to be *for* and

[1]

not *against* them on the question of their permanent freedom. I do not insist upon such temporary arrangement, but only say such would not be objectionable to me. Yours very truly

A. LINCOLN.

[1] ALS, CSmH. See Lincoln to Banks, August 5, *supra.* On October 1 Thomas J. Durant wrote Lincoln that, "By your letter to General Banks, you appear to think that a Registration of voters is going on under my superintendence, with the view of bringing on the election of delegates to a Constitutional Convention; but such is not the case. The means of communicating with a large portion of the state, are not in our power, and before the commencement of a Registration we ought to have undisturbed control of a considerable territory, at least the two congressional districts proclaimed as not being in rebellion. . . ." (Enclosed with Durant to Stanton, October 5, 1863, DLC-RTL).

On December 11 Benjamin F. Flanders wrote:

"I have shown the copy, which you permitted me to take, of your letter to General Banks, to Mr. Durant   Mr. Hahn, Judge Whitaker and a few others of our prominent union men, and it gives to all of them great encouragement and satisfaction.

"The letter has had the desired effect upon the Military leaders; they are stimulated to action by it.

"There is now, and I believe there will continue to be a commendable zeal and entire unity of action among the friends of the Government and its officers civil & military in the movement to form a State, a *free* State government for Louisiana. The measures taken for this great object will I think be stamped with prudence, and we hope their result will meet your expectations." (DLC-RTL).

To Joseph Holt[1]

Execution suspended till further orders.

Nov. 5. 1863   A. LINCOLN

[1] AES, DNA WR RG 153, Judge Advocate General, MM 1061. Lincoln's endorsement is written on a telegram from Andrew G. Curtin, November 5, 1863, asking respite for Samuel Wellers. See Lincoln to Meade, November 3, *infra.*

To George G. Meade[1]

Major-General Meade,   Executive Mansion,
Army of Potomac: Washington, D.C., November 5, 1863.

Please suspend the execution of Samuel Wellers, Forty-ninth Pennsylvania Volunteers, until further orders.   A. LINCOLN.

[1] Tarbell (Appendix), p. 398. See Lincoln to Holt, *supra.*

To Edwin M. Stanton[1]

Let private Noble be discharged.   A. LINCOLN.
Nov. 6. 1863.

[1] AES, owned by Carl Tollefsen, Brooklyn, New York. Private Noble has not been identified.

To Edwin M. Stanton[1]

If Gen. Whipple is entitled to have an Assistant Adjutant General
appointed, let the appointment be made as within requested.

Nov. 6. 1863   A. LINCOLN

1 AES-P, ISLA. Lincoln's endorsement appears on a letter of Brigadier General William D. Whipple, Pottsville, Pennsylvania, October 2, 1863, to Adjutant General Lorenzo Thomas, requesting that Second Lieutenant Robert H. Ramsey, Forty-fifth Pennsylvania Militia, be appointed assistant adjutant general of Volunteers with the rank of captain. Ramsey was appointed on December 5, 1863, and was confirmed by the Senate on February 29, 1864.

To Isaac R. Diller[1]

Capt. Isaac R. Diller   Executive Mansion,
Dear Sir: Washington, Nov. 7, 1863.

I must decline to take charge of Dr. Wetherell's interests. If he
presents a claim to congress, or the court of Claims, I shall be ready
to testify the whole truth, so far as within my knowledge. As to my
ordering him back to the Agricultural Department, and fixing his
Salary as you and he may think right, it is wholly inadmissable.
The law does not authorize me to do any of these things   Yours
truly   A. LINCOLN

1 ADfS, DLC-RTL. See note to Lincoln's memorandum of November 2, *supra*. On November 4 Diller wrote Lincoln from Willard's Hotel: "I find that my health is suffering by remaining here, and I beg you to accept this as my excuse for troubling you with this letter.

"It is important that I should be placed in possession of the views of Your Excellency with regard to this powder matter, at your earliest convenience, in order that many expenses, such as the rent of the building at Westville, N.J. the services of a watchman, &c &c. may be stopped. There is plenty of powder already made to test its merits . . . and with your permission will join my family in Illinois and there await the result. . . ." Diller continued with an expression of hope that Dr. Charles M. Wetherill would not "suffer in consequence" of his services on the powder project: "Should it be the pleasure of Your Excellency to remand him to the Department from which he was detailed, and he is now in this City awaiting that pleasure, I beg that the Commissioner of Agriculture may be informed of your wishes in regard to his future position. . . . The Commissioner should issue to Dr. Wetherill, a salary upon which he can live respectably with his family in Washington. . . ." (DLC-RTL).

Concerning Wetherill's dismissal from his post as chief chemist of the Department of Agriculture, Representative-elect Godlove S. Orth of Lafayette, Indiana, wrote Lincoln on October 16, 1863:

"I regret to learn that a constituent of mine, Dr. C. M. Wetherill 'Chemist of the Dept. of Agriculture,' has received from the Agricultural Comr. under date of Oct. 1, a rather summary dismissal from that Department.

"Dr. W. was specially detailed by your order, of date April 4, '63, for 30 days to make certain experiments in Gunpowder, which detail was afterwards on the 2nd. day of May extended by the Comr. 'until notified to the contrary.'

"Under this state of facts Dr. W. and his friends regard the action of the

Commissioner as harsh and arbitrary and look with confidence to your kind sense of Justice to see that Dr. W. is not thus summarily dealt with. . . ." (DLC-RTL).

Apparently Lincoln took some sort of action, for a contemporary copy of Isaac Newton's letter to Wetherill, dated "Novr. 1863" reads as follows:

"Your salary as Chemist of the Department of Agriculture will be fixed at the rate of $2500 per annum, to commence from November 1st. of the current year.

"I will grant you a furlough of two weeks from the date of your remand to this Department for the purpose of bringing your family from the West." (DLC-RTL).

To Edwin M. Stanton[1]

November 7, 1863

Please have an enquiry made at once, whether Dr. E. Z. Baird may not be allowed to return to his home in Mississippi.

[1] Copy, DNA WR RG 107, Secretary of War, Letters Received, P 203, Register notation. The copy of Lincoln's note preserved in the register indicates referral to General Robert C. Schenck.

To William B. Astor and Robert B. Roosevelt[1]

William B. Astor & Robt. B. Rosevelt   Washington City,
New-York   Nov. 8 1863

I shall be happy to give the interview to the committee as you request.   A. LINCOLN.

[1] ALS, RPB. Astor and Roosevelt telegraphed on November 7 that "a committee of Merchants & citizens of New York ask an interview with the President on Monday morning . . . on important business." (DLC-RTL). See Lincoln to Astor and Roosevelt, November 9, *infra*.

To Samuel C. Pomeroy[1]

Private.   Executive Department
Hon. S. C. Pomeroy   Washington City
My dear Sir: Nov. 8th. 1863

I have examined Killingworths evidence in Capt. Levy's case, and I must say it makes too bad a record to admit of my interference—in fact, it could not be worse. In the nature of the case, K. alone, of all competent witnesses, can know whether Capt. L's hypothesis is true or false; and he most fully disproves it. He fully proves also that Capt. L. sought to have him testify falsely. To interfere, under the circumstances, would blacken my own character. Yours truly   A. LINCOLN

[1] ALS-P, ISLA. No correspondence with Pomeroy in regard to this case has been located, and Killingworth has not been identified. Captain Cheme M. Levy

of New York, assistant quartermaster of Volunteers, convicted of signing a false certificate relating to pay of men under his command, was cashiered on October 9, 1863 (AGO, *General Orders No. 332*).

To John J. Astor, Jr., and Others[1]

Private, except to Gen. Dix

Executive Mansion Washington DC. Nov. 9. 1863

Gentlemen   Upon the subject of your letter I have to say that it is beyond my province to interfere with New-York City politics; that I am very grateful to Gen. Dix for the zealous and able Military, and quasi civil support he has given the government during the war; and that if the people of New-York should tender him the Mayoralty, and he accept it, nothing on that subject could be more satisfactory to me. In this I must not be understood as saying ought against any one, or as attempting the least degree of dictation in the matter. To state it in another way, if Gen. Dix' present relation to the general government lays any restraint upon him in this matter, I wish to remove that restraint. Yours truly

Messrs. J. J. Astor, Jr.   A. LINCOLN
R. B. Roosevelt
Nathl Sands.

[1] ADfS, DLC-RTL. A petition bearing twenty-one signatures, including those of the men addressed, November 7, 1863, reads as follows: "The undersigned representing in the City of New York both political parties have offered Gen Dix the nomination for Mayor and finding some hesitation on his part arising from his official position ask President Lincoln in view of the great national importance of the matter to request Gen. Dix to accept the nomination." (DLC-RTL).

John A. Dix wrote Lincoln on November 10: "Your letter in regard to the Mayoralty of this City reached me after I had declined the nomination. There were many insurmountable objections of a personal character to my acceptance; but I was also of the opinion that I could be more useful to your administration where I am, and many of your most discreet friends coincide with me. I did not understand your letter as expressing any opinion or wish on the subject, but merely as an intimation that, so far as depended on you, obstacles would be removed, should I deem an acceptance advisable. If I could have a few minutes' conversation with you, I know you would be satisfied that my decision is right. I am only anxious to be where you think I can be most useful to the country. . . ." (*Ibid.*).

To Ambrose E. Burnside[1]

Major Gen. Burnside   Washington, D.C.,
Knoxville, Tenn.   Nov. 9. 1863.

Have seen despatch from Gen. Grant about your loss at Rogersville.[2] *Per-contra*, about the same time Averell & Duffie got considerable advantage of the enemy at and about Lewisburg Va;[3] and on

Saturday, the 7th. Meade drove the enemy from Rappahannock-station, and Kellys-ford, capturing 8 battle-flags, four guns, and over eighteen hundred prisoners, with very little loss to himself. Let me hear from you.   A. LINCOLN

[1] ALS, RPB. Burnside replied at 1 A.M. on November 12: "Your dispatch received. The Telegraph lines have been down since Saturday night, so that we could not communicate with Genl Grant. Our loss at Rogersville was about five hundred (500) old troops and one hundred & fifty (150) new troops. Four (4) pieces of artillery and thirty six (36) wagons with all the baggage & ammunition of two (2) Regts & a battery the principal loss was in the Second Tennessee mounted Infantry. The Seventh Ohio Cavalry lost about one hundred (100) men & Phillips Illinois Battery about forty (40). The force at that point consisted of these two (2) Regts & the Phillips Battery with some recruits for a new Tennessee Regt. The rebel attacking force amounted to thirty five hundred (3500) mounted men under Gen Sam Jones. They captured about six hundred horses & equipment & as many stand of small arms. An investigation is being made as to the cause of defeat. I at first thought it was the result of carelessness on the part of the Comdg Officer Col Garrard & want of steadiness on the part of the men but as the Investigation progresses I am becoming satisfied that it is result of the necessity for holding so long a line between two formidable forces of the Enemy. It seems to be impossible to be sufficiently watchful to prevent trouble when so many points are assailable. We were holding the line from Washn. on the Tenn. River to the Watauga. The troops of this command have behaved so well that I shall be glad to find that no one was censurable for the defeat. I send you a cipher dispatch. We were all rejoiced to hear of the Successes in Western Virginia & in the Army of the Potomac." (DLC-RTL).

[2] This sentence was revised by Lincoln. He originally wrote: "Have just seen your despatch to Mrs. B. about your loss at Rogersville. Had before seen substantially the same in a despatch from Gen. Grant." The despatch to "Mrs. B." has not been found, but Grant's despatch to Halleck of 1:30 P.M., November 7, is printed in the *Official Records* (I, XXXI, III, 74).

[3] William W. Averell and Alfred N. Duffie.

To Benjamin F. Flanders[1]

Hon. B. F. Flanders   Executive Mansion
My dear Sir: Washington, D.C. Nov. 9. 1863

In a conversation with Gen. Butler he made a suggestion which impressed me a good deal at the time. It was that, as a preliminary step, a vote be taken, yea or nay, whether there shall be a State convention to repeal the Ordinance of secession, and remodel the State constitution. I send it merely as a suggestion for your consideration, not having considered it maturely myself. The point which impressed me was, not so much the questions to be voted on, as the effect of chrystallizing, so to speak, in taking such popular vote on any proper question. In fact, I have always thought the act of secession is legally nothing, and needs no repealing. Turn the thought over in your mind, and see if in your own judgment, you can make any thing of it. Yours very truly   A. LINCOLN

[1] ADfS, DLC-RTL. No specific reply from Flanders has been discovered, but see the note to Lincoln's letter to Banks, November 5, *supra,* for the text of Flanders' letter of December 11, 1863.

To Stephen T. Logan[1]

Executive Mansion,
Dear Judge   Washington, Nov. 9, 1863.

Col. Lamon had made his calculation, as he tells me, to go to Illinois and bring Mrs. L. home this month, when he was called on to act as Marshal on the occasion of dedicating the Cemetery at Gettysburg Pa on the 19th. He came to me, and I told him I thought that in view of his relation to the government and to me, he could not well decline. Now, why would it not be pleasant for you to come on with Mrs. L. at that time? It will be an interesting ceremony, and I shall be very glad to see you. I know not whether you would care to remain to the meeting of congress, but that event, as you know, will be very near at hand. Your friend as ever

A. LINCOLN.

[1] ALS, owned by Mrs. Logan Hay, Springfield, Illinois. No reply has been found. Stephen T. Logan was Ward H. Lamon's father-in-law.

To George G. Meade[1]

Washington,
Major-General Meade: November 9, 1863– 7.30 p.m.

I have seen your dispatches about operations on the Rappahannock on Saturday, and I wish to say, "Well done." Do the 1,500 prisoners reported by General Sedgwick include the 400 taken by General French, or do the whole amount to 1,900?

A. LINCOLN.

[1] OR, I, XXIX, II, 443. No reply has been located. Meade's telegram to Halleck of 8 P.M., November 8 stated that "Major-General Sedgwick reports officially the capture of . . . over 1,500 prisoners. Major-General French took over 400 prisoners . . ." (*Ibid.*, p. 435). Official figures for Confederate losses to Sedgwick at Rappahannock Station on November 7 were 1674 lost, captured and missing; at Kelly's Ford, Confederate losses to French were 359 captured and missing.

To John E. Mulford[1]

Major Mulford   Washington, D.C.,
Fort Monroe   Nov. 9th 1863

Let Mrs. Clark go with Mrs. Todd   A. LINCOLN

[1] ALS, RPB. "9th" and "Fort Monroe" are not in Lincoln's handwriting. See Lincoln to Todd, October 15, *supra.* "Mrs. Clark" was probably Mrs. Abraham

Lincoln, who is known to have used the name "Mrs. Clarke" in later years when she wished to travel incognito (see Carl Sandburg and Paul M. Angle, *Mary Lincoln, Wife and Widow*, pp. 263, 275).

Order Concerning Export of Tobacco[1]

Executive Mansion, Nov. 10, 1863.

In consideration of peculiar circumstances, and pursuant to the comity deemed to be due to friendly Powers, any tobacco in the United States, belonging to the Government either of France, Austria, or any other State with which this country is at peace, and which tobacco was purchased and paid for by such Government prior to the 4th day of March, 1861, may be exported from any port of the United States, under the supervision and upon the responsibility of naval officers of such Governments, and in conformity to such regulations as may be prescribed by the Secretary of State of the United States, and not otherwise.

ABRAHAM LINCOLN.

[1] New York *Times*, January 20, 1864. No official copy or original document has been located for this order.

To John M. Schofield[1]

Gen. Schofield   Washington, D.C.,
St. Louis, Mo.   Nov. 10. 1863

I see a despatch here from St. Louis which is a little difficult for me to understand. It says "Gen. Schofield has refused leave of absence to members in Military service to attend the Legislature. All such are radical and Administration men. The election of two Senators from this *place* on Thursday will probably turn upon this thing"

What does this mean? Of course members of the Legislature must be allowed to attend it's sessions. But how is there a session before the recent election returns are in? And how is it to be at *"this place"*—that is—St Louis? Please inform me.

A. LINCOLN

[1] ALS, RPB. General Schofield replied the same day, "The legislature meets at Jefferson City today. The recent election was not for members of the Legislature except perhaps to fill vacancies. I have not authority to grant leaves of absence to officers except in case of sickness. The orders of the War Dept. expressly forbid it. I have informed members of the Legislature who are in the Military service that I will accept their resignations to enable them to attend the session of the Legislature. There are but few of them & they are about equally divided between radicalls & conservatives. If authorized to do so I will grant the leaves of absence long enough to elect senators but I would not think it proper for them to be absent all winter and still retain their commissions in the army." (DLC-RTL). See Lincoln to Schofield, November 11, *infra*.

To Hiram Barney[1]

Hon. Hiram Barney   Executive Mansion
New-York.   Washington, D.C. Nov. 11. 1863

I would like an interview with you. Can you not come?

A. LINCOLN

[1] ALS, RPB. Charles P. Clinch, assistant collector of customs, replied at 1:30 P.M., "Mr Barney had left for Washington before the receipt of your message" (DLC-RTL).

To Montgomery Blair[1]

Hon. M. Blair   Executive Mansion Washington D.C.
My dear Sir   Nov. 11. 1863

Mr. Crisfield's letter which you inclose, is received. Let Mr. S.[2] procure the sworn statement of the election judges at any voting place, as to what may be deemed the misconduct of any military officer, and present it to me, and I will call any such officer to account who shall by such statement appear to have violated, or transcended his orders. Yours truly   A LINCOLN

[1] ADfS, DLC-RTL. The letter from defeated congressman John M. Crisfield, November 8, 1863, enclosed by Blair with a note dated November 11, is as follows:

"Order No 53 of Gen. Schenck is already known to you. In obedience to that order, large bodies of troops were moved into this Congressional District on Monday last; and between that and Wednesday morning, the day of the election, they were distributed to all the voting places, where they remained during the day, watching and interfering with the election.

"In my own County, (Somerset), some two or three hundred cavalry, fully armed, with carbines, swords, & pistols, and well mounted, were marched through various parts of the County on Tuesday; and at the hour of opening the polls on Wednesday morning, they were found at each voting place, in squads, numbering from 5 to 30 each. They at once took control of the election, and had it all their own way. . . . in the Union districts, where I was supposed to be strong, their control was exercised in the most absolute way. In one Election District, (Tangier), the officer pulled from his pocket a yellow, or Cresswell [John A. J. Creswell] ticket, and said that no other was to be voted there . . . and every man approaching the polls, with any other ticket, was turned back by an armed force. . . . In . . . other districts . . . the same thing was done . . . many persons who offered to take the oath prescribed by Order No. 53, and were legally qualified voters, were turned down. . . . In . . . Hungary Neck, the officer in command at the opening of the Polls, ordered every ticket to be examined, before it was put into the box; and if it had my name on it, the voter was required to take the oath before the ballot could go in. . . . The consequence was, not over 50 pr. ct. of the vote of the District was cast. . . . In this election District (Princess Anne) the polls were surrounded by the cavalry dismounted, and armed as stated; and each voter was obliged to come up, one at a time, through files of soldiers, to the box, where stood the commanding officer, (Capt [Charles C.] Moore 3rd Md. Cavalry) challenging each as he came up, and requiring oath to be administered to him, before the vote was received. One vote was so received; when the next came

[9]

up, who happened to be my son, the Captain challenged him, and before the oath was put to him, commenced a series of questions as to his loyalty, and political opinions, the means of suppressing the rebellion, his willingness to give up *all his property* to put down the rebellion, &c. and when he had got through, he turned to the judges, and ordered the oath to be administered. At this point the judges said, 'we do not approve of this mode of conducting the election—, we must adhere to the laws of the state; and if we are not permitted to do so, we submit to arrest.' (The Capt had previously told them that unless they obeyed his orders, he would arrest them), and thereupon he did arrest them, and sent them off, under guard, to Gen. Schenck's Head-Quarters, and the election was broken up. The judges were on the bench just 12 minutes, and had taken but one vote. They proceeded to Salisbury, under guard, to take the train for Baltimore, and while waiting for that purpose, were put into the Guard House. After remaining there awhile, by the interference of Gen Lockwood, as was understood, they were released and reached home at one o'clock, on the following morning. . . . Capt. Moore said he had orders for his act but he did not exhibit them, as far as I know. I was an eye witness to this scene. . . .

"Proceedings of the same general nature, occurred in . . . every County. . . . In regard to this county authentic statements, verified by the most respectable witnesses, have been prepared; the originals of which have been sent to the Governor, and copies will be published in the County paper, a copy of which will be sent to you.

"It is not for me to suggest what can, or ought to, be done, but . . . public indignation is very highly aroused and will not be appeased, unless the proceedings of these military officers be disavowed and rebuked, and some assurance be given, that the outrage is not to be repeated. . . ." (DLC-RTL).

See Lincoln to Schenck, November 20, *infra*.

[2] The initial "S" may be in error. Crisfield would be the person meant, and he did in fact procure affidavits.

To John Milderborger[1]

John Milderborger   Executive Mansion
Peru, Indiana.   Washington D.C. Nov. 11. 1863

I can-not comprehend the object of your despatch. I do not often decline seeing people who call upon me; and probably will see you if you call.   A. LINCOLN.

[1] ALS, RPB. John Milderborger telegraphed on November 11, "Can I speak with you if I come. Answer quick." (DLC-RTL). No further reference has been found.

To John M. Schofield[1]

Gen. Schofield   Washington, D.C.,
St. Louis, Mo   Nov. 11 1863

I believe the Secretary of War has telegraphed you about members of the Legislature. At all events, allow those in the service to attend the session; and we can afterwards decide, whether they can stay through the entire session.   A. LINCOLN

[1] ALS, RPB. See Lincoln to Schofield, November 10, *supra*. No telegram from Stanton to Schofield about members of the legislature has been located.

To Edwin M. Stanton[1]

Hon. Secretary of War.   Executive Mansion,
My dear Sir: Washington, Nov. 11, 1863.
    What is there about Major, or Capt. Beckwith? Signs appear that
an unusual commotion is to occur somehow in this connection.
Yours truly   A. LINCOLN

[1] ALS, NHi; ADfS, DLC-RTL. An undated note from First Assistant Post-
master General Alexander W. Randall to Montgomery Blair is as follows:
"Col. Beckwith of the Commissary Bureau here has been ordered by the Secy.
of War, to the West. No cause of complaint against him. I am intimately acquainted with him and he is of service to the President's friends here . . . Can
you not speak to the President on the subject. He has means of getting hold of
a good deal of information that our friends will need." (DLC-RTL).
    Blair endorsed Randall's note, "The within is from Govr. Randall & explains
itself. . . . I believe that it is intended to get some one here in other interests.
I know Beckwith well & I suspect others will agree with me that he is a good
officer. *Burn this.*"
    No reply from Stanton or further reference has been located. Colonel (not
Major) Amos Beckwith was certainly the officer referred to. He was transferred
to St. Louis, Missouri (New York *Tribune*, November 12, 1863), and later ordered to Nashville, Tennessee, becoming after March, 1864, chief commissary
of subsistence for the Military Division of the Mississippi.

To Edwin M. Stanton[1]

Hon. Secretary of War.   Executive Mansion,
My dear Sir: Washington, Nov. 11, 1863.
    I personally wish Jacob R. Freese, of New-Jersey to be appointed
a Colonel for a colored regiment—and this regardless of whether
he can tell the exact shade of Julius Caesar's hair. Yours truly
                                                        A. LINCOLN

[1] ALS, IHi. Jacob R. Freese, formerly a doctor of medicine in Bloomington,
Illinois, was appointed captain and assistant adjutant general of Volunteers on
August 24, 1861. He resigned on December 31, 1863, and there is no record of
his further appointment, but see Lincoln to Stanton, February 24, 1864, and to
Ten Eyck, September 19, 1864, *infra*.

To Edwin M. Stanton[1]

Please let Gen. Harrow withdraw his resignation, & return to the
service.   A. LINCOLN
    Nov. 11. 1863.

[1] AES-P, ISLA. Lincoln's endorsement appears on a letter from James Hughes,
November 5, 1863, asking that the resignation of Brigadier General William
Harrow of Indiana, late of the Army of the Potomac, be revoked: "Gen. Harrow
was compelled to resign by domestic affairs which required his presence in Indiana, but which will now permit him to return to the public service. He left the

army with regret, and is, I believe a valuable and efficient officer." Succeeding endorsements indicate that Harrow's resignation was cancelled. See Lincoln to Stanton, January 7, 1864, *infra.*

To John D. Defrees[1]

Mr. Defrees—Please see this girl who works in your office, and find out about her brother, and come and tell me.

November 12, 1863.   A. LINCOLN

[1] Charles B. Boynton, *History of the Great Western Sanitary Fair* (1864), p. 183. The source also prints a letter from Defrees, December 15, transmitting Lincoln's note as an autograph to be sold at the Fair, which reads in part as follows: "A poor girl in the employment of the Government printing-office had a brother impressed into the rebel service, and was taken prisoner by our forces. He desired to take the oath of allegiance, and to be liberated. She sought an interview with the President, who wrote the note, asking me to inquire into the facts, which I did, and the young man *was* liberated on the President's order." The girl has not been identified.

To Richard C. Vaughan or Officer in Command at Lexington, Missouri[1]

Gen. Vaughan, or   Executive Mansion,
Officer in Command   Washington,
Lexington, Mo.   Nov. 12. 1863.

Let execution of William H. Ogden be suspended until further order from me.   A. LINCOLN

[1] ALS, RPB. No reply has been found, and William H. Ogden has not been identified. Colonel James McFerran was in command of the Department of the Missouri with headquarters at Warrensburg. Presumably Captain Horace B. Johnson of Company L, First Missouri State Militia Cavalry was in command at Lexington.

To Edward Bates[1]

Hon. Edward Bates   Executive Mansion,
My dear Sir.   Washington, Nov. 13, 1863.

Herewith I return the papers of the Western Sanitary Commission. You see an indorsement thereon, made by the Secretary of War, which expresses his view. While I approve heartily the object of the commission, I wish to do nothing unsatisfactory to the War Department, in a matter pertaining to it's business. Yours truly   A. LINCOLN

[1] ALS-P, ISLA. The papers referred to in this letter have not been located, and no further reference has been found.

To E. H. E. Jameson[1]

E. H. & E. Jameson   Washington, D.C.,
Jefferson City, My [sic]   Nov. 13. 1863

Yours saying Brown and Henderson are elected Senators, is received. I understand, this is one and one. If so, it is knocking heads together to some purpose.   A. LINCOLN

[1] ALS, RPB. Lincoln's telegram is addressed to "E. H. & E. Jameson," because the following telegram received from Jameson on November 13 was incorrectly transmitted: "The radicals of Missouri have elected B. Gratz Brown & John B. Henderson U.S. Senators." (DLC-RTL). E. H. E. Jameson was a member of the state legislature from St. Louis.

Reply to John Conness
upon Presentation of a Cane[1]

November 13, 1863

The President then accepted the cane, and, with much emotion, replied that he never personally knew the Senator's friend, Mr. Broderick, but he had always heard him spoken of as one sincerely devoted to the cause of human rights. Testimony to this point of his character had been borne by those whom he had not intimately known, as also by those with whom he was personally and intimately acquainted, and, with all of them, the testimony had been uniform. The memento which was presented him by Senator Conness was of that class of things, the highest honor that could be conferred upon him. If, in the position he had been placed, he had done anything that entitled him to the honor the Senator had assigned him, it was a proud reflection that his acts were of such a character as to merit the affiliation of the friends of a man like David C. Broderick. Whether remaining in this world or looking down upon the earth from the spirit land, to be remembered by such a man as David C. Broderick was a fact he would remember through all the years of his life. The proudest ambition he could desire was to do something for the elevation of the condition of his fellow-man. In conclusion, he returned his sincere thanks for the part the Senator bore in this presentation, and to the memory of his great friend.

[1] Cincinnati *Gazette*, November 17, 1863. Senator John Conness of California, "accompanied by a number of gentlemen, most of them citizens of Pennsylvania, called upon the President of the United States for the purpose of asking his acceptance of a cane which was the gift to him of his great predecessor and exemplar, David Colbert Broderick."

To William S. Rosecrans[1]

Major General Rosecrans   Washington, D.C.,
Cincinnati, O.   Nov. 14 1863 [12:15 P.M.]

I have received and considered your despatch of yesterday. Of
the Reports you mention I have not the means of seeing any except
your own. Besides this the publication might be improper in view
of the Court of Inquiry which has been ordered. With every disposition, not merely to do justice, but to oblige you, I feel constrained
to say I think the publication better not be made now.

                                                A. LINCOLN

[1] ALS, RPB. The time of this telegram is not on the manuscript, but is taken
from the *Official Records*, I, XXXI, III, 144. AGO, *General Orders No. 337*,
October 16, 1863, created the Military Division of the Mississippi, incorporating
the Departments of the Ohio, Cumberland, and Tennessee, under General Grant,
and replaced Rosecrans with General George H. Thomas. Rosecrans telegraphed
from Cincinnati on November 13, "Will you permit me to publish a certified
copy of my official report of the Battle of Chicamauga also those of Generals
Thomas, McCook, Crittenden & Granger. It is an act of justice I solicit from
one in whose justice I confide." (DLC-RTL). Courts of inquiry referred to
were those ordered to meet January 29, 1864, on conduct of James S. Negley,
Thomas L. Crittenden, and Alexander M. McCook at Chickamauga.

To Ambrose E. Burnside[1]

Major General Burnside   Washington City,
Knoxville, Tenn.   Nov. 16. 1863
            What is the news?   A. LINCOLN

[1] ALS, RPB. On November 17 Burnside replied to Lincoln's telegram:
"Longstreet crossed the Tennessee River on Saturday at Huff's Ferry six
miles below Loudon with about 15,000 men. We have resisted the advance
steadily repulsing every attack, holding on, till our position was turned by superior numbers, and then retiring in good order.
"He attacked us yesterday about eleven o'clock at Campbell's Station and
heavy fighting has been going on all day, in which we have held our own and
inflicted serious loss on the enemy.
"No fighting since dark. We commenced retiring, and the most of the command is now within the lines of Knoxville. . . ." (DLC-RTL).

Memorandum Concerning Edward L. Hale[1]

                                 Executive Mansion, Washington,
            Copy.   November 16, 1863.

On condition that Edward L. Hale, named within, faithfully serves
in his present position, until honorably discharged, he is fully pardoned for the desertion mentioned.   A LINCOLN

Nov. 16. 1863

[1] Copy, DLC-RTL. Edward L. Hale has not been identified.

[14]

To Edward Bates[1]

Hon. Attorney General   Executive Mansion,
My dear Sir   Washington, Nov. 17, 1863.
  Please send me an appointment for Richard Busteed of N. Y. to
be Judge in Northern Alabama, in place of ——— Lane deceased.
Yours truly   A. LINCOLN

  [1] ALS, DNA GE RG 60, Papers of Attorney General, Segregated Lincoln
Material. George W. Lane of Huntsville, Alabama, had been appointed in 1861,
but being a strong Unionist he had been forced to leave the state and never
held court. Busteed's appointment was confirmed by the Senate on January
20, 1864.

To Salmon P. Chase[1]

Hon. Secretary of the Treasury   Executive Mansion,
My dear Sir: Washington, Nov. 17. 1863.
  I expected to see you here at Cabinet meeting, and to say something about going to Gettysburg. There will be a train to take and
return us. The time for starting is not yet fixed; but when it shall
be, I will notify you. Yours truly   A. LINCOLN.

  [1] ALS, NBuG. Chase did not go to Gettysburg.

To Salmon P. Chase[1]

Hon. Sec. of Treasury please see and hear Mr. M. V. Hall one of
the best men in northern Illinois.   A. LINCOLN.
  Nov. 17. 1863.

  [1] Copy, IHi-Nicolay and Hay Papers. Myron V. Hall was editor of the
Aurora, Illinois, *Beacon.*

Memorandum: Appointment of Philo P. Judson[1]

Good recommendations for a Quarter-Master, or Commissary
  Nov. 17. 1863.   A. LINCOLN

  [1] AES, RPB. Lincoln's endorsement is written on the recommendation of
Commissary Sergeant Philo P. Judson signed by officers of the Eighth Illinois
Cavalry, November 13, 1863. Judson was appointed first lieutenant and quartermaster of the Seventeenth Illinois Cavalry on December 2, 1863. He was
confirmed as commissary of subsistence of the Eighth Illinois Cavalry with rank
of captain on April 20, 1864.

[15]

Order Concerning Union Pacific Railroad[1]

Executive Mansion, Washington, November 17. 1863.

In pursuance of the fourteenth Section of the act of congress, entitled "An act to aid in the construction of a Railroad and Telegraph Line from the Missouri river to the Pacific ocean, and to secure to the Government the use of the same for postal, military, and other purposes" Approved July 1, 1862, I, Abraham Lincoln, President of the United States, do hereby fix so much of the Western boundary of the State of Iowa as lies between the North and South boundaries of the United States Township, within which the City of Omaha is situated, as the point from which the line of railroad and telegraph in that section mentioned, shall be constructed.

ABRAHAM LINCOLN.

[1] ADS, IHi. See Lincoln's order of March 7, and communication to the Senate of March 9, 1864, *infra.*

To Edwin M. Stanton[1]

[November 17, 1863]

I do not like this arrangement. I do not wish to so go that by the slightest accident we fail entirely, and, at the best, the whole to be a mere breathless running of the gauntlet. But, any way.

A. LINCOLN.

[1] NH, IX, 208. Nicolay and Hay give this as an endorsement on the following letter from Stanton dated November 17:
"*Mr. President:* It is proposed by the Baltimore and Ohio road—
First, to leave Washington Thursday morning at 6 A.M.; and
Second, To leave Baltimore at 8 A.M., arriving at Gettysburg at 12 noon, thus giving two hours to view the ground before the dedication ceremonies commence.
Third, To leave Gettysburg at 6 P.M., and arrive in Washington, midnight; thus doing all in one day.
Mr. Smith says the Northern Central road agrees to this arrangement.
Please consider it, and if any change is desired, Iet me know, so that it can be made."
Stanton replied later in the day: "The arrangement I proposed has been made The train will leave the Depot at 12 oclock. I will assign the Adjutant General or Col. Fry to accompany you as personal escort and to control the train. A carriage will call for you at 12. Please furnish me the names of those whom you may invite that they may be furnished with tickets and unauthorized intrusion prevented." (DLC-RTL).

Remarks to Citizens of Gettysburg, Pennsylvania[1]

November 18, 1863

I appear before you, fellow-citizens, merely to thank you for this compliment. The inference is a very fair one that you would hear me for a little while at least, were I to commence to make a speech. I do not appear before you for the purpose of doing so, and for several substantial reasons. The most substantial of these is that I have no speech to make. [Laughter.] In my position it is somewhat important that I should not say any foolish things.

A VOICE—If you can help it.

Mr. LINCOLN—It very often happens that the only way to help it is to say nothing at all. [Laughter.] Believing that is my present condition this evening, I must beg of you to excuse me from addressing you further.

[1] New York *Tribune*, November 20, 1863. "After supper the President was serenaded by the excellent band of the 5th New-York Artillery. After repeated calls, Mr. Lincoln at length presented himself, when he was loudly cheered." (*Ibid.*).

Address Delivered at the Dedication of the Cemetery at Gettysburg[1]

November 19, 1863

FIRST DRAFT[2]

Executive Mansion, Washington,   , 186

Four score and seven years ago our fathers brought forth, upon this continent, a new nation, conceived in liberty, and dedicated to the proposition that "all men are created equal"

Now we are engaged in a great civil war, testing whether that nation, or any nation so conceived, and so dedicated, can long endure. We are met on a great battle field of that war. We have come to dedicate a portion of it, as a final resting place for those who died here, that the nation might live. This we may, in all propriety

[1] Sources of the various drafts and reports of this speech are given in the succeeding footnotes.

[2] The fact that the first page of this draft was written in ink on Executive Mansion stationery indicates that this page was written at Washington before Lincoln went to Gettysburg. Since the page ends in an incomplete sentence, it may be inferred that there was also a second page written in Washington. The only extant second page, however, written in pencil on lined paper, shows indications of being a copy, presumably of an original page so completely revised and overwritten that Lincoln threw it away. It is also possible, however, that this copy was made from the second draft (see note 3), or possibly from a still different draft of which we have no knowledge.

When he made the copy is another matter of uncertainty. According to John G. Nicolay, he wrote it at Gettysburg on the morning of November 19 (for Nicolay's complete account, see *Century Magazine*, new series, XXV, 596-608); but it is also possible that he wrote this page on the night of November 18 and the second draft on the 19th (see William E. Barton, *Lincoln at Gettysburg*, pp. 68 ff.).

do. But, in a larger sense, we can not dedicate—we can not consecrate—we can not hallow, this ground. The brave men, living and dead, who struggled here, have hallowed it, far above our poor power to add or detract. The world will little note, nor long remember what we say here; while it can never forget what they did here.

It is rather for us, the living, ~~to stand here,~~ we here be dedica-[3]

[Second Page]

ted to the great task remaining before us—that, from these honored dead we take increased devotion to that cause for which they here, gave the last full measure of devotion—that we here highly resolve these dead shall not have died in vain; that the nation, shall have a new birth of freedom, and that government of the people by the people for the people, shall not perish from the earth.

SECOND DRAFT[4]

Four score and seven years ago our fathers brought forth, upon this continent, a new nation, conceived in Liberty, and dedicated to the proposition that all men are created equal.

Now we are engaged in a great civil war, testing whether that nation, or any nation, so conceived, and so dedicated, can long en-

[3] The last three words written in ink on the first page, "to stand here," were deleted by Lincoln and "we here be dedica-" inserted in pencil. If the extant second page of the first draft is a copy, in making the copy Lincoln presumably erred in beginning the revision at the end of page one with the word "dedicated" which appears in line 17 of the second draft, instead of beginning with the word "dedicated" in line 15.

[4] ADf, DLC. This draft is written on lined paper similar to the extant second page of the first draft. The emendations which appear in this draft and the important revisions from the first draft are indicated in succeeding notes.

The exact relationship between the first and second drafts cannot now be established beyond question, for certain emendations in the second draft restore the reading of the first draft. Some of these emendations, however, must have been made after Lincoln delivered the speech, for the newspaper versions follow in some instances the original wording of this draft rather than the emendations (notes 6, 7, 8, 12). Thus it would seem that although Lincoln spoke from the second draft as first written, and perhaps partially revised, he did not read it verbatim. He probably made further changes in this draft after the address to make it conform to what he said.

Nicolay states that Lincoln prepared "a new autograph copy" after he consulted newspaper reports of the address. Possibly Nicolay referred to the Everett copy (infra), which we do not know to have been prepared after rather than before receipt of Everett's letter of January 30, 1864. It has also been supposed that there was once an autograph copy prepared for Judge David Wills, at whose home Lincoln stayed on the night before the dedication ceremony, but this supposed copy has never been located. In any event Nicolay's account is incomplete and vague, and shows no acquaintance with the second draft.

dure. We are met here[5] on a great battle-field of that war. We have come[6] to dedicate a portion of it as a[7] final resting place for[8] those who[9] here gave their lives that that nation might live. It[10] is altogether fitting and proper that we should do this.

But in a larger sense we can not dedicate—we can not consecrate—we can not hallow this ground. The brave men, living and dead, who struggled here, have consecrated[11] it far above our poor[12] power to add or detract. The world will little note, nor long remember, what we say here, but[13] can never forget what they did here. It is[14] for us, the living, rather to be dedicated here to the unfinished work which they have, thus far, so nobly carried on. It is rather for us to be here dedicated to the great task remaining before us—that from these honored dead we take increased devotion to that[15] cause for which they here gave the last full measure of devotion—that we here highly resolve that[16] these dead shall not have died in vain; that this[17] nation shall have a new birth of freedom; and that this[18] government of the people, by the people, for the people, shall not perish from the earth.

NEWSPAPER VERSION[19]

Four score and seven years ago our fathers brought forth upon this continent a new Nation, conceived in Liberty, and dedicated to the proposition that all men are created equal. [Applause.] Now

[5] "Here" does not appear in the first draft.

[6] Lincoln wrote "are met," deleted the words, and inserted "have come," as in the first draft.

[7] Lincoln wrote "the," deleted the word, and substituted "a," as in the first draft.

[8] Lincoln wrote "of," deleted the word, and substituted "for" as in the first draft.   [9] First draft reads "who died here, that the nation might live."

[10] See first draft for first version of this sentence.

[11] First draft reads "hallowed."

[12] "Poor," as in the first draft, purposely or inadvertently omitted, is inserted above the line.   [13] First draft reads "while it can never."

[14] See note 3.

[15] Lincoln wrote "the," deleted the word, and substituted "that," as in first draft.   [16] "That" does not appear in the first draft.

[17] "The nation," in first draft.

[18] "This" does not appear in the first draft.

[19] New York *Tribune*, *Times*, and *Herald*, November 20, 1863. Except for minor differences in punctuation and capitalization, the text is the same in all three papers and is the Associated Press version prepared by Joseph L. Gilbert. According to Gilbert's later account, his text was prepared partly from his shorthand notes and partly from Lincoln's manuscript (see Barton, *op. cit.*, pp. 189-92). Since this version follows closely the second draft prior to its having been emended, down to the final sentence, we have to account chiefly for the variants between the newspaper text and the second draft in this final sentence. All of these variants may be explained by the hypothesis that Lincoln did not

we are engaged in a great civil war, testing whether that Nation or any Nation so conceived and so dedicated can long endure. We are met on a great battle-field of that war. We are met to dedicate a portion of it as the final resting-place of those who here gave[20] their lives that that nation might live. It is altogether fitting and proper that we should do this. But in a larger sense we cannot dedicate, we cannot consecrate, we cannot hallow this ground. The brave men living and dead who struggled here have consecrated it far above our power[21] to add or detract. [Applause.] The world will little note nor long remember what we say here, but it can never forget what they did here. [Applause.] It is for us, the living, rather to be dedicated here to the refinished[22] work that they have thus far so nobly carried on. [Applause.] It is rather for us to be here dedicated to the great task remaining before us, that from these honored dead we take increased devotion to that cause for which they here gave the last full measure of devotion; that we here highly resolve that the[23] dead shall not have died in vain [applause]; that the nation shall, under God, have a new birth of

---

read his manuscript verbatim, and hence Gilbert's shorthand followed the spoken word. Some of them may be accounted for as errors, which in spite of having access to the manuscript Gilbert did not correct, or which occurred in transcription. In any event Gilbert seems not to have relied on the manuscript for Lincoln's last sentence.

Aside from Gilbert's text there are several independent newspaper texts, of varying degrees of reliability, such as those in the Chicago *Tribune* and Philadelphia *Inquirer*. Inferior in general, they are important chiefly in establishing one word, "poor," omitted by Gilbert, which Lincoln assuredly must have spoken and which appears in both first and second drafts. "Our poor power," rather than Gilbert's "our power," appears in the Chicago *Tribune*, and the Philadelphia *Inquirer* has "our poor attempts," in texts prepared independently of each other, and also independently of the Associated Press text. These papers corroborate Gilbert's version, however, in having the phrase "under God," which Lincoln must have used for the first time as he spoke.

Barton (*op. cit.*, pp. 80-83) credits the text taken down in shorthand by Charles Hale of the Boston *Advertiser* as being "what Lincoln actually said," and gives it preference over Gilbert's text chiefly on the ground that Gilbert consulted Lincoln's manuscript, whereas Hale relied solely on his shorthand notes. The few particulars in which Hale's version differs from Gilbert's have been indicated in footnotes. In one particular, however, it may be questioned whether Hale was accurate—along with Gilbert he omits "poor" from "our poor power." It is difficult to comprehend how "poor" found its way into other newspaper reports unless Lincoln spoke the word, and yet both Gilbert and Hale omitted it.

20 Hale's text and that of the Chicago *Tribune* are "have given."

21 Philadelphia *Inquirer* has "our poor attempts" and Chicago *Tribune* has "our poor power."

22 A obvious error in Gilbert's text in all three New York papers. Hale's version and the Chicago *Tribune* have "unfinished."

23 Hale's version has "these" as in the drafts.

freedom; and that Governments[24] of the people, by the people, and[25] for the people, shall not perish from the earth. [Long-continued applause.]

EDWARD EVERETT COPY[26]

Four score and seven years ago our fathers brought forth upon this continent, a new nation, conceived in Liberty, and dedicated to the proposition that all men are created equal.

Now we are engaged in a great civil war, testing whether that nation, or any nation so conceived, and so dedicated, can long endure. We are met on a great battle-field of that war. We have come to dedicate a portion of that field,[27] as a final resting place for those who here gave their lives, that that nation might live. It is altogether fitting and proper that we should do this.

But, in a larger sense, we can not dedicate—we can not consecrate—we can not hallow—this ground. The brave men, living and dead, who struggled here, have consecrated it, far above our poor power to add or detract. The world will little note, nor long remember, what we say here, but it[28] can never forget what they did here. It is for us, the living, rather, to be dedicated here to the unfinished work which they who[29] fought here, have, thus far, so nobly advanced. It is rather for us to be here dedicated to the great task remaining before us—that from these honored dead we take increased devotion to that cause for which they here gave the last full measure of devotion—that we here highly resolve that these dead shall not have died in vain—that this nation, under God,[30] shall have a new birth of freedom—and that, government of the people, by the people, for the people, shall not perish from the earth.

[24] The plural appears only in Gilbert's text, so far as is known, and may well be an error of transcription.

[25] Hale's version omits "and" as in the drafts, but the *Inquirer* text also has "and."

[26] AD, IHi. This manuscript was sent to Edward Everett, to be bound in a volume with the manuscript of Everett's address and sold at the Sanitary Fair in New York. For particulars see the note to Lincoln's letter to Everett, February 4, 1864, *infra.* It is not certain that this copy was made specifically for this purpose after receipt of Everett's letter of January 30, and quite probably it may have been made earlier. In either case, comparison of the Everett copy with the first and second drafts and with the newspaper versions shows it to have been made as a careful revision, incorporating the phrase "under God" and other minor changes from the newspapers, and making additional revisions as indicated in the succeeding notes, but in general following the revised second draft.   [27] "That field" replaced "it" of the earlier versions.

[28] "It" was adopted from the newspaper version.

[29] The remainder of this sentence was completely revised from the earlier versions.   [30] "Under God" was incorporated from the newspaper versions.

GEORGE BANCROFT COPY[31]

Four score and seven years ago our fathers brought forth, on[32] this continent, a new nation, conceived in Liberty, and dedicated to the proposition that all men are created equal.

Now we are engaged in a great civil war, testing whether that nation, or any nation so conceived, and so dedicated, can long endure. We are met on a great battle-field of that war. We have come to dedicate a portion of that field, as a final resting-place for those who here gave their lives, that that nation might live. It is altogether fitting and proper that we should do this.

But, in a larger sense, we can not dedicate—we can not conse-crate—we can not hallow—this ground. The brave men, living and dead, who struggled here, have consecrated it far above our poor power to add or detract. The world will little note, nor long re-member what we say here, but it can never forget what they did here. It is for us the living, rather, to be dedicated here to the un-finished work which they who fought here have thus far so nobly advanced. It is rather for us to be here dedicated to the great task remaining before us—that from these honored dead we take in-creased devotion to that cause for which they here gave the last full measure of devotion—that we here highly resolve that these dead shall not have died in vain—that this nation, under God, shall have a new birth of freedom—and that government of the people, by the people, for the people, shall not perish from the earth.

FINAL TEXT[33]

Address delivered at the dedication of the Cemetery at Gettys-burg.

[31] AD, NIC. This copy was prepared upon request of George Bancroft for reproduction in facsimile in *Autograph Leaves of Our Country's Authors* (1864), a volume to be sold by the Baltimore Sanitary Fair. For particulars see Lin-coln's letter to Bancroft, February 29, 1864, *infra*. This text is notable chiefly for Lincoln's change of "upon this continent" to "on this continent." Written on both sides of a single sheet of paper, the manuscript was not suitable for reproduction, and hence Lincoln prepared the final copy, *infra*.

[32] "On" replaced "upon" of the earlier versions.

[33] ADS, owned by Oscar Cintas, Havana, Cuba. Generally known as the "Bliss Copy" from its long possession by the family of Alexander Bliss, a member of the committee which obtained the volume of original autographs to provide facsimiles for *Autograph Leaves of Our Country's Authors*, this was Lincoln's final text. Only one change in wording, as noted, was made in this copy from the Bancroft copy. The exact date that Lincoln prepared this final manuscript is not known, but was sometime later than March 4, 1864, when John P. Kennedy wrote on behalf of the Baltimore Sanitary Fair to explain that the Bancroft copy would not do because it could not be fitted to the pages of the proposed volume.

Four score and seven years ago our fathers brought forth on this continent, a new nation, conceived in Liberty, and dedicated to the proposition that all men are created equal.

Now we are engaged in a great civil war, testing whether that nation, or any nation so conceived and so dedicated, can long endure. We are met on a great battle-field of that war. We have come to dedicate a portion of that field, as a final resting place for those who here gave their lives that that nation might live. It is altogether fitting and proper that we should do this.

But, in a larger sense, we can not dedicate—we can not consecrate—we can not hallow—this ground. The brave men, living and dead, who struggled here, have consecrated it, far above our poor power to add or detract. The world will little note, nor long remember what we say here, but it can never forget what they did here. It is for us the living, rather, to be dedicated here to the unfinished work which they who fought here have thus far so nobly advanced. It is rather for us to be here dedicated to the great task remaining before us—that from these honored dead we take increased devotion to that cause for which they[34] gave the last full measure of devotion—that we here highly resolve that these dead shall not have died in vain—that this nation, under God, shall have a new birth of freedom—and that government of the people, by the people, for the people, shall not perish from the earth.

November 19. 1863.   ABRAHAM LINCOLN.

[34] "Here" is omitted from the phrase "they here gave," which appears in preceding versions.

To Henry B. Blood[1]

Capt. Blood furnish one Horse for bearer
Nov. 19. 1863   A LINCOLN

[1] ALS-P, ISLA. Captain Henry B. Blood was assistant quartermaster of Volunteers. The bearer has not been identified.

To Zachariah Chandler[1]

Private

Hon. Z. Chandler   Executive Mansion,
My dear Sir: Washington, Nov. 20. 1863.

Your letter of the 15th. marked *"private"* was received to-day. I have seen Gov. Morgan and Thurlow Weed, separately, but not together, within the last ten days; but neither of them mentioned the forthcoming message, or said anything, so far as I can remember, which brought the thought of the Message to my mind.

I am very glad the elections this autumn have gone favorably, and that I have not, by native depravity, or under evil influences, done anything bad enough to prevent the good result.

I hope to "stand firm" enough to not go backward, and yet not go forward fast enough to wreck the country's cause. Yours truly

A. LINCOLN

1 ALS, DLC-Chandler Papers. On November 15, Senator Chandler wrote Lincoln protesting published reports that " 'Thurlow Weed and Gov Morgan & other distinguished Republicans are here [Washington] urging the President to take bold conservative ground in his message.' I have been upon the stump more than two months this fall & have certainly talked to more than 200,000 people in Illinois Ohio & New York . . . & have yet to meet the first Republican or *real* War Democrat who stands by Thurlough Weed or Mr Blair. *All* denounce them. . . . You are today Master of the situation if you stand firm. The people endorsed you gloriously in every state save one & New Jersey could have been carried by a bold *radical* campaign. . . . Conservatives & traitors are buried together, for Gods sake dont exhume their remains in Your Message. They will smell worse than Lazarus did after he had been buried three days (Chandler to Lincoln, November 15, 1863, *ibid.*).

To Edward Everett[1]

Hon. Edward Everett.   Executive Mansion,
My dear Sir: Washington, Nov. 20, 1863.

Your kind note of to-day is received. In our respective parts yesterday, you could not have been excused to make a short address, nor I a long one. I am pleased to know that, in your judgment, the little I did say was not entirely a failure. Of course I knew Mr. Everett would not fail; and yet, while the whole discourse was eminently satisfactory, and will be of great value, there were passages in it which trancended my expectation. The point made against the theory of the general government being only an agency, whose principals are the States, was new to me, and, as I think, is one of the best arguments for the national supremacy. The tribute to our noble women for their angel-ministering to the suffering soldiers, surpasses, in its way, as do the subjects of it, whatever has gone before.

Our sick boy, for whom you kindly inquire, we hope is past the worst. Your Obt. Servt.   A. LINCOLN

1 ALS, MHi. On November 20, Edward Everett wrote Lincoln:
"Not wishing to intrude upon your privacy, when you must be much engaged, I beg leave, in this way, to thank you very sincerely for your great

thoughtfulness for my daughter's accommodation on the Platform yesterday, & much kindness otherwise to me & mine at Gettysburg.

"Permit me also to express my great admiration of the thoughts expressed by you, with such eloquent simplicity & appropriateness, at the consecration of the cemetery. I should be glad, if I could flatter myself that I came as near to the central idea of the occasion, in two hours, as you did in two minutes. My son who parted from me at Baltimore & my daughter, concur in this senti-ment. . . ."

"I hope your anxiety for your child was relieved on your arrival." (DLC-RTL).

"Tad" Lincoln had been sick when Lincoln went to Gettysburg on November 18, and Lincoln was ill with varioloid for several days following his return to Washington.

To George G. Meade[1]

Major General Meade   Executive Mansion
Army of Potomac   Washington D.C. Nov. 20. 1863

If there is a man by the name of King under sentence to be shot, please suspend execution till further order, and send record.

A. LINCOLN

[1] ALS, THaroL. See Lincoln to Meade, *infra*.

To George G. Meade[1]

Major Gen. Meade   Executive Mansion,
Army of Potomac   Washington, Nov. 20, 1863.

An intelligent woman [in] deep distress, called this morning, saying her husband, a Lieutenant in the A.P. was to be shot next Monday for desertion; and putting a letter in my hand, upon which I relied for particulars, she left without mentioning a name, or other particular by which to identify the case. On opening the letter I found it equally vague, having nothing to identify by, ex-cept her own signature, which seems to be "Mrs. Anna S. King" I could not again find her. If you have a case which you shall think is probably the one intended, please apply my despatch of this morning to it.   A. LINCOLN

[1] ALS-P, ISLA. No reply either to this communication or the telegram, *supra*, has been found. The sentence of First Lieutenant Edward King, Company H, Sixty-sixth New York Infantry, was commuted to imprisonment on the Dry Tortugas, May 13, 1864. Letters from Hay and Nicolay to Joseph Holt, Jan-uary 8, 1864, and May 13, 1864 (DNA WR RG 153, Judge Advocate General, MM 1182) relate how Mrs. King was swindled by "an officer who gave his name as Captain Parker Co. M. 12th Pa Cavalry, who promised for $300 to get her husband pardoned—claimed to know you, & got all the money the poor creature had."

Memorandum:
Appointment of Richard S. Hayes[1]

West-Point—   [November 20, 1863]
Richard Somers Hayes—is Grandson of Com. Bainbridge, and
Grandnephew of Coms. Barry & Somers. His mother, now a widow,
is daughter of Com. Bainbridge.

[1] AE, DNA WR RG 94, U.S. Military Academy, 1861, No. 886. Lincoln's
endorsement is on an envelope with recommendations for Richard S. Hayes,
grandson of William Bainbridge and grandnephew of John Barry and Richard
Somers. No record of Hayes' appointment has been found.

To Robert C. Schenck[1]

Major General Schenck   Executive Mansion,
Baltimore, Md.   Washington, Nov. 20, 1863.
   It is my wish that neither Maynadier, nor Gordon, be executed
without my further order. Please act upon this.

                                                    A. LINCOLN

[1] ALS, RPB. No reply has been found. Private John H. Maynadier, First
Virginia Cavalry, CSA, was sentenced to be shot on November 25 for being a
spy. William F. Gordon, private in the Thirty-third Virginia Cavalry who had
been commissioned a captain to raise a company (never regularly commissioned) was sentenced for recruiting within Union lines.

To Robert C. Schenck[1]

                                            November 20, 1863
Major General Schenck will put on trial before a Military commission, Capt. Moore, mentioned within for having transcended
General Order No. 53, in arresting the Judges of election, and for
having hindered Arthur Crisfield, from voting, notwithstanding his
willingness to take the oath in said order prescribed. Let Hon. John
W. Crisfield be notified of time and place, and witnesses named by
him as well as by Capt. Moore, be examined. Let time and place
be reasonably convenient to witnesses, and full record kept & preserved.   A. LINCOLN
   Nov. 20. 1863.

[1] AES, DNA WR RG 153, Judge Advocate General, MM 1277. See Lincoln
to Bradford, November 2, and to Blair, November 11, *supra*. On November 14,
John W. Crisfield wrote Montgomery Blair:
   "Yours of the 12th. covering the President's of the day previous just at hand.
   "I enclose the affidavit of W. H. Fisher, the only judge of election residing in
this village, and immediately accessible to me. I will send others as they can
be obtained.
   "The judges . . . live remote from me. . . . Why will not the affidavits of
other credible persons do as well? . . . .

"I will cause copies of the Presidents letter to be sent to each county in my district, and direct such affidavits as may be procured to be forwarded . . . to you. . . ."

On Crisfield's letter Lincoln endorsed "Affadavit named within, sent to Gen. Schenck, indorsed as follows: [copy of same endorsement as above but not in Lincoln's hand]" (DLC-RTL).

Concerning Captain Charles C. Moore, Third Maryland Cavalry, see further Lincoln to Holt, February 22, 1864.

To Edwin M. Stanton[1]

Hon. Sec. of War   Executive Mansion,
My dear Sir   Washington, Nov. 20, 1863.

Please see and hear the Attorney General, and oblige him in what he will ask in regard to a niece of his who is in distress. Yours truly   A. LINCOLN

[1]ALS, owned by Wilson F. Harwood, Washington, D.C. On the bottom of the letter Stanton endorsed on November 22, "Approved. Mrs Flementine Ball has permission to return to her home with her family necessaries." An accompanying note of Gideon Welles to Commodore Andrew A. Harwood, November 21, 1863, reads as follows: "Comodore Harwood will attend to the request of the Attorney General Bates, who desires that his niece an infirm lady may be conveyed to, and landed at Cone River, or in its vicinity." Other letters preserved with these indicate that Mrs. Flementine Ball, Bates' niece, was successfully transported to Coan River, a tributary of the Potomac in Northumberland County, Virginia, adjoining Lancaster County where she lived.

To Edwin M. Stanton[1]

November 20, 1863

Hon. Sec. of War, please see and hear the Sec. of Interior and Com. of Indian Aff. with Genl. George, Indian Chief and discharge such of the men as the chief applies for & who have not received bounties.

[1] Copy, DNA WR RG 107, Secretary of War, Letters Received, P 206, Register notation. The copy of Lincoln's communication preserved as a notation on the register indicates referral of petition of Samuel George, head chief of the Six Nations, for release of Senecas unlawfully enlisted.

To Edwin M. Stanton[1]

November 21, 1863

Hon. Sec. of War, please see my especial friend, Mr. Judd, now Minister at Berlin, and who wishes his son to go [to] West-Point. I must do this if there [is] any vacancy. Please ascertain, and let him know whether there is a vacancy.   A. LINCOLN

Nov. 21. 1863.

[1] ALS, owned by Mrs. Luther Rossiter, Evanston, Illinois. Lincoln's note is written on both sides of a small card. In reply to a non-extant letter from Lincoln, Norman Judd, minister at Berlin, wrote on October 17, 1863, concerning his son Frank Judd:

"Your kind note is at hand. I do not know enough of naval arrangements to understand whether the position you name offers preferment to the capable and industrious or not. I explained to you my situation, and I believe this will be the turning point in Frank's life, and so important do we regard it that Mrs. J. urges me to go with F. to America and my inclination is to do so.

"To await leave of absence would keep me here a month and I am disposed to venture upon your generosity and secure my leave after I reach Washington. . . ."

On February 11, 1864, Luther Rossiter wrote Lincoln from Lake Forest, Illinois:

"I have charge of Hon. N. B. Judds affairs during his absence. . . .

"Last fall when he was here you gave his son Frank an appointment to West Point . . . which his father expected him to enter next June.

"I understand that he has joined the eighth Illinois cavalry as a private, hoping you would promote him to some office in the regular army. . . .

"I believe also he has written you concerning his appointment at West Point.

"I hope you will take no action in relation to it till you hear from his father." (DLC-RTL).

Young Judd's career in the army seems to have included desertion, and re-enlistment under the alias of "Frank Judson" in the Third Massachusetts Cavalry, from which he also deserted. See Lincoln's communications to Benjamin F. Butler, December 29, 1864, and to Edward O. C. Ord, January 19, 1865.

To Edwin M. Stanton[1]

November 22, 1863

The within is in behalf of the family of Southern, who killed the Lieutenant and fled. It is represented that the family are substantially imprisoned in their house by our soldiers, & are on starvation. I submit that perhaps some attention better be given to the case.

Nov. 22. 1863   A LINCOLN

[1] AES-P, ISLA. Lincoln's endorsement appears on a letter from E. W. Hazard, Chicago, November 11, 1863, introducing "Miss Florence Holcomb of your city. Miss Holcomb has had some friends arrested under military authority, one of whom is a young lady in which Miss Holcomb feels a very deep interest and whom she regards as entirely innocent of any intentional wrong." Succeeding endorsements indicate referral of the letter to Colonel William Birney, Camp Stanton, Bryantown, Maryland, who endorsed on December 4, "Respy. returned with full report of this date." The report has not been found.

Concerning the case of John H. Sothoron and son see Lincoln to Schenck, October 21, supra, and to Stanton, March 18, 1864, infra.

To E. P. Evans[1]

E. P. Evans   Executive Mansion
West-Union, Adams Co. Ohio   Washington, D.C. Nov. 23. 1863

Yours to Gov. Chase in behalf of John A. Welch is before me. Can there be a worse case than to desert and write letters per-su[a]ding others to desert? I can-not interpose without a better showing than you make. When did he desert? When did he write the letters?   A. LINCOLN.

¹ ALS, RPB. See Lincoln's telegram to the officer in command at Covington, Kentucky, December 10, *infra*. E. P. Evans has not been identified, and his communication to Chase has not been located.

To William H. Seward¹

Executive Mansion,
My dear Sir: Washington, D.C. Nov. 23. 1863
    Two despatches since I saw you—one not quite so late on firing as we had before, but giving the points that Burnside thinks he can hold the place, that he is not closely invested, and that he forages across the river. The other brings the firing up to 11. A.M. yesterday, being 23. hours later than we had before. Yours truly
    Hon. Sec. of State   A. LINCOLN

¹ ALS, NAuE. Telegrams from Orlando B. Willcox at Cumberland Gap of 2 P.M. and 8 P.M., November 22, to Halleck, reported firing at Knoxville and information carried by an officer on November 20 that Burnside "still holds out, and had notified the citizens of Knoxville that he would hold the place." (OR, I, XXXI, III, 225-26).

To Green C. Smith¹

Hon. Green Clay Smith   Executive Mansion,
Covington, Ky.   Washington, Nov. 23, 1863.
    I am told that John A. Welch is under sentence as a deserter to be shot at Covington on the 11th. of December. Please bring a copy of the record, and other facts of his case, with you when you come.
                                                  A. LINCOLN

¹ ALS, RPB. No reply from Smith has been found, but see Lincoln's telegram to the officer in command at Covington, Kentucky, December 10, *infra*.

To Seth Eastman¹

Military Officer in   Washington, D.C.,
command at Cincinnati O.   Nov. 24, 1863.
    Please suspend execution of sentence against E. A. Smith, until further order, mean time send me copy of record of his trial
                                                  A. LINCOLN

¹ ALS, RPB. No reply has been found. Lieutenant Colonel Seth Eastman was in command at Cincinnati as of October 31, 1863. On November 24, Richard M. Corwine telegraphed Lincoln from Cincinnati: "I send you . . . petition in behalf of E. A. Smith just convicted by a court martial of fraud in horse contracts and sentenced to pay a heavy fine & suffer twelve months im-

prisonment. I was not his counsel in the trial, but have examined the evidence and am satisfied it is not a just conviction but owing to Gen Burnsides absence no appeal can be made to him & he has not seen & has had no opportunity to revise the proceedings & I respectfully ask you to order the sentence to be suspended until you can examine them. If you do not make the order the sentence will be executed tomorrow." On December 1, 1863, Lincoln referred the petition to Stanton (DNA WR RG 107, Secretary of War, Letters Received, P 208), but the papers are missing from the file. See further Lincoln to Holt, February 4, and to Corwine, March 30, 1864, *infra*.

To William H. Seward[1]

Hon. Sec. of State.   Executive Mansion
My dear Sir.   Washington. Nov. 24. 1863.

A despatch from Foster at Cincinnati received half an hour ago, contains one from Wilcox, at Cumberland Gap without date, saying "fighting going on at Knoxville today." The want of date makes the time of fighting uncertain, but I rather think it means yesterday the 23rd. Yours truly.   A. LINCOLN.

[1] Copy, DLC-RTL. The despatch referred to is in the *Official Records*, I, XXXI, III, 238.

Authorization for Peter H. Watson[1]

War Department Washington City, Nov 25 1863
During the temporary absence of the Secretary of War his duties will be performed by Assistant Secretary P H Watson.

ABRAHAM LINCOLN

[1] DS, ORB.

To Ulysses S. Grant[1]

Major Genl. Grant   Washington, D.C.,
Chattanooga.   Nov. 25 1863

Your despatches as to fighting on Monday & Tuesday are here. Well done. Many thanks to all. Remember Burnside.

A. LINCOLN

[1] ALS, RPB. Grant telegraphed Halleck on November 23: "General Thomas' troops attacked the enemy's left at 2 p.m. to-day, carried the first line of rifle-pits running over the knoll, 1,200 yards in front of Fort Wood, and low ridge to the right of it, taking about 200 prisoners, besides killed and wounded. Our loss small. The troops moved under fire with all the precision of veterans on parade. Thomas' troops will intrench themselves, and hold their position until daylight, when Sherman will join the attack from the mouth of the Chicamauga, and a decisive battle will be fought." (OR, I, XXXI, II, 24).

On November 24 Grant reported again: "The fight to-day progressed favorably. Sherman carried the end of Missionary Ridge, and his right is now at the tunnel, and left on Chicamauga Creek. Troops from Lookout Valley carried

[30]

the point of the mountain, and now hold the eastern slope and point high up. I cannot yet tell the amount of casualties, but our loss is not heavy. Hooker reports 2,000 prisoners taken, besides which a small number have fallen into our hands from Missionary Ridge." (*Ibid.*).

To George G. Meade[1]

Major-General Meade: November 25, 1863.

The sentence in the case of Privt. Moses Giles, Company B, Seventh Maine Volunteers, is suspended until further orders.

A. LINCOLN.

[1] Tarbell (Appendix), p. 401. No further reference has been found.

To George G. Meade[1]

War Department,
Major-General Meade   Washington,
Commanding Army of the Potomac: November 25, 1863.

Suspend execution in case of Adolphus Morse, Seventy-sixth New York, deserter, and send record to me.   A. LINCOLN.

[1] Tarbell (Appendix), p. 401. Meade telegraphed at 10:30 A.M., "Your dispatch of today in relation to Adolphus Morse 76 N.Y. is received. The record will be forwarded by mail tomorrow." (DLC-RTL). Morse's sentence was commuted to imprisonment at hard labor at Fort Jefferson, Florida, where he subsequently died.

To George G. Meade[1]

Major-General Meade: December 2, 1863.

The sentence in the case of Privt. H. Morris Husband, Ninety-ninth Pennsylvania Volunteers, (now of Third Army Corps First Division) is suspended until further orders. Let the record be forwarded to me.   A. LINCOLN.

[1] Tarbell (Appendix), p. 401. The roster of Company I lists Private Henry M. Husband as returned on November 2, 1864, and mustered out with the company on July 1, 1865.

Memorandum
on Construction of Loyal State Governments[1]

[c. December 2, 1863]

It is suggested as proper that in constructing a loyal State government in any State, the name of the State, the boundary, the subdivisions the Constitution and general code of laws, as before the rebellion, be maintained, subject only to the modifications made necessary by the conditions herein before stated, and such others if any, as may be deemed proper in the State, and not contravening said conditions.

[1] ADf, DLC-RTL. This memorandum is written on the back of Lincoln's draft of the letter to Opdyke and others, *infra.*

To George Opdyke and Others[1]

Messrs. George Opdyke, Jos. Sutherland,   Executive Mansion,
Benj. F. Manierre, Prosper M. Wetmore   Washington,
and Spencer Kirby, Committee.   Dec. 2, 1863.

Yours of the 28th. ult. inviting me to be present at a meeting to be held at the Cooper Institute, on the 3rd. Inst. to promote the raising of volunteers, is received. Nothing would be more grateful to my feelings, or better accord with my judgment than to contribute, if I could, by my presence, or otherwise, to that eminently patriotic object. Nevertheless the now early meeting of congress, together with a temporary illness, render my attendance impossible.

You purpose also to celebrate our Western victories. Freed from apprehension of wounding the just sensibilities of brave soldiers fighting elsewhere, it would be exceedingly agreeable to me to join in a suitable acknowledgment to those of the Great West, with whom I was born, and have passed my life. And it is exceedingly gratifying that a portion lately of the Army of the Potomac, but now serving with the great army of the West, have borne so conspicuous a part in the late brilliant triumphs in Georgia.

Honor to the Soldier, and Sailor everywhere, who bravely bears his country's cause. Honor also to the citizen who cares for his brother in the field, and serves, as he best can, the same cause— honor to him, only less than to him, who braves, for the common good, the storms of heaven and the storms of battle. Your Obt. Servt

A. LINCOLN

[1] ADf, DLC-RTL; LS, IHi. The committee's letter of November 28 specifies no more than is paraphrased in Lincoln's reply (DLC-RTL). Lincoln's draft of this letter is on the back of the same sheet as his memorandum, *supra.*

To George G. Meade[1]

Executive Mansion,
Major General Meade,   Washington, December 3, 1863.
Governor Seymour especially asks that Isaac C. White sentenced to death for desertion be reprieved. I wish this done.

(signed) John Hay,   A. LINCOLN.
     a Private Secretary.

¹ Copy, DNA WR RG 153, Judge Advocate General, MM 1142. This official copy attested by Edward D. Townsend is filed with the court-martial record of Private Isaac C. White of the Sixty-first New York Volunteers, sentenced for desertion. No further reference has been found.

To George G. Meade¹

Executive Mansion,
Major-General Meade: Washington, December 3, 1863.
Please suspend execution of Frederick Foster until the record can be examined.   A. LINCOLN.

¹ Tarbell (Appendix), p. 402. Meade's telegram in reply was received at 2:10 P.M.: "Your dispatch of today in relation to Private Frederick Foster ninety-ninth (99th) Penna. Volunteers, is received and has been obeyed. The record will be forwarded for your action by mail tomorrow." (DLC-RTL).

To George G. Meade¹

Major General Meade,   [December 3, 1863]
The sentences in the cases of Brice Birdsill, private, Co. B, 124th N.Y. Vols., and Frederick Foster of 99th Penn. Vols. are suspended until further orders. Let the records be forwarded at once.
                              A. LINCOLN.

¹ Copy, DNA WR RG 153, Judge Advocate General, MM 1147. This official copy attested by Edward D. Townsend, filed with court-martial record of Private Brice E. Birdsall, is without date, but Meade's reply received at 4:40 P.M. on December 3, 1863, establishes the date: "Your dispatch of today in relation to Privates Birdsall & Foster is recd. In obedience to a previous dispatch from you the sentence in the case of Foster has already been suspended   That in the case of Birdsall will be suspended & the records forwarded for your action" (DLC-RTL).
Private Frederick Foster remained in service and was discharged on April 22, 1865. Birdsall's record was returned to the War Department on April 16, 1864, under the order of February 26, 1864, commuting death sentences for deserters to imprisonment on the Dry Tortugas.

To George G. Meade¹

Executive Mansion,
Major-General Meade: Washington, December 3, 1863.
Please suspend execution in case of William A. Gammon, Seventh Maine, and send record to me.   A. LINCOLN.

Send by telegraph and oblige, yours very truly,   JOHN HAY.

¹ Tarbell (Appendix) p. 402. Meade replied on December 4: "Your despatch of today relating to private W. A. Gammon 7th. Maine is rec'd & will be obliged. The record will be forwarded by mail tomorrow for your action."

(DLC-RTL). Lincoln returned the record of Gammon's case to the War Department on April 16, 1864, under the order of February 26, 1864, commuting death sentences for deserters to imprisonment on the Dry Tortugas.

To Mary Todd Lincoln[1]

Mrs. A. Lincoln.   Executive Mansion,
Metropolitan, N.Y.   Washington, Dec. 4. 9½ AM, 1863.
          All going well.   A LINCOLN

[1] ALS, IHi. The case of varioloid which Lincoln contracted following the trip to Gettysburg continued well into December and probably accounts for the series of telegrams sent to Mrs. Lincoln, December 4-7. Mrs. Lincoln telegraphed on December 4: "Reached here last evening. Very tired and severe headache. Hope to hear you are doing well. Expect a telegraph to-day." (Katherine Helm, *Mary, Wife of Lincoln*, p. 234).

To Stephen C. Massett[1]

Mr. Stephen C. Massett.   Washington, Dec. 4, 1863
   My Dear Sir: Allow me to thank you very cordially for your kindness in sending me a copy of your book, "Drifting About." I am very truly, Your Obed't Serv't,   ABRAHAM LINCOLN.

[1] Tracy, p. 236. Stephen C. Massett, a forty-niner from San Francisco, published *Drifting About"; or, What "Jeems Pipes, of Pipesville," Saw-and-Did* (New York, 1863), a comic autobiography which Massett delivered as "lectures," and on one occasion presented in part to President and Mrs. Lincoln at the White House (Carpenter, *Six Months at the White House*, pp. 160-61).

To Edwin M. Stanton[1]

                                        December 4, 1863
Hon. B. J. Clay and Hon. G. C. Smith present this petition and join in it. Therefore let Clifton F. Estill, named within, be discharged, on the conditions stated.   A. LINCOLN.
   Dec. 4. 1863

[1] AES, RPB. Lincoln's endorsement is written on a petition to Governor Bramlette of Kentucky for release of Clifton F. Estill "a prisoner of war at Camp Douglas being a private of John Morgan's command captured in Ohio," whose mother was "one of the most active Union ladies" in Fayette County, signed by numerous citizens and by Brutus J. Clay and Green C. Smith, members of congress. No further reference has been found.

To Mary Todd Lincoln[1]

Mrs. A. Lincoln   Executive Mansion, Washington,
Metropolitan Hotel. New-[York]   Dec. 5. 10 A.M. 1863.
          All doing well   A. LINCOLN

[1] ALS, IHi.

To Mary Todd Lincoln[1]

Mrs. A Lincoln.   Executive Mansion Washington,
Metropolitan Hotel N.Y.   DC. Dec. 6. 1863.
            All doing well   A LINCOLN

[1] ALS, IHi. Mrs. Lincoln telegraphed on December 6: "Do let me know immediately how Taddie and yourself are. I will be home by Tuesday without
fail; sooner if needed." (Katherine Helm, *Mary, Wife of Lincoln*, p. 234).

Announcement of Union Success in Tennessee[1]

Executive Mansion Washington D.C. Dec. 7– 1863
   Reliable information being received that the insurgent force is
retreating from East Tennessee, under circumstances rendering it
probable that the Union forces can not hereafter be dislodged from
that important position; and esteeming this to be of high national
consequence, I recommend that all loyal people do, on receipt of
this, informally assemble at their places of worship and tender
special homage and gratitude to Almighty God, for this great advancement of the national cause.   A LINCOLN

[1] ADS, MH. This press release probably refers to General Grant's despatch
to Halleck, 4:30 P.M., December 6, "Dispatch just received from General Foster
indicates beyond a doubt that Longstreet is retreating toward Virginia. I have
directed him to be well followed up." (OR, I, XXXI, III, 345).

To Mary Todd Lincoln[1]

Mrs. A Lincoln   Executive Mansion, Washington,
Metropolitan Hotel, N.Y.   Dec. 7. 10/20 AM. 1863.
   All doing well. Tad confidently expects you to-night. When will
you come?   A. LINCOLN

[1] ALS, IHi. Mrs. Lincoln replied: "Will leave here positively at 8 a.m.
Tuesday morning. Have carriage waiting at depot in Washington at 6 p.m. Did
Tad receive his book. Please answer." (Katherine Helm, *Mary, Wife of Lincoln*,
p. 235). See Lincoln's telegram of 7 P.M., *infra*.

To Mary Todd Lincoln[1]

Mrs. A. Lincoln   Executive Mansion, Washington,
Metropolitan Hotel N.Y.   Dec. 7. 7 P.M. 1863.
   Tad has received his book. The carriage shall be ready at 6. PM.
tomorrow.   A. LINCOLN

[1] ALS, IHi.

[35]

Annual Message to Congress[1]

December 8, 1863

Fellow citizens of the Senate and House of Representatives:

Another year of health, and of sufficiently abundant harvests has passed. For these, and especially for the improved condition of our national affairs, our renewed, and profoundest gratitude to God is due.

We remain in peace and friendship with foreign powers.

The efforts of disloyal citizens of the United States to involve us in foreign wars, to aid an inexcusable insurrection, have been unavailing. Her Britannic Majesty's government, as was justly expected, have exercised their authority to prevent the departure of new hostile expeditions from British ports. The Emperor of France has, by a like proceeding, promptly vindicated the neutrality which he proclaimed at the beginning of the contest. Questions of great intricacy and importance have arisen out of the blockade, and other belligerent operations, between the government and several of the maritime powers, but they have been discussed, and, as far as was possible, accommodated in a spirit of frankness, justice, and mutual good will. It is especially gratifying that our prize courts, by the impartiality of their adjudications, have commanded the respect and confidence of maritime powers.

The supplemental treaty between the United States and Great Britain for the suppression of the African slave trade, made on the 17th. day of February last, has been duly ratified, and carried into execution.[2] It is believed that, so far as American ports and American citizens are concerned, that inhuman and odious traffic has been brought to an end.

I shall submit, for the consideration of the Senate, a convention for the adjustment of possessory claims in Washington Territory, arising out of the treaty of the 15th. June, 1846, between the United States and Great Britain, and which have been the source

[1] DS, DNA RG 233, Thirty-eighth Congress, First Session, House of Representatives Executive Document No. 1; ADf (partial), DLC-RTL. The preliminary draft, partly in Lincoln's autograph but incomplete and differing from the official signed copy in numerous instances, indicates that considerable revision took place before the official copy was made. No intervening draft or copy, however, has been located. The official copy generally follows the draft in matters of style but differs in order of passages and in portions which were added later than the text of the draft. There are also certain passages in the draft which were omitted in the official copy and in the printed text (Thirty-eighth Congress, First Session, *House of Representatives Executive Document No. 1*). These omitted passages have been given in succeeding footnotes, as they occur. For the various reports of cabinet members submitted with this message and to which Lincoln makes repeated reference, see *Executive Document No. 1*.

[2] See Lincoln's communication to the Senate, February 18, *supra*.

of some disquiet among the citizens of that now rapidly improving part of the country.[3]

A novel and important question, involving the extent of the maritime jurisdiction of Spain in the waters which surround the island of Cuba, has been debated without reaching an agreement, and it is proposed in an amicable spirit to refer it to the arbitrament of a friendly power. A convention for that purpose will be submitted to the Senate.[4]

I have thought it proper, subject to the approval of the Senate, to concur with the interested commercial powers in an arrangement for the liquidation of the Scheldt dues upon the principles which have been heretofore adopted in regard to the imposts upon navigation in the waters of Denmark.[5]

The long pending controversy between this government and that of Chili touching the seizure at Sitana, in Peru, by Chilian officers, of a large amount in treasure belonging to citizens of the United States, has been brought to a close by the award of His Majesty, the King of the Belgians, to whose arbitration the question was referred by the parties.[6] The subject was thoroughly and patiently examined by that justly respected magistrate, and although the sum awarded to the claimants may not have been as large as they expected, there is no reason to distrust the wisdom of his Majesty's decision. That decision was promptly complied with by Chili, when intelligence in regard to it reached that country.

The joint commission, under the act of the last session, for carrying into effect the convention with Peru on the subject of claims, has been organized at Lima, and is engaged in the business intrusted to it.[7]

Difficulties concerning inter-oceanic transit through Nicaragua are in course of amicable adjustment.[8]

In conformity with principles set forth in my last annual message, I have received a representative from the United States of Colombia, and have accredited a minister to that republic.[9]

[3] See Lincoln's communication to the Senate, December 17, *infra*.

[4] No convention seems to have been submitted. The current dispute arose when the U.S.S. *Reaney* was stopped six miles out of Havana by a Spanish warship on January 23, 1863.

[5] See Lincoln's communication to the Senate, December 22, *infra*.

[6] See Lincoln's letter to Leopold, June 13, *supra*.

[7] See Lincoln's communication to the Senate, February 5, *supra*.

[8] The Nicaraguan revolution of 1863 had increased existing difficulties of transit across the Isthmus of Panama on the inter-ocean route from New York to California and return.

[9] Following the revolution in 1863, New Granada became the United States of Colombia. Eustorgio Salgar was accredited minister to the United States, and Allen A. Burton, U.S. minister to Colombia.

Incidents occurring in the progress of our civil war have forced upon my attention the uncertain state of international questions, touching the rights of foreigners in this country and of United States citizens abroad.[10] In regard to some governments these rights are at least partially defined by treaties. In no instance, however, is it expressly stipulated that, in the event of civil war, a foreigner residing in this country, within the lines of the insurgents, is to be exempted from the rule which classes him as a belligerent, in whose behalf the government of his country cannot expect any privileges or immunities distinct from that character. I regret to say, however, that such claims have been put forward, and, in some instances, in behalf of foreigners who have lived in the United States the greater part of their lives.

There is reason to believe that many persons born in foreign countries, who have declared their intention to become citizens, or who have been fully naturalized, have evaded the military duty required of them by denying the fact, and thereby throwing upon the government the burden of proof. It has been found difficult or impracticable to obtain this proof from the want of guides to the proper sources of information. These might be supplied by requiring clerks of courts, where declarations of intention may be made or naturalizations effected, to send, periodically, lists of the names of the persons naturalized, or declaring their intention to become citizens, to the Secretary of the Interior, in whose department those names might be arranged and printed for general information.

There is also reason to believe that foreigners frequently become citizens of the United States for the sole purpose of evading duties imposed by the laws of their native countries, to which, on becoming naturalized here, they at once repair, and though never returning to the United States, they still claim the interposition of this government as citizens. Many altercations and great prejudices have heretofore arisen out of this abuse. It is therefore, submitted to your serious consideration. It might be advisable to fix a limit, beyond which no Citizen of the United States residing abroad may claim the interposition of his government.[11]

The right of suffrage has often been assumed and exercised by aliens, under pretences of naturalization, which they have disavowed when drafted into the military service. I submit the expediency of such an amendment of the law as will make the fact of voting an estoppel against any plea of exemption from military

---

[10] See Lincoln's proclamation of May 8, *supra.*

[11] No action on this suggestion seems to have been taken by this session of congress.

service, or other civil obligation, on the ground of alienage.[12]

In common with other western powers, our relations with Japan have been brought into serious jeopardy, through the perverse opposition of the hereditary aristocracy of the empire, to the enlightened and liberal policy of the Tycoon designed to bring the country into the society of nations. It is hoped, although not with entire confidence, that these difficulties may be peacefully overcome. I ask your attention to the claim of the Minister residing there for the damages he sustained in the destruction by fire of the residence of the legation at Yedo.[13]

Satisfactory[14] arrangements have been made with the Emperor of Russia, which, it is believed, will result in effecting a continuous line of telegraph through that empire from our Pacific coast.[15]

I recommend to your favorable consideration the subject of an international telegraph across the Atlantic ocean; and also of a telegraph between this capital and the national forts along the Atlantic seaboard and the Gulf of Mexico.[16] Such communications, established with any reasonable outlay, would be economical as well as effective aids to the diplomatic, military, and naval service.

The consular system of the United States, under the enactments of the last Congress, begins to be self-sustaining;[17] and there is

---

[12] An act to amend the "act for enrolling and calling out the National Forces" of March 3, 1863, approved February 24, 1864, provided that no person of foreign birth should be exempted from the enrollment who had held office or voted in any election held under the laws of a state or territory.

[13] The American legation at Yedo was destroyed by fire on May 24, 1863. Incendiarism was suspected. On September 1, 1863, Secretary Seward directed Robert H. Pruyn, minister to Japan, to submit losses by himself and his staff. No action seems to have been taken at this session of congress.

[14] Deleted from the message before the official copy was made, the following passage appears in the preliminary draft, just preceding this sentence: "There are indications that the establishment of commercial steam lines of communication with the ports of Spanish America and Brazil, would be rewarded with a large increase of commerce; and the growth of strong, sincere and reliable national attachments throughout the States of Central and Southern America. The policy, though less essential, might be advantageously extended to the commercial states of Western Europe."

[15] An act approved July 1, 1864, "to facilitate Telegraphic communication between the Eastern and Western Continents," gave to Perry M. Collins of California the right to construct lines north to Canada and authorized the Army and Navy to aid Collins' concern, the Russian and American Telegraph Company, chartered to construct a line from the Amur River across the Bering Sea and to San Francisco.

[16] The act approved June 15, 1864, for Army appropriations, provided $275,000 for construction, extension, and operation of the telegraph.

[17] Lincoln may refer to the act of March 3, 1863, "to prevent and punish frauds upon the revenue," which stipulated that all goods exported to the U.S. must be invoiced and a certificate issued by the consul at the port from which shipment was made, thereby increasing collection of import duties.

reason to hope that it may become entirely so, with the increase of trade which will ensue whenever peace is restored. Our ministers abroad have been faithful in defending American rights. In protecting commercial interests, our Consuls have necessarily had to encounter increased labors and responsibilities, growing out of the war. These they have, for the most part, met and discharged with zeal and efficiency. This acknowledgment justly includes those Consuls who, residing in Morocco, Egypt, Turkey, Japan, China, and other oriental countries, are charged with complex functions and extraordinary powers.

The condition of the several organized Territories is generally satisfactory, although Indian disturbances in New Mexico have not been entirely suppressed. The mineral resources of Colorado, Nevada, Idaho, New Mexico, and Arizona are proving far richer than has been heretofore understood. I lay before you a communication on this subject from the governor of New Mexico.[18] I again submit to your consideration the expediency of establishing a system for the encouragement of immigration. Although this source of national wealth and strength is again flowing with greater freedom than for several years before the insurrection occurred, there is still a great deficiency of laborers in every field of industry, especially in agriculture and in our mines, as well of iron and coal as of the precious metals. While the demand for labor is thus increased here, tens of thousands of persons, destitute of remunerative occupation, are thronging our foreign consulates, and offering to emigrate to the United States if essential, but very cheap, assistance can be afforded them. It is easy to see that, under the sharp discipline of civil war, the nation is beginning a new life. This noble effort demands the aid, and ought to receive the attention and support of the government.[19]

Injuries, unforseen by the government and unintended, may, in some cases, have been inflicted on the subjects or citizens of foreign countries, both at sea and on land, by persons in the service of the United States. As this government expects redress from other powers when similar injuries are inflicted by persons in their service upon citizens of the United States, we must be prepared to do justice to foreigners. If the existing judicial tribunals are inadequate to this purpose, a special court may be authorized, with power to hear and decide such claims of the character referred to as may have arisen under treaties and the public law. Conventions

[18] On August 23, 1863, Governor Henry Connelly of New Mexico Territory reported to Secretary Seward on the discovery of gold fields in Arizona.
[19] An act to encourage immigration was approved on July 4, 1864.

for adjusting the claims by joint commission have been proposed to some governments, but no definitive answer to the proposition has yet been received from any.

In the course of the session I shall probably have occasion to request you to provide indemnification to claimants where decrees of restitution have been rendered, and damages awarded by admiralty courts; and in other cases where this government may be acknowledged to be liable in principle, and where the amount of that liability has been ascertained by an informal arbitration.

The proper officers of the treasury have deemed themselves required, by the law of the United States upon the subject, to demand a tax upon the incomes of foreign consuls in this country. While such a demand may not, in strictness, be in derogation of public law, or perhaps of any existing treaty between the United States and a foreign country, the expediency of so far modifying the act as to exempt from tax the income of such consuls as are not citizens of the United States, derived from the emoluments of their office, or from property not situated in the United States, is submitted to your serious consideration.[20] I make this suggestion upon the ground that a comity which ought to be reciprocated exempts our Consuls, in all other countries, from taxation to the extent thus indicated. The United States, I think, ought not to be exceptionally illiberal to international trade and commerce.

The operations of the treasury during the last year have been successfully conducted. The enactment by Congress of a national banking law[21] has proved a valuable support of the public credit; and the general legislation in relation to loans has fully answered the expectations of its favorers. Some amendments may be required to perfect existing laws; but no change in their principles or general scope is believed to be needed.

Since these measures have been in operation, all demands on the treasury, including the pay of the army and navy, have been promptly met and fully satisfied. No considerable body of troops, it is believed, were ever more amply provided, and more liberally and punctually paid; and it may be added that by no people were the burdens incident to a great war ever more cheerfully borne.

The receipts during the year from all sources, including loans and the balance in the treasury at its commencement, were $901,125,674 86, and the aggregate disbursements $895,796,630.65, leaving a balance on the 1st. July, 1863, of $5,329,044.21. Of the

[20] Section 8 of the act "to increase the Internal Revenue," approved on March 7, 1864, provided exemption for foreign consuls.
[21] The act of February 25, 1863.

receipts there were derived from customs, $69,059,642.40; from internal revenue, $37,640,787.95; from direct tax, $1,485,103.61; from lands, $167,617.17; from miscellaneous sources, $3,046,615.-35; and from loans, $776,682,361.57; making the aggregate, $901,-125,674.86. Of the disbursements there were for the civil service, $23,253,922.08; for pensions and Indians, $4,216,520.79; for interest on public debt, $24,729,846.51;[22] for the War Department, $599,298,600.83; for the Navy Department, $63,211,105.27; for payment of funded and temporary debt, $181,086,635.07; making the aggregate, $895,796,630.65, and leaving the balance of $5,329,-044.21. But the payment of funded and temporary debt, having been made from moneys borrowed during the year, must be regarded as merely nominal payments, and the moneys borrowed to make them as merely nominal receipts; and their amount, $181,-086,635 07, should therefore be deducted both from receipts and disbursements. This being done, there remains as actual receipts $720,039,039.79; and the actual disbursements, $714,709,995.58, leaving the balance as already stated.

The actual receipts and disbursements for the first quarter, and the estimated receipts and disbursements for the remaining three quarters, of the current fiscal year, 1864, will be shown in detail by the report of the Secretary of the Treasury, to which I invite your attention. It is sufficient to say here that it is not believed that actual results will exhibit a state of the finances less favorable to the country than the estimates of that officer heretofore submitted; while it is confidently expected that at the close of the year both disbursements and debt will be found very considerably less than has been anticipated.

The report of the Secretary of War is a document of great interest. It consists of—

1. The military operations of the year, detailed in the report of the general-in-chief.

2. The organization of colored persons into the war service.

3. The exchange of prisoners, fully set forth in the letter of General Hitchcock.

4. The operations under the act for enrolling and calling out the national forces, detailed in the report of the provost marshal general.

5. The organization of the invalid corps; and

6. The operation of the several departments of the quartermaster general, commissary general, paymaster general, chief of engineers, chief of ordnance, and surgeon general.

[22] This figure reads "$24.729.846.61" in the preliminary draft.

It has appeared impossible to make a valuable summary of this report except such as would be too extended for this place, and hence I content myself by asking your careful attention to the report itself.[23]

The duties devolving on the naval branch of the service during the year, and throughout the whole of this unhappy contest, have been discharged with fidelity and eminent success. The extensive blockade has been constantly increasing in efficiency, as the navy has expanded; yet on so long a line it has so far been impossible to entirely suppress illicit trade. From returns received at the Navy Department, it appears that more than one thousand vessels have been captured since the blockade was instituted, and that the value of prizes already sent in for adjudication amounts to over thirteen millions of dollars.

The naval force of the United States consists at this time of five hundred and eighty-eight vessels, completed and in the course of completion, and of these seventy-five are iron-clad or armored steamers.[24] The events of the war give an increased interest and importance to the navy which will probably extend beyond the war itself.

The armored vessels in our navy completed and in service, or which are under contract and approaching completion, are believed to exceed in number those of any other power. But while these may be relied upon for harbor defence and coast service, others of greater strength and capacity will be necessary for cruising purposes, and to maintain our rightful position on the ocean.

The change that has taken place in naval vessels and naval warfare, since the introduction of steam as a motive-power for ships-of-war, demands either a corresponding change in some of our existing navy yards, or the establishment of new ones, for the construction and necessary repair of modern naval vessels. No inconsider-

[23] See *House of Representatives Executive Document No. 1*, V, 3-510.

[24] The next sentence replaced a long passage in the preliminary draft which read as follows: "As this government is destined to occupy a leading position among maritime powers it is a primary duty to provide the means and adequate establishments for a navy commensurate with its wants. The improvements which have been made in naval architecture and naval armament, and the services which the new class of vessels have already rendered and are destined hereafter to perform are among the marked events which have their origin in the exigencies of the war and the necessities of the times. Other governments have been making large expenditures for years in experiments with a view to attain naval supremacy, but the condition of the country and the emergencies of the period have stimulated the inventive genius of our countrymen into great activity, and the Navy Department, successfully availing itself of what was useful, has applied with effect the novel principles which modern inventions and improvements have developed."

able embarrassment, delay, and public injury have been experienced from the want of such governmental establishments. The necessity of such a navy yard, so furnished, at some suitable place upon the Atlantic seaboard, has on repeated occasions been brought to the attention of Congress by the Navy Department, and is again presented in the report of the Secretary which accompanies this communication. I think it my duty to invite your special attention to this subject, and also to that of establishing a yard and depot for naval purposes upon one of the western rivers.[25] A naval force has been created on those interior waters, and under many disadvantages, within little more than two years, exceeding in numbers the whole naval force of the country at the commencement of the present administration. Satisfactory and important as have been the performances of the heroic men of the navy at this interesting period, they are scarcely more wonderful than the success of our mechanics and artisans in the production of war vessels which has created a new form of naval power.

Our country has advantages superior to any other nation in our resources of iron and timber, with inexhaustible quantities of fuel in the immediate vicinity of both, and all available and in close proximity to navigable waters. Without the advantage of public works the resources of the nation have been developed and its power displayed in the construction of a navy of such magnitude which has, at the very period of its creation, rendered signal service to the Union.

The increase of the number of seamen in the public service, from seven thousand five hundred men, in the spring of 1861, to about thirty four thousand at the present time has been accomplished without special legislation, or extraordinary bounties to promote that increase. It has been found, however, that the operation of the draft, with the high bounties paid for army recruits, is beginning to affect injuriously the naval service, and will, if not corrected, be likely to impair its efficiency, by detaching seamen from their proper vocation and inducing them to enter the Army.[26] I

---

[25] Several resolutions on the subject of navy yards failed of adoption, but a joint resolution approved on June 30, 1864, authorized the secretary of the navy to appoint a commission to select a site for a navy yard on the Mississippi and to report to congress.

[26] The next sentence replaced a long passage in the preliminary draft which read as follows: "It is of paramount importance that the naval service, which must always give strength and renown to the Union, should be cherished and sustained. I therefore think it proper to authorise mariners or professional seamen who may enlist under the late call for 300,000 volunteers to enter the naval or army service at their election; and in view of the exactions which may be made upon the maratime communities, if compelled to furnish the full

therefore respectfully suggest that Congress might aid both the army and naval services by a definite provision on this subject, which would at the same time be equitable to the communities more especially interested.[27]

I commend to your consideration the suggestions of the Secretary of the Navy in regard to the policy of fostering and training seamen,[28] and also the education of officers and engineers for the naval service. The Naval Academy is rendering signal service in preparing midshipmen for the highly responsible duties which in after life they will be required to perform. In order that the country should not be deprived of the proper quota of educated officers, for which legal provision has been made at the naval school, the vacancies caused by the neglect or omission to make nominations from the States in insurrection have been filled by the Secretary of the Navy.

The school is now more full and complete than at any former period, and in every respect entitled to the favorable consideration of Congress.[29]

During the past fiscal year the financial condition of the Post

---

complement of army recruits in addition to those of their citizens who may enter the navy, I [respectfully(?)] suggest that the townships and states should each be credited on their respective quotas with the number who may hereafter enter the navy. If in the judgment of congress any further legislation be needed to authorise this policy and give it effect, then I recommend such legislative action."

[27] Section 9 of the act to amend the enrollment act of March 3, 1863, approved on February 24, 1864, provided that navy and marine enlistments be credited to the locality of enrollment as part of the draft quota.

[28] See *House of Representatives Executive Document No. 1*, IV, xviii-xx. Secretary Welles suggested that steam engineering be a part of every officer's training and that a special class be set up at Annapolis to provide two years' training for a class of officers to be third assistant engineers.

[29] An additional paragraph appears in the preliminary draft as follows: "The depredations committed upon American commerce by a class of semi piratical vessels, built, armed and manned abroad, and with no recognised nationality, have naturally excited our countrymen, and sometimes even seemed likely to endanger our friendly relations with other countries. From the protection and assistance extended to them by governments which recognised the insurgents as belligerents and equals, and entitled to all the priviliges of the public national vessels of the United States, these predatory rovers have as yet escaped our cruisers, and are capturing and destroying our merchant vessels upon the high seas without sending them in to any port for adjudication. The general policy of nations in the interest of peace and the moral sentiment of mankind are averse to such lawless proceedings. Governments seem disposed to discountenance the conduct of those who, without a country or port to which they can resort, are depredating on the peaceful commerce of a country with which those governments are in amity. The action recently taken by them indicates a determination to permit no armed vessel with hostile preparation and purpose against our commerce and people to go forth from their shores. These manifestations have, I trust, tranquilized whatever excitement may have at any time existed."

office Department has been one of increasing prosperity, and I am gratified in being able to state that the actual postal revenue has nearly equalled the entire expenditures; the latter amounting to $11,314,206.84, and the former to $11,163,789 59, leaving a deficiency of but $150,417 25. In 1860, the year immediately preceding the rebellion the deficiency amounted to $5,656,705 49, the postal receipts of that year being $2,645,722 19 less than those of 1863. The decrease since 1860 in the annual amount of transportation has been only about 25 per cent, but the annual expenditure on account of the same has been reduced 35 per cent. It is manifest, therefore, that the Post Office Department may become self-sustaining in a few years, even with the restoration of the whole service.

The international conference of postal delegates from the principal countries of Europe and America, which was called at the suggestion of the Postmaster General, met at Paris on the 11th of May last, and concluded its deliberations on the 8th of June. The principles established by the conference as best adapted to facilitate postal intercourse between nations, and as the basis of future postal conventions, inaugurate a general system of uniform international charges, at reduced rates of postage, and cannot fail to produce beneficial results.[30]

I refer you to the report of the Secretary of the Interior, which is herewith laid before you, for useful and varied information in relation to the public lands, Indian affairs, patents, pensions, and other matters of public concern pertaining to his department.[31]

The quantity of land disposed of during the last and the first quarter of the present fiscal years was three million eight hundred and forty one thousand five hundred and forty nine acres, of which one hundred and sixty one thousand nine hundred and eleven acres were sold for cash, one million four hundred and fifty six thousand five hundred and fourteen acres were taken up under the homestead law, and the residue disposed of under laws granting lands for military bounties, for railroad and other purposes. It also appears that the sale of the public lands is largely on the increase.

It has long been a cherished opinion of some of our wisest statesmen that the people of the United States had a higher and more enduring interest in the early settlement and substantial cultivation of the public lands than in the amount of direct revenue to be derived from the sale of them. This opinion has had a controlling influence in shaping legislation upon the subject of our national

30 See *House of Representatives Executive Document No. 1*, V.
31 *Ibid.*, III.

domain. I may cite, as evidence of this, the liberal measures adopted in reference to actual settlers; the grant to the States of the overflowed lands within their limits in order to their being reclaimed and rendered fit for cultivation; the grants to railway companies of alternate sections of land upon the contemplated lines of their roads which, when completed, will so largely multiply the facilities for reaching our distant possessions. This policy has received its most signal and beneficent illustration in the recent enactment granting homesteads to actual settlers.

Since the first day of January last the before-mentioned quantity of one million four hundred and fifty-six thousand five hundred and fourteen acres of land have been taken up under its provisions. This fact and the amount of sales furnish gratifying evidence of increasing settlement upon the public lands, notwithstanding the great struggle in which the energies of the nation have been engaged, and which has required so large a withdrawal of our citizens from their accustomed pursuits. I cordially concur in the recommendation of the Secretary of the Interior suggesting a modification of the act in favor of those engaged in the military and naval service of the United States. I doubt not that Congress will cheerfully adopt such measures as will, without essentially changing the general features of the system, secure to the greatest practicable extent, its benefits to those who have left their homes in the defence of the country in this arduous crisis.[32]

I invite your attention to the views of the Secretary as to the propriety of raising by appropriate legislation a revenue from the mineral lands of the United States.[33]

The measures provided at your last session for the removal of certain Indian tribes have been carried into effect. Sundry treaties have been negotiated which will, in due time, be submitted for the constitutional action of the Senate. They contain stipulations for extinguishing the possessory rights of the Indians to large and valuable tracts of land. It is hoped that the effect of these treaties will result in the establishment of permanent friendly relations

[32] Section 1 of "An act amendatory of the Homestead Law" approved on March 21, 1864, provided that men in the armed services could make affidavit before a commissioned officer of the service, that wives or other relatives residing on land to be entered might file the affidavit with the register, and extended the time for filing in cases where men were called from actual settlement to enter the service.

[33] See *House of Representatives Executive Document No. 1,* III, iv, for the suggestion of a small tax on net profits of gold and silver mines. An act amendatory to the internal revenue act of June 30, 1864, approved on March 3, 1865, provided for a license fee of ten dollars on all who employed others in mining, but no profits tax seems to have been levied.

with such of these tribes as have been brought into frequent and bloody collision with our outlying settlements and emigrants.

Sound policy and our imperative duty to these wards of the government demand our anxious and constant attention to their material well-being, to their progress in the arts of civilization, and, above all, to that moral training which, under the blessing of Divine Providence, will confer upon them the elevated and sanctifying influences, the hopes and consolation of the Christian faith.

I suggested in my last annual message the propriety of remodelling our Indian system. Subsequent events have satisfied me of its necessity. The details set forth in the report of the Secretary evince the urgent need for immediate legislative action.[34]

I commend the benevolent institutions, established or patronized by the government in this District, to your generous and fostering care.

The attention of Congress, during the last session, was engaged to some extent with a proposition for enlarging the water communication between the Mississippi river and the northeastern seaboard, which proposition, however, failed for the time. Since then, upon a call of the greatest respectability a convention has been held at Chicago upon the same subject, a summary of whose views is contained in a memorial addressed to the President and Congress, and which I now have the honor to lay before you. That this interest is one which, ere long, will force its own way, I do not entertain a doubt, while it is submitted entirely to your wisdom as to what can be done now.[35] Augmented interest is given to this subject by the actual commencement of work upon the Pacific railroad, under auspices so favorable to rapid progress and completion. The enlarged navigation becomes a palpable need to the great road.

I transmit the second annual report of the Commissioner of the Department of Agriculture, asking your attention to the developments in that vital interest of the nation.

When[36] Congress assembled a year ago the war had already

[34] Bills introduced by Alexander Ramsey in the Senate (April 29, 1864) and by William Windom in the House (January 29, 1864) failed to become law.

[35] No action was taken. A resolution introduced in the House by Isaac N. Arnold on December 16, 1863, calling for the printing of 10,000 copies of the Memorial from the National Canal Convention, was defeated on December 22.

[36] The preliminary draft is in Lincoln's autograph from this point on. Although the draft is incomplete, we infer that the remainder of the message was Lincoln's composition, while the preceding portions were originally prepared by the various members of the cabinet, with the exception of the opening paragraph, which does not appear in the draft, and which was probably composed by Lincoln.

lasted nearly twenty months, and there had been many conflicts on both land and sea, with varying results.

The rebellion had been pressed back into reduced limits; yet the tone of public feeling and opinion, at home and abroad, was not satisfactory. With other signs, the popular elections, then just past, indicated uneasiness among ourselves, while amid much that was cold and menacing the kindest words coming from Europe were uttered in accents of pity, that we were too blind to surrender a hopeless cause. Our commerce was suffering greatly by a few armed vessels built upon and furnished from foreign shores, and we were threatened with such additions from the same quarter as would sweep our trade from the sea and raise our blockade. We had failed to elicit from European governments anything hopeful upon this subject. The preliminary emancipation proclamation, issued in September, was running its assigned period to the beginning of the new year. A month later the final proclamation came, including the announcement that colored men of suitable condition would be received into the war service. The policy of emancipation, and of employing black soldiers, gave to the future a new aspect, about which hope, and fear, and doubt contended in uncertain conflict. According to our political system, as a matter of civil administration, the general government had no lawful power to effect emancipation in any State, and for a long time it had been hoped that the rebellion could be suppressed without resorting to it as a military measure. It was all the while deemed possible that the necessity for it might come, and that if it should, the crisis of the contest would then be presented. It came, and as was anticipated, it was followed by dark and doubtful days. Eleven months having now passed, we are permitted to take another review. The rebel borders are pressed still further back, and by the complete opening of the Mississippi the country dominated by the rebellion is divided into distinct parts, with no·practical communication between them. Tennessee and Arkansas have been substantially cleared of insurgent control, and influential citizens in each, owners of slaves and advocates of slavery at the beginning of the rebellion, now declare openly for emancipation in their respective States. Of those States not included in the emancipation proclamation, Maryland, and Missouri, neither of which three years ago would tolerate any restraint upon the extension of slavery into new territories, only dispute now as to the best mode of removing it within their own limits.

Of those who were slaves at the beginning of the rebellion, full one hundred thousand are now in the United States military service, about one-half of which number actually bear arms in the ranks; thus giving the double advantage of taking so much labor from the insurgent cause, and supplying the places which otherwise must be filled with so many white men. So far as tested, it is difficult to say they are not as good soldiers as any. No servile insurrection, or tendency to violence or cruelty, has marked the measures of emancipation and arming the blacks. These measures have been much discussed in foreign countries, and contemporary with such discussion the tone of public sentiment there is much improved.[37] At home the same measures have been fully discussed, supported, criticised, and denounced, and the annual elections following are highly encouraging to those whose official duty it is to bear the country through this great trial. Thus we have the new reckoning. The crisis which threatened to divide the friends of the Union is past.

Looking now to the present and future, and with reference to a resumption of the national authority within the States wherein that authority has been suspended, I have thought fit to issue a proclamation, a copy of which is herewith transmitted.[38] On examination of this proclamation it will appear, as is believed, that nothing is attempted beyond what is amply justified by the Constitution. True, the form of an oath is given, but no man is coerced to take it. The man is only promised a pardon in case he voluntarily takes the oath. The Constitution authorizes the Executive to grant or withhold the pardon at his own absolute discretion; and this includes the power to grant on terms, as is fully established by judicial and other authorities.

It is also proffered that if, in any of the States named, a State government shall be, in the mode prescribed, set up, such government shall be recognized and guarantied by the United States, and that under it the State shall, on the constitutional conditions, be protected against invasion and domestic violence. The constitutional obligation of the United States to guaranty to every State in the Union a republican form of government, and to protect the State, in the cases stated, is explicit and full. But why tender the benefits of this provision only to a State government set up in this particular way? This section of the Constitution contemplates a case wherein the element within a State, favorable to republican

---

[37] The preliminary draft includes at this point the following sentence: "The governments of England and France have prevented war vessels, built on their shores to be used against us, from sailing thence."

[38] See Lincoln's proclamation of December 8, *infra*.

government, in the Union, may be too feeble for an opposite and hostile element external to, or even within the State; and such are precisely the cases with which we are now dealing.

An attempt to guaranty and protect a revived State government, constructed in whole, or in preponderating part, from the very element against whose hostility and violence it is to be protected, is simply absurd. There must be a test by which to separate the opposing elements, so as to build only from the sound; and that test is a sufficiently liberal one, which accepts as sound whoever will make a sworn recantation of his former unsoundness.

But if it be proper to require, as a test of admission to the political body, an oath of allegiance to the Constitution of the United States, and to the Union under it, why also to the laws and proclamations in regard to slavery? Those laws and proclamations were enacted and put forth for the purpose of aiding in the suppression of the rebellion. To give them their fullest effect, there had to be a pledge for their maintenance. In my judgment they have aided, and will further aid, the cause for which they were intended. To now abandon them would be not only to relinquish a lever of power, but would also be a cruel and an astounding breach of faith. I[39] may add at this point, that while I remain in my present position I shall not attempt to retract or modify the emancipation proclamation; nor shall I return to slavery any person who is free by the terms of that proclamation, or by any of the acts of Congress. For these and other reasons it is thought best that support of these measures shall be included in the oath; and it is believed the Executive may lawfully claim it in return for pardon and restoration of forfeited rights, which he has clear constitutional power to withhold altogether, or grant upon the terms which he shall deem wisest for the public interest. It should be observed, also, that this part of the oath is subject to the modifying and abrogating power of legislation and supreme judicial decision.

The proposed acquiescence of the national Executive in any reasonable temporary State arrangement for the freed people is made with the view of possibly modifying the confusion and destitution which must, at best, attend all classes by a total revolution of labor throughout whole States. It is hoped that the already deeply afflicted people in those States may be somewhat more ready to give up the cause of their affliction, if, to this extent, this vital matter be left to themselves; while no power of the national Executive to prevent an abuse is abridged by the proposition.

[39] This sentence is not in the preliminary draft.

The[40] suggestion in the proclamation as to maintaining the political framework of the States on what is called reconstruction, is
made in the hope that it may do good without danger of harm. It
will save labor and avoid great confusion.

But why any proclamation now upon this subject? This question
is beset with the conflicting views that the step might be delayed
too long or be taken too soon. In some States the elements for resumption seem ready for action, but remain inactive, apparently
for want of a rallying point—a plan of action. Why shall A adopt
the plan of B, rather than B that of A? And if A and B should
agree, how can they know but that the general government here
will reject their plan? By the proclamation a plan is presented
which may be accepted by them as a rallying point, and which they
are assured in advance will not be rejected here. This may bring
them to act sooner than they otherwise would.

The objections to a premature presentation of a plan by the national Executive consists in the danger of committals on points
which could be more safely left to further developments. Care has
been taken to so shape the document as to avoid embarrassments
from this source. Saying that, on certain terms, certain classes will
be pardoned, with rights restored, it is not said that other classes,
or other terms, will never be included. Saying that reconstruction
will be accepted if presented in a specified way, it is not said it
will never be accepted in any other way.[41]

The movements, by State action, for emancipation in several
of the States, not included in the emancipation proclamation, are
matters of profound gratulation. And while I do not repeat in detail what I have hertofore so earnestly urged upon this subject, my
general views and feelings remain unchanged; and I trust that
Congress will omit no fair opportunity of aiding these important
steps to a great consummation.

In the midst of other cares, however important, we must not
lose sight of the fact that the war power is still our main reliance.
To that power alone can we look, yet for a time, to give confidence

[40] This paragraph was revised by Lincoln from a longer paragraph in the
preliminary draft as follows: "The suggestion in the proclamation, as to maintaining the general old frame-work of the States, on what is called re-construction, is made in the hope that it may do good, without danger of harm.
The question whether these States have continued to be States in the Union, or
have become territories, out of it, seems to me, in every present aspect, to be of
no practical importance. They all have been States in the Union; and all are
to be hereafter, as we all propose; and a controversy whether they have ever
been out of it, might divide and weaken, but could not enhance our strength, in
restoring the proper national and State relations."

[41] The preliminary draft does not go beyond this point.

to the people in the contested regions, that the insurgent power will not again overrun them. Until that confidence shall be established, little can be done anywhere for what is called reconstruction. Hence our chiefest care must still be directed to the army and navy, who have thus far borne their harder part so nobly and well. And it may be esteemed fortunate that in giving the greatest efficiency to these indispensable arms, we do also honorably recognize the gallant men, from commander to sentinel, who compose them, and to whom, more than to others, the world must stand indebted for the home of freedom disenthralled, regenerated, enlarged, and perpetuated.   ABRAHAM LINCOLN

Washington, December 8, 1863.

To Ulysses S. Grant[1]

Major General Grant   Executive Mansion,
Chattanooga, Tenn.   Washington, Dec. 8. 1863.

Understanding that your lodgment at Chattanooga and Knoxville is now secure, I wish to tender you, and all under your command, my more than thanks—my profoundest gratitude—for the skill, courage, and perseverance, with which you and they, over so great difficulties, have effected that important object. God bless you all.   A. LINCOLN

1 ALS, RPB. Grant incorporated this dispatch in his *General Orders No. 7,* Military Division of the Mississippi, December 8, 1863.

Proclamation of Amnesty and Reconstruction[1]

December 8, 1863
By the President of the United States of America:

A Proclamation.

Whereas, in and by the Constitution of the United States, it is provided that the President "shall have power to grant reprieves and pardons for offences against the United States, except in cases of impeachment;" and

Whereas a rebellion now exists whereby the loyal State governments of several States have for a long time been subverted, and

1 DS, DNA FS RG 11, Proclamations; ADS, OCHP; ADfS, DLC-RTL. Unlike most of Lincoln's proclamations, this one is preserved in an autograph draft and an autograph copy, as well as in the official signed copy filed in the Archives. The autograph copy was obtained by Senator John Sherman to be sold at auction by the Great Western Sanitary Fair which was held in Cincinnati, Ohio, beginning on December 21, 1863.

many persons have committed and are now guilty of treason against the United States; and

Whereas, with reference to said rebellion and treason, laws have been enacted by Congress declaring forfeitures and confiscation of property and liberation of slaves, all upon terms and conditions therein stated, and also declaring that the President was thereby authorized at any time thereafter, by proclamation, to extend to persons who may have participated in the existing rebellion, in any State or part thereof, pardon and amnesty, with such exceptions and at such times and on such conditions as he may deem expedient for the public welfare; and

Whereas the congressional declaration for limited and conditional pardon accords with well-established judicial exposition of the pardoning power; and

Whereas, with reference to said rebellion, the President of the United States has issued several proclamations, with provisions in regard to the liberation of slaves; and

Whereas it is now desired by some persons heretofore engaged in said rebellion to resume their allegiance to the United States, and to reinaugurate loyal State governments within and for their respective States; therefore,

I, Abraham Lincoln, President of the United States, do proclaim, declare, and make known to all persons who have, directly or by implication, participated in the existing rebellion, except as hereinafter excepted, that a full pardon is hereby granted to them and each of them, with restoration of all rights of property, except as to slaves, and in property cases where rights of third parties shall have intervened, and upon the condition that every such person shall take and subscribe an oath, and thenceforward keep and maintain said oath inviolate; and which oath shall be registered for permanent preservation, and shall be of the tenor and effect following, to wit:

"I, ———, do solemnly swear, in presence of Almighty God, that I will henceforth faithfully support, protect and defend the Constitution of the United States, and the union of the States thereunder; and that I will, in like manner, abide by and faithfully support all acts of Congress passed during the existing rebellion with reference to slaves, so long and so far as not repealed, modified or held void by Congress, or by decision of the Supreme Court; and that I will, in like manner, abide by and faithfully support all proclamations of the President made during the existing rebellion having reference to slaves, so long and so far as not modified or declared void by decision of the Supreme Court. So help me God."

[54]

The[2] persons excepted from the benefits of the foregoing provisions are all who are, or shall have been, civil or diplomatic officers or agents of the so-called confederate government; all who have left judicial stations under the United States to aid the rebellion; all who are, or shall have been, military or naval officers of said so-called confederate government above the rank of colonel in the army, or of lieutenant in the navy; all who left seats in the United States Congress to aid the rebellion; all who resigned commissions in the army or navy of the United States, and afterwards aided the rebellion; and all who have engaged in any way in treating colored persons or white persons, in charge of such, otherwise than lawfully as prisoners of war, and which persons may have been found in the United States service, as soldiers, seamen, or in any other capacity.

And I do further proclaim, declare, and make known, that whenever, in any of the States of Arkansas, Texas, Louisiana, Mississippi, Tennessee, Alabama, Georgia, Florida, South Carolina, and North Carolina, a number of persons, not less than one-tenth in number of the votes cast in such State at the Presidential election of the year of our Lord one thousand eight hundred and sixty, each having taken the oath aforesaid and not having since violated it, and being a qualified voter by the election law of the State existing immediately before the so-called act of secession, and excluding all others, shall re-establish a State government which shall be republican, and in no wise contravening said oath, such shall be recognized as the true government of the State, and the State shall receive thereunder the benefits of the constitutional provision which declares that "The United States shall guaranty to every State in this union a republican form of government, and shall protect each of them against invasion; and, on application of the legislature, or the executive, (when the legislature cannot be convened,) against domestic violence."

And I do further proclaim, declare, and make known that any provision which may be adopted by such State government in relation to the freed people of such State, which shall recognize and declare their permanent freedom, provide for their education, and which may yet be consistent, as a temporary arrangement, with their present condition as a laboring, landless, and homeless class, will not be objected to by the national Executive. And[3] it is sug-

[2] This paragraph, appearing as an insertion in the autograph draft and autograph copy, was based on a list of exceptions furnished by the War Department and revised by Lincoln (DLC-RTL).

[3] The remainder of this paragraph appears as an autograph insertion in the autograph draft and the autograph copy.

gested as not improper, that, in constructing a loyal State government in any State, the name of the State, the boundary, the subdivisions, the constitution, and the general code of laws, as before the rebellion, be maintained, subject only to the modifications made necessary by the conditions hereinbefore stated, and such others, if any, not contravening said conditions, and which may be deemed expedient by those framing the new State government.

To avoid misunderstanding, it may be proper to say that this proclamation, so far as it relates to State governments, has no reference to States wherein loyal State governments have all the while been maintained. And for the same reason, it may be proper to further say that whether members sent to Congress from any State shall be admitted to seats, constitutionally rests exclusively with the respective Houses, and not to any extent with the Executive. And still further, that this proclamation is intended to present the people of the States wherein the national authority has been suspended, and loyal State governments have been subverted, a mode in and by which the national authority and loyal State governments may be re-established within said States, or in any of them; and, while the mode presented is the best the Executive can suggest, with his present impressions, it must not be understood that no other possible mode would be acceptable.

Given under my hand at the city, of Washington, the 8th. day of December, A.D. one thousand eight hundred and sixty-
[L.S.]   three, and of the independence of the United States of America the eighty-eighth.   ABRAHAM LINCOLN

By the President:

WILLIAM H. SEWARD, Secretary of State.

To the Senate[1]

To the Senate of the United States: December 8, 1863

Congress, on my recommendation, passed a Resolution, approved 7th. February 1863, tendering its thanks to Commander D. D. Porter "for the bravery and skill displayed in the attack on the Post of Arkansas on the 10th. January 1863," and in consideration of those services, together with his efficient labors and vigilance subsequently displayed in thwarting the efforts of the rebels to obstruct the Mississippi and its tributaries, and the important part rendered by the Squadron under his command, which led to the surrender of Vicksburg.

I do therefore, in conformity to the 7th. Section, of the Act approved 16th. July 1862, nominate Commander D. D. Porter, to be a Rear Admiral in the Navy, on the Active List, from the 4th. July 1863, to fill an existing vacancy.   ABRAHAM LINCOLN

Washington, D.C. ⎱
8th. December 1863. ⎰

¹ DS, DNA RG 46, Senate 38B A2. David D. Porter's appointment was confirmed by the Senate on February 2, 1864.

To the Senate and House of Representatives¹

December 8, 1863

To the Senate and House of Representatives.

In conformity to the Law of 16 July, 1862, I most cordially recommend that Captain John Rodgers, U.S. Navy, receive a vote of thanks from Congress for the eminent skill and gallantry exhibited by him in the engagement with the Rebel armed Iron Clad Steamer "Fingal," *alias* "Atlanta," whilst in command of the U.S. Iron Clad Steamer "Weehawken," which led to her capture on the 17 June, 1863, and also for the zeal, bravery and general good conduct shown by this Officer on many occasions.

This recommendation is specially made in order to comply with the requirements of the 9th. Section of the aforesaid Act, which is in the following words, viz:—

"That any line officer of the navy or marine corps may be advanced one grade, if, upon recommendation of the President by name, he receives the thanks of Congress for highly distinguished conduct in conflict with the enemy, or for extraordinary heroism in the line of his profession."   ABRAHAM LINCOLN

Washington, D.C.,
8 December, 1863.

¹ DS, DNA RG 46, Senate 38A F2; DS, DNA RG 233, House Executive Document. The resolution of thanks to Captain John Rodgers was approved on December 23, 1863, and Rodgers' appointment as commodore was confirmed by the Senate on February 2, 1864.

To Andrew G. Curtin¹

His Excellency A. G. Curtin   Executive Mansion,
Governor of Pennsylvania   Washington, Dec. 9, 1863.

My dear Sir   I have to urge my illness and the preparation of the Message in excuse for not having sooner transmitted you the inclosed from the Secretary of War and Provost Marshal-General in response to yours in relation to recruiting in Pennsylvania. Though not quite as you desire, I hope the grounds taken will be

[57]

reasonably satisfactory to you. Allow me to exchange congratulations with you on the organization of the H.R. and especially on recent military events in Georgia & Tennessee. Yours very truly

A. LINCOLN.

[1] ADfS, DLC-RTL. On November 24 Governor Curtin had written that it had become evident the draft could not be successful and had suggested a plan for raising volunteers through state authorities. Lincoln referred the letter to the War Department, and on December 1 James B. Fry returned it with a letter accepting Curtin's suggestions in part, which Lincoln enclosed to Curtin on December 9. Curtin's reply of December 10 was in part as follows: "I would . . . observe that the delay of your reply to my letter (the cause of which I sincerely regret) has brought us so near to the 5th of January that I much fear that little can be done in raising volunteers if the new draft is to be then gone on with. . . ." (OR, III, III, 1163-64).

To George G. Meade[1]

Major-General Meade: [December 9, 1863]

The sentences in the cases of Private John L. Keatly, and James Halter, Company I, Second Delaware Volunteers, are suspended until further orders. Let the records be at once forwarded.

A. LINCOLN.

[1] Tarbell (Appendix), p. 402. This telegram is printed without date in the source, but a note from John Hay to Joseph Holt on December 9 instructed Holt to "order the execution of these men to be suspended until the records can be examined, using the President's signature to your dispatch." (Ibid., p. 403). There is no other telegram to which Hay's note can refer, and Meade replied on December 9 as follows: "Your dispatch of today, suspending the sentences in the cases of Privates John L. Keatly and James Haller, Second Delaware Vols., is received. No proceedings of a court martial in these cases have yet reached me; as soon as communicated with, and as soon as this reply is received I will telegraph you again in the matter." (DLC-RTL).

On January 8, 1864, Meade telegraphed Lincoln, "You telegraphed me on the 9th. Dec. suspending the execution of private Keatley of the 2d. Del. The record in his case has just reached me and as the proceedings are disapproved by the division commander there is no case for my action. Private Keatly will be returned to duty." (Ibid.).

No further reference has been found to James Halter or "Haller."

Memorandum:
Appointment of Ferdinand Brewster[1]

Executive Mansion, Washington, Dec. 9, 1863.

Gen. Cameron wishes Ferdinand Brewster to go to West-Point, and for his sake & that of Mr. Brewster,[2] I wish to do it.

A. LINCOLN

[1] ADS, DNA WR RG 94, U.S. Military Academy, 1863, No. 199. No record of Ferdinand Brewster's appointment has been found.
[2] Benjamin H. Brewster.

To Benjamin F. Butler[1]

Major-General Butler   Washington,
Fort-Monroe, Va.   Dec. 10. 1863.

Please suspend execution in any and all sentences of death in
your Department until further orders.   A. LINCOLN

[1] ALS, RPB. On December 8 General Butler telegraphed, "Do you see any
reason for delaying any longer the execution in the cases referred to you by
Col Shaffer my Chief of Staff" (DLC-RTL). A notation on the telegram, not
Lincoln's, gives the names Peter Donnelley, John Flinn, and Charles Leach.

To Andrew Johnson[1]

South-Western Telegraph Company. Dec 10 1863
By Telegraph from Washington 10 30 am
To Hon Andw Johnson

I still desire very much to see you   can you not come

A LINCOLN

[1] Copy, DLC-Johnson Papers. Governor Johnson replied on December 11, "I
will come." (DLC-RTL).

To Officer in Command at Covington, Kentucky[1]

Officer in Military Command,   Executive Mansion
at Covington, Kentucky   Washington, D.C. Dec. 10. 1863

Let the execution of John A. Welch, under sentence to be shot
for desertion to-morrow, be suspended until further order from
here.   A. LINCOLN.

[1] ALS, RPB. See Lincoln's communications to Evans and to Smith, November
23, *supra*. No further reference to John A. Welch has been discovered. As of
October 31, 1863, Colonel Chauncey G. Hawley was in command at Covington,
Kentucky.

To the Senate and House of Representatives[1]

To the Senate of the United States.   December 10, 1863

I transmit, herewith, a report dated the 9th instant, with the
accompanying papers, received from the Secretary of State, in
compliance with the requirements of the sixteenth and eighteenth
sections of the Act entitled "An Act to regulate the diplomatic and
consular systems of the United States," approved August 18, 1856.

Washington. December 10. 1863.   ABRAHAM LINCOLN

[1] DS, DNA RG 46, Senate 38A F3, Executive Document No. 2; DS, DNA
RG 233. The same communication was sent to each house transmitting copies
of Seward's report, which may be found printed in Thirty-eighth Congress, First
Session, *Senate Executive Document No. 2.*

To Edwin M. Stanton[1]

We will consider this a few days, and prepare instructions. In the mean time, no harm will be done.   A. LINCOLN

Dec. 10. [11 ?] 1863.

[1] AES, NHi. Lincoln's endorsement is written on the back of the following note from Stanton dated December 11, 1863: "General Augur reports that applications for the amnesty are already pouring in upon him!! and he has applied for instructions." Either Stanton's date is incorrect or Lincoln misdates his endorsement. General Christopher C. Augur was in command of the Department of Washington, D.C.

To Salmon P. Chase[1]

December 11, 1863

Hon. Sec. of Treasury please see the bearer Mr. Morrison, of Illinois, who is personally known to me to be a most worthy gentleman.   A. LINCOLN

Dec. 11, 1863

[1] ALS, owned by R. E. Crane, Ford City, Pennsylvania. The bearer of Lincoln's note was perhaps James L. D. Morrison.

To Henry H. Lockwood[1]

December 11, 1863

[Brigadier-General Lockwood, Baltimore, Md.:]

The sentences in the cases of privates William Irons co. D, & Jesse Lewis, co E. 5th. Maryland vols ordered to be carried into execution to day, is hereby suspended until further orders.

Decr. 11th. 1863   A. LINCOLN

[1] LS, RPB. Chief of Staff Donn Piatt replied at 11:25 A.M., "Telegram suspending execution of private Wm Irons Co D & Jesse Lewis Co E 5th Md received 11:15 am today" (DLC-RTL). Both soldiers remained in service, Irons being mustered out on June 14, 1865, and Lewis on December 3, 1864.

To George G. Meade[1]

Executive Mansion, Washington, December 11, 1863.

Major-General Meade, Army of the Potomac:

Lieut. Col. James B. Knox, Tenth Regiment Pennsylvania Reserves, offers his resignation under circumstances inducing me to wish to accept it. But I prefer to know your pleasure upon the subject. Please answer.   A. LINCOLN.

[60]

1 Tarbell (Appendix), p. 404. No reply has been located. The roster of the Thirty-ninth Pennsylvania Volunteers (Tenth Reserve) lists Lieutenant Colonel James B. Knox as resigned on November 23, 1863.

To John M. Schofield[1]

"Cypher"

Gen. J. M. Schofield   Executive Mansion,
St. Louis, Mo.   Washington, Dec. 11. 1863.
    Please come to see me at once.   A LINCOLN

1 ALS, RPB. General Schofield's telegram in reply, "I start this evening," was sent at 10:30 A.M. on December 12 but was not received at Washington until December 13. (DLC-RTL). See Lincoln to Schofield, December 13, *infra*.

To George G. Meade[1]

Executive Mansion, Washington,
Major-General Meade: December 12, 1863.
    Please suspend execution of sentence in case of William F. Goodwin, Company B, Seventeenth Infantry, and forward the record for my examination.   A. LINCOLN.

1 Tarbell (Appendix), p. 404. Meade's reply was received at 4:20 P.M.: "Your telegram in relation to private Wm. F. Goodwin Co "B" 17th. Infy has been recd. and the order to suspend the execution of the sentence till your orders are received, the proceedings will be forwarded." (DLC-RTL). No further reference has been found.

To Edwin M. Stanton[1]

December 12, 1863
Gen. Palmer's resignation was not accepted by me. You remember I promised to write him on the subject, which however I have neglected to do. I do not want him to resign, unless there be some reason not yet known to me.   A. LINCOLN.
    Dec. 12. 1863

1 AES, DLC. Lincoln's endorsement is written on a note from Stanton dated December 12: "Will you please to inform me whether General Palmers resignation was accepted by your direction."
    On October 8, 1863, believing that the order dissolving the Twenty-first Corps, of which his Second Division was a part, was a censure, General John M. Palmer submitted his resignation. Halleck recommended acceptance of the resignation and Stanton endorsed the letter of resignation "to take effect December 1st." On October 28 Palmer was notified of his assignment to command the Fourteenth Army Corps, and after a short leave took over the command (*Personal Recollections of John M. Palmer*, pp. 191 ff.).

[61]

To John M. Schofield[1]

Gen. J. M. Schofield   Executive Mansion.
St. Louis, Mo   Washington, D.C. Dec. 13. 1863.
    On the 11th. I telegraphed, asking you to come here and see me.
Did you receive the despatch?   A. Lincoln

[1] ALS, RPB. See Lincoln to Schofield, December 11, *supra,* and to Stanton, December 18, *infra.*

To Edward Bates[1]

                  Executive Mansion,
My Dear Sir   Washington, December 14, 1863.
    If upon examination of this case you find that the facts are in
accordance with the statement of the petition and that Dr. Ratcliffe
took the oath of allegiance at the invitation of our military authorities & has since kept it inviolate, let him be pardoned for any
treasonable practice previous to such recantation, and freed from
the penalties now hanging over him. Your Obt. Servt
    The Hon   The Attorney Gen'l.   A. Lincoln

[1] LS, DNA RG 204, U.S. Pardon Attorney, A 495. This note is filed with the
case of Charles T. Ratcliffe. No further reference has been found.

Agreement Signed by Samuel L. Casey[1]

                  Washington D.C. Dec. 14. 1863.
    In consideration that the President of the United States to-day
delivers to me a paper of which the within is a copy, I pledge him
my word of honor that whatever I may do thereunder shall be at
my own expence, and risk of person and property, with no claim
upon him, or upon the government in any contingency whatever;
that I will take absolutely nothing into the insurgent lines, which
could be of value to them, except the boats, tows, and provisions, as
stated; and that I will not take said boats, tows, and provisions, or
any of them into said insurgent lines, unless I shall first have the
personal pledge of Gen. Kirby Smith,[2] given directly by him to
me, that said boats and tows shall, without condition, safely return
to our military lines.   S. L. Casey

[1] AD, DLC-RTL. The agreement is in Lincoln's autograph except for the
signature and insertion noted.
[2] On a separate page appears a phrase, not in Lincoln's handwriting, which
was intended as an insertion at this point: "or the officer in chief command."

Order Concerning Samuel L. Casey[1]

Executive Mansion, Washington, December 14, 1863.

All Military and Naval commanders will please give to the Hon. Samuel L. Casey, of Kentucky (with any number of inferior Stern-wheel-Steam-Boats not exceeding three taking in tow any number of barges, scows, flats, and the like, not having Steam-power, which they may be able to so take, without money, and without cargoes outgoing, and only with crews to navigate the whole, and necessary provisions for himself and said crews) protection and safe-conduct from Cairo to Red River, and up said river, and it's tributaries, till he shall pass beyond our Military lines, and also give him such protection and safe conduct, on his return to our lines, back to Cairo with any cargoes he may bring; and on his safe return from beyond our lines, with said boats and tows, allow him to repeat once or twice if he shall desire.   A. LINCOLN

[1] ADfS, DLC-RTL. A copy of this order preserved in the Nathaniel P. Banks Papers (Essex Institute, Salem, Massachusetts) preserves endorsements by Rear Admiral David D. Porter and Major General Banks ordering all officers to respect the president's wishes. Casey and others owned a large amount of cotton which they wished to bring North. See further Lincoln's order of February 29, 1864, *infra.*

Amnesty to Emily T. Helm[1]

Executive Mansion, Washington, December 14. 1863.

Mrs. Emily T. Helm, not being excepted from the benefits of the proclamation by the President of the United States issued on the 8th. day of December. 1863, and having on this day taken and subscribed the oath according to said proclamation, she is fully relieved of all penalties and forfeitures, and remitted to all her rights, all according to said proclamation, and not otherwise; and, in regard to said restored rights of person and property, she is to be protected and afforded facilities as a loyal person.

ABRAHAM LINCOLN

P.S. Mrs. Helm claims to own some cotten at Jackson, Mississippi, and also some in Georgia; and I shall be glad, upon either place being brought within our lines, for her to be afforded the proper facilities to show her ownership, and take her property.

A. LINCOLN.

[1] ADS copy, DLC-RTL. Although the widow of Ben Hardin Helm signed her name "Emily" other sources are unanimous in giving it as "Emilie." See also Lincoln's communication to whom it may concern, *infra.* Orville H. Browning's *Diary* records under date of December 14: "The President told me his sister in

law, Mrs Helm was in the house, but he did not wish it known. She wished an order for the protection of some Cotton she had at Jackson, Mississippi. He thought she ought to have it, but he was afraid he would be censured if he did so."

When Mrs. Helm arrived at the White House is not certain. Some time after October (see Lincoln to Todd, October 31, *supra*), she arrived at Fort Monroe, where upon her refusing to take the oath of allegiance, an officer is supposed to have telegraphed Lincoln, who replied, "Send her to me." (Katherine Helm, *Mary, Wife of Lincoln,* p. 221). No trace of these telegrams has been discovered.

Oath of Emily T. Helm[1]

District of Columbia ⎱
Washington County ⎰ SS   [December 14, 1863]

I, Emily T. Helm, do solemnly swear in presence of Almighty God that I will henceforth faithfully support, protect and defend the Constitution of the United States, and the union of the States thereunder; and that I will, in like manner, abide by, and faithfully support all acts of Congress passed during the existing rebellion with reference to slaves, so long and so far as not repealed, modified, or held void by Congress, or by decision of the Supreme Court; and that I will, in like manner, abide by, and faithfully support all proclamations of the President, made during the existing rebellion, having reference to slaves so long and so far as not modified, or declared void by the Supreme Court. So help me God.

[1] AD copy, DLC-RTL.

To Whom It May Concern[1]

Executive Mansion,
Whom it may concern   Washington, December 14. 1863.

It is my wish that Mrs. Emily T. Helm, (widow of the late Gen. B. H. Helm, who fell in the Confederate service) now returning to Kentucky, may have protection of person and property, except as to slaves, of which I say nothing.   A. LINCOLN

[1] ADS copy, DLC-RTL.

To George G. Meade[1]

Executive Mansion,
Major-General Meade: Washington, December 14, 1863.

Please suspend execution in case of William Gibson, Fourth Maine Regiment until further order and send record.

A. LINCOLN.

[1] Tarbell (Appendix), p. 405. No later reference has been discovered.

To George G. Meade[1]

Executive Mansion,
Major-General Meade: Washington, December 14, 1863.
Please suspend execution of Lewis Beers, Fourteenth U.S. Infantry, and of William J. Hazlett, One hundred and nineteenth Pennsylvania Volunteers and send record. A. LINCOLN.

[1] Tarbell (Appendix), p. 405. No later reference has been discovered.

Memorandum and Endorsement
Concerning James B. Rodgers[1]

December 14, 1863
It is sought in this case that, Lieut. Rodgers, having offered his resignation, because of physical disability, the sentence of reprimand, be revoked.

The Recommendation of Gen. Geary is approved. A. LINCOLN
Dec. 14. 1863.

[1] AE and ES, DNA WR RG 153, Judge Advocate General, MM 858. Lincoln's undated memorandum is written on a medical certificate that Rodgers is sick and unfit for duty. The endorsement, in Hay's hand but signed by Lincoln, is written at bottom of the record. Lieutenant James B. Rodgers of the One Hundred Ninth Pennsylvania Volunteers was cashiered for being absent without leave. General Geary recommended commutation to forfeiture of pay for period of absence. Rodgers was discharged April 9, 1864.

Recommendation for John Alexander[1]

I believe Mr. Alexander is a very worthy gentleman, and a very competent one in the line in which he proposes to be engaged
Dec. 14. 1863. A. LINCOLN

[1] AES-P, ISLA. Lincoln's endorsement is written on a letter from Mrs. Lincoln to Clerk of the House of Representatives Edward McPherson, recommending Alexander as "an applicant for the upholstering under you and from the work done at the Executive Mansion by him I can certify to his competency. . . ."

To Edwin M. Stanton[1]

December 14, 1863
Let Henry N. Warfield, named within, be paroled and delivered to the custody,—bailed, so to speak,—to his brother-in-law, Dr. L. W. Brown, who and whose brothers are very near friends of mine in Illinois. A. LINCOLN.
December 14, 1863.

¹ Leslie J. Perry, "Appeals to Lincoln's Clemency," *The Century Magazine,* LI (December, 1895), 252. Lloyd W. Brown, the brother of James N. Brown, married Rebecca P. Warfield. According to Perry, "Henry N. Warfield of Lexington, Ky., a prisoner of war at Camp Douglas, Chicago, in company with other Confederate prisoners made his escape from that military prison on the night of December 2, 1862 [1863?], and made his way to the house of his brother-in-law, Dr. L. W. Brown, who resided thirteen miles east of Jacksonville, Morgan County, Ill. Dr. Brown was a loyal man, and advised Warfield, who was a lad of only eighteen, to surrender himself to the Union military authorities and then take the oath of allegiance. This he did at Jacksonville, after which a petition signed by Governor Yates, Senator Trumbull, E. B. Washburne, I. N. Arnold, and several other political notabilities, was forwarded to the President for his release." Orville H. Browning's *Diary* records under date of December 14, 1863, that he visited Lincoln with Dr. Brown "to try and get Henry Warfield, a lad of 18 years old, a rebel Prisoner at Camp Douglas, and a brother in law of Dr Brown, committed to the custody of the Dr. Got a preliminary order which was finally completed after passing thro several offices to the Commissary of Prisoners. . . ."

To Thomas Cottman¹

Dr. Thomas Cottman   Executive Mansion,
My Dear Sir   Washington, December 15, 1863.

You were so kind as to say this morning that you desire to return to Louisiana, and to be guided by my wishes, to some extent, in the part you may take in bringing that state to resume her rightful relation to the general government.

My wishes are in a general way expressed as well as I can express them, in the Proclamation issued on the 8th of the present month, and in that part of the annual message which relates to that proclamation. It there appears that I deem the sustaining of the emancipation proclamation, where it applies, as indispensable; and I add here that I would esteem it fortunate, if the people of Louisiana should themselves place the remainder of the state upon the same footing, and then, if in their discretion it should appear best, make some temporary provision for the whole of the freed people, substantially as suggested in the last proclamation. I have not put forth the plan in that proclamation, as a Procrustean bed, to which exact conformity is to be indispensable; and in Louisiana particularly, I wish that labor already done, which varies from that plan in no important particular, may not be thrown away.

The strongest wish I have, not already publicly expressed, is that in Louisiana and elsewhere, all sincere Union men would stoutly eschew cliqueism, and, each yielding something in minor matters, all work together. Nothing is likely to be so baleful in the great work before us, as stepping aside of the main object to consider who will get the offices if a small matter shall go thus, and who else will get them, if it shall go otherwise. It is a time now for real patriots to rise above all this. As to the particulars of what I may think best to be done in any state, I have publicly stated certain points, which I have thought indispensable to the reestablishment and maintenance of the national authority; and I go no further than this because I wish to avoid both the substance and the appearance of dictation.

¹ Copy, DLC-RTL.

To William P. Fessenden¹

December 15, 1863

Mr. Fessenden will see the objection to the pardon applied for, as made at the Attorney General's office. Could not he & the others of the Maine delegation fortyfy me a little stronger? Something from the Judge & jury or District Attorney would be in point.

Dec. 15. 1863   A. LINCOLN

Atty. Genl. please file.   A. LINCOLN
April 8. 1864

¹ AES, DNA RG 204, U.S. Pardon Attorney, A 495. Lincoln's endorsements are written on the envelope containing Fessenden's letter of December 4, 1863, transmitting a petition for pardon of Josiah M. Sargent sentenced to nine years' imprisonment for robbing a post office. On Fessenden's letter appears the following endorsement by John Hay dated December 11: "The President directs me to request that you will cause a pardon to be prepared in this case, unless there appear to you reasons to the contrary."

To Mother Mary Gonyeag¹

Mother Mary Gonyeag   Executive Mansion
Sup. Academy of Visitation   Washington D.C.
Keokuk, Iowa   Dec. 15. 1863

The President has no authority as to whether you may raffle for the benevolent object you mention. If there is no objection in the Iowa laws, there is none here.   A. LINCOLN.

¹ ALS, RPB. No communication from Mother Mary Gonyeag has been found.

To Ogden Hoffman¹

Hon. Ogden Hoffman   Executive Mansion
U.S. District Judge   Washington, D.C.
San Francisco, California   Dec. 15. 1863.

The oath in the proclamation of Dec. 8th. is intended for those who may *voluntarily* take it, and not for those who may be *con-*

strained to take it, in order to escape actual imprisonment or punishment. It is intended that the latter class shall abide the granting or withholding of the pardoning power in the ordinary way.

A. LINCOLN.

1 ALS, RPB. No prior communication from Judge Hoffman has been located, but on December 15 Hoffman replied to Lincoln's telegram: "Your Excellency's dispatch is received. I most respectfully suggest inasmuch as the Proclamation does not in terms refer to by you in your dispatch & as it is a public official document which a court is compelled to construe according to its terms whether it be not expedient to declare by our equally formal document the intention of the Executive in making it." (DLC-RTL).

To the Senate[1]

To the Senate of the United States: December [15], 1863

I lay before the Senate, for its constitutional action thereon, a treaty concluded at the city of Washington on the sixth day of April, 1863, between John P. Usher, commissioner on the part of the United States, and the chiefs and headmen of the Comanche, Kiowa, and Apache tribes of Indians, duly authorized thereto.

A letter of the Secretary of the Interior of the 12th instant accompanies the treaty.   ABRAHAM LINCOLN.

Executive Mansion, Washington,
December, 1863.

1 *Executive Journal*, XIII, 313. On April 5, 1864, the treaty was reported from the Committee on Indian Affairs without amendment, but no further action was taken.

To the Senate[1]

To the Senate of the United States: December [15], 1863

I lay before the Senate, for its constitutional action thereon, a treaty concluded at LeRoy, Kansas, on the twenty-ninth day of August, 1863, between William P. Dole, Commissioner of Indian Affairs, and William G. Coffin, superintendent of Indian affairs of the Southern Superintendency, commissioners on the part of the United States, and the chiefs and headmen of the Great and Little Osage tribe of Indians of the State of Kansas.

A communication from the Secretary of the Interior, dated the 12th instant, accompanies the treaty.   ABRAHAM LINCOLN.

Executive Mansion, Washington,
December, 1863.

1 *Executive Journal*, XIII, 313. The treaty was ratified with amendments on July 2, 1864.

To the Senate[1]

To the Senate of the United States: December [15], 1863

I lay before the Senate, for its constitutional action thereon, a treaty concluded at the Sac and Fox Agency, in Kansas, on the 2d day of September, 1863, between William P. Dole, Commissioner of Indian Affairs, commissioner on the part of the United States, and the New York Indians, represented by duly authorized members of the bands of said tribe.

A letter of the Secretary of the Interior of the 12th instant accompanies the treaty.   ABRAHAM LINCOLN.

Executive Mansion, Washington,
December, 1863.

[1] *Executive Journal*, XIII, 313. On December 15, 1863, the treaty was referred to the Committee on Indian Affairs, but no further action was taken.

To the Senate[1]

To the Senate of the United States: December [15], 1863

I lay before the Senate, for its constitutional action thereon, a treaty concluded at the Sac and Fox Agency in Kansas on the 3d day of September, 1863, between William P. Dole, Commissioner of Indian Affairs, and William G. Coffin, superintendent of Indian affairs for the Southern Superintendency, on the part of the United States, and the Creek Nation of Indians, represented by its chiefs.

A letter from the Secretary of the Interior, dated the 12th instant, accompanies the treaty.   ABRAHAM LINCOLN.

Executive Mansion, Washington,
December, 1863.

[1] *Executive Journal*, XIII, 314. The treaty was ratified with amendments on March 8, 1864.

To the Senate[1]

To the Senate of the United States: December [15], 1863

I lay before the Senate, for its constitutional action thereon, a treaty concluded at the Sac and Fox Agency, in Kansas, on the fourth day of September, 1863, between William P. Dole, Commissioner of Indian Affairs, and Henry W. Martin, agent for the Sacs and Foxes, commissioners on the part of the United States, and the united tribes of Sac and Fox Indians of the Mississippi.

A letter from the Secretary of the Interior, dated the 12th instant, accompanies the treaty. ABRAHAM LINCOLN.
Executive Mansion, Washington,
December, 1863.

[1] *Executive Journal*, XIII, 314. The treaty was ratified with amendments on July 2, 1864.

To the Senate[1]

To the Senate of the United States: December [15], 1863
I lay before the Senate, for its constitutional action thereon, a treaty concluded on the 7th day of October, 1863, at Conejos, Colorado Territory, between John Evans, governor and *ex-officio* superintendent of Indian affairs of said Territory, Michael Steck, superintendent of Indian affairs for the Territory of New Mexico, Simeon Whitely and Lafayette Head, Indian agents, commissioners on the part of the United States, and the chiefs and warriors of the Tabequache band of Utah Indians.
I also transmit a report of the Secretary of the Interior, of the 12th instant, submitting the treaty; an extract from the last annual report of Governor Evans, of Colorado Territory, relating to its negotiation; and a map upon which is delineated the boundaries of the country ceded by the Indians, and that retained for their own use. ABRAHAM LINCOLN.
Executive Mansion, Washington,
December, 1863.

[1] *Executive Journal*, XIII, 314. The treaty was ratified with amendments on March 25, 1864.

To the Senate[1]

To the Senate of the United States: December 15, 1863
In answer to the Resolution of the Senate of the 11th. of March last, requesting certain information touching persons in the service of this Government, I transmit a report from the Secretary of State, to whom the resolution was referred.
Washington, 15th. Decr. 1863. ABRAHAM LINCOLN

[1] DS, DNA RG 46, Senate 38A F3. Lincoln's letter together with Seward's report was referred to the Committee on the Judiciary, which on January 25, 1864, was discharged from further consideration of the report. The resolution of March 11, 1863, called for a report on the aggregate number of civil employees of the government subject to removal by the president or any other officer, and the aggregate amount of pay received by them.

Memorandum Concerning Louisiana Affairs[1]

December 16, 1863

On very full consideration I do not wish to say more than I have publicly said, and said in the letter delivered to Dr. Cottman yesterday.   A. LINCOLN

Dec. 16. 1863.

[1] AES, DLC-RTL. Lincoln's endorsement is written on a letter from John L. Riddell, noted chemist, botanist, and professor in the medical department of University of Louisiana, New Orleans, December 15, 1863, requesting that the president so instruct military authorities in Louisiana "that our loyal efforts . . . may be facilitated and not discouraged or prevented. It is proper to state, that a comparatively small party of over zealous men . . . ignoring and contravening the constitution of the state . . . are laboring to call a state convention, whose delegates are to be voted for by residents of six months, instead of a year, the constitutional time; and by free negroes, who do not possess the right of voting under the constitution. . . ."

Pardon of Alfred Rubery[1]

[December 16, 1863?]

Whereas one Alfred Rubery was convicted on or about the twelfth day of October 1863, in the Circuit Court of the United States for the District of California, of engaging in, and giving aid and comfort to the existing rebellion against the Government of this country, and sentenced to ten years' imprisonment, and to pay a fine of ten thousand dollars;

And whereas, the said Alfred Rubery is of the immature age of twenty years, and of highly respectable parentage;

And whereas, the said Alfred Rubery is a subject of Great Britain, and his pardon is desired by John Bright, of England;

Now therefore, be it known that I, Abraham Lincoln, President of the United States of America, these and divers other considerations me thereunto moving, and especially as a public mark of the esteem held by the United States of America for the high character and steady friendship of the said John Bright, do hereby grant a pardon to the said Alfred Rubery, the same to begin and take effect on the twentieth day of January, 1864, on condition that he leave the country within thirty days from and after that date.

[1] George M. Trevelyan, *The Life of John Bright*, p. 296. Although undated and unsigned as given in the source, this pardon has been dated from a despatch of December 16, 1863, appearing in the New York *Times* for December 17:

"The President to-day pardoned Alfred Rubers [*sic*], a young Englishman, convicted of high treason for having fitted out a secesh privateer at San Francisco in October and sentenced to ten years imprisonment and a fine of $10,000. The pardon was solicited by John Bright through Senator Sumner, and the President in the body of it expresses his high gratification at having been able to oblige a devoted English friend of the Union."

Proclamation Concerning Discriminating Duties[1]

December 16, 1863

By the President of the United States of America:

A Proclamation.

Whereas, by an act of the Congress of the United States of the 24th. of May, one thousand eight hundred and twenty-eight, entitled "An Act in addition to an act entitled 'An act concerning discriminating duties of Tonnage and Impost' and to equalize the duties on Prussian vessels and their cargoes," it is provided that, upon satisfactory evidence being given to the President of the United States, by the government of any foreign nation, that no discriminating duties of tonnage or impost are imposed or levied in the ports of the said nation, upon vessels wholly belonging to citizens of the United States, or upon the produce, manufactures, or merchandise, imported in the same from the United States, or from any foreign country, the President is thereby authorized to issue his proclamation, declaring that the foreign discriminating duties of tonnage and impost within the United States are, and shall be, suspended and discontinued, so far as respects the vessels of the said foreign nation, and the produce, manufactures or merchandise, imported into the United States in the same from the said foreign nation, or from any other foreign country; the said suspension to take effect from the time of such notification being given to the President of the United States, and to continue so long as the reciprocal exemption of vessels, belonging to citizens of the United States, and their cargoes, as aforesaid, shall be continued, and no longer.

And whereas, satisfactory evidence has lately been received by me, through an official communication of Señor Don Luis Molina, Envoy Extraordinary and Minister Plenipotentiary of the Republic of Nicaragua, under date of the 28th. of November, 1863, that no other or higher duties of tonnage and impost have been imposed or levied since the second day of August, 1838, in the ports of Nicaragua upon vessels wholly belonging to citizens of the United States, and upon the produce, manufactures, or merchandize imported in the same from the United States, and from any foreign country whatever, than are levied on Nicaraguan ships and their cargoes, in the same ports under like circumstances:

Now, therefore, I, Abraham Lincoln, President of the United States of America, do hereby declare and proclaim, that so much of the several acts imposing discriminating duties of tonnage and impost within the United States are, and shall be, suspended and discontinued, so far as respects the vessels of Nicaragua, and the produce, manufactures, and merchandise, imported into the United States in the same, from the dominions of Nicaragua, and from any other foreign country whatever, the said suspension to take effect from the day above mentioned, and to continue thenceforward, so long as the reciprocal exemption of the vessels of the United States, and the produce, manufactures, and merchandise imported into the dominions of Nicaragua, in the same as aforesaid, shall be continued on the part of the government of Nicaragua.

Given under my hand, at the city of Washington, the sixteenth day of December, in the year of our Lord one thousand [L.S.] eight hundred and sixty-three, and the eighty-eighth of the Independence of the United States.

By the President: ABRAHAM LINCOLN
WILLIAM H SEWARD Secretary of State.

[1] DS, DNA FS RG 11, Proclamations.

To Worthington G. Snethen[1]

W. G. Snethen   Executive Mansion,
My dear Sir   Washington, December 16. 1863.

The application filed by you in behalf of Samuel K. Boyd, to be a Captain in the regular Army has been received, and referred to the War Department. You may not be aware that the application is directly in the teeth of a rule which we have felt constrained to adopt. Suppose your relative were now a First Lieut. in the regular Army, and the Captaincy directly above him were vacant, he would be entitled to be promoted to that vacancy. But suppose I should say to him "Stand back sir; I want that place for outsider" what would you and he think of it? And yet that is precisely the way you you [sic] now ask me to treat some other Lieutenant. I suppose you have not thought of this. Yours truly

A. LINCOLN

[1] ALS, owned by Foreman M. Lebold, Chicago, Illinois. Worthington G. Snethen was a merchant at Baltimore. No record has been found of Samuel K. Boyd's appointment.

To Edwin M. Stanton[1]

It is said Gen. Buford can not live through this day; and it [is] suggested that he be nominated as a Major General.

Dec. 16. 1863.   A. LINCOLN

[1] ALS, NWM. Brigadier General John Buford died at Washington on December 16 a few hours after his commission as major general had been put in his hands.

To Edwin M. Stanton[1]

Hon. Sec. of War   Executive Mansion,
My dear Sir   Washington, December 16. 1863.

I am so repeatedly applied to for leave to Mrs. Upshur, (widow of Sec. Upshur[2]) her sister, and grand-child to come on the flag-of truce boat from City Point, that I shall be obliged if you will permit it. Yours truly   A. LINCOLN

[1] ALS, NNC. Stanton endorsed on the bottom of the letter, "Let the pass be issued by order of the President." A letter from John F. Lee, Upper Marlboro, Maryland, to Montgomery Blair, November 22, 1863, is as follows:

"Will you get from the President, a pass for *Mrs. E. A. B. Upshur*, her sister *Miss Sally Upshur*, and her grandchild *James Ringgold*, to come on the flag of truce boat to Old point comfort, (there is no other way of coming) and thence to their home in Washington.

"They went before the war to the mountains of Va, as always before in summer, and did not come back.

"I am executor of the child's father, administrator of his mother, and hold his property . . . Mrs. Upshur's age & health make it necessary that her sister should live with her. I beleive the President will willingly grant the permission. He said before, that he wished good people to return. . . ." (DLC-RTL).

[2] Abel P. Upshur, secretary of the Navy (1841-1843) and secretary of State (1843-1844).

To Edward Bates[1]

December 17, 1863

In addition to the within letter, I have personal knowledge of this case, and have concluded to ask the Attorney General to make out a pardon at once. I believe the sentence was for eight years.

[Dec. 17, 1863   A. LINCOLN]

[1] AES, DNA RG 204, U.S. Pardon Attorney, A 428. The date and signature have been clipped from the endorsement, which is written on a letter signed by John Dougherty, December 16, 1863, asking pardon of Newton F. Jones, convicted of robbing the mail at Anna, Illinois, and sentenced in 1859 to eight years' imprisonment.

To James H. Hoes[1]

Executive Mansion,
My Dear Sir   Washington, December 17, 1863.
I have received from the Sanitary Commission of Chicago, the Watch which you placed at their disposal, and I take the liberty of conveying to you my high appreciation of your humanity and generosity, of which I have unexpectedly become the beneficiary. I am very truly yours   A. LINCOLN
    James H. Hoes Esq

[1] LS, CSmH. As managers of the Northwestern Sanitary Fair at Chicago, Mrs. Abraham H. Hoge and Mrs. David P. Livermore, wrote Lincoln on November 26, 1863: "Among the many remarkable incidents of our recent Fair, not one has been more pleasant, than the duty that devolves upon us, of consigning to you, on this National Thanksgiving Day, the accompanying watch; of asking you to accept it, as a memorial of the Ladies N. Western Fair. During the progress of the Fair, Mr. James H. Hoes, Jeweller of Chicago, a most loyal and liberal man, after giving very largely himself, in order to stimulate donations from others, proposed through the columns of the Tribune, to give a gold watch to the largest contributor to the Fair. . . . Emancipation Proclamation . . . was sold for $3,000, the largest benefaction of any individual. . . ." (DLC-RTL).

To Stephen A. Hurlbut[1]

"*Cypher*"

Major General Hurlbut   Executive Mansion
Memphis, Tenn.   Washington, D.C. Dec. 17. 1863.
I understand you have, under sentence of death, a tall old man, by the name of Henry F. Luckett. I personally knew him, and did not think him a bad man. Please do not let him be executed, unless upon further order from me, and, in the mean time, send me a transcript of the record.   A. LINCOLN
    "Henry F Luckett"

[1] ALS, RPB. On December 22 General Hurlbut replied to Lincoln's telegram: "The record in Lucketts case has been sent to Gen Grant long since He is guilty of smuggling percussions caps to the enemy but his friends say is insane Mr Luckett is in prison here awaiting action on his case." Henry F. Luckett was a former resident of Springfield, Illinois. See Lincoln's order for pardon of Luckett, March 30, 1864, *infra*.

Memorandum: Removal of James L. Ridgely[1]

Executive Mansion, Washington, Dec. 17, 1863.
To-day Hon. Mr. Webster, M.C. with Messrs Hoffman, Lester, Poteat, Lusby, representing that Gen. Pierce, Mr. Wright, and

Mr. Given, Senator, agree with them, call, and ask that James L. Ridgely, be restored as Collector of Internal Revenue, in the 2nd. District. They say the grounds of his removal were misrepresentations, and that Mr. Stuart, sought nominations in several conventions, & failing bolted the nominations made this year. The States Attorney for Baltimore Co. also concurs, & in fact, they say the entire county organization concurs. These members are all for emancipation.

¹ AD, DLC-RTL. James L. Ridgely had been appointed collector of internal revenue at Baltimore, but was not so actively in favor of emancipation as a faction of the party thought he should be. He was replaced by Joseph J. Stewart, whose nomination was confirmed by the Senate on April 20, 1864. On April 21, 1864, Ridgely's nomination as tax commissioner for North Carolina was also confirmed by the Senate, doubtless as compensation for his removal from his previous Maryland post. Of the persons named by Lincoln, Henry W. Hoffman, Edwin H. Webster, and State Senator John S. Given were certainly three, but the others have not been positively identified.

To the Senate¹

To the Senate of the United States: December 17, 1863

I transmit to the Senate, for consideration with a view to its ratification, a Convention between the United States and Her Britannic Majesty, for the final adjustment of the claims of the Hudson's Bay and Puget Sound Agricultural Companies, signed in this City, on the first day of July, last.   ABRAHAM LINCOLN

Washington, 17th. December, 1863.

¹ DS, DNA RG 46, Senate 39B B3. The treaty was ratified by the Senate on January 18, 1864.

To the Senate and House of Representatives¹

December 17, 1863

To the Senate, and House of Representatives

Herewith I lay before you a letter addressed to myself by a Committee of gentlemen representing the Freedman's Aid Societies in Boston, New-York, Philadelphia and Cincinnati. The subject of the letter, as indicated above, is one of great magnitude, and importance, and one which these gentlemen, of known ability and high character, seem to have considered with great attention and care. Not having the time to form a mature judgment of my own, as to whether the plan they suggest is the best, I submit the whole subject to Congress deeming that their attention thereto is almost imperatively demanded. ABRAHAM LINCOLN

Dec. 17. 1863.

[1] ADS, NNP; DS, DNA RG 46, Senate 38A F2. The letter of December 1, 1863, which Lincoln transmitted, signed by Stephen Colwell and others, proposed establishment of a "Bureau of Emancipation" to assist those freed by the Emancipation Proclamation (See *Senate Executive Document No. 1*). On December 8, Representative Thomas D. Eliot of Massachusetts introduced a bill to establish a Bureau of Emancipation, which was referred to a select committee on December 14, reported by Eliot on December 22, and sent back to the committee. No further action is recorded.

To Edwin M. Stanton and James B. Fry[1]

December 17, 1863

Will the Secretary of War, and Provost Marshal General please consider this application, and make good all that has been promised, as applicable to it, and even beyond promises, etc. equity, so far as practically connected with the public service.

Dec. 17, 1863. A. LINCOLN.

[1] Copy, ISLA. The original document has not been located, but a transcript provided by an autograph dealer describes the item as an ADS, accompanied by a manuscript petition of the city of New Bedford, Massachusetts, signed by Mayor George Howland, "enumerating certain military conditions, solemn promises made to them, that had been broken. . . ."

To Thurlow Weed[1]

Hon. T. Weed. Executive Mansion, Dec 17, 1863.

Dear Sir: Allow me to introduce my friends, Joshua F. Speed and Joshua Tevis of Kentucky. You may rely implicitly on whatever they may tell you; and I think their mission an important one. Yours very truly. A. LINCOLN.

[1] Tracy, p. 236. The mission of Speed and Tevis has not been discovered.

To Edward Bates[1]

Will the Attorney General, please make out and send me a pardon in this case. A. LINCOLN

Dec. 18. 1863.

[1] AES, DNA RG 204, U.S. Pardon Attorney, A 497. Lincoln's endorsement is written on the jacket of papers in the case of William H. Knapp, convicted of defrauding the government in the enlistment of soldiers.

Memorandum:
Appointment of William M. Albin[1]

[c. December 18, 1863]

Gen. Loan recommends William M Albin to be Superintendent of Indian Affairs located at St. Joseph, Mo.

[1] AES, DNA RG 48, Applications, Indian Agencies, Box 1266. Lincoln's endorsement is written on the envelope of a letter signed by Benjamin F. Loan and others, December 18, 1863. William M. Albin's appointment was confirmed by the Senate on March 2, 1864.

To Edwin M. Stanton[1]

Hon. Sec. of War: Executive Mansion,
My dear Sir Washington, Dec. 18. 1863.

I believe Gen. Schofield must be relieved from command of the Department of Missouri, otherwise a question of veracity, in relation to his declarations as to his interfering, or not, with the Missouri Legislature, will be made with him, which will create an additional amount of trouble, not to be overcome by even a correct decision of the question. The question itself must be avoided. Now for the mode. Senator Henderson, his friend, thinks he can be induced to ask to be relieved, if he shall understand he will be generously treated; and, on this latter point, Gratz Brown will help his nomination, as a Major General, through the Senate. In no other way can he be confirmed; and upon his rejection alone, it would be difficult for me to sustain him as Commander of the Department. Besides, his being relieved from command of the Department, and at the same time confirmed as a Major General, will be the means of Henderson and Brown leading off together as friends, and will go far to heal the Missouri difficulty.

Another point. I find it is scarcely less than indispensable for me to do something for Gen. Rosecrans; and I find Henderson and Brown will agree to him for the commander of their Department.

Again, I have received such evidence and explanations, in regard to the supposed cotten transactions of Gen. Curtis, as fully restores in my mind the fair presumption of his innocence; and, as he is my friend, and, what is more, as I think, the countries friend, I would be glad to relieve him from the impression that I think him dishonest, by giving him a command. Most of the Iowa and Kansas delegations, a large part of that of Missouri, and the delegates from Nebraska, and Colorado, ask this in behalf of Gen. C. and suggest Kansas and other contiguous territory West of Missouri, as a Department for him.

In a purely military point of view it may be that none of these things is indispensable, or perhaps, advantageous; but in another aspect, scarcely less important, they would give great relief, while, at the worst, I think they could not injure the military service much. I therefore shall be greatly obliged if yourself and Gen. Halleck can give me your hearty co-operation, in making the arrangement. Perhaps the first thing would be to send Gen. Schofield's nomination to me. Let me hear from you before you take any actual step in the matter. Yours very truly   A. LINCOLN

[1] ALS, DLC-Stanton Papers. Under date of December 13, John Hay's *Diary* records the following:

"The President, speaking today about Missouri matters, said he had heard some things of Schofield which had very much displeased him: that while Washburne was in Missouri he saw or thought he saw that Schofield was working rather energetically in the politics of the State, and that he approached Schofield and proposed that he should use his influence to harmonize the conflicting elements so as to elect one of each wing, Gratz Brown and Henderson. Schofield's reply was that he would not consent to the election of Gratz Brown.

"Again when Gratz Brown was about coming to Washington he sent a friend to Schofield to say that he would not oppose his confirmation if he (S.) would so far as his influence extended, agree to a convention of Missouri to make necessary alterations in her State constitution. Schofield's reply, as reported by Brown to the President, was that he would not consent to a State convention. These things, the President says, are obviously transcendent of his instructions and must not be permitted. He has sent for Schofield to come to Washington and explain these grave matters. . . ."

See further Lincoln to Stanton, December 21, *infra*.

To Elihu B. Washburne[1]

Hon. E. B. Washburne   Executive Mansion,
My dear Sir   Washington, Dec. 18. 1863.

The Joint Resolution of thanks to Gen. Grant & those under his command, has been before me, and is approved. If agreeable to you, I shall be glad for you to superintend the getting up of the Medal, and the making of the copy to be be [sic] engrossed on parchment, which I am to transmit to the General. Yours truly

A. LINCOLN

[1] ALS, IHi. The joint resolution introduced by Washburne on December 8 and approved by Lincoln on December 18, requested the president to "cause a gold medal to be struck, with suitable emblems, devices, and inscriptions" and to "cause a copy of this joint resolution to be engrossed on parchment" to be transmitted to General Grant.

To Edward Bates[1]

Let a pardon be made out for the unexecuted part of the sentence in this case.   A. LINCOLN

Dec. 19. 1863.

[1] AES, DNA RG 204, U.S. Pardon Attorney, A 498. Lincoln's endorsement is written on a petition signed by David K. Cartter, clerk of the District of Columbia Criminal Court, for the pardon of Maria Coffman, alias Philips, sentenced by the court to pay a fine of fifty dollars and costs, in default of which she was committed to jail.

To Edward Bates[1]

Attorney General, please make out a pardon for Mr. Burnam, in this case.   A. LINCOLN
Dec. 19. 1863.

[1] AES, CSmH. Lincoln's endorsement is written on a printed envelope from the "Collector's Office, U.S. Internal Revenue, First District, Kentucky." The case has not been identified, but F. H. Sweet Catalog 53 lists a presidential pardon for "John Burnam, a Kentucky rebel," dated December 21, 1863.

To Ulysses S. Grant[1]

"Cypher"

Major General Grant   Executive Mansion
Chattanooga, Tenn.   Washington, D.C. Dec. 19. 1863.
    The Indiana delegation in Congress, or at least a large part of them, are very anxious that Majr. Gen. Milroy shall enter active service again, and I share in this feeling. He is not a difficult man to satisfy, sincerity and courage being his strong traits. Believing in our cause, and wanting to fight in it, is the whole matter with him. Could you, without embarrassment, assign him a place, if directed to report to you.   A. LINCOLN.

[1] ALS, RPB. No reply from Grant has been discovered. AGO, *Special Orders No. 169*, May 6, 1864, sent General Milroy to Nashville, Tennessee, to report to General George H. Thomas for duty in receiving and organizing militia regiments and for assignment to the command of Indiana troops when organized (OR, I, XXXVIII, IV, 54).

To Edwin M. Stanton[1]

Will the Sec. of War, please allow Charles Alexander, named within, to go home with his relatives.   A. LINCOLN
Dec. 19. 1863.

[1] AES, owned by Dale Carnegie, New York City. Lincoln's endorsement is written on a petition of Mrs. Mary C. Alexander of Jefferson County, Virginia, to Commissary of Prisoners William Hoffman, November 12, 1863, asking release of her son Private Charles A. Alexander, Twelfth Virginia Cavalry, CSA, a prisoner of war at Point Lookout, who was dying of consumption.

To Gideon Welles[1]

Hon. Secretary of the Navy   Executive Mansion,
My dear Sir: Washington, Dec. 20. 1863.

Gen. Gilmore, believing that a joint movement of the Army and Navy is not likely to be made against Charleston very soon, has written asking leave to operate independently of the Navy for a time. As this application comes to me, I will thank you to inform me how long, according to any plan or reasonable calculation of the Navy, it will be before it will need the actual co-operation of the Army before Charleston. Yours very truly   A. Lincoln

[1] ADfS, DLC-RTL. General Quincy A. Gillmore was in command of the Department of the South. For Welles' reply see Lincoln to Stanton, December 21, *infra.*

To Henry C. Wright[1]

Executive Mansion, Washington, Dec 20th, 1863.

"I shall not attempt to retract or modify the emancipation proclamation; nor shall I return to slavery any person who is free by the terms of that proclamation, or by any of the acts of Congress."

Henry C. Wright   ABRAHAM LINCOLN
    Care of Wendell Philips
    221. Washington St.
    Boston– Mass.

[1] ADS-F, ISLA. Henry C. Wright, a lecturing agent of the Massachusetts Anti-Slavery Society, wrote Lincoln on December 16, 1863:
"God bless thee, Abraham Lincoln! With all my heart, & bless thee, in the name of God & Humanity.
"But—*mark!* I want nothing of you—you can do nothing for me—*except*—this one favor . . . that you will write for me, & subscribe your name to it —with your own hand—this sentence in your late Message—i.e.
" 'I shall not attempt to retract or modify the emancipation proclamation; nor shall I return to slavery any person, who is free by the terms of the proclamation, or by any of the acts of Congress.'
"I have given 30 years of my life to the Abolition of slavery—by lecturing, by public & private discussions, & by scattering, broad cast, tracts & pamphlets bearing on that subject. I regard the American Republic as the God-appointed Messiah of Liberty to the great family of Nations. . . ." (DLC-RTL).

To Edward Bates[1]

Hon. Attorney General   Executive Mansion,
My dear Sir   Washington, Dec. 21, 1863.

Please send me a nomination for Henry Hammond, as Marshal of Connecticut. Yours truly   A. Lincoln

[1] ALS, DNA GE RG 60, Papers of Attorney General, Segregated Lincoln Material. See Lincoln's letter to Foster and Dixon, *infra.* Henry Hammond's appointment was confirmed by the Senate on January 18, 1864.

To Benjamin F. Butler[1]

Major Gen. Butler   Executive Mansion
Fort-Monroe, Va.   Washington D.C. Dec. 21. 1863.

It is said that William H. Blake is under sentence of death at Fort-Magruder, in your Department. Do not let him be executed without further order from me, & in the mean time have the record sent me. He is said to belong to the 1st. or 2nd. Pennsylvania Artillery.   A. LINCOLN

[1] ALS, RPB. General Butler replied on December 22: "Private Wm. H. Blake Batty *E* 1st. Penn Artillery, is under sentence of death by hanging for murder. In my judgment a very deliberate one. He will not be executed without further orders from you. The records were forwarded on the 19th. inst. to Col Holt."

William H. Blake's sentence for the murder of Stephen Redson, Battery E, First Pennsylvania Artillery, was commuted to life imprisonment (AGO, *Special Orders No. 14*, January 11, 1864), and on April 27, 1864, he received a presidential pardon (DNA WR RG 153, Judge Advocate General, MM 1201).

To Lafayette S. Foster and James Dixon[1]

Hon. Senators   Executive Mansion,
Foster & Dixon.   Washington, Dec. 21, 1863.

The Marshalship of Connecticut has given me some trouble. Of the Sec. of the Navy, Gov. of the State, two Senators, and three Representatives in Congress, who have made recommendations, two are for Mr. Nichols, two for Mr. Hammond, two for Mr. Barnum, and one for Mr. Phelps.[2] Nothing has been said to me against the integrity or capacity of any of these candidates. So far as stated, three of them are equally well presented. Something more than a year ago Mr. Hammond was so well presented to me for one of the Internal Revenue offices, that it was with great regret I felt constrained to decline giving it to him; and I then wrote one of his friends substantially that I would be glad of a future opportunity to recognize him. I think I should now do this when he stands at least the equal of any competitor, on other grounds. Accordingly I send up his nomination. Please show, or state this to the other gentlemen. Your Obt. Servt.   A. LINCOLN

Since writing the above I have seen letters from six different, and as I understand, respectable and influential citizens of Connecticut, protesting against the appointment of Mr. Hammond.

Also a very respectable recommendation of Mr. Barnum, by citizens.

Also a letter of Mr. Barnum himself, saying "If Mr. Hammond of this State receives the Appt. I am fully satisfied, but I am not willing to withdraw in favor of any other person"

Also a letter of Gov. Buckingham, adhering to his recommendation of Mr. Nichols, but speaking in very high terms of Mr. Hammond.

These things, taken together, do not change my purpose.

A. LINCOLN.

[1] ALS, owned by Newton C. Brainard, Hartford, Connecticut. See Lincoln's letter to Bates, *supra.*

[2] Philo F. Barnum was a resident of Bridgeport, Connecticut. Nichols and Phelps have not been identified.

To Francis H. Peirpoint[1]

Governor Pierpoint   Executive Mansion
Alexandria, Va.   Washington, D.C. Dec. 21. 1863

Please come up and see me to-day.   A. LINCOLN

[1] ALS, RPB. Peirpoint had been elected governor of the "Restored Government" of Virginia, with its capital at Alexandria. Lincoln may have wished to consult him in connection with the calling of a constitutional convention to abolish slavery, or concerning the Amnesty Proclamation of December 8, 1863. John Hay's *Diary* under date of December 25, records:

"The President today got up a plan for extending to the people of the rebellious districts the practical benefits of his proclamation. He is to send record books to various points to receive subscriptions to the oath, for which certificates will be given to the man taking the oath. He has also prepared a placard himself giving notice of the openings of the books and the nature of the oath required.

"He sent the first of these books to Peirpoint to use in Virginia. The second he will probably send to Arkansas."

Permit to Mr. and Mrs. Charles Craig[1]

Executive Mansion, December 21, 1863.

Mr. and Mrs. Craig, of Arkansas, whose plantation, situated upon the Mississippi River a few miles below Helena, has been desolated during the present war, propose returning to reoccupy and cultivate said plantation; and it is my wish that they be permitted to do so, and that the United States military forces in that vicinity will not molest them or allow them to be molested, as long as the said Mr. and Mrs. Craig shall demean themselves as peaceful, loyal citizens of the United States.   ABRAHAM LINCOLN.

[1] NH, IX, 268. Mrs. Charles Craig was related to John T. Stuart, who wrote to his wife from Washington on December 20, 1863, ". . . Last night Sue ac-

companied by Mr. [Henry T.] Blow of St. Louis who is an old friend called upon Mr Lincoln to arrange her business matters. She wants a pass & protection for Craig & herself to go to Arkansas to occupy their farm and raise a crop of cotton next year. The farm is now in possession of some Illinois preacher so Sue says. Mr. Lincoln as I am informed granted all Sue's wishes and promised to have the papers made out for her by tomorrow. . . ." (ALS, IHi-Stuart Papers).

To Edwin M. Stanton[1]

Hon. Sec. of War, please hear Mr. Browning, and grant his request about the Lady going to her husband, if you consistently can.

Dec. 21. 1863.   A. LINCOLN

[1] ALS, InU. Lincoln's note is written on both sides of a small card. The lady has not been identified.

To Edwin M. Stanton[1]

Private

Hon. Sec. of War   Executive Mansion,
My dear Sir   Washington, December 21, 1863.

Sending a note to the Secretary of the Navy as I promised, he called over and said that the strikes in the Ship-yards had thrown the completion of vessels back so much, that he thought Gen. Gilmores proposition entirely proper. He only wishes (and in which I concur) that Gen. Gilmore will courteously confer with and explain to Admiral Dahlgren.

In regard to the Western matter, I believe the programme will have to stand substantially as I first put it. Henderson and especially Brown believe that the social influences of St. Louis would inevitably tell injuriously upon Gen. Pope, in the particular difficulty existing there; and I think there is some force in that view. As to retaining Gen. S. temporarily, if this should be done, I believe I should scarcely be able to get his nomination through the Senate. Send me over his nomination, which however I am not yet quite ready to send to the Senate. Yours as ever   A. LINCOLN

[1] ALS, owned by D. N. Heineman, New York City. See Lincoln to Stanton, December 18, and to Welles, December 20, *supra*. Under date of December 23, 1863, John Hay's *Diary* records:

"I took to the Senate today the nomination of Schofield as Major General. The President had previously spoken to some of the Senators about it. He is anxious that Schofield shd be confirmed so as to arrange this Missouri matter properly. I told Sherman, Wilson, Harris and Doolittle. Senator Foote also agreed to do all he could to put the matter properly through. But on the nomination being read in executive session, Howard of Michigan objected to its consideration and it was postponed. Sherman and Doolittle tell me it will certainly go through when it is regularly taken up.

"Lane came up to see the President about it, and told him this. Lane is very anxious to have the Kansas part of the plan at once carried out.

"Morgan says that Gratz Brown gave to Sumner to present to the Senate the Radical protest against Schofield's confirmation, and that Sumner presented it today. The President sent for Sumner but he was not at his lodgings. . . ."

AGO, *General Orders No. 28*, January 22, 1864, assigned Rosecrans to command the Department of the Missouri replacing Schofield and ordered Schofield to report to Grant at Chattanooga.

To Oliver D. Filley[1]

O. D. Filley   Executive Mansion,
St. Louis, Mo.   Washington, Dec. 22. 1863.

I have just looked over a petition signed by some three dozen citizens of St. Louis, and three accompanying letters, one by yourself, one by a Mr. Nathan Ranney, and one by a Mr. John D. Coalter, the whole relating to the Rev. Dr. McPheeters. The petition prays, in the name of justice and mercy that I will restore Dr. McPheeters to all his ecclesiastical rights.

This gives no intimation as to what ecclesiastical rights are withheld. Your letter states that Provost Marshal Dick, about a year ago, ordered the arrest of Dr. McPheters, Pastor of the Vine Street Church, prohibited him from officiating, and placed the management of the affairs of the church out of the control of it's chosen Trustees; and near the close you state that a certain course "would insure his release." Mr. Ranney's letter says "Dr. Saml. S. McPheeters is enjoying all the rights of a civilian, but can not preach the gospel!!!" Mr. Coalter, in his letter, asks "Is it not a strange illustration of the condition of things that the question of who shall be allowed to preach in a church in St. Louis, shall be decided by the *President* of *the United States?*"

Now, all this sounds very strangely; and withal, a little as if you gentlemen making the application, do not understand the case alike, one affirming that the Dr. is enjoying all the rights of a civilian, and another pointing out to me what will secure his *release!* On the 2nd. day of January last I wrote Gen. Curtis in relation to Mr. Dick's order upon Dr. McPheeters, and, as I suppose the Dr. is enjoying all the rights of a civilian, I only quote that part of my letter which relates to the church. It is as follows: "But I must add that the U.S. government must not, as by this order, undertake to run the churches. When an individual, in a church or out of it, becomes dangerous to the public interest, he must be checked; but the churches, as such must take care of themselves. It will not do for the U.S. to appoint Trustees, Supervisors, or other agents for the churches." This letter going to Gen. Curtis, then in command there I supposed of course it was obeyed, especially as I heard no further complaint from Dr. M. or his friends for nearly an entire year.

I have never interfered, nor thought of interfering as to who shall or shall not preach in any church; nor have I knowingly, or believingly, tolerated any one else to so interfere by my authority. If any one is so interfering, by color of my authority, I would like to have it specifically made known to me.

If, after all, what is now sought, is to have me put Dr. M. back, over the heads of a majority of his own congregation, that too, will be declined. I will not have control of any church on any side. Yours Respectfully   A. LINCOLN

1 ALS, owned by Mr. and Mrs. Thomas McPheeters, St. Louis, Missouri. Filley's letter to Lincoln, November 9, 1863, as well as that of Nathan Ranney of the same date to Edward Bates, petitioned for restoration of Samuel B. McPheeters as pastor of the Pine (not Vine) Street Church at St. Louis. (DLC-RTL). John D. Coalter's letter to Bates, December 13, 1863, asked the attorney general to use his influence with the president to see that he "shall actually read the petition." (*Ibid.*). See Lincoln's endorsement, *infra*.

Endorsement on Petition
Concerning Samuel B. McPheeters[1]

December 22, 1863

The assumptions of this paper, so far as I know, or believe are entirely false. I have never deprived Dr. McPheters of any ecclesiastical right, or authorized, or excused its' being done by any one deriving authority from me. On the contrary, in regard to this very case, I directed, a long time ago, that Dr. McPheters was to be arrested, or remain at large, upon the same rule as any one else; and that, in no event, was any one to interfere by my authority, as to who should, or should not preach in any church. This was done, I think, in a letter, in the nature of an order, to Mr. Dick. The assumption that I am keeping Dr. M. from preaching in his church is monstrous. If any one is doing this, by pretense of my authority, I will thank any one who can, to make out and present me, a specific case against him. If, after all, the Dr. is kept out by the majority of his own parishioners, and my official power is sought to force him in over their heads, I decline that also.

Dec. 22. 1863.   A. LINCOLN

1 AES, DLC-RTL. Lincoln's endorsement is written on a petition signed by John Whitehill and other members of the Pine Street Church, asking restoration of Dr. Samuel B. McPheeters to his pulpit. Concerning the removal of McPheeters, see Lincoln to Curtis, December 27, 1862, *supra*.

To Gilman Marston[1]

Military Commander at

Point-Lookout, Md.

Executive Mansion,

Washington, Dec. 22, 1863.

If you have a prisoner by the name Linder—Daniel Linder, I think, and certainly the son of U. F. Linder, of Illinois, please send him to me by an officer.   A. LINCOLN

[1] ALS, RPB. For General Marston's reply see Lincoln to Stanton, December 26, *infra.*

To the Senate[1]

To the Senate of the United States.   December 22, 1863

I transmit to the Senate, for its consideration with a view to ratification, two Conventions between the United States and His Belgian Majesty, signed at Brussels on the 20th of May and the 20th of July last, respectively, and both relating to the extinguishment of the Scheldt Dues, &c. A copy of so much of the correspondence between the Secretary of State and Mr. Sanford, the Minister Resident of the United States at Brussels, on the subject of the Conventions as is necessary to a full understanding of it, is also herewith transmitted.   ABRAHAM LINCOLN

Washington, December 22nd, 1863.

[1] DS, DNA RG 46, Senate 38B B1. Both treaties were ratified on February 26, 1864. The correspondence transmitted is not filed with Lincoln's message and has not been located.

To Gideon Welles[1]

[December 22, 1863]

I fear that the publication of a part of the intercepted correspondence just now may do harm, and I have to request you that, so far as in your power, you will suppress any further publication of any part of it, either here, at New York or elsewhere, for a few days.   A. LINCOLN.

[1] Hertz, II, 949, misdated 1862. A bundle of letters captured aboard the Confederate ship *Ceres* had been turned over by Welles to his chief clerk William Faxon, for publication. Welles' *Diary* under date of December 21, records a meeting at which the letters were read: "When we met at eight, Faxon proceeded to read them. Those from Trowbridge [N. C. Trowbridge of New York] to young Lamar [Colonel Charles A. L. Lamar, who had been a confederate agent in England] made some singular disclosures, and one of them made mention of a nephew of William H. Seward as being concerned in a cargo for running the blockade. This disturbed Seward more than I should have supposed,—for it was not asserted as a fact,—and if, as he remarked, there were among

[87]

twenty or thirty nephews one traitor it would not be strange. It was thought best to stop the publication. I proposed that a portion . . . should be made public. . . . But I was overruled by the others, and Faxon was sent off to stop the publication. He was too late, however, for a portion of them had already been printed. . . ."

To the Senate and House of Representatives[1]

December 23, 1863

To the Senate and House of Representatives.

I transmit to Congress a copy of the Report to the Secretary of State of the Commissioners on the part of the United States under the Convention with Peru of the 12th. of January last, on the subject of claims. It will be noticed that two claims of Peruvian citizens on this Government have been allowed. An appropriation for the discharge of the obligations of the United States in these cases is requested. ABRAHAM LINCOLN

Washington, 23d. December, 1863.

[1] DS, DNA RG 46, Senate 38A F3; DS, DNA RG 233, House Original Executive Document No. 18. Seward's report may be found in Thirty-eighth Congress, First Session, *House of Representatives Executive Document No. 18*. An act approved on June 1, 1864, appropriated to Stephen G. Montano $41,782.38, and to Juan del Carmen Vergel $1,170.

To Edwin M. Stanton[1]

Hon. Sec. of War.   Executive Mansion
My dear Sir:—   Washington Dec. 23, 1863
   Please see this Lady who is a Sister to our gallant and brave friend, Gen. Reynolds, who fell at Gettysburg. Please oblige her if you can. Yours truly   A. LINCOLN.

[1] Copy, ISLA. A note on the bottom of Lincoln's letter reads as follows: "She applies that Charles H. Veil 9th Penn Reserve orderly to Genl [John F.] Reynolds may be appointed 2nd Lieut in a regular regt." Charles H. Veil's appointment as second lieutenant in the First U.S. Cavalry was confirmed by the Senate on April 7, 1864.

To Edwin M. Stanton[1]

Hon. Sec. of War   Executive Mansion,
Sir.   Washington, Dec. 23, 1863.
   Please see Gen. Schenck, and if you can, appoint for him, the Additional Pay-Master he will ask. Yours truly   A LINCOLN

[1] ALS, owned by Horace A. Hayday, Philadelphia, Pennsylvania.

To Edwin M. Stanton[1]

Executive Mansion,

Hon. Sec. of War   Washington, Dec. 23, 1863.

Let James C. Gates, a prisoner of War at Fort-Delaware, take the oath of allegiance & be discharged. Yours truly   A. LINCOLN

[1] ALS-F, ISLA. James C. Gates, captured at Gettysburg, was from Selma, Alabama.

To Whom It May Concern[1]

Executive Mansion,

Whom it may concern   Washington, Dec. 23, 1863.

The bearer, William Henry Craft, a corporal in Co. C. in the 82nd. N.Y. Volunteers, comes to me voluntarily, under apprehension that he may be arrested, convicted, and punished as a deserter; and I hereby direct him to report forthwith to his regiment for duty, and, upon condition that he does this, and faithfully serves out his term, or until he shall be honorably discharged for any cause, he is fully pardoned for any supposed desertion heretofore committed.   A. LINCOLN.

[1] ALS, IHi. On the inside page of this letter is the following order from Colonel Daniel C. McCallum.

"Transportation by rail from Maryland Avenue Depot to the front-Army of the Potomac will be given to Corporal Wm Henry Craft—[in Citizens clothing]

"This paper must not be taken up by the Conductors."

Brackets are in the source.

To Nathaniel P. Banks[1]

Executive Mansion,

Major General Banks   Washington, December 24. 1863.

Yours of the 6th. Inst. has been received, and fully considered. I deeply regret to have said or done anything which could give you pain, or uneasiness. I have all the while intended you to be *master*, as well in regard to re-organizing a State government for Louisiana, as in regard to the military matters of the Department; and hence my letters on reconstruction have nearly if not quite all been addressed to you. My error has been that it did not occur to me that Gov. Shepley or any one else would set up a claim to act independently of you; and hence I said nothing expressly upon the point. Language has not been guarded at a point where no danger was thought of. I now tell you that in every dispute, with whomsoever, you are master. Gov. Shepley was appointed to *assist* the

Commander of the Department, and not to thwart him, or act independently of him. Instructions have been given directly to him, merely to spare you detail labor, and not to supersede your authority. This, in it's liability to be misconstrued, it now seems was an error in us. But it is past. I now distinctly tell you that you are master of all, and that I wish you to take the case as you find it, and give us a free-state re-organization of Louisiana, in the shortest possible time. What I say here is to have a reasonable construction. I do not mean that you are to withdraw from Texas, or abandon any other military measure which you may deem important. Nor do I mean that you are to throw away available work already done for re-construction; or that war is to be made upon Gov. Shepley, or upon any one else, unless it be found that they will not co-operate with you, in which case, and in all cases, you are master while you remain in command of the Department.

My thanks for your successful and valuable operations in Texas. Yours as ever   A. LINCOLN

¹ ALS, IHi. General Banks wrote on December 6, 1863:

"Your letter dated Nov. 5th. relating to the organization of Government in Louisiana, I recd. upon my return from Texas Dec. 2d. Your letter of the 5th. August, upon the same subject, was also duly received, and answered. My reply expressed a cordial concurrence in your views, and an earnest desire to co-operate in their execution. From the first I have regarded reorganization of government here as of the highest importance, and I have never failed to advocate every where the earliest developement of this interest by congressional elections and by initiatory measures for state, organization. . . . In the initial reconstruction, the basis should be that of a free state beyond the possibility of failure. Having secured this other states, will easily follow. . . . So strong has been my conviction on this subject that I requested Governor Boutwell to press upon your attention my views—when I returned from the Teche Country in October. . . . I addressed to you a lengthy letter, and also wrote to Governor Shepley, and to Mr. Durant, Attorney General and other gentlemen, urging the completion of this duty by the quickest methods: but I found most of these gentlemen so interested in topics, that seemed to me disconnected with the general subject, and so slightly disposed to encourage my participation in the affair that I retained the letter I had written, and turned my attention, not unwillingly, to matters more likely to be accomplished, though not more important. The restoration of our Flag in Texas from Ringold Barracks on the Rio Grande to the Brasos on the coast, rewarded my change of purpose.

"You will judge my surprise, leniently, I hope, when I learned by your letter of the 5th. of Nov. that you attached responsibility to my actions in regard to the execution of your wishes. I assure you it is not so understood here. I do not so understand it. All the officers of the government are officially informed, that it has been committed by special instructions from Washington, to Governor Shepley. When the crazy project of an unauthorized election in November was made known, upon the rumor that I had given it my countenance and my approval Governor Shepley and Honorable Mr Durant both notified me by official letters, that the subject of an election or state organization had been exclusively committed to him, the military Governor. I so understood it myself. I have had neither authority, influence, or recognition as an officer entrusted with this duty. My suggestions are respectfully, but silently received by the Governor and his associates. In that I supposed they were right. How then can I be in any just sense responsible for the result? I beg your just consideration of these facts! Since I received your letter—the reply to which is made with extreme solicitude —I have recurred to my orders from your government. . . . Had the organization of a *free* state in Louisiana been committed to me under general instructions only, it would have been complete before this day. It can be effected now in sixty days—let me say, even in *thirty* days, if necessary. . . . But it should be undertaken only by those who have authority to act: who know what to do, who have no personal interests in addition or superior to the creation of a FREE STATE, and who can harmonize the action of individuals without the sacrifice of public interest. I do not suppose I have the qualifications for this duty; certain I am that I have not the authority. How then can I be held responsible for the failure to satisfy your expectations?. . ."

See further Lincoln to Banks, December 29, *infra*.

To Edward Bates[1]

Attorney General please make out a pardon in the within case.
Dec. 24. 1863   A. LINCOLN

[1] AES, DNA RG 204, U.S. Pardon Attorney, A 500. Lincoln's endorsement is written on a letter from Representative George H. Yeaman, December 21, 1863, enclosing an application for pardon of William Murray Brown of Kentucky.

Endorsement[1]

December 24, 1863

Comrs. to appraise Negroes in Missouri. These recommendations were very urgently pressed by those M.C's whose names appear.

I have given no attention to the subject; & did not even know of the order No. 135.   A. LINCOLN
Dec. 24. 1863.

[1] AES, owned by John F. Reed, Upper Darby, Pennsylvania. The endorsement has been clipped from attendant papers.

To Gilman Marston[1]

Military Commander, at   Executive Mansion
Point Lookout, Md.   Washington D.C. Dec. 24. 1863

If you send Linder to me as directed a day or two ago, also send Edwin C. Claybrook, of 9th. Virginia, rebel cavalry.

A. LINCOLN

[1] ALS, RPB. Bates' *Diary* under date of December 24, 1863, records concerning the son of Colonel R. A. Claybrook of Northumberland, Virginia:

"The Prest, being abt. to send for young Linder of Ills: at my instance, ordered up young Claybrook also . . . . to release them, if they will only accept the boon, or any reasonable terms.

"The Prest: is anxious to gratify Linder, the father, who is his old friend; and I am very desirous to make a New Year's gift of Claybrook, to his father and family. . . ."

See Lincoln to Bates, December 30, *infra*.

To Edwin M. Stanton[1]

December 24, 1863

If there is a vacancy of Lieutenant in the 5th Artillery, oblige Judge Clifford by appointing Samuel Gilman, Jr. now a private in that Regiment, to that vacancy unless you know some substantial reason to the contrary. A. LINCOLN.

[1] Stan. V. Henkels Catalog 1494, November 20, 1935, No. 52. Judge Nathan Clifford of the New York Supreme Court wrote William Whiting, solicitor of the War Department, December 19, 1863, to call attention to "young Samuel Gilman Jr—of New York City. . . . What I want is to get him a commission. . . ." (DLC-RTL). Gilman was appointed second lieutenant in the Fifth Artillery, April 7, 1864, and dismissed on December 6, 1864.

To Edwin M. Stanton[1]

Will the Sec. of War please re-consider this case, and oblige Mr. Rice and the Vice-President, if he consistently can? A. LINCOLN

Dec. 24. 1863

[1] AES-P, ISLA. Lincoln's endorsement appears on a letter of Major George Fuller, Sixth Maine Volunteers, November 22, 1863, to Brigadier General Seth Williams, Assistant Adjutant General, Army of the Potomac, requesting that First Sergeant William H. Coan be mustered into service as second lieutenant of Company H. for gallant and meritorious service and because of the shortage of lieutenants. The accompanying letters of Representative John H. Rice and Vice-president Hamlin are no longer with Fuller's letter. Succeeding endorsements by Thomas M. Vincent and others indicate that the request was not granted: "The provisions of General Orders No. 182, C.S. cannot be departed from."

To John D. Stiles[1]

December 24, 1863

Will Hon. Mr. Stiles please inform me, of what crime Becker was convicted—in what court—when—how long he has served under the sentence—and whether he has behaved well? A. LINCOLN

Dec. 24. 1863

[1] AES, DNA RG 204, U.S. Pardon Attorney, A 466. Lincoln's endorsement is written on a letter from John D. Stiles, member of congress from Pennsylvania, December 16, 1863, asking pardon for George S. Becker, convicted of passing counterfeit money and sentenced in Washington to the penitentiary at Albany, New York. See Lincoln to Bates, January 5 and 25, 1864, *infra*.

To Bayard Taylor[1]

Hon. Bayard Taylor:　　　　　　　　　Executive Mansion,
My dear Sir:　　　　　　　　　Washington, Dec. 25. 1863.

I think a good lecture or two on "Serfs, Serfdom, and Emancipation in Russia" would be both interesting and valuable. Could not
you get up such a thing? Yours truly　　　　A. LINCOLN.

[1] ALS, OClWHi. Recently returned from his post as secretary of legation at
St. Petersburg, Bayard Taylor replied on December 28:
"I have just received your Christmas suggestion, and with all the more pleasure because I think quite as you do with regard to the interest and importance
of the subject you propose. I intended, at first, to devote a part of my present
lecture to Russian serfdom and its abolishment, but found that it would make
my discourse altogether too long. I therefore decided to give, first of all, a general account of Russia and the people, concerning which I had many things to
say which are not only new to our people, but advantageous for them to know.
My own short experience has satisfied me that no country (except, perhaps, our
own) has been as misrepresented as Russia.
"It is rather late, this winter, to prepare a new lecture, especially as I have engaged to deliver that on 'Russia and Her People' in some thirty different cities;
but I fully understand the interest of the subject you propose, and desire to
present it, in some way, to the public. There are only slight resemblances between Russian serfdom and slavery in the southern states, although they rest
on the same basis—property in Man—but the complete success of the scheme
of emancipation in Russia has much significance for this nation at the present
time.
"I am very much gratified by the manifestation of your personal interest in
the subject, and hope that I may be able to contribute, though so indirectly, to
the growth of truer and more enlightened views among the people. . . ."
(DLC-RTL).

To Ambrose E. Burnside[1]

Major General Burnside　　　　　　　　Executive Mansion,
Providence, R.I.　　　　　　　　Washington, Dec. 26, 1863.

Yours in relation to Privates Eaton & Burrows, of the 6th. N.H.
is received. When you reach here about New-Year, call on me,
and we will fix it up—or I will do it sooner if you say so.

A. LINCOLN

[1] ALS, RPB. Burnside's communication to which Lincoln replied has not
been discovered. The roster of the Sixth New Hampshire lists Abel Eaton of
Company C, mustered November 27, 1861, and re-enlisted January 24, 1864;
and Daniel Burrows, Company G, mustered November 28, 1861, re-enlisted
January 24, 1864. See further Lincoln to Burnside, December 29, and to Boyle,
January 5, 1864, *infra.*

To Joseph Holt[1]

Let the Surgeon General be put upon trial by a court, as suggested by the Judge Advocate General.　　　　A. LINCOLN

Dec. 26. 1863.

[93]

¹ AES, DNA WR RG 153, Judge Advocate General, MM 1430. Lincoln's endorsement is written on the envelope containing the report of a military commission ordered July 2, 1863, to investigate purchases and disbursements of Surgeon General William A. Hammond. The court-martial tried Hammond on charges of irregularities in letting contracts and sentenced him to be dismissed on August 18, 1864. From September 3, 1863 to August 18, 1864, Joseph K. Barnes was acting surgeon general during the investigation and trial of Hammond, and was appointed to replace Hammond upon the latter's dismissal. By act of congress, March 15, 1878, a re-investigation was ordered, and Hammond was restored as a brigadier general on the retired list without pay or allowances, as of August 27, 1879.

To Usher F. Linder[1]

Hon. U. F. Linder   Executive Mansion
Chicago, Ills.   Washington DC. Dec. 26. 1863

Your son Dan. has just left me, with my order to the Sec. of War, to administer to him the oath of allegiance, discharge him & send him to you.   A. LINCOLN

¹ ALS, RPB. See Lincoln to Stanton, *infra*.

To George G. Meade[1]

Major General Meade   Executive Mansion,
Army of the Potomac   Washington, Dec. 26, 1863.

If Christopher Delker of the 61st. Penn. Vols. is under sentence of death, do not execute him till further order.

Whenever it shall be quite convenient I shall be glad to have a conference with you about this class of cases.   A. LINCOLN

¹ ALS, owned by Robert B. Davis, Bridgeport, Connecticut. Meade's reply to Lincoln's telegram was received at 10:05 P.M.: "The sentence in the case of private Christopher Delker 61st. Penna. Vols tried for desertion was forfeiture of pay & two years service after expiration of his original term, then to be dishonorably discharged. I will try next week to get up to Washn. and confer with you as you request. I am quite busy now with the re enlistment of veteran volunteers." (DLC-RTL). The roster of Company B lists Christian Delker as returned to service and mustered out with his company on June 28, 1865.

Memorandum:
Appointment of Benjamin F. Hoffman[1]

[December 26, 1863]
Gov. Tod asks *a Judgeship* for Benj. F. Hoffman.

¹ AE, IHi. Lincoln's endorsement is written on the envelope of a telegram from David Tod, December 26, 1863, recommending his private secretary Benjamin F. Hoffman. No record of Hoffman's appointment has been found.

To Edwin M. Stanton[1]

December 26, 1863

Daniel W. Linder, the Daniel Linder named within, is the son of my friend U. F. Linder, at Chicago, Ills. Please administer the oath of allegiance to him, discharge him, and send him to his father.

Dec. 26, 1863.   A. LINCOLN.

[1] John Heise Catalog No. 2464, pp. 17-18. According to the catalog description, Lincoln's endorsement is written on a telegram from Brigadier General Gilman Marston, December 25, 1863, as follows: "In compliance with your request of the 22nd. inst. received last evening I send to you . . . a prisoner of war named Danl. Linder, son of U. F. Linder of Illinois." Beneath Lincoln's endorsement Stanton referred the matter to Edward D. Townsend to administer the oath and execute the order.

To Edwin M. Stanton[1]

Hon. Sec. of War   Executive Mansion,
My dear Sir: Washington, Dec. 26. 1863.

Shall we go down the river to-morrow? And if so, at what hour shall we leave the wharf? and which wharf?

Mrs. L. & Tad, perhaps would go. I am not at all urgent about it, & would not have you incur the least inconvenience for it. I merely mean now that if we go, the details better be fixed. Yours as ever

A. LINCOLN

[1] ALS, NHi. No reply has been located. Lincoln's return from Point Lookout on the evening of December 28 was reported in the New York *Tribune* for December 29: "The President and Secretary of War returned to-night from a short visit to the encampment of Rebel prisoners at Point Lookout. It is understood that they satisfied themselves that not less than a thousand, or about a tenth of the whole number, are ready to enter the service of the United States."

To Nathaniel P. Banks[1]

Executive Mansion
Major Gen. Banks   Washington, Dec. 29. 1863.

Yours of the 16th. is received; and I send you, as covering the ground of it, a copy of my answer to yours of the 6th. it being possible the original may not reach you. I intend you to be master in every controversy made with you. Yours truly

A. LINCOLN

[1] ALS, IHi. This letter is written on the back of a copy of Lincoln's letter of December 24, *supra*, in John Hay's handwriting signed by Lincoln. On December 16 Banks wrote as follows:

"Earnest and continued reflection upon the subject of your letter of the 5th.

November induces me to make a further reply than my answer of the 6th instant contained. It is apparent that you do not view public affairs in this Department precisely as they are presented to me and other officers representing your administration.

"I am only in partial command here: There are not less than *four* distinct governments here, claiming and exercising original and independent powers based upon instructions received directly from Washington, and recognizing no other authority than their own. . . . I have never asked increase of authority: but as your letter implies a responsibility in some matters which I did not understand were commited to me, I think it my duty to you personally, and to your government officially, to represent my position and the difficulties I encounter in other relations than those referred to in my letter of the 6th. instant which relates to the re-construction of the state government in Louisiana only. . . ." (DLC-RTL).

To Ambrose E. Burnside[1]

Major Gen. Burnside   Executive Mansion
Providence, R.I   Washington D.C. Dec. 29, 1863

You may telegraph Eaton and Burrows that these cases will be disposed of according to your request when you come to Washington.   A. LINCOLN

[1] ALS, RPB. See Lincoln to Burnside, December 26, *supra*. Burnside's telegram of December 29 was received at 8 P.M.: "The necessary papers in the case of Private Eaton & Burrows of the Sixth . . . New Hampshire can be made out after my arrival in Washn. Am I authorized to telegraph to the Commanding Officer that the sentence will not be carried into effect? I feel that it is best to decide at once in order to avoid mistakes." (DLC-RTL). See Lincoln to Boyle, January 5, 1864, *infra*.

To George G. Meade[1]

Majr. Gen. Meade.   Executive Mansion,
Army of Potomac   Washington, Dec. 29, 1863

I am appealed to in behalf of Joseph Richardson of 49th. Penn. and Moses Chadbourne (in some New-Hampshire regt.) said to be under sentence for desertion. As in other cases do not let them be executed till further order.   A LINCOLN

[1] ALS-F, ISLA. Meade's reply to Lincoln's telegram was received at 12:50 P.M.: "Telegram recd. The execution of the sentence in the case of private Joseph Richardson Co 'A' 49th. Pa Vols has been suspended till further orders, and the proceedings will be immediately sent to you. There is no such case before me as that of Moses Chadbourn of a New Hampshire regt as referred to by you." (DLC-RTL). The roster of the Forty-ninth Pennsylvania lists Richardson as "discharged by order of the President—date unknown." The roster of the Second New Hampshire lists Private Moses Chadbourn, Company D, as deserted on July 7, 1862, apprehended on November 8, 1863, and discharged at Fredericksburg, Virginia, on October 20, 1865. See further Lincoln to Meade, January 3, 1864, *infra*.

Memorandum Concerning Joseph J. Stewart[1]

Executive Mansion, Washington, Dec. 29, 1863.

To-day Mr. Sterling, State Senator for Baltimore City, and Mr. Silverwood, Rep. of same city, Mr. Newnes Deputy States Atty for same city, and Judge King of Common Pleas of same city, call & protest against the removal of Joseph J. Stuart, as Collector of 2nd. District. The District includes seven wards of the city, & Mr. Silverwood resides in the Districts, but the others do not

[1] AD, DLC-RTL. See Lincoln's memorandum concerning the removal of James L. Ridgely, December 17, *supra*. Archibald Stirling, William Silverwood, Albert A. Nunes, whose name Lincoln misspelled, and John C. King were the men named by Lincoln.

To Edwin M. Stanton[1]

December 29, 1863

Senator Browning, personally knows, and vouches for the writer of this letter. Let William T. Dazey, named within, take the oath prescribed in the proclamation of Dec. 8th. and be bailed to his brother the writer of this letter.   A. LINCOLN

Dec. 29. 1863

[1] AES, IHi. Lincoln's endorsement is written on a letter of Mitchell Dazey, Quincy, Illinois, to Senator Orville H. Browning, December 22, 1863, asking release of his brother William T. Dazey of Mississippi, imprisoned at Alton, Illinois.

To Edwin M. Stanton[1]

If the within request can be lawfully granted, let it be done.

Dec. 29. 1863.   A. LINCOLN

[1] AES, DLC-RTL. Lincoln's endorsement is written on a letter of J. H. Puleston to John G. Nicolay, "Gov. Curtin writes me anxiously about his Brother-in-law Capt. William Wilson of whom he spoke to you at Gettysburgh. . . . Wilson is now detached from his Regt . . . and as he is liable at any time to be sent back to his Regt. Mrs. Curtin is very desirous to have him apptd. A.A.G. or something else with rank of Captain, so that he may be sure to remain with [Winfield S.] Hancock who wants him. . . ." No further appointment for Captain William P. Wilson of the One Hundred Forty-eighth Pennsylvania Infantry seems to have been made until he was appointed aide-de-camp with rank of captain for the First Army Corps (Veteran) on January 23, 1865.

To Edward Bates[1]

Hon. Attorney General,   December 30, 1863

Herewith I send you Edwin C. Claybrook, as you requested. I now place him at your control. Yours truly,   A. LINCOLN

Dec. 30, 1863.

[1] AES, owned by Frederick M. Dearborn, New York City. Lincoln's endorsement is written on the back of a communication from General Gilman Marston, December 29, 1863: "In obedience to your dispatch of the 24th inst. . . . I send to you . . . Edwin C. Claybrook of 9 Va rebel cavalry. Said Claybrook declines to take the oath of allegiance. . . ."

Bates' *Diary* records under date of December 30, 1863:

"To day was delivered to me, by written order of the President, Edwin C. Claybrook. . . . Afterwards Jany. 5., I took his parole, . . . and sent him down the Potomac . . . he got home on the 9th. on which day, he wrote me a very manly and gentlemanly letter. . . ."

To Jeremiah T. Boyle[1]

Gen. Boyle   Executive Mansion,
Louisville, Ky.   Washington, Dec. 30, 1863.

It is said that Corporal Robert L. Crowell, of Co. E. 20 Ky, Vol. Infy. is under sentence to be shot on the 8th. of January, at Louisville. Do not let the sentence be executed until further order from me.   A. LINCOLN

[1] ALS, RPB. See further Lincoln to Boyle, January 5, 1864, *infra*.

To Benjamin F. Butler[1]

Major General Butler   Executive Mansion
Fort-Monroe, Va.   Washington, D.C. Dec. 30. 1863

Jacob Bowers is fully pardoned for past offence, upon condition that he returns to duty, and re-enlists for three years or during the war.   A. LINCOLN

[1] ALS, RPB. General Butler telegraphed Lincoln on December 30: "Jacob Bowers was sentenced to imprisonment for life by Genl. Order No. 37, from these Head Qrs which sentence was approved by me Nov. 24th. for desertion. I now believe that he simply acted under a misapprehension of his duty, being a German not understanding his duty. Please permit me to remit this sentence if he returns to duty and re enlists during the war. I suppose I have the power now to do so but the papers are in Washington. This is the first time I have ever asked you to pardon any body." (DLC-RTL).

Additional Instructions
to Direct Tax Commissioners[1]

December 31, 1863

Additional instructions to the Direct tax Commissioners for the District of South Carolina in relation to the disposition of lands:

1. You will allow any loyal person of twenty one years of age, or upwards, who has at any time since the occupation by the national forces resided for six months, or now resides upon, or is

engaged in cultivating any lands in your district owned by the United States to enter the same for preemption to the extent of one, or at the option of the preemptor, two tracts of twenty acres each, paying therefor one dollar and twenty five cents per acre. You will give preference in all cases to heads of families, and married women whose husbands are engaged in the service of the United States, or are necessarily absent.

2 You will permit each soldier, sailor or marine actually engaged in the service of the United States, or any who may have been, or hereafter shall be honorably discharged to preempt and purchase in person, or by authorized agents, at the rate of one dollar, twenty five cents per acre, one tract of twenty acres of land, if single and, if married, two tracts of twenty acres each, in addition to the amount, a head of family, or married woman in the absence of her husband, is allowed to preempt and purchase under the general privilege to loyal persons.

3 Each preemptor on filing his claim and receiving a certificate of preemption must pay in United States notes, two fifths of the price, and the residue on receiving a deed for the parcels of land preëmpted, and a failure to make complete payment on receipt of the Deed will forfeit all rights under the preemption, as well as all partial payments for the land.

4 When persons authorized to purchase by preemption desire to enter upon, and cultivate lands not yet surveyed, they may do so, but they will be required to conform in their selection, as nearly as possible, to the probable lines of the surveys, and to take and occupy them subject to correction of title and occupation by actual surveys when made.

5. In making surveys, such reservations for paths and roadways will be made as will allow easy and convenient access to the several subdivisions entered for sale and occupancy by preemption or otherwise.   Approved December 31. 1863.

A. LINCOLN.

[1] Copy, DNA FI RG 58, Direct Tax Commission of South Carolina.

To George G. Meade[1]

Will Gen. Meade please suspend execution, in this, case, as in others.   A. LINCOLN

Dec. 31. 1863.

[1] AES, DNA WR RG 153, Judge Advocate General, NN 831. Lincoln's endorsement is written on the papers in the case of Corporal David McGahan, Forty-ninth Pennsylvania Volunteers, sentenced for desertion.

To Edwin M. Stanton[1]

Will the Secretary of War please have early attention given to this subject?   A. LINCOLN

Dec. 31. 1863.

[1] AES, DNA WR RG 156, Office of Chief of Ordnance, N 145. Lincoln's endorsement is written on a petition from employees at the Watertown Arsenal (Massachusetts) setting forth grievances, chiefly longer working hours than were in force at Navy Yards. An endorsement by General George D. Ramsay, January 7, 1864, instructed that "working hours now in force at the Charlestown Navy Yard" be conformed to at the arsenal.

To Edwin M. Stanton[1]

Hon. Sec. of War.   Executive Mansion,
Sir: Washington, Dec. 31, 1863.

John Tipton, an acquaintance of mine, in the county of my residence, represents that he has lost one brother, and had another crippled for life, in our service, and that he has a nephew—*M. P. Davis,*—who was conscripted in the rebel service and is now our prisoner at Camp Douglas. He asks that the nephew, may be discharged on taking the oath. Let it be done. Yours truly

A. LINCOLN

[1] ALS, owned by Mrs. Jennie G. Curl, Eureka, California. Brothers of John P. Tipton of Springfield, Illinois, were: Private Landon P. Tipton, Company I, Seventh Illinois Volunteers, and Sergeant Isaac H. Tipton of the same company who died at Louisville, Kentucky, on April 2, 1862. No further reference has been found to his nephew, M. P. Davis.

To Edwin M. Stanton[1]

Hon. Sec of War.   Executive Mansion,
Sir: Washington, Dec 31st. 1863

Please fix up the Dept. to which Curtis is to go without waiting to wind up the Missouri matter. Lane is very anxious to have Fort Smith in it, and I am willing unless there be decided Military reasons the contrary, in which case of course I am not for it.

It will oblige me to have the Curtis Department fixed at once. Yours truly,   A. LINCOLN.

[1] Copy, DNA WR RG 108, Headquarters of the Army, Letters Received, No. 179. AGO, *General Orders No. 1,* January 1, 1864, assigned General Samuel R. Curtis to command the Department of Kansas, consisting of Kansas, Nebraska, Colorado, and the Indian territories, including the post of Fort Smith, Arkansas.

To Edwin M. Stanton[1]

1864

The Hon. Secretary of War: Please see and hear Mrs Kennedy and oblige her if you can find a place for her son. 1864

[1] Copy, CSmH. Mrs. Kennedy has not been identified.

To Thomas T. Eckert[1]

[c. January, 1864]

Private Please send the above. A. Lincoln

[1] AES, RPB. Lincoln's endorsement is written on the following undated telegram:

"C. P. Johnson, Esq.   Jefferson City Mo.
"Dont let the convention bill be pressed to a vote for some days after it comes up. I will write you at length.   B. Gratz Brown"

Charles P. Johnson of St. Louis, Missouri, was a member of the state legislature. The first ballot on the bill calling for an election to be held in November, 1864, for election of delegates to a constitutional convention, was taken in the Missouri legislature on January 14, 1864, and the act was finally approved on February 13, 1864.

To James S. Wadsworth[1]

[January, 1864?]

You desire to know, in the event of our complete success in the field, the same being followed by a loyal and cheerful submission on the part of the South, if universal amnesty should not be accompanied with universal suffrage.

Now, since you know my private inclinations as to what terms should be granted to the South in the contingency mentioned, I will here add, that if our success should thus be realized, followed by such desired results, I cannot see, if universal amnesty is granted, how, under the circumstances, I can avoid exacting in return universal suffrage, or, at least, suffrage on the basis of intelligence and military service.

How to better the condition of the colored race has long been a study which has attracted my serious and careful attention; hence I think I am clear and decided as to what course I shall pursue in the premises, regarding it a religious duty, as the nation's guardian of these people, who have so heroically vindicated their manhood on the battle-field, where, in assisting to save the life of the Republic, they have demonstrated in blood their right to the ballot, which is but the humane protection of the flag they have so fearlessly defended.

[101]

The restoration of the Rebel States to the Union must rest upon the principle of civil and political equality of both races; and it must be sealed by general amnesty.[2]

[1] New York *Tribune*, September 26, 1865; *Scribner's Magazine*, January, 1893. This extract was widely reprinted in newspapers from the source indicated in the *Tribune* as follows:

"*The Southern Advocate* of the 18th inst. says:

" 'The following extract, which has just been published, is from the late President Lincoln's letter to Gen. Wadsworth, who fell in the battle of the Wilderness. The letter, which is of a private character, is to be sent to Gen. Wadsworth's family.

" 'It shows that Mr. Lincoln, who desired the bestowal of the elective franchise upon the blacks, was also, at an early day, in favor of granting universal amnesty, which, for some strange and unaccountable reason, is still withheld from the South, notwithstanding it is known that it was his intention to grant, without any exception, a general pardon.

" 'His wishes, in this particular, the American people cannot afford to disregard. Congress will, no doubt, exact the right of suffrage for the blacks. Why universal amnesty should be withheld until that time, we are unable to see. This, certainly, was not Mr. Lincoln's plan, whose intentions all parties should sacredly observe.

" 'The following is the extract referred to, in which Mr. Lincoln says: [extract as given above].' "

The Southern Advocate has not been located, and no other reference has been found to the original letter to Wadsworth. The contents of the excerpt is, however, closely in keeping with views expressed by Lincoln elsewhere (see Fragment, August 26, 1863, *supra*), and seems to be genuine. The date assigned is based upon the fact that General Wadsworth returned from his tour of inspection of freedmen in the Mississippi Valley on December 3, 1863, and on the supposition that Lincoln's letter would probably have been written some time thereafter, but in any case prior to May, 1864, since Wadsworth was killed in the Battle of the Wilderness, May 5-7, 1864.

[2] This paragraph does not appear in the newspaper accounts, but is included in the article by Marquis de Chambrun in *Scribner's Magazine*.

To Edwin M. Stanton[1]

Let this appointment be made, if the service can be made useful.

Jan. 1, 1864   A. LINCOLN

[1] City Book Auction Catalog No. 523, April 28, 1951, No. A22. According to the catalog description, Lincoln's endorsement is written on a letter from five officers recommending promotion of David McKinney. First Lieutenant David McKinney, regimental quartermaster of the Seventy-seventh Illinois Infantry, was promoted to captain and assistant quartermaster on March 5, 1865.

To Jeremiah C. Sullivan[1]

Gen. Sullivan   Washington, D.C.,
Harper's Ferry.   Jan. 1. 3/30 PM 1864

Have you anything new from Winchester, Martinsburg, or thereabouts?

A. LINCOLN

[1] ALS, RPB. On December 31, 1863, General Sullivan had reported to General Benjamin F. Kelley that General Jubal Early would attack within twenty-four hours (OR, I, XXIX, II, 591). His reply to Lincoln's telegram was received at 5:30 P.M. on January 1, 1864:

"I have ordered a force to Winchester strong enough to develop anything that may be there. I believe the reports from Martinsburg this morning were premature. I am now leaving for Martinsburg to see for myself." (DLC-RTL).

To Benjamin F. Butler[1]

Executive Mansion,
Major Gen. Butler   Washington, Jan. 2, 1864.

The Secretary of War and myself have concluded to discharge, of the prisoners at Point Lookout, the following classes.

1 Those who will take the oath prescribed in the proclamation of Dec. 8., and, by the consent of Gen. Marston will enlist in our service.

2. Those who will take the oath, and be discharged, and whose homes lie safely within our military lines.

I send by Mr. Hay, this letter, and a blank Book & some other blanks, the way of using which, I propose for him to explain verbally, better than I can in writing. Yours very truly

A. LINCOLN

[1] ALS-P, ISLA. This letter is incorrectly dated "January 2, 1863" by Nicolay and Hay (VIII, 167). Concerning the blanks prepared by Lincoln for the oath of December 8, 1863, see the note to Lincoln's communication to Peirpoint, December 21, 1863, *supra*. Hay's *Diary* records under date of January 2, 1864, his trip to Point Lookout with the blanks.

To Joseph Holt[1]

Judge Advocate General please examine and report on this case.
Jan. 2. 1864.   A. LINCOLN

[1] AES, RPB. Lincoln's endorsement has been clipped from attendant documents and cannot be further identified.

To Francis H. Peirpoint[1]

Gov. Peirpoint.   Executive Mansion
Alexandria, Va.   Washington D.C. Jan. 2. 1864

Please call and see me to-day, if not too inconvenient.

A. LINCOLN

[1] ALS, RPB. Peirpoint's reply, misdated "Jan 2 1863," is as follows:
"Your telegram asking me to call on you to day is recd. I returned from Norfolk on Wednesday morning last and regret that I was so near sick that I have not been out of my room but once since. It is severe cold. The first day I can venture out I will call on you.
"I found things" (DLC-RTL).

To Edwin M. Stanton[1]

January 2, 1864

The writer of this is a good man, and P.M. at Chicago. Webster, from whom he quotes, is also a good man, and the *locus in quo*, as you know, is under Gen. Hurlbut. I submit this case to the Sec. of War.   A. LINCOLN

Jan. 2. 1864.

[1] AES, DLC-Stanton Papers. Lincoln's endorsement is written on a letter from John L. Scripps, December 30, 1863, quoting an extract from a letter of Brigadier General Joseph D. Webster at Memphis, Tennessee, saying that "corruption is openly and constantly charged upon officers in that Department. The President should order a Court of Inquiry."

To Stephen A. Hurlbut[1]

Major-General Hurlbut,   Executive Mansion,
Memphis, Tenn.:   Washington, January 3, 1864.

Suspend execution of sentence of Privt. Peter Fingle of Fourteenth Iowa Volunteers, and forward record of trial for examination.   A. LINCOLN.

[1] Tarbell (Appendix), p. 407. Hurlbut replied on January 11, "The sentence of Peter Wingle [Fingle] fourteenth (14) Iowa Infantry has been recalled & the record sent to Genl Sherman for his approval, Col Holt having decided that I do not command our army in the field" (DLC-RTL). The roster of Company G, Fourteenth Iowa, lists Peter Fingle as deserted at Corinth, Mississippi, May 7, 1862. No further record has been found.

To George G. Meade[1]

Executive Mansion,
Major-General Meade: Washington, January 3, 1864.

Suspend the execution of Prvt. Joseph Richardson, Forty-ninth Pennsylvania Volunteers, who is sentenced to be shot to-morrow, and forward record of trial for examination.   A. LINCOLN.

Major Eckert:
Please send above dispatch.   JNO. G. NICOLAY.

[1] Tarbell (Appendix), p. 408. See Lincoln to Meade, December 29, *supra.* Meade's reply was received at 3:10 P.M.: "Your dispatch of today in reference to private Joseph Richardson, 49th P.V., is received. In obedience to orders recd. from you the execution of the sentence in this case was suspended on the 29th. ultimo. The record was forwarded for your orders on the 30th. ult." (DLC-RTL). Richardson's sentence was commuted to imprisonment in Dry Tortugas by AGO *Special Orders No. 166,* May 3, 1864.

To Edward Bates[1]

Attorney General, please make out a pardon in this case.

Jan. 4. 1864.   A. LINCOLN

[1] AES, IHi. Lincoln's endorsement is written on a letter from L. M. Bentley, Clarksville, Tennessee, December 21, 1863, asking pardon for having served briefly in 1862 as postmaster at Lawrenceburg under Confederate appointment.

To Edward Bates[1]

Attorney General please make out a pardon in the case which Hon. Mr. Grider will request.   A. LINCOLN

Jan. 4. 1864.

[1] AES, DNA RG 204, U.S. Pardon Attorney, A 504. Lincoln's endorsement is written on an envelope filed with the papers of Josiah Pillsbury of Kentucky, convicted of treason.

Recommendation[1]

I personally know nothing of this Lady; and yet I shall be very glad if she can get some suitable employment.   A. LINCOLN

Jan. 4. 1864.

[1] ADS, IHi.

To Edward Bates[1]

Attorney General please examine & report upon this case.

Jan. 5, 1864.   A. LINCOLN

[1] AES, DNA RG 204, U.S. Pardon Attorney, A 466. Lincoln's endorsement is written on the papers in the case of George S. Becker. See Lincoln to Stiles, December 24, 1863, *supra*, and to Bates, January 25, *infra*.

To Henry T. Blow[1]

                              Executive Mansion   Washington,
My Dear Mr Blow   5 January, 1864.

I have received the photograph of Mr. Schaerpp's picture which you have had the kindness to deliver, and I beg that you will express to the artist my thanks for his courtesy   I am yours very truly

Hon. H. T. Blow.   A. LINCOLN.

[1] Copy, ISLA. The present location of the original letter is not known, and the only available transcript seems to be in error as to the artist's name. John W. Schaerff was an artist and lithographer at St. Louis, Missouri. Henry T. Blow as president of the Western Academy of Art probably sent Lincoln an example of Schaerff's work, possibly a lithograph of Lincoln, but the picture has not been identified.

To Jeremiah T. Boyle[1]

General Boyle
Camp-Nelson, Ky

Executive Mansion
Washington D.C. Jan. 5. 1864

Execution in the cases of Burrows and Eaton, is suspended, as stated by Gen. Burnside. Let this be taken as an order to that effect. I do not remember receiving any appeal in behalf of Goddard, Crowell, Puckett, or Smith, and yet I may have sent a despatch in regard to some of them A. LINCOLN

[1] ALS, RPB. See Lincoln to Burnside, December 26 and 29, 1863, *supra*, and to Boyle, January 6, *infra*. AGO *Special Orders No. 16*, January 12, 1864, commuted sentences of Daniel Burrows, Company D, and Abel Eaton, Company C, Sixth New Hampshire Volunteers, to hard labor for the balance of their term of enlistment, but remitted this sentence and returned them to duty "upon condition they re-enlist in their regiment." The same order remitted sentence of Corporal Robert L. Crowell, Twentieth Kentucky Volunteers and returned him to duty. See Lincoln to Boyle concerning Crowell, December 30, 1863, *supra*.

To Mary Todd Lincoln[1]

Mrs. A Lincoln—Continental Hotel.
Philadelphia, Pa.

Washington, D.C.,
Jany. 5. 1864

All very well. A LINCOLN

[1] ALS, IHi. "Continental Hotel" is not in Lincoln's handwriting.

To George G. Meade[1]

Major General Meade

Executive Mansion,
Washington, Jan. 5, 1864

If not inconsistent with the service, please allow Gen. William Harrow as long a leave of absence as the rules permit, with the understanding that I may lengthen it, if I see fit. He is an acquaintance and friend of mine, & his family matters, very urgently require his presence. A. LINCOLN

[1] Copy, DNA WR RG 94, Adjutant General, Letters Received, P 3. See Lincoln's endorsement to Stanton, January 7, *infra*.

To the Senate and House of Representatives[1]

Gentlemen of the Senate, and   January 5, 1864
House of Representatives.

By a Joint Resolution of your Honorable bodies, approved December 23. 1863. the paying of bounties to veteran volunteers, as now practiced by the War Department, is, to the extent of three hundred dollars in each case, prohibited after this fifth day of the present month. I transmit, for your consideration, a communication from the Secretary of War, accompanied by one from the Provost-Marshal-General to him, both relating to the subject above mentioned. I earnestly recommend that the law be so modified as to allow bounties to be paid as they now are, at least until the ensuing first day of February.

I am not without anxiety lest I appear to be importunate, in thus re-calling your attention to a subject upon which you have so recently acted; and nothing but a deep conviction that the public interest demands it, could induce me to incur the hazard of being misunderstood on this point. The executive approval was given by me to the Resolution mentioned; and it is now, by a closer attention, and a fuller knowledge of facts, that I feel constrained to recommend a re-consideration of the subject.

January 5. 1864.   ABRAHAM LINCOLN

[1] ADf, DLC-RTL; DS, DNA RG 46, Senate 38A F4; DS, DNA RG 233, House Executive Document. The letter of James B. Fry to Stanton, January 2, 1864, is as follows:

"After great labor the volunteer recruiting service under the President's call of October 17th is fairly in progress. Letters all dated between the 20th & 24th of December from the Superintendents of Recruiting Service in Sixteen states are in the main very encouraging as to the prospect of getting a large number of recruits by volunteer enlistments. Several of the states were in a fair way to raise the quotas assigned them. The Act approved December 23d. 1863, forbidding after January 5th the payment to volunteers of all bounties except $100 authorized by the Act of 1861 was not known at the time these favorable reports were made to me. I have no doubt the effect of that act will be to check if it does not stop enlistments. Of the $100 bounty provided by Act of 1861 but $25 can be paid in advance, $75 being due only after two years service.

"It took some time after October 17th to get the people aroused to the subject of volunteering; they are now in most states earnestly engaged in it, & I have reports for October, November & part of December showing that 42,529 men have been enlisted, & the daily average of enlistments is increasing. Under these circumstances I respectfully suggest the propriety of a reconsideration of the Act forbidding bounties after January 5th. I enclose herewith copy of my report to you of the 25th December. . . ."

Stanton's letter of January 5, 1864, is as follows:

"I beg to submit to your consideration the accompanying letter of the Provost Marshal General. . . . No one seems to doubt the necessity of increasing the military force . . . and, although much difference of opinion exists in respect to the merits of the system of raising troops by volunteers and the payment of bounties, and the system of raising an adequate force by draft, yet two things are certain—

"First—That, whatever may be the weight of argument or the influence of individual opinion, a large portion of the people . . . prefer the method of contributing their proportion of the military force by bounty to volunteers rather than by draft.

"Second—that veteran soldiers who have become inured to service, even when paid bounty, constitute a cheaper force than raw recruits or drafted men without bounty.

"The information received by this Department from the armies in the field, prior to the passage of the resolution . . . indicated that a very large proportion of the forces now in service would have cheerfully re-enlisted for three years under the terms authorized by the order of this Department, and that such enlistments have been checked, and will in great measure be put an end to, by the restriction imposed by the act of Congress. It is believed that if any limitation should be imposed upon the payment of bounties to encourage the enlistment of the veteran forces now in the field, it ought not to be sooner than the 1st of February. It is respectfully submitted to your consideration, therefore, whether the attention of Congress might not again well be called to the subject, so that the resolution may be reconsidered."

A joint resolution approved January 13, 1864, extended the payment of bounties until March 1, and the joint resolution approved March 3, provided further extension to April 1, 1864.

To Edwin M. Stanton and Henry W. Halleck[1]

January 5, 1864.

I ask the respectful attention and consideration of the Secretary of War and General-in-Chief.   A. LINCOLN.

[1] AES, DNA WR RG 108, H.Q.A., S 256, Box 70. Lincoln's endorsement is on a resolution of the Kentucky General Assembly, December 14, 1863, asking the president to convene a court of inquiry on the conduct of General Thomas L. Crittenden at the Battle of Chickamauga. (See OR, I, XXX, 619.) Stanton endorsed to Halleck with directions "to detail a Court of Inquiry as speedily as possible." The court, convened at Nashville on January 29 and dismissed on February 23, 1864, found Crittenden not censurable.

To Frederick Steele[1]

Executive Mansion,
Major General Steele   Washington, January 5, 1864.

I wish to afford the people of Arkansas an opportunity of taking the oath prescribed in the proclamation of Dec. 8, 1863, preparatory to re-organizing a State-government there.

Accordingly I send you, by Gen. Kimball, some blank-books and other blanks, the manner of using which will, in the main, be suggested by an inspection of them; and Gen. Kimball will add some verbal explanations. Please make a trial of the matter immediately at such points as you may think likely to give success.

I suppose Helena and Little Rock are two of them. Detail any officer you may see fit to take charge of the subject at each point; and which officer, it may be assumed, will have authority to administer the oath. These books of course, are intended to be permanent records. Report to me on the subject. Yours very truly,

A. LINCOLN

[1] ADfS, DLC-RTL; LS, owned by William W. Steele, Pescadero, California. Concerning the blank books carried by Brigadier General Nathan Kimball, see the note to Lincoln's letter to Peirpoint, December 21, 1863, *supra.*

To Jeremiah T. Boyle[1]

Gen. Boyle.   Executive Mansion
Camp Nelson, Ky.   Washington D.C. Jan. 6. 1864
     Let executions in the cases of Goddard, Crowell, Puckett & Smith, mentioned by you be suspended till further order.

A LINCOLN

[1] ALS, RPB. See Lincoln to Boyle, January 5, *supra.* Boyle's telegram has not been discovered.

To Thomas E. Bramlette[1]

Gov. Bramlette   Executive Mansion,
Frankfort, Ky.   Washington, Jan– 6. 1864.
     Yours of yesterday received. Nothing is known here about Gen. Foster's order, of which you complain, beyond the fair presumption that it comes from Gen. Grant, and that it has an object which if you understood, you would be loth to frustrate[2]

True, these troops are, in strict law, only to be removed by my order; but Gen. Grant's judgment would be the highest incentive to me to make such order. Nor can I understand how doing so is bad faith or dishonor; nor yet how it exposes Kentucky to ruin.

Military men here do not perceive how it such [*sic*] exposes Kentucky, and I am sure Grant would not permit it, if it so appeared to him.   A. LINCOLN

[1] ALS, IHi. Governor Bramlette's telegram of January 5 is as follows: "Maj Gen [John G.] Foster has ordered all the organized forces in Kentucky to Knoxville. This will take the forces raised under act of Congress for defense of Kentucky & expose us to Ruin The Act reserved to you at once the power to remove these troops It is due to us, to good faith, to honor & to humanity that this order as to these troops be countermanded" (DLC-RTL). For Bramlette's reply of January 8, see Lincoln to Bramlette, January 17, *infra.*

[2] Grant's command of the Military Division of the Mississippi included the Department of the Ohio, in which John G. Foster had succeeded Burnside.

[109]

To Luiz I[1]

January 6, 1864

Abraham Lincoln
President of the United States of America.

To His Majesty Dom Luis I.
King of Portugal.

Great & Good Friend, I have received the letter which your majesty was pleased to address to me on the 22 day of October last, imparting intelligence of the birth on the 28th of the preceding month of a Prince, who had received in baptism the names of Carlos Fernando.

Your majesty does no more than justice to the friendly feelings of the United States, in believing that they participate with Your Majesty and your Royal Family in the joy consequent upon this event; and I beg your Majesty to accept my sincere congratulations

I pray God to have Your Majesty and Family in His holy keeping   Your Good Friend   ABRAHAM LINCOLN.

Washington, Jan 6 1864.
By the President
WILLIAM H. SEWARD   Secretary of State.

[1] Copy, DNA FS RG 59, Communications to Foreign Sovereigns and States, III, 223.

Memorandum:
Appointment of David D. Johnson[1]

[c. January 6, 1864]
I think I will make this appointment.

[1] AE, DLC-RTL. Lincoln's endorsement is written on a letter from Henry C. Johnson, speaker of the Pennsylvania legislature, to U.S. Representative Amos Myers, January 6, 1864, requesting appointment of his son David D. Johnson to West Point. Entering the academy in July, 1864, David D. Johnson graduated in 1868.

To Edward Bates[1]

Attorney General please make out a pardon in this case.

Jan. 7. 1864.   A. LINCOLN

[1] AES, OClWHi-Palmer Collection. This endorsement has been removed from attendant papers and cannot be identified.

To Christian IX[1]

January 7, 1864

Abraham Lincoln
President of the United States of America

To His Majesty Christian IX.
          King of Denmark
     Great and Good Friend I have recd. the letter which Your
Majesty was pleased to address to me on the 17th day of Nov last,
communicating intelligence of the demise on the 15th of that
month of His late Majesty Frederick VII, and of your accession to
the throne of the Kingdom.

     Assuring you of my deep sympathy at the death of your august
Cousin, who like his predecessors was the constant & steady friend
of the U. States, I beg leave to offer to Your Majesty my sincere
and hearty congratulations upon your accession to the throne,
with my best wishes, that your reign may be happy and glorious
to yourself, and prosperous to your realm. Permit me also to assure Your Majesty of my constant and earnest desire to maintain
the amity and good correspondence which has always subsisted
and still prevails between the two nations and that nothing shall
ever be omitted on my part to cultivate and promote maintain?[2]
towards Your Majesty the friendly relations always, entertained
& cherished by this Government in its relations with his late Majesty and so I recommend your Majesty to the protection of the
Almighty. Your Good Friend   ABRAHAM LINCOLN

     Washington City Jan 7 1864.
          By the President
          WILLIAM H. SEWARD, Secretary of State.

1 Copy, DNA FS RG 59, Communications to Foreign Sovereigns and States,
III, 232-33.
2 "Maintain?" is written above "promote," but "promote" is not deleted.

Endorsement Concerning Henry Andrews[1]

[January 7, 1864]

     The case of Andrews is really a very bad one, as appears by the
record already before me. Yet before receiving this I had ordered
his punishment commuted to imprisonment for during the war at
hard labor, and had so telegraphed. I did this, not on any merit
in the case, but because I am trying to evade the butchering
business lately.   A. LINCOLN.

1 NH, IX, 279. As given in the source Lincoln's endorsement is written on a communication to Salmon P. Chase, January 7, 1864: "One Andrews is to be shot for desertion at Covington, to-morrow. The proceedings have never been submitted to the President. Is this right? Governor Hoadley." The source is obviously in error in having Chase's law partner George Hoadly sign himself as "Governor Hoadley" when he was not elected governor of Ohio until many years later. See Lincoln to Hawley, *infra*.

To Chauncey G. Hawley[1]

Officer in command at Executive Mansion
Covington, Ky. Washington, D.C. Jan. 7. 1864
The death sentence of Henry Andrews is commuted to imprisonment at hard labor during the remainder of the war.

A. LINCOLN

1 ALS, RPB. See Lincoln's endorsement on the telegram from Hoadly, *supra*. AGO *Special Orders No. 11*, January 8, 1864, commuted the sentence of Private Henry Andrews, Company I, One Hundred Twenty-fourth Ohio Volunteers, to imprisonment at hard labor during the remainder of the war.

To Mary Todd Lincoln[1]

Mrs. A. Lincoln Executive Mansion,
Philadelphia, Pa. Washington, Jan. 7, 1864.
We are all well, and have not been otherwise.

A. LINCOLN

1 ALS, IHi.

To the Senate[1]

To the Senate of the United States: January [7], 1864
I herewith lay before the Senate, for its constitutional action thereon, the following described treaties, viz:

A treaty made at Fort Bridger, Utah Territory, on the 2d day of July, 1863, between the United States and the chiefs, principal men, and warriors of the eastern bands of the Shoshonee Nation of Indians.

A treaty made at Box Elder, Utah Territory, on the 30th day of July, 1863, between the United States and the chiefs and warriors of the northwestern bands of the Shoshonee Nation of Indians.

A treaty made at Ruby Valley, Nevada Territory, on the 1st day of October, 1863, between the United States and the chiefs, principal men, and warriors of the [western bands of the] Shoshonee Nation of Indians.

A treaty made at Tuilla Valley, Utah Territory, on the 12th day of October, 1863, between the United States and the chiefs, principal men, and warriors of the Goship bands of Shoshonee Indians.

A treaty made at Soda Springs, in Idaho Territory, on the 14th day of October, 1863, between the United States and the chiefs of the mixed bands of Bannacks and Shoshonees, occupying the valley of the Shoshonee River.

A letter of the Secretary of the Interior of the 5th instant, a copy of a report of the 30th ultimo, from the Commissioner of Indian Affairs, a copy of a communication from Governor Doty, superintendent of Indian affairs, Utah Territory, dated November 10, 1863, relating to the Indians, parties to the several treaties herein named, and a map furnished by that gentleman are herewith transmitted.   ABRAHAM LINCOLN.

Executive Mansion, Washington, January, 1864.

[1] *Executive Journal*, XIII, 323. The treaties were submitted to the Senate on January 7 and ratified on March 7, 1864. The treaty of October 1, 1863, with the western bands was reconsidered, however, and was not finally ratified until June 26, 1866.

To the Senate and House of Representatives[1]

January 7, 1864

To the Senate and House of Representatives:

I transmit to Congress a copy of the Decree of the Court of the United States for the Southern District of New York, awarding the sum of seventeen thousand one hundred and fifty dollars and sixty-six cents for the illegal capture of the British schooner "Glen"; and request that an appropriation of that amount may be made as an indemnification to the parties interested.

Washington, 7th. January, 1864.   ABRAHAM LINCOLN

[1] DS, DNA RG 233, House Executive Document No. 19. An act approved on February 13, 1864, appropriated $17,150.66 to owners of the schooner *Glen*.

To Edwin M. Stanton[1]

Will the Secretary of War please order Gen. Harrow to report to Gen. Grant.   A. LINCOLN

Jan. 7, 1864.

[1] AES, owned by Gordon A. Block, Philadelphia, Pennsylvania. See Lincoln to Stanton, November 11, 1863, and to Meade, January 5, 1864, *supra*. Lincoln's endorsement is written on the back of AGO *Special Orders No. 522 (Extract)*, November 24, 1863, assigning Brigadier General William Harrow to report to Major General Meade. Below Lincoln's endorsement Stanton wrote "Adjt Genl

will issue the order directed by the President." Following Stanton's endorsement, another unsigned endorsement appears: *"No order to be issued."* The final unsigned endorsement is "Letter to Genl [Francis J.] Herron, Jany. 7/64."

To Edwin M. Stanton[1]

If the request of Governor Buckingham and Senator Foster, within, can consistently be granted, let it be done.

Jany. 7. 1864.   A. LINCOLN

[1] AES, owned by C. Norton Owen, Glencoe, Illinois. Lincoln's endorsement is written on a letter of December 29, 1863, signed by William A. Buckingham and endorsed by Lafayette S. Foster, January 7, 1864, recommending Major Hiram B. Crosby of the Twenty-first Connecticut Volunteers for appointment as assistant adjutant general of an army corps. Stanton endorsed as follows: "By the regulations of the Service the Staff officers of Corps Commanders are nominated by the Commander & if there be no objection to the individual it is approved by the Dept."

To Crafts J. Wright and Charles K. Hawkes[1]

Executive Mansion,
Gentlemen: Washington, Jany. 7, 1864.

You have presented me a plan for getting cotten and other products, from within the rebel lines, from which you think the United States will derive some advantage.

Please carefully and considerately, answer me the following questions.

1. If now, without any new order or rule, a rebel should come into our lines with cotten, and offer to take the oath of Dec. 8th. what do you understand would be done with him and his cotten?

2. How will the physical difficulty, and danger, of getting cotten from within the rebel lines be lessened by your plan? or how will the owners motive to surmount that difficulty and danger, be heightened by it?

3. If your plan be adopted, *where* do you propose putting the cotten &c. into market? how assure the government of your good faith in the business? and how be compensated for your services?

Very Respectfully   A. LINCOLN

Messrs. Crafts J. Wright & C. K. Hawkes.

[1] ALS, IHi; LS copy, DLC-RTL. On January 4, 1864, Hawkes and Wright wrote Lincoln:

"We have the honor to refer you to the application of the Hon B F Flanders special Agt of the Treasury Dept., Mr. Geo S. Denison Collector of Customs— Mr Wm. H. Higgins Assessor of U.S. Internal Revenue, the Hon B Rush Plumby Hon Jno. Hutchins—and also that of Maj Gen Banks commanding the department of the Gulf and His Excellency Gov Shepley. This application is for a special permit to obtain supplies on terms & conditions designated. . . .

We may also add that very many worthy union people on each side are looking to the granting of this as the only hope of relieving them from want.

"We may briefly say the request is that you, with whom the power is placed, will grant to Geo. B. Waldron—Crafts J. Wright & Charles K Hawks a permit.

"1st. To recieve from persons beyond the lines of our actual military occupation—such cotton—sugar—other stores as parties beyond our lines may desire to consign to us, to be conveyed & sold within our lines on the terms & according to the rules of the Treasury Department.

"2d. That the proceeds of sales, less the government dues & current expenses, shall be invested in the securities of the Government.

"3d. That such an amount of said securities purchased as aforesaid shall be deposited with some officer of the Treasury Department, until the consignee shall prove his loyalty by taking the oath according to the recent proclamation. . . .

"On recommendation of Gen Banks—Gen Shepley—& others we have come from New Orleans to the city to answer any questions as well as to satisfy you of our loyalty. . . ." (DLC-RTL).

Enclosed with their letter was the following document, signed by John Hutchins, George S. Denison, William H. Higgins and B. Rush Plumly, approved by Benjamin F. Flanders, "provided the holders of the Bonds shall deposit fifty per centum thereof with the Treasurer of the United States until the close of the war:"

"The undersigned are advised that a large number of persons are within the Rebel lines who have cotton—sugar and other stores—which they have been and are concealing from the Rebel authorities as confiscable property. That these parties are anxious to place these supplies within the United States Military lines—not only as a place of safety, but to secure for their families a means of support and a means of satisfying their debts to Loyal Union citizens. Many of these parties desire to leave the so-called Confederacy so soon as they can place their property on which they depend—on a place of safety.

"They do not ask to have the proceeds of their property returned in supplies—but are willing to invest the net proceeds—less the current Government dues and the expenses attending the getting to market and selling—in United States Bonds.

"They have designated George B. Waldron of New York—Crafts J. Wright of Cincinnati and Charles K. Hawkes of New York as Loyal Union citizens to whom they will consign their property and who shall invest the proceeds as above—and in whom they and the Government can confide. . . .

"We therefore urgently recommend that the authority be given to the above named . . . to receive from within the Rebel lines at such points as may be designated—such cotton sugar, and other stores, as it may be desired to convey within the United States Military lines for sale—and to invest the proceeds—less the expenses—in Government securities, that protection be afforded by the military and naval authorities—unless there be imperative military objections at the time." (*Ibid.*).

On January 8, Wright and Hawkes replied to Lincoln's questions:

"Before proceeding to reply specifically to the several questions which you have put to us, we deem it proper, to a better understanding of the difficulties now in the way of the increase of Union people & the protection of Union property, to make, with your permission, a preliminary observation statement. . . .

[Question 1:]

"1st. If he has not *previously* bribed the pickets, they would siese and confiscate it. . . .

"2d. Not having a permit previously obtained it would be, by officers of the Treasury Dept, at once seised & confiscated. . . .

"3d. The *Rebel* would be seperated from his property—arrested—& confined, until he took the oath and *satisfied* the officer . . . to 'keep and maintain' said oath. . . .

"4th. Admitting that after detention . . . he takes the oath . . . gets his property released . . . yet, ignorant of forms . . . must assuredly fall into the hands of Jews . . .

"5th. Cotton is a heavy article to be transported. . . . If the Rebel came to our lines, *he could* bring only *one* load; to secure that load, he must take the *oath.* He cannot get back to rebel lines for other loads.

[Question 2:]

"1st. We have removed all the danger of confiscation & difficulties on *our side of the lines.* . . .

"2d. We give him such assurance & present to him, a *working plan,* clear & distinct, which *induces* effort to. . . .

[Question 3:]

". . . . We answer in New Orleans—Cincinnati—St. Louis, the great cotton markets. We propose only to sell it, at public auction, to make ourselves free of all charge of unfairness. . . . All the officers of the Treasury Department . . . vouch for us, by their recommendations which we present. . . . The *commanding Officers* of the *Department of the Military Government,* vouch for us . . . Some of us have shewn our faith in battle fields. . . . We recommend that the collector of customs have a supervision over . . . affairs . . . The permit granted, if it is found we do not keep faith, or the method works badly, . . . will . . . be revokable at pleasure . . . Our *interest* will induce Faith . . . We are merchants and make our own arrangements as such—our fees & commissions are regulated by the customs of trade, long established in New Orleans, governing all transactions. . . ." (*Ibid.*).

On January 9, Wright and Hawkes sent a supplementary reply and enclosed a suggested form of the order which they hoped the president would issue. Although some of the suggestions made by Wright and Hawkes were adopted in the new regulations issued for Treasury Agents (see Order of January 26, *infra*), no special arrangement with the gentlemen concerned seems to have been made. Efforts on the part of George Ashmun to have Hawkes appointed agent of the Treasury also failed (Ashmun to Lincoln, January 20 and February 2, 1864, DLC-RTL).

To the Senate[1]

To the Senate of the United States: January [8], 1864

I herewith lay before the Senate, for its constitutional action thereon, a treaty made at the Old Crossing of Red Lake River, in the State of Minnesota, on the 2d day of October, 1863, between Alexander Ramsey and Ashley C. Morrill, commissioners on the part of the United States, and the chiefs, headmen, and warriors of the Red Lake and Pembina bands of Chippewa Indians.

A letter of the Secretary of the Interior, of the 8th instant, together with a communication from the Commissioner of Indian Affairs, of the 5th instant, and copies of Mr. Ramsey's report and journal, relating to the treaty, and a map showing the Territory ceded, are herewith transmitted.   ABRAHAM LINCOLN.

Executive Mansion.

Washington, January–, 1864.

To Edwin M. Stanton[1]

Executive Mansion, Washington, Jan. 8. 1864.

To-day Senator Grimes calls and asks that I may particularly examine the recommendations on file for Grenville M. Dodge for Major Genl. & Edward Hatch of 2nd. Iowa Cav. & Henry C. Caldwell of the 3rd. Iowa. Cav. for Brig. Gens. which I promise to do.

Will the Sec. of War please have these papers sent me, which, after examining, I will return?   A. LINCOLN

1 ADS, DLC-RTL. Stanton endorsed on the bottom of the sheet, "There is no vacancy for Major or Brigadier General." Grenville M. Dodge was appointed major general as of June 7, 1864; Edward Hatch was appointed brigadier general as of April 27, 1864; Henry C. Caldwell resigned on June 25, 1864. See Lincoln to Grimes, January 11, *infra*.

To Mrs. Esther Stockton[1]

Executive Mansion,
Mrs. Esther Stockton.   Washington [Jany.] 8, 1864.

Madam: Learning that you who have passed the eighty-fourth year of life, have given to the soldiers, some three hundred pairs of stockings, knitted by yourself, I wish to offer you my thanks. Will you also convey my thanks to those young ladies who have done so much in feeding our soldiers while passing through your city? Yours truly,   A. LINCOLN

1 Tracy, p. 243. This letter is misdated "July" in the source, probably as a misreading for Lincoln's "Jany." The *Illinois State Journal* for January 28, 1864, notes that "President Lincoln has sent a letter of thanks to the widow of Rev. Joseph Stockton, of Pittsburg, Pa., a lady of eighty-five years of age for knitting a great number of stockings for the soldiers, and also thanking the young ladies of that city for feeding the large number of troops passing through." There is an undated reply from Mrs. Stockton (incorrectly supplied with the date of August 5, 1864, probably on the basis of the date of Lincoln's letter in Tracy), as follows:

"Your very kind letter was duly received. My labours in behalf of our gallant soldiers—I fear are some what exaggerated. I have endeavored to do what I could for those who battle to crush this wicked rebellion. . . .

"And now my dear Sir in concluding . . . permit me to say that my earnest prayer for you is, that you may long be spared to enjoy the blessing of a grateful nation. . . ." (DLC-RTL).

To Simon Cameron[1]

Hon: Simon Cameron   Executive Mansion
Harrisburg, Penn.   Washington D.C. Jan. 9. 1864
Your two letters, one of the 6th and the other of the 7th. both
received.   A. LINCOLN

[1] ALS, RPB. Cameron's letters of January 6 and 7 have not been discovered,
but John Hay's *Diary* records on January 9, 1864, that "Cameron has written
to the President that the entire Union force of the Pa. Legislature, House and
Senate, have subscribed a request that the President will allow himself to be
reelected, and that they intend visiting Washington to present it. . . ."

To John A. Dahlgren[1]

Admiral Dahlgren   Executive Mansion,
My dear Sir   Washington, Jan. 9. 1864.
Capt. Lavender wishes to show you a contrivance of his for discovering, and aiding to remove, under-water obstructions to the
passage of vessels, and has sufficiently impressed me to induce me
to send him to you. He is sufficiently vouched to me as a worthy
gentleman; and this known, it needs not my asking for you to
treat him as such. Yours truly   A. LINCOLN

[1] ALS, owned by J. Coleman Scal, New York City. On January 8, 1864,
Senator Edwin D. Morgan wrote Lincoln: "Capt Lavender of New York
eighteen years a sea captain at that Port comes to me from so good a source,
that I cannot refuse to comply with his request to be introduced to you. Such
then is the object of this note, and I hope you may be able to spare him a
few moments. He does not want an office. . . ." (DLC-RTL).
On January 23, Admiral Dahlgren replied to Lincoln's letter:
"Captain Lavender arrived duly with your note, which I was much pleased
to receive, and gave it my immediate attention;—There seems to me no objection to a a [*sic*] trial of his project, and I beg leave, therefore, to recommend that such be made at some Navy Yard under the eye of one or more
experienced persons.
"It would be almost impossible to make the machine here, as material and
mechanics are already unequal to the daily pressing wear and tear of the vessels of the Squadron. . . ." (*Ibid.*).
No further identification of Lavender or his invention has been found.

Order for Observance of Mourning
for Caleb B. Smith[1]

Executive Mansion, January 9th. 1864.
Information having been received that Caleb B. Smith, late Secretary of the Interior, has departed this life, at his residence in
Indiana, it is ordered that the Executive Buildings at the seat of
the Government be draped in mourning, for the period of fourteen
days, in honor of his memory as a prudent and loyal counsellor

and a faithful and effective coadjutor of the Administration in a time of public difficulty and peril. The Secretary of State will communicate a copy of this order to the family of the deceased together with proper expressions of the profound sympathy of the President and Heads of Departments in their great and irreparable bereavement.   ABRAHAM LINCOLN

1 DS, DNA FS RG 59, Miscellaneous Letters, January, 1864.

To Edwin M. Stanton[1]

January 9, 1864.
Let General Blunt have leave to come to Washington.
                         A. LINCOLN.

1 OR, I, XXXIV, II, 52. Lincoln's endorsement is on a letter from James H. Lane and Abel C. Wilder, January 9, 1864, requesting permission for General James G. Blunt to come to Washington to consult with them "on the subject of moving the Kansas Indians to the Indian Territory and the early return of the refugees. . . ."

To Edwin M. Stanton[1]

Hon. Sec. of War   Executive Mansion,
My dear Sir: Washington, Jan. 9. 1864.
    Please send me, to be returned, the testimonials, in favor of Col. Wickliffe Cooper, of Ky, to be a Brigadier General. Yours truly
                         A. LINCOLN.

1 ALS, NHi. Colonel Wickliffe Cooper of the Fourth Kentucky Cavalry was not appointed brigadier general.

To Edwin M. Stanton[1]

Hon. Sec. of War.   Executive Mansion,
Sir: Washington, Jan. 9. 1864.
    Please see Senator Lane, and if you can appoint his man a chaplain, I shall be indeed very glad. Yours truly   A. LINCOLN

1 ALS, owned by L. E. Dicke, Evanston, Illinois. Senator Lane's man has not been identified.

To Ethan A. Hitchcock[1]

Executive Mansion
Washington City, January 10th. 1864.
Major General Hitchcock, Commissioner of Exchanges, is authorized and directed to offer Brigadier-General Trimble now a

prisoner of war in Fort McHenry, in exchange for Major White, who is held as a prisoner at Richmond. He is also directed to send forward the offer of exchange by Henry M. Warfield, Esq. of Baltimore, under a flag of truce, and give him a pass to City Point.

ABRAHAM LINCOLN

[1] John Heise Catalog 2477, No. 28. "Major White" was probably Major Harry White of the Sixty-seventh Pennsylvania Infantry and a Republican senator in the Pennsylvania legislature. See Lincoln to Cameron, October 17, 1863, *supra*. The exchange seems to have been refused by the Confederates, for White was not exchanged until September 29, 1864, and General Isaac R. Trimble remained a prisoner of war until April, 1865.

To Timothy P. Andrews[1]

January 11, 1864

Submitted to the Pay-Master, General—
Major Whitney is a friend I would like to oblige, but not to the prejudice of the service.   A. LINCOLN
Jan. 11. 1864.

[1] AES, IHi. Lincoln's endorsement is written on a letter of Henry C. Whitney to Judge David Davis, January 5, 1864, asking his influence to get transferred from the pay department at Louisville, Kentucky, to that at Fort Leavenworth, Kansas. Davis endorsed, "I suppose he wants to be transferred to Leavenworth, because he wants to live there after war is over. You know whether it is right to interfere and whether you can do it. . . ." Stanton endorsed "No change should be made to the prejudice of the service." Whitney was transferred to Chattanooga, Tennessee, rather than to Fort Leavenworth, Kansas.

To Salmon P. Chase[1]

Executive Mansion,
Hon. Secretary of Treasury: January 11, 1864.
My Dear Sir: I am receiving letters and dispatches indicating an expectation that Mr. Barney is to leave the Custom House, at New York. Have you anything on the subject? Yours very truly,
A. LINCOLN.

[1] Robert B. Warden, *Account of the Private Life and Public Services of Salmon Portland Chase* (1874), p. 556. Secretary Chase replied on January 12, "Nothing at all, except urgent representatives of the necessity of reform, which do not, at all impeach Mr. Barney, in whose integrity I have undiminished confidence." (DLC-RTL).

The many communications on this subject from January to September, 1864, when Barney resigned and Lincoln appointed Simeon Draper in his place, indicate that the issue was not only "reform" but Barney's purported activity in support of Chase's candidacy for the Republican nomination for president.

To James W. Grimes[1]

January 11, 1864

In pursuance of my promise to you I sent for the papers in the three cases mentioned, which were brought to me with a note from the Sec. of War, saying: "There is no vacancy of a Major or Brigadier General."

[1] Parke-Bernet Catalog 451, April 5-6, 1943, No. Z 404. According to the catalog description, this is an autograph letter signed. See Lincoln to Stanton, January 8, *supra*, and to Grimes, January 21, *infra*.

To Robert Todd Lincoln[1]

R. T. Lincoln.   Executive Mansion,
Cambridge, Mass.   Washington, Jany. 11 1864.

I send your draft to-day. How are you now? Answer by telegraph at once.   A. LINCOLN.

[1] ALS, RPB. No reply has been discovered.

Memorandum: Appointment of Henry P. Wade[1]

Senator Wade must be obliged in this matter before long—a West-Point case.   A. LINCOLN

Jan. 11. 1864

[1] AES, DNA WR RG 94, U.S. Military Academy, 1864, No. 176. Lincoln's endorsement is written on a memorandum from Senator Benjamin F. Wade, January 9, 1864, giving qualifications of his son Henry P. Wade. No record of the appointment has been found.

To Edwin M. Stanton[1]

What does this mean?
Sec. of War, please call up subject when we meet
Jan. 11. 1864   A. LINCOLN

[1] AES, NHi. Lincoln's endorsement is written on a telegram from General Jeremiah T. Boyle, January 10, 1864, as follows:

"My superior officers have shown distrust of me I cannot therefore with proper regard to the public interest & my own character serve the public under their command Some one else must go in command I have issued all the orders preparatory to movement I ask to be relieved & that my resignation be accepted I can take this course with true devotion to the government and consistently with good of the service I respectfully request the acceptance of my resignation."

No reply from Stanton has been found. On January 14 Bland Ballard wrote Lincoln advising acceptance of Boyle's resignation or transfer to Burnside's command: "His unfortunate political aspirations have undoubtedly done him injury. . . . But, had he been less conscious of purity, he could not have failed to see he could not discharge the delicate duties of his responsible office while a candidate for popular favor—without being the victim of innumerable slanders. . . ." (DLC-RTL). See further Lincoln to Bramlette, January 31, *infra*.

To Ulysses S. Grant or George H. Thomas[1]

Major General Grant, or   Executive Mansion
Major General Thomas   Washington, D.C.
Chattanooga, Tenn.   Jan. 12, 1864

Let execution of the death sentence upon William Jeffries, of Co. A. Sixth Indiana Volunteers, be suspended until further order from here.   A. LINCOLN

[1] ALS, RPB. The roster of Company A, Sixth Indiana, lists William F. Jeffres as "missing at Louisville, Ky. Oct. 1, 1862." See Lincoln to Morton, *infra*.

To Oliver P. Morton[1]

Gov. O. P. Morton   Executive Mansion,
Indianapolis, Ia.   Washington, Jan. 12, 1864.

I have telegraphed to Chattanooga suspending execution of William Jeffries until further order from me.   A LINCOLN

[1] ALS, RPB. See Lincoln's telegram to Grant or Thomas, *supra*. No communication from Governor Morton concerning this matter has been discovered.

Order Fixing Western Base of Union Pacific Railroad[1]

Executive Mansion, Washington, January 12, 1864.

In pursuance of the eleventh section of the act of congress entitled "An Act to aid in the construction of a Railroad and Telegraph line from the Missouri River to the Pacific Ocean, and to secure to the Government the use of the same for Postal, Military, and other purposes" Approved July 1, 1862, the point where the line of the Central Pacific Railroad crosses Arcade creek in the Sacramento valley is hereby fixed as the western base of the Sierra Nevada mountains.   ABRAHAM LINCOLN

[1] ADS, The Rosenbach Company, Philadelphia and New York. The act provided that the Central Pacific Railroad would receive sixteen $1,000 U.S. bonds per mile and treble this number of bonds per mile for the portion "most mountainous and difficult of construction, to wit: one hundred and fifty miles westwardly from the eastern base of the Rocky Mountains, and one hundred and fifty miles eastwardly from the western base of the Sierra Nevada mountains, said points to be fixed by the President. . . ."

To the Senate[1]

To the Senate of the United States: January 12, 1864

In accordance with the request of the Senate conveyed in their Resolutions of the 16th of December 1863, desiring any information in my possession relative to the alleged exceptional treatment of Kansas troops when captured by those in rebellion, I have the honor to transmit a communication from the Secretary of War, accompanied by reports from the General-in-Chief of the Army, and the Commissary-General of Prisoners, relative to the subject matter of the Resolutions.   ABRAHAM LINCOLN

Executive Mansion
January 12. 1864

[1] DS, DNA RG 46, Senate 38A F4. The enclosures printed in *Senate Executive Document No. 4* indicate no information that Kansas troops were being "invariably put to death" as charged in Senator James H. Lane's resolution of December 16, 1863.

To Edward and Henry T. Anthony[1]

Executive Mansion,
Dear Sirs   Washington, Jan. 13, 1864.

Please accept my thanks for your pretty and acceptable present just now placed in my hands by Mr. Speaker Colfax. Yours truly
E & H.T. Anthony & Co N. Y.   A. LINCOLN

[1] ALS, IHi. On January 7, 1863[4], Edward and Henry T. Anthony, manufacturers and importers of photographic materials, albums, stereoscopes, and views, wrote Lincoln:

"As the President . . . cannot be expected to visit every place that is worth seeing, the places must follow the example of the people and send their Representatives.

"We take pleasure therefore in sending you some views of beautiful bridges, lakes, and landscapes which may be looked upon as the constituents of the New York Central Park.

"Trusting that the society of these quiet visitors may sometimes afford you a relaxation from the turmoil and cares of office, we request that you will accept them with the best wishes of Your Friends and Fellow Citizens" (DLC-RTL).

To Nathaniel P. Banks[1]

Executive Mansion, Washington,
Major General Banks   January 13, 1864.

I have received two letters from you which are duplicates, each of the other, except that one bears date the 27th. and the other the 30th. of December. Your confidence in the practicability of constructing a free state-government, speedily, for Louisiana, and your zeal to accomplish it, are very gratifying. It is a connection, than in which, the words *"can"* and *"will"* were never more precious. I am much in hope that, on the authority of my letter, of December 24th. you have already begun the work. Whether you shall have done so or not, please, on receiving this, proceed with all possible despatch, using your own absolute discretion in all matters which may not carry you away from the conditions stated in your letters to me, nor from those of the Message and Proclamation of December 8th. Frame orders, and fix times and places, for this, and that, according to your own judgment.

I am much gratified to know that Mr. Dennison, the Collector at New-Orleans, and who bears you this, understands your views, and will give you his full, and zealous co-operation. It is my wish, and purpose, that all others, holding authority from me, shall do the like; and, to spare me writing, I will thank you to make this known to them. Yours very truly   A. LINCOLN.

[1] ALS, IHi; ADfS, DLC-RTL. Banks' letter of December 27 has not been located, but that of December 30 is as follows:

"Your message and proclamation can not fail to produce great national results. They offer an escape to many classes of people in the South, who will not fail to yield their assent to the conditions imposed. . . .

"Much reflection, and frank conversation with many persons who know the southern character, thoroughly confirm me in the opinion. I expressed in my recent letters, that the immediate restoration of a State government upon the basis of an absolute extinction of slavery at the start, with the general consent of the people, is practicable. . . . I have been greatly surprised to find how readily my conclusions have been accepted by men of strongest southern sympathies, attachments and interests.

"If, as you have declared in your letter of November the 5th., an early organization in this State be desirable, I would suggest as the *only speedy and certain* method of accomplishing your object, that an election be ordered, of a State Government, under the Constitution and Laws of Louisiana, except so much thereof as recognizes and relates to slavery, which should be declared by the authority calling the election, and in the order authorizing it, *inoperative and void.* The registration of voters to be made in conformity with your Proclamation. . . . A convention of the People for the Revision of the Constitution, may be ordered as soon as the government is organized, and the election of members might take place on the same, or a subsequent day, with the general election. The People of Louisiana will accept such a proposition with favor. . . .

"Let me assure you that this course will be far more acceptable to the citizens of Louisiana, than the submission of the question of slavery to the chances of an election. Their self-respect, their *amour propre* will be appeased if they are not required to vote for or against it. Offer them a Government without slavery, and they will gladly accept it as a necessity resulting from the war. . . .

"Upon this plan, a government can be established whenever you wish—in 30, or 60 days. . . . Defeat is impossible, and the dangers attending delay, are avoided. I would unhesitatingly stake my life upon the issue.

"If this plan be accepted in Louisiana, . . . it will be adopted by general concurrence, in Texas, Arkansas, and Mississippi, and in every other southern state, as rapidly as you choose to accord to them the privilege of self-government. If it be accepted in one State, the World will see that not only the method, but the fact of restoration is accomplished.

"I am opposed to any settlement, and have been from the beginning, except upon the basis of immediate emancipation, but it is better to secure it by consent, than by force, better still by consent *and* force. . . .

"I need not repeat what I have already said, that I shall cordially and earnestly sustain any plan you may adopt for the restoration of government here. It is my duty, and my desire. With very great reluctance, and sense of public duty, I have made the suggestion herein contained, upon the same principle that I would impart important military information. . . .

"The plan of restoration contemplated here by the officers charged with that duty, does not seem to promise results so speedy or certain. It proceeds upon the theory of constitutional convention to frame an organic law. . . . The election of delegates cannot be called before March. . . . The convention could not sit before April. It could scarcely occupy less than two months. Its action could hardly be submitted to the People . . . before July. . . .

"The advantages secured by this course, will be:

1st.   An immediate State organization.
2nd.   The active & general consent of the People of the State.
3rd.   The certainty of immediate emancipation from Slavery.
4th.   The Revision of the Constitution—*pari passu*—by a Convention.
5th.   The exhibition to the World of moral, as well as military power, in the suppression of Rebellion and the reconstruction of government by consent and participation of the different classes of People.
6th.   The certainty that it will be followed in *four* States immediately, and in others as soon as you desire it with the same certainty as to emancipation.
7th.   It places in your hands the means of the restoration of States, as well as the destruction of armies—independent of the possible results of party or political contests.

"The fact of restoration is, however, more important than the means, and I shall cordially sustain any policy you may indicate." (DLC-RTL).

Banks acknowledged receipt of Lincoln's letter of December 29, 1863, *supra*, on January 11: "I have the honor to acknowledge the receipt of your letter of the 29th [24th]. December and a duplicate of the same with an endorsement dated the 29th. of December. They give to me all the authority I can desire. . . . Enclosed you will find an order to be published tomorrow, authorizing an election of state officers on the 22d. of February. It does not contemplate an election of the Legislature or Judges until November at the regular election. . . . I am confident that it will receive a very general support of all classes of people, and a strength at the Polls that will surprise as well as gratify the friends of the government elsewhere. . . ." (DLC-RTL).

To Benjamin F. Butler[1]

Major-General Butler,   Executive Mansion,
Fortress Monroe, Va.:   Washington, January 13, 1864.

Let Wilson B. Kevas [Kerns], Third Pennsylvania Artillery, be respited until further orders.   A. LINCOLN.

[1] Tarbell (Appendix), p. 409. The source is in error as to the name. Wilson B. Kerns, Battery B, Third Pennsylvania Artillery, was dishonorably discharged on January 10, 1865.

To Simeon Draper[1]

Nothing yet about the cotton matter, although I am still considering it.

A. LINCOLN

Jan. 13, 1864

[1] Emily Driscoll Catalog 6, 1948, No. 59. According to the source, Lincoln replied to a note from Draper, cotton agent at New York. See Lincoln to Wright and Hawkes, January 7, *supra*.

To Quincy A. Gillmore[1]

Executive Mansion,
Major General Gillmore   Washington, January 13, 1864.

I understand an effort is being made by some worthy gentlemen to reconstruct a loyal state government in Florida. Florida is in your department, and it is not unlikely that you may be there in person. I have given Mr. Hay a commission of Major, and sent him to you with some blank books and other blanks, to aid in the reconstruction. He will explain, as to the manner of using the blanks, and also my general views on the subject. It is desirable for all to cooperate; but if irreconcileable differences of opinion shall arise, you are master. I wish the thing done in the most speedy way possible, so that, when done, it lie within the range of the late proclamation on the subject. The detail labor, of course, will have to be done by others; but I shall be greatly obliged if you will give it such general supervision as you can find consistent with your more strictly military duties   Yours very truly

A LINCOLN

[1] Copy, DLC-RTL. Major General Gillmore replied from Hilton Head, South Carolina, on January 21, 1864:

"I have received your letter of the 13th inst. by Major Hay, & the matter therein referred to will receive my hearty support. There will not be an hour's delay after the major is ready. I understand from him that his blanks have not arrived here yet.

"What I propose to do for Florida will render it necessary for me to be there in person to inaugurate the work. I have every confidence in the success of the enterprise." (DLC-RTL).

On January 30, Gillmore reported that Major Hay "has been ordered to enter upon the special duties assigned to him without delay." (*Ibid.*). Hay remained in Florida until March. His *Diary* records on March 1 that, "I am very sure that we cannot get the President's 10th. . . ." (referring to the specification of the proclamation of December 8, 1863, that one-tenth of the number of voters qualified in the presidential election of 1860 might, upon taking the oath, establish a state government). Hay was back in Washington on March 24, without having effected the purpose of his mission.

To Theodore T. S. Laidley[1]

Executive Mansion,
Major Laidley   Washington, Jan. 13, 1864.
Please make a trial of the Absterdam projectile, and report to
the Secretary of War. Yours truly   A. Lincoln

[1] ALS, RPB. Patent No. 41,668, issued to John Absterdam of New York City
in 1864, was for an invention consisting "in applying to an elongated projectile one or more bands of a composition of metal similar to 'type metal,'
for the purpose of securing a more accurate and uniform gauge of
calibre. . . ." (Thirty-eighth Congress, Second Session, *House Executive Document No. 51*, I, 299).

To Edwin M. Stanton[1]

I shall be glad for General Crittenden to have permission to go to
New-York, as he desires   A. Lincoln
Jan. 13. 1864

[1] AES-P, ISLA. Lincoln's endorsement is written on an undated note from
Green Clay Smith requesting permission for Major General Thomas L. Crittenden to visit New York and stop by Washington. Stanton endorsed, "Referred
to Genl in Chief to issue order permitting Genl Crittenden to go to New York
as directed by the Prest."

To Edwin M. Stanton[1]

Please see & hear the bearer, Mr. Pirsson.
Jan. 13, 1864   A. Lincoln

[1] Stan. V. Henkels Catalog 1442, April 10, 1930, No. 86. According to the
catalog description, this message is an autograph note written on a card.
Pirsson has not been identified.

To Edwin M. Stanton[1]

Private
Hon. Sec of War   Executive Mansion
Sir   Washington, Jan 13, 1864.
Gen. Green Clay Smith, in order to take his seat in Congress,
had to give up his Military Commission; but he thinks he may
wish to ask to have it back, and go to the field again after a few
months, and in view of which he would like to have his Asst. Adjt
Genl William Cassius Goodloe kept on foot, and asks that, to this

end, he may be ordered to report to the Commanding officer at Louisville, Ky. If this can be lawfully done let it be done. Yours truly   A. LINCOLN.

[1] Angle, p. 339. Representative Smith did not re-enter service, and Captain William C. Goodloe resigned his commission as of January 31, 1864.

To Edward Bates[1]

Hon. Attorney General   Executive Mansion,
My dear Sir: Washington, Jan. 14, 1864.
    Herewith I send to be filed, the papers in regard to the Indiana Judgeship. Besides what is in the papers, Senator, Lane, Speaker Colfax, Rep. Orth   Sec. Usher, Bank Com. McCullough, Mr. Defrees & others, all Indianians, verbally expressed their preference for Mr. White. Yours truly   A. LINCOLN

[1] ALS, DNA GE RG 60, Papers of Attorney General, Segregated Lincoln Material. Ex-congressman Albert S. White's appointment as judge of the U.S. District Court, to succeed Caleb B. Smith, was confirmed by the Senate on January 18, 1864.

To Benjamin F. Butler[1]

                                                     Executive Mansion,
Major Gen. Butler   Washington, Jan. 14, 1864.
    This will introduce Thomas Stackpole, whom I found in the White-House when I came, having been brought from New-Hampshire by Mr. Pierce. I have found him a straight, energetic man. He desires to go into some business about oysters in your vicinity; and so far as you can consistently facilitate him, I shall be glad. Yours truly   A. LINCOLN

[1] ALS, CCamStJ.

To Charles P. McIlvaine[1]

                                                     Executive Mansion,
Dear Bishop McIlvaine   Washington, Jan. 14, 1864.
    I send herein what you have requested. Yours very truly
                                                             A. LINCOLN

[1] ALS, owned by Harvard B. Emery, Lincoln, Maine. On January 6, 1864, Bishop McIlvaine sent New Year's greetings and requested two autographs (DLC-RTL).

To George G. Meade[1]

	Executive Mansion,
Major-General Meade,	Washington, D.C.,
Army of the Potomac:	January 14, 1864.

Suspend execution of the death sentence in the case of Allen G. Maxson, corporal in Company D, in First Michigan Volunteers, until further order.   A. LINCOLN.

[1] Tarbell (Appendix), p. 410. The record in the case of Private Allen G. Maxson was returned by Lincoln to the Judge Advocate General on April 16, 1864, along with a great number of other cases of desertion commuted under AGO *General Orders No. 76*, February 26, 1864.

Memorandum Concerning Edward Haggard[1]

Executive Mansion,
Washington, Jan. 14, 1864.

To-day Hon. Brutus J. Clay calls with Mrs. Haggard, and asks that her son, Edward Haggard, now in his nineteenth year, and a prisoner of War at Camp Douglas, may be discharged. Let him take the oath of Dec. 8. and be discharged.   A. LINCOLN

Do the same for William H. Moore.   A. LINCOLN

[1] ADS-P, ISLA. No further reference has been found.

Recommendation for Miss Weirman[1]

January 14, 1864

This lady, Miss. Weirman, wants employment, and [I] shall be obliged to any Head of a Department or Bureau who can give it to her.   A. LINCOLN

Jan. 14. 1864

[1] THaroL. Miss Weirman has not been identified.

To Edwin M. Stanton[1]

| Hon. Sec. of War | Executive Mansion, |
| Sir. | Washington, Jan. 14, 1864. |

I herewith return the papers in the cases of Dodge, Hatch & Caldwell. Please send me now a petition of members of West-Virginia Legislature, asking to have Gen. Sigel put in command there.
Yours truly   A LINCOLN

[1] ALS, DLC-Stanton Papers. See Lincoln to Stanton, January 8, and to Grimes, January 11, *supra*. AGO *General Orders No. 80*, February 29, 1864, assigned Major General Franz Sigel to command of the Department of West Virginia.

To John Brough[1]

Gov. Brough   Executive Mansion,
Columbus, Ohio   Washington, Jan. 15. 1864.
    If private William G. Toles, of 59th. Ohio Volunteers, returns
to his regiment and faithfully serves out his term, he is fully pardoned for all Military offences prior to this.   A. LINCOLN

[1] ALS, RPB. No communication from Governor Brough in this connection
has been located.

To Andrew Johnson[1]

[c. January 15, 1864.]
    I send by Judge John S. Brien a blank book and some other
blanks to facilitate the taking oath of Dec. 8. He will verbally explain the mode of using them. He particularly wishes to have Mr.
Benjamin C. Robertson to take the oath. I hope you may find
Judge Brien useful, in carrying forward the work generally. I assume that anyone in military commission may administer the
oaths. Yours truly,   A. LINCOLN.

[1] Hertz, II, 872. The date assigned to this undated communication is supplied on the basis of John S. Brien's letter to Lincoln of January 26, 1864:
    "You will see by the inclosed slip [newspaper clipping] that my fears as
to the death of Benjamin C. Robertson have been realized. He died on 22nd.
inst. which was two days before I reached home. It is said to me today by a
friend who was at his bedside when he died, that his greatest regret was, that
he had not the opportunity afforded him to take the oath before his death. . . .
    "But he is gone—his estate is also well-nigh gone. And his good wife and
children will feel ever grateful to you, that you have saved that little to them
by his pardon. Please inclose the pardon to me upon receipt of this.
    "There is great rejoicing here that your book has arrived. I delivered the
book and letter to Gov. Johnson on yesterday morning." (DLC-RTL).
    On January 30, Brien wrote Lincoln again:
    "On my arrival in this city, on the 25th instant, I presented your book and
letter of instructions to Gov. Johnson and made the suggestions as directed by
you.
    "It was soon known all over the city that the book had arrived, and that an
opportunity would be afforded the citizens to manifest their desire for the
establishment of law and order and the Government of the United States, and
to place upon record the evidence of their true and hearty return to the old
Government and to once more enjoy the rights of freemen. . . .
    "The next day or two, . . . Gov. Johnson issued the enclosed proclamation,
in which you observe, he prescribed an oath to be taken by every citizen in
order to [establish] his qualification to vote. This produced considerable confusion. . . .
    "Now, Mr. President, what I ask of you is to state, in some form which may
be made public, the necessary steps to be taken by the people of Tennessee to
entitle them to the exercise of the elective franchise.
    "Does the taking . . . the oath prescribed . . . restore the party to his orig-
inal status. . . ? If not, to what extent is he benefitted?

"Are the elections to be held under the laws of Tennessee, until they are changed by the people in some proper form? As a matter of course, they must be held under the laws of the state passed prior to the rebellion, or then by some rule established by you.

"I need not say that you will see the importance of settling these questions promptly. . . .

"May I ask of you to state as an order what you stated in the letter to Gov. Johnson: that any commissioned officer is qualified to administer the oath, and that he do so whenever called upon by those entitled to its benefits.

"Please let me hear from you at once, as I write on behalf of the people of the State." (*Ibid.*).

See Lincoln to Johnson, January 25, *infra.*

Memorandum Concerning John Racey[1]

[c. January 15, 1864]

Dont pardon Racey.

[1] AE, DLC-RTL. Lincoln's endorsement is written on an envelope addressed to him by Senator John Sherman enclosing a letter of Charles J. Albright, Cambridge, Ohio, to Sherman, January 15, 1864, advising that "friends of Racey, the leading Noble County conspirator . . . are petitioning President Lincoln for his pardon. . . ." Sherman endorsed "I herewith concur in the request that Racey be not pardoned." John Racey was convicted as one of the leaders of "The Hoskinsville Rebellion" (Cincinnati *Daily Gazette*, December 5, 1863).

To Lorenzo Thomas[1]

Executive Mansion,

Adjutant General Thomas,   Washington, Jan. 15. 1864.

It is represented that Mrs. Eugenia P. Bass, owner of plantations in Missippi about seventy miles above Vicksburg, having taken the oath of allegiance, leased and gave possession of said plantations to parties of unquestionable loyalty; and that you, acting perhaps in some mistake of facts, have leased the plantations to other parties. Please ascertain how this is, and if loyal lessees of hers, had rights there prior to any action of yours, do not let them be disturbed. Of course I know nothing certainly about this matter.

Yours truly   A. LINCOLN.

[1] ALS, IHi. On January 15, 1864, Mrs. Eugenia P. Bass wrote Secretary Seward:

"I have returned to Washington, to make an effort to obtain the release of my brother, Major Henry C. Bate, of the first Confederate Cavalry, now a prisoner at Johnson's Island. . . . I am deeply interested in rescuing my brother from all connection with the rebellion, in which he has so unfortunately and . . . reluctantly, become involved, and in reclaiming the relative on whose support and protection, now more than ever needed by me, I have relied for years past. . . . I am now called by the care of my property, and an imperative sense of duty to my family, to undertake the perils of a journey home. . . . I have suffered much, very much, from the Union army, by the loss of my property, and I feel that I have a claim to the protection of the government, and its favor, which it can be accorded without injury to the public.

"I beg you to present my appeal to the President. . . ." (DLC-RTL).

See Lincoln to Grant, January 25, *infra.*

To William Crosby and Henry P. Nichols[1]

Messrs Crosby & Nichols.   Executive Mansion,
Gentlemen   Washington, January 16, 1864.

The number for this month and year of the North American Review was duly received, and, for which, please accept my thanks. Of course I am not the most impartial judge; yet with due allowance for this, I venture to hope that the artical entitled the "Presidents Policy" will be of value to the country. I fear I am not quite worthy of all which is therein kindly said of me personally.

The sentence of twelve lines commencing at the top of page 252, I could wish to be not exactly as it is.[2] In what is there expressed, the writer has not correctly understood me. I have never had a theory that secession could absolve States or people from their obligations. Precisely the contrary is asserted in the inaugeral address; and it was because of my belief in the continuation of these *obligations*, that I was puzzled, for a time, as to denying the legal *rights* of those citizens who remained individually innocent of treason or rebellion. But I mean no more now than to merely call attention to this point. Yours Respectfully

A. LINCOLN

[1] ALS, NNP. On December 31, 1863, the publishers of *The North American Review* wrote Lincoln: "The subscribers respectfully request, that the President will accept the January number of The North American Review, sent by this mail; and they venture to hope that the article upon '*The President's Policy,*' written by James Russell Lowell, (one of the editors,) will meet with his approval. . . ." (DLC-RTL).

On January 22, they wrote Nicolay in appreciation of Lincoln's letter and with the request that they be allowed to publish the letter "to remove any erroneous impression that may have been given with regard to The President's designs. . . ." (*Ibid.*). In the April issue the letter appeared, together with the announcement: "Nothing could have been further from the intention of the Editors than to misrepresent the opinions of the President. They merely meant that, in their judgment, the policy of the Administration was at first such as practically to concede to any rebel who might choose to profess loyalty, rights under the Constitution whose corresponding obligations he repudiated." (p. 630).

[2] James Russell Lowell had written, "Even so long ago as when Mr. Lincoln, not yet convinced of the danger and magnitude of the crisis, was endeavoring to persuade himself of Union majorities at the South, and to carry on a war that was half peace in the hope of a peace that would have been all war,—

while he was still enforcing the Fugitive Slave Law, under some theory that Secession, however it might absolve States from their obligations, could not escheat them of their claims under the Constitution, and that slaveholders in rebellion had alone among mortals the privilege of having their cake and eating it at the same time,—the enemies of free government were striving to persuade the people that the war was an Abolition crusade. . . ." (p. 252).

To George G. Meade or John Sedgwick[1]

Major-General Meade
or Major-General Sedgwick,
Army of the Potomac:

Executive Mansion,
Washington, D.C.,
January 16, 1864.

    Suspend execution of death sentence of Joseph W. Clifton, of Sixth New Jersey Volunteers, until further order.

A. LINCOLN.

[1] Tarbell (Appendix), p. 410. Joseph W. Clifton's sentence for desertion was commuted to imprisonment in Dry Tortugas by AGO *Special Orders No. 166*, May 3, 1864.

To Edwin D. Morgan[1]

Will Senator Morgan please present my compliments to Judge Edmonds, & say to him the books will be gratefully accepted by me.
Jan. 16. 1864.   A. LINCOLN

[1] ALS-F, The Collector, December, 1951, p. 236. Senator Morgan wrote on January 16, 1864, "Please read the letter of Judge Edmonds and return it to me that I may tell him you will accept of his Books." (DLC-RTL). No indication is given of the titles of the books, but Judge John W. Edmonds published *An Address to His Law Students* . . . , New York, 1864, and *Spiritualism* (with George T. Dexter), New York, 1854.

To Edwin M. Stanton[1]

Hon. Sec. of War
Dear Sir

Executive Mansion,
Washington, Jan. 16. 1864.

    Some days ago, upon the unanamous request of our friends in congress from Connecticut, and upon what appeared to be good reason, I ordered a change of Provost Marshal & commissioner, under the enrolment law in one of the Districts—the 4th; and they are complaining now that it is not done. Let it be done. Yours truly   A. LINCOLN

[1] ALS, owned by Edward C. Stone, Boston, Massachusetts. William H. Riley, appointed provost marshal on September 9, 1863, was replaced by Leverett W. Wessels on January 9, 1864; Frederick Ellsworth, appointed commissioner on September 9, 1863, was replaced by Edward J. Alvord on January 9, 1864.

To Jeremiah C. Sullivan[1]

Gen. Sullivan   Executive Mansion,
Harper's Ferry   Washington, Jan. 16. 1864.

Please state to me the reasons of the arrest of Capt. William
Firey, of Major Coles Battalion, at Charlestown.   A. LINCOLN

[1] ALS, RPB. General Sullivan's reply was received at 1 P.M.: "Capt. Ferry
was arrested for failing to enforce discipline while in command of a scout,
allowing his men to straggle into private houses and commit depredations.
Owing to the gallantry displayed by Maj [Henry A.] Coles comdg at the recent attack on his camp, I had restored Capt Ferry to duty before your dispatch was received." (DLC-RTL). Captain William Firey, Company B, First
Regiment, Potomac Home Brigade Cavalry of the Maryland Volunteers, was
finally dismissed from the service on May 30, 1864.

To Thomas E. Bramlette[1]

Governor Bramlette   Executive Mansion,
Frankfort, Ky.   Washington, Jan. 17, 1864.

Your letter of the 8th. is just received. To your question "May
I not add Q.E.D.?" I answer, "no" because you omit the "premise"
in the law, that the President may, in his discretion, send these
troops out of Kentucky and I take it that if he shall do so on the
judgment of Gen. Grant, as to it's propriety, it will be neither
cruelty, bad faith or dishonor. When I telegraphed you, I knew,
though I did not say so to you, that Gen. Grant was, about that
time, with Gen. Foster at Knoxville, and could not be ignorant of
or averse to the order which alarmed you. I see he has since passed
through Kentucky, and I hope you have had a conference with
him.   A. LINCOLN

[1] ALS, IHi. On January 8, Governor Bramlette replied to Lincoln's communication of January 6, *supra:*

"I did not intend by any expression in my telegram, to impugn the motives
of any one. I only intended . . . to express my conviction of the effect of the
order. . . . My confidence in Genl Grant has been continuous. . . . I regard
him as the first Genl of the age. . . . Had I believed that the order emanated
from or was sanctioned by Genl Grant, my great confidence in him would
have prevented me from telegraphing to you. I had reasons to believe that
Genl Grant did not know of the order. . . . This order necessarily exposes his
communications and supplies to destruction. . . . If this order was with the
approbation of Genl Grant I will await the denouement before I venture a
judgment of condemnation. Though I cannot now see any good in it, yet if
it be his plan, I will await, with confidence the result, without forming any
opposing judgment. . . ."

After quoting his previous telegram and amplifying each point, the governor
continued:

"May I not add—Q.E.D.

"In all candor and with the kindest feelings I ask what reliance can our
people place upon any pledge of the Government and its functionaries, if this

[134]

be not observed. . . . Kentucky loyalty cannot be driven from its secure lodge-
ment in the hearts of the people, by any bad faith of others. We are in and
of the Union and will live and die there. Rebel outrages cannot drive us, nor
federal injustice divert us from the true line of patriotism. . . ." (DLC-RTL).

To Thomas B. Bryan[1]

Executive Mansion,
My Dear Sir. Washington, January 18th, 1864.
I have recieved the two copies of the lithographed fac-simile of
the original draft of the Emancipation Proclamation, which you
have had the kindness to send me, and in answer to your question,
I have to say that although I have not examined it in detail, yet
it impresses me favorably as being a faithful and correct copy.
Yours truly, A LINCOLN.
Thos B Bryan Esq
Chicago, Illinois.

[1] Copy, DLC-RTL. Thomas B. Bryan wrote on January 7, 1864:
"I mail herewith . . . the two *first* copies of the lithographed Facsimile of
your Proclamation of Freedom. Have the kindness to inform me if the copy
impress you favorably as an exact Fac-simile. . . .
"It may interest you to know that the Original Manuscript . . . will be held
by our Soldiers Home in trust for the benefit of the sick & disabled soldiers of
the Union Army. Although I purpose donating a share of the avails of my
copyright to the Home as mentioned in the certificate on the face of the print,
yet at the voluntary suggestion of Dr. Bellows of New York, all copies sold
in the East will yield a fund for the U.S. Sanitary Commission, of which he
is Prest. . . . The caption will therefore be changed. . . ." (DLC-RTL).
Numerous copies of the facsimiles issued by Bryan are extant. Comparison
with the photographic copies of the Proclamation preserved in the Lincoln
Papers (see note to Proclamation, January 1, 1863, *supra*) show the Bryan
facsimile to be accurate as to text, but inferior to the photographs as an exact
reproduction.

To Benjamin F. Butler[1]

Major General Butler [January 18, 1864]
Fort-Monroe.
Gov. Pierpoint has been, from the first, a zealous and efficient
supporter of the government. He now understands that you have
ordered all the municipal officers of Norfolk and Portsmouth to
report to you in detail the amounts of all money received by them,
&c. and also that you have constituted a commission to investigate
the condition of the Savings Funds and Banking institutions there;
and he, as Governor, feels agrieved by these measures. The President directs me to request you to suspend these measures, until

[135]

you can state to him, in writing or otherwise, your views of the necessity or propriety of them.   EDWIN M STANTON
Sec of War

[1] AL-F, ISLA. This communication was written by Lincoln and signed by Stanton. General Butler wrote Lincoln on February 23, 1864, a forty-page report enclosing voluminous reports and summaries from his subordinates, which explained the necessities that had dictated the issuing of his *General Orders No. 40* and clarified misstatements made by Governor Peirpoint (DLC-RTL). The bracketed date is established by related communications in the Butler Papers and the Lincoln Papers (DLC).

Endorsement Concerning A. Z. Boyer[1]

Let A. Z. Boyer, named within, take the oath of December 8th. 1863, upon doing which he is pardoned and to be discharged.
Jan. 18. 1864   A. LINCOLN

[1] AES, DNA WR RG 153, Judge Advocate General, MM 1027. Lincoln's endorsement is written on the court-martial record of A. Z. Boyer, Company C, Second Kentucky Cavalry, CSA, sentenced to be hanged as a spy. Letters from James Speed, January 12, and Brutus J. Clay, January 14, 1864, requested Lincoln's favorable consideration of the case (DLC-RTL). AGO *Special Orders No. 45*, January 29, 1864, directed Boyer's discharge from custody.

Endorsement Concerning Charles T. Hagan[1]

January 18, 1864
At the request of the Hon. Mr. Harding of Kentucky it is ordered that the within named Charles Thomas Hagan may take the oath of Dec. 8 & be discharged   A. LINCOLN
Jan. 18. 1864

[1] AES, owned by John M. Holcombe, Jr., Hartford, Connecticut. Lincoln's endorsement is written on a letter of Charity Mudd to Representative Aaron Harding, Springfield, Kentucky, January 6, 1864, asking that her son Charles Thomas Hagan, captured with John H. Morgan and imprisoned at Camp Chase, be released. A portion of the letter, presumably bearing Harding's endorsement, has been cut off.

To Edwin M. Stanton[1]

Let a pass be allowed in this case.   A. LINCOLN
Jan. 18, 1864

[1] AES, DNA WR RG 107, Secretary of War, Letters Received, P 27. Lincoln's endorsement is written on a letter from Hiram Shaw, Jr., Washington, D.C., January 14, 1864, requesting a pass for his sister, Mrs. B. P. Truman o join her mother's family in Kentucky.

[136]

To Whom It May Concern[1]

Executive Mansion
Whom it may concern: Washington, January 18, 1864
    The bearer, John P. W. [M.] Thornton, a private in Co. E 61st
New York volunteers, comes to me voluntarily under apprehension
that he may be arrested, convicted, and punished as a deserter;
and I hereby direct him to report forthwith to his regiment for
duty, and upon condition that he does this, and faithfully serves
out his term, or until he shall be honorably discharged for any
cause, he is fully pardoned for any supposed desertion heretofor
committed.   A. LINCOLN.

[1] William D. Morley Catalog, January 28, 1944, No. 84. AGO *Special Orders
No. 26*, January 18, 1864, ordered Private John P. M. Thornton to report to his
regiment for duty.

To John Clark[1]

Col. John Clark.   Executive Mansion,
Of 3rd. Regt. of Penn. Reserves   Washington,
Alexandria, Va.   Jan. 19, 1864.
    Where is, John Wilson, under sentence for desertion, of whom
you wrote Hon Mr. Thayer yesterday?   A. LINCOLN

[1] ALS, RPB. No reply has been discovered. See Lincoln to Sedgwick, January 20, *infra*.

To Robert T. Lincoln[1]

R. T. Lincoln,   Executive Mansion,
Cambridge, Mass: Washington, January 19, 1864.
    There is a good deal of small-pox here. Your friends must judge
for themselves whether they ought to come or not.
                                                 A. LINCOLN.
Major Eckert:
    Please send above dispatch.   JNO. G. NICOLAY.

[1] Tarbell (Appendix), p. 410. No communication from Robert T. Lincoln
has been found in this connection.

To Edwin M. Stanton and Henry W. Halleck[1]

Executive Mansion
Washington Dec. [*sic*] Jan 19./64
To-day Hon. Joshua R. Giddings calls and says his son, Major Gro-
tius R. Giddings, of the 14th. Regular Infantry, wishes his name

to be remembered, if Brigadier Generals shall be appointed for colored troops. A. LINCOLN

Submitted to the Sec. of War & General-in-Chief.
Jan. 19. 1864. A. LINCOLN

[1] ADS and AES, IHi. Major Grotius R. Giddings was appointed lieutenant colonel as of May 18, 1864, but not brigadier general.

To Benjamin F. Butler[1]

Executive Mansion
Major General Butler. Washington D.C. Jan. 20. 1864.
If Henry C. Fuller, of Co. C. 118th. N.Y. Vols. under sentence of death for desertion, has not been executed, suspend his execution until further order. A. LINCOLN

[1] ALS, RPB. Henry C. Fuller's sentence was commuted to imprisonment for three years.

To Benjamin F. Butler[1]

Major General Butler Executive Mansion
Fort-Monroe Washington D.C. Jan. 20. 1864.
Please suspend executions, until further order, in the cases of private Henry Wooding, of Co. C. 8th. Conn. Vols. and private Albert A. Lacy of Co. H. 4th. Rhode-Island Vols.

A. LINCOLN

[1] ALS, RPB. Henry Wooding was dishonorably discharged on May 27, 1865; Albert A. Lacy was released from prison on May 27, 1869.

Endorsement Concerning Charles M. Shelton[1]

January 20, 1864
Hon. James E. English, endorses the writer of the within, and states that he personally knows much of what is set forth to be true. The said Charles M. Shelton, is pardoned for the unexecuted part of his punishment, and is to be fully discharged.
Jan. 20. 1864. A. LINCOLN

[1] AES, IHi. Lincoln's endorsement is written on a statement signed by Harry Peck, principal of Greenwich Institute, Greenwich, Connecticut, October 17, 1863, concerning Charles M. Shelton, an epileptic. One Charles M. Shelton of Company H, Second Connecticut Volunteers, had been discharged for disability after one month's service on June 26, 1861. The roster of Company K, Eleventh Connecticut Volunteers, lists the same name as enlisted on February 11, 1863, and dishonorably discharged as of August 28, 1863. AGO *Special*

Orders No. 30, January 20, 1864, directed that Charles M. Shelton "be released from confinement, and discharged." James E. English was U.S. representative from New Haven, Connecticut.

Memorandum:
Appointment of John D. C. Hoskins[1]

[c. January 20, 1864]

John D. C. Hoskins—18 years of age. Jan. 19. 1864.

West-Point–

Gen. Hitchcock, will present a paper.

I have seen this boy's discharge, by which it appears that he has served thirty days during this war.   A. LINCOLN

Jan. 20. 1864

[1] AE and AES, DNA WR RG 94, U.S. Military Academy, 1861, No. 395. The first endorsement is written on the envelope containing recommendations for John D. C. Hoskins of North Carolina. The second is written on a letter of H. L. Kendrick, West Point, New York, to Colonel William A. Nichols, Adjutant General's Office, recommending that the son of Charles Hoskins (adjutant of the Fourth U.S. Infantry, killed September 21, 1846, at the Battle of Monterey) be appointed to West Point. John D. C. Hoskins entered West Point July 1, 1864, and graduated in 1868.

Memorandum Concerning Thomas J. Kellinger[1]

January 20, 1864

Thomas J. Kellinger, having been pardoned upon condition of his entering the Naval service, and having been rejected as physically unfit for that service, his pardon is now made absolute and unconditional.   A. LINCOLN

Jan. 20. 1864

[1] AES, owned by Julius E. Haycraft, Fairmont, Minnesota. Lincoln's endorsement has been removed from attendant papers. AGO *Special Orders No. 35*, January 23, 1864, ordered discharge of Private Thomas J. Kellinger, One Hundred Forty-fifth New York Volunteers.

Order Concerning W. D. Walker[1]

January 20, 1864

Let this man take the oath of December 8th. & be discharged. It is not improbable he is already discharged by Gen. Marston[2] on these terms.   A. LINCOLN

Jan. 20. 1864

[1] AES, owned by R. E. Burdick, New York City. Lincoln's endorsement appears on a letter from John B. S. Todd, January 9, 1864, asking release of "W. D. Walker, a prisoner of war, now at Point Lookout, Maryland, & belonging to Company C, 3d Missouri Vol's. rebel Service."   [2] Gilman Marston.

To John Sedgwick[1]

Executive Mansion, Washington,

Major General Sedgwicke   Jan. 20, 1864

Suspend execution till further order, in case of private James Lane, Co. B. 71st. N.Y vols.   A. LINCOLN

[1] ALS-F, ISLA. General Sedgwick's telegram in reply was received at 8 P.M.: "Your dispatch directing the suspension of the execution of the sentence in the case of Private James Lane of Co B. 71st N.Y. Vols received." (DLC-RTL). Private James Lane's sentence for desertion was commuted to imprisonment along with numerous others on April 18, 1864, under the order of February 26, 1864. See further, Lincoln to Sedgwick, January 26, *infra*.

To John Sedgwick[1]

Major-General Sedgwick,   Executive Mansion,

Army of the Potomac: Washington, January 20, 1864.

Please suspend execution of John Wilson, of Seventy-first Pennsylvania, under sentence for desertion, till further order.

A. LINCOLN.

[1] Tarbell (Appendix), p. 411. See Lincoln to Clark, January 19, *supra*. John Wilson's sentence was commuted to imprisonment. See further Lincoln to Sedgwick, January 26, *infra*.

To the Senate and House of Representatives[1]

January 20, 1864

Gentlemen of the Senate and House of Representatives

In accordance with a letter addressed by the Secretary of State, with my approval, to the Hon. Joseph A. Wright, of Indiana, that patriotic and distinguished gentleman repaired to Europe and attended the International Agricultural Exhibition held at Hamburg last year, and has, since his return made a report to me, which it is believed, can not fail, to be of general interest, and especially so to the agricultural community. I transmit, for your consideration, copies of the letter and report. While it appears by the letter that no re-imbursement of expences, or compensation, was promised him, I submit whether reasonable allowance should not be made him for them.   ABRAHAM LINCOLN

January 20th. 1864.

[1] ADf, DLC-RTL; DS, DNA RG 46, Senate 38A F2; DS, DNA RG 233, House Executive Document No. 28. The enclosures may be found in *House Executive Document No. 28*. No record has been found of compensation or reimbursement for Joseph A. Wright.

To Edwin M. Stanton[1]

January 20, 1864

Submitted to Sec. of War. If another Assistant Quarter-Master—is needed to serve in Central Illinois, or with Illinois troops, let Mr. Lawrence be appointed.   A. LINCOLN

Jan. 20, 1864.

[1] AES, IHi. Lincoln's endorsement is written on an envelope endorsed in an unidentified hand "R. D. Lawrence Recomd for Asst Qr Mr of Vols." A further unidentified endorsement reads: "Left by Hon W. Jayne delegate from Dakota." Lawrence was probably Rheuna D. Lawrence, a merchant of Springfield, Illinois. No record of his appointment has been found.

To Frederick Steele[1]

Executive Mansion Washington, D.C.

Major General Steele   Jan. 20. 1864.

Sundry citizens of the State of Arkansas petition me that an election may be held in that State, at which to elect a Governor thereof;

that it be assumed at said election, and thenceforward, that the constitution and laws of the State, as before the rebellion, are in full force, except that the constitution is so modified as to declare that "There shall be neither slavery nor involuntary servitude, except in the punishment of crime whereof the party shall have been duly convicted; but the General Assembly may make such provision for the freed-people as shall recognize and declare their permanent freedom, provide for their education, and which may yet be consistent, as a temporary arrangement, with their present condition as a laboring, landless, and homeless class"; and also except that all now existing laws in relation to slaves are inoperative and void; that said election be held on the twentyeighth day of March next, at all the usual voting places of the State, or all such as voters may attend for that purpose; that the voters attending at each place, at eight o'clock in the morning of said day, may choose Judges and Clerks of election for that place; that all persons qualified by said constitution and laws, and taking the oath prescribed in the Presidents proclamation of December the 8th. 1863, either before or at the election, and none others, may be voters provided that persons having the qualifications aforesaid, and being in the Volunteer military service of the United States, may vote once wherever this may be at voting places; that each sett of Judges and Clerks may make return directly to you, on or before the eleventh day of

April next; that in all other respects said election may be conducted according to said modified constitution, and laws; that, on receipt of said returns, you count said votes, and that, if the number shall reach, or exceed, five thousand four hundred and six, you canvass said votes and ascertain who shall thereby appear to have been elected Governor; and that on the eighteenth day of April next, the person so appearing to have been elected, and appearing before you at Little Rock, to have, by you, administered to him, an oath to support the constitution of the United States and said modified constitution of the State of Arkansas, and actually taking said oath, be by you declared qualified, and be enjoined to immediately enter upon the duties of the office of Governor of said State; and that you thereupon declare the constitution of the State of Arkansas to have been modified and amended as aforesaid, by the action of the people as aforesaid.

You will please order an election immediately, and perform the other parts assigned you, with necessary incidentals, all according to the foregoing. Yours truly   A. LINCOLN

¹ ALS, CSmH; LS, owned by William W. Steele, Pescadero, California. See Lincoln's remarks to Arkansas Delegation, January 22, and his letters to Steele, January 27 and 30, *infra*.

To Benjamin F. Butler¹

Major General Butler   Executive Mansion,
Fort-Monroe, Va   Washington, Jan. 21. 1864.

Suspend until further order, the execution of James C. Gratton, of Co. F. 11th. Penn. Cavalry, and send record of his case.

A. LINCOLN

¹ ALS, RPB. See Lincoln to Butler, January 26, *infra*. The roster of Company F, Eleventh Pennsylvania Cavalry lists James C. Gratton as deserted on August 7, 1863, returned on October 30, 1863, wounded May 14, 1864, and discharged August 26, 1864. AGO *Special Orders No. 55*, February 4, 1864, announced the president's pardon of "James C. Grattan" [*sic*].

To James W. Grimes¹

Hon. J. W. Grimes   Executive Mansion
My dear Sir   Washington, January 21, 1864

Yours of yesterday about vacancies of Generalships was received today and referred to the War-Department for further information. I did not give you my *understanding*, but the Secretary's *distinct statement* that "There is no vacancy of a Major, or Brigadier General." Yours very truly   A. LINCOLN.

[142]

[1] John Heise Catalog 2467, No. 78. See Lincoln to Grimes, January 11, *supra.* Senator Grimes' letter of January 20, 1864, endorsed by Lincoln "Submitted to the Sec. of War for further information," is as follows:

"Your note of the 15th inst in which you informed me that you understood there were no vacancies in the grades of Major & Brigadier Genls. came duly to hand. I suspect that there must be some misapprehension about this for I saw to day in the hands of the chairman of the Military Committee of the Senate in executive session a list prepared for him at the War Department which showed that whilst there were no vacancies in grade of Major Genl. there were thirteen vacancies in the grade of Brigadier" (ALS, NHi).

Memorandum:
Appointment of Alexander D. B. Smead[1]

West-Point—

This is a very strong case.　　　　A. LINCOLN

Jan. 21. 1864

[1] AES, DNA WR RG 94, U.S. Military Academy, 1864, No. 415. Lincoln's endorsement is written on a letter from Major General Ethan A. Hitchcock, January 21, 1864, recommending Alexander D. B. Smead. No record of Smead's appointment has been found.

To the Senate[1]

To the Senate of the United States.　　　　January 21, 1864

In compliance with the resolution of the Senate of yesterday respecting the recent destruction by fire of the church of the Compañia at Santiago, Chile, and the efforts of citizens of the United States to rescue the victims of the conflagration, I transmit a report from the Secretary of State, with the papers accompanying it.　　　　ABRAHAM LINCOLN

Washington, January 21, 1864.

[1] DS, DNA RG 46, Senate 38A F3. The enclosures are printed in Thirty-eighth Congress, First Session, *Senate Executive Document No. 10.* The report of Thomas H. Nelson, minister to Chile, related the part played by Americans in helping to try to put out the fire and in rescuing victims when the church burned on December 8, 1863. Nearly 2,500 persons lost their lives in the fire.

To Commander at Fort Independence[1]

Military commander, at　　　　Executive Mansion,
Fort-Independence　　　　Washington, January 22, 1864.

Suspend until further order, execution of Charles R. Betts of 12th. Massachusetts, and send me the record of his trial.

A. LINCOLN

[1] ALS, RPB. No reply has been located. Charles R. Betts of Company A, Twelfth Massachusetts Volunteers, sentenced for desertion, was released on May 30, 1864, on condition that he join the Navy. He enlisted in the Navy for two years, but deserted on September 3, 1864.

Endorsement[1]

January 22, 1864

Let the within named, except Yocum, take the oath of Dec 8 & be discharged. Yocum is in the Old Capitol, not as a prisoner of war, but for an offence for which he has suffered enough & should, as I think, be discharged.   A. LINCOLN.

Jan. 22, 1864.

[1] Stan. V. Henkels Catalog 1379, October 15, 1925, No. 32. According to the catalog description this is an autograph endorsement signed, but no account of the document is given. Concerning William Yocum, see Lincoln to Holt, February 3, 1864, *infra.*

Remarks to Arkansas Delegation[1]

January 22, 1864

The President announced to the Arkansas delegation, this afternoon, that he had determined not to appoint a separate Military Governor, but to entrust to General Steele, the recently appointed Commander of the Department of Arkansas, with both the military and civil administration of the State.

He stated the reason to be that the experience of the past had proved that there was constant conflict between military governors and military commanders, which was injurious to the interests under their charge. He expressed hopes that a formal organization of the State Government under the terms of the Amnesty Proclamation would speedily be made by the people of Arkansas. The delegation was fully satisfied with the President's action.

[1] *Illinois State Journal,* January 27, 1864. See Lincoln's letters to Steele, January 20, *supra,* and January 27 and 30, *infra.*

To Edwin M. Stanton[1]

Secretary of War, please send me nominations according to the within, irrespective of whether there are any vacancies

Jan. 22. 1864   A. LINCOLN

[1] AES, InHi. Lincoln's endorsement is written on a letter from Governor Oliver P. Morton, January 17, 1864, calling attention to past promises of promotions for Colonel John T. Wilder, Seventeenth Indiana, Colonel Silas Colgrove, Twenty-seventh Indiana, Colonel William Grose, Thirty-sixth Indiana, and Colonel Benjamin F. Scribner, Thirty-eighth Indiana. All four were nominated on January 23, 1864, but their nominations were returned to the president on February 8, for lack of vacancies.

To Edward Bates[1]

Hon. Attorney General   Executive Mansion,
My dear Sir   Washington, Jan. 23, 1864.
I do not quite understand the little difficulty about the Marshal
of Ky; but if you understand it is now, clear, send me a nomination of Mr. William A. Meriwether, for that office. Yours truly
                                        A. LINCOLN

[1] ALS, DNA GE RG 60, Papers of Attorney General, Segregated Lincoln
Material. William A. Merriwether, whose name Lincoln misspells, was confirmed by the Senate on February 3, 1864.

To Alpheus Lewis[1]

Alpheus Lewis, Esq.   Executive Mansion,
My dear Sir   Washington, January 23. 1864.
You have enquired how the government would regard and treat
cases wherein the owners of plantations, in Arkansas, for instance,
might fully recognize the freedom of those formerly slaves, and
by fair contracts of hire with them, re-commence the cultivation
of their plantations. I answer I should regard such cases with
great favor, and should, as the principle, treat them precisely as I
would treat the same number of free white people in the same relation and condition. Whether white or black, reasonable effort
should be made to give government protection. In neither case
should the giving of aid and comfort to the rebellion, or other
practices injurious to the government, be allowed on such plantations; and in either, the government would claim the right to take
if necessary those of proper ages and conditions into the military
service. Such plan must not be used to break up existing leases or
arrangements of abandoned plantations which the government
may have made to give employment and sustenance to the idle
and destitute people. With the foregoing qualifications and explanations, and in view of it's tendency to advance freedom, and restore peace and prosperity, such hireing and employment of the
freed people, would be regarded by me with rather especial favor.
Yours truly   A. LINCOLN

P.S. To be more specific I add that all the Military, and others acting by authority of the United States, are to favor and facilitate
the introduction and carrying forward, in good faith, the free-
labor system as above indicated, by allowing the necessary supplies therefor to be procured and taken to the proper points, and
by doing and forbearing whatever will advance it; *provided* that

[145]

existing military and trade regulations be not transcended thereby. I shall be glad to learn that planters adopting this system
shall have employed one so zealous and active as yourself to act
as an agent in relation thereto.   A.L.

This P.S. is in the body of the letter given[2]

[1] ADfS, DLC-RTL. On January 20, 1864, Green C. Smith wrote Lincoln:
"Mr. Lewis obtained when here some time since a permit to purchase cotton. He proceeded south for that purpose but found that the planters in side
of our lines refused to let him have cotton unless he would furnish a . . . proportion of supplies in lieu of the cotton purchased. These people are bound to
live, must live, & they can only live on supplies furnished by our people. . . .
Therefore would it be improper to allow Mr. Lewis this privilege. I will stand
as sponsor for him that he will not abuse this privilege, but in connexion with
it, obtain more valuable information upon which the govt. can act than any
man you can have to operate. . . ." (DLC-RTL).
    A letter from Brutus J. Clay of January 21 gives supplemental information:
"From our conversation last night it seemed probable, Mr. Lewis would leave
for the South soon, and stop at Bolivar, Mississippi, and see my Brother-in-law,
C. F. Field. I thought I would act at once for him & in behalf of those he
represents, as well as of my son Christopher F. Clay, for permission to hire
voluntary Labour to carry on their plantations . . . under such restrictions
as you may require. Also the right to purchase and carry to the plantations
all needful supplies . . . and receive the proper protection from the Military
Authorities for carrying on their legitimate business. . . . The season is approaching for putting in a crop. . . . Therefore despatch is necessary, & I
would like for Mr. Lewis to carry all proper authority to Mr. Field when he
goes." (Ibid.).
    A draft of an order dated January 21, 1864, is as follows:
"The Supervising Special Agents of Treasury for 1st Agency, or proper
Treasury Agents at Memphis or Vicksburg will grant to Alpheus Lewis Esq,
necessary authority to purchase at, and ship from either place, family supplies,
to the residence and plantations of such well disposed persons as he may name,
within the lines of national military occupation, who will adopt the voluntary
labor system.
    "And the Surveyor of Customs at either place will clear all boats containing
such supplies to any place or places within our lines, for the purpose of trans-
porting said supplies and bringing back cotton or other produce he may receive
in exchange.
    "The Military and Naval authorities are requested to allow Mr Lewis to
proceed to and from such places as he may desire with his boats, for the purpose of carrying out the above." (Ibid.).
[2] The letter given has not been located.

Permit to Christopher F. Field and Christopher F. Clay[1]

Executive Mansion,
Washington, [January 23?], 1864.

Confiding in the representations and assurances made and given
by Hon. Brutus J. Clay of Kentucky, that if permitted, and afforded reasonable protection and facilities by the government, his

brother-in-law, Christopher F. Field, and his son, Christopher F. Clay, having, prior to the rebellion, had ownership and lawful control, of several plantations in Mississippi and Arkansas would put said plantations into cultivation, upon the system of free hired labor, recognizing and acknowledging the freedom of the laborers, and totally excluding from said plantations, the slave system of labor and all actual slavery, and would neither do or permit anything on said plantations which would aid the rebellion, it is hereby ordered that said Christopher F. Field, and Christopher F. Clay, or either of them, be permitted to so put said plantations, or any of them, into cultivation; and that the Military, and all others acting by the authority of the United States, are to favor and facilitate said Field and Clay in the carrying forward said business in good faith, by giving them protection, and allowing them to procure, and take to the proper points, the necessary supplies of all kinds, and by doing and forbearing in whatever way will advance the object aforesaid; *provided* that existing Military or Trade regulations, nor any military necessity, be transcended or over-ridden thereby. ABRAHAM LINCOLN

I have made the representations and given the assurances as within indicated. BRUTUS J. CLAY

Feb. 1. 1864

1 ADfS, DLC-RTL. The bracketed portion of the date has been supplied on the basis of the letter to Lewis, *supra*. The certificate in Lincoln's handwriting signed by Brutus J. Clay is on a separate page, and was probably drawn up on the date given.

To the Senate[1]

To the Senate of the United States: January 23, 1864

I transmit to the Senate a copy of a dispatch of the 12th. of April, last, addressed by Anson Burlingame, Esquire, the Minister of the United States to China, to the Secretary of State, relative to a modification of the 21st. article of the Treaty between the United States and China of the 18th. of June 1858, a printed copy of which is also herewith transmitted. These papers are submitted to the consideration of the Senate with a view to their advice and consent being given to the modification of the said Twenty-first article as explained in the said dispatch and its accompaniments.

Washington, 23d. January, 1864. ABRAHAM LINCOLN

1 DS, DNA RG 46, Senate 38B B2. The communication from Burlingame transmitted an agreement of April 7, 1863, with the government of China that the twenty-first article of the treaty of June 18, 1858, "shall be so modified as to permit duties to be paid when goods are re-exported from any one of the

free ports of China, at the port into which they are finally imported; and that drawbacks shall be substituted for exemption certificates at all the ports, which drawbacks shall be regarded as negotiable and transferable articles, and be accepted by the custom-house from whatsoever merchant who may tender them, either for import or export duty to be paid by him." The Senate advised and consented to this modification by resolution of February 4, 1864; and it was accepted, ratified, and confirmed by the President, February 22, 1864. (Sixty-first Congress, Second Session, *Senate Executive Document No. 357, Treaties . . . 1776–1909,* I, 221.)

To Cadwallader C. Washburn[1]

Major General C. C. Washburn.   Executive Mansion,
[Care of C. & G. Woodman   Washington,
No. 33 Pine Street, N.Y. City][2]   Jan. 23, 1864.

Your brother wishes you to visit Washington, and this is your authority to do so.   A. LINCOLN

[1] ALS, RPB. General Washburn was the brother of Representative Elihu B. Washburne. General Nathaniel P. Banks wrote Lincoln on January 15:

"Major General C. C. Washburn, who visits Washington upon leave of absence, given by you, will be able to state to you more fully than it can be presented in despatches, the condition of affairs in Texas. I have requested him to call upon you for that purpose. Although dated in October he has declined to avail himself of the privelege granted to him, until now, when the public service justifies his temporary absence.

"You will allow me to express the hope that he return to this Department upon the termation of his furlough. He is a valuable officer and in his service here, has exhibited the most commendable energy and capacity in the discharge of his duties fully justifying the high confidence you have reposed in him." (DLC-RTL).   [2] The bracketed address was inserted by a clerk.

To Edward Bates[1]

Hon. Attorney General please make out & send me a pardon in this case.   A. LINCOLN

Jan. 25. 1864.

[1] AES, DNA RG 204, U.S. Pardon Attorney, A 466. Lincoln's endorsement is written on a letter of B. Milburn to John D. Stiles, January 22, 1864, testifying to the good behavior of George S. Becker while a prisoner in the District of Columbia jail. See Lincoln to Stiles, December 24, 1863, *supra.*

To Salmon P. Chase[1]

Executive Mansion,
Washington, D.C., January 25, 1864.

My dear Sir: Not intending to hurry you, may I ask if the new provisions about trade in cotton and sugar are nearly ready to go into effect? Yours truly,   A. LINCOLN.

[1] NH, IX, 295. Chase replied on the same day: "Will you have the goodness to name an hour today, either at the Executive Mansion or here, which you will give to the final revision of the new regulations of trade, with me." (DLC-RTL). See Lincoln's order of January 26, and letter to Chase of January 28, *infra*.

Endorsement[1]

January 25, 1864

Senator Powell says that of the many applications he has, he thinks the within named may safely be allowed to take the oath and be discharged. He says those designated as officers have resigned, as they write to him and he believes.

Let them all take the oath of Dec. 8. and be discharged.

Jan. 25. 1864.   A. LINCOLN

[1] Angle, p. 340. Lincoln's endorsement having been cut from the attendant document, Senator Lazarus W. Powell's recommendation is not available.

To Ulysses S. Grant[1]

January 25, 1864

I have declined to sign the within; and yet I do desire that an examination of Mrs. Bass' losses may be made by those having the means of doing so; and that she be paid, or her account forwarded to the War Department, in due form, accordingly as the rules of the service may apply to her case.   A. LINCOLN

Jan. 25. 1864

Majr. Genl. Grant.

[1] AES-F, American Art Association Anderson Galleries Catalog 2823, February 25-26, 1930, No. 240. See Lincoln to Lorenzo Thomas, January 15, *supra.* Lincoln's endorsement is written on an order for an inquiry into the claims of Mrs. Eugenia P. Bass for supplies taken from her plantation for use of U.S. troops. The document is also endorsed by Grant and by Andrew Johnson on June 10, 1865. Grant wrote: "The endorsement herein will be executed by the present commander of Vicksburg." President Johnson wrote: "The endorsement of Gen'l. Grant hereon is approved, and will be carried into execution."

To Andrew Johnson[1]

Gov. Johnson   Executive Mansion,
Nashville, Tenn.   Washington, Jan. 25, 1864.

The oath in the proclamation may be administered by the Military Governor, the Military commander of the Department, and by all persons designated by them for that purpose. Loyal as well as disloyal should take the oath, because it does not hurt them, clears all question as to their right to vote, and swells the aggregate number who take it, which is an important object. This[2] is the President's reply to your questions of the 14th. I intend to start for Nashville in the morning. Will go directly through—stopping a few hours in Cincinnati, where a dispatch will reach me.   HORACE MAYNARD

Please send the above as public business.   A. LINCOLN

[1] AL and AES, RPB. The manuscript telegram is in Lincoln's autograph excepting the portion noted. See Lincoln to Johnson, January 15, *supra*.

[2] The remainder down to and including Maynard's signature is in Maynard's autograph.

To George G. Meade[1]

                                          Executive Mansion, Washington,
Major-General Meade: January 25, 1864.
    Suspend execution of death sentence of Robert Gill, ordered to be shot on the 29th instant, and forward record for examination.
                                                        A. LINCOLN.

Major Eckert:
    Please send above dispatch.   JNO. G. NICOLAY.

[1] Tarbell (Appendix), p. 412. No reply has been found. See Lincoln to Stanton, January 28, *infra*.

To George G. Meade[1]

                                          Executive Mansion, Washington,
Major-General Meade: January 25, 1864.
    Suspend execution of sentence Samuel Tyler, of Company G, Third Regiment New Jersey Volunteers, in First Brigade, First Division, Sixth Corps, and forward record for examination.
                                                        A. LINCOLN.

Major Eckert:
    Please send above dispatch   JNO. G. NICOLAY.

[1] Tarbell (Appendix), p. 412. No reply has been found. Samuel Tyler, sentenced for desertion, was transferred to Company C, Fifteenth New Jersey Volunteers and served until mustered out with the company on September 23, 1864. His pardon was announced in AGO *Special Orders No. 68*, February 11, 1864.

Recommendation for Henry R. Green[1]

                                          Washington Jan 25. 1864
This is to show that Henry R. Greene Esq of Illinois is an upright, honorable and worthy man. I have known him and his family for many years.

Mr Greene goes to New Orleans intending to establish himself in some business there. For several years before the commencement of the Rebellion, he spent his winters there and is acquainted with the customs of the South.

I hope the various commanders, agents and employees of the Government will extend to Mr Greene such aid and facilities as are[2] proper and consistent with the interests of the service.

A. LINCOLN

[1] DS-P, ISLA. Henry R. Green was a resident of Delavan, Illinois.
[2] "Is" corrected to "are" by Lincoln.

To Benjamin F. Butler[1]

Major General Butler   Executive Mansion,
Fort-Monroe   Washington, Jan. 26. 1864.

Some days ago a despatch was sent to stay execution of James C. Gratton, & perhaps some others, which has not been answered. Please answer.   A. LINCOLN

[1] ALS, RPB. No reply has been discovered. See Lincoln to Butler, January 21, *supra.*

Memorandum[1]

I find this bundle of somewhat old papers upon my table, & can not remember for what object they were left. Please file them.

Jan. 26. 1864   A. LINCOLN

[1] ADS, owned by Robert R. Spaulding, Providence, Rhode Island. The bundle of papers has not been identified.

Order Approving Trade Regulations[1]

Executive Mansion,
Washington, January 26, 1864.

I, Abraham Lincoln, President of the United States, having seen and considered the Additional Regulations of Trade prescribed by the Secretary of the Treasury, and numbered LI, LII, LIII, LIV, LV, and LVI, do hereby approve the same; and I further declare and order that all property brought in for sale in good faith, and actually sold in pursuance of said Regulations LII, LIII, LIV, LV, and LVI, after the same shall have taken effect and come in force as provided in Regulation LVI, shall be exempt from confiscation or forfeiture to the United States.   ABRAHAM LINCOLN.

[1] *Additional Regulations Concerning Commercial Intercourse with and in States Declared in Insurrection*, January 26, 1864. The Treasury regulations referred to are printed in the same pamphlet. See Lincoln to Chase, January 25, *supra*, and January 28, *infra*; also the orders of February 2 and May 20, 1864, *infra*.

To John Sedgwick[1]

Executive Mansion, Washington,
Major-General Sedgwick: January 26, 1864.

Your letter of January 22, received. Suspend execution of sentence in all the capital cases mentioned in General Orders No. 1 and 2, where it has not already been done. I recapitulate the whole list of capital cases mentioned in said orders including those cases in which execution has been heretofore, as well as those on which it is now suspended.

Private John Wilson, Company D, Seventy-first Pennsylvania; Private James Lane, Company B, Seventy-first New York; Private Joseph W. Clifton, Company F, Sixth New Jersey; Private Ira Smith, Company I, Eleventh New Jersey; Private Allen G. Maxson, Company D, First Michigan; Private John Keatly, Company I, Second Delaware; Private Daniel P. Byrnes, Company A, Ninety-eighth Pennsylvania; Private Samuel Tyler, Company G, Third New Jersey; Private Robert Gill, Company D, Sixth New York Cavalry.

Forward the records in these cases for examination.

A. LINCOLN.

Major Eckert:
Please send above dispatch.   JNO. G. NICOLAY.

[1] Tarbell (Appendix), pp. 412-13. General Sedgwick wrote on January 22: "Enclosed I have the honor to transmit copies of General Court Martial Orders Nos. 1 & 2 current series from these Head Quarters.

"The execution of the sentence in all the capital cases mentioned in General Orders No. 1, except that of Private Ira Smith, 11th New Jersey, has been suspended by your order and the records in the cases forwarded for your action.

"The orders will be carried out in the cases of Private Smith and those men mentioned in General Orders No 2 unless you interpose." (DLC-RTL).

To Edward Bates[1]

Attorney General please make out a pardon in this case.
Jan. 27. 1864   A. LINCOLN

[1] AES, CSmH. Lincoln's endorsement is written on a letter from Representative Austin A. King, January 27, 1864, asking pardon for John B. Corner of Ray County, Missouri, indicted for conspiracy against the government.

To Edward Bates[1]

January 27, 1864

This is a good recommendation for a territorial Judgeship, embracing both sides in Missouri & many other respectable gentlemen.   A. Lincoln

Jan. 27, 1864

[1] AES-P, ISLA. Lincoln's endorsement is written on a letter from Austin A. King and others, January 5, 1864, recommending Judge Solomon P. McCurdy of Missouri. McCurdy's appointment as associate justice for Utah Territory was confirmed by the Senate on April 21, 1864.

To John G. Foster[1]

Majr. Gen. Foster   Washington, D.C.,
Knoxville, Tenn.   January 27 1864

Is a supposed correspondence between Gen. Longstreet and yourself, about the amnesty proclamation, which is now in the newspapers, genuine?   A. Lincoln

[1] ALS, RPB. General Foster had sent copies of his correspondence with Longstreet to Halleck and Grant on January 26, and replied to Lincoln's telegram on January 30, 1864: "Telegram of twenty seventh (27th) received. I have had a correspondence with Genl Longstreet upon the subject of the amnesty proclamation, but cannot say whether the newspapers have the correct version as I have not seen them. Copies of the letters are on their way to Washington." (DLC-RTL).

The letters as printed in the New York *Tribune* for January 25, 1864, were substantially correct. The text from the *Tribune* as given below corresponds with that of the *Official Records* (III, IV, 50-51) except for the variants given in brackets. In addition to the two letters as given by the *Tribune*, Longstreet's further letter of January 11 and Foster's reply of January 17 appear in the *Official Records*, but since they add little to the facts of the story or the humor of the situation they are not reproduced.

COPY OF LETTER RECEIVED FROM LIEUT-GEN. J. LONGSTREET,
AT HEADQUARTERS DEPARTMENT OF THE OHIO, AND
REPLY OF MAJ. GEN. J. G. FOSTER, COMMANDING
DEPARTMENT OF THE OHIO, KNOXVILLE, TENN.

Headquarters Confederate Forces, East Tenn.,
To the Commanding General U.S. Forces, East Tenn.   Jan. 3, 1864.

Sir: I find the Proclamation of President Lincoln of the 8th of December last, in circulation in handbills among our soldiers. The immediate object of this circulation appears to be to induce our soldiers to quit our ranks and to take the oath of allegiance to the United States Government. I presume, however, that the great object and end in view is to hasten the day of peace.

I respectfully suggest, for your consideration, the propriety of communicating any views that your Government may have upon this subject through me, rather than by handbills circulated among our soldiers. The few men who may desert under the promise held out in the Proclamation can not be men of character or standing. If they desert their cause they degrade [disgrace] themselves in the eyes of God and of man. They can do your cause no good, nor can they injure ours.

As a great nation, you can accept none but an honorable peace; as a noble people, you could have us accept nothing less. I submit, therefore, whether the mode that I suggest would not be more likely to lead to an honorable end than such a circulation of a partial promise of freedom [pardon].

I am, Sir, very respectfully, your most obedient servant,

J. LONGSTREET, Lieut-Gen. Commanding

REPLY OF MAJ-GEN. JNO. G. FOSTER, COMMANDING
DEPARTMENT OF THE OHIO.

Headquarters Department of the Ohio,
Knoxville, E.T.,
Lieut.-Gen. Commanding Forces in East Tennessee: Jan. 7, 1864.

Sir: I have the honor to acknowledge the receipt of your letter dated Jan. 3, 1864: you are correct in the supposition that the great object in view in the circulation of the President's Proclamation, is to induce those now in Rebellion against the Government, to lay aside their arms, and return to their allegiance as citizens of the United States, thus securing the re-union of States now arrayed in hostility against one another and restoration of peace. The immediate effect of the circulation may be to cause many men to leave your ranks, to return home, or come within our lines, and, in view of this latter course, it has been thought proper to issue an order announcing the favorable terms on which deserters will be received.

I accept, however, your suggestion that it would have been more courteous to have sent these documents to you for circulation, and I embrace with pleasure the opportunity thus afforded to enclose to you twenty (20) copies of each of these documents and rely upon your generosity and desire for peace, to give publicity to the same among your officers and men.

I have the honor to be, General, Very Respectfully,

J. G. FOSTER, Maj.-Gen. Commanding

Memorandum:
Appointment of Edward L. Wooden[1]
West-Point

Edward L. Wooden, of Conn—18 in Augt. 1863, is 5. feet 10. and has served 9 months in the War—upon the Mississippi.

Jan. 27. 1864   A. LINCOLN

[1] AES, DNA WR RG 94, U.S. Military Academy, 1864, No. 196. Lincoln's endorsement is written on a letter of Edward L. Wooden to Stanton, January 22, 1864, applying for appointment to West Point and setting forth that he had served from September 2, 1862, to August 30, 1863, in the Twenty-third Connecticut Volunteers. No appointment is of record.

To Frederick Steele[1]

Executive Mansion, Washington,
Major General Steele: January 27, 1864.

I have addressed a letter to you, and put it in the hands of Mr. Gantt and other Arkansas gentlemen, containing a programme for an election in that State. This letter will be handed you by some of these gentlemen. Since writing, it I see that a convention in Arkansas, having the same general object, has taken some action, which I am afraid may clash somewhat with my programme. I therefore can do no better than to ask you to see Mr. Gantt immediately on his return, and with him, do what you and he may deem necessary to harmonize the two plans into one, and then put it through with all possible vigor. Be sure to retain the free State constitutional provision in some unquestionable form, and you and he can fix the rest. The points I have made in the programme have been well considered. Take hold with an honest heart and a strong hand. Do not let any questionable man control or influence you. Yours truly   A. LINCOLN

¹ ALS, owned by William W. Steele, Pescadero, California. See Lincoln's letter to Steele, January 20, *supra*, which was carried by Edward W. Gantt. Isaac Murphy, chosen provisional governor of Arkansas by convention in January, 1864, was elected by popular vote in March and inaugurated on April 18, 1864. See further Lincoln to Steele, January 30, *infra*.

To George L. Andrews[1]

Executive Mansion, Washington, January 28, 1864.
To the Commanding Officer at Fort Preble, Portland, Me.:
   Suspend the execution of death sentence of Charles Caple, until further orders, and forward record for examination.

                                        A. LINCOLN.

Major Eckert:
   Please send above dispatch. I infer from the letter on which the reprieve is granted that Fort Preble is in Maine, but do not certainly know. Please inquire of Colonel Hardee. As the execution was set for to-morrow, it is important that the dispatch should go at once.   JNO. G. NICOLAY,
                                        Private Secretary.

¹ Tarbell (Appendix), p. 413. Major George L. Andrews replied on the same day: "Charles G. Capell was enlisted at this post June 1, 1863, he was born in England aged 22 years, occupation Laborer. June 6, 1863 he was assigned to Company 'C' 2d Battalion 17th Infy. U.S.A. and bore a good character until Aug. 12. 1863 at which time he was 'absent without leave' Aug 15, 1863, having been absent three days he was reported a deserter. Nothing more was known of him until Nov 15. 1863 when notice was received of his arrest as a deserter and Nov. 30, 1863 he was delivered at this post. About the 1st. of Jany., inst. by the connivance of his guard he escaped from confinement, but a few days after was arrested at Camp Perry (by a Sergt. Geo. F. Adams from this command, who was sent in search of him) having enlisted and received the bounty in one of the Maine Cavalry Regts. about leaving for the field. No information as regards his trial or sentence, has ever been received at this post until your telegram of this date; and he has been held as awaiting trial." (DLC-RTL).

To Edward Bates[1]

Attorney General please make out pardons in these cases.

Jan. 28. 1864   A. LINCOLN

[1] AES, RPB. Lincoln's endorsement is written on a letter of James E. Wright and G. T. Blakey, Russellville, Kentucky, to Representative Henry Grider, January 20, 1864, asking his influence to obtain pardons for William M. Clark and James McCallen, indicted for treason.

To Salmon P. Chase[1]

Executive Mansion, January 28, 1864.

My dear Sir: Herewith I return this proof-sheet of the new rules. I suggest two points, but do not urge them. First, that as the trust and emoluments of the agents are to be increased, should not their bonds be increased?[2] Secondly, might it not be well to fix a maximum, as is sometimes done in acts of Congress, beyond which the one per cent. compensation shall not go in a year?[3]

If the increase of business should necessitate the appointment of an additional agent, I would be glad for Charles K. Hawkes to be appointed. He is one of the three so favorably mentioned by the treasury and other officers at New Orleans, in the letter I read in your hearing twice or thrice, I believe.[4] I have some reason to believe it would please General Banks, though he has not said so, that I have heard. I *have* heard that he and General Banks are old acquaintances and friends. Yours truly,   A. LINCOLN.

[1] NH, IX, 298. See the Orders of January 26, *supra*, and February 2, *infra*.
[2] Chase replied on the same day, "I have prepared the amendments suggested by you. . . ." (DLC-RTL). Regulation LIII as revised set the amount of bond required of supervising special agents and assistant special agents at $50,000.
[3] Regulation LIII as revised provided that the "aggregate compensation of no Supervising Special Agent or Assistant Special Agent shall exceed the sum of five thousand dollars per annum, or at that rate for a less period."
[4] See note to Lincoln's letter to Wright and Hawkes, January 7, *supra*. No record of Hawkes' appointment has been discovered.

To Salmon P. Chase[1]

January 28, 1864

This boy says he knows Secretary Chase, and would like to have the place made vacant by William Johnson's death. I believe he is a good boy and I should be glad for him to have the place if it is still vacant.   A. LINCOLN

Jan. 28, 1864

¹ ADS, DNA WR RG 56, Treasury Department, Personnel Records. The
Negro boy was Solomon James Johnson (see John E. Washington, *They Knew
Lincoln*, pp. 135-41). See also Lincoln's note to Chase concerning a promotion
for Solomon J. Johnson, March 15, 1865. In addition to working as messenger
for the Treasury Department, William H. Johnson had been Lincoln's personal
barber and valet.

To Commanding Officer at Fort Mifflin[1]

Executive Mansion, Washington,

Commanding Officer, Fort Mifflin: January 28, 1864.

Suspend execution of death sentence of Bernard Develin, Company E, Eighty-first Pennsylvania Volunteers, until further orders, and forward record for examination. A. LINCOLN.

Major Eckert:

Please send above dispatch. JNO. G. NICOLAY,
Private Secretary.

[1] Tarbell (Appendix), p. 413. No reply has been discovered. AGO *Special Orders No. 41*, January 27, 1864, directed that the original order for Develin's execution on February 5, 1864, issued by the Department of the Susquehanna (*General Orders No. 25*, December 22, 1863) "will be executed under the orders of the Commanding General of the Army of the Potomac." No further record has been found. The roster of Company E lists Bernard Develin as absent by court-martial at muster-out on June 29, 1865.

To John W. Forney[1]

Will see the gentlemen at 7. P.M. this evening. A. LINCOLN
Jan. 28. 1864

[1] AES, RPB. Lincoln's endorsement is written on a letter from John W. Forney, January 28, 1864, asking for an interview on the part of Simon Cameron, Henry C. Johnson, Speaker of the Pennsylvania House of Representatives, and himself.

To Henry W. Halleck[1]

Executive Mansion, Washington,

Maj Genl Halleck. Jany 28th. 1864.

Some citizens of Missouri—vicinity of Kansas City—are apprehensive that there is special danger of renewed troubles in that neighbourhood and thence on the route toward New-Mexico. I am not impressed that the danger is very great or imminent, but I will thank you to give Genls Rosecrans and Curtis respectively such orders as may turn their attention thereto and prevent as far as possible the apprehended disturbances. Yours truly,

A. LINCOLN.

¹ Copy, DNA WR RG 108, Headquarters of the Army, Letters Received, Document File 1864, 183/L. General Samuel R. Curtis had been assigned to command the Department of Kansas on January 1, 1864, and General William S. Rosecrans had been assigned to command the Department of the Missouri on January 22. On January 29, Halleck sent the following despatch to each: "Some citizens of Missouri having represented to the President that there is special danger of renewed troubles in the neighborhood of Kansas City and on the route toward New Mexico, he directs that your attention be called to the matter, so that, if necessary, measures may be taken to prevent the apprehended disturbance." (OR, I, XXXIV, II, 184).

To Edward Stanly¹

Hon. Edward Stanley   Executive Mansion, Washington,
San Francisco. Cal.   January 28, 1864.

Yours of yesterday received. We have rumors similar to the despatch received by you, but nothing very definite from North Carolina. Knowing Mr. Stanley to be an able man, and not doubting that he is a patriot, I should be glad for him to be with his old acquaintances South of Virginia, but I am unable to suggest anything definite upon the subject.   A. LINCOLN

¹ ALS, RPB. Edward Stanly, who resigned as military governor of North Carolina on January 15, 1863, and moved to San Francisco, telegraphed Lincoln on January 27, 1864: "I recd. the following message from a loyal, well informed man. 'Newburn 19th. and New York 25th. Jany. Important movements on foot in interior. Your friends want you to come here. C. B. Dabblee.' When the Country needs my service not as Governor, I am ready to come." (DLC-RTL).

To Edwin M. Stanton¹

Hon. Sec. of War.   Executive Mansion,
Sir   Washington, Jan. 28. 1864.

Col. Thomas C. Devin represents that Robert Gill, now of Co. D. 6th. N.Y. Cavalry, of which he Col. D. is the Colonel, is under sentence of death for desertion & that since his desertion, he has fought at Gettysburg and in several other battles, & has otherwise behaved well; and he asks that said Gill may be pardoned and sent to his Regiment. Let it be done. Yours truly   A. LINCOLN

¹ ALS, owned by Charles W. Olsen, Chicago, Illinois. Concerning Robert Gill, see Lincoln to Meade, January 25, 1864. AGO *Special Orders No. 43*, January 28, 1864, announced Gill's pardon.

To George S. Boutwell[1]

Hon. George S. Boutwell   Executive Mansion,
My dear Sir   Washington, January 29, 1864.
Please call and see me this morning, and as soon after receiving this as convenient. Yours truly   A. LINCOLN

[1] ALS, IHi. No clue has been found as to Lincoln's business with Representative Boutwell.

To Henry W. Halleck[1]

Executive Mansion, Washington,
Major General Halleck,   January 29, 1864.
The New Mexico people here understand that Gen. Joseph R. West, has asked to be relieved of his command in that part of the country; and they say they are for his being relieved. Let it be done unless you know some reason to the contrary. Yours truly,
A. LINCOLN.

[1] Thomas F. Madigan, *A Catalogue of Lincolniana* (1929), p. 28. AGO *Special Orders No. 49*, February 1, 1864, relieved Joseph R. West from duty in the Department of New Mexico and directed him to report for duty in the Department of Arkansas.

Memorandum:
Appointment of Henry O. Ryerson[1]

Executive Mansion, Washington, Jan. 29, 1864.
This morning I am impressed with the belief that the appointment of Col. Henry O. Ryerson of 10th. New-Jersey, as a Brig. Genl. would be, perhaps the best that can be made for the State. He has been in the war almost or quite from the beginning; and has been severely wounded, having been in nearly all the battles of the A.P.
A. LINCOLN

[1] ADS, IHi. No appointment is of record. Ryerson died on May 12, 1864, of wounds received in the Battle of the Wilderness on May 6.

To John Sedgwick[1]

Major General Sedgwick   Executive Mansion
Army of Potomac   Washington D.C. Jan. 29. 1864
Suspend execution of George Sowers, Co. E. 4th. Ohio Vols. & send record.   A. LINCOLN

[1] ALS, IHi. No reply has been found.

To the Senate[1]

To the Senate of the United States: January 29, 1864

I transmit herewith a report from the Secretary of State, in answer to the resolution of the Senate, respecting the correspondence with the authorities of Great Britain, in relation to the proposed pursuit of hostile bands of the Sioux Indians into the Hudson Bay Territories   ABRAHAM LINCOLN.

Washington, 29th. Jany. 1864.

[1] DS, DNA RG 46, Senate 38A F3. The enclosures are printed in Thirty-eighth Congress, First Session, *Senate Executive Document No. 13.* After the uprising in Minnesota in 1862, the Sioux Indians fled to the Red River country in Canada. On January 21, 1864, Seward asked that U.S. troops be allowed to pursue them or that the British use U.S. troops to restrain them from raids across the border. Lord Lyons replied on January 22 that the request had been forwarded to London.

To Daniel E. Sickles[1]

Major General Sickles   Executive Mansion,
New-York: Washington, January 29, 1864.

Could you, without it's being inconvenient, or disagreeable to yourself, immediately take a trip to Arkansas for me?

A. LINCOLN.

[1] ALS, RPB. General Sickles wrote Lincoln on January 27, 1864, that he could walk without crutches by use of an artificial leg and was anxious for duty (DLC-RTL). On January 29 he replied to Lincoln's telegram, "Your telegram received this afternoon. I am ready to go at once. Shall I wait here for orders or proceed to Washington?" (*Ibid.*). On February 2, he wrote:

"Since replying to your telegram in reference to Arkansas—to the effect that I was ready to go—I have waited here for orders presuming that if you wished me to report to you in person in Washington your wish would be made known . . . by telegram or letter. I write now lest there might be a different expectation on your part.

"Here I am making good use of my time in learning the use of my artificial limb . . . and . . . as soon as I am advised that I am fit for . . . duty will proceed to Washington. . . .

"My *first* wish is to resume command of my Corps—next to that, the command of Washington—but I shall be entirely satisfied to undertake any duty which you think I can be most useful to the Government,—whether in the field, or at Washington, Arkansas or elsewhere." (*Ibid.*).

See further, Lincoln to Sickles, February 10, *infra.*

To Joseph Holt[1]

January 30, 1864

In accordance with the recommendation of Major General Meade, the sentence of Capt. Jesse Armstrong, 7th Indiana Volunteers is commuted to forfeiture of one months pay proper.

Jan. 30, 1864.   A. LINCOLN

[160]

¹ ES, DNA WR RG 153, Judge Advocate General, MM 810. Lincoln's endorsement is written on the court-martial record of Jesse B. Armstrong, Company K, Seventh Indiana Volunteers, dismissed for conduct prejudicial to good order and military discipline and conduct unbecoming an officer and gentleman.

To Joseph Holt¹

January 30, 1864

In consideration of the recommendation made by Major General Schofield and the long period of time this officer has already been under arrest, his sentence is hereby remitted.   A. LINCOLN

January 30, 1864

¹ ES, DNA WR RG 153, Judge Advocate General, MM 905. Lincoln's endorsement is written on the court-martial record of Captain Samuel M. Logan, First Colored Cavalry, cashiered for violation of Fourteenth and Fifteenth Articles of War.

To Frederick Steele¹

Executive Mansion, Washington,

Major General Steele   January 30. 1864.

Since writing mine of the 27th. seeing still further accounts of the action of the convention in Arkansas, induces me to write you yet again. They seem to be doing so well, that possibly the best you can do would be to help them on their own plan—but of this, you must confer with them, and be the judge. Of all things, avoid if possible, a dividing into cliques among the friends of the common object. Be firm and resolute against such as you can perceive would make confusion and division. Yours truly   A. LINCOLN

¹ ALS, owned by William W. Steele, Pescadero, California; ADfS, DLC-RTL. See Lincoln to Steele, January 20 and 27, *supra*.

To Nathaniel P. Banks¹

Executive Mansion, Washington,

Major General Banks   January 31, 1864.

Yours of the 22nd. Inst. is just received. In the proclamation of Dec. 8. and which contains the oath that you say some loyal people wish to avoid taking, I said:

And² still further, that this proclamation is intended to present the people of the States wherein the national authority has been suspended, and loyal State governments have been subverted, a mode in and by which the national authority and loyal State governments may be re-established within said States, or in any of them; and, while the mode presented is the best the Executive can suggest, with his present impressions, it must not be understood that no other possible mode would be acceptable.

And speaking of this in the Message, I said:

Saying[3] that reconstruction will be accepted if presented in a specified way, it is not said it will never be accepted in any other way.

These things were put into these documents on purpose that some conformity to circumstances should be admissable; and when I have, more than once, said to you in my letters that available labor already done should not be thrown away, I had in my mind the very class of cases you now mention. So you see it is not even a modification of anything I have heretofore said when I tell you that you are at liberty to adopt any rule which shall admit to vote any unquestionably loyal free-state men and none others. And yet I do wish they would all take the oath. Yours truly,

A. LINCOLN

[1] ALS, IHi; ADfS, DLC-RTL. On January 22, Banks wrote Lincoln:

"It gives me great pleasure to report the progress making in the state election. All parties participate in the selection of candidates, and a very handsome vote will be given. Not a word is heard from any one in favor of a restoration of slavery, and no objection is made to the free state basis upon which the election is based. The indications are very strong that Mr. Hahn will be elected governor. By the middle of April, you will receive a full delegation in both houses of Congress, composed not only of loyal men but earnest supporters of your administration. This will be accomplished in ninety days from the receipt of your letter embracing your instructions for a free state organization in the shortest possible time, and it will give in its results I am sure satisfaction to the People. Officers selected will be from the established residents of the state. The only part I take in the affair is to discourage nominations from the army of which none will be attempted.

"The only ground of hesitation on the part of the most conservative men is in regard to the oath required which is that of your proclamation of the 8th. December. Prominent Union men, who have never sympathized with or aided the rebellion directly or indirectly, . . . who support your administration, . . . have taken the oath, and complied with the conditions of your proclamation . . . say, that having been established in their rights as citizens, and voted in election of members of congress they ought not to be compelled to take an additional oath in order to vote at this election. The exception taken refers . . . to the clauses referring to the laws of congress &c. relating to slavery and the confiscation of property. There is perhaps a professional interest in the case. Some of the most prominent and steadfast are lawyers of high standing. They have discussed the statutes of confiscation in the District court here and expect to argue their causes in Washington. They interpret the oath so as to forbid this exercise of their professional privileges. . . . It has seemed to me that the oath prescribed in the late proclamation was intended to apply to states in which no elections have been held, and that if it were so construed as to allow loyal men to vote who had qualified under the conditions of the Proclamation of   no harm could be done. It would not change the results of the election, but affect only the aggregate of votes. . . .

"You will have heard of some objections to the speedy organization of the state which I have proposed. It proceeds . . . from those who did not desire an immediate restoration of the state . . . but the mass of the people are entirely satisfied. . . ." (DLC-RTL).

2 In the ALS this passage is a printed clipping pasted on the letter.

3 Ditto.

To Thomas E. Bramlette[1]

Governor Bramlette   Executive Mansion.
Frankfort, Ky.   Washington, D.C. Jan. 31. 1864

Gen. Boyles resignation is accepted, so that your Excellency can give him the appointment proposed.   A. LINCOLN

1 ALS, RPB. See Lincoln to Stanton, January 11, *supra.* On January 30, Governor Bramlette telegraphed Lincoln: "Has Brig Genl Boyles resignation been accepted. If so I wish to give him an appointment. Answer." (DLC-RTL). Boyle's resignation took effect on January 26. Afterwards he helped organize the Louisville City Railroad and became president of the company.

To John A. Dix[1]

Executive Mansion, Washington,
Major-General Dix, New York: February 1, 1864.

Suspend execution of death sentence of Frank W. Parker, of one of the Maine regiments, sentenced to be shot for desertion on the 5th instant, and forward record for examination.   A. LINCOLN.

Major Eckert:
Please send above dispatch.   JNO. G. NICOLAY,
                                 Private Secretary.

1 Tarbell (Appendix), p. 414. No reply has been found. Lincoln returned the record in the case to Judge Advocate General Holt on April 16, 1864, under the order of February 26, *infra* (DNA WR RG 153, Judge Advocate General, NN 802).

To Caleb Lyon[1]

Hon. Caleb Lyon   Executive Mansion,
My dear Sir   Washington, February 1, 1864

Gov. Wallace of Idaho is very anxious for a different man to be appointed Gov. of that Territory. I told him my promise to you was absolute, but if he could persuade you out of it, all right, but that I should keep my word with you. See the Governor, and then call and see me. Yours truly   A. LINCOLN

[1] ALS, THaroL. No reply has been found, but ex-congressman Lyon was appointed to succeed William H. Wallace. See Lincoln to Seward, February 2, *infra*.

Order for Draft of 500,000 Men[1]

Executive Mansion
Ordered: February 1st. 1864.
That a draft for five hundred thousand men to serve for three years or during the war, be made on the tenth day of March next, for the military service of the United States, crediting and deducting therefrom, so many as may have been enlisted or drafted into the service prior to the first day of March, and not heretofore credited. ABRAHAM LINCOLN

[1] DS, owned by Harry MacNeill Bland, New York City. The original order is in the hand of a clerk with emendations by Stanton and signed by Lincoln.

To Edwin M. Stanton[1]

Executive Mansion, February 1, 1864.
Sir: You are directed to have a transport (either a steam or sailing vessel as may be deemed proper by the Quartermaster-General) sent to the colored colony established by the United States at the island of Vache, on the coast of San Domingo, to bring back to this country such of the colonists there as desire to return. You will have the transport furnished with suitable supplies for that purpose, and detail an officer of the Quartermaster's Department who, under special instructions to be given, shall have charge of the business. The colonists will be brought to Washington, unless otherwise hereafter directed, and be employed and provided for at the camps for colored persons around that city. Those only will be brought from the island who desire to return, and their effects will be brought with them. ABRAHAM LINCOLN.

[1] OR, III, IV, 75. This order was enclosed by Stanton to Meigs on February 3, 1864. On February 4, Meigs reported to Stanton:
"The ship Maria L. Day has been chartered in the port of New York. She is being fitted, victualed, and watered as for a voyage to Aspinwall by the Windward Passage, to bring to Boston 500 troops.
"I have directed Major Van Vliet, quartermaster at New York, to hold the ship ready to take on board the officer who may be designated to go in her, and to obey his orders to stop at any other port than Aspinwall, and to proceed in any direction he may order.
"I respectfully name Edward L. Hartz, assistant quartermaster, U.S. Army, as the officer to receive the special instructions. . . .
"I propose to order Captain Hartz to proceed at once to New York to report to Major Van Vliet and receive from him the charge of the ship. . . .

"I respectfully suggest the propriety of ordering an assistant surgeon and a guard of a subaltern and twenty men and non-commissioned officers of the Invalid Corps to proceed on the ship. . . ." (*Ibid.*, p. 76).
Concerning the colonization of Isle A'Vache see Lincoln to Seward, January 6, 1863, and the proclamation of April 16, 1863, *supra*.

To Kamehameha V[1]

To His Majesty Kamehameha, V,   February 2, 1864
  King of the Hawaiian Islands.

Great and Good Friend: I have read with feelings of profound sorrow your Majesty's letter of the 5th. December last announcing the death on the 30th. of the preceding month, of His Majesty, your Brother, Kamehameha IV, and conveying also the pleasing intelligence of your Majesty's constitutional succession to the Throne of the Hawaiian Kingdom.

Your Majesty's anticipations of sympathy from me in the double bereavement which you have experienced in the decease of your Sovereign and Brother are fully realized. Not only I, but the whole American People are deeply moved by the intelligence of the event with which God in His infinite wisdom has afflicted your Majesty and the Hawaiian nation; for whom this Government and people have ever entertained sentiments of almost paternal regard, as well as of sincere friendship and unchanging interest.

It is gratifying to know that His Majesty's place on the Throne and in the hearts of the Hawaiian people is occupied by one who was allied to him by the closest ties of blood, and by a long participation in the affairs of the Kingdom. These influences, controlled by the Supreme Ruler of the Universe whose guidance your Majesty invokes, and by those aspirations which your Majesty cherishes for the good of your subjects, cannot fail to assure the well-being and prosperity of the Hawaiian Kingdom.

Your Majesty may ever firmly rely upon my sincere sympathy and cordial support and upon the abiding friendship of the people of the United States in the execution of the lofty mission entrusted to you by Providence.

Commending your Majesty, and the bereaved Widow and People of the late King to the Fatherly protection and comfort of the Almighty, I remain Your Majesty's Good Friend,

By the President: ABRAHAM LINCOLN.
  WILLIAM H. SEWARD, Secretary of State.
Washington, February 2d. 1864.

[1] Copy, DNA FS RG 59, Communications to Foreign Sovereigns and States, III, 211-12.

Order Approving Regulations of Trade[1]

Executive Mansion
Washington, February 2, 1864.

I, Abraham Lincoln, President of the United States, having seen and considered the Additional Regulation of Trade prescribed by the Secretary of the Treasury, and numberd LVII, do hereby approve the same.   ABRAHAM LINCOLN.

[1] *Additional Regulations Concerning Commercial Intercourse with and in States Declared in Insurrection,* January 26, 1864. Additional Regulation LVII modified the Twenty-sixth Regulation established on September 11, 1863, in so far as to annul restrictions on trade in the State of West Virginia within the Union lines, with the exception that no products could be shipped into any state in insurrection. See Lincoln's orders of January 26, *supra,* and May 20, *infra.*

To William H. Seward[1]

Hon. Sec. of State,   Executive Mansion,
Dear Sir: Washington, Feb. 2, 1864.

Please send me a nomination for Hon. Caleb Lyon, as Governor of Idaho Territory. Yours truly,   A. LINCOLN.

[1] Thomas F. Madigan, *A Catalogue of Lincolniana* (1929), p. 28. See Lincoln to Lyon, February 1, *supra.* Lyon's nomination went to the Senate on February 2, and was confirmed on February 26, 1864. See Lincoln to Roscoe Conkling, February 19, *infra.*

To Charles A. Dana[1]

[February 3, 1864]

Will Mr. Dana please see and hear this man and do the best for him he can?   A. LINCOLN

[1] AES, DNA WR RG 107, Secretary of War, Personnel Appointments, Box 29. Lincoln's endorsement is written on a letter from Francis S. Macnamara, Washington, D.C., February 3, 1864, reminding the president of a promise made at Judiciary Square Hospital after the Seven Days Battle, to give him an appointment. F. G. McNamara, listed in the *U.S. Official Register,* 1865, as a clerk in the pay department, may or may not be the same man.

Endorsement[1]

Upon the refunding all bounties and other expenses, let this boy be discharged.   A. LINCOLN

Feb. 3. 1864

[1] AES, owned by Mrs. Ethel M. Nauman, Baltimore, Maryland. The endorsement has been removed from attendant papers and cannot be further identified.

To Joseph Holt[1]

Executive Mansion Washington,
Judge Advocate General   Feb. 3. 1864
    Please obtain the record, examine & report upon it, in the case
of ——— Yocum, mentioned in the accompanying letter. Yours
truly   A. LINCOLN

[1] ALS, DNA WR RG 153, Judge Advocate General, MM 1217. William
Yocum, employee in charge of contrabands at Cairo, Illinois, had been sen-
tenced to five years at hard labor for aiding in kidnapping employees of the
U.S. See Lincoln's endorsements, January 22, *supra*, and February 16, *infra*.

To William H. Seward[1]

Hon. Sec. of State   Executive Mansion,
My dear Sir   Washington, February 3, 1864.
    Please see Hon. Wm. R. Morrison, and oblige him about the
pass-ports for Mr. Merrick if you consistently can. Yours truly
                                               A. LINCOLN

[1] ALS, IHi. Merrick has not been positively identified, but as a guess, Democratic Representative William R. Morrison may have sought passports for
Democrat Richard T. Merrick of Chicago, who moved to Washington in 1864.

To Richard Yates[1]

Gov. Yates   Executive Mansion,
Springfield, Ills.   Washington, Feb. 3, 1864.
    The U.S. government lot in Springfield, can be used for a Sol-
diers Home, with the understanding that the government does
not incur any expence in the case.   A. LINCOLN

[1] ALS, RPB. Governor Yates telegraphed on January 28: "A Soldier's home
is very much needed here & the San. Com. have donated two thousand dolls.
for that purpose. Can the Commission have for that purpose the use of lot
purchased of Maj. Iles by the Govt. for Court house?" (DLC-RTL).
    The site of the present Federal Building at Sixth and Monroe Streets in
Springfield was the lot in question. A frame building, with lounge and sleeping rooms for furloughed soldiers, was promptly erected after receipt of Lincoln's telegram. See Lincoln to Woods, April 25, *infra*.

To Edward Everett[1]

                                           Executive Mansion,
My dear Sir   Washington, February 4, 1864.
    Yours of Jan. 30th. was received four days ago; and since then
the address mentioned has arrived. Thank you for it. I send here-

with the manuscript of my remarks at Gettysburg, which, with my note to you of Nov. 20th. you are at liberty to use for the benefit of our soldiers as you have requested. Yours very truly

Hon. Edward Everett. A. LINCOLN.

[1] ALS, MHi; ADfS, DLC-RTL. Edward Everett wrote on January 30: "I shall have the honor of forwarding to you by Express . . . a copy of the Authorized Edition of my Gettysburg Address & of the Remarks made by your-self, & the other matters connected with the Ceremonial of the Dedication of the Cemetery. It appeared, owing to unavoidable delays, only yesterday.

"I have promised to give the Manuscript of my address to Mrs. Governor [Hamilton] Fish of New-York, who is at the head of the Ladies' Committee of the Metropolitan fair. It would add very greatly to its value, if I could bind up with it the manuscript of your dedicatory Remarks, if you happen to have preserved them.

"I would further venture to request, that you would allow me also to bind up in the volume the very obliging letter of the 20 Nov. '63, which you did me the favor to write to me . . . . as its insertion would greatly enhance the value of the volume. . . ." (DLC-RTL).

The manuscript of Lincoln's letter of November 20 was not bound up with the manuscripts of the two addresses as proposed, but is in the Everett Papers at the Massachusetts Historical Society. The manuscript address which Lincoln enclosed on February 4, known as "the Everett Copy," was probably prepared in November, 1863, shortly after the ceremony. See the notes to the Gettysburg Address, November 19, 1863, *supra*.

To Joseph Holt[1]

If the Judge Advocate General has made report as within indicated, please send me the report and record. A. LINCOLN

Feb. 4. 1864.

[1] AES, OFH. Lincoln's endorsement is written on a letter from Richard M. Corwine, February 4, 1864, asking the president to review the case of E. A. Smith, convicted of fraud against the government. See Lincoln to Eastman, November 24, 1863, *supra*, and to Corwine, March 30, *infra*.

To the Senate[1]

To the Senate: February 4, 1864

In compliance with the Resolution of the Senate of the 26th ultimo, requesting "a copy of all the correspondence between the authorities of the United States and the Rebel authorities on the exchange of prisoners, and the different propositions connected with that subject," I transmit herewith a report from the Secretary of War, and the papers with which it is accompanied.

Washington, ABRAHAM LINCOLN

February 4, 1864.

[1] DS, DNA RG 46, Senate 38A F2. Stanton's report of February 4 with enclosures is printed in Thirty-eighth Congress, First Session, *Senate Executive Document No. 17*.

To Green Adams[1]

February 5, 1864

You see the ladys name is not given in this letter. Judge Adams, may, in his discretion, send the enclosed card—blank to be filled by who can. A. LINCOLN

Feb. 5, 1864

[1] AES, owned by John S. Adams, Sr., Wayne, Pennsylvania. Lincoln's endorsement is written on a letter of Hiram Shaw, Jr., Lexington, Kentucky, to Green Adams, January 27, 1864, asking a pass for his sister in Macon, Georgia, "allowing her to come, with her *two small children*." A note, not by Lincoln, Shaw, or Adams, is written on the top of the letter: "Sent pass in letter Feb. 6. 1864."

To the Senate[1]

To the Senate of the United States. February 5, 1864

In answer to the Resolution of the Senate of yesterday on the subject of a Reciprocity Treaty with the Sandwich Islands, I transmit a Report from the Secretary of State, to whom the Resolution was referred. ABRAHAM LINCOLN.

Washington, 5 February 1864.

[1] DS, DNA RG 46, Senate 38A F3. Seward's report of February 5 indicated that "application has been made for a revival of a similar treaty which was negotiated here during the administration of President Pierce, but which was not approved by the Senate. After due consideration, however, especially in connexion with the probable effect of such a measure on the public revenue at this juncture, it has not been deemed advisable further to entertain the subject. It is not deemed expedient at present to communicate the correspondence called for by the resolution. . . ." (Thirty-eighth Congress, First Session, *Senate Executive Document No. 16*).

To Edwin M. Stanton[1]

February 5, 1864

Submitted to the Sec. of War. On principle I dislike an oath which requires a man to swear he *has* not done wrong. It rejects the Christian principle of forgiveness on terms of repentance. I think it is enough if the man does no wrong *hereafter*. A. LINCOLN

Feb. 5. 1864

[1] AES, DLC-RTL. Lincoln's endorsement is written on a letter of Colonel Richard M. Edwards, Fourth Tennessee Cavalry, to Stanton, January 29, 1864, as follows:

"Sir: Under authority of Gov Johnson of Tennessee I have raised a Regiment of cavalry known as the 4th East Tennessee cavalry. I began the organization of the Regiment at Cumberland Gap previous to receiving a copy of the newly prescribed oath of office requiring persons to swear that they have 'not sought nor accepted nor attempted to exercise the functions of any office whatever under any authority or pretended authority in hostility to the

United States.' As I had held the position of Representative in the state legislature of Tennessee after the so-called act of secession, it has been seriously urged by some, that the terms of the oath were intended to debar all holding state offices in a seceded state as well as those holding confederate offices. Hence desiring to be mustered in as Colonel of my Regiment, I desire a settlement of the question as to my eligibility to that position

"About twenty other union men served in the same legislature with me who have maintained their positions as loyal men to the present time. Some of them in fact like myself are organizing Regiments for our service, and I suppose the same question will be presented in their behalf. The question is one of very great importance to a very large portion of the loyal men of Tennessee, reaching as it does from a constable or justice of a civil district to the Judge of the supreme court. The Union men of East Tennessee, held nearly all the state offices in that section, maintaining as we all do, that the state was *not out of the Union;* and that only a portion of her citizens were in hostility to the Government. Nearly all those officers were forced by the Rebel authorities to take an oath 'to support the confederate constitution, and the constitution of Tennessee,' a very extraordinary oath considering the constitution of Tennessee not changed according to its own provisions, which expressly provides that members of the legislature & other officers shall take an oath to support the constitution of the United States. The two clauses of their oath, being inconsistent were of course void. Further there was no law of Tennessee requiring such an oath we having succeeded in defeating that measure in the legislature. The oath then was not only void on account of inconsistent terms, and in direct conflict with the provisions of our own constitution of Tennessee, but also wanting legal sanction. Yet the so called confederate Government through their military control of the state, required all civil officers as well as military to take said oath; in default of which the offender was forced off to Tuscaloosa, there to lie and sicken and die as numbers from East Tennessee have done, in a prison, the loathsomeness of which was scarce equalled by the famous Blackhole of Calcutta. Having then held a state office, in a *state not out of the Union* (for if out the doctrine of secession must be true which we can not agree to) and having been forced under military power to take an illegal unconstitutional, void oath, am I as well as all other state officers of Tennessee disqualified for holding a Federal office? Having raised a good Regiment many of whom voted for me for the aforesaid office, & now desire me to lead them I only await a decision of the above question   I am Very Respy."

Charles A. Dana returned the letter to the president on February 19, 1864, with the following communication:

"In regard to the case of R. M. Edwards Colonel of the 4th. Tennessee Cavalry whose letter, objecting to the oath of allegiance was by you submitted to the Secretary of War on the 5th instant. . . . I am directed to say that the oath to which Colonel Edwards objects is verbally the same as that prescribed by Act of Congress approved July 2d 1862 to be taken by 'every person elected or appointed to any office of honor or profit under the government of the United States, either in the civil, military or naval departments of the public service excepting the President of the United States.' " (*Ibid.*).

Final disposition of the problem has not been learned.

To Nathaniel P. Banks[1]

Executive Mansion, Washington,

Majr. Gen. N. P. Banks: February 6th, 1864.

The bearer, Gen. G. A. Scroggs, of Buffalo, has been appointed colonel of a colored regiment, and is to report with it to you at

New Orleans. The object of moving in this matter is to have Col. Scroggs sent by you, with his regiment, to Texas, charged to collect and organize the colored men of that State, it being believed that such a nucleus as this regiment, and such an experienced organizer of troops as Col. Scroggs has shown himself, will prove highly successful. I hope this purpose will meet with your approval, and that, by such orders as your judgment will dictate, you will put Col. S. in the way of executing his mission. Yours truly,   A. LINCOLN.

¹ George H. Stowits, *History of the One Hundredth Regiment of New York Volunteers* (1870), p. 385. Brigadier General Scroggs of the New York Militia and provost marshal of the Thirtieth District of New York, arrived in New Orleans on May 5, 1864, but upon the withdrawal of Union troops from Texas, resigned on July 6, 1864.

To Henry D. Terry¹

Executive Mansion, Washington, February 6, 1864.
Commanding Officer at Sandusky, Ohio:

Suspend the execution of death sentence of George Samuel Goodrich, Jr., One hundred and twenty-second Regiment New York Volunteers, and forward record for examination.

                                                                              A. LINCOLN.
Major Eckert:

Send above dispatch.   JNO. G. NICOLAY,
                                        Private Secretary.

¹ Tarbell (Appendix), p. 415. No reply or further reference has been discovered. Brigadier General Henry D. Terry assumed command of the post at Sandusky and Johnson's Island, Ohio, on January 14, 1864.

Endorsement: Release of A. H. Gray¹

Mr. Baxter of Vermont is very anxious to have the request granted at once.   A. LINCOLN

Feby 7, 1864

¹ Stan. V. Henkels Catalog 1373, May 19, 1925, No. 140. According to the catalog description Lincoln's endorsement is written on a letter of A. H. Gray, a Union man impressed into service by the Confederates, asking for his release from prison. No further reference has been found.

Endorsement: Request of C. T. Benton¹

This is the Canada lady's case about which Mr. Baxter is so anxious as I told Sec. of War.   A. LINCOLN

Feb. 7. 1864

[171]

[1] AES, owned by Harold L. Watt, Los Angeles, California. Lincoln's endorsement is written on a letter of C. T. Benton to Representative Portus Baxter of Vermont, Rock Island, Illinois, February 2, 1864. Benton's son, a rebel prisoner at Rock Island, had been in Kentucky at the outbreak of war and "was caught there and thinking it would be better to enter as a volunteer than as a conscript" had enlisted in the Confederate forces. No further reference has been found.

To George L. Andrews[1]

Commanding Officer, Portland, Me.,
care of Israel Washburne, Jr.:

Executive Mansion,
Washington,
February 8, 1864.

Suspend execution of death sentence of James Taylor until further orders, and forward record of trial for examination.

A. LINCOLN.

Major Eckert:

Please send above dispatch.   JNO. G. NICOLAY,
                                              Private Secretary.

[1] Tarbell (Appendix), p. 415. No reply from Colonel George L. Andrews, commanding officer at Portland, Maine, has been located, and James Taylor has not been positively identified. The death sentence of one James Taylor, for disloyalty and for being a spy, was commuted to imprisonment on recommendation of General Schofield on April 27, 1864 (DNA WR RG 153, Judge Advocate General MM 959), but the James Taylor referred to in Lincoln's telegrams to Dix and Cabot, February 12, *infra*, was sentenced for desertion. See also Lincoln to Sedgwick, *infra*.

To John D. Defrees[1]

Our own friends have this under consideration now, and will do as much without a Message as with it   A. L.

Feb. 8. 1864.

[1] AES, owned by F. L. Pleadwell, Honolulu, Hawaii. Lincoln's endorsement is written on a letter from John D. Defrees, February 7, 1864:

"The last Session of the 36th. Congress proposed to so amend the Constitution of the U.S. as to prohibit any interference with slavery, (by the General Government) where it then existed.

"It was disregarded, and the slave states resorted to war to separate from the free states.

"Now, why not send a message to Congress recommending the passage of a joint resolution proposing an amendment to the Constitution forever prohibiting slavery in the States and territories?

"It would be *your* measure and would be passed by a two thirds vote, and, eventually, three fourths of the states, through their Legislatures, would consent to it.

"If not done very soon the proposition *will* be presented by the Democracy and claimed by them as *their* proposition. This may look strange to those who do not remember with what *facility* that party can change front.

"Is it not right in itself and the best way to end Slavery!

"It would have a beneficial influence on our election next fall.

"Those who deny the justice of a second term to you are attempting to

[172]

weaken the faith of the people in your plan of reorganizing the state Governments of the rebel states. *They* say, suppose a state does so change its constitution as to prohibit slavery, why may it not, in a few years, hereafter, change back again?

"The proposed amendment would answer that cavil.

"A single amendment, thus submitted to the Legislatures of the several states, would not open the whole constitution to amendment—and no harm can come of it, even should it fail to receive the sanction of the constitutional number of states.

"If done, it would be in accordance with the mode provided by the constitution itself for its amendment—to which no one could reasonably object.

"Many reasons could be given in its favor—but I only desire to call your attention to the subject, and not to trouble you with an argument.

"Should you submit such a proposition I think it would be heartily endorsed by our State Convention on the 22d. inst.

"I think it a great *move* on the political chess-board."

A joint resolution (S. 16), introduced by Senator John B. Henderson on January 11, 1864, was amended and passed by the Senate on April 11. In the House it failed to receive the necessary two-thirds majority until January 31, 1865. Approved by President Lincoln on February 1, 1865, the resolution was adopted by the requisite three-fourths of the states and became the Thirteenth Amendment to the Constitution.

To Joseph Holt[1]

February 8, 1864

In consederation of the recommendation referred to, and that the party has already suffered much he is hereby pardoned for the rest. A. LINCOLN

Feb. 8. 1864

[1] AES, DNA WR RG 153, Judge Advocate General, LL 506. Lincoln's endorsement is written on the court-martial record of Private Michael Nash, Sixty-fifth Ohio Volunteers, sentenced to be shot for desertion. Officers of his regiment testified to his good conduct and questioned the severity of the penalty.

To Isaac Murphy[1]

Gov. Isaac Murphy
Little-Rock, Arkansas

Washington, D.C.,
February 8. 1864

My order to Gen. Steele about an election was made in ignorance of the action your convention had taken or would take. A subsequent letter directs Gen. Steele to aid you on your own plan, and not to thwart or hinder you. Show this to him.

A. LINCOLN.

[1] ALS, RPB. This telegram is misdated by Nicolay and Hay "February 6, 1864" (NH, IX, 304). A telegram signed by Isaac Murphy, William M. Fishback, Lafayette Gregg, and E. D. Mayers was received at 7:35 P.M. on February 8: "We understand that you have authorized Maj Gen. Steele to order an election on the 24th of March as you have doubtless seen the convention had appointed the fourteenth This call has gone into parts of the state to

which a new call cannot go before the 24th unless you change to the fourteenth Neither election will have one tenth Please change by telegraph"
(DLC-RTL).

To John Sedgwick[1]

Executive Mansion, Washington,
Major-General Sedgwick: February 8, 1864.
Suspend execution of death sentence of James Taylor until fur-
ther orders and forward record of trial for examination.

Major Eckert: A. LINCOLN.
Please send above dispatch. JNO. G. NICOLAY,
Private Secretary.

[1] Tarbell (Appendix), p. 415. No reply has been located. See telegrams to
Andrews, *supra*, and to Dix, February 12, *infra*.

To Edwin M. Stanton[1]

Hon. Sec. of War Executive Mansion,
My dear Sir Washington, Feb. 8, 1864.
Allow Gen. Benham to simply publish Mr. Holt's report in his
case. Yours truly A. LINCOLN

[1] ALS, THaroL. Stanton endorsed on the bottom of the letter "Approved &
referred to the Adjt Genl to furnish copy for publication." Concerning General
Henry W. Benham's case see Lincoln to Holt, January 3, 1863, *supra*.

To Edwin M. Stanton[1]

Hon. Sec. of War: Executive Mansion—
My dear Sir: Washington. Feb. 8. 1864.
I saw Doolittle and made your views known to him. He is altogether tractable on the question and thinks there is no danger of
precipitate action. Yours truly A. LINCOLN.

[1] Copy, DLC-RTL. No clue has been found as to the import of this note.

To Edwin M. Stanton[1]

Lieut. Monroe is a son of an old friend of mine, and I desire him
to have the promotion sought, if the service admits of it.
Feb. 8, 1864 A. LINCOLN

[1] Copy, ISLA. Lincoln's endorsement appears on a letter of Brigadier General Nathan Kimball recommending First Lieutenant George Monroe of the
Fifty-fourth Illinois Volunteers for promotion to captain and assistant quartermaster. George Monroe, son of Byrd Monroe of Coles County, Illinois, was appointed captain to rank from September 30, 1864. The appointment was confirmed by the Senate on February 20, 1865.

[174]

To Joseph Holt[1]

Action to relieve in this declined   A. LINCOLN
Feb. 9. 1864

[1] AES, DNA WR RG 153, Judge Advocate General NN 111. Concerning Joseph M. Bushfield, see Lincoln to Holt, August 28, 1863, *supra*, and March 31, 1864, *infra*. Only one of sixty-three court-martial cases reviewed by Lincoln on this date, this one is included because of previous references. Sentences in other cases were approved, remitted, commuted, or pardons were ordered in routine endorsements.

To John Brough[1]

Gov. Brough   Washington, D.C.,
Columbus, Ohio   Feb. 10 1864

Robert Johnson, mentioned by you, is hereby fully pardoned, for any supposed desertion, up to date   A. LINCOLN

[1] ALS, RPB. Governor Brough telegraphed on February 9, 1864: "Robert Johnson a private in the ninety second regt. O.V.I. surrenders himself to me as a deserter. The circumstances are peculiar & I respectfully ask his full pardon. Please send by telegraph as he is now in custody. I send papers by mail showing an interesting case." (DLC-RTL). No further reference has been found.

To Joseph Holt[1]

Order of dismissal set aside, and party to stand as honorably discharged.   A. LINCOLN
Feb. 10. 1864

[1] AES, DNA WR RG 153, Judge Advocate General, MM 1214. Lincoln's endorsement is written on the court-martial record of Captain Conrad Eberhardt, First Battalion, Pennsylvania Six-Months Cavalry, sentenced to be dismissed for signing muster rolls containing false statements and misapplying provisions. The record showed that Eberhardt could not read English. In addition to the three court-martial endorsements reproduced of this date there are forty-three other cases reviewed by Lincoln on February 10, bearing routine endorsements of pardon, approval, remission, or commutation of sentence.

To Joseph Holt[1]

Dennis McCarty—   February 10, 1864
Sentence of death at Cumberland, Md.
Sentence commuted to imprisonment at hard labor in the Penitentiary for five years.   A. LINCOLN
Feb. 10. 1864

[1] AES, DNA WR RG 153, Judge Advocate General, MM 372. See Lincoln to Kretz, October 15, 1863, *supra*. Lincoln's endorsement is written on the

court-martial record of Private Dennis McCarty, sentenced to death on charges of assault with intent to kill. AGO *Special Orders No. 107*, March 5, 1864, announced the commutation of McCarty's sentence, to be done at Albany, New York.

To Joseph Holt[1]

Boy discharged and mustering officer rebuked
Feb'y 10, 1864.   A LINCOLN

[1] ES, DNA WR RG 153, Judge Advocate General, LL 334. Lincoln's endorsement is written on the court-martial record of Private John S. Lounsberry, Company I, Second U.S. Artillery, sentenced for desertion. An appeal for clemency sets forth that the boy was a minor under seventeen years of age.

To Daniel Sickles[1]

Major General Sickles   Washington, D.C.,
New-York   Feb. 10 1864
    Please come on at your earliest convenience, prepared to make the contemplated trip for me.   A. LINCOLN

[1] RPB, ALS. See Lincoln to Sickles, January 29, *supra*, and to Steele, February 11, to Sickles, February 15, and to Steele, February 25, *infra*. Sickles' reply was received at 8 P.M.: "Your telegram recd. Will go on tomorrow afternoon." (DLC-RTL).

To Edwin M. Stanton[1]

Sec. of War, please see Col. Alger, who has come up on our invitation in regard to the proclamation.   A. LINCOLN
    Feb. 10. 1864

[1] ALS, MiU-C. Colonel Russell A. Alger, Fifth Michigan Cavalry, wrote Nicolay on February 9, 1864:

"Obeying your instructions of this date, I have the honor to submit the following suggestion, together with plan, of carrying into effect, the circulation of the Presidents Amnesty Proclamation within the enemy's lines.

"Almost invariably, the first questions asked by deserters coming within our lines, are, 'What are you going to do with us?' 'Are we to be shut up in prison?' 'Are we to be pressed into your army?' &c.

"This, they are taught by their officers, will be, if they desert to us.

"They also ask, 'What privileges can we have, if we take the oath. . . .'

"These questions the Proclamation does not answer so plainly to all as not to admit of a doubt.

"Could an order be made, and affixed to the Proclamation, answering them as far as possible. . . .

"The plan I would suggest for distributing is: let scouts carry it within the Enemy's lines; let Cavalry expeditions be sent out, supplied with it; leave copies at every house possible, and scatter wherever the enemy will be likely to find it. . . . Many will be found by rebel soldiers, and many will be sent to them by mail from their friends. . . .

"If a Reg't of Cavalry can be furnished to me, at different points along the enemy front, I will, if permitted, volunteer to, as far as is in my power, see this carried into effect personally." (DLC-RTL).

Edward D. Townsend wrote Nicolay on February 23 that "Col. Alger has gone to Genl. Butler's Department with some of those small print Proclamations. . . ." (*Ibid.*).

To Lyman Trumbull[1]

Hon. Lyman Trumbull   Executive Mansion,
My dear Sir   Washington, Feb. 10, 1864.

This morning I sent the nomination of ——— Pieper to the Senate for Assessor in the 12th. District of Illinois. If you see no objection, I wish you would write to Mr. Flagg, asking him to give Shiel the place Pieper now has. Yours truly   A. LINCOLN

[1] ALS, IHi. On February 12, 1864, Senator Trumbull endorsed on the bottom of the page to Willard C. Flagg, collector of internal revenue: "If young Mr Schiel is competent, & qualified in all respects, I hope you will consult the President's wishes."

John Schiel (Scheil, Scheel, or Schell), deceased brother-in-law of Gustave Koerner, was followed by Frederick Pieper of Belleville, Illinois, as assessor. Presumably Lincoln's reference to giving Schiel the place formerly held by Pieper meant Schiel's son, Frederick E. Schiel, and referred to a minor position as clerk.

To Edward Bates[1]

Let a pardon be made out in this case.   A. LINCOLN
     Feb. 11. 1864

[1] AES, DNA RG 204, U.S. Pardon Attorney, A 496. Lincoln's endorsement is written on a letter from Judge A. B. Orin, of Washington, D.C., February 10, 1864, asking pardon for D. Henry Burtinett (Burtnete), imprisoned for keeping a bawdy house: "In consequence of his good behavior since he has been imprisoned and for other reasons, I ask his immediate and unconditional pardon. I presided at the trial of his case is the reason I sign this application."

To Edward Bates[1]

Attorney General please make out and send me a pardon in this case.   A. LINCOLN
     Feb. 11. 1864.

[1] AES, RPB. Lincoln's endorsement is written on an envelope marked in a different hand "James Speed asks pardon of Combs." The case has not been further identified.

To Salmon P. Chase[1]

Hon. Sec. of Treasury, please see & hear my townsman & friend
Mr. Van Duyn.   A. LINCOLN
Feb. 11. 1864

[1] ALS-P, ISLA. Robert Irwin of Springfield wrote Lincoln on February 6,
1864, "The bearer Mr. G. A. Van Duyn, of our city visits Washington to try
and get a permit to trade South. Mr. Van Duyn is of the firm of G. A. Van
Duyn & Co. a House of good standing here. (I have no doubt you will recol-
lect him). Any assistance you can render him will be appreciated by Your
Friend Robt. Irwin" (DLC-RTL).

Endorsement Concerning Pennsylvania Militia[1]

I fully indorse the within statement, and shall be glad if Congress
shall see fit to act promptly in the case.   A. LINCOLN
Feb. 11, 1864

[1] Parke-Bernet Catalog 223, October 30-November 1, 1940, No. 584. According to the catalog description, Lincoln's endorsement is written on a letter from
Stanton as follows: "The Department has this day received returns of the
amounts required for the payment of the militia called out for the defence of
the State of Pennsylvania on the 26th of June 1863, against the invasion of
the rebel forces under command of General Lee. There being no appropriation out of which these payments could be made at the time they were required patriotic citizens of Philadelphia advanced the money, and it is proper
that they should be reimbursed without delay. I would respectfully recommend therefore that an immediate appropriation for that purpose be
made. . . ." An act approved April 12, 1866, appropriated $800,000 to reim-
burse Pennsylvania for expenditures in payment of militia in the U.S. service.

To John Sedgwick[1]

Major Gen. Sedgwick   Washington,
Army of Potomac   Feb. 11. 1864
Unless there be strong reason to the contrary, please send Gen.
Kilpatrick to us here, for two or three days.   A. LINCOLN

[1] ALS-P, ISLA. General Sedgwick replied to Lincoln's telegram at 9:25 P.M.,
"Gen. [Judson] Kilpatrick has been ordered to proceed at once to Washington
and report to you." (DLC-RTL).

To Edwin M. Stanton[1]

Hon. Secretary of War   Executive Mansion,
My dear Sir   Washington, Feb. 11, 1864.
In January 1863, the Provost-Marshal at St. Louis, having taken
the control of a certain church from one set of men and given it
to another, I wrote Gen. Curtis on the subject, as follows:
"the U.S. Government must not, as by this order, undertake to

run the churches. When an individual, in a church or out of it, becomes dangerous to the public interest, he must be checked; but the churches, as such, must take care of themselves. It will not do for the U.S. to appoint trustees, Supervisors, or other agents for the churches."

Some trouble remaining in this same case, I, on the 22nd. of Dec. 1863, in a letter to Mr. O. D. Filley, repeated the above language; and, among other things, added "I have never interfered, nor thought of interfering as to who shall or shall not preach in any church; nor have I knowingly, or believingly, tolerated any one else to so interfere by my authority. If any one is so interfering by color of my authority, I would like to have it specifically made known to me. . . . I will not have control of any church on any side."

After having made these declarations in good faith, and in writing, you can conceive of my embarrassment at now having brought to me what purports to be a formal order of the War Department, bearing date Nov. 30th. 1863, giving Bishop Ames control and possession of all the Methodist churches in certain Southern Military Departments, whose pastors have not been appointed by a loyal Bishop or Bishops, and ordering the Military to aid him against any resistance which may be made to his taking such possession and control. What[2] is to be done about it? Yours truly

A. LINCOLN

[1] ALS, DLC-Stanton Papers; LS copy, DLC-RTL. The circular letter of November 30, 1863, signed by Edward D. Townsend by order of the Secretary of War, is as follows:

"To the Generals commanding the Departments of the Missouri, the Tennessee, and the Gulf, and all Generals and officers commanding armies, detachments, and posts, and all officers in the service of the United States in the above mentioned Departments:

"You are hereby directed to place at the disposal of Rev. Bishop Ames all houses of worship belonging to the Methodist Episcopal Church South in which a loyal minister, who has been appointed by a loyal Bishop of said church, does not now officiate.

"It is a matter of great importance to the Government, in its efforts to restore tranquility to the community and peace to the nation, that Christian ministers should, by example and precept, support and foster the loyal sentiment of the people.

"Bishop Ames enjoys the entire confidence of this Department, and no doubt is entertained that all ministers who may be appointed by him will be entirely loyal. You are expected to give him all the aid, countenance, and support practicable in the execution of his important mission.

"You are also authorized and directed to furnish Bishop Ames and his clerk with transportation and subsistence when it can be done without prejudice to the service, and will afford them courtesy, assistance and protection." (Edward McPherson, *The Political History of the United States . . . During the Great Rebellion*, p. 521).

According to McPherson, the Reverend John Hogan, acting for the loyal

Methodists of Missouri, brought the matter to Lincoln's attention and procured an explanatory order to General William S. Rosecrans from Townsend on February 13, as follows:

"I am directed by the Secretary of War to say that the orders from the Department placing at the disposal of the constituted Church authorities in the Northern States houses of worship in other States, is designed to apply only to such States as are by the President's Proclamation designated as being in rebellion and is not designed to operate in loyal States, nor in cases where loyal congregations in rebel States shall be organized and worship upon the terms prescribed by the President's Amnesty." (*Ibid.*, p. 523).

See further Lincoln's endorsement to John Hogan, February 13, *infra*.

[2] Lincoln originally wrote: "Is this supposed order genuine? And if so, what is to be done about it?" It appears deleted in both the ALS and LS copy.

To John B. Steele[1]

February 11, 1864

It is not proposed to send Gen. Sickles, with any authority to control Gen. Steele in any matter; but only to confer with him and give him my views more fully than I can do by writing or by telegraph.   A. LINCOLN

Feb. 11, 1864

[1] AES, owned by Frederick M. Dearborn, New York City. Lincoln's endorsement is written on the back of a note reading as follows: "I want to state why I think it would not be wise to send Gen Sickles to Arkansas—John B. Steele." See communications to Sickles, February 10, *supra*, and February 15, *infra*. John B. Steele was the brother of General Frederick Steele.

To John P. Usher[1]

Hon. Sec. of Interior—Please see and hear my friend, S. M. Cullom.   A. LINCOLN

Feb 11, 1864

[1] Copy, ISLA.

To Stephen Cabot[1]

Military Commander   Executive Mansion
Boston, Mass.   Washington Feb. 12. 1864

If there is anywhere in your command, a man by the name of James Taylor under sentence of death for desertion, suspend execution till further order   A. LINCOLN

[1] ALS, RPB. No reply from Major Stephen Cabot, commanding at Fort Warren, Boston, Massachusetts, has been discovered. See Lincoln's telegram to Andrews, February 8, *supra*, and to Dix, *infra*.

To Salmon P. Chase[1]

Hon. Secretary of the Treasury   Executive Mansion,
My dear Sir: Washington, [February 12], 1864.

I have felt considerable anxiety concerning the Custom House at New-York. Mr. Barney has suffered no abatement of my confidence in his honor and integrity; and yet I am convinced that he has ceased to be master of his position. A man by the name of Bailey,[2] whom I am unconscious of ever having seen, or even having heard of, except in this connection, expects to be, and even now assumes to be, Collector *de facto*, while Mr. Barney remains nominally so. This Mr. Bailey as I understand having been summoned as a witness to testify before a committee of the House of Representatives which purposed investigating the affairs of the New-York Custom-House, took occasion to call on the Chairman in advance, and to endeavor to smother the investigation, saying among other things, that whatever might be developed, the President would take no action, and the committee would thereby be placed unpleasantly. The public interest can not fail to suffer in the hands of this irresponsible and unscrupulous man.[3] I propose sending Mr. Barney Minister to Portugal, as evidence of my continued confidence in him; and I further propose appointing ———[4] Collector of the Customs at New-York. I wrote the draft of this letter two weeks ago, but delayed sending it for a reason which I will state when I see you. Yours truly   A. LINCOLN

1 ADfS, DLC-RTL. Although the bracketed portion of the date does not appear on the draft, the envelope in which the draft was filed bears Lincoln's endorsement "To Sec. of Treasury. Feb. 12, 1863." The year date in the endorsement is Lincoln's obvious error. Chase replied on February 13, 1864: "I was surprised and pained by your letter this morning. Misrepresentations, I am sure, must have been made to you about the New York Custom House. I regret that I was not earlier consulted in a matter which so deeply concerns this Department & still trust, that before you take any definitive action, you will confer with me fully on the subject. I shall be ready at any hour which may suit your convenience." (DLC-RTL). See further letters to Chase, February 13, 15, 20, and 25, *infra*.

2 J. F. Bailey, special agent of the Treasury at New York.

3 The following sentence was deleted by Lincoln at this point: "This can go no further."   4 "Hon. Preston King" was deleted by Lincoln.

To Salmon P. Chase[1]

         Executive Mansion,
To the Secretary of War [*sic*].   Washington, Feby 12, 1864.

Dear Sir: Herewith is the resignation of Mr. McElroth [*sic*], as General Appraiser at New York. Send me a nomination for James

Freeland as his successor unless you know some reason to the contrary. Yours truly,   A. Lincoln

P.S. The recommendations of **Mr.** Freeland which seem good
and ample are herewith.   A. L.

¹ Tracy, p. 238. The source is obviously in error in giving this letter as "To
the Secretary of War." Thomas McElrath was succeeded by John T. Hogeboom, not by James Freeland, but no reply from Chase (or Stanton) has been
discovered.

To John A. Dix¹

Major Gen. Dix   Executive Mansion,
New-York   Washington, Feb. 12, 1864.

If there is anywhere in your command, a man by the name of
James Taylor under sentence of death for desertion, suspend execution till further order.   A. Lincoln

¹ ALS, RPB. No reply has been discovered. See the telegrams to Andrews
and Sedgwick, February 8, *supra.* In this telegram and the one to Cabot, *supra,*
the specification "for desertion" further complicates the identification of Taylor. No such case has been discovered.

To Salmon P. Chase¹

                        Executive Mansion, Washington,
Hon. Secretary of Treasury: February 13, 1864.

My dear Sir: On coming up from the reception, I found your
note of to-day. I am unwell, even now, and shall be worse this
afternoon. If you please, we will have an interview Monday.
Yours truly,   A. Lincoln

¹ Robert B. Warden, *Account of the Private Life and Public Services of Salmon Portland Chase* (1874), p. 572. See Lincoln to Chase, February 12, *supra,*
and February 15, *infra.*

Endorsement to John Hogan¹

                                        February 13, 1864
Indorsed on the modifying Methodist order & sent to Rev John
Hogan.

"As you see within, the Secretary of War modifies his order so
as to exempt Missouri from it. Kentucky was never within it; nor,
as I learn from the Secretary, was it ever intended for any more

[182]

than a means of rallying the Methodist people in favor of the Union, in localities where the rebellion had disorganized and scattered them. Even in that view, I fear it is liable to some abuses, but it is not quite easy to withdraw it entirely, and at once.

["]Feb. 13. 1864.   A. Lincoln["]

¹ ADS, DLC-RTL. The original endorsement written on an order of February 13 has not been discovered, and there is some question as to the precise document which Lincoln endorsed and gave to Hogan. On February 28 General Rosecrans notified Stanton as follows:

"On the 12th of the present month the Rev. Bishop Ames presented at these headquarters a circular letter from War Department, dated November 30, 1863, copy of which is hereto annexed, marked A, directing that— 'All houses of worship belonging to the Methodist Episcopal Church South, in which a loyal minister appointed by a loyal bishop of said church does not now officiate, are placed at the disposal of the Right Rev. Bishop Ames—' and asked that an order be issued in conformity thereto. I immediately issued a circular to commanding officers of troops of the department . . . directing that 'they furnish Bishop Ames every facility and assistance compatible with the interests of the service' under the order mentioned. Saturday, Mr. John Hogan called with a letter dated February 13, 1864 (copy inclosed, marked C), bearing the official signature of James A. Hardie . . . directed to Major-General Rosecrans . . . with an indorsement in the handwriting and bearing the signature of the President . . . intended, as he (Hogan) claimed, to abrogate entirely in this State the circular order printed by Bishop Ames. As no official copy of the letter to me of the 13th . . . has been received . . . and as there is a doubt in my mind as to the policy the War Department intends to adopt as regards church property in this State . . . I would respectfully request that more definite instructions be furnished. . . ." (OR, I, XXXIV, II, 452-53).

A footnote in the source states that neither the order of November 30, 1863, nor the letter from Hardie of February 13, 1864, could be found at the time the *Official Records* were compiled. As given by McPherson (see note to Lincoln's letter to Stanton, February 11, *supra*), both the order of November 30 and the modifying order of February 13, were issued over the signature of Edward D. Townsend rather than that of James A. Hardie. It seems probable, however, from the contents of Lincoln's endorsement, that the order was substantially the same.

To Horace Maynard¹

Hon. Horace Maynard   Executive Mansion
Nashville, Tenn.   Washington, Feb. 13. 1864.

Your letter of 2nd. received. Of course Gov. Johnson will proceed with re-organization as the exigencies of the case appear to him to require. I do not apprehend he will think it necessary to deviate from my views to any ruinous extent. On one hasty reading, I see no such deviation in his programme which you send

A. Lincoln

¹ ALS, RPB. On February 2, Tennessee's Attorney General Maynard wrote Lincoln:

"In the first interview I had the honor to hold with your Excellency, during my recent visit to Washington, I informed you that during the brief interval between the arrival here of your Proclamation of Decr. 8, & my departure, I had heard two criticisms . . .

"1. Its excessive liberality to rebels.

"2. Its placing in the same category repentant rebels & men always loyal. "Since my return I found the same criticisms . . . especially the latter. . . . The expressions of repugnance are too strong to be disregarded.

"Gov. Johnson has attempted, in solution of the difficulty, in a manner quite satisfactory to the Union men, but greatly to the disgust of secesh & semi-secesh. I will enclose you a copy of his Proclamation for our March election. In all probability you will be solicited to interfere. This I hope you *will not do*." (DLC-RTL).

Pass for Mrs. Samuel P. Hamilton[1]

Allow this lady to pass to Nashville Tenn. to report to Gov. Johnson, and be heard by him & be disposed of as he shall decide.

[Feby] 14, 1864   A. LINCOLN

[1] AES-F, Louisville, Kentucky, *Times*, February 12, 1945. The facsimile shows the month blotted, but seems to read "Feby." According to the account given in the source, Mrs. Samuel P. Hamilton had been dispossessed of her home for refusing to give up a Confederate flag which she had flown from her roof during the occupation of Knoxville by Federal forces in September, 1863.

To Salmon P. Chase[1]

Hon. Secretary of Treasury: February 15, 1864

My Dear Sir: I have just called to see you on the matter mentioned Saturday, and am pained to learn you are suffering too much to be out. I hope you will soon be relieved; meanwhile, have no uneasiness as to the thing to which I am alluding, as I shall do nothing in it until I shall [have] fully conferred with you. Yours truly,   A. LINCOLN.

[1] Robert B. Warden, *Account of the Private Life and Public Services of Salmon Portland Chase* (1874), p. 573. See Lincoln to Chase, February 12 and 13, *supra*. Chase replied on February 15:

"I thank you for your very kind note & the assurance it contains.

"I was coming to see you this morning; for really I do not suffer at all. My right eye won't bear much light; but I can get on pretty well with the left. So I could come with no other inconvenience than having one eye under bandage. With the permission of your note, however, I will wait till tomorrow." (DLC-RTL).

On February 18, Chase wrote again: "My eye is so much better that I was able to do a little work at the Department yesterday, and am here again this afternoon. Whenever you summon me I shall attend you for conference about New York matters or any other." (*Ibid*).

See further Lincoln to Chase, February 20 and 25, *infra*.

To Daniel E. Sickles[1]

Executive Mansion, Washington,

Major General Sickles: February 15. 1864.

I wish you to make a tour for me (principally for observation and information) by way of Cairo and New-Orleans, and returning by the Gulf and Ocean. All Military and Naval officers are to facilitate you with suitable transportation, and by conferring with you, and imparting, so far as they can, the information herein indicated, but you are not to command any of them. You will call at Memphis, Helena, Vicksburg, New-Orleans, Pensacola, Key-West, Charleston-Harbor, and such intermediate points as you may think important. Please ascertain at each place what is being done, if anything, for reconstruction—how the Amnesty proclamation works, if at all—what practical hitches, if any, there are about it—whether deserters come in from the enemy, what number has come in at each point since the Amnesty, and whether the ratio of their arrival is any greater *since* than before the Amnesty —what deserters report generally, and particularly, whether, and to what extent, the Amnesty is known within the rebel lines. Also learn what you can as to the colored people—how they get along as soldiers, as laborers in our service, on leased plantations, and as hired laborers with their old masters, if there be such cases. Also learn what you can about the colored people within the rebel lines. Also get any other information you may consider interesting, and, from time to time, send me what you may deem important to be known here at once, and be ready to make a general report on your return. Yours truly   A. LINCOLN

[1] ALS-P, ISLA; ADfS, DLC-RTL. See Lincoln to Steele, February 11, *supra,* and February 25, *infra.*

To John M. Thayer[1]

Gen. Thayer   Washington, D.C.,

Fort Smith, Arkansas   Feb. 15. 1864

Yours received. Whatever of conflict there is between the convention and me is accidental, not designed, I having acted in ignorance that the convention would act. I yield to the convention, and have so notified Gen. Steele, who is master, and is to cut any knots which can not be untied. Correspond with him.

A. LINCOLN

[1] ALS, RPB. General Thayer, in command at Fort Smith, Arkansas, telegraphed on February 14: "The state convention which formed a free constitu-

tion for Arkansas appointed a General Election on the fourteenth of March next. The people of Western Arkansas respectfully request you to modify your order, so as to have the election on the fourteenth, for the reason that notice has been circulated, through Arkansas that, it will be held on that day. They desire to know, at the earliest moment if you make the change." (DLC-RTL). See Lincoln to Murphy, February 8, *supra*, and to Steele, February 17, *infra*.

To Nathaniel P. Banks[1]

Executive Mansion, Washington,

Major General Banks.   February 16, 1864.

Mrs. J. Q. A. Fellows has come all the way here to make complaint about a certain dwelling house from which she says she has been ejected. Of course I can have no accurate knowledge of the merits of the case. I can do no more than ask you, which I cheerfully do, that you will have the case carefully investigated, and do justice in it. Yours truly   A. LINCOLN

[1] ALS, IHi. General Banks replied on March 26, 1864:

"Your letter relating to the case of Mrs. J. Q. A. Fellows, who was dispossessed of her House by order of the Treasury Agent in New Orleans, was given to me by Mrs Fellows, before I left New Orleans. The case is as follows: —All the real estate in New Orleans belonging to active Rebels was seized by the military authorities as far as it could be identified. It was all made to pay rent to the government, when not in use by the government itself: and carefully protected, until the courts under the law of confiscation should decide the rights of the claimants for repossession. Pending this decision, by an order from the war department, I turned over all this property in the Department, Plantations and other estates to Honble. B. F. Flanders, Treasury agent, who assumed possession, collected the rents, controlled the occupancy, and when it seemed to him proper, restored these estates . . . to the Rebels who claimed them:—the cases still pending in the District court of the United States. The only control over any of this property that I have relates to that which is required for miliary uses. The rest is under the exclusive control of the Treasury Agent, and I am required to assist with military force, the execution of any order he gives concerning the disposition of this property by the same general order No: 88 of the War Department.

"Mr: Fellows is an honorable and perfectly loyal man, as thoroughly so as Mr: Flanders or any man in New Orleans, but he is weak enough to believe that the constitution of Louisiana can be restored as it was. . . . He was active in the Riddell election which took place when I was in Texas. . . . There can be . . . no other cause for the ejectment of his family, than that this course was politically unacceptable to Mr: Flanders, and his friends. He assigned this house to an officer of the army who was to pay rent as Mr Fellows had done, and made a demand upon me in writing for the support I was required to give him by war Dept: orders No: 88, which with the greatest reluctance I gave him—hence the visit of Mrs Fellows to Washington. She had a good case, but it concerns the Treasury officers, not the war Department. When she presented me your letter directing an investigation of the case, I immediately requested Brigadier General [James] Bowen to present the case in person to Mr Flanders, and requested his attention to your request. He replied that when Colonel Dudley, the occupant surrendered the house, he would assign it to Mrs Fellows, and not till then. Colonel Dudley is now commanding a Brigade of Cavalry in front of the enemy here It is very hard for me to order the family of a soldier, who is in the field, out of a house which is assigned to him by the officers of the Treasury who have by orders of the War & Treasury Departments exclusive control over it.

"The Secretary of the Treasury should be required to give such orders to his agent in New Orleans as may be required in this case. . . . I enclose copies of all the papers in this case, and have written to Mrs Fellows, and to Senator Foote, a full statement of the facts involved. . . ." (DLC-RTL).

Endorsement Concerning W. Marshall Swayne[1]

I indorse what is said above of Mr. Swayne.   A. LINCOLN

Feb. 16. 1864

[1] AES, owned by Mrs. Isaac G. Roberts, West Chester, Pennsylvania. Lincoln's endorsement is written on a letter of Salmon P. Chase, January 17, 1864: "Mr. W. Marshall Swayne, a clerk in the Internal Revenue Bureau, wishes to contribute to the Fair to be held in this city for the benefit of the Christian Commission a Series of bas reliefs heads of the President and the Heads of Departments. Mr. Swayne has modeled a head of myself and I think of Governor Seward, which are said to be good. His object is certainly a good one, and if you will give him a sitting or two to enable him to accomplish it, you will help it and at the same time gratify a very worthy gentlemen [*sic*]. He devotes only his spare hours to the work, not allowing it to interfere at all with his official duties." The bust sculptured by Swayne was finally sent to the Great Central Fair at Philadelphia (New York *Tribune*, June 15, 1864).

Endorsement Concerning William Yocum[1]

William Yocum, within named, is hereby pardoned.

February 16, 1864.   A. LINCOLN.

[1] Thirty-eighth Congress, First Session, *Senate Executive Document No. 51*, p. 20. Lincoln's endorsement is given as appearing on a petition signed by Lucian Anderson, Brutus J. Clay, W. H. Randall, S. L. Casey, and G. Clay Smith. See Lincoln to Holt, February 3, *supra*, and to the Senate, June 13, *infra*.

To the House of Representatives[1]

February 16, 1864

To the House of Representatives, of the United States.

In answer to the resolution of the House of Representatives of the 8th instant requesting information touching the arrest of the United States Consul General to the British North American Provinces, and certain official communications respecting Canadian commerce, I transmit a report from the Secretary of State, and the documents by which it was accompanied.

[Washington, February 16, 1864.]   [ABRAHAM LINCOLN.]

[1] DS, DNA RG 233, House Executive Document No. 39. The date and signature have been cut off the document. The enclosures are printed in Thirty-eighth Congress, First Session, *House Executive Document No. 39*. William

G. L. Redpath of New York brought suit against Joshua R. Giddings, consul general at Montreal, charging kidnapping, imprisonment, and forcible return to the United States from Canada. Giddings was arrested upon returning to Ohio on leave of absence.

To the Senate and House of Representatives[1]

February 16, 1864

To the Senate and House of Representatives:

I transmit to Congress a Report from the Secretary of State, with the accompanying papers, relative to the claim on this Government of the owners of the French ship "La Manche"; and recommend an appropriation for the satisfaction of the claim, pursuant to the award of the arbitrators.   ABRAHAM LINCOLN

Washington, 16th. February, 1864.

[1] DS, DNA RG 46, Senate 38A F3; DS, DNA RG 233, Original Executive Document. An act approved March 22, 1864, appropriated "a sufficient amount to purchase a bill of exchange . . . for the sum of one hundred and forty thousand seven hundred and thirty-five and fifteen one-hundredths francs, with interest . . ." as indemnity to the owners of the *La Manche,* seized on August 23, 1862, and released by the Prize Court.

To William H. Seward[1]

Hon. Sec. of State   Executive Mansion,
Sir: Washington. Feb. 16. 1864.

Hon. W. H. Wallace, formerly of Washington Territory, and now of Idaho, says that Elwood Evans, Secretary of Washington T. was appointed at his—Mr. W's. recommendation, and that he has gone wholly over to the enemy, using the patronage to establish and uphold a paper to oppose & embarrass the Administration.[2]

[1] AL and AES, NAuE. No reply has been discovered. Evans remained in office as secretary of Washington Territory.

[2] The letter is unsigned, but a small slip bearing "File—A.L. Sep. 27. 1864," is pasted on the bottom.

To Edwin M. Stanton[1]

February 16, 1864

Will the Sec. of War please oblige Judge Catron in the matter.

A. LINCOLN

[1] Parke-Bernet Catalog 611, December 4-5, 1944, No. 269. According to the catalog description, Lincoln's endorsement is written on a letter from John Catron about an order from the War Department for release of a prisoner which had been wrongly directed. No further reference has been discovered.

To Edwin M. Stanton[1]

Hon. Sec. of War, please see and hear Mr. Marshall, of St.
Louis.   A. LINCOLN
Feb. 16, 1864.

[1] Copy, ISLA. Representative William R. Morrison wrote on February 11,
1864: "I write this to introduce to you the bearer George Marshall Esqr of St.
Louis in the absence of Mr. Blair his representative & friend. Mr. Marshall is
a *friend* of yours & desires to see you on business. See him if possible." (DLC-
RTL).

To Edward Bates[1]

I will thank the Attorney General to enquire into this case and
report upon it.   A. LINCOLN
Feb 17. 1864

Let the pardon be made out.   A. LINCOLN.
March. 2, 1864.

[1] AES, CSmH. Lincoln's endorsements are written on a letter from James
S. Rollins and others, February 8, 1864, asking pardon of Porter Jackman of
Howard County, Missouri, imprisoned and fined by a military commission for
disloyalty. Bates endorsed on March 2, 1864, "I have no doubt of your *power*
to exonerate the man *by a pardon*. And, in view of the within Statement, I
advise it to be done.

"If you determine to grant the pardon, please send your order, endorsed on
this paper."

To William M. Fishback[1]

William Fishback   Washington, D.C.,
Little Rock, Arkansas   Feb. 17 1864
    When I fixed a plan for an election in Arkansas I did it in ig-
norance that your convention was doing the same work. Since I
learned the latter fact, I have been constantly trying to yield my
plan to them. I have sent two letters to Gen. Steele, and three or
four despatches to you and others, saying that he—Gen. Steele—
must be master, but that it will probably be best for him to merely
help the convention on it's own plan. Some single mind must be
master, else there will be no agreement in anything, & Gen. Steele,
commanding the Military, and being on the ground, is the best
man to be that master. Even now, citizens are telegraphing me to
postpone the election to a later day than either that fixed by the
convention or by me. This discord must be silenced.
                                                         A. LINCOLN

¹ ALS, RPB. See Lincoln to Murphy, February 8, *supra*, and to Steele, *infra*. Fishback was elected U.S. Senator when the Arkansas legislature convened on April 25 under the new constitution.

To Edwin M. Stanton[1]

Please see and hear Mr. Gibbs, on the subject of the within letter of Gov. Andrew.   A. LINCOLN

    Feb. 17, 1864

    Hon. Sec. of War

¹ AES, DLC-RTL. Lincoln's endorsement is written on the following letter from Governor John A. Andrew, February 12, 1864:

"I respectfully introduce . . . Mr. O[liver]. C. Gibbs, Postmaster of Wareham, Mass. who on many occasions during the past three years has been detailed to visit various camps and Hospitals of the army, as a Messenger of charity and relief to Massachusetts soldiers. I have learned through Mr Gibbs and otherwise, that persons of color, both freemen and refugees from slavery, desiring to pass northward from Washington, seeking to better their fortunes and support their families by reaching Massachusetts, are forcibly and against their will detained. I am at a loss to understand by what color of pretended authority people not charged with crime, and not being engaged in the military service, and being in the peace of the law, are thus subjected to hardship and wrong. Aside from the oppressiveness of such treatment against which I respectfully remonstrate, I appeal in behalf of the Commonwealth of Massachusetts, whose right to receive immigrants from all parts of the Union choosing to come here is thus unlawfully interfered with. Suppose the passage of Germans and Irishmen seeking to buy land and make their homes in the great land states of the West was denied, and they were compelled to remain in New England or New York, how long would such an embargo on population be endured by Illinois, and her neighboring States. . . . The industry of Massachusetts imperatively demands every laborer now on her soil or willing to come. The people of Massachusetts, in addition to furnishing her quota of soldiers, manufacture one third of all the woollen goods in the country, without which the army cannot live a day. And notwithstanding the shoe contracts in which she directly participates, many of the shoes contracted for by . . . other States are farmed out at a profit to her shoemakers . . . hold at least one twelfth of the National Loan. How long then can we continue to furnish soldiers, help clothe the army, fabricate ships, machinery and munitions of war, subscribe to the National Loans, and furnish internal revenue if persons desiring to make their way hither are forbidden to come? . . ." (DLC-RTL).

See Lincoln's reply to Andrew, February 18, *infra*.

To Frederick Steele[1]

Major General Steele   Executive Mansion,

Little-Rock, Ark.   Washington, Feb. 17, 1864.

The day fixed by the Convention for the election is probably the best, but you, on the ground, and in consultation with gentlemen there, are to decide. I should have fixed no day for an election

—presented no plan for reconstruction—had I known the convention was doing the same things. It is probably best that you merely assist the convention on their own plan, as to election day & all other matters. I have already written and telegraphed this half a dozen times.   A. LINCOLN

1 ALS, RPB. General Steele telegraphed on February 16: "On what day have you ordered the election in this State & do your instructions to me correspond with the action of the Convention?" (DLC-RTL). See Lincoln to Murphy, February 8, *supra*.

To John A. Andrew[1]

His Excellency. John A. Andrew   Executive Mansion,
Governor of Massachusetts   Washington, February 18. 1864.

Yours of the 12th. was received yesterday. If I were to judge from the letter, without any external knowledge, I should suppose that all the colored people South of Washington were struggling to get to Massachusetts; that Massachusetts was anxious to receive and retain the whole of them as permanent citizens; and that the United States Government here was interposing and preventing this. But I suppose these are neither really the facts, nor meant to be asserted as true by you. Coming down to what I suppose to be the real facts, you are engaged in trying to raise colored troops for the U.S. and wish to take recruits from Virginia, through Washington, to Massachusetts for that object; and the loyal Governor of Virginia, also trying to raise troops for us, objects to your taking his material away; while we, having to care for all, and being responsible alike to all, have to do as much for him, as we would have to do for you, if he was, by our authority, taking men from Massachusetts to fill up Virginia regiments. No more than this has been intended by me; nor, as I think, by the Secretary of War. There may have been some abuses of this, as a rule, which, if known, should be prevented in future.

If, however, it be really true that Massachusetts wishes to afford a permanent home within her borders, for all, or even a large number of colored persons who will come to her, I shall be only too glad to know it. It would give relief in a very difficult point; and I would not for a moment hinder from going, any person who is free by the terms of the proclamation or any of the acts of Congress.

1 ADf, DLC-RTL. Andrew's letter of February 12 is given in the note to Lincoln's endorsement to Stanton, February 17, *supra*. See also Lincoln to Stanton, February 25, *infra*.

Memorandum Concerning John A. Andrew[1]

[c. February 18, 1864 ?]

I have not yet my letter ready for Gov. Andrew.   A. L.

[1] ADS, DLC-Nicolay Papers. The date has been supplied on the supposition that this memorandum refers to the unfinished draft of Lincoln's letter to Andrew, *supra.*

Proclamation Concerning Blockade[1]

February 18, 1864

By the President of the United States of America:

A Proclamation.

Whereas, by my Proclamation of the nineteenth of April, one thousand eight hundred and sixty-one, the ports of the States of South Carolina, Georgia, Alabama, Florida, Mississippi, Louisiana and Texas, were, for reasons therein set forth, placed under blockade; and whereas, the port of Brownsville in the district of Brazos Santiago in the State of Texas, has since been blockaded, but as the blockade of said port may now be safely relaxed with advantage to the interests of commerce:

Now, therefore, be it known that I, Abraham Lincoln, President of the United States, pursuant to the authority in me vested by the fifth section of the act of Congress approved on the 13th. of July 1861, entitled, "an act further to provide for the collection of duties on imports, and for other purposes," do hereby declare that the blockade of the said port of Brownsville shall so far cease and determine from and after this date, that commercial intercourse with said port, except as to persons, things and information hereinafter specified, may, from this date, be carried on, subject to the laws of the United States, to the regulations prescribed by the Secretary of the Treasury, and until the rebellion shall have been suppressed, to such orders as may be promulgated by the General Commanding the Department, or by an officer duly authorized by him and commanding at said port. This Proclamation does not authorize or allow the shipment or conveyance of persons in or intending to enter the service of the insurgents, or of things or information intended for their use, or for their aid or comfort, nor except upon the permission of the Secretary of War or of some officer duly authorized by him, of the following prohibited articles, namely—cannon, mortars, firearms, pistols, bombs, grenades, powder, saltpetre, sulphur, balls, bullets, pikes, swords, boarding-caps, (always excepting the quantity of the said articles which may be necessary for the defence of the ship and those who compose the crew) saddles, bridles, cartridge-bag material, percussion and other caps, clothing adapted for uniforms, sail cloth of all kinds, hemp and cordage, intoxicating drinks, other than beer and light native wines.

To vessels clearing from foreign ports, and destined to the port of Brownsville, opened by this Proclamation, licenses will be granted by Consuls of the United States upon satisfactory evidence that the vessels so licensed will convey no persons, property or information excepted or prohibited above, either to or from the said port; which licenses shall be exhibited to the Collector of said port immediately on arrival, and if required, to any officer in charge of the blockade; and on leaving said port, every vessel will be required to have a clearance from the Collector of the Customs, according to law, showing no violation of the conditions of the license. Any violations of said conditions will involve the forfeiture and condemnation of the vessel and cargo, and the exclusion of all parties concerned from any further privilege of entering the United States during the war for any purpose whatever.

In all respects, except as herein specified, the existing blockade remains in full force and effect as hitherto established and maintained, nor is it relaxed by this Proclamation except in regard to the port to which relaxation is or has been expressely applied.

In witness whereof, I have hereunto set my hand, and caused the seal of the United States to be affixed.

Done at the city of Washington, this eighteenth day of February, in the year of our Lord one thousand eight hundred [L.S.] and sixty-four, and of the Independence of the United States the eighty-eighth. ABRAHAM LINCOLN

By the President:
WILLIAM H. SEWARD, Secretary of State.

1 DS, DNA FS RG 11, Proclamations.

To A. Robinson[1]

A. Robinson: Executive Mansion
Leroy, N.Y.   Washington, Feb. 18. 1864

The law only obliges us to keep accounts with States, or, at most, Congressional Districts; and it would overwhelm us to attempt in counties, cities and towns. Nevertheless we do what we can to oblige in particular cases. In this view I send your despatch to the Provost-Marshall-General, asking him to do the best he can for you. A. LINCOLN

[1] ALS, RPB. Robinson's message has not been discovered. It probably had to do with draft quotas.

To George S. Blake[1]

Com. Geo. S. Blake.   Executive Mansion.
Comdt. Naval Academy   19 Feb. 1864.
Newport, R.I.

I desire the case of Midshipman C. Lyon re-examined and if not clearly inconsistent I shall be much obliged to have the recommendation changed. A. LINCOLN.

[1] LS, RPB. Acting Midshipman Caleb Lyon (Jr.?) is listed as having resigned at Annapolis, February 10, 1862. No further reference has been found.

To Roscoe Conkling[1]

Hon. R. Conkling   Executive Mansion,
My dear Sir   Washington, February 19, 1864.

I have just received the letter of yourself and others in relation to Caleb Lyon. I understood he was once a member of Congress; his nomination to some respectable office was repeatedly urged upon me certainly by two, if not three Senators of the highest standing; and your letter contains the first imputation I ever heard against his moral character. Yours very truly A. LINCOLN

[1] ALS-P, ISLA. Ex-congressman Roscoe Conkling's letter has not been discovered. See Lincoln's letter to Lyon, February 1, and to Seward, February 2, *supra*.

To Edwin M. Stanton[1]

February 19, 1864

The writer of this, Hon. Mr. Nelson of Tennessee, is a man of mark, and one whom I would like to have obliged. I am in favor of discharging his son, with pledge that he shall not be conscripted, upon his taking the oath of December 8. A. LINCOLN.

February 19, 1864.

[1] Leslie J. Perry, "Appeals to Lincoln's Clemency," *The Century Magazine*, LI (December, 1895), 253. According to Perry, Lincoln's endorsement was written on the back of a letter from Thomas A. R. Nelson, but the name of Nelson's confederate son is not given.

[194]

To Edward Bates[1]

Attorney General please make out a pardon in this case.

Feb. 20. 1864.   A. LINCOLN

[1] AES, DNA RG 204, U.S. Pardon Attorney, A 517. Lincoln's endorsement is written on a letter from George F. Brown, D.D., "Moral Instructor to the N.J. State Prison," Trenton, New Jersey, December 23, 1863, recommending pardon of James Ackerman serving sentence for making counterfeit coin.

To Salmon P. Chase[1]

Executive Mansion, Washington,
Hon. Secretary of Treasury: February 20, 1864.

My Dear Sir: Herewith I return the affidavit you handed me. In glancing it over I do not perceive anything necessarily inconsistent with the practice of detectives, and others, engaged in the business of "rascal-catching;" but a closer consideration might show it. It seems to me that *August,* the month within which the affiant fixes his first interview with Hanscomb, was really before Hanscomb left Boston and came to New York. Yours truly,

A. LINCOLN.

[1] Robert B. Warden, *Account of the Private Life and Public Services of Salmon Portland Chase* (1864), p. 573. Chase replied on February 22:

"The Solicitor informs me that Hanscomb went to New York before August: but, also, shows me a letter from Mr. Bailey in which he says he does not put much confidence in its statements.

"You were kind enough to say you would see Mr. Bailey: but he will not be here till the latter part of this week or the first of next." (DLC-RTL).

Albert Hanscom, deputy collector in the Boston Custom House, was transferred to the same post in the New York Custom House in 1863. The affidavit referred to has not been discovered. See Lincoln to Chase, February 25, *infra.*

To Edwin M. Stanton[1]

I specially request that you will see Judge Cooper and allow him to take his brother home with him.   A. LINCOLN

Feb. 20. 1864

Hon. Sec. of War.
Feb. 20. 1864   A. LINCOLN

[1] AES, DLC-Hitchcock Papers. Lincoln's endorsement is written on a letter from Edward Cooper and Judge Henry Cooper of Shelbyville, Tennessee, February 19, 1864, asking release of their brother F. F. Cooper, a prisoner of war at Camp Morton, Indiana, ill with tuberculosis. Stanton endorsed directing General Ethan A. Hitchcock to "issue the order for discharge of the within named prisoner on his taking the oath."

To Warren Jordan[1]

Warren Jordan   Washington, D.C.,
Nashville, Tenn.   February 21 [20?] 1864
   In county elections you had better stand by Gov. Johnson's plan. Otherwise you will have conflict and confusion. I have seen his plan.   A. LINCOLN

  [1] ALS, RPB. The date numeral "21" of this manuscript is not in Lincoln's handwriting. As printed by Nicolay and Hay (X,17) the date of the telegram is "February 20." Since February 21 was Sunday, Nicolay and Hay may have the correct date, but no corroboration has been discovered. Concerning Warren Jordan, see further Lincoln's communication to East, February 27, *infra*.

To George S. Boutwell[1]

Thanks for the privilege of reading.
Feb. 22. 1864.   A. L.

  [1] AES, owned by L. E. Dicke, Evanston, Illinois. Lincoln's endorsement is on an envelope addressed to George S. Boutwell from Nathaniel P. Banks, postmarked at New York, February 20, contents unknown.

To John Brough[1]

His Excellency   Executive Mansion,
Governor Brough   Washington,
Columbus, Ohio   Feb. 22. 1864.
   As you request, Clinton Fuller, charged as a deserter, is pardoned.   A. LINCOLN

  [1] ALS, RPB. No communication from Governor Brough in this connection has been discovered, and Clinton Fuller has not been identified.

To William P. Dole[1]

Commissioner of Indian Affairs, please examine and report upon this case.   A. LINCOLN
Feb. 22. 1864

  [1] AES, ORB. Lincoln's endorsement is written on a letter from John Ross, Principal Chief of the Cherokee Nation, February 18, 1864, presenting a petition of the Cherokees "sent . . . by the hands of the Hon. Lewis Ross, the Treasurer of the Nation" asking government aid in alleviating "the extreme destitution to which the people of the Cherokee Nation have been reduced by the disasters of the present war. . . ." The appropriation approved June 25, 1864, for expenses of the Indian Department, authorized the Secretary of Interior to extend relief to refugee Indians, including Cherokees, "reduced to want on account of their friendship to the United States."

To Joseph Holt[1]

This is a peculiar case, & I will thank the Judge Advocate General to have made for me a good abstract of the evidence

Feb. 22. 1864   A. LINCOLN

1 AES, DNA WR RG 153, Judge Advocate General, MM 1277. Lincoln's endorsement is written on the papers in the case of Captain Charles C. Moore, tried by a military commission on Lincoln's order to Robert C. Schenck, November 20, 1863, *supra.* Captain Moore was acquitted and died a prisoner of the enemy on August 31, 1864.

To Benjamin F. Loan[1]

Hon. B. Loan   War Department
Dear Sir: Washington, Feb. 22, 1864

At your instance I directed a part of the advertising for this Department to be done in the St. Joseph Tribune. I have just been informed that the Tribune openly avows it's determination that in no event will it support the re-election of the President. As you probably know, please inform me whether this is true. The President's wish is that no objection shall be made to any paper respectfully expressing it's preference for the *nomination* of any candidate; but that the patronage of the government shall be given to none which engages in cultivating a sentiment to oppose the *election* of any when he shall have been fairly nominated by the regular Union National Convention.

1 ADf, DLC-Stanton Papers. Lincoln presumably drafted this letter for Stanton to sign. A complimentary close "Yrs truly" has been added to the document in Stanton's handwriting. It has not been established that Stanton sent the message. No reply from Representative Loan or from D. K. Abeel, proprietor of the St. Joseph, Missouri, *Tribune,* has been discovered.

Remarks at Opening of Patent Office Fair[1]

February 22, 1864

Loud calls being made then for the President, Mr. Lincoln stepped forward, and said that he appeared before the audience to apologize for not speaking rather than to speak.

He thought that the Committee had practiced a little fraud on him, for they did not intimate when they came to see him in the morning, that they expected him to speak, therefore he had come before the audience totally unprepared to say anything; that was taking one at great disadvantage after the eloquent speech of Mr. Chittenden and the poem of Mr. French.

There was great objection to his saying anything, for necessarily, in consequence of his position, everything went into print. [Laughter and applause.] If he made any mistake it might do both himself and the nation harm. [Applause.] It was very difficult to say sensible things. [Laughter.] He therefore hoped that the audience would excuse him after expressing his desire that the charitable enterprise in which we were engaged might be abundantly successful. [Applause.]

[1] New York *Tribune*, February 24, 1864. Lincoln's remarks followed a speech by Lucius E. Chittenden and a patriotic poem read by Benjamin B. French.

To William S. Rosecrans[1]

Major General Rosecrans   Washington, D.C.,
St. Louis, Mo   Feb. 22 1864

Col. Sanderson will be ordered to you to-day—a mere omission that it was not done before. The other questions in your despatch I am not yet prepared to answer   A. LINCOLN

[1] ALS, RPB. General Rosecrans telegraphed on February 12, asking that Colonel John P. Sanderson of the Thirteenth Infantry "now on recruiting service at Newport, Ky. be ordered to report to me" for duty as provost marshal (DLC-RTL). On February 20, Rosecrans telegraphed again: "Will the law provide that the pay of colored troops shall be the same as for other? Will the families of these men be made free? It is important and just that they should be so. Will you give me Colonel Sanderson? I beg an early reply." (OR, I, XXXIV, II, 381). AGO *Special Orders No. 88*, February 23, 1864, directed Colonel Sanderson to report to General Rosecrans without delay.

To the Senate and House of Representatives[1]

February 22, 1864

To the Senate and House of Representatives:

I transmit to Congress the copy of a correspondence which has recently taken place between Her Britannic Majesty's Minister accredited to this Government and the Secretary of State, in order that the expediency of sanctioning the acceptance, by the Master of the American schooner "Highlander," of a present of a watch which the Lords of the Committee of Her Majesty's Privy Council for Trade propose to present to him in recognition of services rendered by him to the crew of the British vessel "Pearl," may be taken into consideration.   ABRAHAM LINCOLN

Washington, 22d. Feby. 1864.

[1] DS, DNA RG 46, Senate 38A F2; DS, DNA RG 233, House Executive Document No. 43. The correspondence transmitted concerned the request (December 31, 1863) of the British Privy Council for Trade for permission to present a gold watch to the master of the *Highlander* (unnamed), in recognition of his rescue of the crew of the British vessel *Pearl*. Secretary Seward replied

on February 20, 1864, that congressional assent was necessary (Thirty-eighth Congress, First Session, *Executive Document No. 43*). On March 1, Senator Sumner reported a joint resolution giving assent, which was tabled on March 3. On March 9, Sumner offered a resolution which was passed, to the effect that the master of the *Highlander* was not an officer of the U.S. Navy and held no office of trust or profit such as contemplated by the Constitution for congressional consent for acceptance of gifts.

To Edwin M. Stanton[1]

I believe it was agreed some days ago that Gen. Sigel should be assigned to West-Virginia.   A. LINCOLN

Feb. 22. 1864.

[1] AES, DLC-Stanton Papers. Lincoln's endorsement is written on a letter from Sigismund Kaufman and others, New York, February 12, 1864, urging assignment of General Franz Sigel.

To Edwin M. Stanton[1]

[c. February 22, 1864]

I propose that the husband's parole be enlarged so that he may occasionally visit Washington.

[1] Copy, DNA WR RG 107, Secretary of War, Letters Received, P 123, Register notation. Although the letter bearing Lincoln's endorsement is missing, a notation on the register quotes the above as appearing on the application of Mrs. V. C. K. Neagle.

To Frederick Steele[1]

Major General Steele   Washington, D.C.,
Little Rock, Arkansas   Feb. 22. 1864

Yours of yesterday received. Your conferrence with citizens approved. Let the election be on the fourteenth of March, as they agreed.   A. LINCOLN

[1] ALS, RPB. See Lincoln to Steele, February 17, *supra*. General Steele's telegram of February 21 is as follows: "I called together the prominent citizens who telegraphed you opposite opinions in regard to the day on which the election should be held and they agree unanimously on the fourteenth (14) of March. Your written instructions are not yet rec'd. It is probable that several thousand votes will be polled in excess of the required number. A. A. C. Rogers of Pine Bluff is announced as opposing candidate for governor." (DLC-RTL).

To Gideon Welles[1]

February 22, 1864

These extracts from letters of Admiral Foote show Commander Stembel to be a very meritorious officer; unless the Sec. of the Navy knows some reason to the contrary, I propose that a vote of thanks be asked of Congress for him. If there be nothing in the way, please send me the papers to sign.   A. LINCOLN

Feb. 22, 1864.

[1] Stan V. Henkels Catalog 1328, May 25, 1923, No. 271. According to the catalog description, Lincoln's endorsement is written on the back of extracts from letters of Admiral Andrew H. Foote, recommending Commander Roger N. Stembel. No record has been found of Stembel's having received a congressional vote of thanks.

To Montgomery Blair[1]

February 23, 1864

Post-Master General please see the bearer Mr. Miller, now of Washington Territory, and son of an old friend of mine in Illinois, who originally went from Kentucky. He comes well recommended by his neighbors on the Pacific.   A. LINCOLN

Feb. 23. 1864

[1] ALS-P, ISLA. This note is written on both sides of a small card. On November 18, 1863, Anson G. Henry wrote to Lincoln, introducing Miller: "This will be handed you by my good friend Genl. W. W. Miller of this place. He is a son of our old friend Major [William] Miller of Jacksonville. He is the best specimen of a Union Democrat of the Andy Johnson stamp, we have in this Territory, and I know you will like to make his acquaintance." (DLC-RTL).

To Salmon P. Chase[1]

Hon. Sec. of Treasury   Executive Mansion,
My dear Sir   Washington, Feb. 23. 1864.

Yours of yesterday in relation to the paper issued by Senator Pomeroy was duly received; and I write this note merely to say I will answer a little more fully when I can find the leisure to do so. Yours truly   A. LINCOLN

[1] ALS (copy or ADfS?), DLC-RTL. The printed circular opposing the renomination of President Lincoln and advocating nomination of Secretary Chase was issued over the signature of Samuel C. Pomeroy. On February 22 Chase wrote Lincoln:

"It is probable that you have already seen a letter printed in the *Constitutional Union* Saturday afternoon, & reprinted in the *Intelligencer* this morning, written by Senator Pomeroy, as Chairman of a Committee of my political friends.

"I had no knowledge of the existence of this letter before I saw it in the *Union*.

"A few weeks ago several gentlemen called on me & expressed their desire, which, they said, was shared by many earnest friends of our common cause, that I would allow my name to be submitted to the consideration of the people in connexion with the approaching election of Chief Magistrate. I replied that I feared that any such use of my name might impair my usefulness as Head of the Treasury Department & that I much preferred to continue my labors where I am & free from distracting influences, until I could honorably retire from them. We had several interviews. After consultation, and conference with others, they expressed their united judgment that the use of my name as proposed would not affect my usefulness in my present position, and that I ought to consent to it. I accepted their judgment as decisive; but at the same time told them distinctly that I could render them no help, except what might come incidentally from the faithful discharge of public duties, for these must have my whole time. I said also that I desired them to regard themselves as not only entirely at liberty, but as requested, to withdraw my name from consideration wherever, in their judgment the public interest would be promoted by so doing.

"The organization of the Committee, I presume, followed these conversations; but I was not consulted about it; nor have I been consulted as to its action; nor do I even know who compose it. I have never wished that my name should have a moment's thought in comparison with the common cause of enfranchisement & restoration or be continued before public a moment after the indication of a preference by the friends of that cause for another.

"I have thought this explanation due to you as well as to myself. If there is anything in my action or position which, in your judgment, will prejudice the public interest under my charge I beg you to say so. I do not wish to administer the Treasury Department one day without your entire confidence.

"For yourself I cherish sincere respect and esteem; and, permit me to add, affection. Differences of opinion as to administrative action have not changed these sentiments; nor have they been changed by assault upon me by persons who profess themselves to spread representations of your views and policy. You are not responsible for acts not your own; nor will you hold me responsible except for what I do or say myself.

"Great numbers now desire your reelection. Should their wishes be fulfilled by the suffrages of the people I hope to carry with me, into private life the sentiments I now cherish, whole and unimpaired." (DLC-RTL).

Chase's statement that he had no knowledge of the circular before it appeared in print is contradicted by a statement of James M. Winchell, author-in-fact of the circular, who wrote, in reply to Jacob W. Schuckers' *Life and Public Services of Salmon Portland Chase* (1874), a detailed account of the Pomeroy Committee which included the following: "*Mr. Chase was informed of this proposed action and approved it fully.* He told me himself that the arraignment of the Administration . . . was one which he thoroughly indorsed and would sustain. The circular was, therefore, sent out." (J. M. Winchell to editor, September 14, 1874, New York *Times*, September 15, 1874. Italics are in the source.)

See further, Lincoln to Chase, February 29, *infra*.

To Ozias M. Hatch[1]

"Cypher"

Hon. O. M. Hatch   Executive Mansion,
Springfield, Ills.   Washington, Feb. 23, 1864.

I would be very glad, but really I do not perceive how I can reconcile the difficulty you mention. Will try to write you soon.

                                   A. LINCOLN

[1] ALS, RPB. Lincoln's telegram was sent in reply to a "confidential" letter from Hatch, February 16, 1864:

"Several of the friends of General [Richard J.] Oglesby, and Mr Dubois, —Uncle Jesse—would dislike very much to see an ugly contest between them, before the convention, for the nomination as candidate for governor.

"*They* now appear to be more prominent than other candidates,—both are qualified . . . but *one* can be nominated. The succeeding four years may be as pregnant with great events as the last three years . . . and it is of the utmost importance to the *Government* as well as to the *State*, that the interests of both, be entrusted to experienced hands. . . .

"For me, I feel certain, that Illinois is loyal, and will demonstrate it, not only in the convention, but at the polls—in November. I am certain that Jesse desires the nomination much,—and knowing . . . there is no man more conversant, with the affairs, or interests, of the state than he is—I feel that they would be entirely safe, in his hands. . . . We are certain that you can, if you will, reconcile these difficulties, and hope you will do so. I say *we*, because I have conversed with many of our friends upon the subject." (DLC-RTL).

General Oglesby was nominated on May 25 by the Republican state convention and was subsequently elected governor of Illinois over the Democratic candidate James C. Robinson.

To Willie Smith[1]

Executive Mansion, Washington,

Master Willie Smith: February 23, 1864

Your friend, Leroy C. Driggs, tells me you are a very earnest friend of mine, for which please allow me to thank you. You and those of your age are to take charge of this country when we older ones shall have gone; and I am glad to learn that you already take so lively an interest in what just now so deeply concerns us. Yours truly,   A. LINCOLN

[1] Angle, p. 343. Angle's note is as follows: "Willie Smith was a lad some twelve years of age who had conceived an unusually strong admiration for Lincoln. Among his father's friends was Leroy C. Driggs, who told Lincoln of the boy's feeling for him." No further information has been found.

Endorsement Concerning John Dickson[1]

February 24, 1864

Owing to Mr. Dickson being a respectable citizen of Illinois, I suppose it was, that this claim or case, was brought to my notice even before the receipt of the corn was finally refused. I only remember generally that my impression was that Mr. D. was being hardly dealt with. I think Major Belger himself so represented to me. I can only say now that I wish full and speedy justice to be done him.   A. LINCOLN

Feb. 24. 1864

[1] AES, owned by Harold C. Brooks, Marshall, Michigan. Lincoln's endorsement is written on a copy of H.R. 756, "A Bill for the benefit of John Dickson, of Illinois. . . . That the sum of twenty-three thousand dollars be paid to John Dickson . . . to compensate him for the damages he sustained by reason of the failure of J. W. Belger, quartermaster of United States volunteers, to receive one hundred thousand bushels of corn tendered . . . under a contract therefor. . . ." The bill passed and was approved by the president on March 11, 1864.

Pass for Simon Cameron[1]

Executive Mansion,
Washington, February 24, 1864.

Pass Hon. Simon Cameron and friends to Fortress Monroe and return.   A. LINCOLN

[1] DS, DLC-Cameron Papers. On February 8, Cameron wrote General Benjamin F. Butler, "Your letter of the 15th did not reach me till the 28th, and since my return home I have not been well enough to say when I can make you a visit. But I will try to come some time before this month ends. . . ." (*Private and Official Correspondence of Benjamin F. Butler*, III, 395. Butler's letter of the 15th has not been located.)

To Edwin M. Stanton[1]

Hon. Sec. of War   Executive Mansion,
Dear Sir.   Washington, Feb. 24. 1864.

I will be personally obliged if the appointment of an Additional PayMaster shall be given to J. R. Freese, of New-Jersey. Yours truly   A. LINCOLN

[1] ALS, THaroL. No record of an appointment for Freese has been found.

To Joseph K. Barnes[1]

February 25, 1864

Surgeon General please have an examination made of Michael Mullins, Co. C Harris Light Cavalry, now at Army Square Hospital, with reference to his discharge for disability.
Feb. 25. 1864   A. LINCOLN

[1] ALS, NHi. No reply or further reference has been found.

To Benjamin F. Butler[1]

February 25, 1864

Major General Butler please see and hear Judge Pitts of Eastern Shore of Virginia. He wishes to do right, but meets some difficulty at a point which it is probable you can obviate.   A. LINCOLN
Feb. 25. 1864

[1] ALS, RPB. Reverdy Johnson wrote Lincoln on February 24: "I take pleasure in introducing to you, Judge E. P. Pitts, of Va. who desires to see you on official business that he will explain. As a loyal gentleman he is most deserving of your regard." (DLC-RTL). Judge Edward P. Pitts of Northampton County, Virginia, had sent a memorial to the rebel legislature of Virginia in 1861 stating his loyalty to the South (see OR, II, II, IV, 39-40, and *passim*).

To Salmon P. Chase[1]

Will see Mr. Bailey at 7. this evening
Feb. 25, 1864   A.L.

[1] AES, DLC-RTL. Lincoln's endorsement is written on a note from Secretary Chase, "Mr. Bailey has arrived and will wait on you this morning. I hope it will be convenient for you to see him." See Lincoln to Chase, February 12 and 20, *supra*.

To Edwin M. Stanton[1]

February 25, 1864
Let John Hatton, within alluded to, and in prison at Alton, be discharged.

[1] Copy, DNA WR RG 107, Secretary of War, Letters Received, P 101, Register notation. This missing endorsement, according to the notation in the register, referred a letter of Francis P. Blair, Jr., requesting Hatton's release.

To Edwin M. Stanton[1]

February 25, 1864
I am told there are one hundred colored men at Alexandria, Va. who wish to go to Massachusetts; with their own consent and the consent of Gov. Pierpoint, let them go.   A. LINCOLN
Feby 25. 1864.

[1] Copy, DNA WR RG 94, AGO, Colored Troops Division, W 456. The copy of Lincoln's endorsement is preserved on a copy of the following letter from Governor Francis H. Peirpoint February 23, 1864:
"Oliver C. Gibbs Esq of Massachusetts, by request of Gov. Andrew as he informs me, desires to recruit colored troops in Virginia: to fill a Massachusetts regiment in that state. I dont see that I ought to object to it. I have no means to pay this or any other class of soldiers a bounty; and Mr Gibbs informs me that Massachusetts will pay them $300. Bounty.
"There are other parties here, recruiting for other states, who I learn, appropriate or receive one half of the bounty given by their states, for enlisting. I think I ought to require all these parties to report to me and make satisfactory arrangements to secure to these helpless men their full bounty. Unless you advise otherwise I shall issue a notice to this effect—and will respectfully ask that you will give aid in carrying it out if the parties prove refractory."
See Lincoln to Andrew, February 18, *supra*.

To Frederick Steele[1]

Major General Steele   Washington, D.C.,
Little Rock, Arkansas.   Feb. 25 1864
   General Sickles is not going to Arkansas. He probably will make a tour down the Mississippi, and home by the Gulf and ocean, but

he will not meddle in your affairs. At one time I did intend to have him call on you and explain more fully than I could do, by letter or Telegraph, so as to avoid a difficulty coming of my having made a plan here while the convention made one there, for re-organizing Arkansas, but even his doing that, has been given up for more than two weeks. Please show this to Gov. Murphy to save me Telegraphing him.　　　A. LINCOLN

[1] ALS, RPB. See Lincoln to Sickles, February 15, *supra*. On February 24, Provisional Governor Isaac Murphy telegraphed Lincoln, "I hope you will not send General Sickles here, and if an order has been made to that effect that it may be revoked. His coming here would only be an annoyance and will do no good. Everything is working well. General Steele is doing everything that can be done." (OR, III, IV, 127-28). A second telegram of the same date signed by Murphy and Freeman Warner, chairman of the Executive Committee of Arkansas, reiterated the request (*ibid.*).

To Telegraph Office[1]

Executive Mansion,
Telegraph Office　　　　　　Washington, Feb. 25, 1864.
　Please show Gov. Johnson my despatch to some at at [*sic*] Nashville, Tenn. saying the oath prescribed by Gov. Johnson was to be followed—& let the Gov. have a copy　　A. LINCOLN

[1] ALS, DLC-Johnson Papers. See Lincoln's telegram to Jordan, February 21, *supra*.

To Henry D. Terry[1]

Commanding Officer,　　　　　　Executive Mansion,
Johnson's Island:　　　　Washington, February 25, 1864.
　Suspend execution of death sentence of John Marrs until further orders and forward record for examination.　　A. LINCOLN.

Major Eckert:
　Please send the above dispatch.　　JNO. G. NICOLAY,
　　　　　　　　　　　　　　　　　Private Secretary.

[1] Tarbell (Appendix), p. 417. No reply or further reference has been found.

To Benjamin F. Butler[1]

Major General Butler　　　　　　Executive Mansion
Fort-Monroe, Va.　　　　　Washington, Feb. 26, 1864
　I can not remember at whose request it was that I gave the pass to Mrs. Bulkley. Of course detain her, if the evidence of her being a spy is strong against her.　　　A. LINCOLN

[1] ALS, RPB. General Butler telegraphed on February 25: "Mrs Bulkley, to whom you gave a pass to go through the lines, is charged upon strong evidence of being a spy. I have detained her for investigation. Is this right?" (DLC-RTL). Mrs. Bulkley has not been identified.

To Benjamin F. Butler[1]

Major-General Butler,   Executive Mansion,
Fort Monroe: Washington, February 26, 1864.

If it has not already been done, suspend execution of death sentence of William K. Stearns, Tenth New Hampshire Volunteers, until further orders and forward record.   A. LINCOLN.

Major Eckert:
Please send the above dispatch.   JNO. G. NICOLAY,
                                        Private Secretary.

[1] Tarbell (Appendix), p. 418. Butler replied on the same day: "The Pres. is respy informed that no death sentence will be executed in this Dept. for desertion only without his assent
"As I understand it to be his policy not to have such executions
"The record in the Stearns case is already forwarded." (DLC-Butler Papers).
The roster of Company A, Tenth New Hampshire Volunteers, lists William K. Stearns as mustered out June 21, 1865.

Endorsements Concerning Robert T. Van Horn[1]

Submitted to Gen. Rosecrans.   A. LINCOLN
Feb. 26. 1864

As the Sec. of War does not approve the above submission, let the paper be filed.   A. LINCOLN
March 2. 1864

[1] AES, IHi. Lincoln's endorsements are written on a letter from Governor Willard P. Hall of Missouri, February 9, 1864, asking that Lieutenant Colonel Robert T. Van Horn, Twenty-fifth Missouri Infantry, who was also a member of the State senate from Jackson County, be authorized to raise a brigade.

To William Jayne[1]

Hon. W. Jayne   Executive Mansion,
Dear Sir: Washington, February 26, 1864.

I dislike to make changes in office so long as they can be avoided. It multiplies my trouble and harrassment immensely. I dislike to make two appointments when one will do. Send me the name of some man, not the present Marshal, and I will nominate him to be Provost-Marshal for Dakota. Yours truly   A. LINCOLN

1 ALS, owned by Perry Jayne, Springfield, Illinois. Petitions for the removal of George P. Waldron, provost marshal for Dakota Territory, were submitted by unconditional Union men of Dakota on September 9, 1863, and January 11, 1864 (DLC-RTL). Letters from William Jayne, congressional delegate from the territory (February 3), Representative Asahel W. Hubbard of Iowa (February 27), and James M. Edmunds of the General Land Office (February 28), recommended appointment of George M. Pinney, U.S. Marshal for the Territory, to replace Waldron as provost marshal. Although orders removing Waldron and appointing Pinney under date of March 2 were sent to Lincoln by James B. Fry on March 4, Lincoln merely filed the letter with the endorsement "William Jayne—about Dakotah affairs." On April 21, Fry wrote Nicolay, "I enclose herewith, a letter from Capt. George M. Pinney, dated Yankton D.T. April 1st. 1864, by which it will be seen, that his appointment as Provost Marshal, Dakota Territory, had not reached him at that date. It was forwarded to His Excellency the Present, on the 4th. of March last, and the revocation of the appointment of Mr Waldron as Provost Marshal of Dakota Territory, was also forwarded at the same time, as directed by the President. Can you give me any information as to when and where they were mailed. . . ." (*Ibid.*).

No reply has been found, but Waldron remained in office until honorably discharged on May 20, 1865. See Lincoln to Bates, March 1, *infra*, concerning the replacement of Pinney as U.S. marshal.

Memorandum Concerning Benjamin F. Butler[1]

February 26, 1864

Col Shaffer has been conversing with me and I have said to him that Genl Butler has my confidence in his ability and fidelity to the country *and to me* and I wish him sustained in all his efforts in our great common cause subject only to the same supervisions which the Government must take with all Department Commanders   A LINCOLN

Feby 26. 1864

1 Copy, DLC-Butler Papers. The copy of Lincoln's memorandum was enclosed with a letter to Butler from Colonel John W. Shaffer, Butler's chief of staff, dated "Saturday Morning" (February 27, 1864):

"I yester[day] had a long and very satisfactory talk with Mr Lincoln and I think I have done all I came to do. I inclose you a copy of the statement Mr L. made on paper. he talked very decidedly in your favor

"I will try and arrange business at War Office to day, and get home Monday or Tuesday."

As printed in *Private and Official Correspondence of Benjamin F. Butler*, IV, 547-48, Shaffer's letter is dated July 27, 1864, and Lincoln's enclosure July 26, 1864. In the absence of Lincoln's original memorandum, the date cannot be certified, but a letter from Butler to Lincoln, February 24, 1864, seems to confirm the February date by requesting a statement of Lincoln's confidence. Jared D. Thompson of New Haven, Connecticut, had sworn under oath that Lincoln said "I think you agree with me that General Butler is not fit to have a command." Butler continued, "My only desire is that the President will say that this supposed conversation did not take place, so that I may properly punish this retailer of slander. . . ." (*Op. cit.*, III, 464-65).

Order Commuting Sentence of Deserters[1]

General Orders, No. 76.
War Department, Adjutant-General's Offi
Washington, February 26, 1864.

Sentence of Deserters.

The President directs that the sentences of all deserters, who have been condemned by Court Martial to death, and that have not been otherwise acted upon by him, be mitigated to imprisonment during the war, at the Dry Tortugas, Florida, where they will be sent under suitable guards by orders from army commanders.

The Commanding Generals, who have power to act on proceedings of Courts Martial in such cases, are authorized in special cases to restore to duty deserters under sentence, when in their judgment the service will be thereby benefited.

Copies of all orders issued under the foregoing instructions will be immediately forwarded to the Adjutant General and to the Judge Advocate General.

By order of the Secretary of War: E. D. Townsend,
Assistant Adjutant-General.

[1] AGO *General Orders No. 76*, February 26, 1864. If Lincoln issued his direction in writing, the document has not been discovered, but the explicit nature of the order dictates its inclusion here.

To Edwin M. Stanton[1]

Hon. Sec. of War   Executive Mansion,
My dear Sir.   Washington, Feb. 26, 1864.

Allow Howard D. O'Neill, now a prisoner at Old Capitol Prison to take the oath of Dec. 8. and be discharged. Yours truly

A. Lincoln

[1] ALS, DLC-Hitchcock Papers. The letter is endorsed by Stanton referring to "Major Genl Hitchcock to execute this order." Howard D. O'Neill of Ohio was a supporter of Clement L. Vallandigham.

To John W. Davidson[1]

Gen. Davidson   Washington, D.C.,
Cairo, Ills.   Feb. 27. 1864

Whether you shall visit Washington I must submit to the General-in-chief   A Lincoln

[1] ALS, RPB. Brigadier General John W. Davidson was relieved of his command at Little Rock, Arkansas, by request of General Frederick Steele to Halleck, January 28, 1864: ". . . I ask authority to relieve General Davidson

from my command. He is the only discordant element in it. He will intrigue against me." (OR, I, XXXIV, II, 175). On February 26, Davidson telegraphed Lincoln from Cairo, Illinois:

"I desire to come to Washn. I have facts to lay before the Judge Advocate General I have been relieved of a command I had formed & no reason assigned known to me. I have to send you the following telegram from Gov. Murphy I did not send it from Little Rock because I did not wish to add to your anxiety about the discords there—'Little Rock Ark, Feby 15th. 1864— To A. Lincoln Prest U.S.—

"'Genl Davidson is a true man & soldier a patriot in whom the unconditional Union men of Arkansas trust with unlimited confidence any action against him will be against the Union Element here & against your own policy. This, an investigation will show. Isaac Murphy Pro. Gover. of Arkansas' I cannot do duty with Honor until this question of the insult put upon me by Genl Steele be investigated. . . ." (DLC-RTL).

On June 26, 1864, General Davidson was placed in command as chief of cavalry in the Military Division of the West Mississippi.

To Edward H. East[1]

Hon E. H. East   Washington,
Secretary of State, Nashville, Tenn.:   February 27, 1864.

Your telegram of the 26th instant asking for a copy of my dispatch to Warren Jordan, esq., at Nashville Press office, has just been referred to me by Governor Johnson. In my reply to Mr. Jordan, which was brief and hurried, I intended to say that in the county and State elections of Tennessee the oath prescribed in the proclamation of Governor Johnson on the 26th of January, 1864, ordering an election in Tennessee on the first Saturday in March next, is entirely satisfactory to me as a test of loyalty of all persons proposing or offering to vote in said elections, and coming from him would better be observed and followed. There is no conflict between the oath of amnesty in my proclamation of 8th December, 1863, and that prescribed by Governor Johnson in his proclamation of the 26th ultimo. No person who has taken the oath of amnesty of 8th December, 1863, and obtained a pardon thereby, and who intends to observe the same in good faith, should have any objection to taking that prescribed by Governor Johnson as a test of loyalty. I have seen and examined Governor Johnson's proclamation, and am entirely satisfied with his plan, which is to restore the State government and place it under the control of citizens truly loyal to the Government of the United States.

A. LINCOLN.

Please send above for Governor Johnson.[2]   A. L.

[1] OR, III, IV, 141. See Lincoln's note to the Telegraph Office, February 25, and telegram to Jordan, February 21, *supra*.

[2] In the source Lincoln's telegram to East is followed by a certification

signed by Charles A. Tinker, March 1, 1864, and a postscript by Andrew Johnson:

"I certify that the above telegram is a verbatim copy of a dispatch forwarded this day to Nashville, Tenn., and now on file in this office.

"CHAS. A. TINKER,
"Cipher Clerk.

"P.S.—Please send copy of foregoing telegram to James B. Bingham, Memphis, Tenn., and oblige, ANDREW JOHNSON
"Military Governor of Tennessee."

Memorandum: Appointment of George W. Pyle[1]

I specially desire this case to be called to my attention when we act upon this class of cases. A. LINCOLN

Feb. 27. 1864

West-Point.

[1] AES, DNA WR RG 94, U.S. Military Academy, 1864, No. 128. George W. Pyle of College Hill, Ohio, appointed at large, entered West Point on July 1, 1864, and graduated in 1868.

To Edwin M. Stanton[1]

Hon. Secretary of War. Executive Mansion,
Sir Washington, Feb. 27, 1864.

You ask some instruction from me in relation to the Report of Special Commission,[2] constituted by an order of the War Department, dated Dec. 5 1863, "to revise the enrolment & quotas of the City & State of New-York, & report whether there be any & what errors, or irregularities therein, and what corrections, if any should be made." [The aspect of this case, as presented by this order and report, is entirely new to me, I having personally known nothing of the order, commission, or report, until now presented for my consideration.] In the correspondence between the Governor of New-York and myself last summer, I understood him to complain that the enrolments in several of the Districts of that State had been neither accurately nor honestly made; and, in view of this I for the draft then immediately ensuing, ordered an arbitrary reduction of the quotas in several of the Districts, wherein they seemed too large, [for the draft then immediately ensuing,] and said "After this drawing these four Districts and also the seventeenth and twentyninth shall be carefully re-enrolled, and, if you please, agents of yours may witness every step of the process" In a subsequent letter I believe some additional Districts were put into the list of those to be re-enrolled. My idea was to do the work over, according to the law, in presence of the complaining party, and thereby to correct anything which might be found amiss. The

Commission, whose work I am considering, seem to have proceeded upon a totally different idea. Not going forth to find men at all, they have proceeded altogether upon paper examinations and mental processes. One of their conclusions, as I understand is, that as the law stands, and attempting to follow it, the e[n]rolling officers could not have made the enrolments much more accurately than they did. The report, on this point, might be useful to Congress.

The Commission conclude that the quotas for the draft should be based upon entire population, and they proceed upon this basis to give a table for the State of New-York, in which some districts are reduced, and some increased. For the now ensuing draft, let the quotas stand as made by the enrolling officers, in the Districts wherein this table requires them to be increased; and let them be reduced according to the table, in the others. This to be no precedent for subsequent action; but as I think this report may, on full consideration, be shown to have much that is valuable in it, I suggest that such consideration be given it; and that it be especially considered whether it's suggestions can be conformed to without an alteration of the law. Yours truly   A. LINCOLN

[1] ALS, DLC-Stanton Papers. Portions enclosed in brackets appear as deleted in the manuscript, presumably by Lincoln. As printed in the *Official Records* (III, IV, 139-40) this letter is endorsed by Stanton on February 27, 1864: "Referred to Colonel Fry . . . with directions to make the ensuing draft in New York in conformity with the instructions of the President, herein contained."

[2] Members of the commission were: William F. Allen of New York, John Love of Indiana, and Chauncey Smith of Massachusetts.

To George H. Thomas[1]

Maj. Gen. George H. Thomas,   Executive Mansion,
Department of Cumberland: Washington, February 27, 1864.

Suspend execution of death sentence of F. W. Lanferseick, first[2] corporal, Company D, One hundred and sixth Regiment Ohio Volunteers, until further orders, and forward record for examination.   A. LINCOLN.

Major Eckert:
Please send the above dispatch.   JNO. G. NICOLAY,
                                   Private Secretary.

[1] Tarbell (Appendix), p. 418. Headquarters Department of the Cumberland, *General Orders No. 10*, January 10, 1864, lists Corporal F. W. Lanferseick to be shot for desertion.

[2] An error which occurred because Corporal Lanferseick was listed first of the two men sentenced: "1st. Cpl. F. W. Lanferseick."

To Lorenzo Thomas[1]

Gen. L. Thomas   Washington, D.C.,
Louisville, Ky.   Feb. 28. 1864..

I see your despatch of yesterday to the Sec. of War. I wish you would go to the Mississippi river at once, and take hold of, and be master in, the contraband and leasing business. You understand it better than any other man does. Mr. Mellen's[2] system doubtless is well intended; but, from what I hear, I fear that, if persisted in, it would fall dead within it's own entangling details. Go there, and be the judge. A Mr. Lewis[3] will probably follow you with something from me on this subject, but do not wait for him. Nor is this to induce you to violate or neglect any Military order from the General-in-Chief, or Secretary of War.   A. LINCOLN

[1] ALS, RPB. On February 27, Lorenzo Thomas telegraphed Stanton: "I arrived here this morning. In my letter of the 1st instant I requested instructions respecting the First Artillery Regiment Colored Troops, to be raised at Paducah, Ky. Shall I proceed with its organization? I will await your instructions here. It is very important that I should proceed down the Mississippi as soon as possible. . . . If the Treasury agent should insist on carrying out his regulations for leasing abandoned plantations and furnishing hands, none of the blacks can be provided for. If, however, the scale of wages and the regulations adopted by Superintendent Eaton [John Eaton, superintendent of Freedmen], approved by Major-General Grant and myself, be adopted, and the control be continued by the military authorities, there is yet time to lease plantations by the Treasury agent and provide for a vast amount of labor. May I request an early reply? . . ." (OR, III, IV, 138).

[2] William P. Mellen, treasury agent.

[3] See Lincoln's letter to Alpheus Lewis, January 23, *supra*.

To George Bancroft[1]

Hon. George Bancroft   Executive Mansion,
My dear Sir: Washington, Feb. 29. 1864.

Herewith is the copy of the manuscript which you did me the honor to request. Yours truly   A. LINCOLN.

[1] ALS-P, ISLA. No letter of Bancroft requesting the manuscript of the Gettysburg Address has been discovered. Perhaps he made the request in person, on behalf of the committee for the Baltimore Sanitary Fair. See notes to the Gettysburg Address, November 19, 1863, *supra*.

To Salmon P. Chase[1]

Hon. Secretary of the Treasury   Executive Mansion,
My dear Sir: Washington, February 29. 1864.

I would have taken time to answer yours of the 22nd. sooner, only that I did not suppose any evil could result from the delay, especially as, by a note, I promptly acknowled[ged] the receipt of yours, and promised a fuller answer. Now, on consideration, I find there is really very little to say. My knowledge of Mr. Pomeroy's letter having been made *public* came to me only the day you wrote; but I had, in spite of myself, known of it's *existence* several days before. I have not yet read it, and I think I shall not. I was not shocked, or surprised by the appearance of the letter, because I had had knowledge of Mr. Pomeroy's Committee, and of secret issues which I supposed came from it, and of secret agents who I supposed were sent out by it, for several weeks. I have known just as little of these things as my own friends have allowed me to know. They bring the documents to me, but I do not read them —they tell me what they think fit to tell me, but I do not inquire for more. I fully concur with you that neither of us can be justly held responsible for what our respective friends may do without our instigation or countenance; and I assure you, as you have assured me, that no assault has been made upon you by my instigation, or with my countenance.

Whether you shall remain at the head of the Treasury Department is a question which I will not allow myself to consider from any stand-point other than my judgment of the public service; and, in that view, I do not perceive occasion for a change. Yours truly   A. LINCOLN

[1] ALS (copy or ADfS?), DLC-RTL. See Lincoln to Chase, February 23, *supra*.

To John A. Dix[1]

Major General Dix   Executive Mansion,
New-York   Washington, Feb. 29, 1864.

Do you advise that John McKee, now in Military confinement at Fort-Lafayette, be turned over to the Civil authorities?

                                  A. LINCOLN

[1] ALS, RPB. No reply or further reference to John McKee has been discovered.

Draft of Order Concerning Samuel L. Casey[1]

Washington D.C. Feb 29 1864

Whereas Samuel L Casey of Kentucky has made the following statements to me that John Bishop   John Ray, S. Baker   S. C. Floyd   Thos M Watts and John B Shepard of Louisiana   Thos. S. Halloway and Joseph Turnage of Arkansas—William Butler of Illinois and him self and Peter Casey all Loyal men are the owners of a large amount of cotton on the Red River and its tributaries. Some of the cotton is with in our Military lines and a good deal within our trading lines, but all will have to pass into the Red River to reach a market or a place of safety and as orders have been given by the commander of the confederate forces of that Department to destroy all the cotton should the Federal army attempt to occupy that part of the country. believing that it would be a public injury to have the cotton destroyed, and having confidence in the integrity and ability of William Butler of Illinois and Samuel L Casey of Kentucky they are hereby authorised to take charge of—by the consent of the owners—and to convey to market or a place of safety said cotton under the regulations governing trade in the insurrectionary states adopted 23 of January 1864 and may sell the same receiving payment in full except the fees and taxes charged by the Treasury Department and all Military and Naval commanders are hereby directed to give all Steam Boats in charge of said Butler or Casey all necessary protection to and from their places of destination

¹ Df, DLC-RTL. The draft is by Casey. Although there is no record of Lincoln's having issued such an order, the order given to Casey on December 14, 1863, *supra*, and a letter from Casey to Lincoln February 25, 1864 (DLC-RTL) suggest the probability that Lincoln may have signed such an order on February 29, 1864.

To the House of Representatives¹

To the House of Representatives: February 29, 1864
In answer to the Resolution of the House of Representatives of the 26th. instant, I transmit herewith a report from the Secretary of War relative to the re-enlistment of Veteran Volunteers.
Washington, ABRAHAM LINCOLN
February 29th. 1864.

¹ DS, DNA RG 233, House Executive Document No. 44. Stanton reported that "it would be prejudicial to the public service to transmit . . . at the present time, the information requested."

To Frederick F. Low¹

Gov. Lowe. Executive Mansion, Washington,
My dear Sir Feb. 29, 1864.
Judge Hughes of the Claims Court here, has a Step-Son—William B. Barnes,—a private in a California regiment, and now at Benicia Barracks, whom he wishes appointed a Captain in his regiment or some other if possible; and I shall be personally obliged if you will make the appointment. Yours truly
A LINCOLN

[1] ALS, Archives and Central Record Depository, Sacramento, California. William B. Barnes, stepson of Judge James Hughes, was promoted to second lieutenant of Company E, Sixth California Infantry on May 23, 1864, and resigned on November 15, 1864.

To the Senate[1]

To the Senate of the United States: February [29], 1864

I communicate to the Senate herewith, for its constitutional action thereon, the articles of agreement and convention made and concluded at the city of Washington, on the 25th day of the present month, by and between William P. Dole as commissioner on the part of the United States, and the duly authorized delegates of the Swan Creek and Black River Chippewas, and the Munsees or Christian Indians in Kansas.   ABRAHAM LINCOLN.

Executive Mansion, February—, 1864.

[1] *Executive Journal*, XIII, 427. This communication was received by the Senate on February 29, 1864. Referred to the committee on Indian affairs the treaty was reported without amendment on April 7, 1864, but failed to be ratified.

To Cadwallader C. Washburn[1]

Maj. Genl. C. C. Washburne
La Crosse, Wis.
          Your leave is extended twenty days.   A. LINCOLN
Feb. 29. 1864

[1] LS-P, ISLA. Only the date and signature of this telegram are in Lincoln's handwriting. See Lincoln to Washburn, January 23, *supra*.

To Edward Bates[1]

Hon. Attorney General   Executive Mansion,
My dear Sir: Washington, March 1, 1864.

Please send me a nomination for John C. Smart to be Marshal for Dakota Territory in place of George M. Pinney, transferred to be Provost-Marshal. Yours truly   A. LINCOLN

[1] ALS, DNA GE RG 60, Papers of the Attorney General, Segregated Lincoln Material. See Lincoln to Jayne, February 26, *supra*. On February 27, J. P. Williston, U.S. Judge, Dakota Territory, recommended John C. Smart to William Jayne, and Jayne forwarded Williston's letter to Lincoln with his own endorsement that "He has been the deputy marshal for five years past—he will make an honest & efficient officer." (DLC-RTL). A letter of nomination for Smart, March 2, 1864, never signed or sent to the Senate, is in the Lincoln Papers.

To James G. Benton[1]

I do not sign the above in the form written; and yet if it can be conveniently done I shall be obliged.　　　　　A. LINCOLN

March 1. 1864

[1] AES, owned by Louis B. Souter, Long Beach, California. Lincoln's endorsement is written on an order to Captain James G. Benton, Washington Arsenal, which is as follows: "You will finish the trial of the Absterdam projectile by fireing the shell with time fuses for my friend A. C. Dickson and report immediately to Brigr Genl Ramsey." See further, Lincoln to Ramsay, March 7 and 10, *infra.*

Memorandum: Appointment of Henry P. Torsey[1]

[c. March 1, 1864]

The Vice-President says I promised to make this appointment, & I suppose I must make it.

[1] AE, DNA FS RG 59, Appointments, Box 393. Lincoln's endorsement is written on a letter from Hannibal Hamlin, March 1, 1864, recommending Henry P. Torsey of Readfield, Maine, for appointment as secretary of "one of the Territories." Torsey's appointment as secretary of Montana was confirmed by the Senate on June 22, 1864.

Memorandum Concerning Charles Garretson[1]

[c. March 1, 1864]

A

York Union League says G. is *"ultra copperhead"* & has no sympathy with the Government. Appoints under him, "bitter enemies"—Calvin B. Rhoads, George L. Jacoby, William Garretson, Martin Quinn & Joseph Ruby.

B

Hon. Thadeus Stevens says he is well acquainted with G. & subordinates—that he has always been disloyal since the war began.

C

Union League says G's bondsmen are copperheads—that he, G, left the State rather than vote for Curtin—and was outspoken, loud-mouthed copperhead—has made money out of his position.

D.

H. H. Jacobs says, G's partizans knocked down and dragged to prison, soldiers for cheering for Lincoln and Curtin, and that Calvin Rhoads and Martin Quinn were Marshals & participated in it—that George L. Jacoby painted carricatures of L & C, that William Garretson cheered Early's men when they marched

through York—that G. very well knew these men & got his bondsmen by promising to take these men in his employ, that G's own
language proves him as disloyal as any man can be.

E

Resolutions of Copperhead conventions not naming G.

F.

Mr. Edmunds letter transmitting papers.

[1] AD, DLC-RTL. James M. Edmunds, Grand President, Union League of
America, wrote Stanton on March 1, 1864, forwarding testimony concerning
the disloyalty of Captain Charles Garretson, assistant quartermaster, furnished
by the Union League of York, Pennsylvania, and others. On March 5, Garretson was "By direction of the President . . . dismissed the service of the United
States . . . for disloyalty to the Government" (AGO *Special Orders No. 107*).
See further, Lincoln's note to Stanton, March 7, *infra*.

To Edwin M. Stanton[1]

Hon. Sec. of War—   Executive Mansion,
My dear Sir: Washington, March. 1, 1864.

A poor widow, by the name of Baird, has a son in the Army,
that for some offence has been sentenced to serve a long time
without pay, or at most, with very little pay. I do not like this
punishment of withholding pay—it falls so very hard upon poor
families. After he has been serving in this way for several months,
at the tearful appeal of the poor Mother, I made a direction that
he be allowed to enlist for a new term, on the same conditions as
others. She now comes, and says she can not get it acted upon.
Please do it. Yours truly   A LINCOLN

[1] ALS, IHi. See Lincoln to Stanton, August 12, 1863, *supra*. Isaac P. Baird
was transferred to the One Hundred Eighty-third Pennsylvania Volunteers on
July 19, 1864, and served until discharged on May 30, 1865.

To Lorenzo Thomas[1]

                                    Executive Mansion,
Genl. L. Thomas: Washington, March 1, 1864.

This introduces Mr. Lewis, mentioned in my despatch sent you
at Louisville some days ago. I have but little personal acquaintance with him; but he has the confidence of several members of
Congress here who seem to know him well. He hopes to be useful,
without charge to the government, in facilitating the introduction
of the free-labor system on the Mississippi plantations. He is acquainted with, and has access to, many of the planters who wish

to adopt this system. He will show you two letters of mine on this subject, one somewhat general, and the other relating to named persons. They are not different in principle. He will also show you some suggestions coming from some of the planters themselves. I desire that all I promise in these letters so far as practicable, may be, in good faith, carried out, and that suggestions from the planters may be heard, and adopted, so far as they may not contravene the principles stated, nor justice, or fairness to the laborers. I do not herein intend to over-rule your own mature judgment on any point. Yours truly   A. LINCOLN

¹ ADfS, DLC-RTL. See Lincoln's letters to Thomas, February 28, and to Lewis, Field and Clay, January 23, *supra*. On March 30, Lorenzo Thomas wrote Lincoln as follows:

"A short time since Mr A. Lewis presented a letter from you to me at Vicksburg introducing him as a capable person to facilitate me in my operations regarding the plantation system, as carried on in this region of country I conferred with Mr Lewis at length and assured him that any arrangement that he and Mr [William P.] Mellen, the Supervising agent might make to carry out the views of the Administration would be sustained by me. With this understanding Mr Lewis proceeded up the river to confer with Mr Mellen. To-day I received a second visit from Mr Lewis, and also a communication from Mr. Mellen. From the letter I understand that Mr Lewis has promised to insure planters owning their own estates protection, but that he proposes to tax each of them five per cent on the crops raised by them in consideration of such protection being given, and for his services in consideration therewith.

"My plan is to encourage all to cultivate their estates, and to afford protection as far as it can properly be given, they working under the system adopted; and I cannot admit the policy of their paying for any protection given, to any individual, and therefore I cannot sanction Mr Lewis' plan Indeed I desire no assistance outside of the Treasury Agents, and the Military authorities now charged with the work. It seems to me that Mr Lewis' plan is a selfish one, having his own interest at stake, and I can hardly suppose he fully explained his views to you" (DLC-RTL).

On April 13, John Hay wrote Thomas:

"The President directs me to acknowledge the receipt of your favor of the 30th March, and to state in reply that Mr Lewis has no authorization from him for any such purpose as you mention. He gave to Mr Lewis a letter introducing him to you, at the request of some very respectable gentlemen from Kentucky, and here his responsibility for Mr Lewis terminated.

"The President does not wish you to be hampered in the execution of your duties by any consideration of the letter given by himself to Mr. Lewis." (*Ibid.*)

To Edward Bates¹

If Attorney-General concurs, let a pardon be made out in this case.

March. 2. 1864   A. LINCOLN

¹ AES, CSmH. Lincoln's endorsement is written on a letter of Reuben Shultz, Gentry County, Missouri, to Representative Austin A. King, January 21, 1864, asking executive clemency. Shultz had been a member of the Secession Legislature at Neosho, Missouri, in 1861.

To Edward Bates[1]

Attorney General please send nomination according to the within
March 2. 1864.   A. LINCOLN

[1] AES, DNA GE RG 60, Papers of Attorney General, Segregated Lincoln
Material. Lincoln's endorsement is written on a letter signed by Henry B.
Anthony and others, March 2, 1864, asking appointment of Robert Sherman of
Pawtucket, Rhode Island, as U.S. Marshal. See Lincoln to Bates, March 5,
infra.

To Daniel Breck[1]

Judge D. Breck   Executive Mansion
Richmond, Ky   Washington, March 2, 1864
I have directed the officer at Knoxville to allow Mrs. Rumsey[2] to
come to you.   A. LINCOLN

[1] ALS, RPB. Judge Daniel Breck wrote Representative William H. Randall
on February 22, 1864: "My Daughter, Anna Maria Ramsey, the wife of Dr.
F. A. Ramsey, with her six daughters, . . . is now at his residence in Knoxville, Ten. Her Husband is a Medical Director their only son an officer in the
Rebel Army. She has been ordered to leave with her children & go South
within the rebel lines, having failed to take the oath. . . . The order has been
temporarily suspended. She was willing to take the oath with the consent of
her husband, but being a *loyal* wife she doubted the propriety of doing so
without it. To obtain his consent is impracticable, for even if willing, he could
not safely give it in his present situation. I think the most desirable & natural
shelter for her & her children under the circumstances is her father's roof—
and indeed the safest for the Union cause, as you know her father is a Union
man. . . ." (DLC-RTL). See Lincoln to Tillson, *infra.*
[2] Presumably Lincoln misspelled the name here as well as in the telegram
to Tillson. Judge Breck's letter clearly reads "Ramsey."

To Joseph Holt[1]

Judge Advocate General please examine and report on this case.
March 2. 1864   A. LINCOLN

[1] AES, DNA WR RG 153, Judge Advocate General, MM 977. Lincoln's endorsement is written on the record of John O'Connell of Cincinnati, sentenced
to be hanged for disloyal practice. O'Connell claimed to be an alien. See further, Lincoln's endorsement to Holt, April 27, *infra.*

To George G. Meade[1]

                                                     Executive Mansion,
Major-General Meade: Washington, March 2, 1864.
Suspend execution of the death sentence of James Whelan, One
hundred and sixteenth Pennsylvania Volunteers, until further orders and forward record for examination.   A. LINCOLN

Major Eckert:

Please send the above dispatch.   JNO. G. NICOLAY,
                                             Private Secretary.

¹ Tarbell (Appendix), p. 419. On March 3, General Meade replied to Lincoln's telegram:

"You telegraphed me yesterday to suspend the death sentence of private James Wheelan 116th Penna Vols. & to forward the records for examination.

"I have ascertained that Wheelan has been tried by court martial & acquitted." (DLC-RTL).

To the New England Kitchen¹

Executive Mansion, March 2, 1864.

To the New-England Kitchen, connected with the
Brooklyn Sanitary Fair:

It is represented to me that my autograph, appended to this note, may somewhat augment, through the means you are so patriotically employing, the contributions for the benefit of our gallant and suffering soldiers, and for such an object I am glad to give it. Yours, truly,   A. LINCOLN.

¹ *The Drum Beat* (Brooklyn Sanitary Fair), March 5, 1864. According to the source, Lincoln's original autograph letter was sold at the Fair on March 4, 1864, for one hundred dollars, to C. H. Mallory, Mystic Bridge, Connecticut.

To Davis Tillson¹

Officer in Command   Executive Mansion,
at Knoxville, Tenn.   Washington, March 2. 1864.

Allow Mrs. Anne Maria Rumsey, with her six daughters, to go to her father, Judge Breck, at Richmond, Kentucky.

                                             A. LINCOLN

¹ ALS, RPB. Brigadier General Davis Tillson was the ranking officer at Knoxville and was assigned to command the defenses of Knoxville in April. See Lincoln to Breck, *supra*.

To Edward Bates¹

Hon. Attorney General   Executive Mansion,
My dear Sir: Washington, March 3. 1864.

Please send me a nomination for James S. Emory of Kansas to be District Attorney for Kansas. Yours truly   A. LINCOLN

¹ ALS, DNA GE RG 60, Papers of Attorney General, Segregated Lincoln Material. James S. Emory's appointment was confirmed by the Senate on March 18. As listed in the *U.S. Official Register*, 1865, his name is given as "James S. Amory."

To Edwin M. Stanton[1]

If the Secretary of War concurs, let Coln E W Serrell visit
Washington to examine Pontoons.   A LINCOLN.
March 3d. 1864.

[1] Copy, DLC-RTL. The copy is preserved in a letter from Joseph Francis,
March 4, 1864, relating that on the other side of the card bearing Lincoln's
note, Stanton wrote as follows: "The Secretary does not deem it expedient to
permit Coln Serrell to visit Washington for the purpose within mentioned, but
on the contrary thinks it highly injurious to the service to grant such applications." Colonel Edward W. Serrell was in command of the First New York
Engineers. Joseph Francis has not been identified.

To Frederick Steele[1]

Major General Steele   Washington, D.C.,
Little-Rock, Ark.   March 3. 1864

Yours including Address to People of Arkansas, is received. I
approve the address and thank you for it. Yours in relation to
Willard M. Randolph also received.[2] Let him take the oath of Dec.
8 and go to work for the new constitution, and on your notifying
me of it, I will immediately issue the special pardon for him.

                                          A. LINCOLN

[1] ALS, RPB. The text of Steele's address contained in his telegram of
March 2 is as follows:
"To the People of Arkansas:
"It affords the Genl commanding the highest gratification to be able to say
that, by the conduct of the army under his command, in connection with the
Administration of the Government by its officers at Washington, peace has, so
far been restored in your midst as to enable you to institute proceedings for
the restoration of the civil government, by which order may be firmly established and the rights of persons and property secured against violence and the
dangers of anarchy.
"The convention of your citizens held at Little Rock during the last month,
has adopted a constitution and submitted it to you for your approval or rejection. That constitution is based upon the principles of freedom and it is for
you now to say by your voluntary and unbiased action whether it shall be
your fundamental law, while it may have deficits in the main in accordance
with the views of that portion of the people who have been resisting the
fratricidal war which has been made during the last three years to overthrow
the government of our country.
"The convention has fixed the 14th day of March next on which to decide
this great question and the General commanding is only following the instructions of his government when he says to you that every facility will be
affixed for the expression of your sentiments uninfluenced by any considerations save those which effect your own interests and those of your posterity.
If you will now institute a government of your own, he feels great confidence
in assuring you that quiet and security will soon be restored to your Eastern
borders. Those who have been unwisely led by the counsel of bad men to en-
gage in the unjustifiable and wicked rebellion will speedily return and ac-

knowledge the rightful sovereignty of the state as well as the supremacy of the national Govt. over the whole dominion and peace will prevail. . . . The election will be held and the returns made in accordance with the Schedule adopted by the convention interference from any quarter will be allowed to prevent free expression of the loyal men of the state on that day. The schedule will be hereto appended. To render the election valid there must be cast five thousand four hundred & six (5406) votes." (DLC-RTL).

² Steele's telegram, received at 9:20 P.M. on March 2, recommended that "Willard M Randolph late Attorney Genl of the Confederate states for the Eastern district of Ark be pardoned, he only accepted office to keep out the rebel army. He is a man of talent—will be true to the U.S. He will assist in the election." (*Ibid.*). See Lincoln's endorsement to Bates concerning Randolph, March 7, *infra*.

To Joseph K. Barnes[1]

If the Surgeon General has the means will he please give the information sought in this letter. A. LINCOLN

March 4, 1864

¹ American Art Association Catalog, December 3, 1923, No. 553. According to the catalog description Lincoln's endorsement is written on a letter from Mrs. W. R. Twitchell, contents not specified.

To Benjamin F. Butler[1]

Major General Butler   Executive Mansion,
Fort-Monroe, Va   Washington, March 4, 1864.

Admiral Dahlgren is here, and of course is very anxious about his son. Please send me at once all you know, or can learn of his fate. A. LINCOLN

¹ ALS, RPB. General Butler forwarded news received from General Judson Kilpatrick that "Colonel Dahlgren was directed to make a diversion with 500 men on the James River. He attacked at 4 p.m. Tuesday evening; drove the enemy in on Richmond. The main attack having failed, Colonel Dahlgren attempted to rejoin me. . . . He and Colonel [Major Edwin F.] Cooke were with the advance guard . . . ; became separated from his main force, since which nothing has been heard. . . ." (OR, I, XXXIII, 197-98). Concerning Colonel Ulric Dahlgren's death, see Lincoln to Butler, March 7, *infra*.

To Salmon P. Chase[1]

Hon. Secretary of the Treasury.   Executive Mansion,
My dear Sir: Washington, March 4, 1864.

In consequence of a call Mr. Villard makes on, me, having a note from you to him, I am induced to say I have no wish for the publication of the correspondence between yourself and me in relation to the Pomeroy Circular—in fact, rather prefer to avoid an unnecessary exhibition—yet you are at liberty, without in the least offending me, to allow the publication, if you choose. Yours truly   A. LINCOLN

1 ALS copy (ADfS?), DLC-RTL. Henry Villard's despatch of March 6, is in part as follows: "In consequence of the stir made by the secret circular of Senator Pomeroy the Secretary addressed a letter to the President, inquiring whether there was anything in his action or position that would prejudice the public interests under his charge, and added that he did not wish to administer the affairs of the Treasury Department without the President's entire confidence. The President replied in a spirit equally frank and friendly, stating in substance that he did not perceive any occasion for any change in their official relations. This is the substance of the correspondence. . . ." (New York *Herald*, March 7, 1864).

To Joseph Holt[1]

Judge Advocate General please report on this case if the record is accessible.   A. LINCOLN
    March 4. 1864

              Sentence approved   A. LINCOLN
              April 21. 1864

1 AES, DNA WR RG 153, Judge Advocate General, MM 1212. Lincoln's endorsements are written on papers in the case of Joseph R. Hammill, engineer and detective, sentenced to two years' imprisonment and to refund public money embezzled. Holt reported that the sentence was in accord with Maryland laws.

Memorandum about Churches[1]

March 4, 1864

I have written before, and now repeat, the United States Government must not undertake to run the churches. When an individual in a church or out of it becomes dangerous to the public interest he must be checked, but the churches as such must take care of themselves. It will not do for the United States to appoint trustees, supervisors, or other agents for the churches. I add if the military have military need of the church building, let them keep it; otherwise let them get out of it, and leave it and its owners alone except for causes that justify the arrest of any one.

A. LINCOLN.

1 NH, X, 30. See also Lincoln to Rosecrans, April 4, and the memorandum of May 13, *infra*, and the endorsement to John Hogan, February 13, *supra*. The original of the memorandum of March 4, has not been located, and the occasion which necessitated Lincoln's repetition of aims has not been determined.

To William S. Rosecrans[1]

Executive Mansion Washington,

Major General Rosecrans   March 4. 1864

I shall be obliged if you will examine the question, and give me your opinion whether, on the whole, it would be advantageous to our military operations for the United States to furnish iron for completing the South West Branch of the Pacific Railroad, all, or any part of the way, from Rolla to Springfield Missouri, so fast as the Company shall do all the other work for the completion; and to receive pay for said iron, in transportation upon said newly made part of said road. It is understood that the Company will, on these terms, speedily put the road into working order. Yours truly

A. LINCOLN

[1] ALS and LS, DLC-RTL. This letter was never sent, but the letter to Rosecrans, March 10, *infra*, was drafted instead. See Lincoln's order of July 11, 1862, and communications to Curtis, October 12, 1862, and to Glover, January 20, 1863, *supra*. On January 20, 1864, Nicolay returned the order of July 11, 1862, after making a copy of it for the president (ALS, DNA RG 60, Papers of Attorney General, Box 116). Sometime *circa* March 4-10, 1864, a letter was drafted, possibly by Bates, although the undated copy in the Lincoln Papers is not in Bates' autograph:

"Applications have been frequently made to me to order the completion of the South West Branch of the Pacific Railroad. The measure has been recommended by four or five of the Major Generals commanding at different times in that section. I made an order for its completion to Lebanon in June 1862, which order still remains unexecuted.

"Mr. Gibson [Charles Gibson, solicitor of U.S. Court of Claims] on behalf of the Railroad Company now proposes that if the General Government will furnish the iron, the company will grade, & otherwise complete the road & furnish it with rolling stock.

"While I desire to see Missouri prosper I can only view this subject from a strictly national stand point.

"You will examine into the matter & if you should be of the opinion that the interests of the United States would be promoted by furnishing this iron, you may enter into an agreement with the company to do so, & may in that event order the Quartermaster at St. Louis to purchase it, being very particular in such agreement to guard well the interests of the National Government.

"From the lights before me I am inclined to the opinion it would be well to secure the early completion of the road as far as Springfield" (DLC-RTL, 2901-2, misdated "[1863]").

Bates *Diary* under date of March 9 and 10, 1864, records the following:

"The Govr. and Gibson are not content with the Presidents letter to Genl. Rosecrans, about completing the S.W. Branch of our Pacific R.R. and want me to try to get him to make it stronger. It only directs the Genl. to enquire into the subject and report. We want it to authorise the Genl. if he finds that the road would be advantageous to the military service, to act definitively, and furnish the iron, as fast as the company can lay it down.

"I hope to convince the President that the latter is the better course—better for the service, better for the State and better for himself. . . .

"Mar. 10   The Prest has changed his letter to Genl Rosecrans so as to allow him to proceed at once. . . ."

To Edwin M. Stanton[1]

I send this over as a reminder in relation to allowing the "Thomas Colyer" to run between here & Mount-Vernon.   A. LINCOLN

March 4, 1864

[1] AES, NHi. Lincoln's endorsement is written on a letter from Harriet V. Fitch, Vice Regent of the Mount Vernon Association, February 26, 1864, requesting that the steamboat *Thomas Collyer* be permitted to run between Washington and Mount Vernon: "We have through much labor bought, and paid for, the, home and grave of Washington, and but for the national troubles, would long since have collected a sum, equal to its restoration, and future keeping. *Now*, we have no means to keep it—no revenue but such as this boat will bring us. With that we will be enabled to go on another year, at least, and at the end of that time, let us hope for brighter days, when we can add to our fund; by further collections in the States."

Stanton's endorsement follows Lincoln's: "The Secretary of War does not deem it expedient to allow a Steamboat to run to Mt Vernon at present."

To John P. Usher[1]

Send nomination.   A. LINCOLN

March. 4. 1864

[1] AES, DNA NR RG 48, Indian Agencies, Box 1274. Lincoln's endorsement is written on an undated letter from James R. Doolittle and others, recommending appointment of John G. McMynn of Wisconsin as superintendent of Indian affairs for Washington Territory. McMynn's appointment was confirmed by the Senate on March 30, 1864.

To Edward Bates[1]

Hon. Attorney General   Executive Mansion,
My dear Sir: Washington, March 5. 1864.

Send me a nomination for Robert Sherman, as Marshal for the District of Rhode-Island.   [A. LINCOLN]

[1] ALS, DNA GE RG 60, Papers of Attorney General, Segregated Lincoln Material. The signature has been clipped from the letter. Sherman's appointment was confirmed by the Senate on March 7, 1864.

To Edward Bates[1]

Gov. Johnson. Attorney-General please make out pardons in these cases in the forms Gov. Johnson [will] request.

March 7, 1864.   A. LINCOLN.

[1] Anderson Auction Company Catalog 941, February 27, 1912, No. 608. According to the catalog description, Lincoln's endorsement is written on a letter relative to pardon of David T. Patterson, J. C. Grant, and S. J. W. Luckey, of Tennessee.

To Edward Bates[1]

March 7, 1864

The name is Willard M. Randolph. He was an attorney for the Rebel Government, but now taking the oath and going to work to carry the free State Constitution at the election on the 14th. I wish a special pardon for him. Please send me the document.

March 7, 1864   A. LINCOLN

[1] Anderson Galleries Catalog 1658, May 2, 1922, No. 802. According to the catalog description Lincoln's endorsement is written on the back of a military telegram. See Lincoln to Steele, March 3, *supra*.

To Benjamin F. Butler[1]

Major General Butler   Executive Mansion,
Fort-Monroe   Washington, March 7. 1864.

Gen. Meade has Richmond Sentinel, saying that Col. Dahlgren was killed, and ninety of his men captured at King & Queen C.-H. *When* did Kilpatrick's informant last see Col. Dahlgren?

A. LINCOLN

[1] ALS, RPB. See Lincoln to Butler, March 4, *supra*, and March 17, *infra*.

To John A. J. Creswell[1]

Hon. John A. J. Creswell   Executive Mansion,
My dear Sir: Washington, March 7, 1864.

I am very anxious for emancipation to be effected in Maryland in some substantial form. I think it probable that my expressions of a preference for *gradual* over *immediate* emancipation, are misunderstood. I had thought the *gradual* would produce less confusion, and destitution, and therefore would be more satisfactory; but if those who are better acquainted with the subject, and are more deeply interested in it, prefer the *immediate*, most certainly I have no objection to their judgment prevailing. My wish is that all who are for emancipation *in any form*, shall co-operate, all treating all respectfully, and all adopting and acting upon the major opinion, when fairly ascertained. What I have dreaded is the danger that by jealousies, rivalries, and consequent ill-blood—driving one another out of meetings and conventions—perchance from the polls—the friends of emancipation themselves may divide, and lose the measure altogether. I wish this letter to not be

[226]

made public; but no man representing me as I herein represent myself, will be in any danger of contradiction by me. Yours truly

A. LINCOLN.

1 ALS and ADfS, DLC-RTL. The envelope in which the letter was sent bears Lincoln's endorsement "Returned." The Maryland legislature had enacted a bill calling an election on April 6 for delegates to a constitutional convention to be held on April 27, 1864. See Lincoln to Hoffman, October 10, 1864.

To Joseph Holt[1]

Judge Advocate General please examine & report on this case at once.   A. LINCOLN

March 7, 1864

Sentence approved, and execution fixed for Friday, April 22nd 1864.   A. LINCOLN

April 14, 1864

Sentence commuted to imprisonment in the Penitentiary at hard labor for ten years.   A. LINCOLN

Jan. 25, 1865

1 AES, DNA WR RG 153, Judge Advocate General, LL 1431. Lincoln's endorsements are written on the papers in the case of Lorenzo C. Stewart (alias Shear), Fourteenth New York Artillery, sentenced to be hanged for desertion and murder (poisoning soldiers). A petition from citizens of Elmira, New York, asking clemency, bears the endorsement of April 14, 1864, and a report by Dr. John P. Gray, January 25, 1865, on the mental condition of Stewart, bears the commutation of sentence of that date. See Lincoln to Gray, April 25, 1864, infra.

To William A. Merriwether[1]

U.S. Marshal   Executive Mansion,
at Louisville Ky   Washington, March 7, 1864.

Until further orders, suspend sale of property and further proceedings in cases of the United States against Dr John B English and S. S. English, et al. sureties for John L Hill

Also same against same sureties for Thomas A. Ireland

A. LINCOLN.

Major Eckert
Please send the above dispatch   JNO. G. NICOLAY
Priv: Sec

1 Copy, DLC-Nicolay Papers. On February 26, 1864, Jeremiah T. Boyle wrote Lincoln from Louisville:
"This will be handed to you by Col. S. S. English, of this city, a loyal citizen

and true union man, who desires to see you relative to business which he will explain.

"I can say that it is within my knowledge that Dr. English, brother of the colonel, entered as security and procured the colonel to unite with him as security for Hill and Ireland (who afterward violated their oath and bond) with the view . . . of inducing the said Hill and Ireland to resign and vacate the offices of County Judge and County Clerk of Owen County, Ky, in order that loyal men should fill the offices, and thus that the power and influence of the government might be increased in the county. I believe the main purpose was to increase the loyal union influence, and such I believe was the result of the action of Dr. English and the colonel. I trust you may feel that it would be right to relieve them from the penalty of the bond.

"Colonel English is a true and reliable gentleman and will make a statement to you on which you can fully rely. . . ." (DLC-RTL).

Order Designating Starting Point of Union Pacific Railroad[1]

March 7, 1864

In pursuance of the provisions of Section 14, of the Act of Congress entitled "An Act to aid in the construction of a Rail Road and Telegraph Line from the Missouri River to the Pacific Ocean, and to secure to the Government the use of the same for Postal,—Military, and other purposes," Approved July 1st. 1862, authorizing and directing the President of the United States, to fix the point on the Western boundary of the State of Iowa, from which the Union Pacific Rail Road Company is by said section authorized and required to construct a single line of Rail Road, and Telegraph, upon the most direct and practicable route, subject to the approval of the President of the United States, so as to form a connection with the lines of said Company, at some point on the one hundre[d]th meridian of longitude in said section named: I, Abraham Lincoln President of the United States do, upon the application of the said Company, designate and establish such first above named point, on the Western boundary of the State of Iowa, east of, and opposite to the East line of Section 10, in Township 15, North, of Range 13, East of the sixth principle meridian, in the Territory of Nebraska

Done at the City of Washington this, seventh, day of March, in the year of our Lord, one thousand eight hundred and sixty four

ABRAHAM LINCOLN

[1] Copy, DNA RG 46, Senate 38A F6. The original order has not been located. The copy in the Senate files was enclosed with Lincoln's communication to the Senate of March 9, *infra*. See also Lincoln's order of November 17, 1863, *supra*.

Order in Regard to Export of Tobacco[1]

Executive Mansion
Washington, 7th March, 1864.

Whereas by an Executive Order on the 10th of November last, permission was given to export certain tobacco belonging to the French Government from insurgent territory, which tobacco was supposed to have been purchased and paid for prior to the 4th March 1861; but whereas, it was subsequently, ascertained that a part at least, of the said tobacco had been purchased subsequently to that date, which fact made it necessary to suspend the carrying into effect of the said order; but whereas, pursuant to mutual explanations a satisfactory understanding on the subject has now been reached, it is directed that the Order aforesaid may be carried into effect; it being understood that the quantity of French tobacco so to be exported, shall not exceed Seven thousand hogsheads, and that it is the same tobacco respecting the exportation of which application was originally made by the French Government.

ABRAHAM LINCOLN.

[1] Copy, DLC-Butler Papers.

To George D. Ramsay[1]

Executive Mansion,
Gen. Ramsay.   Washington, March 7, 1864.

Will a number of the Absterdam Shells, or projectiles, be placed in the hands of the troops for trial, as recommended by Capt. Benton, in his report of March 3rd? Yours truly   A LINCOLN

[1] ALS, ORB. See Lincoln to Benton, March 1, *supra*. On the bottom of Lincoln's note is the following endorsement by General Ramsay: "I should like to preserve this note and therefore beg it may be returned to me." See further, Lincoln's endorsement to Ramsay, March 10, *infra*.

To Edwin M. Stanton[1]

Executive Mansion,
Washington, March 7, 1864.

I think it is but fair that Quarter-Master-General Allen, should be allowed to fix the rate of rent of Col. Mondays property now used by the Government at Mound-City; and I shall be glad if the Sec. of War will direct him to do so.   A. LINCOLN

[1] ALS, THaroL. Colonel Marcellus Mundy, Twenty-third Kentucky Infantry, whose signature is incorrectly indexed as "M. Murray" in the Lincoln

Papers, wrote Lincoln from Willard's Hotel on March 8, 1864: "I had the honor this morning to present your respectful request to the Secretary of War, that he would refer the matter at issue between the government and me regarding the rental of my property at Mound City, Illinois, used by the government for hospital, to Brig. Gen. [Robert] Allen A.Q.M. at Louisville Kentucky for settlement,—and I regret to inform you that the Hon. Secretary declines to comply with your request. Without detailing the interview I will say to you that I feel compelled to abandon my property as I am satisfied that whatever fair claims I may have as citizen or soldier will be disregarded by the present administration and the urging of them further would but subject me to further discourtesy. I thank you for the courtesy extended to me in our last interview. . . ." (DLC-RTL).

To Edwin M. Stanton[1]

Hon. Sec. of War: Executive Mansion,
My dear Sir: Washington, March 7, 1864.

It is represented to me that General David B. Birney, who is nominated for a Major General to take rank from June 22nd. 1863, is really entitled, if at all, to take rank from May 3. 1863, for meritorious conduct at Chancellorsville. It is also represented that to make the desired change will not give Gen. Birney rank over any one who now ranks him. I shall be glad to withdraw his present nomination and make the change, if the above is a true and a full statement of the facts. Yours truly   A. LINCOLN

[1] ALS-P, ISLA. Brigadier General David B. Birney's nomination as major general was revised to date from May 20, 1863, rather than from May 3.

To Edwin M. Stanton[1]

Hon. Sec. of War: Executive Mansion,
My dear Sir   Washington, March 7, 1864.

The bearer is Gov. Hall of Missouri, whom I have much pleasure in introducing to you. I shall be glad for yourself and Col. Fry to give him a full hearing on Missouri matters. Yours truly

A. LINCOLN

[1] ALS, IHi. Lieutenant Governor Willard P. Hall succeeded to the governorship following the death of Governor Hamilton R. Gamble on January 31, 1864.

To Edwin M. Stanton[1]

March 7, 1864
Sec. of War, please have a full report of this case sent me. Hon. Mr. Bailey says this man went home last fall on the loyal side, and actually fought for the previlege.   A. LINCOLN
March 7. 1864.

[1] AES, DLC-RTL. Lincoln's endorsement is written on the back of a printed copy of AGO *Special Orders No. 107.* See Lincoln's memorandum concerning Charles Garretson, March 1, *supra.* Representative Joseph Bailey may have obtained modification of Garretson's dismissal, for later references give Garretson as "mustered out" rather than "dismissed" on March 5, 1864.

To Queen Victoria[1]

March 7, 1864

Abraham Lincoln
President of the United States of America.

To Her Majesty Victoria
Queen of the United Kingdom
of Great Britain and Ireland
&c. &c. &c.

Sendeth Greeting:

Great and Good Friend: I have received the letter which Your Majesty addressed to me on the 30th. day of January last, informing me that Her Royal Highness, the Princess of Wales, Daughter of His Majesty, the King of Denmark, Consort of Your Majesty's well-beloved son, His Royal Highness Albert Edward, Prince of Wales, Duke of Saxony, Prince of Saxe Coburg and Gotha &c. &c. was safely delivered of a Prince on the 8th. of that month.

I pray Your Majesty to accept my cordial congratulations upon this event, and to be assured that I take a lively interest in all that concerns the happiness and prosperity of Your Royal House, and so I recommend Your Majesty and Your Royal Family to the protection of the Almighty. Your Good Friend

Washington 7th. March, 1864. ABRAHAM LINCOLN
By the President
WILLIAM H. SEWARD Secretary of State.

[1] Copy, DNA FS RG 59, Communications to Foreign Sovereigns and States, III, 217-18.

Memorandum:
Appointment of William F. Allen[1]

[March 8, 1864]

West-Point.

William F. Allen—Son of Col. who lost his life off, Hatteras—
New-Jersey.

[1] AES, DNA WR RG 94, U.S. Military Academy, 1862, No. 1. Lincoln's endorsement is written on an envelope containing recommendations and pho-

tograph of William F. Allen, son of Colonel Joseph W. Allen, Ninth New Jersey Volunteers, drowned January 15, 1862, on Burnside's expedition. A similar endorsement by Lincoln is on the photograph: "West-Point—Wm. F Allen —son of Col. Allen—drowned at Hatteras Inlet—" There is no record of Allen's appointment.

To Benjamin F. Butler[1]

Major General Butler Executive Mansion,
Fort-Monroe, Va. Washington, March 9. 1864.

What are the facts about the imprisonment of Joseph A. Bilisoly? A. LINCOLN

[1] ALS, RPB. General Butler replied on the same day that the causes of imprisonment of Bilisoly were "first he is a Secessionist, has had eleven children and grandchildren in the confederate army, said he was sorry he hadn't more & has taken the oath of allegiance but says his sympathies are with the South and not with the north. Third—Over two hundred thousand (200 000) dollars of the assets of the Saving Bank of Portsmouth have been traced into his hands & he refuses to give any account of it & lies when he is examined about it. Fourth. He had a secret box made under his daughter's bedroom floor in which he concealed arms & the plate of another secessionist & when called to account for it lied about it. Fifth. He is only committed until he will tell the truth as to the secretion of the Bank property. When he does this he will be brought up for examination. It is the common case of confinement of a witness for contempt." (DLC-RTL).

In the Butler Papers (DLC) is a letter from Bilisoly's daughter, Mrs. George R. Boush, addressed to President Lincoln, March 1, 1864, which states the circumstances of her father's imprisonment somewhat differently: "He is charged with knowing, where some of the most important papers of the Portsmouth Saving's Bank, are concealed. Notwithstanding, he positively denied the charge[,] was taken to prison, and early in the morning, hurried to Fortress Monroe, without breakfast, and not one penny in his pocket. Report says confined in a cell, with nothing to lie down on. My husband Geo. Richard Boush (Master Builder of the Gosport Yard) is now in Alexandria, attending the Convention; therefore I have to act for myself."

To Joseph Holt[1]

Judge Advocate General please examine and report on this case.
March 9, 1864. A. LINCOLN

Pardon, for the unexpired part of the imprisonment.
March 29. 1864 A. LINCOLN

[1] AES, DNA WR RG 153, Judge Advocate General, MM 1253. Lincoln's endorsements are written on the papers in the case of Captain William H. Wickes, One Hundred Sixty-ninth New York Volunteers, dismissed on February 12, 1864, and sentenced to six months' imprisonment for presenting false vouchers. Holt's report indicated no ground justifying interference in the case by the president. The record also indicates an endorsement of Lincoln's

dated April 21, 1864, denying the application for pardon, which has not been found and may have been removed from the file because of Wickes' prior release from prison under AGO *Special Orders No. 134*, April 1, 1864.

To George G. Meade[1]

Major-General Meade,   Executive Mansion,
Army of Potomac: Washington, March 9, 1864.

New York City votes 9,500 majority for allowing soldiers to vote, and the rest of the State nearly all on the same side. Tell the soldiers.   A. LINCOLN.

[1] Tarbell (Appendix), p. 420. Daniel H. Craig of the Associated Press at New York City telegraphed Lincoln on March 8, 1864: "New York City gives ninety five hundred (9500) majority for allowing soldiers to vote. Returns from interior show majorities same every where." (DLC-RTL).

To the Senate[1]

Executive Mansion
To the Senate of the United States: March 9th. 1864.

In compliance with a resolution of the Senate, of the 1st. instant, respecting the points of commencement of the Union Pacific Railroad, on the 100th. degree of West Longitude, and of the branch road, from the Western boundary of Iowa, to the said 100th. degree of Longitude, I transmit the accompanying report from the Secretary of the Interior, containing the information called for.

I deem it proper to add that, on the 17th day of November last, an executive order was made upon this subject, and delivered to the Vice President of the Union Pacific Rail Road Company, which fixed the point, on the western boundary of the State of Iowa from which the Company should construct their Branch-Road to the 100th. degree of West Longitude, and declared it to be within the limits of the township, in Iowa, opposite the town of Omaha in Nebraska. Since then the Company has represented to me, that, upon actual surveys made, it has determined upon the precise point of departure of their said Branch-R road from the Missouri river, and located the same as described in the accompanying report of the Secretary of the Interior, which point is within the limits designated in the order of November last; and inasmuch as that order is not of record in any of the Executive Departments, and the Company having desired a more definite

[233]

one, I have made the order, of which a copy is herewith, and caused the same to be filed in the Department of the Interior.

ABRAHAM LINCOLN

[1] DS, DNA RG 46, Senate 38A F6. See Lincoln's order of March 7, *supra.* Secretary Usher's report of March 8, which Lincoln transmitted, indicated that "the point of commencement of said road on the one hundredth degree of west longitude has not yet been fixed."

Speech to Ulysses S. Grant[1]

General Grant   [March 9, 1864]

The nation's appreciation of what you have done, and it's reliance upon you for what remains to do, in the existing great struggle, are now presented with this commission, constituting you Lieutenant General in the Army of the United States. With this high honor devolves upon you also, a corresponding responsibility. As the country herein trusts you, so, under God, it will sustain you. I scarcely need to add that with what I here speak for the nation goes my own hearty personal concurrence.

[1] AD, owned by Ulysses S. Grant, III, Washington, D.C. On the night of March 8, 1864, General Grant reported to President Lincoln at the White House in obedience to orders received at Nashville, Tennessee, several days before. The president's weekly reception was in progress, but following an ovation to General Grant, Lincoln arranged to meet him later for a private conference. Nicolay's report of the conference is as follows:

"The President here made an appointment with him for the formal presentation next day of his commission as lieutenant-general. 'I shall make a very short speech to you,' said Lincoln, 'to which I desire you to reply, for an object; and that you may be properly prepared to do so I have written what I shall say, only four sentences in all, which I will read from my manuscript as an example which you may follow and also read your reply—as you are perhaps not so much accustomed to public speaking as I am; and I therefore give you what I shall say so that you may consider it. There are two points that I would like to have you make in your answer: First, to say something which shall prevent or obviate any jealousy of you from any of the other generals in the service; and second, something which shall put you on as good terms as possible with the Army of the Potomac. If you see any objection to doing this, be under no restraint whatever in expressing that objection to the Secretary of War.'" (Nicolay and Hay, *Abraham Lincoln: A History,* VIII, 340-41).

The next day at one o'clock the presentation took place "in presence of the Cabinet, General Halleck, two members of Grant's staff, and the President's private secretary. . . ." (*Ibid.*). Following Lincoln's speech, Grant read his pencilled reply as follows:

"Mr. President:

"I accept this commission with gratitude for the high honor confered.

"With the aid of the noble armies that have fought on so many fields for our common country, it will be my earnest endeavor not to disappoint your expectations.

"I feel the full weight of the responsibilities now devolving on me and know that if they are met it will be due to those armies, and above all to the

[234]

favor of that Providence which leads both Nations and men." (AD, DLC-Grant
Papers).

Grant's commission as lieutenant general dated from March 2, 1864.

To Ulysses S. Grant[1]

Lieut. Gen. Grant   Executive Mansion
Army of Potomac   Washington, March 10. 1864

   Mrs. L. invites yourself and Gen. Meade to dine with us Saturday evening. Please notify him, and answer whether you can be
with us at that time.   A. LINCOLN

   [1] ALS, DNA WR RG 107, Presidential Telegrams, I, 1. Grant's reply to
Lincoln's telegram was received at 7:45 P.M.: "Genl. Meade and myself accept
your kind invitation to dine with Mrs. Lincoln on Saturday." (DLC-RTL). A
Washington despatch of March 13 reported, however, that "The sudden return
of Lieut.-Gen. Grant to the West prevented him from participating in the
military dinner at the Executive Mansion last night. However, nearly all, if
not the entire number of Major and Brigadier-Generals now here, including
Gens. Halleck, Meade, Sickles, and McCook, together with the Secretary of
War, dined with the President. . . ." (New York *Tribune*, March 14, 1864).

List of Candidates for West Point[1]

[c. March 10, 1864]

John D. C. Hoskins.— Has served in this war—Gen. Grant's boy.[2]
David Dick Johnson— Penn.[3]
Beverly Allen—   Mo.   Pope's boy.[4]
William Whipple—   Army[5]
Augustus P. Barnard.— Army[6]
          Nesmith.—[7] Oregon.
John B. Engle. Ia. now in Libby—Hon. H. S. Lane.[8]

   [1] AD, DLC-RTL. This list is written on a military telegraph form dated
1864, and appears to be contemporary with the memorandum, *infra*.
   [2] See memorandum of January 20, *supra*.
   [3] See memorandum of January 6, *supra*.   [4] See memorandum, *infra*.
   [5] Charles William Whipple, son of William D. Whipple, entered West Point,
July 1, 1864.   [6] No record of an appointment has been found.
   [7] "George W. Pyle" is written in pencil above "Nesmith," which has been
deleted. See Lincoln's memorandum of February 27, *supra*.
   [8] Corporal John B. Engle, Eighty-sixth Indiana Infantry, was mustered out
in June, 1865, and appointed second lieutenant, Seventeenth Infantry, on February 23, 1866.

Memorandum: Appointment of Beverly Allen[1]

[c. March 10] 1864

Papers used when making West-Point appointments for 1863—
and now some to be used in 1864.

[235]

[1] AE, DLC-RTL. Lincoln's endorsement is written on an envelope containing a letter from Mrs. Lucretia Pope Yeatman, March 10, 1864: "I take liberty of reminding you that in October last you promised to appoint early in March Beverly Allen of St. Louis Missouri to a cadetship at West Point. Lest in the multiplicity of cares it may have passed out of your mind I venture to call your attention to it." No appointment of Beverly Allen is of record.

Order Assigning Ulysses S. Grant to Command of the Armies of the U.S.[1]

Executive Mansion,
Washington, D.C., March [10], 1864.

Under the authority of an act of Congress to revive the grade of lieutenant-general in the United States Army, approved February 29, 1864, Lieutenant-General Ulysses S. Grant, U.S. Army, is assigned to the command of the armies of the United States.

ABRAHAM LINCOLN.

[1] OR, I, XXXII, III, 83. Lincoln's order has not been found. As printed in the *Official Records,* it is dated "March, 1864, but Stanton's telegram to Grant of March 10, 1864, establishes the date: "Pursuant to the authority of the act of Congress . . . the President, by Executive Order of this date, has assigned to you the command of the Armies of the United States." (OR, I, XXX-III, 663).

To George D. Ramsay[1]

March 10, 1864

I think the Absterdam projectile is too good a thing to be lost to the service, and if offered at the Hotchkiss prices, and not in excessive quantities, nor unreasonable terms in other respects, by either or both parties to the patent controversy, take it, so that the test be fully made. I am for the government having the best articles, in spite of patent controversies. A. LINCOLN

March. 10. 1864.

[1] AES, DLC-RTL. See Lincoln to Ramsay, March 7, *supra.* Lincoln's endorsement is written on a letter from Brigadier General Ramsay, March 8, 1864, as follows:

"I had the honor to receive this morning your interrogatory as to placing a number of the Absterdam projectiles in the hands of troops for trial as recommended by Captain Benton in his Report of the 3d instant? In reply, I beg to state that Messrs Dickson & Zane propose to furnish to the U States, for a period of twelve months, and to be delivered in the City of Phila, seven hundred & twenty thousand of the Absterdam projectiles, in the proportion of 1/10 solid shot & 9/10 shell at the following rates, viz:—

10 pds	ea.	two dollars	($2.00)
20 "	"	three 60/	$3.60
4.62 inch	"	four 10/	$4.10

"These prices are greatly in excess of what is now paid for similar projectiles as will be seen by the comparative statement herewith submitted. I would further state that Mr. Absterdam claims that the projectiles tried and reported upon by Capt Benton were made under a patent not covered by the assignment of his projectiles to other parties. It would thus appear that the question of right is involved in controversy; and until this question is satisfactorily adjusted, I should feel unwilling to negotiate with either party. All things harmoniously arranged and the prices agreed upon, I shall be happy to order a sufficient number of these projectiles to fully test their merits by actual trial in the field."

To William S. Rosecrans[1]

Executive Mansion,

Major General Rosecrans   Washington, March 10, 1864.

Please carefully examine and consider the question whether, on the whole, it would be advantageous to our Military operations for the United States to furnish iron for completing the South-West-Branch of the Pacific Railroad all, or any part of the way from Rolla to Springfield, Missouri, so fast as the Company shall do all the other work for the completion, and to receive pay for said iron in transportation upon said newly made part of said road—and if your opinion shall be in the affirmative, make a contract with the company to that effect, subject to my approval or rejection. In any event report the main facts together with your reasoning, to me. Yours truly   A. LINCOLN

[1] ALS (ADfS?), DLC-RTL. See Lincoln to Rosecrans, March 4, *supra.* On September 15, 1864, Rosecrans submitted his report, enclosing the agreement made at St. Louis on July 26, between the Pacific Railroad (by its president, George R. Taylor) and the United States (by Colonel William Myers, assistant quartermaster, acting under Rosecrans' order), which followed Lincoln's instructions of March 10. Exhibit P of the Report is a letter from Bates to Rosecrans, March 19, 1864:

"I venture to address you touching a matter of great importance which has been committed to your discretionary judgment, by a special order of the President. . . . I shall not trouble you . . . with any detailed . . . facts, nor any prolonged argument . . . because my friend, Mr Gibson who will hand you this, is fully possessed of the subject, and has . . . all needful documents . . . I desire however to say that, long ago (perhaps two years—& ever since) I urged upon the government here, the immediate completion of that road, as a military necessity, and as a measure of great and obvious economy, in money, time, and actual force necessary, not only to the defence of that frontier, but also to the reëstablishment of the national authority, still farther south and west. In my judgment, the same necessity and the same motives of economy still exist. . . .

"The measure, if now adopted and promptly acted upon, will, I think, yield immediate fruits—1. It will stranguilize Missouri into order & peace: 2. It will deter the enemy from any attempt, even by guerrillas, to continue the war in S.W. Mo. and N.W. Arkansas: 3. It will set free a large force, now required to guard that region, either to serve in other fields, where the enemy is still in force, or to return to agriculture. . . .

"I know that the President heretofore was favorable to the measure, and I am fully convinced that he believes, with me, now, that if it had been then

carried out, millions of money would have been saved to the treasury. . . ."
(DLC-RTL).

Rosecrans' eight-page letter of September 15 concluded: "Under all the circumstances of the case I would respectfully recommend prompt action and an early anouncement of the approval of the contract. . . ." (*Ibid.*).

To William H. Seward[1]

I would like for Mr. Dudley and Mr. Scovel to be obliged in this matter. A. LINCOLN

March 10. 1864

[1] AES, DNA FS RG 59, Appointments, Box 293. Lincoln's endorsement is written on a letter from Thomas H. Dudley, consul at Liverpool, England, December 29, 1863, recommending George W. Gilbert of Camden, New Jersey. James M. Scovel also recommended Gilbert's appointment, but no record of an appointment has been found.

To Edwin M. Stanton[1]

March 10, 1864

The widow of Commander Ward of the Navy, killed at Mathia's Point early in the war appeals to me to discharge her son, who has enlisted in the New York 6th. . . . For the memory of his father and that his mother is an indigent widdow, let him be discharged.

[1] American Art Association Anderson Galleries Catalog 4115, May 17, 1934, No. 180. According to the catalog description, this partial text is taken from an autograph letter signed. Commander James H. Ward was killed on June 27, 1861, in action at Mathias Point on the Potomac. His son, Frederick B. Ward, is mentioned in his obituary as being present at his father's death, but identification of the son enlisted in the Sixth New York Volunteers has not been made.

To W. F. M. Arny[1]

March 12, 1864

I shall not be hasty about the matter mentioned. Mr. Perea never asked for your removal, at least, never to me, till very recently; and then only as I understood him, because you had left your post and come here to meddle with him and his business. I only wish now you were at your post attending to it's duties.

March 12. 1864 A. LINCOLN

[1] AES, owned by Herman Blum, Blumhaven Library, Philadelphia, Pennsylvania. Lincoln's endorsement is written on a letter from W. F. M. Arny, Secretary of New Mexico, February 11, 1864:

"I understand that Mr. Perea is pressing my removal

"Do me the favor to postpone any action in the matter till I can—prepare my reply to the charges which I will do next week."

Francisco Perea was delegate to congress from New Mexico.

To Benjamin F. Butler[1]

Office U.S. Military Telegraph,
Major General Butler   War Department,
Fort-Monroe, Va   Washington, D.C., March 12 1864.

If Miss Gaston and Miss Manly still refuse to take the oath let
them return South.   A LINCOLN

1 ALS, DNA WR RG 107, Presidential Telegrams, I, 4. General Butler telegraphed on March 11: "Miss Gaston and Miss Manly friends of Mr Blair
have come to this point upon your order. They refuse to take the oath of
allegiance. They understand they are coming on a visit only to their friends
in Maryland, and are soon to return south. What shall be done, wish return
or send them to Baltimore?" (DLC-RTL). Miss Gaston and Miss Manly have
not been further identified.

To William M. Fishback[1]

Office U.S. Military Telegraph,
William Fishback   War Department,
Fort-Smith, Ark.   Washington, D.C., March 12 1864.

I know not that any change of departmental lines is likely to
be made in Arkansas; but if done, it will be for purely military
reasons, to which the good people there can have no just cause of
objection. Get out the largest vote you can, and the largest part
of them on the right side which is possible   A. LINCOLN

1 ALS, DNA WR RG 107, Presidential Telegrams, I, 3. Lincoln received
telegrams on March 12 from William Fishback and Governor Isaac Murphy,
protesting news from Fort Smith that several counties of Northwest Arkansas
were to be attached to the Department of Kansas (DLC-RTL).

General Orders No. 98[1]

War Department
General Orders⎫   Washington City,
    No. 98 ⎭   March 12th, 1864.

The President of the United States orders as follows:

I. Major General H. W. Halleck is, at his own request, relieved
from duty as General-in-Chief of the Army, and Lieutenant General U. S. Grant is assigned to the command of the Armies of
the United States. The Head Quarters of the Army will be in
Washington, and also with Lieutenant General Grant in the field.

II. Major General H. W. Halleck is assigned to duty in Washington as Chief of Staff of the Army, under the direction of the
Secretary of War and the Lieutenant General commanding. His
orders will be obeyed and respected accordingly.

III. Major General W. T. Sherman is assigned to the command of the Military Division of the Mississippi, composed of the Departments of the Ohio, the Cumberland, the Tennessee, and the Arkansas.

IV. Major General J. B. McPherson is assigned to the command of the Department and Army of the Tennessee.

By order of the Secretary of War

¹ D, DNA WR RG 94, Adjutant General, Letters Received, P 1578. Although not written by Lincoln nor signed by him as issued, this order was indubitably drafted at his direction and probably at his personal dictation in response to Halleck's letter to Stanton of March 9, which Stanton referred to the president on the same day with a request for instructions:

"Under the provisions of the Act of April 4th 1862, which authorizes the President to assign to command officers *of the same grade*, without regard to *seniority*, of *rank*, the undersigned, a Major General, was assigned, in July 1862, to the command of the land forces of the United States. Since that time the higher grade of Lieutenant General has been created, and the distinguished officer promoted to that rank has received his armies now and reported for duty. I, therefore, respectfully request that orders be issued placing him in command of the Army and retiring me from that duty. In making this request I am influenced solely by a desire to conform to the provisions of the law, which, in my opinion impose upon the Lieutenant General the duties and responsibilities of General in Chief of the Army." (DLC-RTL).

To Isaac Murphy¹

Office U.S. Military Telegraph,
Gov. Murphy   War Department,
Little Rock, Ark.   Washington, D.C., March 12 1864.

I am not appointing officers for Arkansas now, and I will try to remember your request. Do your best to get out the largest vote possible; and, of course, as much of it as possible on the right side

A. LINCOLN

¹ ALS, DNA WR RG 107, Presidential Telegrams, I, 2. Governor Murphy telegraphed on March 11, 1864: "I respectfully ask you to issue no commissions and to make no appointments of any kind for Ark. until the fate of our present earnest and hopeful efforts to restore our State to the Union is determined and the undoubted union men have time to be heard from." (DLC-RTL).

Pass for Mrs. J. R. Reid¹

Allow Mrs. J. R. Reid, with her child, to take the oath of Dec. 8, 1863, and pass our lines at City-Point, and go North.

March 12, 1864.   A. LINCOLN.

¹ Hertz, II, 923.

To the Senate[1]

Executive Office

To the Senate of the United States: March 12 1864.

In obedience to the resolution of the Senate of the 28th of January last, I communicate herewith a report, with accompanying papers, from the Secretary of the Interior, showing what portion of the appropriations for the colonization of persons of African descent has been expended, and the several steps which have been taken for the execution of the Acts of Congress on that subject.

ABRAHAM LINCOLN

[1] DS, DNA RG 46, Senate 38A F6. The "12" in the date was filled in by Lincoln. On March 14, this communication was read in the Senate and referred to the select committee on slavery and freedmen. No record of Usher's report has been found in published Executive Documents or in the National Archives. See Lincoln's further communication to the Senate on this subject, June 29, *infra*.

To Edwin M. Stanton[1]

Hon. Sec. of War   Executive Mansion,
My dear Sir: Washington, March 12, 1864.

Gov. Smith of Rhode Island brings you this. Please give him a full hearing. After a pretty full talk with him, it seems to me that the one thing most likely to surmount the difficulty there, would be to not consolidate the 1st. & 3rd. Cavalry, but preserve them both, the Governor to exert himself to the utmost to fill both. The consolidation throws out one set of officers, and which ever set it may be, it offends either the Governor or a U.S. Senator. We can not afford to offend either, while we can avoid it. Please try. There is also a difficulty about Capt. Silvey, upon which I hope you will fully hear the Governor.[2] Yours truly   A. LINCOLN

[1] ALS, NHi.
[2] AGO *Special Orders No. 124*, March 22, 1864, ordered Captain Wesley Owens, Fifth U.S. Cavalry, to relieve Captain William Silvey, First U.S. Artillery, as chief mustering and disbursing officer for Rhode Island.

To Lewis Wallace[1]

March 12, 1864

Will Major General Lewis Wallace please join some other General officers to a Dinner at the Executive Mansion at 6-45 o'clock, this evening.   A. LINCOLN

March 12, 1864.

[1] ALS, InHi. See Lincoln's invitation to Grant and Meade, March 10, *supra*. No reply from General Wallace has been found.

To Gideon Welles[1]

[c. March 12, 1864]

Has the Sec. of the Navy any knowledge of this case? and if any, what?   A LINCOLN

[1] AES, DLC-RTL. Lincoln's endorsement is written on a letter of Joshua Hanna, Pittsburgh, Pennsylvania, to Stanton, March 12, 1864:

"The bearer Capt. Lewis F L Vandegrift of this city had his boat taken from him by the Navy under a charge of violating the laws while in the employment of the War department.

"I have known Capt. V. for many years, and have had a business transaction with [him] for several years. I have no doubt of his honesty or loyalty nor do I believe any citizen of Pittsburgh would believe him guilty of the charge. . . ." (DLC-RTL).

Welles replied on March 19: "I would respectfully state that this Department has not been furnished by Rear Admiral Porter with a full report of the seizure. On the 20th ult. . . he forwarded to me an appraisement of the vessel, stating that she had been captured some time since for 'illicit trading, robbing plantations &c.' and that owing to the scarcity of transports he had obtained permission from the Judge of the District to use her for Government service. The 'Volunteer' was appraised at Twenty-five thousand dollars . . . and a requisition for that sum was drawn by this Department for the payment of the same.

"You will thus perceive that the case is in the hands of the District Court at Springfield, Ill., and therefore, no longer under the control of this Department." (DLC-RTL).

To Meredith P. Gentry[1]

Hon. M. P. Gentry   Executive Mansion,
My dear Sir: Washington, March 13. 1864.

Yours by the hand of Gen. Grant is received. Of course I have not forgotten you, Gen. Grant is hereby authorized, in his discretion, to send you South; and it is rather my wish that he may find it not inconsistent with his view of the public interest to oblige you. Yours truly   A. LINCOLN

[1] ADfS, DLC-RTL. Gentry's letter of February 3, 1864, reminded Lincoln of their early acquaintance when they were members of congress. Elected to the Confederate Congress, Gentry was ill at his home in Shelbyville, Tennessee, when Confederate forces retreated. Permitted to remain for some time without taking an oath of allegiance to the Union, he was later ordered to take the oath or go to prison: "They decided that I should either go beyond the Federal lines southward or be sent a Prisoner to Camp Chase. . . . When the case came before Genl Rouseau he took no other action upon it, except to extend the Parol which had been given me at Shelbyville specifically to the 21st of Febr Inst—at which time my term as a member of the Confederate Congress expired. I am now at this City (Nashville) to solicit his final decision. Genl Grants Head Quarters being here Genl Rouseau has introduced me to Genl Grant & I expressed to him my wish to be discharged from arrest and to recieve from him a pass to go south with the privilege of returning when I

shall have attended to business in that region which if *not promptly and suc-cessfully attended to, will* involve me & mine, in complete & entire *pecuniary ruin.* Genl Grant whilst giving a courteous hearing to my application seems to think that it would be irregular for him to decide upon the case, and has suggested that . . . I should apply directly to you . . . and has consented to forward my Letter, with such endorsement upon it as will attract your at-tention. . . ." (DLC-RTL).

To Michael Hahn[1]

Private   Executive Mansion,
Hon. Michael Hahn   Washington,
My dear Sir: March 13. 1864.

I congratulate you on having fixed your name in history as the first-free-state Governor of Louisiana. Now you are about to have a Convention which, among other things, will probably define the elective franchise. I barely suggest for your private consideration, whether some of the colored people may not be let in—as, for in-stance, the very intelligent, and especially those who have fought gallantly in our ranks. They would probably help, in some trying time to come, to keep the jewel of liberty within the family of freedom. But this is only a suggestion, not to the public, but to you alone. Yours truly   A. LINCOLN

[1] ALS, owned by Roger W. Barrett, Chicago, Illinois; ADfS, DLC-RTL. In an election held on February 22, 1864, Michael Hahn defeated Benjamin F. Flanders and J. Q. A. Fellows for governor. The new constitution drafted by the convention which met beginning April 6 and adopted at an election held on September 5, 1864, contained no provisions for Negro suffrage.

To Carl Schurz[1]

Private.   Executive Mansion,
Major General Schurz   Washington,
My dear Sir: March 13, 1864.

Yours of February 29th, reached me only four days ago; but the delay was of little consequence, because I found, on feeling around, I could not invite you here without a difficulty which at least would be unpleasant, and perhaps would be detrimental to the public service. Allow me to suggest that if you wish to remain in the military service, it is very dangerous for you to get tem-porarily out of it; because, with a Major General once out, it is next to impossible for even the President to get him in again. With my appreciation of your ability, and correct principle, of course I would be very glad to have your service for the country

in the approaching political canvass; but I fear we can not properly have it, without separating you from the military. Yours truly
                                                                    A. LINCOLN

[1] LS copy, DLC-RTL. The signed copy preserved in the Lincoln Papers is followed immediately by the autograph draft of Lincoln's letter to Schurz of March 23, *infra*, which explains that the original letter of March 13 was never received by Schurz. On February 29, 1864, Schurz wrote Lincoln from New York:

"Yesterday I arrived here on a short leave of absence. It was my intention to attend the meeting of the National Committee on the 22d but I could not leave my command in time on account of Gen. Howard's absence.

"I should be glad to have a conversation with you about political matters and should already have called upon you but for the necessity of having first the permission of the War Dept. to go to Washington. An arrangement might perhaps be made which might render it possible for me to take an active part in the presidential canvass. Things seem to be in a somewhat confused state, and . . . I . . . fear the consequences of the contest now being carried on inside of the Union-party. . . .

"If it should be agreeable to you to see me at Washington, please let me know as soon as convenient—not to forget the required permission from the War Dept., as I should not like to be arrested.

"I am very glad you gave Sigel the Dept. of West-Virginia. It was a very judicious measure in every respect.

"Have you heard already of the difficulties between Gen. Hooker and myself, of the court of inquiry I demanded and obtained and of the opinion of that court in my favor and against Hooker? If you have been informed of what happened there, you will already have come to the conclusion that it is impossible for me to continue in my command . . . and ardently hope that the rumor about Gen. Hooker's being transferred . . . in consequence of Gen. Grant's and Thomas' representations to the War Dept., prove true. . . ." (DLC-RTL).

On March 8, Schurz wrote again: "Several days ago . . . I wrote you a few lines for the purpose of bringing about an interview with you at which we might exchange our views on pending political questions. I requested you to let me know whether this would be agreeable. . . . I desire to have that interview . . . not only because I am as warm a friend of our common cause as ever, but your friend also. Waiting for a few words in reply in vain, I have come to the conclusion that either you did not receive my letter or do not desire me to visit Washington. If the latter should be the case it would oblige me by simply advising me of it. My leave will soon expire. . . ." (*Ibid.*). See further, Lincoln's letter to Schurz, March 23, *infra*.

To Benjamin F. Butler[1]

Major General Butler   Executive Mansion,
Fort-Monroe, Va.   Washington, March 14, 1864.

1 Lieut, and Adjt. of 6. Wisconsin Volunteers, Edward P. Brooks is a prisoner of War at Richmond; and if you can, without difficulty, effect a special exchange for him, I shall be obliged.
                                                                    A. LINCOLN

[1] ALS, DNA WR RG 107, Presidential Telegrams, I, 5. General Butler's telegram in reply was received at 6:25 P.M.: "Lieut. Brooks will be sent for-

ward for special exchange and I have no doubt the exchange will be effected."
(DLC-RTL). See also Lincoln to Butler, March 18, *infra*.

Draft Order for 200,000 Men[1]

Executive Mansion.
Washington, March 14th 1864.

In order to supply the force required to be drafted for the Navy,
and to provide an adequate reserve force for all contingencies,—
in addition to the five hundred thousand men called for February
1st. 1864, a call is hereby made and a draft ordered for two hundred thousand men for the "military service" (Army, Navy, and
Marine Corps) of the United States.

The proportional quotas for the different wards, towns, townships, precincts or election districts, or counties, will be made
known through the Provost Marshal General's Bureau, and account will be taken of the credits and deficiencies on former
quotas.

The 15th. day of April, 1864, is designated as the time up to
which the numbers required from each "ward of a city, town," &c.
may be raised by voluntary enlistment, and drafts will be made
in "each ward of a city, town," &c. which shall not have filled the
quota assigned to it within the time designated, for the number
required to fill said quotas. The draft will be commenced as soon
after the 15th. of April as practicable.

The Government bounties, as now paid, continue until April
1st, 1864, at which time the additional bounties cease. On and
after that date, one hundred dollars bounty only will be paid, as
provided by the act approved July 22d. 1861.

ABRAHAM LINCOLN

[1] DS, IHi. This order was issued as AGO *General Orders No. 100*, March
15, 1864.

Endorsement[1]

If this womans husband is in our service, let her have transportation home. A LINCOLN

March. 14. 1864

[1] AES, owned by C. Norton Owen, Glencoe, Illinois. Lincoln's endorsement is
written on a letter signed "Mrs. Sterry" and addressed to Mrs. Lincoln, March
15: "The bearer of this note has a Husband in the 153d regt (that have gone
to Texas) and she is left destitute. It will be a deed of charity for you to help
her she wants to get home she has no friends here is stranger in the City
she is a nice respectable Old Lady."

Memorandum:
Appointment of Thornton A. Jenkins, Jr.[1]

Capt. Fox is very anxious for this young man.   A. LINCOLN
March 14, 1864.

[1] AES, DNA WR RG 94, U.S. Military Academy, 1864, No. 309. Lincoln's endorsement is written on a letter of Gustavus V. Fox to Nicolay, March 14, 1864, introducing Thornton A. Jenkins, Jr., and requesting an interview for him. There is no record of an appointment for Jenkins.

To the Senate[1]

To the Senate,   Executive Mansion,
of the United States.   Washington, March [14], 1864.
I transmit, herewith, a report of the Secretary of the Interior, of the 11th instant, containing the information requested in Senate Resolution of the 29th ultimo.   ABRAHAM LINCOLN

[1] DS, DNA RG 46, Senate 38A F6. This communication is docketed by the clerk as read in the Senate on March 14, referred to the committee on Indian affairs, and ordered to be printed, but the *Senate Journal* supplies the date as March 8, which is obviously incorrect in view of enclosures dated March 10 and March 11, 1864. Senator James H. Lane's resolution of February 29, 1864, requested the president to furnish "the amount of money received by the government for the sale of the Wea trust lands in Kansas, and the manner in which said money was invested; if in State bonds, what states, and whether the interest of said State bonds has been paid; and if any of said bonds were stolen, what ones, and what provision has been made for the bonds so stolen." Concerning the so-called "Russell Fraud," see note to Lincoln's letter to Bates, March 11, 1861, *supra*. Secretary Usher's report of March 11, 1864, transmitted with Lincoln's communication *supra*, may be found in *Senate Executive Document No. 28*.

To the Senate and House of Representatives[1]

March 14, 1864
To the Senate and House of Representatives:
I transmit to Congress a copy of a Treaty between the United States and Great Britain, for the final settlement of the claims of the Hudson's Bay and Puget's Sound Agricultural Companies, concluded on the 1st. of July, last, the ratifications of which were exchanged in this City, on the 5th. instant; and recommend an appropriation to carry into effect the first, second, and third articles thereof.   ABRAHAM LINCOLN
Washington, 14th. March, 1864.

[246]

1 DS, DNA RG 46, Senate 38A F2; DS, DNA RG 233, House Executive Document No. 54. The first, second, and third articles of the treaty provided for the appointment of a commissioner to investigate rights of the Hudson Bay and Puget Sound Agricultural Companies. An act approved June 27, 1864, authorized the president to appoint a commissioner and a clerk and appropriated necessary funds.

To the Senate and House of Representatives[1]

March 14, 1864

To the Senate and House of Representatives:

On the 25th. day of November 1862, a Convention for the mutual adjustment of claims pending between the United States and Ecuador, was signed at Quito by the plenipotentiaries of the contracting parties. A copy is herewith enclosed.

This Convention, already ratified by this Government, has been sent to Quito for the customary exchange of ratifications, which it is not doubted will be promptly effected. As the stipulations of the instrument require that the Commissioners who are to be appointed pursuant to its provisions shall meet at Guayaquil within ninety days after such exchange, it is desirable that the legislation necessary to give effect to the Convention on the part of the United States, should anticipate the usual course of proceeding. I therefore invite the early attention of Congress to the subject.   ABRAHAM LINCOLN

Washington March 14, 1864.

1 DS, DNA RG 46, Senate 38A F2; DS, DNA RG 233, House Executive Document No. 55. An act approved March 28, 1864, authorized appointment of a commissioner and appropriated necessary funds.

Endorsement Concerning Churches in New Orleans[1]

March 15, 1864

While I leave this case to the discretion of Gen. Banks, my view is, that the U.S. should not appoint trustees for or in any way take charge of any church as such. If the building is needed for military purposes, take it; if it is not so needed, let its church people have it, dealing with any disloyal people among them, as you deal with other disloyal people.   A. LINCOLN

March 15th. 1864

1 Copy, DLC-RTL. The copy of Lincoln's endorsement is on a copy of a letter from Elijah Guion, Thomas Sloo, and John B. Morison, of New Orleans,

March 5, 1864, complaining of an order by General James Bowen requiring them to surrender the keys and property of St. Paul's Church.

To Ulysses S. Grant[1]

Private   Executive Mansion
Lieut. Genl. Grant   Washington, D.C.
Nashville, Tenn.   March 15. 1864

Gen. McPherson having been assigned to the command of a Department, could not Gen. Frank Blair without difficulty or detriment to the service, be assigned to command the corps he commanded a while last autumn?   A LINCOLN

[1] ALS, DNA WR RG 107, Presidential Telegrams, I, 6. Grant replied on March 16: "General Logan commands the corps referred to in your despatch. I will see General Sherman within a few days and consult him about the transfer, and answer." On March 17 Grant telegraphed again: "General Sherman is here. He consents to the transfer of General Logan to the seventeenth corps and the appointment of General F. P. Blair to the fifteenth corps." On March 26 General John A. Logan telegraphed: "I understand by the papers that it is contemplated to make a change of commanders of the 15th and 17th army corps, so as to transfer me to the 17th. I hope this will not be done. I fully understand the organization of the 15th corps now . . . I . . . earnestly hope that the change may not be made." Finally Grant notified Sherman on March 31 that "General F. P. Blair will be assigned to the seventeenth (17th) corps, and not the fifteenth, (15th.). . . ." (Thirty-eighth Congress, First Session, *House Executive Document No. 80*, pp. 4-5).

AGO *General Orders No. 98*, March 12, 1864, assigned McPherson to command the Department of the Tennessee and Sherman to replace Grant in command of the Military Division of the Mississippi. AGO *General Orders No. 178*, April 23, 1864, assigned Blair to command the Seventeenth Army Corps. See Lincoln to Stanton, April 21, and to the House of Representatives, April 28, *infra*.

To Michael Hahn[1]

His Excellency   Executive Mansion,
Michael Hahn   Washington,
Governor of Louisiana   March 15. 1864.

Until further order, you are hereby invested with the powers exercised hitherto by the Military Governor of Louisiana. Yours truly   ABRAHAM LINCOLN

[1] ALS-P, ISLA. With this letter Lincoln enclosed copies of the commission of General George F. Shepley and War Department instructions to Shepley of June 3, 1862 (OR, III, IV, 182). On April 6 Governor Hahn wrote Lincoln: "Your private letter of . . . the 13th and official letter of the 15th . . . came duly to hand. I thank you sincerely for the kind and confiding manner in which you have always treated me, and I can only promise in return that besides doing all in my power towards the restoration of the Union, I shall feel pleasure in seeing it restored under *your* administration. . . ." (DLC-RTL).

To Edwin M. Stanton[1]

If the vacancy has not been filled, let the within request be granted.   A. LINCOLN

March 15. 1864

[1] AES, owned by Harry E. Blake, Alhambra, California. Lincoln's endorsement is written on a letter from Senator James R. Doolittle and others, March 12, 1864, asking reappointment of Captain Edward Sanford Blake of Wisconsin who had resigned because of illness on October 6, 1863. No record of his reappointment has been found.

To Edwin M. Stanton[1]

Hon. Sec. of War   Executive Mansion,
My dear Sir   Washington, March 15. 1864.

Please see the gallant Drummer-boy, Robert H. Hendershot, whose history is briefly written on the fine drum presented him which he now carries. He must have a chance, and if you can find any situation suitable to him, I shall be obliged. Yours truly

                                   A. LINCOLN

[1] ALS, IHi. Robert H. Hendershot of the Eighth Michigan Volunteers, born in December, 1850, was barely twelve years old when he distinguished himself at the Battle of Fredericksburg on December 13, 1862. He was discharged for disability at Falmouth, Virginia, December 27, 1862, and accounts of his exploits in the Battle of Murfreesboro, are unreliable. Following his discharge, he became something of a celebrity and an attraction at Barnum's Museum. His drum, referred to by Lincoln, was the present of the Tribune Association of New York. There is no record of his appointment by Stanton, but he was eventually employed as messenger in the office of U.S. Treasurer Francis E. Spinner who recommended that he be appointed to West Point on January 1, 1865 (see Lincoln's endorsement of January 1, 1865, *infra*). According to William S. Dodge, *Robert Henry Hendershot; or, The Brave Drummer Boy of the Rappahannock* (Chicago, 1867), his appointment was the last one Lincoln made for West Point, but no record has been found of his entrance. See also Frank Moore, *The Civil War in Song and Story, 1860-1865* (New York, 1889), pp. 245-46.

To Edwin M. Stanton[1]

Hon. Sec. of War   Executive Mansion,
Dear Sir: Washington, March 15, 1864.

I understand a question exists as to the *time* the Pennsylvania Reserve Corps' term expires. Let them have their own way upon that, unless it would cause very considerable injury. Yours truly

                                   A. LINCOLN

[1] ALS, ORB. On March 4, 1864 Governor Curtin wrote Lincoln: "In May, 1861, the Legislature of Pennsylvania directed fifteen regiments to be raised,

subsisted, and instructed by the State, to be called the Pennsylvania Reserve Corps. . . . This division was enlisted for three years, and sworn into the service of the State in . . . June and July, 1861, and was to be turned over to the United States whenever it should be called for. . . . After the battle of Bull Run the whole division was wanted by the United States. . . . The three years for which the men enlisted count from the date of their being mustered into the service of the State. They are now told . . . that they will be held for three years from the date of their being mustered into the service of the United States. The United States may thus gain a few days, or even a month's service, at the expense of creating dissatisfaction and losing the men for a new period of three years. . . ." (OR, I, XXXIII, 636-38).

On April 30 Thomas M. Vincent instructed General Meade to discharge the men as of the date of their state muster. (*Ibid.*, p. 1032).

To Edwin M. Stanton[1]

Private   Executive Mansion,

Hon. Sec. of War   Washington,

My dear Sir,   March 15, 1864..

I shall be personally obliged if you will allow Silas H. Highley to take the oath of Dec. 8. and be discharged. Yours truly

A. LINCOLN

P.S. He is at Alton, Illinois.   A L.

[1] ALS, NHi. Edward Bates' *Diary* under date of March 15, 1864, notes that "I have succeeded, at last, in getting the order for the discharge of young Silas Highley, of St. Joe . . . and his father, the old Captain, has gone home rejoicing, with the order in his pocket."

To Whom It May Concern[1]

Executive Mansion, Washington,

Whom it may concern.   March 15. 1864.

Major General Sickles is making a tour for me from here by way of Cairo, New-Orleans, and returning by the Gulf and Ocean; and all Land and Naval officers and employees, are directed to furnish reasonable transportation and other reasonable facilities to himself and personal Staff, not inconsistent with the public service.   ABRAHAM LINCOLN

[1] ALS copy, DLC-RTL. See Lincoln to Steele, February 25, *supra*.

To Isaac Murphy[1]

Office U.S. Military Telegraph,

Gov. Isaac Murphy   War Department,

Little Rock, Ark   Washington, D.C., March 16th. 1864.

What of your election on the 14th.?   A. LINCOLN

¹ ALS, DNA WR RG 107, Presidential Telegrams, I, 7. Governor Murphy's reply sent on March 16, was received at 1 A.M. on March 17: "Polls close tonight twelve (12) M. We are confident of victory A heavy vote here, not counted, will send results as soon as known." (DLC-RTL).

To Benjamin F. Butler¹

Major General Butler Executive Mansion,
Fort-Monroe, Va Washington, March 17, 1864.
If you obtain the remains of Col. Dahlgren, please notify me instantly, so that I can let his afflicted know A. LINCOLN

¹ ALS, DNA WR RG 107, Presidential Telegrams, I, 9. See Lincoln to Butler, March 7, *supra*. Butler replied the same day, "The President shall be informed of the arrival of Col Dahlgren's remains at the earliest possible moment. Probably on Sunday" (DLC-Butler Papers).

To John A. J. Creswell¹

Hon. John A. J. Creswell Executive Mansion,
My dear Sir: Washington, March 17, 1864.
It needs not to be a secret, that I wish success to emancipation in Maryland. It would aid much to end the rebellion. Hence it is a matter of national consequence, in which every national man, may rightfully feel a deep interest. I sincerely hope the friends of the measure will allow no minor considerations to divide and distract them. Yours truly A. LINCOLN

¹ ALS-F, ISLA; ADfS, DLC-RTL. See Lincoln to Creswell, March 7, *supra*. The new Maryland constitution, drafted by the convention which met at Annapolis on April 27, and adopted at the election of October 12 and 13, 1864, prohibited slavery by its Article Twenty-three.

Order for Discharge of Christopher C. Callan and Daniel R. Payne¹

March 17, 1864
Let Christopher C. Callan and Daniel R. Payne, named within, take the oath of Dec. 8, and be discharged and remain hereabouts for the object within indicated A. LINCOLN
March 17, 1864

¹ AES, owned by R. E. Burdick, New York City. Lincoln's endorsement is written on a letter from Judge John C. Underwood, U.S. District Court, Alexandria, Virginia, March 14, 1864, asking discharge of Captain Christopher C. Callan and Private Daniel R. Payne, Confederate deserters, who had "cheerfully given most important testimony for the government" and would be important witnesses in other cases.

To William S. Rosecrans[1]

Major Gen'l Rosecrans.   Executive Mansion,
St: Louis, Mo.   Washington, March 17th. 1864.
 Suspend execution of death sentence of John T. Abshier, citizen,
until further orders.   A. LINCOLN.

Maj: Eckert
 Please send the above dispatch   JNO. G. NICOLAY
             Priv: Sec

 [1] D, DNA WR RG 107, Presidential Telegrams, I, 8. The telegram is in the
handwriting of Edward Neill, and signed by Nicolay. No reply has been found.
John T. Abshier, citizen of Missouri, was sentenced to be hanged for murder
and "violation of laws and customs of war." General Rosecrans recommended
commutation to imprisonment because of Abshier's youth and the loyalty of
his family. On February 9, 1864, however, Lincoln approved the death sentence (DNA WR RG 153, Judge Advocate General, MM 1001). AGO *Special
Orders No. 134,* April 1, 1864, commuted the sentence to imprisonment.

To Benjamin F. Butler[1]

Major General Butler,   Executive Mansion,
Fortress Monroe.   Washington, March 18th, 1864.
 Edward P. Brooks, 1st Lieutenant 6th Wisconsin, is a prisoner of
war, at Richmond. I desire, that if practicable his special exchange
be effected for a rebel prisoner of same rank. Have you one to
send, and can you arrange it at once?   A. LINCOLN

Maj: Eckert
 Please send the above dispatch   JNO. G. NICOLAY
             Priv: Sec

 [1] D, DNA WR RG 107, Presidential Telegrams, I, 11. The telegram is in
the handwriting of Edward Neill and signed by Nicolay. See Lincoln to Butler,
March 14, *supra.* Butler replied the same day: "The exchange desired has been
proposed. Boat leaves tonight." (DLC-Butler Papers). On March 23 he wrote
further: "I have the honor to report to you the exchange of Edward P. Brooks,
1st. Lieut. 6th. Regt. Wis. Vols, concerning whom you telegraphed me the
other day. He is now on board the Flag of Truce boat which has just returned from City Point. The boat brought down more than nine hundred
(900) men and sixty three (63) officers. I have the honor also to enclose an
open letter sent by the same Flag of Truce directed to yourself. . . ." (DLC-
RTL).

Endorsement Concerning Benjamin A. Watson[1]

            March 18, 1864
The writer of this resides in my town, is an intimate acquaintance
and friend, and is of good character, and good qualification for the

business he seeks to be engaged in. I know nothing of the particular case.   A. LINCOLN

March 18. 1864

1 AES, IHi. Lincoln's endorsement is written on a letter from Benjamin A. Watson of W. W. Watson & Son, confectioners at Springfield, Illinois, March 12, 1864:

"There is some talk about town that there will be a 'Post Sutler' appointed for 'Camp Butler'

"I have an appointment from Gov Yates under which I have bought a stock of goods for the Camp, if there is to be any change made at Camp Butler, am I asking too much of you to say to Mr Stanton to give me the commission of 'Post Sutler' for 'Camp Butler.'"

No further reference has been found.

To Isaac Murphy[1]

Office U.S. Military Telegraph,
Gov. Murphy   War Department,
Little-Rock, Ark.   Washington, D.C. March 18. 1864.

Yours of yesterday received, & thanks for it. Send further returns when you receive them. Will do my best to protect people and new State government, but can act with no better intentions than have always done. Tell Gen. Steele I have Randolph's pardon[2] & will send by mail if he says so.   A. LINCOLN

1 ALS, DNA WR RG 107, Presidential Telegrams, I, 10. Governor Murphy's telegram of March 17 is as follows: "Only eight counties heard from they give 3,556 votes—only 137 votes against constitution. We feel sure of 10,000 when the other counties are heard from & soldiers vote obtained. Guerrillas made immense efforts to hinder the election. The people are full of enthusiasm but much alarmed Will you give them assurance of the energetic protection of the government—praise be to God!" (DLC-RTL).

A telegram from Murphy sent on March 22 but not received until March 27, is as follows: "More than eight Thousand (8000) votes reported, the entire vote will exceed ten thousand (10,000) the people have been enthusiastic in view of the protection of law voting in immense risk of loss of life & property, the guerrilas having threatened to hang every one, that went to the polls. Should the army leave the line of the Arkansas unprotected terror would prevail the state. Will the Gov't accept of two (2) regts. of artillery, one (1) black & a regt of Cavalry armed for pursuit of guerrilas. The swamps & mountains are full of armed rebels waiting for the movement of the army to pounce upon unprotected points. . . . As it is, the risk is great. All may be lost that has been gained by the election. We need arms to arm the loyal. . . ." (DLC-RTL).   2 See Lincoln to Bates, March 7, supra.

Remarks at Closing of Sanitary Fair, Washington, D.C.[1]

March 18, 1864

Ladies and Gentlemen: I appear to say but a word. This extraordinary war in which we are engaged falls heavily upon all

[253]

classes of people, but the most heavily upon the soldier. For it has been said, all that a man hath will he give for his life; and while all contribute of their substance the soldier puts his life at stake, and often yields it up in his country's cause. The highest merit, then, is due to the soldier. [Cheers.]

In this extraordinary war extraordinary developments have manifested themselves, such as have not been seen in former wars; and amongst these manifestations nothing has been more remarkable than these fairs for the relief of suffering soldiers and their families. And the chief agents in these fairs are the women of America. [Cheers.]

I am not accustomed to the use of language of eulogy; I have never studied the art of paying compliments to women; but I must say that if all that has been said by orators and poets since the creation of the world in praise of woman were applied to the women of America, it would not do them justice for their conduct during this war. I will close by saying God bless the women of America! [Great applause.]

[1] Washington *Evening Star*, March 19, 1864. This item is misdated March 16, 1864, by Hertz (II, 923) and Lapsley (VII, 105). This is the most complete report of Lincoln's remarks which has been found. A briefer version appeared in the *Morning Chronicle* and other papers.

To Edwin M. Stanton[1]

Hon. Secretary of War:
My dear Sir:

Executive Mansion,
Washington, March 18. 1864.

I am so pressed in regard to prisoners of war in our custody, whose homes are within our lines, and who wish to not be exchanged, but to take the oath and be discharged, that I hope you will pardon me for again calling up the subject. My impression is that we will not ever force the exchange of any of this class; that taking the oath, and being discharged, none of them will again go to the rebellion, but the rebellion again coming to them, a considerable per centage of them, probably not a majority, would rejoin it; that by a cautious discrimination the number so discharged would not be large enough to do any considerable mischief in any event; would relieve 'distress in, at least some meritorious cases; and would give me some relief from an intolerable pressure.

[1] ALS, DLC-Stanton Papers; ADf, DLC-RTL. The letter sent to Stanton is reproduced as sent, but represents only the first paragraph of the draft. The remainder of the draft is reproduced following Lincoln's signature. Stanton replied on March 19: "Your order for the discharge of any prisoners of war, will be cheerfully & promptly obeyed." (DLC-RTL).

I shall be glad therefore to have your cheerful assent to the discharge of those whose names I may send, which I will only do with circumspection. Yours truly   A LINCOLN

In using the strong hand, as now compelled to do, the government has a difficult duty to perform. At the very best, it will by turns do both too little and too much. It can properly have no motive of revenge, no purpose to punish merely for punishment's sake. While we must, by all available means, prevent the overthrow of the government, we should avoid planting and cultivating too many thorns in the bosom of society. These general remarks apply to several classes of cases, on each of which I wish to say a word.

First, the dismissal of officers when neither incompetency, nor intentional wrong, nor real injury to the service, is imputed. In such cases it is both cruel and impolitic, to crush the man, and make him and his friends permanent enemies to the administration if not to the government itself. I think of two instances. One wherein a Surgeon, for the benefit of patients in his charge, needed some lumber, and could only get it by making a false certificate wherein the lumber was denominated "butter & eggs" and he was dismissed for the false certificate. The other a Surgeon by the name of Owen[2] who served from the beginning of the war till recently, with two servants, and without objection, when upon discovery that the servants were his own *sons,* he was dismissed.

Another class consists of those who are known or strongly suspected, to be in sympathy with the rebellion. An instance of this is the family of Southern,[3] who killed a recruiting officer last autumn, in Maryland. He fled, and his family are driven from their home, without a shelter or crumb, except when got by burthening our friends more than our enemies. Southern had no justification to kill the officer; and yet he would not have been killed if he had proceeded in the temper and manner agreed upon by yourself and Gov. Bradford. But this is past. What is to be done with the family? Why can they not occupy their old home, and excite much less opposition to the government than the manifestation of their distress is now doing? If the house is really needed for the public service; or if it has been regularly confiscated and the title transferred, the case is different.

[2] The only surgeon of this name who has been identified was Joshua J. Owen of Pennsylvania, appointed August 3, 1861, and mustered out on July 27, 1865. No record has been found of his dismissal.

[3] Concerning John H. Sothoron, see the note to Lincoln's telegram to Schenck, October 21, and Lincoln to Stanton, November 22, 1863, *supra.*

Again, the cases of persons, mostly women, wishing to pass our lines, one way or the other. We have, in some cases, been apparantly, if not really, inconsistent upon this subject—that is, we have forced some to go who wished to stay, and forced others to stay who wished to go. Suppose we allow all females, with ungrown children of either sex, to go South, if they desire, upon absolute prohibition against returning during the war; and all to come North upon the same condition of not returning during the war, and the additional condition of taking the oath.

I wish to mention two special cases—both of which you well remember. The first is that of Yocum.[4] He was unquestionably guilty. No one asking for his pardon pretends the contrary. What he did, however, was perfectly lawful, only a short while before, and the change making it unlawful had not, even then been fully accepted in the public mind. It is doubtful whether Yocum did not suppose it was really lawful to return a slave to a loyal owner, though it is certain he did the thing secretly, in the belief that his superiors would not allow it if known to them. But the great point

[4] See Lincoln to Holt, February 3 and endorsement February 16, *supra*. On March 24, Attorney General Bates wrote Secretary Seward:

"I am directed by the President to request you to issue a warrant for the pardon of William Yocum, with the following recital.

" 'Whereas one William Yocum was convicted by a General Court Martial sitting in Washington D.C. in January 1864, of aiding in kidnapping and abstracting an employee of the United States from the military service . . . and was sentenced to confinement at hard labor, for five years, in the Penitentiary at Albany N.Y.

" 'And whereas, previous to his said conviction, the said William Yokum had been a loyal and patriotic citizen, and a faithful and efficient servant of the Government;

" 'And whereas the said William Yokum is an aged man, and has a large family dependent on his labor for support; and has now suffered a sufficient punishment for the offence committed;

" 'And whereas Hon. G. Clay Smith, Hon. Lucian Anderson, Hon. Brutus J. Clay, Hon. W. H. Randall, Hon. S. L. Casey and many other highly respectable citizens have earnestly petitioned for his pardon;

" 'Now therefore &c: &c: &c:. . . . ' " (DLC-RTL).

Seward forwarded a copy to Stanton with a note to the effect that the requisition would not be complied with "until I shall learn your views on the subject." Stanton endorsed: "My views are that the President could commit no greater mistake, and in no way do the military service, his own administration, the sense of public justice & his own reputation so much harm as by granting this pardon and in the name of the Department, and on behalf of the colored people to whom the President has promised protection and emancipation I respectfully protest against the pardon of a man who while in the Military service gave a colored man under his command into the hands of a slave dealer to be sold & held in bondage. His crime in my judgment is greater than that of the African Slave trader and his pardon will in my opinion injure the government in the eyes of all civilized nations and destroy the faith of the colored man in the government." (*Ibid.*).

with me is that the severe punishment of five years at hard labor in the Penitentiary is not at all necessary to prevent the repetition of the crime by himself or by others. If the offence was one of frequent recurrence, the case would be different; but this case of Yocum is the single instance which has come to my knowledge. I think that for all public purposes, and for all proper purposes, he has suffered enough.

The case of Smithson is troublesome.[5] His wife and children are quartered mostly on our friends, and exciting a great deal of sympathy, which will soon tell against us. What think you of sending him and his family South, holding the sentence over him to be re-inforced if he returns during the war.

[5] See Lincoln's endorsement of August 1, 1863, *supra*. William T. Smithson was still in confinement in September, 1864.

To Benjamin F. Butler[1]

Major General Butler   Executive Mansion,
Fort-Monroe, Va   Washington, March 19, 1864.

Please find a Captain amo[ng] the rebel prisoners in your charge and exchange of for Capt. T. Ten Eyck, of 18th. U.S. Infantry, now a prisoner at Richmond.   A. LINCOLN

[1] ALS, DNA WR RG 107, Presidential Telegrams, I, 12. No reply has been located. See Lincoln's telegram to Butler, April 23, *infra*, concerning exchange of Tenodor Ten Eyck at request of Senator John C. Ten Eyck of New Jersey.

Order for Discharge of George B. Ackerman[1]

March 20, 1864

If George B. Ackerman, now a prisoner of War at Camp Douglas, Illinois, shall take the oath of December 8. 1863, and be discharged, I pledge my honor he will keep faith. HENRY WILSON

Let him take the oath and be discharged.   A. LINCOLN
March 20 1864

[1] AD and AES, IHi. The document is in Lincoln's autograph, excepting Wilson's signature.

To Montgomery Blair[1]

Post-Master-General   Executive Mansion,
My dear Sir   Washington, March 21, 1864.

These young ladies, Miss Dugger and Miss Beattie, are from Illinois, & want employment. They are loyal and worthy, and I

shall be very glad indeed if places can be found for them. Yours truly   A. LINCOLN

[1] ALS, owned by Richard F. Lufkin, Boston, Massachusetts. Miss Susan Dugger of Carlinville, Illinois, was given a job in the Post Office Department and later transferred to the Treasury Department, but no record of Miss Beattie's employment has been found.

To Clara and Julia Brown[1]

Executive Mansion Washington
Misses Clara & Julia Brown   March 21 1864

The Afgan you sent is received, and gratefully accepted. I especially like my little friends; and although you have never seen me, I am glad you remember me for the country's sake, and even more, that you remember, and try to help, the poor Soldiers. Yours very truly   A LINCOLN

[1] Copy, DLC-HW. This letter is misdated March 2, 1864, in Tracy (p. 238). The copy was sent to Herndon by H. C. Brown, Nyack on the Hudson, February 13, 1867: "I enclose one [letter] recd by by [sic] my little daughters (then 11 & 13 years old respectively). . . ." (*Ibid.*). A note on the bottom of the copy explains that a photograph of Clara and Julia was sent with the afghan. The letter from Clara and Julia, dated at Buffalo, New York, March 9, 1864, is as follows:

"Please accept this Afghan from your little friends who desire to express their regard. . . . The afghan was exhibited at the 'Central Fair' recently held here, and now we are very happy in sending it to our *Dear President.*

"Please remember that you have little friends in Buffalo who pray for you, that you may be *cheerful, strong* and *wise.*" (DLC-RTL).

Endorsement Concerning George W. Lane[1]

I approve the object of the within.   A. LINCOLN.
March 21, 1864.

[1] *Naval Records*, I, X, 164. Lincoln's endorsement is on a letter from Benjamin F. Butler, March 19, 1864, stating that George W. Lane of the steam tug *Philadelphia* should have permission to trade in Chowan County, North Carolina.

To Henry H. Lockwood[1]

March 21, 1864
So far as I know, the placing of Maj. Gen. Wallace in command at Baltimore, was not in consequence of any objection of any sort, to Gen. Lockwood. This much said in writing, I verbally explain a little further to Lt. Col Massey.   A. LINCOLN
March 21. 1864

[258]

1 AES, NNP. Lincoln's endorsement is written on a letter from Brigadier General Henry H. Lockwood, Headquarters, Middle Department, Baltimore, Maryland, March 21, 1864:

"When I had the honor to see Your excellency, you intimated that I would not be removed from the command of this Dept. except for cause. An order having been issued for my removal, I infer that there exists some cause. My object in troubling you with this letter is to know if this cause be personal military or political. If the latter then I have nothing more to say, as being no politician I cannot pretend to comprehend the operations of the political world. But if the cause be either personal or military, I hold my reputation too dear not to seek, very respectfully an explanation, and set the honored head of the state right, if any one has maligned me. This letter is taken by my confidential officer and friend Lt. Col. [George V.] Massey, who awaits a brief interview with you, and who being privy to all my doings can refute any erroneous impressions you may have recd. respecting me."

AGO *General Orders No. 97*, March 12, 1864, assigned Major General Lewis Wallace to command of the Middle Department.

Reply to New York Workingmen's Democratic Republican Association[1]

Gentlemen of the Committee.   March 21, 1864

The honorary membership in your Association, as generously tendered, is gratefully accepted.

You comprehend, as your address shows, that the existing rebellion, means more, and tends to more, than the perpetuation of African Slavery—that it is, in fact, a war upon the rights of all working people. Partly to show that this view has not escaped my attention, and partly that I cannot better express myself, I read a passage from the Message to Congress in December 1861:

"It continues to develop that the insurrection * * * * * * * * * * till all of liberty shall be lost."[2]

The views then expressed remain unchanged, nor have I much to add. None are so deeply interested to resist the present rebellion as the working people. Let them beware of prejudice, working division and hostility among themselves. The most notable feature of a disturbance in your city last summer, was the hanging of some working people by other working people. It should never be so. The strongest bond of human sympathy, outside of the family relation, should be one uniting all working people, of all nations, and tongues, and kindreds. Nor should this lead to a war upon property, or the owners of property. Property is the fruit of labor —property is desirable —— is a positive good in the world. That some should be rich, shows that others may become rich, and hence is just encouragement to industry and enterprize. Let not him who is houseless pull down the house of another; but let him labor diligently and build one for himself, thus by example assuring that his own shall be safe from violence when built.

¹ D, DLC-RTL. This manuscript, not in Lincoln's autograph, is probably a copy of the original of which no trace has been discovered. The New York *Tribune*, March 22, 1864, reported the occasion but gave an incomplete text of Lincoln's reply:

"A Committee on behalf of the New-York Workingmen's Democratic Republican Association today waited on the President to inform him that their association had elected him an honorary member. The object of the organization is to advance the workingmen of America in morals, position and loyalty; it binds them together in support of the Union, and induces them at all sacrifices to sustain it. They requested Mr. Lincoln to give his views on the subject matter of which their address treated."

² The passage indicated by ellipsis in the document may be found in volume v, 51-3.

To Edwin M. Stanton¹

Hon. Secretary of War.   Executive Mansion,
My dear Sir   Washington, March 21, 1864.

If there is on file a request of Gen. Meigs, that William Alexander may be appointed an Assistant Quarter-Master, with the rank of Captain, let him be appointed. Yours truly A. LINCOLN

¹ ALS-P, ISLA. No record has been found of William Alexander's appointment.

To Benjamin F. Butler¹

Major General Butler   Executive Mansion,
Fort-Monroe, Va   Washington, March 22. 1864.

Hon. W. R. Morrison, says he has requested you by letter to effect a special exchange of Lt. Col. A. F. Rogers, of 80th. Ills. Vols. now in Libby Prison and I shall be glad if you can effect it.

A LINCOLN

¹ ALS, DNA WR RG 107, Presidential Telegrams, I, 13. General Butler replied on the same day: "I had supposed that I had effected the exchange of Lieut Col [Andrew F.] Rogers of the 80th. Illinois, but when the prisoner came down, it was the wrong Col Rogers. However I will try again." (DLC-Butler Papers).

On Slavery¹

I never knew a man who wished to be himself a slave. Consider if you know any *good* thing, that no man desires for himself.
March 22, 1864   A. LINCOLN

1 ADS, CSmH. As first printed by Tracy (p. 239), this item was identified as having been written in an autograph album for a Sanitary Fair. It is no longer in an album, and the circumstances of its composition are unknown.

To the Senate[1]

To the Senate of the United States: March 22, 1864

I herewith lay before the Senate, for its constitutional action thereon, a treaty made and concluded in Washington City on the 18th instant, by and between William P. Dole, commissioner of Indian Affairs, and the Shawnee Indians, represented by their duly authorized delegates.

A report of the Secretary of the Interior and a communication of the Commissioner of Indian Affairs accompany the treaty.

ABRAHAM LINCOLN.

Executive Office, Washington, March 22d, 1864.

1 *Executive Journal*, XIII, 456. The treaty and accompanying documents were referred to the committee on Indian affairs and ordered to be printed, but on May 4, Senator Samuel C. Pomeroy presented a remonstrance against the treaty from the Chilicothe band of Shawnees. No further action seems to have been taken.

To Edwin M. Stanton[1]

If services needed let him be appointed.   A. LINCOLN
March 22. 1864

1 AES, RPB. Lincoln's endorsement is written on a letter of Colonel Lewis A. Grant, commanding the Second Brigade, Second Division, Sixth Corps, to Stanton, March 12, 1864, asking that First Lieutenant John W. Clark, quartermaster of the Sixth Vermont Volunteers, be appointed captain. Clark's appointment was confirmed by the Senate on April 7, 1864.

To George G. Meade[1]

Major General Meade   Executive Mansion,
Army of Potomac   Washington, March 23, 1864.

Please suspend execution of Alanson Orton, under sentence for desertion, until further order   A. LINCOLN

1 ALS, owned by R. E. Burdick, New York City. No reply has been found. See Lincoln to Meade, March 24, *infra. General Court Martial Orders No. 6*, March 4, 1864, ordered execution of "Allison Ortan," First Battalion, Twelfth Infantry, on March 25.

To Robert C. Schenck[1]

March 23, 1864

After the company left last evening, Mrs. L. made known to me a little matter which has annoyed me ever since . . . I beg to assure you that a programme was brought to me, exactly as I carried it out; and that I had not the slightest suspicion of a mistake. I am aware this is no great matter, not going beyond a little temporary embarrassment to any but myself; still I feel that this explanation is due all round, which I am sure you will believe is the truth, and nothing but the truth.

[1] Emily Driscoll Catalog 12, April, 1951, No. 126. The source describes this incomplete text as being from an autograph letter signed. Representative Schenck, chairman of the committee on military affairs, answered on the same day: "I am very sorry that you have felt annoyed in any way, or for a moment, by the little matter of last evening. I did not for an instant suppose that it was any thing but accidental, & without design, that Mrs. Lincoln's arrangement was not carried out; I should not have given it another thought, but for your note which I have just received. I pray you not to think of it again. . . ." (DLC-RTL).

To Carl Schurz[1]

Executive Mansion Washington,

Major General Schurz.   March 23. 1864

My dear Sir: The letter, of which the above is a copy, was sent to you, before Mr. Willmann saw me; and now yours of the 19th. tells me you did not receive it.

I do not wish to be more specific about the difficulty of your coming to Washington. I think you can easily conjecture it. I perceive no objection to your making a political speech when you are where one is to be made; but quite surely speaking in the North, and fighting in the South, at the same time, are not possible. Nor could I be justified to detail any officer to the political campaign during it's continuance, and then return him to the Army

[1] ADf, DLC-RTL. See Lincoln to Schurz, March 13, *supra*, a signed copy of which precedes this letter in the manuscript draft. On March 19 Schurz wrote Lincoln from New York:

"Mr. [Andreas] Willmann of this city, who delivered my last letter . . . was informed . . . that you had written to me in reply, but as I have received no letter whatever from you, there must be some mistake. . . . From what Mr. Willmann told me of his conversation with you I am led to believe that you consider my taking part in the electoral contest this summer as attended with some difficulty in asmuch as it would not be an easy thing to find a proper command and position for me afterwards. This as well as your silence upon my letters I can explain upon no other supposition than that you have entirely hindered my intentions.

"Under present circumstances I do not want to appear to feel bound by any

favor from anybody. If I can take an active part in the political contest consistently, with my position in the army, I shall be glad . . . expecting nothing for myself but to resume my old position . . . after the election. If a political activity be deemed inconsistent with my military position, I shall then have to make my choice. . . . I wish to assure you here emphatically, that in neither case I would make any demands on the administration. . . .

"About this and several other matters of a political nature. I desired to have a conversation with you. At a time like this I would not consider it out of place to volunteering advice and opinion about a few points of some importance. . . . It is somewhat difficult for me to understand why I do not receive this permission in reply to my letter.

". . . . For your information I send you a copy of my argument before the Court of Inquiry which I had printed for my own private use. . . . I would be completely satisfied with the command of a respectable division in some other Dept., Gen. Sigel's for instance, . . . and that, in case the 11th Corps is taken from under Gen. Hooker, I shall be quite content with the command I now have. . . .

"I am quite sick, suffering from all sorts of complaints common in camps. I expect however to be able in a few days to return to the Army. Until then I should be glad to know what I shall have to do, and on my way there to visit Washington, unless my presence there be particularly undesirable." (DLC-RTL).

On March 21 Schurz wrote again:

"At last I have received your letter of the 13th; it was not directed to my hotel and I did, therefore, not hear of it until it was advertised in the papers.

"My letters to you were dictated by the ardent desire to see the unity of the party unimpaired at the next presidential election, for without that unity the prospective result seems to me extremely doubtful. . . . I thought that my opinion and advice upon several points of importance might be entitled to some consideration . . . for there are things which it is better to discuss in private than in public. In believing that a full exchange of views might be desirable not only to me but also to you, it seems I was mistaken. While a number of generals were permitted to visit Washington, it is difficult for me to understand, how my presence there could be attended with unpleasant difficulties or even be detrimental to the public service. I might perhaps claim a right to know, what particular unpleasant difficulty or what detriment to the service is meant, but I apprehend I have to submit not only to an incomprehensible refusal but also to a mysterious hint as to the cause of that refusal. I approached you with the feelings of a friend, not to ask for something but to offer something and I find myself turned off very much like an enemy or a suspicious character. I must confess, I cannot understand this. . . . I did not think it would be as difficult with your assistance to procure me an opportunity to take an active part in the political contest some time in July or August and September; and if you think it is, I shall then have to decide the question of my remaining in the army for myself when the time comes.

"While I regret most sincerely that you deemed best to cut off a full exchange of views, I beg you not to construe this letter as a renewed application for permission to visit Washington. . . ." (*Ibid.*).

To Edwin M. Stanton[1]

March 23, 1864

I would like to oblige Gov. Newell with a note like the within, unless the Sec. of War perceives objection. Will he please answer?

March 23. 1864.   A. LINCOLN

[263]

The Long-Branch and Sea-Shore Railroad Company is hereby authorized to make and use a railroad track on the land of the United States, conforming to the curve dotted line on this map, which line commences at the figure 8, and runs Southward nearly touching the right hand ends of these written lines, and on till it passes off the government lands, upon condition that said railroad track and all possession of the ground shall be removed and surrendered by force if necessary, upon either the order of the President of the United States, or a Joint Resolution of Congress so requiring.

[1] AES and AD, DLC-RTL. Lincoln's endorsement is separated from the memorandum as cataloged in the Lincoln Papers, but they seem obviously to belong together. A note from Governor William A. Newell, dated March 23 (but incorrectly cataloged as "March 25") is as follows: "If your Excellency shall determine to sign the paper which I left with you on yesterday I will be greatly obliged if it can be sent to me at Allentown N. Jersey; I do hope that the favor sought will not be refused. The land is valueless, and on the expression of a wish to that effect the whole works will be removed, or relinquished, without compensation, to the Government. It will contribute vastly to the welfare of that portion of the County in which I live, New Jersey has always responded to the calls of your Excellency & I beg to express the hope that this small request of some of her citizens will be allowed. . . ." (*Ibid.*).

The document which Governor Newell submitted, written on Executive Mansion stationery, reads as follows:

"Permission is hereby given to the Long Branch and Sea-Shore Rail Road Company to use so much of the government property at Sandy Hook, beginning at the Horse Shoe and extending southward, as may be necessary for the construction of suitable dock, depot and track accommodations, with the understanding that the improvements thus designated shall be removed or transfered to the Government whenever it shall be required"

Secretary Stanton referred the matter to General Halleck and Halleck referred to Judge Advocate General Holt, who reported on March 26: "This, like other property belonging to the government, having been acquired by public law, can only be disposed of under the same sanctions. I am aware of no principle or precedent which can be held to authorise the executive, to transfer either the absolute title to or a usufructuary, interest in property, of the U. States, thus acquired, without the express concurrence of Congress. The rule is believed to be the same, without reference to the amount of interest sought to be conveyed. In this particular case, the privilege of using the land described for the purpose mentioned, would probably prove one of great pecuniary value, to the Rail Road company, but whether of great or little value, in its transfer or bestowal, the government must act through a public law, and not through the will of any one of its Departments." (*Ibid.*).

To Edward Bates[1]

Attorney General please send me a nomination as within requested.   A. LINCOLN

March 24. 1864

[1] AES, RPB. Lincoln's endorsement is written on a letter of Edward B. Taylor, March 24, 1864, register of the Land Office at Omaha, Nebraska Territory, recommending Daniel Gantt of Omaha for U.S. District Attorney. Gantt's appointment was confirmed by the Senate on May 10, 1864.

To Benjamin F. Butler[1]

Major Gen. Butler   Executive Mansion,
Fort-Monroe, Va.   Washington, March 24, 1864.
Please, if you can, effect special exchanges, for J. F. Robinson,
1st. Lieut. Co. E, 67, P.V. and C. L. Edmunds, 1st. Lieut. Co. D,
67, P.V.   A. LINCOLN

[1] ALS, DNA WR RG 107, Presidential Telegrams, I, 15. The roster of the
Sixty-seventh Pennsylvania Regiment lists these men as James T Robinson,
discharged on March 24, 1865, and Charles L. Edmonds, mustered out on December 18, 1864.

To James R. Doolittle[1]

Hon. J. R. Doolittle, please call and see me this morning.
March 24, 1864   A. LINCOLN
[1] ALS-P, ISLA.

To Joseph Holt[1]

                         Executive Mansion, Washington,
Judge Advocate General   March 24, 1864.
Please examine and report upon the case of Capt. John Hopper,
Co. D. 21st. Regt. Invalid Corps, said to have been summarily dis-
missed. Yours truly   A. LINCOLN

[1] ALS, DLC-RTL. Holt returned this letter with the following endorsement
dated March 25, 1864: "Respectfully returned to the President. This case has
been heretofore fully examined, & reports upon it made to the President under
dates of 11th. & 28th. of present month. Reference is had to these reports as
expressing the views of this office, on the application for the restoration of
Capt. Hopper to the service." No further record has been found of Lincoln's
action in the case.

To George G. Meade[1]

                                    Executive Mansion,
Major-General Meade, Army of Potomac: March 24, 1864.
Do not change your purpose to send Private Orton, of Twelfth
U.S. Infantry, to the Dry Tortugas.   A. LINCOLN.

[1] Tarbell (Appendix), p. 421. See Lincoln to Meade, March 23, *supra*.

To the Senate[1]

To the Senate of the United States: March 24, 1864
In reply to the Resolution of the Senate of the 15th. instant in
relation to the establishment of monarchical governments in Cen-

[265]

tral and South America, I transmit a report from the Secretary of State, to whom the subject was referred.

Washington 24 March 1864.   ABRAHAM LINCOLN

[1] DS, DNA RG 46, Senate 38A F3. Seward reported on March 24, 1864, that "surmises and jealousies are constantly arising on the subject to which the resolution refers. . . . But there is no correspondence or . . . information which furnishes any reliable facts showing the existence of 'plans' for the accomplishment of the object mentioned."

To John P. Usher[1]

March 24, 1864

If there is such an office, vacant, and ready to be filled, as indicated, the Sec. of the Interior will please send me a nomination, according to the within.   A. LINCOLN

March. 24. 1864

[1] AES, DLC-RTL. Lincoln's endorsement is written on a letter from Marcus Boyd of Missouri, asking appointment as surveyor general of government and Indian lands in Utah Territory. An unsigned endorsement in reply from the Department of Interior called the president's attention to the fact that there was no vacancy.

To Benjamin B. French[1]

Private

Hon. B. B. French

My dear Sir:

Executive Mansion,

Washington,

March 25, 1864.

I understand a Bill is before Congress, by your instigation, for taking your office from the control of the Department of the Interior, and considerably enlarging the powers and patronage of your office. The proposed change may be right for aught I know; and it certainly is right for Congress to do as it thinks proper in the case. What I wish to say is that if the change is made, I do not think I can allow you to retain the office; because that would be encouraging officers to be constantly intriguing, to the detriment of the public interest, in order to profit themselves. Yours truly

A. LINCOLN

[1] ADfS, DLC-RTL. This letter is printed by Hertz (II, 946), without date or addressee. The bill (S.43) did not pass. Commissioner French replied on March 27, 1864:

"Your note of the 25th is recd. and I am greatly surprised at the contents . . . because I have been guilty of no intended impropriety, and of no wrong. I have been cruelly treated by your Secretary of the Interior, and have been *forced by him,* to defend myself, and, because I have done so, you have been appealed to to crush me. I do not believe you will do so when you know all the facts. . . ."

"The Secretary of the Interior, when that excellent man, Caleb B. Smith was Secretary, was charged by Congress, with the supervision and control of the erection of the Capitol Extension and New Dome. He saw fit, of his own accord, to confer upon me the honor and trust of Disbursing Agent. I have bonds in the penalty of $40,000, and entered upon the duty, and performed it, I believe, satisfactorily to Mr. Smith. He resigned, Mr. Usher was appointed . . . removed my Clerk, who was charged with keeping my accounts, and for whose acts, I, alone, was responsible under my bonds, and placed another man in his stead. . . . On the 30th of June, 1863, . . . removing me from the place of disbursing agent, . . . appointed the clerk he had sent . . . with enlarged powers, and a salary of $2500 per annum. At this I felt grieved . . . and addressed to the Secretary, a letter . . . also . . . to you. . . .

"Naturally, I wrote to Senator Foot, informing him of the fact. . . . He replied . . . that as soon as Congress met it was his intention to introduce a bill placing the work on the Extension & Dome under the Commissioner of Public Buildings, where it belonged, & removing the office of Commissioner from any control of the Secy. I drew up a bill which I supposed would carry out what Senator Foot said, and sent it to him, keeping a copy of it. Some time afterwards a friend, to whom I showed the copy, wanted a few copies of it for his own use, and, without the least idea of there being any impropriety in my doing so, having a printing press and type in my office, I printed for him a few copies.

"I had no agency whatever in the introduction of the bill by Senator Foot, as he never mentioned it to me, that I remember, after he came to Washington, before its introduction. I never spoke to a Senator or Representative concerning it, unless spoken to. I had not the least agency in its introduction into the House. . . . After it was . . . referred to the Committee on Public Buildings and Grounds, I was notified by the Chairman . . . to appear before it on a certain day, which I did, and there met the Secretary of the Interior. He was heard fully, and said something to which *I was forced* to reply, and, at a subsequent meeting, I did reply. This is all my personal action in the matter. . . . I have never spoken to a member of the Senate Committee, except Senator Foot, on the subject of it. He submitted to me, unasked, some papers sent him by the Secy. for my answer, and I gave it. . . . I have done, Mr. President, exactly what you would have done in my case, and nothing more, except, perhaps, in the printing of about a dozen copies of the bill. . . .

"As I did not seek the passage of the bill in question, I cannot . . . seek to stop it; but I beg of you not to sacrifice me without granting me a personal interview.

"I have submitted your letter to Senator Foot who expressed much surprise at its contents . . . evidently written . . . under a false impression as to the facts, and that he would call upon you tomorrow and assure you that, so far as he was concerned, I had no agency whatever in the introduction of the bill, except that I drew it up for him, a thing that is done daily by officials about the Capital, at the request of members." (DLC-RTL).

To James H. Lane[1]

March 25, 1864

I have endorsed, as you see, your application for Henry W. Fick to be an Assistant Pay-Master in the Navy. I return it to you to say that, by law, he cannot be appointed. . . .

[1] American Art Association Anderson Galleries Catalog 3850, May 12-13, 1930, No. 198. According to the catalog description, this partial text is from an autograph letter signed.

To Thurlow Weed[1]

Hon. Thurlow Weed
My dear Sir:

Executive Mansion,
Washington, March 25. 1864.

I have been both pained and surprised recently at learning that you are wounded because a suggestion of yours as to the mode of conducting our national difficulty, has not been followed—pained, because I very much wish you to have no unpleasant feeling proceeding from me, and surprised, because my impression is that I have seen you, since the last Message issued, apparently feeling very cheerful and happy. How is this? Yours truly

A LINCOLN

[1] ALS, NRU (on deposit); LS copy, DLC-RTL. On March 30, 1864, John G. Nicolay wrote Lincoln from the Astor House, New York:

"Mr. Weed was here at the Astor House on my arrival last Saturday morning and I gave him the note you sent him.

"He read it over, carefully once or twice and then said he didn't quite understand it. He had written a letter to Judge Davis, which the Judge had probably shown you, but in that he had said nothing except about Custom House matters.

"He said that all the solicitude he had was in your behalf. You had told him in January last that you thought you would make a change in the Collectorship here, but that thus far it had not been done. He had told you he himself had no personal preference as to the particular man who is to be his successor. He did not think Mr. Barney a bad man but thought him a weak one. His four deputies are constantly intriguing against you. Andrews is doing the same. Changes are constantly being made among the subordinates in the Custom House, and men turned out, for no other real reason than that they take active part in primary meetings &c., in behalf of your re-nomination.

"His only solicitude, he said, was for yourself. He thought that if you were not strong enough to hold the Union men together through the next Presidential election, when it must necessarily undergo a great strain, the country was in the utmost danger of going to ruin.

"His desire was to strengthen you as much as possible and that you should strengthen yourself. You were being weakened by the impression in the popular mind that you hold on with such tenacity to men once in office, although they prove to be incapable and unworthy. This feeling among your friends also raises the question, as to whether, if re-elected, you would change your Cabinet. The present Cabinet is notoriously weak and inharmonious—no Cabinet at all—gives the President no support. Welles is a cypher, Bates a fogy, and Blair at best a dangerous friend.

"Something was needed to reassure the public mind and to strengthen yourself. Chase and Fremont, while they might not succeed in making themselves successful rivals might yet form and lead dangerous factions. Chase was not formidable as a candidate in the field, but by the shrewd dodge of a withdrawal is likely to turn up again with more strength than ever.

"He had received a letter from Judge Davis, in which the Judge wrote him that he had read his (Weed's) letter to you, but that you did not seem ready to act in the appointment of a new Collector, and that he (the Judge) thought it was because of your apprehension that you would be merely getting 'out of one muss into another.'

[268]

"A change in the Custom House was imperatively needed because one whole bureau in it had been engaged in treasonably aiding the rebellion.

"The ambition of his life had been, not to get office for himself, but to assist in putting good men in the right places. If he was good for anything, it was as an outsider to give valuable suggestions to an administration that would give him its confidence. He feared he did not have your entire confidence— that you only regarded him with a certain degree of leniency; that you only regarded him as being not quite so great a rascal as his enemies charged him with being.

"The above are substantially the points of quite a long conversation. This morning I had another interview with Mr. Weed.

"He had just received Gov. Morgan's letter informing him of the nomination of Hogeboom to fill McElrath's place, and seemed quite disheartened and disappointed. He said he did not know what to say. He had assured your friends here that when in your own good time you became ready to make changes, the new appointments would be from among your friends; but that this promotion of one of your most active and malignant enemies left him quite powerless. He had not yet told any one, but knew it would be received with general indignation, &c &c.

"I shall remain here a day or two longer." (DLC-Nicolay Papers).

Proclamation About Amnesty[1]

March 26, 1864

By the President of the United States of America:

A Proclamation.

Whereas, it has become necessary to define the cases in which insurgent enemies are entitled to the benefits of the proclamation of the President of the United States, which was made on the eighth day of December, 1863, and the manner in which they shall proceed to avail themselves of those benefits:

And whereas, the objects of that proclamation were to suppress the insurrection and to restore the authority of the United States, and whereas the amnesty therein proposed by the President was offered with reference to these objects alone:

Now, therefore, I, Abraham Lincoln, President of the United States, do hereby proclaim and declare that the said proclamation does not apply to the cases of persons who, at the time when they seek to obtain the benefits thereof by taking the oath thereby prescribed are in military, naval or civil confinement or custody, or under bonds or on parole of the civil, military or naval authorities or agents of the United States as prisoners of war or persons detained for offences of any kind, either before or after conviction, and that, on the contrary, it does apply only to those persons who being yet at large and free from any arrest, confinement or duress, shall voluntarily come forward and take the said oath with the purpose of restoring peace and establishing the national authority. Prisoners excluded from the amnesty offered in the said proclamation may apply to the President for clemency like all other offenders, and their applications will receive due consideration.

I do farther declare and proclaim that the oath prescribed in the aforesaid proclamation of the 8th. of December, 1863, may be taken and subscribed before any commissioned officer, civil, military or naval, in the service of the United States, or any civil or military officer of a State or Territory not in insurrection, who, by the laws thereof, may be qualified for administering oaths. All officers who receive such oaths are hereby authorized to give certificates thereon to the persons respectively by whom they are made. And such officers are hereby required to transmit the original records of such oaths at as early a day as may be convenient to the Department of State, where they will be deposited and remain in the archives of the Government. The Secretary of State will keep a register thereof, and will on application, in proper cases, issue certificates of such records in the customary form of official certificates.

In testimony whereof, I have hereunto set my hand and caused the seal of the United States to be affixed.

Done at the city of Washington, the twenty-sixth day of March, in the year of our Lord one thousand eight hundred and [L.S.] sixty-four, and of the Independence of the United States the eighty-eighth.　　　　　ABRAHAM LINCOLN

By the President:

WILLIAM H. SEWARD Secretary of State.

[1] DS, DNA FS RG 11, Proclamations.

To Edward Bates[1]

March 28, 1864

Will the Attorney General please give me his opinion whether this law relieves the Marshal of the District from the duty of executing the death sentence upon persons under that sentence in the District jail?　　　　　A. LINCOLN

March 28. 1864

[1] AES, DNA GE RG 60, Papers of Attorney General, Segregated Lincoln Material. Lincoln's endorsement is written on S. 86, "A Bill to authorize the appointment of a warden of the jail in the District of Columbia," approved February 29, 1864. Bates' autograph opinion of March 28 is as follows:

"A somewhat troublesome question arises under this bill which requires either the interpretation of the Court or the action of the Executive.

"The President has nominated a Warden of the Jail, but he has not been confirmed by the Senate.

"The Warden of the Penitentiary became *functus officio*, and has neither done service nor received emolument for more than two years.

"There is no Warden of the jail qualified by law; there is no Warden of the Penitentiary recognized by the Executive, or accounting officers of the treasury and no penitentiary in the District of which he could be Warden.

"To remove all doubt I suggest that an order from the President be issued reciting the fact of the removal of the Penitentiary, the vacation of the office of Warden of the penitentiary, and in order to remove all doubt that he be now removed to relate back to the time of the last payment of his salary." (*Ibid.*).

To Joseph Holt[1]

Judge Advocate General
My dear Sir

Executive Mansion,
Washington, March 28. 1864.

I am told there is a man in the Old Capitol Prison by the name of Benedict A. King, on some charge of desertion. He belongs, it is said, to the 153rd. N. Y. Vols.[2] He wishes to be sent to his Regiment. Report me the facts of his case if you can. Yours truly

A. LINCOLN

[1] ALS, Herman Blum, Blumhaven Library, Philadelphia, Pennsylvania. Private Benedict A. King, First Maine Battery, was sentenced February 10, 1864, to death for desertion. General Christopher C. Augur recommended commutation to dishonorable discharge and five years' imprisonment. The records show that Lincoln returned the papers in the case on April 16, 1864, without further action (DNA WR RG 153, Judge Advocate General, MM 773).

[2] He had deserted and re-enlisted.

To Edwin M. Stanton[1]

Hon. Secretary of War.
My dear Sir:

Executive Mansion,
Washington, March 28, 1864.

The letter of Mr. Tho. H. Burrowes, written in behalf of the Common School Teachers of Pennsylvania, and which you left with me as a mode of giving me the notice therein requested, is herewith returned to you. Please present to the writer, and to those he represents, my grateful thanks for this evidence of their patriotic devotion, and this contribution to the great loyal public sentiment of the country, which is, indeed, the foundation of all else that is valuable in this great national trial. The gun tendered you will please accept and dispose of in such way as you may deem proper. Yours truly,
A. LINCOLN.

[1] Copy, DNA WR RG 107, Secretary of War, Letters Received, P 175. No further reference has been found.

To Edwin M. Stanton[1]

Hon. Secretary of War   Executive Mansion,
My dear Sir: Washington, March 28 1864.

The Governor of Kentucky is here, and desires to have the following points definitely fixed:

1. That the quotas of troops furnished, and to be furnished by Kentucky, may be adjusted upon the basis as actually reduced by able bodied men of hers having gone into the rebel service; and that she be required to furnish no more than her just quotas upon fair adjustment on such basis.

2. That to whatever extent the enlistment, and drafting, one or both, of colored troops may be found necessary within the State, it may be conducted within the law of Congress; and, as far as practicable, free from colateral embarrasments, disorders, and provocations.

I think these requests of the Governor are reasonable; and I shall be obliged, if you will give him a full hearing, and do the best you can to effect these objects. Yours very truly

A. LINCOLN.

[1] ALS-F, Parke-Bernet Catalog 643, March 5-6, 1945, No. 411; copy, DLC-RTL. The facsimile lacks the last two words of the body of the letter, the close, and signature. Bates' *Diary* records Governor Bramlette's audience with Lincoln on March 26: "The Govr. says that the draft will not be opposed, if conducted in a simple and honest way—i.e. enlist the men and march them off, without making it a pretence to insult, and rob, and dominate every neighborhood—as in Maryland!"

To Ulysses S. Grant[1]

Lt. Genl. Grant   Executive Mansion
Army of Potomac   Washington, March 29. 1864

Capt. Kinney, of whom I spoke to you as desiring to go on your Staff, is now in your camp in company with Mrs. Senator Dixon. Mrs. Grant and I and some others agreed last night that I should, by this despatch, kindly call your attention to Capt. Kinney.

A. LINCOLN

[1] ALS, DNA WR RG 107, Presidential Telegrams, I, 17. General Grant replied on the same day: "Your dispatch suggesting Capt. Kinney for a staff appointment just recd. I would be glad to accommodate Capt Kinney but in the selection of staff I do not want any one whom I do not personally know to be qualified for the position assigned them." (DLC-RTL). Captain Kinney has not been positively identified. Mrs. Dixon was presumably the wife of James Dixon, U.S. senator (1857-1869).

To Andrew Johnson[1]

Gov. Johnson   Executive Mansion,
Nashville, Tenn.   Washington, March 29. 1864.
   Judge Catron is asking for the discharge of W. M. Bell, now at
Rock-Island, and whom he thinks was arrested as a hostage by
you or by your authority. What say you?   A. LINCOLN

[1] ALS, DNA WR RG 107, Presidential Telegrams, I, 16. Governor Johnson
replied on April 1, "Wm Bell was not arrested by my authority. I presume he
is a prisoner of war. I have not been able to find out much about him. There
are hundreds . . . no doubt, who are more entitled to executive clemency than
he is. . . ." (DLC-RTL).

To George G. Meade[1]

Major General Meade   Executive Mansion,
My dear Sir: Washington, March 29. 1864.
   Your letter to Col. Townsend, inclosing a slip from the Herald,
and asking a Court of Inquiry, has been laid before [me] by the
Secretary of War, with the request that I would consider it. It is
quite natural that you should feel some sensibility on the subject;
yet I am not impressed, nor do I think the country is impressed,
with the belief that your honor demands, or the public interest demands, such an Inquiry. The country knows that, at all events,
you have done good service; and I believe it agrees with me that it
is much better for you [to] be engaged in trying to do more, than
to be diverted, as you necessarily would be, by a Court of Inquiry.
Yours truly   A. LINCOLN

[1] ALS, NHi. On March 15, 1864, General Meade wrote Assistant Adjutant
General Edward D. Townsend:
   "I inclose herewith a slip from the New York *Herald*, containing a communication signed 'Historicus,' purporting to give an account of the battle of
Gettysburg. . . . For the past fortnight the public press . . . has been teeming
with articles, all having for their object assaults upon my reputation as an
officer, and tending to throw discredit upon my operations at Gettysburg. . . .
   "I have not noticed any of these attacks, and should not now . . . but that
the character of the communication . . . bears such manifest proofs that it
was written either by some one present at the battle, or dictated . . . and having access . . . to confidential papers that were never issued to the army,
much less made public.
   "I cannot resist the belief that this letter was either written or dictated by
Maj. Gen. D. E. Sickles. . . .
   "I have to ask, therefore, that the Department will take steps to ascertain
whether . . . Sickles has authorized or indorses this communication, and, in
the event of his replying in the affirmative, I have to request of the President
. . . a court of inquiry. . . ." (OR, I, XXVII, I, 127-28).
   The three-column clipping from the New York *Herald* of March 12, 1864,

[273]

criticized errors in Meade's report of the Gettysburg operations and particularly referred to his failure to heed advice of his corps commanders.

Order for Discharge of Prisoners[1]

March 29, 1864

If the persons whose names follow, now prisoners of war shall take the oath of December 8, 1863, and be discharged, we, the undersigned members of Congress pledge our honor that they will keep faith:

> John F. Rice, at Rock Island, Ill.
> James J. Moore, at Camp Morton, I
> Robert P. Green, at Johnson Island
> James B. McCreary, at Columbus, O.
> J. Miller Turner, at Rock Island, Ill.
> Andrew Moore, at Camp Morton, In.
> (Signed) Lu Anderson M.C.
> W. H. Randall M.C.
> B. J. Clay M.C.

Let the above named prisoners be discharged upon the condition stated.   A. LINCOLN

March 29, 1864.

[1] Angle, p. 346. A note in the source describes this document as having the names of the prisoners and the endorsement in Lincoln's handwriting.

To the Senate and House of Representatives[1]

March 29, 1864

To the Senate, and House of Representatives

Mr Charles B. Stuart, Consulting Engineer, appointed such by me, upon invitation of the Governor of New York, according to a law of that State, has made a Report, upon the proposed improvements to pass Gun-Boats from Tide-water to the Northern and North-Western Lakes, which Report is herewith respectfully transmitted for your consideration.   ABRAHAM LINCOLN

March 29, 1864

[1] DS, DNA RG 46, Senate 38A F2; DS, DNA RG 233, House Executive Document No. 61. Charles B. Stuart's report of March 24, 1864, suggested improvements on canals in New York, Illinois, and Wisconsin, which would enable naval vessels to get from the Atlantic or the Gulf of Mexico to the Great Lakes. Lincoln's communication with enclosures was referred to the House committee on roads and canals (March 29, 1864) and the Senate committee on military affairs (March 30, 1864). No record of further action has been found.

To Richard M. Corwine[1]

Office U.S. Military Telegraph,
Hon. R. M. Corwine   War Department,
New-York.   Washington, D.C., March 30 1864.

It does not occur to me that you can present the Smith case any better than you have done. Of this, however, you must judge for yourself.   A LINCOLN

[1] ALS, DNA WR RG 107, Presidential Telegrams, I, 18. See Lincoln to Holt, February 4, *supra*. Corwine telegraphed from New York on March 30, 1864: "Continued illness required me to leave without seeing you again. If I can be of any further use in the Smith Case I will return otherwise go West Monday" (DLC-RTL).

Order for Pardon of Henry F. Luckett[1]

Let this man, Henry F. Luckett, be pardoned, and sent North.
March. 30. 1864   A. LINCOLN

[1] AES, RPB. See Lincoln to Hurlbut, December 17, 1863, *supra*. Lincoln's endorsement is written on a letter from Luckett's niece, Lizzie L. Rafter, Memphis, Tennessee, February 27, 1864, asking a pardon for her uncle.

On April 30, Henry F. Luckett wrote Lincoln:
"Since it has been by your grace that I have been delivered from the Lions Paw [?] and have been permitted to return home I deem it not only my duty but esteem it a great pleasure and privilege to express to you in this way (the best within my reach) my profound acknowledgements and sincere gratitude for the exercise of your Executive Clemency in releasing me from a condition the sufferings of which were more intolerable than death itself. . . ." (DLC-RTL).

To Lewis Wallace[1]

[c. March 30, 1864]
Will Gen. Wallace call and see me?   A. LINCOLN.

[1] Lew Wallace, *An Autobiography*, II, 684. According to the source, this note was sent on a small card, and General Wallace caught the next train from Baltimore. See Lincoln to Stanton, March 31, *infra*.

To William Windom[1]

Hon. Mr. Windom, please see & hear Rev. Bishop Whipple, about Indians. He has much information on the subject.
March 30. 1864   A. LINCOLN

[1] ALS, DLC. Bishop Henry B. Whipple of Minnesota was noted for his work in behalf of the Indians in his diocese, but precisely what Lincoln wished him to effect through Representative Windom, chairman of the committee on Indian affairs, has not been determined.

To Edward Bates[1]

The Vice-President & Senator Fessenden present this Petition & join in the prayer thereof.   A LINCOLN

March 31. 1864

[1] AES, DNA RG 204, U.S. Pardon Attorney, A 561. Lincoln's endorsement is written on a petition from citizens of Portland, Maine, asking pardon of Franklin B. Furlong, imprisoned for robbery of a post office.

To Joseph Holt[1]

Judge Advocate General please examine & report on this case.

March 31. 1864   A. LINCOLN.

[1] AES, DNA WR RG 153, Judge Advocate General, NN 111. Lincoln's endorsement is written on the record in the case of Joseph M. Bushfield. See Lincoln to Holt, August 28, 1863, and February 9, 1864, *supra*.

Memorandum
Concerning Thomas Worthington[1]

Copy.

Executive Mansion. March 31st. 1864.

Today I verbally told Colonel Worthington that I did not think him fit for a Colonel; and now, upon his *urgent* request, I put it in writing.   A. LINCOLN.

[1] Copy, IHi. See Lincoln to Worthington, *infra*. Colonel Thomas Worthington of the Forty-sixth Ohio Infantry is listed as having resigned on November 21, 1862, but from his letter to Lincoln, April 12, 1864, it seems obvious that he was dismissed: "On full consideration I have declined urging on Gen Schenck, the responsibility of my possible return to the service. . . . I will never reenter the Army while that terrible and degrading law under which *I have had no official notice of being dismissed* continues to disgrace the statute book. . . .

"I saw something of its operation at Memphis . . . where a General . . . scarcely ever clear of liquor staggered into his court room to decide on the cases of men better and abler than himself. . . .

"When however, the last section of the law of July 17th 1862 Chap 200—is repealed, and Judge Holt & Gen Halleck . . . are also, in their proper places, if the war should still be *on hand* I may possibly request a removal of that disability under which by their advice and initiation, I must for the present remain, hoping for better luck next time. With a very respectful request that this document may be referred to either or both of these distinguished '*Field Officers*'. . . ." (DLC-RTL).

To Edwin M. Stanton[1]

Executive Mansion, Washington,

Hon. Sec. of War   March 31, 1864.

Gen. Wallace has been with me; and I think he is getting along with the matter we wished to see him for, very satisfactorily. It is a great point, which he seems to be effecting, to get Gov. B. & Hon. H. W. D.² together. I have told him to be fair, but to give the benefit of all doubts to the emancipationists. Please confer with him, and add any suggestion that may occur to you. Yours truly

A. LINCOLN

¹ ALS, InHi.
² Governor August W. Bradford and Representative Henry Winter Davis.

To Edwin M. Stanton¹

March 31, 1864

I sincerely wish that something satisfactory to Lt. Col. Scates—an old personal friend & most worthy gentleman—may be done for him. A. LINCOLN

March. 31. 1864

¹ AES, IHi. Lincoln's endorsement appears on a letter from General Edward O. C. Ord to Senator Lyman Trumbull, New Orleans, February 1, 1864, recommending that Lieutenant Colonel Walter B. Scates be transferred for reasons of health. An endorsement by Assistant Secretary of War Charles A. Dana, April 8, ordered that Scates be relieved from duty as assistant adjutant general of the Thirteenth Army Corps and report to Washington for court-martial duty.

To Thomas Worthington¹

Executive Mansion,
Col. Worthington Washington, March 31, 1864.

If Major General Schenck will say in writing upon this sheet that he believes the public service would be advanced by your being placed at the head of a Regiment in the field, I will remove any legal disability resting upon you so that the Governor of Ohio may appoint you to so command a Regiment. Yours truly

A. LINCOLN

¹ ALS, RPB. See Lincoln's memorandum concerning Worthington, *supra*. No reply from Schenck has been discovered.

Endorsement Concerning Edward Avery¹

April 1, 1864

Let this man, Edward Avery go to his Company, and upon faithfully serving out his term, he is fully pardoned as to the offence for which he has been convicted. A. LINCOLN

April 1. 1864

¹ AES, owned by R. E. Burdick, New York City. Lincoln's endorsement is written on a letter from Captain Ezekiel R. Mayo, Third Maine Battery, March

29, 1864, requesting pardon of Private Edward Avery, sentenced for desertion, October 29, 1863.

To Frederick A. Farley[1]

Executive Mansion, Washington,
Reverend and Dear Sir:—   April 1, 1864.

Permit me to return my most cordial thanks for the beautiful present transmitted by you, and for the kind and graceful manner in which it was conveyed. I am very truly yours,   A. LINCOLN.

Reverend Frederick A. Farley, D.D.

[1] *History of the Brooklyn and Long Island Fair* (Brooklyn, 1864), p. 166. Reverend Frederick A. Farley, corresponding secretary of the Fair, wrote Lincoln on March 7, 1864, "A few of your fellow-citizens have the honor of offering . . . a silk 'Bed-Spread,' formed of the National Colors, and emblazoned with the Stars and Stripes and the National Eagle." (*Ibid.*).

To Ward H. Lamon[1]

April 1, 1864

In this case of Emanuel Pollard the punishment of death is commuted to imprisonment during life at hard labor in the Penitentiary.   A. LINCOLN

April 1. 1864

[1] AES-P, ISLA. Lincoln's endorsement is written on the writ of execution issued March 31, 1864, in the case of Emanuel Pollard, a colored man. U.S. Marshal Lamon's endorsement of the same date is as follows: "After receiving this writ I proceeded to the preparation for its execution up to April 1st. 1864. When I received the following communication from the President to wit: [as above]. Whereupon I presented the communication to the prisoner and enquired of him whether he accepted the commutation of the President, upon its terms, having fully made them known to him. Upon receiving his affirmative answer I returned him to his place of imprisonment to await the execution of the qualified punishment."

Memorandum:
Appointment of F. Augustus Schermerhorn[1]

Executive Mansion,
Washington, April 1. 1864.

Mr. Stebbins reminds me of Mrs. Schermerhorn's application for her son to West-Point.

[1] AD, DNA WR RG 94, U.S. Military Academy, 1861, No. 782. See Lincoln's memorandum of January 22, 1862, *supra*. Henry G. Stebbins was a member of congress from Staten Island, New York.

To Edwin M. Stanton[1]

Hon. Sec. of War   Executive Mansion,
My dear Sir   Washington, April 1. 1864.

Senator Harlan tells me that the nomination of Col. Chambers
as a Brig. Gen. for Iowa was rejected by the Senate to-day; and he
asks that Col. E. Hatch of the 2nd. Iowa Cavalry be nominated in
the place. I remember Col. Hatch to be very excellently recommended; and I am content if you know nothing to the contrary
If all right send me the nomination. Yours truly

A. LINCOLN

1 ALS, NHi. Alexander Chambers was colonel of the Sixteenth Iowa Volunteers. Colonel Edward Hatch of the Second Iowa Cavalry was appointed brigadier general on April 27, 1864.

Order Prohibiting Export of Salted Provisions[1]

Ordered: Executive Mansion, April, 2d., 1864.

That the Executive Order of September, 4th., 1863, in relation
to the exportation of live stock from the United States, be so extended, as to prohibit the exportations of all classes of salted provisions from any port of the United States to any foreign port, except, that meats, cured, salted or packed in any state or territory,
bordering on the Pacific ocean, may be exported from any port of
such state or territory.   ABRAHAM LINCOLN

1 DS, Saddle and Sirloin Club, Union Stock Yards, Chicago, Illinois. This
order appears in the *Official Records*, III, IV, 212. On April 8 Secretary Chase
wrote Lincoln: "An order signed by you, and prohibiting the exportation of
salted provisions from any port of the United States, excepting any State or
Territory bordering on the Pacific Ocean, has this day been transmitted to me,
for information, by the Secretary of War. Not having been consulted as to
the making of this order, I am necessarily ignorant of the public reasons which
are supposed to require it; but as its effects on our foreign trade, and consequently upon the finances, must be very serious, I respectfully suggest the
suspension of its operation until I can lay before you a statement of the magnitude and relations of the commercial movements affected by it." (DLC-
Nicolay Papers). On the same day Nicolay replied: "In answer to your note of
today the President directs me to say that the order concerning the exportation
of salted provisions has not yet been issued. It was merely printed and sent to
you for examination and will not be issued before a full consultation with
yourself." (DNA FI RG 56, General Records of the Treasury Department,
Letters from Executive Officers, Part I, Volume I, 10.)

To Joseph H. Barrett[1]

J. H. Barrett, Com. of Pensions, please call and see me.
April 3. 1864.   A. LINCOLN

[1] ALS-F, Joseph H. Barrett, *Abraham Lincoln and His Presidency* (1904), II, 370. According to the source, Lincoln conferred with Barrett concerning "the attempted movement to postpone the Baltimore convention, called to meet in June. He wanted this scheme defeated, and, in fact, it never gained much headway. . . ."

To Edward Bates[1]

April 4, 1864

Attorney General please give me your legal opinion whether the Pay-Master should have paid as demanded, and if yea, is it the duty of the President to order him to pay?   A. LINCOLN
April 4. 1864.

[1] AES, DLC-RTL. Lincoln's endorsement is written on a letter from Governor John A. Andrew, March 24, 1864, concerning the case of Samuel Harrison, a Negro chaplain of the Fifty-fourth Massachusetts Volunteers. Although appointed and regularly commissioned by Andrew, Harrison had been refused his pay of $100 per month and two rations per day, on the grounds that the law of July 17, 1862, fixed pay of colored persons at $10 per month and one ration per day, which amount Harrison refused. Bates replied on April 23 that Harrison should have been paid, inasmuch as he had been lawfully appointed and mustered into the U.S. service and his appointment was not based on the law of July 17, 1862. Bates also gave his opinion that the president should direct the War Department to notify all paymasters that such was his view of the case. See Lincoln's communication to the Senate, May 7, *infra*.

To Edward Bates[1]

April 4, 1864

Will the Attorney General please give me his opinion whether the President has legal power to remit the fine in the case as within stated?   A. LINCOLN
April 4. 1864

[1] AES, DNA GE RG 60, Papers of Attorney General, Segregated Lincoln Material. Lincoln's endorsement is written on a communication signed by representatives and senators from Indiana, March 29, 1864, asking that the president remit the fine of $500 assessed against John Caldwell of Morgan County, Indiana, for aiding a deserter. Caldwell had died, leaving a wife and three children in destitute circumstances. See Lincoln to Bates, April 18, *infra*.

To Edward Bates[1]

Hon. W. H. Randall, knows Judge Woodson & concurs in this recommendation.   A. LINCOLN
April 4. 1864. *File*

[1] AES-P, ISLA. Lincoln's endorsement is written on a letter from Samuel F. Miller, Associate Justice of the U.S. Supreme Court, April 4, 1864, recommending Silas Woodson of Missouri for appointment as Chief Justice of Montana Territory. Woodson was not appointed.

Endorsement[1]

I wish this brought to my notice at the right time.

April 4. 1864.   A. LINCOLN

[1] AES, RPB. Lincoln's endorsement has been clipped from attendant papers and mounted between the covers of a book, but bears the notation that "It was given to Genl. [Edward C.] Carrington, when he was U.S. Atty. for W. D.C."

To Albert G. Hodges[1]

A. G. Hodges, Esq   Executive Mansion,
Frankfort, Ky.   Washington, April 4, 1864.

My dear Sir: You ask me to put in writing the substance of what I verbally said the other day, in your presence, to Governor Bramlette and Senator Dixon. It was about as follows:

"I am naturally anti-slavery. If slavery is not wrong, nothing is wrong. I can not remember when I did not so think, and feel. And yet I have never understood that the Presidency conferred upon me an unrestricted right to act officially upon this judgment and feeling. It was in the oath I took that I would, to the best of my ability, preserve, protect, and defend the Constitution of the United States. I could not take the office without taking the oath. Nor was it my view that I might take an oath to get power, and break the oath in using the power. I understood, too, that in ordinary civil administration this oath even forbade me to practically indulge my primary abstract judgment on the moral question of slavery. I had publicly declared this many times, and in many ways. And I aver that, to this day, I have done no official act in mere deference to my abstract judgment and feeling on slavery. I did understand however, that my oath to preserve the constitution to the best of my ability, imposed upon me the duty of preserving, by every indispensable means, that government—that nation—of which that constitution was the organic law. Was it possible to lose the nation, and yet preserve the constitution? By general law life *and* limb must be protected; yet often a limb must be amputated to save a life; but a life is never wisely given to save a limb. I felt that measures, otherwise unconstitutional, might become lawful, by becoming indispensable to the preservation of the constitution, through the preservation of the nation. Right or wrong, I assumed this ground, and now avow it. I could not feel that, to the best of my ability, I had even tried to preserve the constitution, if, to save slavery, or any minor matter, I should permit the wreck of government, country, and Constitution all together. When, early in the war, Gen. Fremont attempted military emancipation, I forbade it, because I did not then think it an indispensable necessity. When a little later, Gen. Cameron, then Secretary of War, suggested the arming of the blacks, I objected, because I did not yet think it an indispensable necessity. When, still later, Gen. Hunter attempted military emancipation, I again forbade it, because I did not yet think the indispensable necessity had come. When, in March, and May, and July 1862 I made earnest, and successive appeals to the border states to favor compensated emancipation, I believed the indispensable necessity for military emancipation, and arming the blacks would come, unless averted by that measure. They declined the proposition; and I was, in my best judgment, driven to the alternative of either surrendering the Union, and with it, the Constitution, or of laying strong hand upon the colored element. I chose the latter. In choosing it, I hoped for greater gain than loss; but of this, I was not entirely confident. More than a year of trial now shows no loss by it in our foreign relations, none in our home popular sentiment, none in our white military force,—no loss by it any how or any[2] where. On the contrary, it shows a gain of quite a hundred and thirty thousand soldiers, seamen, and laborers. These are palpable facts, about which, as facts, there can be no cavilling. We have the men; and we could not have had them without the measure.

["]And now let any Union man who complains of the measure, test himself by writing down in one line that he is for subduing the rebellion by force of arms; and in the next, that he is for taking these hundred and thirty thousand men from the Union side, and placing them where they would be but for the measure he condemns. If he can not face his case so stated, it is only because he can not face the truth.["]

I add a word which was not in the verbal conversation. In telling this tale I attempt no compliment to my own sagacity. I claim not to have controlled events, but confess plainly that events have controlled me. Now, at the end of three years struggle the nation's condition is not what either party, or any man devised, or expected. God alone can claim it. Whither it is tending seems plain. If God now wills the removal of a great wrong, and wills also that we of the North as well as you of the South, shall pay fairly for our complicity in that wrong, impartial history will find therein new cause to attest and revere the justice and goodness of God. Yours truly

A. LINCOLN

[1] ADfS, DLC-RTL. Albert G. Hodges, editor of the Frankfort, Kentucky, *Commonwealth*, and Archibald Dixon, former senator from Kentucky, 1852-1855, met with Lincoln on March 26 to discuss border state problems. Orville

H. Browning's *Diary* under date of April 3, 1864, records the visit: "The President told me that a few days before Govr Bramlett of Ky: Hon Archibald Dixon & Mr Hodges of the same state had called upon him in regard to the enlistment of slaves as soldiers in Ky, in reference to which there has been much dissatisfaction in that State, and that everything had been amicably adjusted between them, and that they had gone home satisfied. He said when they were discussing the matter he asked them to let him make a little speech to them, which he did and with which they were much pleased. That afterwards Mr Hodges came back to him, and asked him to give him a copy of his remarks to take with him to Ky. He told Mr Hodges that what he had said was not written, and that he had not then time to commit it to paper—but to go home and he would write him a letter in which he would give, as nearly as he could all that he had said to them orally. . . ." See further, Lincoln to Hodges, April 22, *infra*.   2 "Any" inserted by an unidentified person.

To Isabel II[1]

April 4, 1864

Abraham Lincoln.
President of the United States of America

To Her Majesty Dona Isabel II,
By the Grace of God and the Constitution of the Spanish Monarchy, Queen of Spain, &c, &c, &c.

Great Good Friend: I have received the letter which your Majesty was pleased to address to me on the 24th. of February last, announcing that Your Majesty had, on the 12th. of that month, safely given birth to an Infanta who had received in baptism the names of Maria, Eulalia, Francisco de Asis, Margarite, Roberta Isabel, Francisca de Paula, Cristina Maria de la Piedad.

Your Majesty does no more than justice to the friendly feelings of the United States in beliveing that they participate with Your Majesty and Royal Family in the joy consequent upon this event: and I beg Your Majesty to accept my sincere congratulations

May God have your Majesty always in His holy keeping   Your Good Friend   ABRAHAM LINCOLN.

Washington April 4th 1864.
By the President
WILLIAM H. SEWARD   Secretary of State.

1 Copy, DNA FS RG 59, Communications to Foreign Sovereigns and States, III, 227.

To William S. Rosecrans[1]

Major General Rosecrans   Executive Mansion,
My dear Sir: Washington, April 4th, 1864.

This is rather more social than official, containing suggestions rather than orders. I somewhat dread the effect of your Special

Order, No. 61 dated March 7. 1864. I have found that men who have not even been suspected of disloyalty, are very averse to taking an oath of any sort as a condition, to exercising an ordinary right of citizenship. The point will probably be made, that while men may without an oath, assemble in a noisy political meeting, they must take the oath, to assemble in a religious meeting.

It is said, I know not whether truly, that in some parts of Missouri, assassinations are systematically committed upon returned rebels, who wish to ground arms, and behave themselves. This should not be. Of course I have not heard that you give countenance to, or wink at such assassinations.

Again, it is complained, that the enlistment of negroes, is not conducted in as orderly a manner, and with as little collateral provocation, as it might be.

So far you have got along in the Department of the Missouri, rather better than I dared to hope; and I congratulate you and myself upon it. Yours very truly   A. LINCOLN.

[1] LS (copy?), DLC-RTL. Bates' *Diary* under date of April 10, 1864, records that this letter was written "at my instance . . . to stop . . . useless and wanton interference with the churches. . . ." See Lincoln's endorsement to John Hogan, February 13, and memorandum about churches, March 4, *supra*.

To the Senate[1]

To the Senate of the United States: April 4, 1864

I herewith lay before the Senate, for its constitutional action thereon, a treaty concluded June 9, 1863, between C. H. Hale, superintendent of Indian affairs, Charles Hutchins, and S. D. Howe, Indian agents, on the part of the United States, and the chiefs, headmen, and delegates of the Nez Percé tribe of Indians in Washington Territory.

A report of the Secretary of the Interior of the 1st instant, with a letter from the Commissioner of Indian Affairs, of the 2d ultimo, proposing amendments to the treaty, together with a report of Superintendent Hale on the subject and a synopsis of the proceedings of the council held with the Nez Percé Indians, are herewith transmitted for the consideration of the Senate.

Executive Office,   ABRAHAM LINCOLN.
Washington April 4, 1864.

[1] *Executive Journal*, XIII, 471. On April 5, the treaty and accompanying papers were referred to the committee on Indian affairs and a remonstrance of "_____ McDaniels and others" against ratification of the ninth article of the treaty was read. The treaty as amended was ratified on June 26, 1866.

To Ambrose W. Thompson[1]

Ambrose W. Thompson   Executive Mansion,
My Dear Sir   Washington, April 4, 1864.

Yours of yesterday is just received. The financial scheme you suggest I shall consider further, but I have not time to form a conclusion which could reach you by the 6th.

I shall be glad to hear from you in Europe as you suggest. Yours truly   A. LINCOLN.

[1] DfS, DLC-RTL. On April 3, Thompson wrote, "In continuation of the conversation of Saturday . . . . I beg to make one suggestion. Negotiate a loan of one hundred millions in Europe upon the condition that the *money or its average amount is to remain there in Bankers hands.* Use this as a credit to break down Exchange. Gold falls with Exchange—prices of Subsistence with gold. . . . If you have the amount named to your credit in Europe, draw against it—sell the exchange at a gradually reducing rate so as not to create ruin of present holders, remit the amount received for sales, to keep the credit intact—and you have control of the markets. Army supplies will be reduced one half. . . . Who would then doubt the skill of the movement, or fail to render praise at the result? It would crush the Chase faction at a blow, and . . . it would also crush out the Confederate negotiations for Capital. . . . If you wish I can make quiet inquiries & write you from England an outline of the whole matter. I shall sail on the morning of the 6th instant. . . ." (DLC-RTL).

To Nathaniel P. Banks[1]

                              Executive Mansion,
Major General Banks   Washington, April 5. 1864.

I have received a letter from Gen. Charles P. Stone, indorsed by yourself, asking that "some act, some word, some order may issue from the Executive which shall place my name clear of reproach &c." Nothing more definite than this is indicated as to what Gen. Stone desires me to do, or supposes I can do in the case. I can only state the facts of the case from memory, and, of course not with great minuteness or accuracy. Gen. Stone was arrested, as I now think, early in February 1862. Owing to sickness in my family, the Secretary of War made the arrest without notifying me that he had it in contemplation. Gen. McClellan was then General-in-chief, with Head Quarters at Washington, and Gen. Stone was commanding a Division twentyfive or thirty miles above on the Potomac. Learning of the arrest I inquired for the cause, and found it, or the evidence constituting it to consist of three classes. First, the evidence taken in writing by the Committee of Congress on the conduct of the War. The point supposed to be made by this against General Stone was that when before the committee at one time, and excusing himself for not having sent a force from one point to another during the battle in which Col. Baker was killed, he stated that the enemy had a redoubt or dirt fort on the route which could not be passed. Afterwards the committee, conceiving that Gen. Stone could have prevented the erection of that fort, and ought to have done so, called him before them again to inquire why he did not, and he then denied that there ever had been a fort at that place. I did not think the evidence, as read to me, made the point conclusively against the general; but that evidence, whatever it is, I suppose is still accessible.

Secondly, evidence taken and put in the form of a report by a detective of Gen. McClellan.

[1] ADf, DLC-RTL. Presumably this letter was never completed or sent. General Stone's letter of February 15, 1864, states:

"As a soldier, I make to you my last appeal for justice. . . . It is now more than two years since I was suddenly taken from the command of one of the largest and finest divisions of the Army, and incarcerated in a prison set aside for traitors. . . .

"I remained in prison one hundred and eighty nine days, as true a soldier of the United States as remained in her armies. . . .

"I will not recal the frequent appeals which I made. . . . Appeals for appearance of accuser—appeals for statement of accusation—appeals for hearing—appeals for opportunity of service.

"It is sufficient that none were ever regarded. . . . I was discharged without ever having seen accusation or the name of an accuser. . . .

"After six months of imprisonment and nine months of forced inactivity . . . I was suddenly ordered . . . to report for duty in the Department of the Gulf. . . .

"A new campaign is now about to open. It may be the last of many which I have had the fortune to participate in. It will perhaps be fortunate for all concerned that it should be so. . . .

"I respectfully ask, for the sake of the Service which I have loved and never dishonored, and for the sake of my name in history to be read by my descendants, that some act, some word, some order shall issue from the Executive which shall place my name clear of reproach, as I know it should be. . . ." (DLC-RTL).

See Lincoln's communications to Hamlin, April 28, 1862, and to the Senate, May 1, 1862, *supra*. General Stone resigned from the army on September 13, 1864.

To Edward Bates[1]

DeWitt. C. Ballou   April 5, 1864
         Pardon.

Will the Attorney General please preserve these papers? It may be easier hereafter than now, to grant a pardon in the case.

April 5. 1864   A.L.

[1] AES, DNA RG 204, U.S. Pardon Attorney, A 528. Lincoln's endorsement is written on an envelope containing a petition for pardon of DeWitt C. Ballou of Missouri, convicted of conspiracy.

Endorsement Concerning John F. Botts[1]

April 5, 1864

I think the Department Commander, with his assistants, should, with reference to the public peace and security on the one hand, and humanity on the other, decide applications of this class.

April 5. 1864   A. LINCOLN

[1] Copy, DNA WR RG 107, Secretary of War, Letters Received, P 207, Register notation. The transcript preserved in the register is of an endorsement by Lincoln on a letter of John S. Clark concerning John F. Botts, banished South from Missouri and wishing to return.

To Mrs. Horace Mann[1]

Mrs. Horace Mann,   Executive Mansion,
Madam,   Washington, April 5, 1864.

The petition of persons under eighteen, praying that I would free all slave children, and the heading of which petition it appears you wrote, was handed me a few days since by Senator Sumner. Please tell these little people I am very glad their young hearts are so full of just and generous sympathy, and that, while I have not the power to grant all they ask, I trust they will remember that God has, and that, as it seems, He wills to do it. Yours truly

A. LINCOLN

[1] ADfS, DLC-RTL; ALS-F, ISLA. See Lincoln to Sumner, *infra*. The "Petition of the Children of the United States; that the President will free all slave children" bears one hundred ninety-five signatures (DLC-RTL). In reply to Lincoln's letter, forwarded by Senator Sumner, Mrs. Mann wrote: "It was wholly without my knowledge that my name was sent to you in connection with the petition of persons under eighteen in Concord . . . but I cannot regret it, since it has given me this precious note from your hand. . . . We intend immediately to scatter fac-similes of your sweet words to the children like apple blossoms all over the country—and we look with more hope than ever for the day when perfect justice shall be decreed, which shall make every able bodied colored man spring to the defence of the nation which it is plain the white man alone cannot save. . . ." (*Ibid.*).

In deference to Mrs. Mann's desire to remain anonymous, the facsimiles, which were widely distributed, show instead of "Mrs. Horace Mann" "Mrs. ——— (of Concord Mass.)."

To Edwin M. Stanton[1]

I leave to the Sec. of War whether this shall be brought to the notice of Gen. Grant   A. LINCOLN

April 5. 1864

[1] AES, NHi. Lincoln's endorsement is written on a telegram from Governor Andrew Johnson, April 5, 1864: "The papers state that Genl Buell is to be sent to Knoxville to take Command. I trust in god that Gen Buell will not be sent

to Tennessee. We have been cursed with him here once and do not desire its repetition. We had a fine meeting at Shelbyville. Went off well General Ro[u]sseau made a fine speech taking high ground on the negro question which will I think do great good in Kentucky and Tennessee If Genl Ro[u]sseau had leave of absence for a short time which would enable him to visit Kentucky and make some speeches in that state such as he made at Shelbyville it would do much good in putting down copperheads and traitors. If this suggestion was made to Genl Thomas I have no doubt he would grant him leave of absence for the present. His services would be invaluable in Kentucky."

General Buell had been before a Military Commission to investigate his Kentucky and Tennessee campaign of November 24, 1862 to May 10, 1863, and was awaiting orders at Indianapolis. On June 1, 1864, he resigned.

To Charles Sumner[1]

If Senator Sumner thinks it would be proper, he may forward the inclosed to Mrs. Mann.

April 5. 1864

A.L.

[1] ALS, CSmH. See Lincoln to Mrs. Horace Mann, *supra.*

To Robert B. Van Valkenburgh[1]

April 5, 1864

If Hon. Mr. Van Valkenburgh will say distinctly in writing that he desires the discharge of Reuben C. Ward, he shall be discharged.
April 5. 1864.

A. LINCOLN

Let said Reuben C. Ward be discharged.   A. LINCOLN
April 5. 1864.

[1] AES, owned by Roy G. Fitzgerald, Dayton, Ohio. Lincoln's first endorsement is written on a letter from Representative Robert B. Van Valkenburgh, April 1, 1864, introducing Mrs. Ward "a widow residing in my district. She has only *two* sons both in the 50th Regt N.Y.V. Since their enlistment her husband has died, and she desires that one of her sons be discharged. . . ." The second endorsement is written on Van Valkenburgh's note of April 5, 1864, asking that Reuben C. Ward be discharged.

To John Catron[1]

Mr. Justice Catron   Executive Mansion,
My dear Sir   Washington, April 6, 1864.

Mrs. Masson comes to me with a note of introduction from you. She asks that James H. McEwen, now a prisoner [of] war at Rock-Island, Illinois [be pardoned]. If you will write below on this sheet that if he shall take the oath of December 8. and be discharged, you pledge your honor he will keep faith, I will order his discharge.
Yours truly   A. LINCOLN

[1] ALS, owned by Henry R. Benjamin, New York City. No reply from Judge Catron has been found, and neither Mrs. Masson nor McEwen has been identified.

To Edwin M. Stanton[1]

If the services can be made available let Hon. Mr. Whaley be
obliged by the appointment within requested   A. LINCOLN
    April 6, 1864

1 AES, IHi. Lincoln's endorsement is written on a letter of U.S. Representative Kellian V. Whaley of West Virginia, to Stanton, April 5, 1864, recommending appointment of J. Mabbett Brown as quartermaster or commissary of subsistence with rank of captain. No record of Brown's appointment has been discovered.

To Benjamin F. Butler[1]

Executive Mansion,
Major General Butler.   Washington, April 7, 1864.
    Mrs. L. and I think we will visit Fort-Monroe some time next
week; meanwhile whatever is to be done on the business-subject[2]
will be conducted through the War Department. Please do not
make public our probable visit.   A LINCOLN

1 ADfS, DLC-RTL; LS, DNA WR RG 107, Presidential Telegrams, I, 22. A telegram from John Hay to Butler, April 6, 1864, authorizing Butler to visit Washington at the president's direction, was amended by Stanton so as to read "you will submit by letter or telegram to the Secretary of War the points in relation to the exchange of prisoners whenever you wish instructions and that it is not necessary for you to visit Washington for the purpose indicated." (DNA WR RG 107, Presidential Telegrams, I, 20). Butler replied on the same day, "I beg leave to assure the President that I have no desire to visit Washington, but wish he should visit Fortress Monroe as expressed in my telegram of Saturday." (*Private and Official Correspondence of General Benjamin F. Butler. . . . ,* IV, 29). See further, Lincoln to Butler, April 11, *infra.*

2 Perhaps Lincoln refers to Butler's confiscation of the estate of John Williams of Portsmouth, Virginia. See Butler to Stanton, April 4, 1864, *op. cit.,* IV, 16.

To Simon Cameron[1]

Hon. Simon Cameron   Executive Mansion,
My dear Sir.   Washington, April 7, 1864.
    I have this moment, only, received yours of March 29th. I will
see you any time it is convenient for you to come. Yours truly
          A. LINCOLN

1 ALS, DLC-Cameron Papers. Cameron's letter of March 29, 1864, is as follows:
    "I had a letter this morning from a very intelligent politician of much influence in N. York urging me to consent to a postponement of the convention till Sept. Some time ago a committee called on me to urge the same matter
    "These things and others that have come to my view, convince me that it will be vigorously urged and that if it is not vigorously resisted, it will succeed.
    "In connection with this it is well known that Mr. Seward has never ceased to think he will succeed you, and that his faithful manager hopes to carry him

into the Presidency next March, by his skill, aided perhaps by the millions made in N. York by army & navy contracts.

"Another, and I think a wiser party, look to the election of Genl. Dix. The least failure this summer, some men think, will evince [?] your defeat, by bringing forward a negative man, with a *cultivated* character such as Dix has acquired by avoiding all responsibility, & always obtaining with every party in *power* a *high* position.

"I am against all postponements & I presume you are, but I look upon this movement as being so formidable that I should like to have a full & free conversation with you concerning it & the campaign. There are many points which would probably enable me to do more service—& as I am in the contest, with no wish saving your success—and with little business to interfere, I desire to guard against all surprizes. You are always so much employed when I am in Washington that I have hesitated to occupy your time—but, if you will drop me a line saying when I can come to your house with a chance of an hours uninterrupted talk, I will obey it.

"I came from Ft. Monroe yesterday after spending three days there, during which time I had much pleasant conversation with Genl. Butler—part of which I would like to communicate to you." (DLC-RTL).

To the House of Representatives[1]

To the House of Representatives: April 7, 1864

I transmit herewith a report from the Secretary of War, in answer to the Resolution of the House of Representatives of the 4th. instant, in relation to Major N. H. McLean.

Washington,   ABRAHAM LINCOLN
April 7th. 1864.

[1] DS, DNA RG 233, House Executive Document No. 67. The resolution passed on April 4, 1864, requested the president to communicate the reasons why Major Nathaniel H. McLean, adjutant general of the Department of the Ohio (August 23, 1862 to December 26, 1863), had been ordered to Fort Vancouver as assistant to the provost marshal general and superintendent of recruiting service in Oregon and Washington Territory. Stanton's report of April 7, transmitted by Lincoln, reads as follows:

"In answer to the resolution of the House . . . dated April 4. . . . I have the honor to state—

"1. That Major McLean was ordered to Vancouver because it was deemed expedient for the service that he should go there.

"2. It has never been the practice of the War Department . . . to furnish copies of changes affecting the capacity or fidelity of its officers upon which no action has been taken. In the present instance it is not deemed compatible with the public interests to make any further answer to the latter branch of the inquiry contained in said resolution. . . ."

To Edwin M. Stanton[1]

Hon. Sec. of War   Executive Mansion,
My dear Sir   Washington, April 7, 1864.

What are the facts in the case of William T. Aud, in the Carroll building prison   Yours truly   A. LINCOLN

[1] ALS, DNA WR RG 107, Secretary of War, Letters Received, P 236. Stanton replied on April 8 that William T. Aud had been found guilty on charges of being in business of conducting persons through Federal lines by rowing them across the Potomac, but that "on application in his behalf one half of his sentence was remitted yesterday." (DLC-RTL). Montgomery Blair wrote on April 7 introducing "Miss Lavania Beers who is sister-in-law of Wm T Aud. . . . I have very little knowledge of Mr. Aud. . . . I know however that he has voted with the Union party. . . ." (*Ibid.*).

Form Order for Release of Prisoners[1]

April 8, 1864

If the persons whose names follow, now Prisoners of War at ———————————, *shall take the oath of December 8, 1863, and be discharged, we, the undersigned Members of Congress, pledge our honor that they will keep faith:*

Joseph Henry Crosster	Fort Deleware
John B. Talbott	Camp Chase
Jefferson M Booth	Camp Chase
William E. Wood	Camp Morton
John Cohen	Camp Douglas
C. D. Nutter	Camp Douglas
J. N. Taylor	Fort Deleware
T. M Combs	Fort Deleware

Brutus J. Clay, *M. C.*
W. H Randall *M. C.*
Lu Anderson *M. C.*

Excepting such as are commissioned officers, let the above named prisoner[s] be discharged on the conditions stated

April 8. 1864. A. LINCOLN

[1] D and AES, IHi. A similar document of this date, bearing the same autograph endorsement by Lincoln, was submitted by members of congress from Missouri (RPB), and presumably numerous others were signed by Lincoln. The printed portions of the document are reproduced in italic type.

To Edwin M. Stanton[1]

If consistent with the public interest, I shall be glad for the within request to be granted. A. LINCOLN

April 8. 1864.

[1] AES, MiU-Hi-Chase Osborn Papers. See Lincoln's memorandum of July 29, 1862. Lincoln's endorsement is written on a letter from Mrs. Hattie Knight asking that her sick husband, Robert T. Knight, "shall have the privilege of selling goods at the Soldiers Rest in Alexandria."

To Gideon Welles[1]

Hon. Sec. of Navy please see & hear Lieut. Merryman, who was raised in the town of my residence A. LINCOLN

April 8. 1864

[1] ALS, owned by Philip R. Davis, Chicago, Illinois. Concerning Lieutenant James H. Merryman, see Lincoln to Chase, May 13, 1863.

To Benjamin F. Butler[1]

April 9, 1864

Mr. Buttz wishes to return to Portsmouth. I will not force him back into Gen. Butler's Department, contrary to his will; but I will be obliged if Gen. Butler will hear him on the question of what his future conduct will be, and restore him if he shall think he safely can. A. LINCOLN.

April 9. 1864

[1] AES, DLC-Butler Papers. Lincoln's endorsement is written on an envelope endorsed by Edward Bates: "The bearer, Mr Butts of Norfolk, Va., begs a short interview, upon a matter of the greatest importance to him.

"Mr Butts, is a Pennsylvanian, late a cavalry officer. Reputed a good lawyer, and stands highly recommended, in this office for Dist: Atty." Charles W. Butts, a lawyer and formerly a lieutenant of Company I, Eleventh Pennsylvania Cavalry (resigned October 28, 1863) wrote Attorney General Bates on March 19, 1864, protesting Butler's confiscation orders, specifically the seizure of the estate of John W. Williams of Portsmouth, Virginia (*Private and Official Correspondence of Benjamin F. Butler*, IV, 18).

To Joseph Holt[1]

Judge Advocate General please examine and report upon this case.

April 9. 1864 A. LINCOLN

[1] AES, DNA GE RG 60, Papers of Attorney General, Segregated Lincoln Material. Lincoln's endorsement is written on an envelope containing papers in the case of J. V. W. Vandenburg formerly a captain in the One Hundred Twenty-fifth New York Volunteers, convicted of presenting false accounts and vouchers, and fined $1,000. Holt's report of April 21, 1864, gave the opinion that the case against Vandenburg was faulty and recommended pardon. An opinion by Attorney General Bates, May 18, 1864, concurred that "the offence is not a *felony.*" On May 9, Lincoln endorsed "Pardon. A. Lincoln."

To Joseph Holt[1]

Judge Advocate General please report on this case.

April 9. 1864. A. LINCOLN

Application denied. A. LINCOLN
April 27, 1864.

[1] AES, DNA WR RG 153, Judge Advocate General, LL 1670. Lincoln's endorsement is written on the record of Nathan W. Stout, late pilot of the steamer *Fulton*, dismissed for intoxication. Holt reported that Stout should not be relieved of sentence.

To George G. Meade[1]

Major General Meade   Executive Mansion,
Army of the Potomac   Washington, April 9. 1864.
    Suspend execution of private William Collins, Co. B. 69th. N.Y. Vols. Irish Brigade, and class him with other suspended cases.

                                         A. LINCOLN

[1] ALS, owned by Joseph L. Block, Chicago, Illinois. See further, Lincoln to Meade, April 17, *infra*.

To Edwin M. Stanton[1]

Let the order in this case be modified as within requested.
    April 9, 1864.   A. LINCOLN

[1] AES, IHi. Lincoln's endorsement appears on a letter of Reverend John A. Spooner, Baltimore, to Montgomery Blair, April 7, 1864. Because of poor health, Spooner had attempted to resign as hospital chaplain at Point Lookout, but had been dismissed instead. AGO *Special Orders No. 144*, April 11, 1864, directed that "So much of . . . Special Orders, No. 99, of March 1st, 1864, from this Office, as dismissed Hospital Chaplain *John A. Spooner*, U.S. Army, for absence without proper authority, is hereby revoked, and his resignation has been accepted by the President, to take effect February 8th, 1864."

To Charles Sumner[1]

Will Senator Sumner please call and see me this morning?
    April 9. 1864   A. LINCOLN
        251. F. Street

[1] ALS, owned by Dale Carnegie, New York City.

To Benjamin F. Butler[1]

                              Office U.S. Military Telegraph,
Major General Butler   War Department,
Fort-Monroe, Va   Washington, D.C., April 11 1864.
    Mrs. L. is so unwell that I now think we will not make the contemplated trip this week. Will notify you in time. Will probably get a Boat here, but will accept yours if necessary. Thanks for your kind interest in the case.   A. LINCOLN

[293]

[1] ALS, DNA WR RG 107, Presidential Telegrams, I, 24. See Lincoln to Butler, April 7, *supra.* On April 10 Butler telegraphed, "Shall I send a boat for yourself and party? If not please telegraph me when you leave, or will arrive" (DLC-RTL).

Endorsement Concerning John Ehler[1]

They say that by the destruction of a bridge this boy has been unable to pass on this. Might it not be renewed for the little fellow.?

April 11. 1864   A. LINCOLN

[1] AES, IHi. Lincoln's endorsement is written on the back of an official War Department pass issued on April 9, 1864, to "John Ehler, a boy 10 years old, to the Army of the Potomac, to join Emery R. Simons, 61st. N.Y. Veteran Vols." See also Lincoln's pass for John Ehler, September 13, *infra.*

To Joseph Holt[1]

Executive Mansion, Washington,
Judge Advocate General   April 11. 1864.

It is understood that in the early part of 1862, or latter part of 1861, Francis G. Young was tried and dismissed by a Court Martial sitting at Poolesville Md. Col. Devens[2] was President of the Court. What I want is the record of the trial, & if you can find it for me I shall be obliged   Yours truly   A. LINCOLN

[1] ALS, owned by Joseph Holt Rose, Pasadena, California. See Lincoln to McClellan, December 6, 1861, *supra.* No reply has been discovered.
[2] Colonel Charles Devens (?) of the Fifteenth Massachusetts Infantry.

Order for Discharge of Prisoners[1]

Excepting commissioned officers, let the within named prisoners be discharged on the conditions stated.   A. LINCOLN
April 11. 1864.

[1] AES, ICU. Lincoln's endorsement is written on a form order for discharge of forty-five prisoners as listed and vouched for by members of congress from Missouri. See similar order, April 8, *supra.*

To William H. Seward[1]

Office U.S. Military Telegraph,
Hon. W. H. Seward   War Department,
Astor-House   Washington, D.C.,
New-York.   April 11, 6/15 PM. 1864.

Nothing of importance since you left.   A. LINCOLN

[1] ALS, DNA WR RG 107, Presidential Telegrams, I, 25.

[294]

To Edwin M. Stanton[1]

April 11, 1864

Hon. Sec. of War, please see L. H. Putnam, whom you will find a very intelligent colored man; and who wishes to talk about our colored forces, their organization, &c   A. LINCOLN.
April 11, 1864.

[1] ALS-F, Brooklyn *Daily Eagle,* February 12, 1928. L. H. Putnam has not been identified.

To Miss Steele[1]

Executive Mansion, Washington,

My Dear Miss Steele   April 11, 1864.
I cannot refuse you so slight a favor for so good a purpose. Yours very truly   A. LINCOLN.

[1] LS, RPAB-Hawkins Collection. Miss Steele has not been identified, but may have been the same Ella Steele to whom Lincoln sent his autograph on February 20, 1865, *infra.*

To John C. Underwood[1]

Executive Mansion,
Washington, April 11. 1864.

If Judge John C. Underwood will say in writing on this sheet that he personally knows Mrs. Keenan, and that he desires her & her little nephew to pass our lines and go to her father in Rockingham, Va, I will direct a pass to be given her accordingly.

A. LINCOLN

[1] ALS, DLC-RTL. John C. Underwood, judge of the U.S. District Court of Virginia at Alexandria, answered on the bottom of the page: "I have long known Mrs Keenan her father husband & children I highly esteem her for her energy integrity & private virtues & since duty calls her to guide & guard her now fatherless children who are with her father in Rockingham Co. Va. I request for her & her little nephew a pass to that place." Mrs. Keenan has not been further identified.

To Whom It May Concern[1]

Executive Mansion,
Whom it may concern   Washington, April 11. 1864.
I know nothing on the subject of the attached letter, except as therein stated. Neither do I personally know Mrs. Hunt. She has,

however, from the beginning of the war, been constantly represented to me as an open, and somewhat influential friend of the
Union. It has been said to me, (I know not whether truly) that her
husband is in the rebel army, that she avows her purpose to not
live with him again, and that she refused to see him when she had
an opportunity during one of John Morgan's raids into Kentucky.
I would not offer her, or any wife, a temptation to a permanent
separation from her husband; but if she shall avow that her mind
is already, independently and fully made up to such separation, I
shall be glad for the property sought by her letter, to be delivered
to her, upon her taking the oath of December 8, 1863.

A. LINCOLN

[1] ALS, ORB; ADfS, DLC-RTL. Mrs. Sallie Ward Hunt, wife of Daniel Hunt,
wrote Mrs. Lincoln on March 31, 1864, requesting her influence in obtaining
furniture and personal effects held by authorities in New Orleans (ALS, ORB).

To Alexander II[1]

April 12, 1864

Abraham Lincoln
President of the United States of America.
To His Majesty Alexander II.
Emperor and Autocrat of all the Russias
&c.   &c.   &c.

Great and Good Friend: I have received the letter which Your
Imperial Majesty was pleased to address to me on the 26th. (14) of
January last, announcing the birth of the 22d (10th) of that month
of a son who has received the name of Pierre to Madame the Grand
Duchess Alexandra Petrovna, Spouse of Your Imperial Majestys
well beloved brother His Imperial Highness Monseigneur the
Grand Duke Nicolas Nicolaewitch.

Your Majesty does but justice to my sentiments in the conviction
which you have been pleased to express that I will take, in an event
so satisfactory to you, and Your Imperial House the same interest
which Your Majesty is ever inclined to take in all that concerns
the prosperity of the United States, and I beg Your Majesty to accept my sincere congratulations upon the occasion: And so I recommend Your Majesty's Imperial Family to the protection of the
Almighty. Your Good Friend   ABRAHAM LINCOLN
Washington, 12th April 1864.
By the President
F. H. SEWARD. Acting Secretary of State.

[296]

1 Copy, DNA FS RG 59, Communications to Foreign Sovereigns and States, III, 218-19.

To Benjamin F. Butler[1]

Major General Butler   Executive Mansion Washington, DC.
Fort-Monroe, Va.   April 12. 1864
 I am pressed to get from Libby, by special exchange, Jacob C. Hagenbuch 1 Lieut. Co. H. 67. Penn. Vols. Please do it, if you can, without detriment or embarrassment.   A. LINCOLN

1 ALS, DNA WR RG 107, Presidential Telegrams, I, 27. Butler replied on the same day that he would "endeavor to effect the proposed exchange." (DLC-Butler Papers). The roster of the Sixty-seventh Pennsylvania Volunteers lists Jacob C. Hagenbuch as mustered out at the expiration of his term on March 24, 1865.

To Benjamin F. Butler[1]

Major Gen. Butler   Executive Mansion,
Fort-Monroe, Va   Washington, April 12. 1864.
 I am appealed to in behalf of Charles Crumblin [Crumpton] said to be under sentence of death, to be executed at Norfolk to-morrow. Please ascertain whether there is any ground for a pardon, or even a respite, and answer me.   A. LINCOLN

1 ALS, DNA WR RG 107, Presidential Telegrams, I, 28. Butler replied on the same day:
 "Telegram recieved. In regard to the question of pardon or respite I send the extract from the General Order which approved the sentence to wit
 " 'In the case of Private Charles Crumpton Co. G. 10th. regt New Hampshire Vols, it appearing that the accused enlisted as a substitute and recieved his bounty in payment therefor, then deliberately procured a rebel uniform with which to aid him in deserting and did desert from his regiment and was detected in the act, and when detected attempted to pass himself off as a rebel deserter, no excuse is left for his acts and indeed none is attempted to be given. He has been tried before a General Court Martial and upon satisfactory evidence although defended by counsel of his own selection he has been found guilty. The proceedings findings and sentence are therefore approved & confirmed'
 "I know nothing which can by possibility be urged in Crumptons favor except that he was defended by one Butts a lawyer who neglected his case, but I examined the record and came to the result above stated
 "Large numbers of the New Hampshire substitutes have deserted from Yorktown yesterday and to day—some have gone to the enemy, some are lurking in swamps and some are attempting to get to Baltimore they are from the regiments lately at Point Lookout which I have had to remove from thence because I found them colluding with the prisoners and escaping. Three (3) having siezed a boat and carried off five (5) prisoners Those that we catch are being tried by Court Martial and I believe it will be necessary to execute quite a number of them." (DLC-Butler Papers).
 See Lincoln to Butler, April 13, infra.

To John A. Dix[1]

Major General Dix.
New York City.

Executive Mansion,
Washington, April 12, 1864.

Suspend execution of death sentence, of William H. Gibney, 7th N.Y. Heavy Artillery, until further orders. A. LINCOLN.

Maj: Eckert.

Please send the above dispatch JNO. G. NICOLAY Priv: Sec:

[1] D, DNA WR RG 107, Presidential Telegrams, I, 26. Nicolay signed both "A. Lincoln" and his own signature. Simeon Draper of New York City wrote Lincoln on April 12 asking clemency for William Gibney, sentenced for desertion. Gibney remained in solitary confinement until June 22, when Lincoln referred to Stanton Gibney's request to be released from heavy irons to work (DNA WR RG 107, Secretary of War, Letters Received, P 375, returned to the president, July 8, 1864). No further record of Lincoln's action has been found.

To Benjamin F. Butler[1]

Major General Butler
Fort-Monroe, Va.

Executive Mansion
Washington D.C. April 13. 1864

Yours in regard to Charles Crumpton received. I have no more to say in the case. A. LINCOLN

[1] ALS, DNA WR RG 107, Presidential Telegrams, I, 29. See note to Lincoln's telegram of April 12, *supra*. No record of Lincoln's further action has been found, but Crumpton seems not to have been executed. The roster of the Tenth New Hampshire Volunteers lists him as discharged on July 12, 1865, at Concord, New Hampshire.

To Joseph Holt[1]

Pardon—proof being insufficient, except for short absence without leave. A. LINCOLN
April 14. 1864

[1] AES, DNA WR RG 153, Judge Advocate General, NN 1204. Lincoln's endorsement is written on the court-martial record of John C. Clevenger, First New Jersey Cavalry, sentenced to two years' imprisonment for absence without leave and for forgery. This is one of sixty-seven cases reviewed by Lincoln on April 14. His endorsements are routine pardons, commutations, remissions, or approvals of sentence with the exception of the two reproduced.

To Joseph Holt[1]

This man is pardoned, and hereby ordered to be discharged from the service. A. LINCOLN
April 14. 1864

1 AES, DNA WR RG 153, Judge Advocate General, MM 761. Lincoln's endorsement is written on the court-martial record of Private Patrick Murphy, Company E, Second California Volunteers, sentenced to be shot for desertion and violation of the Twenty-Third Article of War. The court asked clemency, as the accused was insane.

To the Senate[1]

To the Senate of the United States: April 15, 1864

I herewith lay before the Senate, for its constitutional action thereon, a supplemental treaty negotiated on the 12th of April, 1864, with the Red Lake and Pembina bands of Chippewa Indians.

A report of the Secretary of the Interior of this date and a communication from the Acting Commissioner of Indian Affairs accompany the treaty.   ABRAHAM LINCOLN.

Washington City, April 15, 1864.

1 *Executive Journal*, XIII, 490. See Lincoln's communication to the Senate, January 8, *supra*. The supplemental treaty was ratified by the Senate on April 21, 1864.

To James B. Fry[1]

Executive Mansion   April 16. 1864

The within paper was written at my suggestion by gentlemen representing Philadelphia, to present their views of the subject embraced and to be signed by me if I could approve it. I am not prepared to assent to all that it asks at present, but I do order that the Philadelphia quotas be adjusted for the calls of 1863 and 1864 already made, upon the basis that that City was under no deficit on November 3d. 1862, and allowing full credits for all since that date; and further that all other questions presented on said paper are left open for future adjustment.   A. LINCOLN

1 ES, IHi; ADf, DLC-RTL. The autograph draft is undated and reads: "The within paper was written at my suggestion, by gentlemen representing Philadelphia, to present their views of the subject embraced, & to be signed by me, if I could approve it. I can not sign it, but order for the present, that the Philadelphia quotas be adjusted for the calls of 1863 & 1864 already made, upon the basis that she was under no deficit on Nov. 3, 1862, and allowing full credits for all since that date; and further that all other questions presented on said paper are left open for further adjustment."

The endorsement signed by Lincoln accompanies the following communication dated April 15, 1864, and addressed to Colonel James B. Fry:

"Finding that the quotas assigned to the different Congressional Districts of the State of Pennsylvania, under the calls for men of the years 1863 & 1864, are all affected by distributed portions of a supposed deficiency of that state, under calls of the years 1861 & 1862, when no accounts were kept by your department with Congressional Districts, but only with the state at large; and evidence having been adduced before me tending to shew that persons acting officially, and by authority from the Governor of that state, did, on November 3d. 1862, make a report to him, that, so far as the City of Philadelphia was concerned, she had complied with all calls upon her up to that time; which report was accepted by said Governor, who, acting thereupon, at once ordered that no draft should take place in said City; & now, that we have begun to keep accounts with Congressional Districts, and even smaller localities, I am disposed to regard this report, so accepted and acted upon by said Governor, as conclusive in favor of said City, upon the questions therein decided. You will please direct the officers of your Bureau of Enrolment to act upon this report as follows: viz.

"1st. To strike out all charge against said City of Philadelphia, as for a deficiency under the calls of 1861 & 1862.

"2d. To give said City the benefit of any credit that may result to her, under the present practice of your department to reduce all charges & credits to terms of three years men, from the facts appearing in said report and the accompanying documents, shewing that she furnished three years men who, in said report, are made to stand no better than nine months men furnished by other parts of the state.

"3d. That credit be further given to said City for all men mustered into the service from November 3d. 1862, the date at which her quotas were declared filled by the proper officers, under their existing regulations, until the date when accounts were opened by your Bureau with the several Congressional Districts

"4th. That any credits, resulting from these orders, for surplus troops furnished under the calls of 1861 & 1862, shall be a balance to the credit of Philadelphia under the calls of 1863 & 1864."

To Henry W. Halleck[1]

April 16, 1864

Let it be done.   A. LINCOLN.

[1] OR, I, XXXIV, III, 178. Lincoln's endorsement is written on a despatch from General Grant to Halleck: "Please ask the President to authorize the transfer of Fort Smith and the Indian Territory to the Department of Arkansas. There is every reason why this Territory and the State of Arkansas should be under one man, and that man in the field. In case this change is made I wish General Blunt ordered back to report to General Curtis." AGO *General Orders No. 164*, April 17, 1864, ordered the transfer and also Blunt to report to Curtis.

To John P. Usher[1]

Let the lands be withheld from sale as recommended.

April 16. 1864   A. LINCOLN

[1] ES, DNA NR RG 75, Office of Indian Affairs, Executive Order File. Lincoln's endorsement is written on a letter of William P. Dole to Usher, April 12, 1864, concurring in recommendations of an enclosed letter from D. C. Leach, agent of the Mackinac Indian Agency, Detroit, April 5, 1864, that certain public lands be withdrawn from sale and added to the Little Traverse Indian Reservation.

To George G. Meade[1]

Major-General Meade,   Executive Mansion,
Army of Potomac: Washington, April 17, 1864.

Private William Collins of Company B, of the Sixty-ninth New York Volunteers, has been convicted of desertion, and execution suspended as in numerous other cases. Now Captain O'Neill, commanding the regiment, and nearly all its other regimental and company officers, petition for his full pardon and restoration to his company. Is there any good objection?   A. LINCOLN.

[1] Tarbell (Appendix), p. 422. See Lincoln to Meade, April 9, *supra*. No reply or further reference has been located. Captain Bernard S. O'Neill of the Sixty-ninth New York Volunteers was killed at Petersburg, Virginia, June 16, 1864.

Address at Sanitary Fair, Baltimore, Maryland[1]

April 18, 1864.

Ladies and Gentlemen—Calling to mind that we are in Baltimore, we can not fail to note that the world moves. Looking upon these many people, assembled here, to serve, as they best may, the soldiers of the Union, it occurs at once that three years ago, the same soldiers could not so much as pass through Baltimore. The change from then till now, is both great, and gratifying. Blessings on the brave men who have wrought the change, and the fair women who strive to reward them for it.

But Baltimore suggests more than could happen within Baltimore. The change within Baltimore is part only of a far wider change. When the war began, three years ago, neither party, nor any man, expected it would last till now. Each looked for the end, in some way, long ere to-day. Neither did any anticipate that domestic slavery would be much affected by the war. But here we are; the war has not ended, and slavery has been much affected— how much needs not now to be recounted. So true is it that man proposes, and God disposes.

But we can see the past, though we may not claim to have directed it; and seeing it, in this case, we feel more hopeful and confident for the future.

The world has never had a good definition of the word liberty, and the American people, just now, are much in want of one. We all declare for liberty; but in using the same *word* we do not all mean the same *thing*. With some the word liberty may mean for each man to do as he pleases with himself, and the product of his labor; while with others the same word may mean for some men to do as they please with other men, and the product of other men's labor. Here are two, not only different, but incompatable things, called by the same name—liberty. And it follows that each of the things is, by the respective parties, called by two different and incompatable names—liberty and tyranny.

The shepherd drives the wolf from the sheep's throat, for which the sheep thanks the shepherd as a *liberator,* while the wolf denounces him for the same act as the destroyer of liberty, especially as the sheep was a black one. Plainly the sheep and the wolf are not agreed upon a definition of the word liberty; and precisely the same difference prevails to-day among us human creatures, even in the North, and all professing to love liberty. Hence we behold the processes by which thousands are daily passing from under the yoke of bondage, hailed by some as the advance of liberty, and bewailed by others as the destruction of all liberty. Recently, as it seems, the people of Maryland have been doing something to define liberty; and thanks to them that, in what they have done, the wolf's dictionary, has been repudiated.

It is not very becoming for one in my position to make speeches at great length; but there is another subject upon which I feel that I ought to say a word. A painful rumor, true I fear, has reached us of the massacre, by the rebel forces, at Fort Pillow, in the West end of Tennessee, on the Mississippi river, of some three hundred colored soldiers and white officers, who had just been overpowered by their assailants.[2] There seems to be some anxiety in the public mind whether the government is doing it's duty to the colored soldier, and to the service, at this point. At the beginning of the war, and for some time, the use of colored troops was not contemplated; and how the change of purpose was wrought, I will not now take time to explain. Upon a clear conviction of duty I resolved to turn that element of strength to account; and I am responsible for it to the American people, to the christian world, to history, and on my final account to God. Having determined to use the negro as a soldier, there is no way but to give him all the protection given to any other soldier. The difficulty is not in stating the principle, but in practically applying it. It is a mistake to suppose the government is indiffe[re]nt to this matter, or is not doing the best it can in regard to it. We do not to-day *know* that a colored soldier, or white officer commanding colored soldiers, has been massacred by the rebels when made a prisoner. We fear it, believe it, I may say, but we do not *know* it. To take the life of one of their prisoners, on the assumption that they murder ours, when it is short of certainty that they do murder ours, might be too serious, too cruel a mistake. We are having the Fort-Pillow affair thorough-

ly investigated; and such investigation will probably show conclusively how the truth is. If, after all that has been said, it shall
turn out that there has been no massacre at Fort-Pillow, it will be
almost safe to say there has been none, and will be none elsewhere.
If there has been the massacre of three hundred there, or even the
tenth part of three hundred, it will be conclusively proved; and
being so proved, the retribution shall as surely come. It will be
matter of grave consideration in what exact course to apply the
retribution; but in the supposed case, it must come.

1 AD, The Rosenbach Company, Philadelphia and New York. A preliminary
draft (*infra*) of the opening paragraph of this address is preserved in the Lincoln Papers.
2 See Lincoln's communication to cabinet members and note, May 3, *infra*.

Draft of Address for Sanitary Fair at Baltimore[1]

[c. April 18, 1864]

Mr. Webster once stated the proposition that a President could not
be so applauded, and ministered unto, when his term of office, and
with it, his power to confer favors, drew near to it's close, as he had
been in the hey-day of his inauguration. To illustrate this, he said:
"Politicians—office-seekers—are not sun-flowers; they do not turn
upon their god when he sets, the same look they gave when he
rose." This may be a general truth; but, to my personal knowledge
it is not particularly true in Baltimore. For intance, on the 22nd.
or 23rd. of February 1861 (so near the end of one and the beginning of the other, as to be doubtful which) I passed through
Baltimore, rich with honorable and fat offices, soon to be dispensed,
and not one hand reached forth to greet me, not one voice broke
the stillness to cheer me. Now, three years having past, and offices
having passed away, Baltimore marks my coming, and cheers me
when I come. Traitorous malice has sought to wrong Baltimore
herein, ascribing to one cause what is justly due to another. For instance the Richmond,[2] alluding to that passage through Baltimore,
said: "We have no fear of any bold action by the federal government; we remember Baltimore, and our faith is unwavering in
Lincoln's cowardice" Now this is hugely unjust to Baltimore. I
take it to be unquestionable that what happened here three years
ago, and what happens here now, was contempt of office then, and
is purely appreciation of merit now.

1 AD, DLC-RTL. This fragment would seem logically to have been Lincoln's
opening paragraph for the Baltimore address, abandoned for obvious reasons,
both of politics and sentiment.
2 Lincoln probably intended to insert here the name of a newspaper.

To Edward Bates[1]

Hon. Attorney General   Executive Mansion,
My dear Sir   Washington, April 18, 1864.

Hon Ebenezer Dumont is very desirous that the fine of five hundred dollars assessed in the U.S. District Court of Indiana, against John Caldwell, for aiding a rescue, be remitted, said Caldwell having died, and the fine only operating upon his destitute family. If it be your opinion that the President has the legal *power* so to remit, please prepare the papers, or what is necessary to have it legally done. Yours truly   A. LINCOLN

[1] ALS, DNA RG 204, U.S. Pardon Attorney, A 516. See Lincoln to Bates, April 4, *supra*. Ebenezer Dumont was U.S. representative from Indiana.

To Edward Bates[1]

Attorney General please send nomination for Thomas A. Osborne, in place of McDowell resigned.   A. LINCOLN
April 18. 1864.

[1] AES, DNA GE RG 60, Papers of Attorney General, Segregated Lincoln Material. Lincoln's endorsement is written on a page torn from a letter which has not been found. Thomas A. Osborne's appointment as U.S. marshal for Kansas, replacing James L. McDowell, was confirmed by the Senate on April 20, 1864.

To Edward Bates[1]

Attorney General please examine & report upon this case.
April 18, 1864   A. LINCOLN

[1] AES, DNA RG 204, U.S. Pardon Attorney, A 530. Lincoln's endorsement is written on a petition, November 17, 1863, for pardon of George Ward, signed by jurors who convicted him of highway robbery in the District of Columbia. No further reference has been found.

To Paul Frank[1]

Col. Paul Frank
    of N.Y. 52nd.   Executive Mansion,
Army of Potomac   Washington, April 18. 1864.

Is there, or has there been a man in your Regiment by the name of Cornelius Garvin;? and if so, answer me as far as you know, where he now is.   A. LINCOLN

[1] ALS, DNA WR RG 107, Presidential Telegrams, I, 30. No reply or further reference has been located.

To Stephen Cabot[1]

Officer in Military command,   Executive Mansion
at Fort-Warren.   Washington,
Boston-Harbor, Mass.   April 20. 1864

If there is a man by the name of Charles Carpenter, under sentence of death for desertion, at Fort-Warren, suspend execution until further order, and send the record of his trial. If sentenced for any other offence, telegraph what it is, and when he is to be executed. Answer at all events.   A. LINCOLN.

[1] ALS, DNA WR RG 107, Presidential Telegrams, I, 31. No reply has been discovered. See Lincoln's telegrams to Cabot and to Dix, April 21, *infra*.

Endorsement[1]

April 20, 1864

If the officer commanding this man's regiment, and the officer commanding his company will write on this paper that they desire him to rejoin his regiment, I will send him to them.   A. LINCOLN
April 20, 1864

[1] Thomas A. Madigan, *A Catalogue of Lincolniana* (1929), p. 29. According to the source, this endorsement is written on a petition for pardon, not otherwise identified.

Endorsement Concerning John Oberteuffer[1]

[c. April 20, 1864]

I apprehend the re-organization of the Militia is a far larger job than Lieut. Col. Oberteuffer thinks. I could not enter upon it, now when I have not half time enough for other duties.

[1] American Art Association Catalog 4221, January 14-15, 1936, No. 356. According to the source, Lincoln's endorsement was written on the back of a letter from Lieutenant Colonel John H. Oberteuffer, One Hundred Twelfth Pennsylvania Volunteers (Second Pennsylvania Artillery), April 20, 1864, asking an interview for the purpose of presenting a plan of reorganizing the militia system.

Pass for Miss E. Sharp[1]

Allow Miss E. Sharp, an invalid to pass northward through our line and go to her parents in Norfolk, Va.   A. LINCOLN
April 20, 1864.

[1] Copy, ISLA.

Note[1]

Please ascertain whether the message sent by me yesterday to Fort Warren, Boston-Harbor was delivered.   A. LINCOLN
April 21, 1864

[1] ALS-P, ISLA. This unaddressed note was probably sent to the telegraph officer in the War Department. See Lincoln to Cabot, April 20, *supra*.

To Stephen Cabot[1]

Officer in Military command
at Fort-Warren
Boston-Harbor, Mass.

Executive Mansion,
Washington,
April 21, 1864.

The order I sent yesterday in regard to Charles Carpenter is hereby withdrawn, and you are to act as if it had never existed.

A. LINCOLN

[1] ALS, DNA WR RG 107, Presidential Telegrams, I, 32. See Lincoln to Dix, *infra*.

To John A. Dix[1]

Major General Dix
New-York

Executive Mansion
Washington, D.C. April 21. 1864

Yesterday I was induced to telegraph the officer in military command at Fort-Warren, Boston-Harbor, Massachusetts, suspending the execution of Charles Carpenter, to be executed to-morrow for desertion. Just now, on reading your order in the case, I telegraph the same officer withdrawing the suspension, and leaving the case entirely with you. The man's friends are pressing, me, but I refer them to you, intending to take no further action myself.

A. LINCOLN

[1] ALS, DNA WR RG 107, Presidential Telegrams, I, 33. The New York *Tribune* (April 26, 1864) reported the execution of Carpenter and his accomplice as follows: "Privates Charles Carpenter and Matthew Riley . . . two unassigned recruits of the Vermont volunteers, suffered the extreme penalty of military law on Friday last [April 22], at Fort Warren, Boston Harbor, for the crime of desertion. They deserted the service in December, 1863. Carpenter after deserting, disguised himself, and commenced business as a bounty or substitute broker. . . . They were convicted and sentenced to be shot . . . before a general court martial that met on January 30 . . . which sentence was approved by Gen. Dix. Maj. Cabot was charged with the execution of this order. . . ."

To George G. Meade[1]

April 21, 1864

This case is submitted to Gen. Meade to be disposed of by him, under the recent order[2] upon the subject.   A. LINCOLN

April 21. 1864

If Gen. Warren has recommended the discharge of this man, let him be discharged.   A. LINCOLN

Aug. 20. 1864

[1] AES, DNA WR RG 153, Judge Advocate General, MM 1343. Lincoln's endorsements are written on the court-martial record of Private William T. Evers (alias William J. Evans), Fourteenth New York State Militia, sentenced to ten years' imprisonment for desertion. General Meade had recommended mitigation on General [Gouverneur K.] Warren's recommendation, but for unknown reasons Lincoln's first endorsement was not acted upon. Lincoln reviewed seventy-two court-martial cases on April 21, his other endorsements of this date being routine approvals, mitigations, or remissions of sentence.

[2] AGO *Special Orders No. 154,* April 21, 1864, authorized General Meade "to commute the sentence of death to imprisonment, (with forfeiture of all pay due,) in the Dry Tortugas Fort, during the present war, or to make such other commutation of sentence . . . as in each case justice, and the benefit of the service, may, in his judgment, require."

To Edwin M. Stanton[1]

April 21, 1864

Please have General Halleck make the proper order in this case.
Hon. Secretary of War.   A. LINCOLN.

[1] Thirty-eighth Congress, First Session, *House Executive Document No. 80,* p. 6. Lincoln's endorsement is on a letter from Francis P. Blair, Jr., April 20, 1864:

"You will do me a great favor by giving the order assigning me to the command of the 17th army corps immediately, as I desire to leave Washington the next Saturday to join the command. I also request the assignment of Captain Andrew J. Alexander, of 3d regiment U.S. cavalry, as adjutant general of the 17th corps, with the rank of lieutenant colonel. The present adjutant, or rather the former adjutant . . . has been retained by General McPherson as adjutant general of the department, and the place . . . is necessarily vacant.

"I also request the appointment of George A. Maguire, formerly captain, 31st Missouri volunteer infantry, as major and aide-de-camp, and Lieutenant Logan Tompkins, 21st Missouri volunteer infantry, as captain and aide-de-camp on my staff."

See Lincoln's communications to Grant, March 15, *supra,* and to the House of Representatives, April 28, *infra.*

To Edwin M. Stanton[1]

Hon. Sec. of War   Executive Mansion,
My dear Sir,   Washington, April 21, 1864.

The accompanying letter & papers from Gov. Hahn, came to me with a letter of his to me, requesting me to read these and hand

them to you. Shall we send him his Louisiana citizens named?
Yours truly   A. LINCOLN

[1] ALS, ORB. The accompanying papers have not been found.

To Edwin M. Stanton[1]

Hon. Sec. of War   Executive Mansion,
My dear Sir   Washington, April 21, 1864.
   The Governors of Ohio Indiana, Illinois, and Iowa have just
been with me; and I have made an engagement with them to meet
you, Gen. Halleck and myself at 7. P.M. to-day, at this room. Please
notify Gen. Halleck & you and he attend. Yours truly
                                                        A. LINCOLN

[1] ALS, NHi. See Lincoln to Stanton, April 23, *infra*.

To Mason Brayman[1]

                                Office U.S. Military Telegraph,
Brig Gen Brayman.   War Department,
Comdg Cairo.   Washington, D.C., April 22nd. 1864.
What day did General Corse part with Gen Banks?
                                                        A. LINCOLN

[1] D, DNA WR RG 107, Presidential Telegrams, I, 34. This telegram is not
in Lincoln's handwriting. Brigadier General Brayman had telegraphed Stanton
on April 21: "General [John M.] Corse, who was sent by General Sherman
to recall General A[ndrew] J. Smith's command from Red River, has returned. Banks returned to Grand Ecore, badly injured. He refused to return
Smith's command. The naval force is caught in low water, with shoals above
and below." (OR, I, XXXIV, III, 244). On April 23, Brayman replied to Lincoln's telegram: "General Corse left General Banks on Monday the eleventh
(11) I refer you to my dispatch to Mr Stanton yesterday The word 'severely
injured' referred to Genl Banks Army & not him. Genl Corse left yesterday &
expected to be in Nashville tomorrow" (DLC-RTL).

To Albert G. Hodges[1]

                                Office U.S. Military Telegraph,
A. G. Hodges, Esq   War Department,
Frankfort, Ky   Washington, D.C., April 22. 1864.
        Did you receive my letter?   A. LINCOLN

[1] ALS, DNA WR RG 107, Presidential Telegrams, I, 35. Hodges replied the
same day:

"Yours of the 4th instant was received by due course of mail, and will be given to the people of Kentucky at the proper time. I have shown it to some of the prominent union men . . . and I have met but one as yet who dissents from your reasoning upon the subject of slavery.

"It is with feelings of profound satisfaction I inform you, that every day . . . I have been receiving information of your steady gain upon the gratitude and confidence of the People of Kentucky. . . . My deliberate belief is, that with your name before the people of our State,—to use a homely phrase,—'ye shall "*flax them out handsomely*"'. . . ." (DLC-RTL).

Order for Release of John Connor[1]

April 22, 1864

Let this man, John Connor, go to his regiment; and upon his faithfully serving out his term, making up lost time, or until he is otherwise honorably discharged, he is pardoned for said desertion.

April 22, 1864   A. LINCOLN

[1] ADS, NN. Private John Connor, First District of Columbia Infantry, was ordered released by AGO *Special Orders No. 158*, April 25, 1864. Lincoln's order is explained by a note of appreciation from Sister Emerentiana Bowden, Sisters of Charity, St. Matthew's Academy, April 23, 1864: "Accept our heartfelt thanks for the Pardon of John Connor, prisoner in Fort Delaware, which, at our instance, you were so kind as to grant yesterday. You will ever have the prayers & blessing of the afflicted wife & four almost starving children whom you have relieved. . . ." (DLC-RTL).

To Edwin M. Stanton[1]

Hon. Sec. of War   Executive Mansion,
My dear Sir   Washington, April 22. 1864.

I infer, by Mr. Smith's pencil note that there may be some special reason for not discharging the five prisoners named on the accompanying paper. If so, lay the case aside till I see you. If not, let it take the usual course. Yours truly   A. LINCOLN

[1] ALS, IHi. The verso is endorsed by Stanton, referring the matter to General Ethan A. Hitchcock. The accompanying paper has not been found, but a letter from Green Clay Smith, dated April 19, 1864, is as follows:

"Permit me to call your attention to the paper I left with you in regard to the release of five prisoners—signed by myself & Mr Whaley. The Prisoners are Hopkins, Oldham, Coulter, Fretwell[?], and Emboy. These men I know, and by your own suggestion some time ago I offered this.

"Now as to my signature to the paper presented by Messrs. Grider and Harding, it was alone through politeness and kindness to them, without any purpose of commiting myself to them or their applicants—I desired to return good for evil.

"Please consider my personal claim, & let bearer . . . have the order for them. . . ." (DLC-RTL).

To Edwin M. Stanton[1]

Hon. Sec. of War, please see & hear Hon. Mr. Granger, of the last
House of Representatives.   A. LINCOLN
    April 22, 1864

[1] ALS, DLC. Bradley F. Granger was a Democrat of Ann Arbor, Michigan.

To Benjamin F. Butler[1]

Major General Butler   Executive Mansion
Fort-Monroe, Va.   Washington, April 23. 1864
    Senator Ten-Eyck is very anxious to have a special exchange of
Capt. Frank J. McLean, of 9th. Tennessee Cavalry, now, or lately,
at Johnson's Island, for Capt. T. Ten-Eyck, 18th. U.S. Infantry, &
now at Richmond. I would like to have it done. Can it be?

                                                A. LINCOLN.

[1] ALS, DNA WR RG 107, Presidential Telegrams, I, 37. See Lincoln's pre-
vious telegram to Butler, March 19, *supra*. Butler's reply was received at 3:15
P.M.: "I have no doubt that I can exchange Capt. McLean . . . for Capt. Ten
Eycke. . . ." (DLC-RTL).

To Gustavus V. Fox[1]

                                        [April 23, 1864]
    I do not think I can go. Shall be glad if Captain Fox does.
                                                A. LINCOLN.

[1] *Naval Records,* I, IX, 686. Lincoln's endorsement is on a telegram of Benjamin F. Butler to Fox, April 23, 1864: "I think you can do more good to the
service by coming here for twenty-four hours than anywhere else. Please
breakfast with me to-morrow morning at 9 a.m. Perhaps you can bring the
President with you." Major John Hay accompanied Fox.

To William S. Rosecrans[1]

Major General Rosecrans   Executive Mansion,
St. Louis, Mo.   Washington, April 23. 1864.
    A lady—Mrs. Ward, sister of the late John M. Weimer—is here,
saying she is banished from St. Louis, her home, and asking to be
allowed to return on taking the oath and giving bond. It is exclusively with you to decide; but I will thank you to examine the
case; and shall be glad if you find it consistent with your views to
oblige her.   A. LINCOLN

1 ALS, DNA WR RG 107, Presidential Telegrams, I, 36. Rosecrans telegraphed his reply on April 24: "Mrs. Wards case is a very bad one—she was banished East of Ills, North of the Ohio, which should have kept her from Washn. when it was rumored that there [was] a possibility of Provost Marshal Brohears [James A. Broadhead] yielding to pressure & rescinding the order the union aid society waited on him by committee with resolutions of remonstrance I think the order should stand." (DLC-RTL).

To the Senate[1]

To the Senate of the United States: April 23, 1864

I transmit herewith a report from the Secretary of War, in answer to the Resolutions passed by the Senate in Executive session on the 14th. and 18th. of April, 1864.   ABRAHAM LINCOLN

Washington,
April 23d, 1864.

1 DS, DNA RG 46, Senate 38B A4. Stanton's report of April 22, 1864, is as follows: "In answer to the Senate resolutions of April 14th and April 18th, I have the honor to state that the nominations of Colonel Hiram Burnham, Colonel Edward M. McCook, Colonel Lewis A. Grant, and Colonel Edward Hatch are not either of them made to fill any vacancy in the proper sense of that term. They are not made to fill a command vacated by any other general, but are independent nominations, and if confirmed the officers will be assigned to such command as the General commanding may deem proper. But in consequence of the resignations of Generals [Stephen] Miller, [Jeremiah T.] Boyle, and [John] Beatty, and the death of General [Stephen G.] Champlin, their confirmations will be within the number of brigadiers allowed by law." (*Executive Journal*, XIII, 501). The appointments were confirmed by the Senate on April 27, 1864.

To the Senate and House of Representatives[1]

To the Senate and House of Representatives.   April 23, 1864

I transmit to Congress a copy of a note of the 19th. instant from Lord Lyons to the Secretary of State, on the subject of two British naval officers who recently received medical treatment at the Naval Hospital at Norfolk. The expediency of authorizing Surgeon Solomon Sharp to accept the piece of plate to which the note refers, as an acknowledgement of his services, is submitted to your consideration.   ABRAHAM LINCOLN

Washington,
23d, April, 1864.

1 DS, DNA RG 233, House Executive Document No. 75. Lord Lyons' note of April 19, 1864, expressed his government's thanks for kindness in affording to "Lieutenant Cardale and Sub Lieutenant Dodsworth of her Majesty's ship Greyhound" during their illness the comforts and conveniences of the U.S. hospital at Norfolk, Virginia. Senator Sumner's joint resolution authorizing Surgeon Sharp to accept the piece of plate was approved on June 7, 1864.

To Edwin M. Stanton[1]

Executive Mansion,
Washington, April 23, 1864.

My Dear Sir: According to our understanding with Major General Frank P. Blair, at the time he took his seat in Congress last winter, he now asks to withdraw his resignation as major general, then tendered, and be sent to the field. Let this be done. Let the order sending him be such as shown me to-day by the Adjutant General, only dropping from it the names of Maguire and Tompkins. Yours, truly,   A. LINCOLN.

Hon. Secretary of War.

[1] Thirty-eighth Congress, First Session, *House Executive Document No. 80,* pp. 6-7. See Lincoln's letter to Grant, March 15, and endorsement to Stanton, April 21, *supra.* On April 23 Blair wrote Stanton, "I respectfully request to withdraw my resignation as major general of the United States volunteers, tendered on the 12th day of January, 1864." (*Ibid.*). On the same day AGO *General Orders No. 178* assigned Blair to command the Seventeenth Army Corps and assigned Captain Andrew J. Alexander to be his assistant adjutant general with rank of lieutenant colonel.

To Edwin M. Stanton[1]

The foregoing proposition of the Governors is accepted, and the Secretary of War is directed to carry it into execution.

April 23. 1864.   A. LINCOLN

[1] AES, NN. Lincoln's endorsement is written on a memorandum from Stanton, April 22, 1864, accompanied by a letter from the governors and a telegram from General Grant, as follows:

"An estimate has been made of the probable expense of the force mentioned in the foregoing proposition and it is believed that its cost to the United States will amount to $25,000,000 The views of General Grant are indicated in the telegram a copy of which is annexed and which is a response to my enquiry as to whether he would desire the acceptance of 100 000 men as at first proposed by the Governors. In view of the importance of the ensuing campaign and the judgment of General Grant that the troops offered may be of 'vast importance' I am in favor of accepting the offer. The present estimates are inadequate to meet the expense and additional appropriation will be required."

"To the President   Washington City,
    of the United States: April 21st. 1864.

"I. The Governors of Ohio, Indiana, Illinois, Iowa, and Wisconsin offer to the President infantry troops for the approaching campaign, as follows:

Ohio	30,000
Indiana	20,000
Illinois	20,000
Iowa	10,000
Wisconsin	5,000

"II. The term of service to be one hundred days, reckoning from the date of muster into the service of the United States, unless sooner discharged.

"III. The troops to be mustered into the service of the United States by regiments, when the regiments are filled up, according to regulations, to the minimum strength—the regiments to be organized according to the regulations of the War Department. The whole number to be furnished within twenty days from date of notice of the acceptance of this proposition.

"IV. The troops to be clothed, armed, equipped, subsisted, transported, and paid as other United States infantry volunteers, and to serve in fortifications, or wherever their services may be required, within or without their respective States.

"V. No bounty to be paid the troops, nor the service charged or credited on any draft.

"VI. The draft for three years' service to go on in any State or district where the quota is not filled up; but if any officer or soldier in this special service should be drafted, he shall be credited for the service rendered.

"Jno Brough   W. M. Stone
   Gov. of Ohio   Gov. Iowa
"O. P. Morton   James T. Lewis
   Gov Ind.   Gov Wis"
"Rich. Yates
   Gov. Ills

"Office U.S. Military Telegraph,
"Cipher.   War Department.

"The following Telegram received at Washington, 7 P.M. Apl. 21st. 1864

"Hon. Edwin M. Stanton   From H'd. Qrs. Culpepper.
"Secretary of War.   Dated April 21st. 1864.

"As a rule I would oppose receiving men for a short term, but if 100,000 men can be raised in the time proposed by the Governors of Ohio, Indiana, Illinois and Iowa, they might come at such a crisis as to be of vast importance.

"I would not recommend accepting them in lieu of quotas now due on any previous calls for three years troops, otherwise I would.

"(Signed) U. S. Grant
Lt. Gen."

To John P. Gray[1]

Dr. John P. Gray.   Executive Mansion,
Utica, New York.   Washington, April 25, 1864.

Sir, Private Lorenzo Stewart, 14th regiment New York Volunteer Artillery, is in military custody at Elmira, New York, having been, by a military court, tried for murder, and sentenced to death, his execution awaiting the order of the President of the United States. The record is before me; and a question is made as to the sanity of the accused. You will please proceed to Elmira, New York, and take in writing, all evidence which may be offered on behalf of Private Stewart, and against him, and any, in addition, which you may find within your reach, and deem pertinent; all said evidence to be directed to the question of Private Stewart's sanity or insanity, and not to any other question; you to preside, with power to exclude evidence which shall appear to you clearly not pertinent to the question.

[313]

When the taking of the evidence shall be closed, you will report the same to me, together with your own conclusions as to Private Stewart's sanity, both at the time of the homocide,[2] and at the time of your examination. On reaching Elmira, you will present this letter to the officer then commanding at that Post, and deliver to him a copy of the same, upon which he is hereby directed to notify Clinton Rice, Esqr. and F. B. Swift, Esqr., No. 200 Broadway, New York, of the same; to designate some suitable person in his command to appear for the Government as Judge Advocate, or Prosecuting Attorney: to provide for the attendance of all such witnesses before you as may be desired by either party, or by yourself, and who may be within convenient reach of you; to furnish you a suitable place, or places, for conducting the examination; and to render you such other reasonable assistance in the premises as you may require. If you deem it proper you will examine Private Stewart personally, and you may, in your discretion, require him to be present during the whole, or any part, of the taking of the evidence. The military are hereby charged to see that an escape does not occur. Yours Very Truly,   A. LINCOLN

[1] LS, IHi. See Lincoln to Holt, March 7, *supra.*
[2] Lincoln deleted "murder" and substituted "homocide."

To Joseph Holt[1]

If this Petition is true, as it probably is, these men should be pardoned. Can the J.A.G. throw any light upon it?   A. LINCOLN
April 25. 1864

[1] AES, DNA WR RG 153, Judge Advocate General, LL 1523. Lincoln's endorsement is written on a letter from Salmon P. Chase, April 21, 1864, calling attention to the petition of Major Chambers Baird and citizens of Ripley, Ohio, concerning hardships of enlisted men and misconduct of officers—with particular reference to the cases of Privates Calvin P. Shaw, John Steele, Lucian Stevens, and Henry Washburn, Second Ohio Heavy Artillery, sentenced to imprisonment for mutiny. Holt left the question to the president. On August 16, Lincoln pardoned Stevens, but the records do not show pardons for the others.

To George G. Meade[1]

Major-General Meade,   War Department,
Army of Potomac: Washington City, April 25, 1864.

A Mr. Corby brought you a note from me at the foot of a petition I believe, in the case of Dawson, to be executed to-day. The record has been examined here, and it shows too strong a case for a pardon or commutation, unless there is something in the poor man's favor outside of the record, which you on the ground may know, but I do not. My note to you only means that if you know of any such thing rendering a suspension of the execution proper, on your own judgment, you are at liberty to suspend it. Otherwise I do not interfere. A. LINCOLN.

¹ Tarbell (Appendix), p. 424. Chaplain William Corby, Eighty-eighth New York Volunteers, telegraphed Lincoln on April 24: "General Meade has not the official proceedings relative to the Court Martial of L Dawson who is under sentence of death to take place 25th instant therefore cannot act   Please say what will be done." (DLC-RTL).

General Meade replied to Lincoln's telegram the same day: "I duly received your note by Mr Corby & after examining the case of Dawson could see nothing to justify my reccomending a mitigation The only point is the fact that he has been awaiting sentence for a long period & may have deluded himself into the belief that he would escape   Unless you intervene he will be executed." (DLC-RTL).

Order for Discharge of F. P. Beidler[1]

April 25, 1864

Upon the personal application of Hon. W. R. Morrison & Hon. F. C. Beaman,[2] and on the case within stated, which I believe to be true, let F. P. Beidler, within named be discharged.

April 25. 1864 A. LINCOLN

¹ AES, owned by John S. M. Glidden, Natick, Massachusetts. Lincoln's endorsement is written on a letter from Richard Yates, April 24, 1864: "This lady Mrs. Beidler visited Springfield to see me in relation to discharge of her husband, but not finding me there has come to Washington. I have no doubt after hearing her case, that it is one in which the exception may be made, and I sincerely hope that you will grant the discharge of her husband. He is a minister of the Gospel and his education & state of health have not been such as to fit him for a soldier's life." A Franklin Beidler of Moweaqua, Illinois, Company E, Forty-first Illinois, was mustered out August 20, 1864.

² Representatives William R. Morrison of Illinois and Fernando C. Beaman of Michigan.

To Gideon Welles[1]

Hon. Sec. of Navy
My dear Sir:

Executive Mansion,
Washington, April 25, 1864.

Francis A. Hoffmann our Lieut. Governor of Illinois, has an application on file for his son Francis to be appointed to the Naval School, but finds he is too old. He therefore wishes to substitute the name of a younger son—Julius Hoffmann,—who is now but sixteen. I wish this appointment made so soon as it can be consistently with what I have already said in other cases. Please keep me reminded of it   Yours truly A. LINCOLN

¹ ALS-P, ISLA. This letter is misdated "1861" in Tracy, p. 181. Julius T. C. Hoffmann entered the Naval Academy, September 22, 1864, but resigned.

To John Williams[1]

John Williams,

Springfield, Ills.

War Department
Washington City,
April 25 1864

Yours of the 15th. is just received. Thanks for your kind remembrance. I would accept your offer at once, were it not that I fear there might be some impropriety in it, though I do not see that there would. I will think of it a while.   A. LINCOLN

[1] ALS, DNA WR RG 107, Presidential Telegrams, I, 38. John Williams, president of the First National Bank of Springfield, Illinois, wrote Lincoln on April 15, 1864: "When I returned from Washington to New York I concluded to write you asking if you wished to invest $5000 in the First National Bank of Springfield Illinois. The stock holders would feel proud of your association with them as one of the share holders; If you desire to become so I will sell you 50 shares of my stock which is paid up in full in fact the entire stock is paid up and our organization complete After writing the above it occured to me that possibly your position as President of the United States might make it improper for you to become a stock holder in any of the National Banks if so of course you will understand that the offer is made in all good faith & without any wish that you should do any thing that would compromise your high position" (DLC-RTL).

To John R. Woods[1]

My Dear Sir

Executive Mansion,
Washington, April 25, 1864.

I regret that I cannot be present at the inauguration of your Soldiers Home this week. Accept my thanks for your kind invitation and believe me, very truly   Your Obedient Servant

John R. Woods Esq   A. LINCOLN

[1] LS, owned by Donald A. Woods, Milwaukee, Wisconsin. John R. Woods was secretary of the Illinois Sanitary Commission. Concerning the Soldiers' Home project, see Lincoln to Yates, February 3, *supra.*

To George H. Thomas[1]

Major General Thomas
Chattanooga, Tennessee

Executive Mansion,
Washington, April 26, 1864.

Suspend execution of death sentence of young Perry from Wisconsin condemned for sleeping on his post, until further orders, and forward record for examination.   A. LINCOLN.

Maj Eckert

Please send the above dispatch   JNO. G. NICOLAY Priv. Sec.

[1] D, DNA WR RG 107, Presidential Telegrams, I, 39. This telegram was written and signed by Nicolay. An undated draft of a telegram with an explanatory note from Senator James R. Doolittle accounts for the telegram:

"To Genl Thomas   Chattanooga
"Do not execute sentence upon young Perry from Wisconsin for sleeping at his post until case is reviewed
"This young man is but 16 years old. I know his father well He consented at last to his son's enlisting at last [*sic*]. He is a fine boy, but overcome with fatigue and sleep has incurred the dreadful penalty of death Please telegraph Genl Thomas to suspend execution" (DLC-RTL).
No reply from Thomas has been found, and "Perry from Wisconsin" has not been satisfactorily identified. The court-martial files contain an incomplete record of Private Charles O. Perry, Company B, Third Maine Volunteers, sentenced to death for sleeping on post, but it is uncertain that this is the same soldier (DNA WR RG 153, Judge Advocate General, NN 1355).

Endorsement Concerning Herman Huidekoper[1]

April 27, 1864

I know nothing of the young man within named, except by hearsay, which is all in his favor. His brother Lt-Col. Huidekoper, who lost an arm at Gettysburg, I do know, and for his sake I would be very glad for the advancement of the young man.

April 27, 1864.   A. LINCOLN

[1] Henry S. Huidekoper, *Personal Notes and Reminiscences of Lincoln* (1896), p. 13. According to the source, Lincoln wrote this endorsement on a request presented by Judge S. Newton Pettis of Meadville, Pennsylvania, that Herman Huidekoper be appointed a captain of colored troops. "Through this favor on part of Mr. Lincoln, it fell to the lot of Captain Huidekoper, not yet of age, to organize . . . the One Hundred and Twenty-seventh Regiment U.S.C.T."

To George G. Meade[1]

Major-General Meade,   Executive Mansion,
Army of Potomac: Washington, D.C., April 27, 1864.
Your dispatch about Private Peter Gilner received. Dispose of him precisely as you would under the recent order, if he were under sentence of death for desertion, and execution suspended by me.   A. LINCOLN.

[1] Tarbell (Appendix), p. 425. Meade's despatch has not been located. Private Peter Gilner, Company F, Sixty-second Pennsylvania Volunteers, was sentenced to be shot for neglect of duty, disorderly conduct, and violation of Ninth Article of War. His sentence was commuted to imprisonment in Dry Tortugas, and on October 19 he received a presidential pardon (DNA WR RG 153, Judge Advocate General, MM 948). See Lincoln to Meade, September 20, *infra*.

[317]

To George G. Meade[1]

Major-General Meade,   Executive Mansion,
Army of Potomac: Washington, April 27, 1864.
    John J. Stefke [Siefke], Company I, First New Jersey Cavalry, having a substitute, is ordered to be discharged. Please have him sent here to Washington.   A. LINCOLN.

[1] Tarbell (Appendix), p. 425. Meade telegraphed on the same day that the necessary orders for Siefke's discharge had been given (DLC-RTL).

Memorandum Concerning Joseph L. Savage[1]

[c. April 27, 1864]

Presented by the Mayor of Washington

Peter Force	Thomas P. Morgan	Valentine Blanchard
John H. Simms	B. F. Guy.	John F. Ennis
Lewis Johnson	E. C. Dyer	Wm. E. Spaulding
William Orme	H. A. Chadwick	James Skivving[?]
Francis Mohan	Wm. O'Brien	R. C. Johnson–
Wm. B Todd	James Kelly	Geo. Savage
Geo. H. Plant	Patrick Cowley	

[1] AE, DLC-RTL. Lincoln's endorsement is written on a letter from Charles J. M. Gwinn, Baltimore, April 27, 1864, asking release of prisoner Joseph L. Savage, Navy contractor.

To Isaac Murphy[1]

Governor Murphy   Office U.S. Military Telegraph,
Little-Rock,   War Department,
Arkansas.   Washington, D.C., April 27. 1864.
    I am much gratified to learn that you got out so large a vote, so nearly all the right way, at the late election; and not less so, that your State-Government, including the Legislature, is organized, and in good working order. Whatever I can, I will do, to protect you; meanwhile you must do your utmost to protect yourselves. Present my greeting to all   A LINCOLN

[1] ALS, DNA WR RG 107, Presidential Telegrams, I, 40. Governor Murphy's telegram, sent April 15 and received April 22, is as follows: "Both houses of the Legislature have organized today. . . . The vote for Constitution twelve thousand one hundred and seventy nine against it two hundred & twenty six (226) For Govr Twelve thousand four hundred & thirty We ask your sympathy & aid The country north & south of the Arkansas River is full of guerillas One (1) member killed coming here If reinforcements are not sent soon or Gen Steele ordered to return we are in great danger." (DLC-RTL).

[318]

Endorsement[1]

April 28, 1864

I shall be glad for the Regiment to be filled; and am quite willing that recruits may be obtained therefor in West Virginia. . . .

[1] Anderson Galleries Catalog 2193, November 15, 1927, No. 278. This fragmentary text is described in the source as an autograph endorsement signed, without further identification.

To the House of Representatives[1]

To the House of Representatives   April 28, 1864

In obedience to the Resolution of your Honorable body, a copy of which is herewith returned, I have the honor to make the following brief statement which is believed to contain the information sought.

Prior to, and at the meeting of the present Congress, Robert C. Schenck, of Ohio, and Frank P. Blair, Jr. of Missouri, members elect thereto, by and with the consent of the Senate, held commissions from the Executive, as Major Generals in the Volunteer Army. Gen. Schenck tendered the resignation of his said commission and took his seat in the House of Representatives, at the assembling thereof, upon the distinct verbal understanding with the Secretary of war and the Executive, that he might, at any time during the session, at his own pleasure, withdraw said resignation, and return to the field. Gen. Blair was, by temporary assignment of Gen. Sherman, in command of a corps, through the battles in front of Chattanooga, and in the march to the relief of Knoxville, which occurred in the latter days of November, and early days of December last; and, of course was not present at the assembling of Congress. When he subsequently arrived here, he sought, and was allowed, by the Secretary of War and the Executive, the same conditions, and promise, as allowed and made to Gen. Schenck. Gen. Schenck has not applied to withdraw his resignation; but when Gen. Grant was made Lieut. General, producing some change of commanders, Gen. Blair sought to be assigned to the command of a corps. This was made known to Generals Grant and Sherman and assented to by them, and the particular corps for him designated. This was all arranged and understood, as now remembered, so much as a month ago; but the formal withdrawal of Gen. Blair's resignation, and making the order assigning him to the command of the corps, were not consummated at the War Department until last week—perhaps on the 23rd. of April, Inst. As a summary of

[319]

the whole it may be stated that Gen. Blair holds no military commission or appointment, other than as herein stated; and that it is believed he is now acting as a Major General upon the assumed validity of the commission herein stated, in connection with the facts herein stated, and not otherwise. There are some letters, notes, telegrams, orders, entries, and perhaps other documents, in connection with this subject, which it is believed would throw no additional light upon it; but which will be cheerfully furnished, if desired.   ABRAHAM LINCOLN

April 28. 1864.

[1] ADf, DLC-RTL; DS, DNA RG 233, House Executive Document No. 77. On April 25 Representative Henry L. Dawes of Massachusetts introduced the resolution calling on the president "to communicate to this House whether the Hon. Francis P. Blair, Jr., representing the first congressional district of Missouri in the Present House, now holds any appointment or commission in the military service of the United States; and if so, what that appointment or commission is, and when the said Blair accepted the same; and whether he is now acting under the authority of any such appointment or commission." See Lincoln to Grant, March 15, and to Stanton, April 21, *supra;* and the further communication to the House, May 2, *infra.*

To Mary Todd Lincoln[1]

Mrs. A. Lincoln   Executive Mansion,
Metropolitan Hotel   Washington,
New-York.   April 28. 1864.

The draft will go to you. Tell Tad the goats and father are very well—especially the goats.   A. LINCOLN.

[1] ALS, DNA WR RG 107, Presidential Telegrams, I, 41. Mrs. Lincoln telegraphed on April 28: "We reached here in safety. Hope you are well. Please send me by mail to-day a check for $50 directed to me, care Mr. Warren Leland, Metropolitan Hotel, Tad says are the goats well." (Katherine Helm, *Mary, Wife of Lincoln,* p. 239).

To George G. Meade[1]

Major-General Meade,   Executive Mansion,
Army of Potomac: Washington, April 28, 1864.

If Private George W. Sloan, of the Seventy-second Pennsylvania Volunteers, is under sentence of death for desertion, suspend execution till further order.   A. LINCOLN.

[1] Tarbell (Appendix), p. 425. The roster of the Seventy-second Pennsylvania Volunteers lists George W. Sloane as transferred to the One Hundred Eighty-third Pennsylvania Volunteers on July 20, 1864.

To the Senate and House of Representatives[1]

To the Honorable, the Senate, and   April 28, 1864
House of Representatives,

I have the honor to transmit herewith an Address to the President of the United States, and through him, to both Houses of Congress, on the condition and wants of the people of East Tennessee, and asking their attention to the necessity of some action on the part of the Government for their relief—and which address is presented by a committee of an organization called "The East Tennessee Relief Association."[2]

Deeply commiserating the condition of these most loyal and suffering people, I am unprepared to make any specific recommendation for their relief. The Military is doing, and will continue to do the best for them within its power. Their address represents that the construction of direct Railroad communication between Knoxville and Cincinnati, by way of central Kentucky would be of great consequence in the present emergency. It may be remembered that in the annual Message of December, 1861, such Railroad construction was recommended. I now add that with the hearty concurrence of Congress, I would yet be pleased to construct the road, both for the relief of these people, and for its continuing military importance.   ABRAHAM LINCOLN
April 28, 1864

[1] ADf, DLC-Nicolay Papers; DS, DNA RG 46, Senate 38A F2. A joint resolution reported from the committee on military affairs by Representative Robert C. Schenck on May 25 authorized the president to construct a railroad from the valley of the Ohio to East Tennessee. It passed the House on May 31, but failed to pass the Senate.

[2] The address was signed by William Heiskell, William G. Brownlow, John Baxter, O. P. Semple, John M. Fleming, and Thomas W. Hughes.

To Whom It May Concern[1]

Executive Mansion, Washington,
Whom It May Concern   April 28, 1864.

Charles G. Russell comes to me voluntarily saying he is a private in Co. B. in the 12th Iowa Regiment, and saying he is apprehensive of being arrested and punished as a deserter. Now, on condition that he rejoins his Regiment, and re-enlists with it, and serves out said re-enlistment, or until honorably discharged, for any cause, he is fully pardoned for said supposed desertion.   A. LINCOLN.

[1] Hertz, II, 928. Charles G. Russell wrote Lincoln on April 19, 1864: "I am . . . a member of Company B 12th Iowa Inf. . . . That reg. was . . . engaged

at Fort Henry Donelson Shiloh the latter place we was taken prisoners, retained
some two months . . . paroled . . . then sent to Benton Barracks St. Louis.
. . . Many of us left, went home I suppose most of them went back I did
not I went to Leavenworth Kansas. . . . While there I saw an order in the
papers that all Iowa troops that was paroled was exchanged including those
Benton Barracks and that many of them tired of the ennui of camp life had
left. All would be furnished with transportation from where they happen to
be. I wrote to a privat of company B telling him to show it to the Capt. . . . I
waited some three weeks got no answer then went to Denver City Colorado
Territory have been there ever since up to the 26th day of Feb. Left for the
States. Stayed in Nebraska a short time then came directly here on purpose
to deliver myself up for a deserter I never intended to stay away from the
reg. but force of circumstance some time controls a man when he intends to do
differently. . . . All I ask is to return to the reg. after having a few days to
see my friends. I would have went strait back to it if it had not been for that
for I am very anxious to see my parents if I had went home before going to the
reg. I probably have been arrested. . . ." (DLC-RTL).

To Mason Brayman[1]

Gen. Brayman   Executive Mansion,
Cairo, Ills.   Washington, April 29, 1864.
 I am appealed to in behalf of O. Kellogg, and J. W. Pryor, both
in prison at Cairo. Please telegraph me what are the charges, and
summary of evidence against them.   A. LINCOLN

[1] ALS, DNA WR RG 107, Presidential Telegrams, I, 42. Brayman replied
on April 30: "Orton Kellog is under arrest for furnishing powder & munitions
of war for being within the rebel lines two years & returning as a spy. he was
a citizen of Illinois. his Attorney is in Washington. J W Ryan [sic] is not in
custody here." (DLC-RTL).

To Joseph Holt[1]

At the request of Hon. E. H. Rollins, and in consideration that
Lieut. Snell has already suffered severely, the sentence is remitted.
 April 29. 1864   A. LINCOLN

[1] AES, DNA WR RG 153, Judge Advocate General, MM 129. Lincoln's en-
dorsement is written on the court-martial record of Lieutenant Jason D. Snell,
Company K, Fourteenth New Hampshire Volunteers, who was dismissed from
the service for selling whisky to enlisted men. The roster of the Fourteenth New
Hampshire Volunteers shows that Jason D. Snell died of disease at Carrollton,
Louisiana, on April 26, 1864.

To the Senate[1]

To the Senate of the United States.   April 29, 1864
 In compliance with the Resolution of the Senate of the 27th. instant, requesting information in regard to the condition of affairs
in the Territory, of Nevada, I transmit a copy of a letter of the

25th. of last month addressed to the Secretary of State by James W. Nye, the Governor of that Territory.   ABRAHAM LINCOLN
    Washington,
    29th. April, 1864.

[1] DS, DNA RG 46, Senate 38A F2. This communication and enclosure were printed as *Senate Executive Document No. 41.* Governor Nye's report gives a glowing account of progress in Nevada Territory.

To Edwin M. Stanton[1]

April 29, 1864

Private Daniel P. Clark of 19th Conn. Vols. under sentence for desertion, suspended for action of President, is fully pardoned on condition that he enters and faithfully serves through a new enlistment of three years.

[1] William D. Morley Catalog, April 28, 1944, No. 214. According to the catalog description this is the text of an autograph letter signed. AGO *Special Orders No. 163,* April 30, 1864, conveyed Lincoln's pardon of Clark and ordered that Clark be released and returned to his regiment.

Endorsements Concerning Julius Silversmith[1]

April 30, 1864

I do not personally know Mr. Silversmith but Senator Conness who writes the above is habitually careful not to say what he does not know.   A. LINCOLN
    April 30, 1864

Not personally knowing Mr. Silversmith I cheerfully endorse what Governor Nye says of him.   A. LINCOLN
    April 30, 1864.

[1] Isaac Markens, *Lincoln and the Jews* (1909), p. 55. According to the source, Lincoln's endorsements were written on letters from Senator John Conness of California and Governor James W. Nye of Nevada Territory, introducing Julius Silversmith, a metallurgist, editor and proprietor of the *Mining and Scientific Press* of San Francisco (1860-1862) and author of *Practical Handbook for Miners, Metallurgists and Assayers* (1866).

To James R. Fry[1]

Executive Mansion
My Dear Sir   April 30. 1864
    I thank you heartily for the kind invitation conveyed in your letter of the 26th. and sincerely regret that I cannot make a positive engagement to avail myself of it. My time is subject to such constant and unexpected requisitions that I cannot unreservedly

[323]

accept any such pleasure as that you offer me, at this distance of time.

I shall be most happy to be present at an entertainment which promises so much, especially as it is in aid of so beneficent a charity as that in which you are interested, if my engagements next week will allow it. But I must beg that you will make no special arrangements in view of my presence, as I may be disappointed. If I can come, I will notify you as early as possible. Yours very truly

[A. LINCOLN.]

[1]Df, DLC-RTL. The draft is in John Hay's autograph, without signature, which is as printed in NH, X, 90. A telegram of the same date from Nicolay to Fry reads "The President cannot promise to come. Will write you today." (DNA WR RG 107, Presidential Telegrams, I, 43). James R. Fry of Philadelphia wrote Lincoln on April 26, 1864:

"You will receive, in the course of a few days, a formal invitation from gentlemen representing the Great Central Fair of the Sanitary Commission, the Union League and other bodies of this city, to come hither on Wednesday the 4th day of May to attend the Grand Musical Festival which will inaugurate the Fair. As chairman of the committee having charge of the Festival, while I advise you of the proposed invitation, I solicit your attention to the importance of honoring the occasion by your acceptance of it. . . . If you can favor me with an early reply it will be of moment to enable me to send prompt invitations. . . . P.S. Other departments of the Fair begin in June, but the Musical Festival (as I state above) on Wednesday the 4th of May." (DLC-RTL).

Ulysses S. Grant[1]

Executive Mansion Washington,
Lieutenant General Grant.   April 30, 1864

Not expecting to see you again before the Spring campaign opens, I wish to express, in this way, my entire satisfaction with what you have done up to this time, so far as I understand it. The particulars of your plans I neither know, or seek to know. You are vigilant and self-reliant; and, pleased with this, I wish not to obtrude any constraints or restraints upon you. While I am very anxious that any great disaster, or the capture of our men in great numbers, shall be avoided, I know these points are less likely to escape your attention than they would be mine. If there is anything wanting which is within my power to give, do not fail to let me know it.

And now with a brave Army, and a just cause, may God sustain you. Yours very truly   A. LINCOLN

[1] ALS, CSmH. General Grant replied on May 1:

"Your very kind letter of yesterday is just received. The confidence you express for the future, and satisfaction with the past, in my military administration is acknowledged with pride. It will be my earnest endeavor that you, and the country, shall not be disappointed.

"From my first entrance into the volunteer service of the country, to the present day, I have never had cause of complaint, have never expressed or implied a complaint, against the Administration, or the Sec. of War, for throwing any embarassment in the way of my vigorously prossecuting what appeared to me my duty. Indeed since the promotion which placed me in command of all the Armies, and in view of the great responsibility, and importance of success, I have been astonished at the readiness with which every thing asked for has been yielded without even an explaination being asked. Should my success be less than I desire, and expect, the least I can say is, the fault is not with you." (DLC-RTL).

To Nathan Kimball[1]

Officer in Command at   Executive Mansion,
Little Rock, Ark.   Washington, April 30. 1864..

Please send me the record of trial for desertion of Thadeus A. Kinsloe of Co. D. 7th. Missouri Vol. Cavalry.   A LINCOLN

[1] ALS, DNA WR RG 107, Presidential Telegrams, I, 44. No reply has been found. AGO *Special Orders No. 212*, June 18, 1864, remitted the unexecuted portion of Thaddeus A. Kinsloe's sentence to imprisonment at hard labor for the remainder of his term of service.

Order for Exchange of H. H. Brogden[1]

April 30, 1864

Let H. H. Brogden, now in prison at Fort Delaware, be sent to Major Mulford, at City-Point, to be exchanged for any one of same rank held a prisoner by the rebels.   A. LINCOLN
April 30. 1864

[1] ADS, DLM. Sergeant H. H. Brogden of the Confederate Signal Corps was captured on a visit behind Union lines to see his father who was ill (DNA WR RG 153, Judge Advocate General, MM 1139). Major John E. Mulford was Union agent for exchange of prisoners.

Order for Pardon of Sioux Indians[1]

April 30, 1864

List of Indian prisoners now in confinement at Camp McClellan near Davenport Iowa pardoned and to be liberated and sent to their families

Tapeta Tanka	Wiyaka	Tunkanhuamani
Tahohpi wakan	Kimyan hiotan	Boyaya
Wakanhotito	Oye Muza	Iyasamani
Tate sica	Cinkpa tawa	Icawtuze
Wiyuha	Tunkan Canholiska	Manikiya
Tunkan Oyate yanka	Wakan inapedan alias	Ahotonna
Pantaninniye	Muza kiyemani	Maza adidi
Contidoka duta	Kalpantpan ku	Tate Ibomdu
Kimyan hiyaya	Tahokaye	

The persons named on this list are pardoned and ordered to be sent to their families or relatives. A. LINCOLN

April 30, 1864

[1] D and AES-P, ISLA. Lincoln's endorsement is written in the right-hand margin of the single page containing the list. A copy of the list preserved in the Lincoln Papers contains Lincoln's endorsement "Pardoned to-day, April 30, 1864." (DLC-RTL). Reverend Thomas S. Williamson, missionary to the Sioux, had written to Lincoln on April 27, assigning reasons for pardoning the Sioux imprisoned at Davenport, Iowa, since November, 1862, under sentence of death. Lincoln submitted the letter to William P. Dole, who answered on April 28: "I have read the letter of the Rev. Mr Williamson to you asking the pardon of certain Indians now under the sentence of death at Davenport and wish to say . . . that I do not believe any injury will accrue to the white people if you should exercise the pardoning power in favour of a portion of these people and I have so much confidence in . . . Mr. Williamson that I have no hesitancy in uniting in his recommendation in favor of the particular persons named by him. . . ." (DLC-RTL).

To Francis W. Kellogg[1]

Hon. F. W. Kellogg. Executive Mansion,
My dear Sir: Washington, May 1 1864.

I find the card of yourself and Governor Blair on my table. If you and he please I will call and take you riding at half past 3. Yours truly A. LINCOLN.

[1] ALS-F, ISLA. Francis W. Kellogg of Grand Rapids was representative in congress and Austin Blair was governor of Michigan.

To the California Delegation in Congress[1]

California Delegation Executive Mansion,
in Congress— Washington, May 2. 1864.

Will you gentlemen please take this case off my hands? I really have no time to acquaint myself with it. Yours truly

A. LINCOLN

[1] ALS, owned by M. W. Morrow, San Francisco, California. No clue to the case has been found.

To the House of Representatives[1]

May 2, 1864

To the honorable the House of Representatives:

In compliance with the request contained in your resolution of the 29th ultimo, a copy of which resolution is herewith returned, I have the honor to transmit the following:

[*Executive Document No. 80* here prints: Lincoln to Montgomery Blair, November 2, 1863 (*vide supra*); Robert C. Schenck to Stanton forwarding resignation, November 13, 1863; Edward

D. Townsend, November 21, 1863, to Schenck, accepting resignation; Francis P. Blair, Jr. to Lincoln, January 1, 1864, "I hereby tender my resignation as a major general of the United States Volunteers"; James A. Hardie to Blair, January 12, 1864, accepting resignation; Lincoln to Grant, *re* Blair, March 15, 1864 (*vide supra*); Grant to Lincoln *re* telegram, March 16, 1864; Grant to Lincoln *re* telegram, March 17, 1864; John A. Logan to Lincoln, asking to be retained in Fifteenth Corps, March 26, 1864; Grant to Sherman, March 30, 1864, directing Blair to be assigned to Seventeenth Corps; Grant to Halleck, April 9, 1864, asking if Blair has been sent to Sherman; Blair to Lincoln, April 20, 1864, asking to be assigned immediately to command of Seventeenth Corps, endorsed by Lincoln to Stanton, April 21, 1864 (*vide supra*); Lincoln to Stanton, April 23, 1864 (*vide supra*); Blair to Stanton, April 23, 1864, withdrawing his resignation of January 12, 1864; AGO *General Orders No. 178*, assigning Blair to command of Seventeenth Corps.]

The foregoing constitutes all sought by the resolution, so far as is remembered, or has been found upon diligent search.

May 2. 1864   ABRAHAM LINCOLN

[1] DS (incomplete), DNA RG 233, House Executive Document No. 80; Thirty-eighth Congress, First Session, *House Executive Document No. 80*. On April 29 the House adopted a resolution requesting copies of all "letters, notes, telegrams, orders, entries, and other documents" referred to in Lincoln's communication of April 28, *supra*.

To Stephen A. Hurlbut[1]

Major General Hurlbut.   Executive Mansion
My Dear Sir.   Washington May 2d. 1864

Gen Farnsworth has just been reading to me from your letter to him of the 26th. ult. I snatch a moment to say that my friendship and confidence for you remains unabated, but that Gen's Grant & Thomas[2] cannot be held to their just responsibilities, if they are not allowed to control in the class of cases to which yours belongs.

From one stand point a court of Inquiry is most just, but if your case were my own, I would not allow Gen's Grant and Sherman [to] be diverted by it just now. Yours Truly   A LINCOLN

[1] Copy, DLC-RTL. General John F. Farnsworth, who had resigned his commission on March 4, 1863, to take up his duties as congressman, was pressing Hurlbut's demand for a court of inquiry. On April 16, 1864, General Sherman telegraphed Hurlbut: "There has been marked timidity in the management of affairs since Forrest passed north of Memphis. General Grant orders me to relieve you. You will proceed to Cairo and take command there." (OR, I, XXXII, III, 381).

On April 18 Hurlbut replied: "Portions of your telegram are of such a nature as justify and, in fact, require that I should demand a court of inquiry, where all the facts and circumstances may be developed, and your charge of 'marked timidity' be proven or disproven. When that shall have been done, and the responsibility of the late disasters fixed upon the proper parties, I shall do myself the justice of tendering to the President . . . my resignation of a commission which cannot be advantageously held by me in subordination to officers who entertain and express the opinions contained in your dispatch." (*Ibid.*, p. 405).

Also on April 18 Hurlbut wrote Stanton requesting a court of inquiry and enclosing Sherman's telegram. On April 30 Halleck communicated the request to Grant, and on May 2 Grant declined to order a court of inquiry (*ibid.*, pp. 405-406). [2] George H. Thomas, in command at Nashville, Tennessee.

Order Concerning Alonzo Sheffield[1]

May 2, 1864

Upon a good man being furnished by Alonzo Sheffield, within named, and mustered into the service for the term of three years, said Sheffield is fully pardoned for any supposed desertion.

May 2, 1864   A. LINCOLN

[1] AES, DLC-RTL. Lincoln's endorsement is written on an affidavit of Mary Sheffield, Brooklyn, New York, April 28, 1864, that her husband Alonzo Sheffield had enlisted in the Fifty-first New York Volunteers on August 21, 1861, while intoxicated, that he had left the regiment after two months to return to his business and had never concealed himself until arrested as a deserter on April 1, 1864, and that he was the sole support of his family. On May 16, Colonel Daniel T. Van Buren, assistant adjutant general, Department of the East, enclosed papers in the case to General John A. Dix, who forwarded them to Lincoln with the following endorsement: "Respectfully forwarded with the request that the attention of the President . . . may be called to the case for the purpose of suggesting that his interposition, on the ex parte representations of interested persons, in cases of military crime, is almost always hazardous. In this case the soldier, whom he ordered discharged, while laboring under the charge of desertion, deserted a second time; but the substitute having been provided, it was not deemed proper to suspend the President's order & ask a reconsideration. But it is respectfully suggested that in all future cases, reference may be made to the Comg. Genl. of the Dept. for a report before any final action is taken." (DLC-RTL).

To Cabinet Members[1]

Executive Mansion,
Sir: Washington, May 3, 1864.

It is now quite certain that a large number of our colored soldiers, with their white officers, were, by the rebel force, massacred after they had surrendered, at the recent capture of Fort-Pillow. So much is known, though the evidence is not yet quite ready to be laid before me. Meanwhile I will thank you to prepare, and give me in writing your[2] opinion as to what course, the government should take in the case. Yours truly   A. LINCOLN

1 ADfS, DLC-RTL. The envelope containing the letter is endorsed by Lincoln "Letter to each Member of Cabinet, May 3, 1864." Individual letters sent to the cabinet members are extant as follows: to Blair (DLC-Blair Papers), to Seward (DNA FS RG 59, Miscellaneous Letters), to Welles (owned by George A. Ball, Muncie, Indiana). The lengthy and divergent replies from the cabinet members are in the Lincoln Papers, but limitations of space forbid adequate quotation and summary. A satisfactory summary may be found in Nicolay and Hay, *Abraham Lincoln: A History*, VI, 478 ff. All members agreed that the Confederate government should be called on to avow or disavow the massacre. Seward, Chase, Stanton, and Welles agreed in advising that Confederate prisoners equal in numbers to the Union troops massacred should be set apart as hostages, to be executed if the Confederate government avowed the massacre. Usher, Bates, and Blair advised no retaliation against innocent hostages, but advised that orders be issued to commanders to execute the actual offenders (Forrest and any of his command) if captured. Recommendations of the cabinet were not carried out, but see further Lincoln's instructions to Stanton, May 17, *infra*. For the report of the special committee (Senator Benjamin F. Wade and Representative Daniel W. Gooch) appointed to investigate the massacre, see *House Committee Reports No. 65*, Thirty-eighth Congress, First Session.

Although attempts have been made to absolve General Forrest and although Forrest's own explanation undertook to place the blame on the Union commander, Major Lionel F. Booth, for declining to surrender the fort before it was stormed, the truth contained in Forrest's own reports to Assistant Adjutant General Thomas J. Jack and to General Leonidas Polk on April 15, 1864, is self-evident. Testimony of survivors was that after they had thrown down their arms the Confederates shot most of those who did not jump into the river. Forrest's report to Jack is as follows:

". . . Arrived there [Fort Pillow] on the morning of the 12th and attacked the place with . . . about 1,500 men, and after a sharp contest captured the garrison and all of its stores. A demand was made for the surrender, which was refused. The victory was complete, and the loss of the enemy will never be known from the fact that large numbers ran into the river and were shot and drowned. The force was composed of about 500 negroes and 200 white soldiers (Tennessee Tories). The river was dyed with the blood of the slaughtered for 200 yards. There was in the fort a large number of citizens who had fled there to escape the conscript law. Most of these ran into the river and were drowned.

"The approximate loss was upward of 500 killed, but few of the officers escaping.

"It is hoped that these facts will demonstrate to the Northern people that negro soldiers cannot cope with Southerners. We still hold the fort.

"My loss was about 20 killed and about 60 wounded. . . ." (OR, I, XXXII, I, 610-11).

2 The autograph draft was revised to the present text by an unidentified hand. As Lincoln wrote it, the remainder of this sentence read: "what course, in your judgment the government should take in the case."

Order Concerning William W. White[1]

May 3, 1864

The within order of dismissal is revoked, if no successor to Captain White has been appointed; and if such successor has been appointed, then the order is modified to be an honorable discharge.

May 3. 1864   A. LINCOLN

¹ Copy, DLC-RTL. The copy of Lincoln's endorsement is on a copy of a letter of James B. Fry to White, January 11, 1864, "By direction of the President, you are hereby dismissed from the service of the United States." Provost Marshal William W. White of the Eighteenth Pennsylvania District had been convicted on charges of forgery and presenting a fraudulent claim against the government. White was discharged as of May 4, 1864, but on May 23 Stanton wrote Lincoln, "Your order in relation to Capt W White a copy of which is enclosed, did not direct him to be discharged from the Old Capitol Prison, and until the receipt of your peremptory order of this date I was not aware that he was in the Old Capitol. The order for his discharge was made on receipt of your note." (DLC-RTL). Lincoln's note of May 23 has not been located.

To William H. Seward¹

Hon. Secretary of State   Executive Mansion,
My dear Sir   Washington, May 3., 1864.

Please invite all members of the Cabinet to be [present at the meeting today. Yours truly.   A. LINCOLN]

¹ ALS, NAuE; copy, DLC-RTL. The bracketed portion has been cut off the original manuscript.

To William T. Sherman¹

       Office U.S. Military Telegraph,
Major General Sherman   War Department,
Chattanooga, Tenn.   Washington, D.C., May 4. 1864.

I have an imploring appeal in behalf of the citizens who say your order No. 8 will compel them to go North of Nashville. This is in no sense, an order; nor is it even a request that you will do any thing which in the least, shall be a drawback upon your military operations, but any thing you can do consistently with those operations, for those suffering people, I shall be glad of

       A. LINCOLN

¹ ALS, DNA WR RG 107, Presidential Telegrams, I, 45. Sherman's *General Orders No. 8*, April 19, 1864, read in part: "Provisions will no longer be issued to citizens at military posts south of Nashville. When citizens cannot procure provisions in the country there is no alternative but they must remove to the rear. . . . It is idle for us to be pushing forward subsistence stores if they are lavished and expended on any persons except they belong to the army proper."

On May 5, 1864, Sherman replied to Lincoln's telegram: "We have worked hard with the best talent of the country & it is demonstrated that the railroad cannot supply the army & the people too. one or the other must quit & the army don't intend to unless Joe Johnston makes us. The issues to citizens have been enormous & the same weight of corn or oats would have saved thousands of the mules whose carcasses now corduroy the roads and which we need so much. We have paid back to East Tenn. ten for one of provisions taken in war. I will not change my order and I beg of you to be satisfied that the clamor is partly a humbug & for effect, & to test it I advise you to tell the bearers of the appeal to hurry to Kentucky & make up a caravan of cattle & wagons & to come over by Cumberland Gap and Somerset to relieve their suffering friends on foot as they used to do before a railroad was built Tell them they have no time to lose. We can relieve all actual suffering by each company or regiment giving of their savings. Every man who is willing to fight and work gets all rations & all who won't fight or work should go away and we offer them free transportation" (DLC-RTL).

To Mrs. Abner Bartlett[1]

Mrs. Abner Bartlett   Executive Mansion,
My dear Madam.   Washington, May 5, 1864.

I have received the very excellent pair of socks of your own knitting, which you did me the honor to send. I accept them as a very comfortable article to wear; but more gratefully as an evidence, of the patriotic devotion which, at your advanced age, you bear to our great and just cause.

May God give you yet many happy days. Yours truly

A. LINCOLN

[1] ALS, owned by LeBaron R. Barker, Plymouth, Massachusetts. Mrs. Abner Bartlett of Medford, Massachusetts, born in 1777, had knitted a great many socks for soldiers. No letter from Mrs. Bartlett has been located.

To Salmon P. Chase and Edwin M. Stanton[1]

Executive Mansion,
Washington, 5th May, 1864.

The Secretaries of the Treasury and of War, are hereby authorized and required, so far to relax the order pro[hi]biting the exportation of horses from the United States, as to allow the exportation of such horses, as have been bought for the personal use of the Emperor of the French and the Captain General of Cuba.

ABRAHAM LINCOLN

[1] DS, DNA FS RG 59, Miscellaneous Letters. See Lincoln's order of September 4, 1863, *supra.*

To John A. J. Creswell[1]

Hon. Jno. A. J. Creswell   Executive Mansion,
My dear Sir.   Washington, May 5, 1864.

I shall be pleased to receive the gentlemen named at 2. P.M. today. Yours truly   A. LINCOLN

[1] ALS, CCamStJ. No clue has been found as to the identity of "the gentlemen named."

To Joseph Holt[1]

Executive Mansion   May 5. 1864

Let the disability now resting upon Surgeon McLetchie be removed so that he be rendered eligible for reappointment.   A. LINCOLN.

[1] ES, DNA WR RG 153, Judge Advocate General, LL 1621. Lincoln's endorsement is on the court-martial record of Assistant Surgeon Andrew McLetchie, Seventy-ninth New York Militia, dismissed for drunkenness. AGO *Special Orders No. 200*, June 7, 1864, removed the disability and rendered McLetchie eligible, provided the Governor of New York desired to reappoint him.

Remarks at Marine Band Concert[1]

May 7, 1864

Ladies and gentlemen, you, no doubt, desire to have a speech from me. In lieu of a speech, I propose that we give three cheers for Major General Grant and all the armies under his command.

[1] Washington *Daily Times*, May 9, 1864.

To the Senate[1]

To the Senate of the United States.   May 7, 1864

In compliance with the request contained in a resolution of the Senate, dated April 30. 1864, I herewith transmit to your honorable body a copy of the opinion by the Attorney General on the rights of colored persons in the army or volunteer service of the United States, together with the accompanying papers.

May 7, 1864.   ABRAHAM LINCOLN

[1] DS, DNA RG 46, Senate 38A F5. See Lincoln to Bates, April 4, *supra*.

To Edwin M. Stanton[1]

I have given nothing to any reporter   A. LINCOLN

May 7. 1864

[1] AES, DLC-Stanton Papers. Lincoln's endorsement is written on a communication signed "Berry," addressed to Thomas T. Eckert, asking if a statement on a military engagement, claimed to have been given by the president to a reporter, could be forwarded.

To Hiram Barney[1]

Hon. Hiram Barney.   May 9, 1864

My dear Sir   The bearer, Lt. Millard, wishes to apply to you for some place in the Custom-House; and while I do not personally know much of him, the within, & other vouchers leave no doubt in my mind that he is entirely worthy, & I shall be really pleased if you can find a place for him.   A. LINCOLN

May 9. 1864

[1] AES, RPAB-Hawkins Collection. Lincoln's endorsement is written on a letter from Representative James A. Garfield, May 5, 1864, introducing "H. Millard—late Lieut in the Regular Army," who had been wounded at Chickamauga. Harrison Millard is listed as chief amendment clerk in the New York Custom House, *U.S. Official Register*, 1865.

To the Friends of Union and Liberty[1]

Executive Mansion, Washington,
To the friends of Union & Liberty.   May 9, 1864.

Enough is known of Army operations within the last five days to claim our especial gratitude to God; while what remains undone demands our most sincere prayers to, and reliance upon, Him, without whom, all human effort is vain. I recommend that all patriots, at their homes, in their places of public worship, and wherever they may be, unite in common thanksgiving and prayer to Almighty God.   ABRAHAM LINCOLN

[1] ADfS, DLC-RTL; copy, DNA WR RG 107, Presidential Telegrams, I, 47. This press release appeared in the newspapers on May 10, 1864.

To Mrs. Sarah B. Meconkey[1]

Mrs. Sarah B. Meconkey.   Executive Mansion,
Madam: Washington, May 9. 1864.

Our mutual friend, Judge Lewis tells me you do me the honor to inquire for my personal welfare. I have been very anxious for some days in regard to our armies in the field, but am considerably cheered, just now, by favorable news from them. I am sure you will join me in the hope for their further success; while yourself, and other good, mothers, wives, sisters, and daughters, do all you and they can, to relieve and comfort the gallant soldiers who compose them. Yours truly   A. LINCOLN

[1] ALS, NNC. Commissioner of Internal Revenue Joseph J. Lewis wrote Lincoln on May 7, 1864: "Mrs Sarah B. Meconkey a most estimable and loyal lady of [West Chester] Pennsylvania piously concerned for the health and personal welfare of the President inquires how he sustains the burden of his multiplied cares at this trying period. I have thought it best to refer the inquiry to the President himself for an answer with the assurance that nothing can afford her higher gratification than a cheerful line under your hand, with the addition, if it may be, that you feel that you have just grounds for confidence in a near deliverance of our bleeding country from its present perils and troubles." (DLC-RTL).

Response to Serenade[1]

May 9, 1864

FELLOW-CITIZENS: I am very much obliged to you for the compliment of this call, though I apprehend it is owing more to the good news received to-day from the army than to a desire to see me. I am, indeed, very grateful to the brave men who have been struggling with the enemy in the field, to their noble commanders who have directed them, and especially to our Maker. Our commanders are following up their victories resolutely and successfully. I think, without knowing the particulars of the plans of Gen. Grant, that what has been accomplished is of more importance than at first appears. I believe I know, (and am especially grateful to know) that Gen. Grant has not been jostled in his purposes; that he has made all his points, and to-day he is on his line as he purposed before he moved his armies. I will volunteer to say that I am very glad at what has happened; but there is a great deal still to be done. While we are grateful to all the brave men and officers for the events of the past few days, we should, above all, be very grateful to Almighty God, who gives us victory.

There is enough yet before us requiring all loyal men and patriots to perform their share of the labor and follow the example of the modest General at the head of our armies, and sink all personal considerations for the sake of the country. I commend you to keep yourselves in the same tranquil mood that is characteristic of that brave and loyal man. I have said more than I expected when I came before you; repeating my thanks for this call, I bid you good-bye. [Cheers.]

[1] Washington *National Republican*, May 10, 1864. This response is misdated May 13 in Hertz, II, 929. News that Grant had won a victory in the Battle of the Wilderness and had moved on Spottsylvania Court House brought premature rejoicing in Washington. On the night of May 9, the band of the Twenty-seventh Michigan Volunteers followed by a large crowd marched to the White House lawn and serenaded until Lincoln appeared on the portico to make his response.

To William H. Seward[1]

May 9, 1864

I believe Mr. Snow is a good man; but two things need to be remembered. 1s. Mr. Roger's rival was a relative of Mr. Snow. 2nd. I hear of nobody calling Mr. Rogers a Copperhead but Mr Snow. However, let us watch.   A. L.

May 9, 1864.

[1] ALS, NAuE. This note (misdated "1863" in Lapsley, VI, 292) is written on both sides of a small card, apparently in relation to Arkansas politics. A letter

from J. Snow dated at Little Rock, May 10, addressed to "Dear Governor" (Seward), sheds light on the circumstances referred to:

"Banks going down Red River leaves this state in a bad fix. If [John B.] Magruder concentrates this way, we shall *'go up'* if re-inforcements do not come at once. *No mistake.*

"Judge [Elisha] Baxter elected Senator in [Charles B.] Mitchells place. Balloted three days for [William K.] Sebastian's place. My son Wm D Snow was ahead in 23 ballotings but [William M.] Fishback succeeded

"I am one of the Delegates to Baltimore, &c.

"[Horace B.] Allis, Speaker of House was expelled today for *factiousness* and attempts to disorganize. He is [Anthony A. C.] Roger's leader here. Rogers is one of our Reps. to Congress. He has seven belonging to his side in the House. Allis, was elected to Baltimore Convention, before the *copper* became so conspicuous. After his election shewed his hand more boldly. *He has left here for an office at Washington* He kept out of the House with *all* his party (7) to kill election of Senator, so there should be no quorum." (DLC-RTL).

To Edwin M. Stanton[1]

May 9, 1864

Secy of War please see Chaplain Bristow.

[1] Copy, ISLA. Chaplain Bristow has not been identified.

To Edwin M. Stanton[1]

Hon. Sec. of War   Executive Mansion,
Dear Sir.   Washington, May 10, 1864.

Let Private Thomas Lowery of Co. G. 11th New-Jersey Vols, now in hospital at Philadelphia, be discharged. Yours truly

A. LINCOLN.

[1] Hertz, II, 929. The roster of the Eleventh New Jersey Volunteers gives the name as "Lowrey." Lincoln's order was conveyed in AGO *Special Orders No. 174,* May 11, 1864.

To Lewis Wallace[1]

Office U.S. Military Telegraph,
Major Gen. Wallace   War Department,
Baltimore.   Washington, D.C., May 10 1864.

Please tell me what is the trouble with Dr. Hawks. Also, please ask Bishop Whittington to give me his view of the case.

A. LINCOLN

[1] ALS, DNA WR RG 107, Presidential Telegrams, I, 48. The case of Dr. Francis L. Hawks, rector of Christ Church in Baltimore, was reported by General Wallace's letter of May 11, 1864:

"Your telegram touching 'the trouble with Dr. Hawks,' and requesting me to ask Bishop Whittingham to give you his view . . . reached me so late . . . that I could do nothing . . . until this morning.

"Knowing that Bp. W. knew nothing of the affair, I carried yr. request to him in person. After a full expose, he wrote you a letter in reply, which I have the honor to forward. . . .

"Dr. H. came to Baltimore . . . from New York, imported by the disloyalists. . . . Today his congregation . . . are sympathisers of the highest social *caste*. Publicly the Revd gentleman never says anything exceptionable; hence, his loyal people defend him, and even carry their entreaties to yr. Excellency. They honestly believe him all right, while I feel a positive assurance that he is all wrong. . . .

"I waited patiently till I became satisfied and assured of his dangerous character, abilities, and operations, then directed my Provt. Marshal to notify him that he must either take the oath of allegiance . . . or leave the city within twenty four hours. Would a Union Man hesitate about the alternative to take? . . . .

"The Provt. Marshal found him absent in New York. He is not yet returned; probably on account of notice of the order. . . .

"I beg you to support my action. . . .

"I laid my order at his door, because, being leader among the disaffected Ministers, I hoped his example would, for the present, at least, admonish the rest." (DLC-RTL).

Protestant Episcopal Bishop William R. Whittingham's letter, enclosed by Wallace, reads in part as follows: "There are very strong reasons, personal and official, why I should desire to remain totally unconnected with the case. Nevertheless, I could not, in duty, decline to hear Gen. Wallace's statement of the grounds upon which he acted, nor can I refuse to the President the expression of my conviction, upon hearing that statement, that he had sufficient reasons. . . ."

See Lincoln's letter to Wallace, May 13, *infra*.

To Edward Bates[1]

Attorney General please make out pardons for these two boys.

May 11. 1864   A. LINCOLN

[1] AES, DNA RG 204, U.S. Pardon Attorney, A 535. Lincoln's endorsement is written on an envelope containing a request for pardon of Isaac Baker and Robert Ford, imprisoned at Denver, Colorado, on conviction for assault with intent to kill.

To Christian IX[1]

May 11, 1864

Abraham Lincoln
President of the United States of America

To His Majesty Christian IX.

King of Denmark

Great & Good Friend. I have received the letter which Your Majesty was pleased to address to me on the 7th of last month, announcing the decease on the 28th of the preceding month, of Her Royal Highness Madam the Landgrave Louise Charlotte of Hesse consort of His Highness the Landgrave William.

I deeply sympathise in the grief which has been occasioned by this sad event and I offer to Your Majesty my sincere condolence.

May God have your Majesty always in his safe and holy keeping Your Good Friend   ABRAHAM LINCOLN

Washington. 11th. May. 1864.

> By the President
>
> WILLIAM H. SEWARD   Secretary of State

¹ Copy, DNA FS RG 59, Communications to Foreign Sovereigns and States, III, 233.

To William S. Rosecrans[1]

Major General Rosecrans   Executive Mansion,
St. Louis, Mo.   Washington, May 11. 1864.

Complaints are coming to me of disturbances in Carroll, Platte & Buchanan counties. Please ascertain the truth, correct what is found wrong, and telegraph me.   A. LINCOLN

¹ ALS, DNA WR RG 107, Presidential Telegrams, I, 49. General Alfred Pleasonton replied on May 12, 1864: "Maj Genl Rosecrans is absent. . . . Your dispatch Recd in reference to Disturbances. . . . Brig Genl Clinton B Fisk Commanding that District telegraphs as follows—St Joseph Mo May 12—64 The President of the U S may be assured that there is less disturbance in Carroll Putnam & Buchanan counties in this state than at any previous time during the Rebellion   the Citizens of this this [*sic*] district are very generally engaging earnestly in their legitimate pursuits   I wish the President would give us the source of information He has Received" (DLC-RTL).

To John Birely[1]

                              Executive Mansion, Washington,
My Dear Sir   May 12, 1864.

I have the honor to acknowledge the receipt of your favor of the 11th May and the accompanying cane.

I beg that you will accept the assurance of my cordial gratitude for your kindness.

I am very truly   Your Obedient Servant   A. LINCOLN

John Birely Esq
    (Birely & Son)
    Philadelphia

¹ LS, owned by Charles W. Olsen, Chicago, Illinois. On May 11, 1864, John Birely, shipbuilder of Philadelphia, Pennsylvania, wrote Lincoln: "I send you to-day, by Adams Express, a walking cane, the wood of which was taken from the wreck of the United States ship Alliance, (now lying in the River Delaware.) the first American built man of war, that hoisted the glorious stars and stripes in the War of Independence. . . . It is a relic of the olden times and you would do me an honor by accepting it. It comes from an old soldier and officer in the War of 1812. . . ." (DLC-RTL).

To F. B. Loomis[1]

Executive Mansion, Washington, May 12, 1864.

My Dear Sir: I have the honor to acknowledge the receipt of your communication of the 28th April, in which you offer to replace the present garrison of Fort Trumbull with volunteers, which you propose to raise at your own expense. While it seems inexpedient at this time to accept this proposition, on account of the special duties now devolving upon the garrison mentioned, I cannot pass unnoticed such a meritorious instance of individual patriotism. Permit me, for the Government, to express my cordial thanks to you for this generous and public-spirited offer, which is worthy of note among the many called forth in these times of national trial.

I am very truly your obedient servant.   A. LINCOLN.

F. B. Loomis, Esq.

[1] New York *Times*, May 29, 1864. The letter from F. B. Loomis, New London, Connecticut, is in the Nicolay Papers (DLC).

To Samuel C. Pomeroy[1]

Hon. Senator Pomeroy   Executive Mansion
Sir—   Washington May 12. 1864

I did not doubt yesterday that you desired to see me about the appointment of Assessor in Kansas. I wish you and Lane would make a sincere effort to get out of the mood you are in. I[t] does neither of you any good—it gives you the means of tormenting my life out of me, and nothing else. Yours &c   A. LINCOLN

[1] ADfS, DLC-RTL. Secretary Chase wrote Lincoln on May 11, 1864:
"The office of Assessor for the District of Kansas has become vacant by the resignation of J. M. Leggett. Gov. Carney and Senator Pomeroy recommend the appointment of Mr. Ellsworth Cheeseborough, while Senator Lane and Mr. Wilder of the House recommend the appointment of Thomas Stineburgh.

"I know nothing of the gentlemen recommended . . . and therefore submit the appointment to you without recommendation." (DLC-RTL).

The *U.S. Official Register*, 1865, lists Thomas J. Sternbergh of Lawrence, Kansas, as assessor.

To the Senate[1]

To the Senate of the United States.   May 12, 1864

In answer to the Resolution of the Senate of the 9th. instant, requesting a copy of correspondence relative to a controversy between the Republic of Chile and Bolivia, I transmit a Report from the Secretary of State, to whom the Resolution was referred.

Washington, 12 May, 1864.   ABRAHAM LINCOLN

¹ DS, DNA RG 46, Senate 38 F3. Seward's report of May 12, 1864, transmitted his correspondence with U.S. Minister to Chile, Thomas H. Nelson, relative to Bolivia's declaration of war upon Chile for having appropriated some three degrees latitude of territory comprising the desert of Atacama, and to the suggestion of the United States that Spain should be requested to arbitrate the dispute.

Endorsement Concerning a Church at Memphis, Tennessee¹

May 13, 1864
I believe it is true that with reference to the church within named I wrote as follows:

"If² the Military have Military need of the church building, *let them keep it;* otherwise *let them get out of it,* and leave it and it's owners alone, except for causes that justify the arrest of any one."
March 4. 1864. A. LINCOLN"

I am now told that the Military were not in possession of the building; and yet that in pretended execution of the above they, the Military put one set of men out of and another set into the building. This, if true, is most extraordinary. I say again, if there be no military need for the building, leave it alone, neither putting any one in or out, of it, except on finding some one preaching or practicing treason, in which case lay hands upon him just as if he were doing the same thing in any other building, or in the streets or highways. A. LINCOLN
May 13. 1864

¹ ADfS, DLC-RTL. The envelope containing this draft is endorsed by Lincoln "Church at Memphis." See the memorandum of March 4, *supra.* Apparently the endorsement of May 13, of which Lincoln retained his first draft, was written on a statement or petition of the loyal church members who had been turned out by the secessionist trustees (see note to Lincoln's communication to Cadwallader C. Washburn, July 5, *infra*). A portion of the endorsement has been preserved as noted below, but the remainder, as well as the document on which it was written, has not been located.
² An autograph fragment comprising the quoted portion of the endorsement, which appears to have been cut out of Lincoln's original endorsement written on the petition from the loyal church members, is in the Illinois State Historical Library.

To Lewis Wallace¹

Office U.S. Military Telegraph,
Major General Wallace   War Department,
Baltimore, Md.   Washington, D.C., May 13. 1864.
I was very anxious to avoid new excitements at places where quiet seemed to be restored; but after reading, and considering,

your letter and inclosure, I have to say I leave you to act your careful discretion in the matter. The good news this morning I hope will have a good effect all round.[2]　　　　　A. LINCOLN

[1] ALS, DNA WR RG 107, Presidential Telegrams, I, 50. See Lincoln to Wallace, May 10, *supra.*

[2] Newspapers of May 13 devoted full pages to exceedingly favorable reports on the Battle of the Wilderness, May 5-7.

To Thomas Carney[1]

May 14, 1864

The within letter is, to my mind, so obviously intended as a page for a political record, as to be difficult to answer in a straight-forward business-like way. The merits of the Kansas people need not to be argued to me. They are just as good as any other loyal and patriotic people; and, as such, to the best of my ability, I have always treated them, and intend to treat them. It is not my recollection that I said to you Senator Lane would probably oppose raising troops in Kansas, because it would confer patronage upon you. What I did say was that he would probably oppose it because he and you were in a mood of each opposing whatever the other should propose. I did argue generally too, that, in my opinion, there is not a more foolish or demoralizing way of conducting a political rivalry, than these fierce and bitter struggles for patronage.

As to your demand that I will accept or reject your proposition to furnish troops, made to me yesterday, I have to say I took the proposition under advisement, in good faith, as I believe you know; that you can withdraw it if you wish, but that while it remains before me, I shall neither accept or reject it, until, with reference to the public interest, I shall feel that I am ready. Yours truly

May 14, 1864　　　　　A. LINCOLN

[1] ALS, IHi. This communication was returned to Governor Carney along with Carney's letter of May 13, 1864, which reads:

"Kansas has furnished more men according to her population, to crush this rebellion, than any other State in this Union. Her sons, to day; are scattered over the country, defending the Old Flag, while many of her peaceable citizens at home, are being murdered by lawless Guerrillas. Such is the intelligence I received today.

"The Major General Commanding that Department, informed me, he needed more troops to secure protection to the State. I have tendered you two thousand troops, for One hundred days, such as you have accepted from other States, to be used as you might direct through the Commander of that Department, without other cost to the Government than the pay of Volunteers without bounty.

"You refered the matter to the Secretary of War, for his consideration. I found that officer overburdened with business of such magnatude to the country, that he could not be seen, either upon my request or yours.

"I have to ask that you will either accept or reject the proposition, I made in my communication of the 12th. instant.

"I hope, however, you will not allow the lives & homes of the Citizens of Kansas, to be jeopardised by the objections you suggested in our conversation, 'that Senator Lane would probably oppose the raising of the troops, or if raised, would oppose an appropriation for their pay, in consequence of the patronage thus confered upon the Governor of the State.'

"You will do me the favor to reply at your earliest convenience" (IHi).

On May 16, Carney replied:
"Your note of 14th instant is received. I regret you do not consider the threatening attitude of affairs in Kansas of sufficient public interest to accept at once the offer I made you of two thousand troops. . . .

"I did not intend to advise as to public interest outside of Kansas. . . .

"Kansas has been, and still is, in deep distress, and needs the fostering care of the Government, therefore, I made to you the proposition I did in my communication of the 12th. . . . This care . . . I feel the citizens of my state have a right to claim. . . . Their sufferings and sacrifices have been great . . . because her sons have gone forth to fight the battles of their common country, and left their homes in the care of the Government. Yet their homes have been visited by the assassin, and are again threatened by these murderous outlaws.

"It was to prevent a return of those disasters that I urged the acceptance of the troops offered; and in that spirit, and for that purpose, I again respectfully, but earnestly renew it." (DLC-RTL).

To Joseph Roberts[1]

Officer in Military Command at   Executive Mansion
Fort-Monroe, Va.   Washington, May 14. 1864

If Thomas Dorerty, or Welsh, is to be executed to-day, and it is not already done, suspend it till further order   A LINCOLN

[1] ALS, DNA WR RG 107, Presidential Telegrams, I, 51. General Benjamin F. Butler was in the field, leaving Colonel Joseph Roberts, Third Pennsylvania Heavy Artillery, in command. No reply has been found, and no Thomas Dorerty (Donerty?) or Welsh has been identified.

To the Senate[1]

To the Senate   Executive Mansion,
of the United States.   Washington, May 14. 1864

I transmit, herewith, a report of the Secretary of the Interior, of the 14th instant, and accompanying papers, in answer to a resolution of the Senate of the 14th ultimo, in the following words, viz:

"Resolved, That the President of the United States be requested to communicate to the Senate the reasons, if any exist, why the refugee Indians in the State of Kansas, are not returned to their homes."

ABRAHAM LINCOLN

[1] DS, DNA RG 46, Senate 38A F6. Secretary Usher transmitted a report of William P. Dole, May 11, 1864, that the presence of Confederates and hostile

Indians in the territory made it inadvisable to return the loyal refugees without adequate protection and also because he had no funds to use for the purpose of removal, but that he interpreted the act approved on May 3, 1864, to aid and to return the refugees to their homes, as an order which he would carry out as soon as possible.

Endorsement Concerning Allison C. Poorman[1]

May 15, 1864

Indorsed

The writer of the within is a family connection of mine, & a worthy man; and I shall be obliged if he be allowed what he requests, so far as the rules and exigencies of the public service will permit.   A LINCOLN

May 15. 1864

[1] AES (copy), DLC-RTL. The copy of Poorman's letter of May 9, 1864, in Lincoln's autograph and with the above endorsement, reads as follows: "As I am now out of business I write you for the purpose of making application for a permit to trade within the lines of the Western Army in all kinds of Merchandize, Liquors excepted. I would of course expect to be governed by the rules of Trade as established by the *Treasure* department. If you will grant me this request you will confer a favor that will not be soon forgotten."

Allison C. Poorman married Amanda Hanks, daughter of Dennis Hanks.

Endorsement Concerning William F. Shriver[1]

May 15, 1864

Indorsed

The writer of this is personally unknown to me, though married to a young relative of mine. I shall be obliged if he be allowed what he requests so far as the rules and exigencies of the public service will permit.   A. LINCOLN

May 15. 1864

[1] AES (copy), DLC-RTL. The copy of Shriver's letter of May 9, 1864, in Lincoln's autograph and with the above endorsement, reads as follows: "This will be presented to you by Father Hanks who will more fully lay before you my wants than I can here explain. I will simply say that if consistent with your feelings, and not in any way conflicting with Army regulations I would like a permit to trade within the lines of the Armies of the Cumberland, Mississippi and Arkansas in Cotton & Hides for shipment North. For reference I can only offer Father Hanks."

William F. Shriver (Schriver) married Mary L. Hanks, daughter of Dennis Hanks.

To Orville H. Browning[1]

Will Mr. Browning please look at the card just sent Mr. Ewing?

May 16, 1864   A. LINCOLN

[1] American Art Association Anderson Galleries Catalog 3823, February 25-26, 1930, No. 241. See Lincoln to Ewing, *infra*. Browning and Thomas Ewing acted as defense for Rear Admiral Charles Wilkes in his court-martial for insubordination (unauthorized publication of letters to Gideon Welles). Wilkes was sentenced on April 27, 1864, to three years' suspension and reprimand. Browning's *Diary* under date of April 30, and May 5, 1864, records interviews with the president, in company with Ewing, and Welles' *Diary* under date of December 20, 1864, records Ewing's continued efforts in the case.

To L. J. Cist[1]

L. J. Cist,   Executive Mansion,
Chairman &c.   Washington, May 16. 1864.

Dear Sir   A letter of yours to Hon. Mr. Blow, requesting an autograph note of mine for the benefit of the Mississippi Valley Sanitary Fair, has been laid before me. I am glad to give it, in the hope that it may contribute, in some small degree at least, to the relief and comfort of our brave soldiers. Yours truly   A. LINCOLN

[1] ALS, owned by Robert A. Ramsdell, Wilmington, Delaware. L. J. Cist's letter to Representative Henry T. Blow, May 9, 1864, was forwarded in a letter of Representative Joseph W. McClurg, May 14, 1864:

"From the accompanying letter . . . to the Hon. H. T. Blow, you will please see the anxiety to have your *Photograph* and *Autograph* at the Mississippi Valley Sanitary Fair. I hope you will see proper to gratify those who so much desire them with what they ask and an accompanying letter of encouragement.

"A line from you, to the effect that the request will be granted, will be appreciated. . . .

"Hon. H. T. Blow is *very unwell*." (DLC-RTL).

To Thomas Ewing[1]

Respects to Mr. Ewing; but I am not ready to decide his cases, & I do not wish him to come in [and] scold about it.   A. LINCOLN
May 16. 1864

[1] ALS, DLC-Ewing Papers. This note is misdated May 6 in Hertz, II, 929. See Lincoln to Browning, *supra*, and to Welles, December 26, *infra*.

To Edwin M. Stanton[1]

May 16, 1864
Genl. Curtis had better be asked to look to it.

[1] Copy, DNA WR RG 107, Secretary of War, Letters Received, P 304, Register Notation. The register preserves a copy of Lincoln's endorsement transmitting a letter of Benjamin Holiday about soldiers on the road from Atchison, Kansas, pressing hay and corn. The letter with the endorsement is missing from the file.

Order for Draft of 300,000 Men[1]

Executive Mansion,
Washington, D.C. May 17. 1864.

To increase the active and reserved force of the Army, Navy, & Marine Corps of the United States, a call is hereby made, & a draft ordered for three hundred thousand men to serve for the period of ――― unless sooner discharged.

The proportional quotas for the different wards, towns, townships, precincts, or election districts, or counties, will be made known through the Provost Marshal General's Bureau, & account will be taken of the credits & deficiencies on former quotas.

The 1st. day of July 1864 is designated as the time up to which the numbers required from each ward of a city, town, &c, may be raised by voluntary enlistment, & drafts will be made in each ward of city, town, &c, which shall not have filled the quota assigned to it within the time designated, for the number required to fill said quotas. The drafts will be commenced as soon after the 1st. of July as practicable. ABRAHAM LINCOLN.

[1] DS, InFtwL. This order does not appear in the *Official Records* and seems not to have been issued, perhaps because of the effect on public opinion produced by the bogus proclamation of May 17 (see Lincoln to Dix, May 18, *infra*). The act of congress approved by Lincoln on July 4, 1864, provided similar terms for the call of 500,000 men. See the proclamation of July 18, *infra*.

To Joseph Roberts[1]

Officer in command at
Fort-Monroe, Va.

Executive Mansion,
Washington, May 17, 1864.

If there is a man by the name of William H. H. Cummings, of Co. H. 24th. Mass. Volunteers, within your command, under sentence of death for desertion, suspend execution till further order. A LINCOLN

[1] ALS, DNA WR RG 107, Presidential Telegrams, I, 52. The roster of the Twenty-fourth Massachusetts Volunteers lists William H. Cummings as discharged for disability at Fort Monroe on May 26, 1864. Lincoln probably wrote the second "H" inadvertently.

To the Senate[1]

To the Senate of the United States: May 17, 1864

I herewith lay before the Senate, for its constitutional action thereon, a treaty concluded on the 7th instant, in this city, between William P. Dole, Commissioner of Indian Affairs, and Clark W.

Thompson, superintendent of Indian affairs, Northern Superintendency, on the part of the United States, and the chief Hole-in-the-day and Mis-qua-dace for and on behalf of the Chippewas of the Mississippi, and the Pillager and Lake Winnebagoshish bands of Chippewa Indians in Minnesota.

A communication from the Secretary of the Interior of the 17th instant, with a statement and copies of reports of the Commissioner of Indian Affairs of the 12th and 17th instants, accompany the treaty. ABRAHAM LINCOLN.

Executive Mansion,
Washington, May 17, 1864.

[1] *Executive Journal*, XIII, 548. The treaty was ratified, as amended by the Senate, on February 9, 1865.

To Edwin M. Stanton[1]

Hon. Sec. of War   Executive Mansion,
My dear Sir: Washington, May 17, 1864.

I rather think I have said before, and at all events I say now, I would like for Rev Dr. Robert L. Stanton, of the Theological Seminary at Danville, Ky, to be a Visitor to West-Point, if there be no great obstacle in the way. Yours truly   A. LINCOLN

[1] ALS, NHi. No reply has been discovered. A letter from Brigadier General Richard Delafield to Nicolay, May 25, 1864, lists the "Board of Visitors to the Mily. Academy, so far as they have been appointed," but Robert L. Stanton is not on the list (DLC-RTL).

To Edwin M. Stanton[1]

Hon. Secretary of War: Executive Mansion
Sir.   Washington, D.C. May 17. 1864

Please notify the insurgents, through the proper military channels and forms, that the government of the United States has satisfactory proof of the massacre, by insurgent forces, at Fort-Pillow, on the 12th. and 13th. days of April last, of fully white and colored officers and soldiers of the United States, after the latter had ceased resistance, and asked quarter of the former.

That with reference to said massacre, the government of the United States has assigned and set apart by name   insurgent officers, theretofore, and up to that time, held by said government as prisoners of war.

That, as blood can not restore blood, and government should not act for revenge, any assurance, as nearly perfect as the case

admits, given on or before the first day of July next, that there shall be no similar massacre, nor any officer or soldier of the United States, whether white or colored, now held, or hereafter captured by the insurgents, shall be treated other than according to the laws of war, will insure the replacing of said insurgent officers in the simple condition of prisoners of war.

That the insurgents having refused to exchange, or to give any account or explanation in regard to colored soldiers of the United States captured by them, a number of insurgent prisoners equal to the number of such colored soldiers supposed to have been captured by said insurgents will, from time to time, be assigned and set aside, with reference to such captured colored soldiers, and will, if the insurgents assent, be exchanged for such colored soldiers; but that if no satisfactory attention shall be given to this notice, by said insurgents, on or before the first day of July next, it will be assumed by the government of the United States, that said captured colored troops shall have been murdered, or subjected to Slavery, and that said government will, upon said assumption, take such action as may then appear expedient and just.

¹ ADf, owned by Charles W. Olsen, Chicago, Illinois. See Lincoln's letter to cabinet members and note, May 3, *supra*. Presumably this communication to Stanton was never signed or delivered, and there is some mystery surrounding the fact that it should have been preserved until recently in the papers of Thomas T. Eckert of the War Department telegraph office. No record has been found of a communication from Stanton to the Confederate authorities carrying out Lincoln's instructions. According to Nicolay and Hay, action on the Fort Pillow massacre was "crowded out of view and consideration" by Grant's Wilderness campaign (*Abraham Lincoln: A History*, VI, 483).

To Benjamin F. Butler¹

"Cypher"   Office U.S. Military Telegraph,
Major General Butler.   War Department,
Bermuda Hundreds, Va   Washington, D.C., May 18. 1864.

Until receiving your despatch of yesterday, the idea of Commissions in the Volunteers expiring at the end of three years had not occurred to me. I think no trouble will come of it; and, at all events, I shall take care of it so far as in me lies. As to the Major Generalships in the Regular Army I think I shall not dispose of another, at least until the combined operations now in progress under direction of Gen. Grant, and within which yourself and command are included, shall be terminated. Meanwhile, on behalf of yourself, officers, and men, please accept my hearty thanks for what you and they have so far done.   A. LINCOLN

1 ALS, DNA WR RG 107, Presidential Telegrams, I, 53. On May 17 Butler telegraphed: "On the 16th of May 1861 I was honored by your kindness with a commission as Major General United States Volunteers I have heard that such commission expires by limitation of three years. I by no means desire to quit the service till the war is done. Do you think I have time enough to entitle me to one of the vacant commissions in the army to date from May 16th 61? Otherwise I should prefer my present one if you think me fit to hold either and I can hold on to it" (DLC-RTL).

To Salmon P. Chase[1]

May 18, 1864

I have issued no proclamation lately, I signed a very modest paper last night for the Sec. of War, about drafting 300.000 in July, as I remember, but the document now rampant at New York is a forgery. A. LINCOLN.

May 18. 1864

1 Copy, DLC-Chase Papers. This copy of an endorsement is labeled "Copy of Writing on the back of a Telegram." The telegram bearing Lincoln's endorsement has not been discovered, but it was probably one of many similar communications received on May 18. See Lincoln to Dix, infra.

To Salmon P. Chase[1]

Hon. Secretary of the Treasury: Executive Mansion,
My dear Sir: Washington, May 18, 1864.

Evening before last two gentlemen called on me, and talked so earnestly about financial matters, as to set me thinking of them a little more particularly since. And yet only one idea has occurred, which I think worth while even to suggest to you. It is this: Suppose you change your five per cent loan to six, allowing the holders of the fives already out to convert them into sixes, upon taking each an equal additional amount at six. You will understand, better than I all the reasons pro and con, among which probably will be, the rise of the rate of interest in Europe. Yours truly A. LINCOLN.

1 Copy, DLC-RTL. No reply has been discovered, and the "two gentlemen" have not been identified.

To John A. Dix[1]

To Maj. Gen'l Dix,   Executive Mansion,
Commanding, at New York.—   Washington, May 18. 1864.

Whereas, there has been wickedly and traitorously printed and published this morning, in the "New York World" and New York

"Journal of Commerce," newspapers printed and published in the city of New York,—a false and spurious proclamation, purporting to be signed by the President, and to be countersigned by the Secretary of State, which publication is of a treasonable nature, designed to give aid and comfort to the enemies of the United States, and to the rebels now at war against the Government, and their aiders and abettors: you are therefore hereby commanded forthwith to arrest and imprison in any fort or military prison in your command, the editors, proprietors and publishers of the aforesaid newspapers, and all such persons as, after public notice has been given of the falsehood of said publication, print and publish the same, with intent to give aid and comfort to the enemy;—and you will hold the persons so arrested, in close custody, until they can be brought to trial before a military commission, for their offense. You will also take possession by military force, of the printing establishments of the *"New York World,"* and *"Journal of Commerce,"* and hold the same until further order, and prevent any further publication therefrom.   A. LINCOLN

¹ LS, DNA WR RG 107, Presidential Telegrams, I, 54. Only the date and signature are in Lincoln's handwriting, the telegram having been drafted in the War Department at Stanton's direction. For an account of the hoax perpetrated by Joseph Howard, Jr., the same reporter who had created the hoax story of Lincoln's arrival in Washington in 1861 disguised in "a Scotch cap and long military cloak," see Sandburg, *Abraham Lincoln: The War Years*, III, 53 ff. The spurious proclamation as printed in the New York *World* and *Journal of Commerce*, May 18, 1864, reads:

"Fellow Citizens of the United States:

"Executive Mansion,
May 17, 1864.

"In all seasons of exigency, it becomes a nation carefully to scrutinize its line of conduct, humbly to approach the Throne of Grace, and meekly to implore forgiveness, wisdom, and guidance.

"For reasons known only to Him, it has been decreed that this country should be the scene of unparalleled outrage, and this nation the monumental sufferer of the Nineteenth Century. With a heavy heart, but an undiminished confidence in our cause, I approach the performance of a duty rendered imperative by my sense of weakness before [the] almighty, and of justice to the people.

"It is necessary that I should tell you that the first Virginia campaign under Lieut. Gen. Grant, in whom I have every confidence, and in whose courage and fidelity the people do well to honor, is virtually closed. He has conducted his great enterprise with discreet ability. He has crippled their strength and defeated their plans.

"In view, however, of the situation in Virginia, the disaster at Red River, the delay at Charleston, and the general state of the country, I, Abraham Lincoln, do hereby recommend that Thursday, the 26th day of May, A.D., 1864, be solemnly set apart throughout these United States as a day of fasting, humiliation and prayer.

"Deeming furthermore that the present condition of public affairs presents an extraordinary occasion, and in view of the pending expiration of the service of (100,000) one hundred thousand of our troops, I, Abraham Lincoln, President of the United States, by virtue of the power vested in me by the Constitution and the laws, have thought fit to call forth, and hereby do call forth the citizens of the United States, between the ages of (18) eighteen and (45) forty-five years, to the aggregate number of (400,000) four hundred thousand, in order to suppress the existing rebellious combinations, and to cause the due execution of the laws.

"And, furthermore, in case any State, or number of States, shall fail to furnish by the fifteenth day of June next, their assigned quota, it is hereby ordered that the same be raised by an immediate and peremptory draft.

"The details for this object will be communicated to the State authorities through the War Department.

"I appeal to all loyal citizens to favor, facilitate and aid this effort to maintain the honor, the integrity and the existence of the National Union, and the perpetuity of popular government.

"In witness whereof, I have hereunto set my hand, and caused the seal of the United States to be affixed. Done at the City of Washington this 17th day of May, one thousand eight hundred and sixty-four, and of the independence of the United States the eighty-eighth.

"By the President,   ABRAHAM LINCOLN.
WM. H. SEWARD, Secretary of State."

On May 19, Sidney H. Gay of the *Tribune*, Erastus Brooks of the *Express*, Frederick Hudson of the *Herald*, and M. F. Beach of the *Sun*, telegraphed Lincoln: "The undersigned Editors and publishers of a portion of the daily press of the City of New York respectfully represent that the leading daily journals of this city sustain very extended telegraphic news arrangements under an organization established in 1848 & known as the N York associated Press which is controlled by the members acting through an executive committee a general Agent in this city & Assistant Agents immediately responsible to the association at every important news centre throughout this country & Europe   Under the above named organization the rule has always been to transmit by telegraph all intelligence to the Office of the General Agent in this city & by him the same is properly prepared for publication & then written out by manifold process on tissue Paper & a copy of the same is sent simultaneously in sealed envelopes to each of the Editors who are entitled to receive the same. From foregoing statement of facts your excellency will readily perceive that an ingenious rogue knowing the manner in which the editors were supplied with much of their telegraphic news could by selecting his time & opportunity easily impose upon Editors or compositors the most wicked & fraudulent reports. On wednesday morning at about three oclock a messenger who well counterfeited the regular messenger of the Associated Press presented himself at all save one of the editorial rooms of the Papers connected with the associated Press and delivered to the foreman in the absence of the night editors sealed envelopes containing manifold Paper similar in all respects to that used by the association upon which was written a fraudulent Proclamation purporting to be signed by your Excellency and countersigned by the honorable Secy of State. The very late hour at which the fraud was perpetrated left no time for consideration as to the authenticity or genuineness of this document & the copy in most of the offices was at once cut up into small pieces and given into the hands of the compositors & in two cases the fraud was not discovered or suspected even till after the whole morning edition of the Papers were printed off & distributed The undersigned beg to state to your excellency that the fraud which succeeded with the World and the Journal of Commerce was one which from the circumstances attending it & the practices of the associated Press was extremely natural and very liable to have succeeded in any daily newspaper establishment in this city & inasmuch as in the judgement of the undersigned the editors and proprietors of the World were innocent of any knowledge of wrong in the publication of the fraudulent document and also in view of the fact that the suspension by your excellencys order of two Papers last evening has had the effect to awaken editors & publishers and news agent telegraph companies etc. to the propriety of increased vigilance in their several duties the undersigned respectfully request that your excellency will be pleased to rescind the order under which the World and the Journal of Commerce were suppressed. . . ." (DLC-RTL).

The editors were released, and the *World* and *Journal of Commerce* resumed publication after two days, but Joseph Howard remained in prison at Fort Lafayette until August 23, 1864. See Lincoln to Stanton, August 22, *infra*.

To Ulysses S. Grant[1]

Lieut. General Grant   Executive Mansion,
Army of Potomac   Washington, May 18, 1864.

An elderly gentleman—Dr. Winston—is here, saying he is well acquainted with the ground you are on, and trying to get on, and having letters from Gov. Morton, Senator Lane, and one from your Father, and asking to be allowed to go to you. Shall we allow him to go to you?   A. LINCOLN

[1] ALS, DNA WR RG 107, Presidential Telegrams, I, 56. On May 19 Grant telegraphed in reply: "Dr Winston may be of great service to us, please send him along." (DLC-RTL). Dr. Winston has not been further identified. See Lincoln to Stanton, May 20, *infra*.

To Thomas H. Hicks[1]

May 18, 1864

If Governor Hicks will examine this case, and say in writing below this he thinks Mr. Sherberne should be pardoned, I will pardon him.   A. LINCOLN
May 18, 1864.

[1] AES, DLC-RTL. Lincoln's endorsement is written on an envelope containing a printed copy of AGO *General Orders No. 147*, April 5, 1864, sentencing William L. Shurburne of Newport, Maryland, to five years' imprisonment for trading with the enemy. Hicks did not answer "below this" or elsewhere so far as has been discovered.

Response to Methodists[1]

Gentlemen.   May 18, 1864

In response to your address, allow me to attest the accuracy of it's historical statements; indorse the sentiments it expresses; and thank you, in the nation's name, for the sure promise it gives.

Nobly sustained as the government has been by all the churches,

I would utter nothing which might, in the least, appear invidious against any. Yet, without this, it may fairly be said that the Methodist Episcopal Church, not less devoted than the best, is, by it's greater numbers, the most important of all. It is no fault in others that the Methodist Church sends more soldiers to the field, more nurses to the hospital, and more prayers to Heaven than any. God bless the Methodist Church—bless all the churches—and blessed be God, Who, in this our great trial, giveth us the churches.

May 18, 1864   A. LINCOLN

¹ ADS, DLC; DS copy, owned by Mrs. Arthur Wendell, Rahway, New Jersey. The copy signed by Lincoln was originally in the papers of Joseph A. Wright. As printed by Nicolay and Hay (X, 99-100) the response is misdated "May 14," perhaps because the address to which Lincoln replied bore that date in the newspapers (Washington *Morning Chronicle*, May 19, 1864), and was followed by the undated text of Lincoln's response. The address from the General Conference of the Methodist Episcopal Church, presented by a committee composed of Bishop Edward R. Ames, Reverend Joseph Cummings, Reverend Granville Moody, Reverend Charles Elliott, and Reverend George Peck, pointed to the Methodist record of loyalty to the Union and support of the administration and pledged a continuation of prayers for the "preservation of our country undivided, for the triumph of our cause, and for a permanent peace, gained by the sacrifice of no moral principles, but founded on the Word of God, and securing, in righteousness, liberty and equal rights to all."

To Richard Yates¹

His Excy. Richd Yates   Executive Mansion,
Springfield Illinois   Washington, May 18, 1864.
   If any such proclamation has appeared, it is a forgery.
                                                  A. LINCOLN

¹ LS, DNA WR RG 107, Presidential Telegrams, I, 55. Yates telegraphed on May 18, 1864: "Is the proclamation in New York World purporting to be your recommendation for fasting & prayer with announcement of close of Virginia Campaign & call for four hundred thousand (400000) fresh troops a genuine document Please answer immediately." (DLC-RTL). See Lincoln to Dix, *supra*.

To Andrew Johnson¹

                              Office U.S. Military Telegraph,
Hon. Andrew Johnson   War Department,
Nashville, Tenn.   Washington, D.C., May 19 1864.
   Yours of the 17th. was received yesterday. Will write you on the subject within a day or two   A. LINCOLN

¹ ALS, DNA WR RG 107, Presidential Telegrams, I, 57. Governor Johnson's telegram of May 17 stated: "I am thoroughly satisfied that the amnesty will

be serious detriment in organizing the State Govt & that Tenn should be made an exception so far as the army is concerned We have gained all the benefit that can result from it let all the pardons granted to Tennesseans be upon the applications of those deserving it, made directly to the President The influence will be better & they will feel a much greater obligation to the Govt as it now operates its main tendency is to keep alive the Rebel spirit in fact reconciling none this is the opinion of every Real union man here" (DLC-RTL). If Lincoln wrote a letter "within a day or two," it is presumably not extant.

Proclamation Revoking Recognition of Charles Hunt[1]

May 19, 1864

Abraham Lincoln,
President of the United States of America.

To all whom it may concern:

An Exequatur bearing date the third day of May, 1850, having been issued to Charles Hunt, a citizen of the United States, recognizing him as Consul of Belgium, for Saint Louis, Missouri, and declaring him free to exercise and enjoy such functions, powers, and privileges, as are allowed to the Consuls of the most favored nations in the United States; and the said Hunt having sought to screen himself from his military duty to his country in consequence of thus being invested with the Consular functions of a foreign power in the United States, it is deemed advisable that the said Charles Hunt should no longer be permitted to continue in the exercise of said functions, powers, and privileges:

These are, therefore, to declare, that I no longer recognize the said Charles Hunt as Consul of Belgium for Saint Louis, Missouri, and will not permit him to exercise or enjoy any of the functions, powers or privileges allowed to Consuls of that Nation; and that I do hereby wholly revoke and annul the said Exequatur heretofore given, and do declare the same to be absolutely null and void, from this day forward.

In testimony whereof, I have caused these letters to be made patent, and the Seal of the United States of America to be hereunto affixed.

Given under my hand at Washington, this Nineteenth day of May, in the year of our Lord 1864, and the Independence of the United States of America the Eighty-eighth.

By the President: ABRAHAM LINCOLN

WILLIAM H. SEWARD, Secretary of State.

[1] DS, DNA FS RG 11, Proclamations.

Endorsement Concerning William B. Slack[1]

Presented by Gov. Newell in behalf Major Slack for Commandant of Marine Corps. Gov. Newell recommends in highest terms.

May 20, 1864.   A. LINCOLN

[1] AES, DLC-RTL. Lincoln's endorsement is written on the application of Major William B. Slack for appointment as commandant of the Marine Corps to succeed Colonel John Harris, deceased May 12, 1864. Major Jacob Zeilin was appointed colonel and commandant on June 10, 1864.

To Joseph Holt[1]

Judge Advocate General please examine & report upon this case.

May 20. 1864.   A. LINCOLN

[1] AES, IHi. Lincoln's endorsement is written on a letter from Commissary General W. W. Irwin, Pennsylvania Militia, Harrisburg, May 13, 1864, asking reinstatement of Captain George H. Smith, late commissary of subsistence in the U.S. Army, discharged March 23, 1864. Holt forwarded the record of Smith's dismissal and endorsed with recommendation that no further action be taken.

To Alfred Mackay[1]

Alfred Mackay   Executive Mansion,
Sec. of Fair   Washington,
St. Louis, Mo.   May 20, 1864.

Your despatch received. Thanks for your greeting, and congratulations for the successful opening of your Fair. Our soldiers are doing well, and must, and will be well done by.   A. LINCOLN

[1] ALS, DNA WR RG 107, Presidential Telegrams, I, 59. Mackay telegraphed Lincoln on May 19: "The officers & executive committees of Ladies & Gentlemen of the fair greet you warmly & desire that your endeavors to suppress the rebellion will be crowned with success. Our fair has opened splendidly The Mississippi Valley will do her full share to aid the sick & wounded soldiers. God bless you" (DLC-RTL).

Memorandum:
Appointment of Josiah W. Morris[1]

Executive Mansion,
Washington, May 20. 1864.

To-day Mr. Thomas E. Morris of New-Jersey calls and asks that his son, Josiah W. Morris, born Aug. 17. 1844, be appointed a Cadet. He entered the Anderson Troupe, now 15th. Penn. Cavalry

—in Sep. 1862, where he has remained and still is, and is one of the boys recommended by Gen. Rosecrans for West-Point

[1] AD, DNA WR RG 94, U.S. Military Academy, 1864, No. 117. No appointment of Josiah W. Morris has been discovered.

Order Concerning Trade[1]

May 20, 1864

No person engaged in trade, and proceeding in strict accordance with the published Regulations of the Treasury Department, upon that subject, *and promulgated according to the Regulation numbered LVI, and being the last on page 6, to the left opposite this,* shall be hindered or delayed therein, by the Army or Navy, or any person or persons connected therewith.　　　　A. LINCOLN

May 20, 1864

[1] AES, OClWHi; AES, DLC. In addition to the two copies extant, Lincoln may have written this order on other copies of the Treasury pamphlet *Additional Regulations Concerning Commercial Intercourse with and in States Declared in Insurrection,* January 26, 1864. The autograph endorsement is written on the bottom of the unnumbered inside back page of both copies, opposite the following regulation: "LVI. The foregoing Regulations, numbered LII, LIII, LIV, LV, shall take effect and be in force within the lines of the several military departments in the insurrectionary States, whenever the Generals commanding said departments shall, respectively, under authority from the President, and by proper orders promulgate the same."

See also the orders of January 26 and February 2, *supra.*

To Felix Schmedding[1]

Felix Schmedding　　　　　　　　　　　　Executive Mansion
St. Louis, Mo.　　　　　　　　Washington, May 20. 1864
　　The pleasure of attending your fair is not within my power.
　　　　　　　　　　　　　　　　　　　A. LINCOLN

[1] ALS, DNA WR RG 107, Presidential Telegrams, I, 58. Schmedding telegraphed on May 19, 1864, "Will you attend our Fair" (DLC-RTL).

To Edwin M. Stanton[1]

Hon. Sec. of War. Please provide for Dr. Winston going forward according to the within.　　　　　　　　　　　A. LINCOLN

May 20, 1864.

[1] Copy, DLC-RTL. The copy of this communication is written on Grant's telegram of May 19, 1864. See Lincoln to Grant, May 18, note, *supra.*

To Edward Bates[1]

Executive Mansion,
Dear Sir.   Washington, May 21st. 1864.
The Bill for Montana has passed, and I will thank you to have
the applications for offices there, which are in your Department,
briefed at once. Yours truly.   A. LINCOLN
Hon. Attorney General

[1] LS, DNA GE RG 60, Papers of Attorney General, Segregated Lincoln Material. In addition to his signature, Lincoln also wrote "Hon. Attorney General."
See the similar letter to Seward, *infra*. The "act to provide a temporary Government for the Territory of Montana" as amended by the Senate was approved
by Lincoln on May 26, 1864. The nominations from Bates' department were:
Hezekiah L. Hosmer of New York, chief justice; Ammi Giddings of Connecticut,
associate justice; Asa Bartlett of Illinois, associate justice; Lorenzo P. Williston
of Dakota Territory, associate justice; Edward B. Neally of Iowa, U.S. attorney;
Cornelius Buck of Minnesota, U.S. marshal. All were confirmed by the Senate
on June 25, except Hosmer, who was confirmed on June 30.

Endorsement Concerning Miss Gilbert[1]

May 21, 1864
These are very excellent testimonials, & I shall be glad for this
[woman] to get a place, if it can be [done] consistently with the
service.   A. LINCOLN
May 21. 1864

[1] AES, ICHi. Lincoln's endorsement has been removed from the attendant
papers, but is followed by an endorsement of General Joseph Hooker dated
February 1, 1865: "I fully concur with the within & recommend that employment be given Miss Gilbert." Miss Gilbert has not been identified.

To Gustavus V. Fox[1]

Capt. Fox, please see and hear the bearer, Mr. Sawyer.
May 21, 1864.   A. LINCOLN

[1] Tracy, p. 241. Mr. Sawyer has not been identified.

To Oliver P. Morton[1]

Executive Mansion,
Gov. O. P. Morton.   Washington, May 21, 1864.
The getting forward of hundred day troops to sustain Gen. Sherman's lengthening lines promises much good. Please put your best
efforts into the work.   A. LINCOLN

Same to   Governor Yates—Springfield.
            Stone—Davenport.
            Lewis—Madison.

[1] ALS, RPB; D, DNA WR RG 107, Presidential Telegrams, I, 61. The autograph original does not contain the notation appearing on the bottom of the copy filed in the volume of Presidential telegrams. Governor Morton replied the same day: "I started one Regiment of one hundred (100) day men yesterday, another today. Shall send one tomorrow, another on Monday, another on Tuesday, another on Wednesday, and another on Thursday. Am organizing and sending forward as rapidly as possible." (DLC-RTL).

Governor James T. Lewis replied on May 24: "Your telegram of twenty first (21st) inst recd I am doing all I can to forward hundred (100) day troops have two Regiments reported full they will be mustered and ready to leave as soon as arms are provided for them Two more Regiments are nearly full hope to be able to give you five Regiments very soon." (DLC-RTL).

No replies from Governor Richard Yates or Governor William M. Stone have been located.

To Christiana A. Sack[1]

Office U.S. Military Telegraph,
Christiana A. Sack   War Department,
Baltimore, Md.   Washington, D.C., May 21 1864.

I can not postpone the execution of a convicted spy, on a mere telegraphic despatch signed with a name I never heard before. Gen. Wallace may give you a pass to see him, if he chooses.

A. LINCOLN

[1] ALS, DNA WR RG 107, Presidential Telegrams, I, 62. Christiana A. Sack telegraphed Lincoln on May 21: "My brother Henry Sack is sentenced to be hung on Monday next at Eastville in Genl Butlers Dept on charge of being a spy. I think I can prove that he is not a spy Please postpone the execution of the sentence & give me permission to see him" (DLC-RTL). The sentence of Henry Sack, citizen of C.S.A., convicted of acting as a spy and transgressing laws and customs of war, was commuted on May 24, 1864, to imprisonment at hard labor for duration of the war (DNA WR RG 153, Judge Advocate General, MM 1448). See further Lincoln's telegrams to Joseph Roberts, May 23 and 24, *infra*.

To William H. Seward[1]

Executive Mansion,
Dear Sir   Washington, May 21., 1864.

The Bill for Montana has passed, and I will thank you to have the applications for offices there, which are in your Department, briefed at once. Yours truly   A. LINCOLN

[1] ALS, DLC-RTL. Although cataloged in the Lincoln Papers as an ALS to Seward, this may be Lincoln's autograph draft of the communication he wished to send both Bates and Seward. See Lincoln to Bates, *supra*. On June 20, Lincoln

nominated Sidney Edgerton of Idaho Territory to be governor and Henry P. Torsey of Maine to be secretary of Montana Territory. Both were confirmed by the Senate on June 22.

To ——— Stansbury[1]

War Department
Mr Stansbury   Washington City
U.S. San Com   May 21 1864
Principal Musician John A Burke 14th U.S Infy has permission to accompany Capt W. R. Smedburg 14th Infy. (wounded) to New York   A. LINCOLN

[1] D, DNA WR RG 107, Presidential Telegrams, I, 60. This telegram, including the signature, is not in Lincoln's handwriting. At the top of the telegram is written "Fredericksburg," presumably the location of the hospital in which Colonel William R. Smedburg was convalescing from wounds received in the Battle of the Wilderness. Stansbury has not been positively identified, but may have been E. A. Stansbury of New York City.

To Edwin M. Stanton[1]

If the services of another Additional Pay-Master can be made useful, let this appointment be made.   A. LINCOLN
May 21. 1864

[1] AES, owned by Emanuel A. Gardiner, New York City. Lincoln's endorsement is written on a communication signed by members of the Pennsylvania Senate and House of Representatives, February 25, 1864, recommending appointment of William H. Postlethwaite of Somerset County as paymaster. Stanton endorsed "File the foregoing application." No record of Postlethwaite's appointment has been found.

To Joseph Holt[1]

Judge Advocate General please examine & report on this case
May 23. 1864   A. LINCOLN

[1] AES, DNA WR RG 153, Judge Advocate General, NN 1514. Lincoln's endorsement is written on the record of Fountain J. Brown, citizen of Arkansas, sentenced to five years' imprisonment for selling freedmen into slavery. Holt approved the sentence, and the application for pardon was denied.

To Joseph Roberts[1]

United States Military Telegraph,
To the Commanding Officer   War Department.
at Fort Monroe   May 23. 1864
Is a man named Henry Sack to be executed tomorrow at noon? If so, when was he condemned and for what offense?
A. LINCOLN

[1] D, DNA WR RG 107, Presidential Telegrams, I, 63. The telegram was written and appears to have been signed by John Hay. See Lincoln to Christiana A. Sack, May 21, *supra*, and to Roberts, May 24, *infra*.

To Edwin M. Stanton[1]

May 23, 1864

Understanding that Mr. John J. Chew, of Fredericksburg Va—is now in arrest as a hostage for our wounded soldiers, carried by citizens from Fredericksburg into the rebel hands at Richmond, and understanding that Mr. Chew, so far from doing anything to make him responsible for that act, or which would induce the rebels to give one of our men for him, he actually ministered, to the extent of his ability, to the relief of our wounded in Fredericksburg, it is directed that said John J. Chew be discharged and allowed to return to his home.

[1] Copy, DNA WR RG 107, Secretary of War, Letters Received, P 309, Register. The application for release of John J. Chew bearing Lincoln's endorsement is missing from the file, but a transcript of the endorsement is preserved in the register.

To Edwin M. Stanton[1]

May 23, 1864

I am informed that Charles Case was nominated and confirmed as an Additional Pay-Master, but taking the Colonelcy of a Regiment, he never qualified.

[1] *The Collector*, November, 1950, No. D 2196. According to the source, this incomplete text is from an autograph letter signed, in which Lincoln further "directs that the place be given to William Williams of Warsaw, Ind." Williams' appointment was confirmed by the Senate on June 30, 1864. Charles Case was colonel of the One Hundred Twenty-ninth Indiana Infantry.

To Timothy P. Andrews[1]

May 24, 1864

I also know Major Holbrook to be a man of high character; and I therefore direct that he be allowed the thirty days to get the money.   A. LINCOLN

May 24, 1864

[1] AES, owned by C. Norton Owen, Chicago, Illinois. Lincoln's endorsement follows an endorsement by Senator Lyman Trumbull on a letter of Paymaster James C. Holbrook, Washington, May 24, 1864, explaining that he needed thirty-days' leave to raise $2,500 to cover a shortage in his accounts, occasioned by loss or theft while paying troops on Red River.

To John Brough[1]

Gov. Brough   War Department Washington City,
Columbus, O.   May 24. 1864

Yours to Sec. of War asking for something cheering. We have nothing bad from any where. I have just seen a despatch of Grant, of 11 P.M. May 23, on the North Anna, and partly accross it, which ends as follows: "Every thing looks exceedingly favorable for us."[2] We have nothing later from him.   A. LINCOLN

[1] ALS, DNA WR RG 107, Presidential Telegrams, I, 65. Governor Brough telegraphed Stanton on May 24: "Have you anything cheering or consoling that you can give me, either confidentially or publicly, as to the position of army affairs? Are things working smoothly . . . . ? Do you still retain your perfect confidence in the result?" (OR, III, IV, 405).

[2] Grant to Halleck, 11 P.M., May 23, OR, I, XXXVI, III, 113-14.

To the House of Representatives[1]

To the House of Representatives.   May 24, 1864

In answer to the Resolution of the House of Representatives of yesterday on the subject of the Joint Resolution of the 4th. of last month relative to Mexico, I transmit a Report from the Secretary of State to whom the Resolution was referred.

Washington. 24th. May, 1864.   ABRAHAM LINCOLN

[1] DS, DNA RG 233, House Executive Document No. 92. The resolution of the House, May 23, 1864, requested copies of "any explanations given by the government of the United States [to France] respecting the sense and bearing of the joint resolution relative to Mexico, which passed the House of Representatives unanimously on the 4th of April, 1864." Seward's report of May 24, 1864, transmitted his correspondence with Minister William L. Dayton (April 7 and 22, and May 2, 9, and 21, 1864) instructing Dayton to inform the French government that the joint resolution of April 4, 1864, expressing opposition to recognition of a monarchy in Mexico, would have to pass the Senate and be approved by the president, that it arose in the House and not with the executive, and that in event of any change in U.S. policy the French government would be duly notified. See Thirty-eighth Congress, First Session, *House Executive Document No. 92.*

To Joseph Roberts[1]

                  Executive Mansion
To the Commanding Officer at   Washington D.C.
Fort Monroe. Va   May 24. 1864

Let the execution of Henry Sack be suspended. I have commuted his sentence to imprisonment during the war.   A. LINCOLN

Major Eckert

Please send this at once Yrs JOHN HAY Major & AAG

[1] LS, DNA WR RG 107, Presidential Telegrams, I, 64. See Lincoln's telegrams to Roberts, May 23, and to Christiana A. Sack, May 21, *supra*.

To the Senate[1]

To the Senate of the United States: May 24, 1864

I recommend Lieutenant-Commander Francis A. Roe for advancement in his grade five numbers, to take rank next after Lieutenant-Commander John H. Upshur, for distinguished conduct in battle in command of the U.S. steamer Sassacus in her attack on and attempt to run down the Rebel iron-clad ram Albermarle on the 5th of May, 1864.

I also recommend that First Assistant Engineer James M. Hobby[2] be advanced thirty numbers in his grade for distinguished conduct in battle and extraordinary heroism, as mentioned in the report of Lieutenant-Commander Francis A. Roe, commanding the U.S. steamer Sassacus in her action with the Rebel ram Albermarle on the 5th May, 1864. ABRAHAM LINCOLN.

Washington, D.C., May 24, 1864.

[1] *Executive Journal*, XIII, 559.
[2] James M. Hobby had been badly scalded by steam from a broken boiler.

To Edwin M. Stanton[1]

E. A. Paul.

The Times I believe is always true to the Union, and therefore should be treated at least as well as any. A. LINCOLN

May 24. 1864

[1] AES, DLC-RTL. Lincoln's endorsement is written on a letter from E. A. Paul, Times Bureau, Washington, D.C., May 23, 1864, enclosing a pass to the Army of the Potomac, May 21, 1864, which Stanton had refused to approve. Below Lincoln's endorsement Stanton endorsed:

"Respectfully returned to the President. The Times is treated by this Department precisely as other papers are treated. No pass is granted by the Department to any paper except upon the permission of General Grant or General Meade. Repeated applications by Mr Forney and by other editors have been refused on the same ground as the Times until the correspondent is approved by the Commanding General. This is the regulation of all the armies and the Secretary of War declines to do for the Times what is not done for other papers. EDWIN M STANTON

"May 24. 1864 Sec of War

"P.S. Since writing the above I perceive a paper purporting to be a pass from [William W.] Beckwith which I have not before seen. It was shown to Col Hardie who refused to approve it on account of the condition[?] of the army & transportation. I think he did right & that as soon as it is known where the army is a pass may be given if authorised by General Meade or Grant but not without their express or personal authority."

To Isaac N. Arnold[1]

Hon. I. N. Arnold.   Executive Mansion,

My dear Sir.   Washington, May 25, 1864.

In regard to the order of General Burnside suspending the Chicago Times now nearly a year ago, I can only say I was embarrassed with the question between what was due to the Military service on the one hand, and the Liberty of the Press on the other, and I believe it was the despatch of Senator Trumbull and yourself, added to the proceedings of the meeting which it brought me, that turned the scale in favor of my revoking the order. I am far from certain to-day that the revocation was not right; and I am very sure the small part you took in it, is no just ground to disparage your judgment, much less to impugn your motives. I take it that your devotion to the Union and the Administration can not be questioned by any sincere man. Yours truly   A. LINCOLN

1 ADfS, DLC-RTL. It would be logical to assume that this draft was used for Lincoln's reply to Arnold's letter of April 24, 1864, if it were not for the fact that Arnold published a somewhat different letter from Lincoln dated May 27, *infra*. Arnold wrote Lincoln on April 24:

"My friends . . . write to me, that in the canvass now going on in my district for Congress, the principal charges used against me, are: First that I am responsible for the revocation of the order of Genl. Burnside suppressing the Chicago Times, & that *You* are indifferent or more than indifferent about my re-election. . . . I am desirous in case of your re-election (which for the sake of the country may God grant) of remaining in congress. . . .

"If you would address a note . . . stating how far I was responsible for the Burnside order, & whether I had been a faithful friend, I am sure it would be discreetly used, would probably secure my election, & be ever gratefully remembered. . . ." (DLC-RTL).

To George G. Meade[1]

Major-General Meade,   Executive Mansion,

Army of Potomac: Washington, May 25, 1864.

Mr. J. C. Swift wishes a pass from me to follow your army to pick up rags and cast-off clothing. I will give it to him if you say so, otherwise not.   A. LINCOLN.

1 Tarbell (Appendix), p. 428. On March 4 and March 9, 1864, John C. Swift had written Lincoln offering to pay $200 per month to the Sanitary Commission for the exclusive privilege of picking up clothing cast off by Grant's army (DNA WR RG 107, Secretary of War, Letters Received, P 311 and P 134, Register notation. Both letters are missing from the file). No reply from Meade has been found.

To Edwin M. Stanton[1]

May 25, 1864

If it is true that Major Miller made payments under express orders of the Secretary of War; as a matter of equity, he, Major Miller, should not be made to lose the money; but the accounting office having settled the matter, I doubt both the legality and propriety of interference by the President.

1 Copy, DNA WR RG 107, Secretary of War, Letters Received, P 318, Register notation. The letter of Major Morris S. Miller bearing Lincoln's endorsement is missing from the file, but the register preserves a transcript of Lincoln's endorsement as given above. Miller served as quartermaster at Washington, D.C., May, 1861 to September, 1864.

To Edward Bates[1]

Hon. Attorney General   Executive Mansion,
Dear Sir: Washington, May 26. 1864.

Please allow the Secretary of War to withdraw the record in the case of William Yokum, he to furnish you a transcript of it if you deem it necessary. Yours truly,   A. LINCOLN

1 ALS, DNA GE RG 60, Papers of Attorney General, Segregated Lincoln Material. See Lincoln to Stanton, March 18, *supra*, and communication to the Senate, June 13, *infra*.

To Edwin M. Stanton[1]

Hon. Sec. of War   Executive Mansion,
Dear Sir: Washington, May 26, 1864.

Let Stephen C. Campbell, now held as a prisoner of War at Johnson's Island,[2] be discharged on taking the oath. This is a special case, and not a precedent, the man having voluntarily quitted the rebel service, and also being subject to fits. Yours truly
                              A LINCOLN

1 ALS, IHi. No reply or further reference has been discovered.
2 "Point Lookout" as written by Lincoln is corrected to "Johnson's Island."

To Edwin M. Stanton[1]

I had these letters some days ago, but so far have not attended to them. Will the Sec. of War please look into them?   A. LINCOLN
    May 26. 1864.

[1] AES, DNA WR RG 107, Secretary of War, Letters Received, P 317. Lincoln's endorsement is written on a letter from Governor Augustus W. Bradford of Maryland, enclosing a statement of Dr. Thomas K. Carroll, Jr., of Dorchester County, concerning impressment of Negroes by recruiting parties. James A. Hardie endorsed on May 29, calling for an investigation and report from General Lewis Wallace, in command at Baltimore. No further reference has been found.

To Whom It May Concern[1]

Executive Mansion,
Whom it may concern.   Washington, May 26. 1864.
    I am again pressed with the claim of Mr. Marshall O. Roberts, for transportation of what was called the Naval Brigade from New-York to Fortress Monroe. This force was a special organization got up by one Bartlett, in pretended pursuance of written authority from me, but in fact, pursuing the authority in scarcely any thing whatever. The credit given him by Mr. Roberts, was given in the teeth of the express declaration that the government would not be responsible for the class of expences to which it belonged. After all some part of the transportation became useful to the government, and equitably should be paid for; but I have neither time or means to ascertain this equitable amount, or any appropriation to pay it with if ascertained. If the Quarter-Master at New-York can ascertain what would compensate for so much of the transport[at]ion as did result usefully to the government, it might be a step towards reaching justice. I write this from memory; but I believe it is substantially correct.   A. LINCOLN.

[1] ALS, IHi. Concerning the "Naval Brigade," see Lincoln to Washington Bartlett, May 27, 1861, supra.

To Isaac N. Arnold[1]

Executive Mansion,
Hon. Isaac N. Arnold: Washington, May 27, 1864.
    My Dear Sir: I hear you are assailed for your action in regard to General Burnside's order suppressing the Chicago *Times*. All

you did was to send me two dispatches. In the first you jointly with Senator Trumbull, very properly asked my serious and prompt consideration, for a petition of some of your constituents, praying for a revocation of the order. In the second you said you did *not* in the first dispatch intend to express an opinion that the order should be abrogated. This[2] is absolutely all that ever came to me from you on the subject. I am far from certain to-day that the resolution [revocation][3] was not right, and I am very sure the small part you took in it is no proper ground to disparage your judgment, much less to impugn your motives.

Your devotion to the Union and the Administration cannot be questioned by any sincere man. Yours truly,

ABRAHAM LINCOLN.

[1] Chicago *Tribune*, July 15, 1864. This letter is reproduced as printed in a report of Arnold's speech to a Republican mass meeting on July 14. In introducing the letter Arnold spoke as follows: "General Burnside . . . issued an order for its [Chicago *Times*] suppression. That order was revoked by the President. The President was petitioned by prominent and good citizens of Chicago to revoke the order. I was requested to join in such a petition. I refused. I was asked to transmit their message to the President. This I did, as I do for all petitions sent through me, asking for his prompt and careful consideration. Exactly what I did will appear from the following copy of a note addressed to me from the President on this subject: [text of letter as reproduced above]."

Although the manuscript of Lincoln's letter, as quoted by Arnold, has not been found, it seems reasonable to accept the text as authentic, especially since a draft of the letter, in Arnold's autograph and written on Executive Mansion stationery, is preserved in the Lincoln Papers along with Arnold's letter to Lincoln dated April 24. The precise relationship of Lincoln's autograph draft of May 25, *supra*, to Arnold's draft of the present letter is not entirely clear. A reasonable assumption would be that Lincoln showed Arnold the draft of May 25, that Arnold revised it to the more specific statement in Arnold's draft, and that Lincoln thereupon copied and signed the letter on May 27, according to Arnold's wishes. Variations in the *Tribune* text and Arnold's draft are indicated in succeeding footnotes.

[2] This sentence does not appear in Arnold's draft.
[3] "Revocation" in Arnold's draft is certainly correct.

To Richard W. Thompson[1]

Hon. R. W. Thompson   Executive Mansion,
Terre Haute, Ia.   Washington, May 27, 1864.

Your letter in relation to Gen. Hunter and your son, just received. If Gen. Hu[nter] should ask to have your son on his staff, the requ[est] would be granted; but the General is now actively moving in the field, and is beyond telegraph. I doubt whether the promotion you think of is legally possible   A LINCOLN

[1] ALS, DNA WR RG 107, Presidential Telegrams, I, 66. Richard W. Thompson wrote Lincoln on May 21, 1864: "I find by telegram to day that Maj. Gen.

Hunter has been assigned to the command of the District of Western Virginia. For more than a year my son, Capt R. W. Thompson, was on his staff, & the Genl has expressed a wish that he should be returned to him again when placed upon active duty. I presume he will ask his transfer from Commissary duties with the army of the Potomac. In that event I respectfully request that the transfer may be made. And if made I make the additional request that he be promoted. . . ." (DLC-RTL). No record has been found of the transfer of Captain Richard W. Thompson, Jr.

Reply to Delegation of Baptists[1]

May 28, 1864

In the present very responsible position in which I am engaged, I have had great cause of gratitude for the support so unanimously given by all Christian denominations of the country. I have had occasion so frequently to respond to something like this assemblage, that I have said all that I had to say. This particular body is in all respects as respectable as any that have been presented to me. The resolutions I have merely heard read, and I therefore beg to be allowed an opportunity to make a short response in writing.

[1] New York *Tribune*, May 30, 1864. On May 28 a delegation representing the American Baptist Home Missionary Society presented a set of resolutions adopted "at the session recently held by them in Philadelphia. The resolutions indorse the course of President Lincoln, and express the warmest wishes for his welfare and the welfare of the country." (*Ibid.*). As printed by Nicolay and Hay (X, 101-102), Lincoln's reply is misdated "[May 14, 1864?]." For Lincoln's formal reply see the communication to Ide, Doolittle, and Hubbell, May 30, *infra*.

To the Senate[1]

To the Senate of the United States.   May 28, 1864

In reply to a Resolution of the Senate of the 25th. instant, relating to Mexican Affairs I transmit a partial report from the Secretary of State of this date; with the papers therein mentioned.

Washington, 28 May 1864.   ABRAHAM LINCOLN

[1] DS, DNA RG 46, Senate 38A F2. The documents transmitted may be found in Thirty-eighth Congress, First Session, *Senate Executive Document No. 47*.

To Cornelius A. Walborn[1]

Hon. C. A. Walborn.   Executive Mansion
Philadelphia, Pa.   Washington D.C. May 28. 1864

Yours received. I have felt constrained to answer repeated invitations to attend the great Fair at your city, that I can not be present at it's opening, and that whether I can during it's continuance must depend on circumstances.   A. LINCOLN

1 ALS, DNA WR RG 107, Presidential Telegrams, I, 67. Cornelius A. Walborn, postmaster at Philadelphia, telegraphed on May 27, 1864: "The Hon John Welsh, Chairman of the Executive Committee of Great Central fair has requested me to ask if you have received his letter in relation to attending the fair—an immediate answer will oblige the committee" (DLC-RTL). Welsh's telegram (not letter) of May 23, 1864, is also in the Lincoln Papers

To Gideon Welles[1]

This introduces Hon. Mr. Ingersoll, successor to our lamented friend Lovejoy. Please see him.   A. LINCOLN
    [May] 28, 1864

1 ALS, IHi. On May 7, 1864, Ebon C. Ingersoll of Peoria, Illinois, was elected to fill the vacancy caused by death of Representative Owen Lovejoy on March 25. The date of this note is partly burned off.

To John H. Bryant[1]

Hon. John H Bryant   Executive Mansion,
My dear Sir.   Washington, May 30, 1864.

Yours of the 14th. Inst. inclosing a card of invitation to a preliminary meeting contemplating the erection of a Monument to the memory of Hon. Owen Lovejoy, was duly received.

As you anticipate, it will be out of my power to attend. Many of you have known Mr. Lovejoy longer than I have, and are better able than I to do his memory complete justice. My personal acquaintance with him commenced only about ten years ago, since when it has been quite intimate; and every step in it has been one of increasing respect and esteem, ending, with his life, in no less than affection on my part. It can be truly said of him that while he was personally ambitious, he bravely endured the obscurity which the unpopularity of his principles imposed, and never accepted official honors, until those honors were ready to admit his principles with him. Throughout my heavy, and perplexing responsibilities here, to the day of his death, it would scarcely wrong any other to say, he was my most generous friend. Let him have the marble monument, along with the well-assured and more enduring one in the hearts of those who love liberty, unselfishly, for all men. Yours truly   A. LINCOLN

1 ALS-P, ISLA. On May 14, 1864, John H. Bryant of Princeton, Illinois, wrote Lincoln: "I enclose a card of invitation which will explain itself. It is

not of course to be expected that one occupying the responsible station that you do . . . can leave his post of duty to attend the meeting. . . . But knowing as I do the warm friendship that existed between yourself and Mr. Lovejoy . . . I feel that we should not do justice to either our departed brother or the honored President . . . did we not at least call your attention to the movement we are about to make in honor of our mutual friend. A letter approving our object with such remarks as you might be pleased to add, to be read at our meeting would be received with great satisfaction and would do much to further our plans. . . ." (DLC-RTL).

To Arthur H. Dutton[1]

[Dutton]   Executive Mansion
[Old Point Comfort Va.][2]   Washington, May 30. 1864
    Col. Dutton is permitted to come from Fort-Monroe to Washington.   A. LINCOLN

[1] ALS, DNA WR RG 107, Presidential Telegrams, I, 68. Colonel Arthur H. Dutton of the Twenty-first Connecticut Infantry died June 5, 1864, of wounds received May 26 while on reconnaissance before Bermuda Hundred, Virginia.
[2] The bracketed address is in the handwriting of a clerk.

Endorsement Concerning A. Barton Holcomb[1]

I wish to consider this case.   A LINCOLN
        May 30. 1864.

[1] AES, DNA WR RG 94, U.S. Military Academy, 1864, No. 227. Lincoln's endorsement is written on a letter from General Burnside, May 26, 1864, recommending A. Barton Holcomb, Third New York Cavalry, for appointment to West Point: "He . . . has been with me as personal orderly since June 1862. . . ." There is no record of Holcomb's appointment.

To Thomas H. Hicks[1]

This little gentleman has seen me, and now carries my respects back to his good father, Gov Hicks.   A. LINCOLN
    May 30, 1864.

[1] ALS, IHi. Thomas H. Hicks wrote from the Metropolitan Hotel, May 30, 1864:
    "Will you allow my little boy (son) to see and shake hands with you before he leaves for Home at 3 oclock. he is quite anxious to see you. I shall be glad for my man to go with him as he is small.
    "I sit at yr door in carriage until I hear your determination. wish I could climb the stair way as formerly, and see yr Honor myself" (DLC-RTL).
    Hicks' foot had been amputated in 1863. Which of his several children called on Lincoln is uncertain, but only one son of Hicks' third wife has been identified, B. Chapin Hicks.

To George B. Ide, James R. Doolittle, and A. Hubbell[1]

Rev. Dr. Ide ⎫   Executive Mansion,
Hon. J. R. Doolittle ⎬ Committee   Washington,
& Hon. A. Hubbell ⎭   May 30, 1864.

In response to the preamble and resolutions of the American Baptist Home Mission Society, which you did me the honor to present, I can only thank you for thus adding to the effective and almost unanamous support which the Christian communities are so zealously giving to the country, and to liberty. Indeed it is difficult to conceive how it could be otherwise with any one professing christianity, or even having ordinary perceptions of right and wrong. To read in the Bible, as the word of God himself, that "In the sweat of *thy* face shalt thou eat bread,["] and to preach therefrom that, "In the sweat of *other mans* faces shalt thou eat bread," to my mind can scarcely be reconciled with honest sincerity. When brought to my final reckoning, may I have to answer for robbing no man of his goods; yet more tolerable even this, than for robbing one of himself, and all that was his. When, a year or two ago, those professedly holy men of the South, met in the semblance of prayer and devotion, and, in the name of Him who said "As ye would all men should do unto you, do ye even so unto them" appealed to the christian world to aid them in doing to a whole race of men, as they would have no man do unto themselves, to my thinking, they contemned and insulted God and His church, far more than did Satan when he tempted the Saviour with the Kingdoms of the earth. The devils attempt was no more false, and far less hypocritical. But let me forbear, remembering it is also written "Judge not, lest ye be judged."

[1] ADf, DLC-RTL. See Lincoln's reply to a delegation of Baptists, May 28, *supra*. The preamble and resolutions to which Lincoln replied have not been discovered. Reverend George B. Ide was a prominent Baptist author and minister at Springfield, Massachusetts. "A. Hubbell" has not been identified.

To Edwin M. Stanton[1]

May 30, 1864

On principle an officer who resigns should receive his pay until he receives notice that his resignation is accepted. Let this be done in this case, if the law will admit of it.

[1] Copy, DNA WR RG 107, Secretary of War, Letters Received, P 319, Register. The copy of this endorsement is preserved in a notation in the register which indicates that it was written on a letter from Austin A. King concerning

the complaint of Thomas Allin on refunding pay. The letter bearing Lincoln's endorsement is missing from the file. The resignation of Captain Thomas Allin, commissary of subsistence, was accepted on May 31, 1864.

Endorsement Concerning a Purported Forgery[1]

May 31, 1864

I got the impression that a forgery was charged, but I can not say, nor do I think I have said, that it was distinctly charged, or that the gentlemen intended me to understand it as being charged.

May 31. 1864.   A. LINCOLN

[1] AES, DLC-RTL. Lincoln's endorsement is written on a letter from John H. Oliver and E. J. More, Washington, May 28, 1864:

"The undersigned having this day transmitted to the Department of Internal Revenue a letter of Samuel McHose Esq, asking leave to recall his resignation of the office of Assessor of Internal Revenue for the Sixth District of Penna., beg leave to submit the following statement in reference to the charge of the forgery of a certain letter of Benjamin T Hagenbuch of date of March 13th. 1863, on file in the office of Internal Revenue at Washington.

"We are responsible for the genuineness of that letter and in justice to ourselves expect that you shall satisfy your own mind as to whether it is genuine or not, in order that our own character be vindicated, and that you may form a correct estimate of the value of statements made by persons alleging the forgery. . . ."

Although Lincoln had nominated Henry J. Saeger as successor to McHose on May 19, he withdrew the nomination on May 25. McHose's resignation was eventually accepted, however, and Saeger was renominated on December 10, 1864, and confirmed by the Senate on January 13, 1865.

To Mrs. Field[1]

Executive Mansion,
Mrs. Field   Washington, May 31, 1864.

Mr. Sedgwick informs me that you desire an autograph of mine, to finish a collection for the Sanitary Fair. It gives me great pleasure to comply with your request. Yours truly   A. LINCOLN

[1] ALS, PHi. Charles B. Sedgwick wrote Nicolay on May 31, 1864: "I enclose a note received by me from Mrs. Field of Phila. a daughter of the late Judge Peters. She desires as you will see an autograph of the President to be sold with others at their Fair which opens tomorrow. If the President will thus favor the ladies of Phila. please enclose to me & I will forward to Mrs. F." (DLC-RTL). Mrs. Field has not been further identified. The collection of autographs of the presidents had been donated to the Fair by F. J. Dreer.

To James B. Fry[1]

Will the Provost Marshal please give the bearer, James Johnson and J. C. Lucas, both colored, a pass to visit Camp Casey?

May 31, 1864   A. LINCOLN.

[1] Copy, ISLA.

To Stephen A. Hurlbut[1]

Major Gen. Hurlbut   Executive Mansion
Belvidere, Ills.   Washington, May 31, 1864
    You are hereby authorized to visit Washington and Baltimore
                                                          A. LINCOLN

[1] ALS, DNA WR RG 107, Presidential Telegrams, I, 69. See Lincoln to
Hurlbut, May 2, *supra.*

To the Senate[1]

To the Senate of the United States.   May 31, 1864
    I transmit to the Senate, in answer to their Resolution of the
28th instant, a report from the Secretary of State, with accompanying documents.   ABRAHAM LINCOLN
    Washington, May 31st. 1864.

[1] DS, DNA RG 46, Senate 38A F2. The resolution of May 28 called upon
the president to "inform the Senate . . . whether he has, and when, authorized
a person alleged to have committed a crime against Spain or any of its dependencies to be delivered up to officers of that government, and whether such
delivery was had, and if so, under what authority of law or of treaty it was
done."
    Seward transmitted documents in the case of José A. Argüelles, a Spanish
officer in Cuba, who had seized a cargo of over 1,000 negroes landed on the
coast from a slaver, and had received over $15,000 in prize money. Obtaining
twenty days' leave to visit New York, he was discovered during his absence to
have falsely reported the deaths of 141 of the negroes and sold them for himself. No treaty of extradition between Spain and the United States then being
in existence, Spanish officials requested that he be returned for trial. He was
sent back to Havana and turned over to officials there.
    Seward's report of May 30 concludes:
    "There being no treaty of extradition between the United States and Spain,
nor any act of Congress directing how fugitives from justice in Spanish dominions shall be delivered up, the extradition in the case referred to . . . is understood by this department to have been made in virtue of the law of nations and
the Constitution of the United States.
    "Although there is a conflict of authorities concerning the expediency of
exercising comity towards a foreign government by surrendering, at its request,
one of its own subjects charged with the commission of crime within its territory . . . yet a nation is never bound to furnish asylum to dangerous criminals
who are offenders against the human race. . . ." (Thirty-eighth Congress, First
Session, *Senate Executive Document No. 48*).
    See further, Lincoln's communication to the Senate, June 18, *infra.*

To William H. Seward[1]

Hon. Sec. of State   Executive Mansion,
Dear Sir   Washington, May 31. 1864.
    The attached is an application for the Consul-Generalship at
Montreal. Yours truly   A. LINCOLN

[1] ALS, DNA FS RG 59, Appointments, Box 403. A slip pasted on the letter reads "with Letter from Genl [Thomas S. ?] Mather of Springfield, Ill.," and bears the name of the person applying, "A. F. Williams/Conn." John F. Potter of Wisconsin received the appointment as consul general at Montreal to succeed Joshua R. Giddings, deceased May 27, 1864.

List of Applicants for Montana Appointments[1]

[c. June, 1864]

GOVERNOR OF MONTANA.

William Cumback.	Ia	M. N. Wisewell.	N.J.
R. T. Van Horn.	Mo.	Charles H. Morgan.	Nevada.
Joseph C. McKilbin.	Cal.	Sidney Edgerton.	Idaho.
James M. Clarke.	R.I.	Jesse H. Leavenworth.	
Daniel E. Somes.	Me.	James L. Campbell.	Idaho.
Alexander Cummings.		Penn.	

SECRETARY OF MONTANA.

C. De Witt Smith.	N Y.	Elisha M. Wright.	Ia.
Silas W. Burr.	O.	William F. Shaffer.	Colorado.
James M. Campbell.	Idaho.	Henry W. De Puy.	
Thomas J. Pickett.	Ills.	Samuel T. Hauser.	Mont.
Ebenezer Moore.	Ills.	Henry P. Torsey.	Maine
Clement W. Rice.	Nevada.	Ammi Giddings.	Conn. (Misplaced)

Judgeships in Montana.

Thomas J. Logan.	Kan.	William Hemingway.	Mich.
A. Bartlett.	Ills.	Henry O'Connor.	Iowa.
Theodore J. Burnett.	N.Y.	Lorenzo K. Haddock.	N.Y.
Dennis S. Sweany.	Md.	Thomas S. Briscoe.	Md.
Silas Woodson.	Mo.	Moses B. Hopkins.	Mich.
George J. Parsons.	Mich	L. P. Williston.	Dakota
Henry L. Jennings.	Minn.	Hez. L. Hosmer.	N.Y. Ashley.
H. Miles Moore.	Kan.	Stephen P. Twiss.	Mass.
Eviend Brierer.	Pa	Leonard G. Hall.	Mich
Dolphus S. Paine		N. W. Davis.	N.Y.
William C. Rheim		Charles McClure.	Minn.
J. Warren Bell.	Mo.	Charles M. Runk.	Penn.
J. K. Hoed.		Ammi Giddings.	Conn.

DISTRICT ATTORNEY, for Montana

Edward B. Nealley,	Iowa.	George C. Bates.	Ills.
Robert Martin.	Ohio.	E. C. Gobin.	Pa.
Charles P. Leslie.	N.Y.		

Marshall for Montana

C. F. Buck.	Minn.
P. W. Norris.	Ohio.

Surveyor General

Nathaniel P. Langford.	Montana.
Boyd.	Mo.

Nathan Shipley, Jr.	Md. ⎫ Something
John Coons.	Va ⎭ in Territories.

[1] AD, DLC-RTL. This document is incorrectly assigned the date of April, 1861, as cataloged in the Lincoln Papers. See memorandum, *infra*.

Memorandum of Appointments[1]

[c. June, 1864]

Consul at Montreal—	John F. Potter.	Wis.
Judge Advocate General.	⎧ Joseph Holt	
	⎩ William McKee Dunn.	Ia.
Montana—Governor.	Sidney Edgerton.	Idaho.
" Secretary.	Henry P. Torsey.	Me.
" C. J.	Hezikiah L. Hosmer.	N.Y.
" As. J.	Ammi Giddings.	Conn.
" As. J.	Lorenzo P. Williston.	Dakota.
Vacancancy [*sic*] in Idaho.	Silas Woodson.	Mo.
Do " Dakota.	A[sa]. Bartlett.	Ills.
Attorney.	Edward B. Neally.	Iowa.
Marshal.	C[ornelius]. F. Buck.	Minn.
Surveyor G.	Marcus Boyd.	Mo.

[1] AD, DLC-RTL. This document is incorrectly assigned the date of April, 1861, as cataloged in the Lincoln Papers, and bears a pencil notation, "Jan. 1863 (?)." The men and the appointments listed were not, as a group, possible earlier than June, 1864. Hosmer, Giddings, Williston, Neally, and Buck were nominated to the Senate on June 15; Potter, Edgerton, Torsey, Woodson, Bartlett, and Boyd, on June 20; Holt was reappointed, with Dunn as assistant judge advocate general, on June 22. Woodson replaced Edgerton as chief justice for Idaho, and Bartlett replaced Williston as associate justice for Dakota.

To Edwin M. Stanton[1]

[June, 1864?]

Dear Sir: The bearer of this, William J. [B?] Post, a member of the 140th Pennsylvania Regiment, wants to go to his home in Washington, Pa. As you can see, he is nothing but a boy, has been sick in the hospital, but I believe he is made of the right kind of stuff. Please see to his release and that he gets transportation home.

A. LINCOLN.

[1] Hertz, II, 868. According to a note in the source, this undated letter was written in June, 1862. This date cannot be corroborated, however, and the content of this letter is open to question. The roster of the One Hundred Fortieth Pennsylvania lists no William J. Post, but lists a William B. Post. The regiment

was not organized until September 8, 1862. William B. Post's record shows him wounded at Spottsylvania Court House, May 12, 1864, and transferred to the Fifty-third Pennsylvania Regiment on May 30, 1865.

To José M. Medina[1]

June 1, 1864

Abraham Lincoln,
President of the United States of America,
To His Excellency
Señor General Don José Maria Medina
President of the Republic of Honduras

Great and Good Friend: I have had the honor to receive your Excellency's letter of the 20 February, last, announcing your elevation by constitutional forms to the Presidency of the Republic of Honduras, and expressing your determination to maintain and extend the friendly relations which happily exist between our two countries.

Accept, your Excellency, my congratulations upon this event, and be assured that on my part your friendly disposition and efforts will be warmly and cordially reciprocated.

I sincerely pray the Almighty to give you a peaceful and successful administration and to grant to the people of Honduras prosperity, and happiness; and so commending you to His safe and Holy keeping, I am your good friend,   ABRAHAM LINCOLN.

By the President:
WILLIAM H. SEWARD, Secretary of State.
Washington, June 1, 1864.

[1] Copy, DNA FS RG 59, Communications to Foreign Sovereigns and States, III, 219-20.

Order for Parole of Charles H. Jonas[1]

June 2, 1864

Allow Charles H. Jonas, now a prisoner of war at Johnson's Island, a parole of three weeks to visit his dying father, Abra[ha]m Jonas, at Quincy, Ill.   A. LINCOLN.

June 2, 1864.

[1] Leslie J. Perry, "Appeals to Lincoln's Clemency," *The Century Magazine*, December, 1895, p. 254. Under date of June 2, 1864, Orville H. Browning's *Diary* records: "Went to the President and got Chas H Jonas, a rebel prisoner at Johnson's Island, paroled for three weeks to visit his father, who is dying." On June 10 Browning wrote: "I went to the Presidents and got his promise to appoint Mrs Jonas Post Mistress at Quincy in place of her decd husband" (*ibid.*).

To Edwin M. Stanton[1]

If the Sec. of War, can find the legal authority and means to give the protection sought by the within, let it be done.

June 2. 1864.   A. LINCOLN

[1] AES, IHi. Lincoln's endorsement is written on a petition signed by Reverend Adam Wallace, presiding elder, Snow Hill District, Philadelphia Conference of the Methodist Episcopal Church, and others, May 21, 1864, asking appointment of Captain Henry C. McCoy as military officer for Somerset County on the Eastern Shore of Maryland, where loyal ministers were being threatened and prevented from holding church services among Negroes. Below Lincoln's endorsement Stanton endorsed as follows: "It is the duty of the General commanding the Department to offer a protection to loyal persons of whatever color or age against Disloyal, & secessionist and their aiders and abettors." No record of McCoy's appointment has been found.

To Frederick A. Conkling and Others[1]

Hon. F. A. Conkling   Executive Mansion,
and others.   Washington, June 3, 1864.

Gentlemen: Your letter inviting me to be present at a mass meeting of loyal citizens to be held at New York on the 4th inst., for the purpose of expressing gratitude to Lieutenant General Grant for his signal services, was received yesterday. It is impossible for me to attend. I approve, nevertheless, whatever may tend to strengthen and sustain Gen. Grant and the noble armies now under his direction. My previous high estimate of Gen. Grant has been maintained and heightened by what has occurred in the remarkable campaign he is now conducting; while the magnitude and difficulty of the task before him does[2] not prove less than I expected. He and his brave soldiers are now in the midst of their great trial, and I trust that at your meeting you will so shape your good words that they may turn to men and guns moving to his and their support. Yours truly   A. LINCOLN

[1] LS, NHi; Df, DLC-RTL. The letter of May 31, 1864, signed by Conkling and nineteen other prominent New Yorkers is as follows:

"The loyal citizens of New-York, without distinction of party, will convene in Mass Assemblage, on Union Square, on Saturday next, the Fourth of June, at 6 o'clock, P.M. to give an expression of their gratitude to Lieutenant General Grant, for his signal services in conducting the National armies to victory; to reaffirm their devotion to the sacred cause of the Union, and to pledge their united energies to the support of the Government for the complete suppression of the Rebellion.

"Lieutenant-General Scott has been invited to preside.

"The undersigned have been instructed to solicit the honor of your presence and influence on an occasion of so much interest to the Country." (DLC-RTL).

[2] The draft shows Lincoln's emendation of the remainder of this sentence to the present reading from "is not at all lessened in my view." Although Lincoln first wrote "does," the draft has been corrected to "do," apparently by Lincoln. The signed letter, however, reads "does."

To John A. Dix[1]

Major General Dix   Executive Mansion,
New-York.   Washington, June 4. 1864.
 Please inform me whether Charles H. Scott, of 8th. U.S. Infantry is under sentence of death in your Department, & if so, when to be executed & what are the features of the case.

A. LINCOLN

[1] ALS, DNA WR RG 107, Presidential Telegrams, I, 70. No reply or further reference has been found.

Endorsement Appointing Green C. Goodloe[1]

Let this re-appointment be made.   A. LINCOLN
June 4. 1864

[1] AES, DNA WR RG 94, U.S. Military Academy, 1863, No. 76. Lincoln's endorsement is written on a copy of the joint resolution approved May 20, 1864, "that nothing in an act entitled An Act making appropriations for the support of the Military Academy . . . approved April first, eighteen hundred and sixty-four, shall be so construed as to prevent the re-appointment of Green Clay Goodloe. . . ." Representative Green Clay Smith enclosed the copy of the resolution with the following undated note:
 "The resolution is enclosed and I respectfully ask the President to act, as the first of June is close at hand when it must be done.
 "The President will remember that he & the scty. of War agreed with me, that young Goodloe should have been appointed, but for the law of April 1st./64. Therefore I succeeded in having this law passed to remove the difficulty."
 Green Clay Goodloe is listed at West Point in 1863, but not later.

To William H. Seward[1]

Please file—written I suppose by Gen. Cameron, though not signed.
June 4. 1864.   A. LINCOLN

[1] AES, DNA FS RG 59, Appointments, Box 383. Lincoln's endorsement is written on an unsigned letter dated at Harrisburg, Pennsylvania, June 2, 1864, recommending appointment of P. Frazer Smith of Chester County, Pennsylvania, as consul general at Montreal to succeed Joshua R. Giddings, deceased.

To Edwin M. Stanton[1]

Hon. Sec. of War   Executive Mansion,
Dear Sir.   Washington, June 4, 1864.
 When we shall next meet please try to remember to call up for conference the Hurtt case. Yours truly   A. LINCOLN

[1] ALS, NHi. No further reference has been found. Lincoln probably referred to Captain Francis W. Hurtt, assistant quartermaster, dismissed on June 17, 1864.

To Salmon P. Chase[1]

I will try to call at your office at 3 P.M., to-day, June 6, 1864.

Hon. Sec. of Treasury   A. LINCOLN.

[1] Robert B. Warden, *Account of the Private Life and Public Services of Salmon Portland Chase* (1874), p. 600. According to Warden, Lincoln's note was penciled on a note from Chase in regard to business before congress.

Endorsement
Concerning Discharge of Volunteers[1]

The Secretary of War says this attempt, if successful, would reach forty thousand of the Army.   A. LINCOLN

June 6. 1864.

[1] AES, RTL. Lincoln's memorandum is written on a letter from Charles E. Sherman, attorney for men enlisted in the Fifteenth New York Volunteer Engineers, June 6, 1864, as follows:

"If, from your Examination of the Evidence in favor of the discharge of the Recruits to fill up the 15th N.Y. Vol. Engineers, you are Enabled to inform me whether they will be *presently* discharged according *to their* contract of Enlistment, as *interpreted* to them by *word & Certificate of honor*, by *all the Federal & State Officers at the time of their Enlistment;*—or Even that they will be discharged in *a short time*, after their present duties are performed, in the Existing Crises, I shall be exceedingly obliged to you if you will do so, as I wish to leave the city tomorrow.

"On the 17th. inst., these men will have been *illegally* detained, one year. . . .

"P.S. I am sure there is no other case like that of these men, & their number is but ab[o]ut 186 in all."

The Fifteenth New York Engineers had been mustered on May 9, 1861, and men who enlisted in June, 1862, to fill the ranks thought they were enlisting for the unexpired portion of the three-year enlistment, which would have ended May 9, 1864.

Endorsement
Concerning Leonard Swett and Joseph Holt[1]

[June 6, 1864]

Swett is unquestionably all right. Mr. Holt is a good man, but I had not heard or thought of him for V.P. Wish not to interfere about V.P. Can not interfere about platform. Convention must judge for itself.

[1] AE, DLC-Nicolay Papers. Lincoln's endorsement is written on a letter of John G. Nicolay to John Hay, Eutaw House, Baltimore, June 5, 1864:

"Arrived here safely—find quite a number of delegates already in, but have not yet talked much with them.

"One of the first men I met was B. C. Cook, who stands at the head of our Illinois delegation, and had quite a long and confidential talk with him. He told me he had thought of going to Washington tomorrow, but seeing me he concluded he could sufficiently post himself.

"He premised by telling me that the milk-and-water Lincoln resolution which was first reported to the Illinois State Convention, was cooked up by a few plotters, to the utter surprise and astonishment of nine-tenths of the convention, and by only a part of the committee, and was with the others reported to the convention when there was but a small attendance, it being late at night, but that the convention very handsomely repudiated them, referred them to a new committee, which introduced and passed others of the right stripe. Cook does not seem to know thoroughly who were at the bottom of the matter. He thinks [Thomas J.] Turner was the chief manager. [Joseph] Medill is understood to have declared himself opposed to the resolution in committee but seems to have contented himself with the mere expression of his dissent, after which he went away without further active opposition. Strangely enough one or two men have told me that Wm A Grimshaw, either of his own volition or under the influence of others, was in the scheme. Jack [Jackson Grimshaw] on the contrary, Cook told me, was open and hearty for Lincoln.

"Cook says there will be three or four disaffected members in the delegation from Illinois, but that nevertheless the delegation will vote and act as a unit, under the instructions of the convention and also the will of the large majority of the delegation. He says the delegation will in good faith do everything they can for Lincoln that is in arranging the Vice P., the Committees, Platform &c. taking his own nomination of course as beyond question.

"What transpired at home, and what he has heard from several sources, have made Cook suspicious that Swett may be untrue to Lincoln. One of the straws which lead him to this belief is that Swett has telegraphed here urging the Illinois delegation to go for Holt for Vice President.

"I told Cook that I thought Lincoln would not wish even to indicate a preference for V.P. as the rival candidates were all friendly to him.

"There will be some little trouble in arranging the matter of the contested seats from Missouri. The Radicals seem to have the technical right to be admitted. They threaten to withdraw from the convention if the conservatives are also admitted; but promise to abide the action of the convention if they (the Radicals) obtain the seats. Cook says they intimated to him that they would even promise to vote for Lincoln in the convention, for the promise of an admission to seats.

"Whitelaw Reid is here and told me this evening that the Radicals conceded Lincoln's re-nomination, but their present game was to make a very radical platform.

"Cook wants to know confidentially whether Swett is all right—whether in urging Holt for V.P. he reflects the Presidents wishes—whether the President has any preference, either personally or on the score of policy—or whether he wishes not even to interfere by a confidential indication. Also whether he thinks it would be good policy to give the Radical delegates from Missouri the seats, on their promising to vote for him.

"Please get this information for me, if possible. Write and send your letter by express so that it will reach me by the earliest practicable hour on tomorrow (Monday). This will go to you by express by the 7 A.M. train tomorrow so that you ought to have it by ten A.M.

"Address me at Eutaw House."

In accord with Lincoln's instructions, Hay answered on June 6:

"Yours of yesterday just received & read to the President. Swett is unquestionably all right in regard to the President, but his presentation of Col. Holt's name is entirely of his own suggestion. He seemed not to have considered the bad effect of the contiguity of Illinois & Kentucky. . . . He has never even mentioned Col. Holt's name to the Prest. for the place. . . .

"The President wishes not to interfere in the nomination even by a confidential suggestion. He also declines suggesting anything in regard to platform or the organization of the Convention. . . .

"Do not infer from what I have said above that the President objects to Swett presenting Col. Holt's name. He is, and intends to be absolutely impartial. . . ." (Tyler Dennett, ed., *Lincoln and the Civil War in the Diaries and Letters of John Hay*, p. 186).

To George G. Meade[1]

Major General Meade   Executive Mansion,
Army of the Potomac.   Washington, June 6, 1864.

Private James McCarthy of the 140th. N.Y. Vols. is here under sentence to the Dry Tortugas for an attempt to desert. His friends appeal to me, and if his Colonel and you consent, I will send him to his regiment.

Please answer.   A. LINCOLN

[1] ALS, IHi. On June 2, 1864, Joseph Henry wrote Lincoln as follows: "I beg leave to introduce to your attention my much esteemed friends Professor Horsford of Cambridge and Mr. Morgan of Rochester, who desire to place before you, a case of military discipline." (DLC-RTL). Professor Horsford was probably Eben N. Horsford, professor of chemistry at Harvard University, and Mr. Morgan of Rochester was probably the famous anthropologist Lewis H. Morgan. For General Meade's reply see note to Lincoln's communication to Henry, June 10, *infra*.

To Henry W. Slocum[1]

Executive Mansion, Washington,
Major General Slocum   June 6. 1864.

My friend, Thomas A. Marshall, who will hand you this, informs me that he has some difficulty in managing a plantation in your Department. It may be that you withhold nothing from him which can safely be granted; and I do not make any order in the case; but simply wish to say I personally know, so far as such things can be known, that Mr. Marshall is loyal, truthful, and honorable; and that I shall be glad for him to be obliged in any not unreasonable way. Yours truly   A. LINCOLN

[1] ALS, CSmH. Thomas A. Marshall wrote Lincoln from Vicksburg, Mississippi, May 27, 1864:

"Will you do me the favor to write a letter to Genl Slocum to the following effect.

"Maj. Genl. H. W. Slocum

"Sir   Will you oblige me by granting to my friend T. A. Marshall such facilities, as he may desire consistent with the public interest, in working the plantation he has leased from the Treasury Agents, and in passing to & from the same, with supplies for it, & its products, his loyalty I will vouch for & that he will not in any way abuse such priviledges as you may grant him.

"(& sign it) A. LINCOLN

"The reason I ask this is because Genl Slocums orders have stopped all passing on the only road by which I can without great inconvenience get to the place. . . . I have been using this road all this Spring, & but for the expectation of getting the use of it would not have leased the place. It leads no where but to my place. . . ." (DLC-RTL).

To Edwin M. Stanton[1]

Secretary of War.   [c. June 6, 1864?]

Sir: Without an if or an and, let Colonel Elliott W. Rice be made a Brigadier-General in the United States Army.   A. LINCOLN.

[1] NH, XI, 133. The text of this undated note, described in the source as "Card to Secretary of War," is dubious. On June 6, 1864, Lincoln nominated Colonel Elliott W. Rice, Seventh Iowa Volunteers, for appointment as brigadier general of Volunteers, and the Senate confirmed the appointment on June 20. No record has been found of Rice's appointment as brigadier general in the Regular Army, and it seems improbable that Lincoln would have attempted to jump a colonel of Volunteers to brigadier general in the Regular Army.

To William S. Rosecrans[1]

United States Military Telegraph,
Major General Rosecrans   War Department.
St. Louis, Mo.   Washington, June 7. 1864

When your communication shall be ready send it by Express. There will be no danger of it's miscarriage.   A. LINCOLN.

[1] ALS, DNA WR RG 107, Presidential Telegrams, I, 71. General Rosecrans telegraphed Lincoln on June 2, 1864:
"After hearing from Genl [James A.] Garfield I shall write you, but detailed information of high national importance, of a plot to overthrow the Government, which you should know, can not be entrusted to the mails.
"To convey the facts to you, and avoid such an outrage on my messenger as was perpetrated on Major [Frank S.] Bond, I respectfully request an order from you to forward the documents by a Staff Officer."
See further, Lincoln's communications to Rosecrans, June 8 and 10, *infra*.

To William S. Rosecrans[1]

Cypher   United States Military Telegraph,
Major Gen. Rosecrans   War Department.
St. Louis, Mo.   Washington June 8. 1864

Yours of to-day received. I am unable to conceive how a message can be less safe by the Express than by a Staff-officer. If you send a verbal message, the messenger is one additional person let into the secret.   A. LINCOLN

[1] ALS, DNA WR RG 107, Presidential Telegrams, I, 72. On June 8, Rosecrans replied to Lincoln's telegram of June 7, *supra*, as follows: "The nature of the information is too grave involving the interests of the country & the safety of individuals to admit of transacting the business through the express a sense of duty obliges me to refrain from so transmitting it." (DLC-RTL). See further, Lincoln to Rosecrans, June 10, *infra*.

[379]

To the Senate and House of Representatives[1]

To the Senate, and   June 8, 1864
House of Representatives

I have the honor to submit, for the consideration of Congress, a letter and inclosure from the Secretary of War, with my concurrence in the recommendation therein made.

June 8. 1864   ABRAHAM LINCOLN
Washington D.C.

[1] ADf, DLC-RTL; DS, DNA RG 46, Senate 38A F4; DS, DNA RG 233, House Executive Document No. 97. Lincoln transmitted Stanton's letter of June 7, 1864, recommending repeal of the "clause in the enrolment act known as the three hundred dollar clause," which allowed persons to pay that amount in lieu of personal service. Stanton enclosed a report of James B. Fry, June 6, 1864, showing that more than half of those actually drafted were paying the commutation money. Fry concluded, "I see no reason to believe that the army can be materially strengthened . . . so long as the $300 clause is in force. . . ." (Thirty-eighth Congress, First Session, *House Executive Document No. 97*, p. 2).

Reply to Committee Notifying Lincoln of His Renomination[1]

June 9, 1864

[Mr. Chairman and][2] Gentlemen of the Committee: I will neither conceal my gratification, nor restrain the expression of my gratitude, that the Union people, through their convention, in their[3] continued effort to save, and advance the nation, have deemed me not unworthy to remain in my present position.

I know no reason to doubt that I shall accept the nomination tendered; and yet perhaps I should not declare definitely before reading and considering what is called the Platform.

I will say now, however, [that][4] I approve the declaration in favor of so amending the Constitution as to prohibit slavery throughout the nation. When the people in revolt, with a[5] hundred days of[6] explicit notice, that they could, within those days, resume their allegiance, without the overthrow of their institution, and that they could not so resume it afterwards, elected to stand out, such [an][7] amendment of the Constitution as [is][8] now proposed, became a fitting, and necessary conclusion to the final success of the Union cause. Such alone can meet and cover all cavils. Now,[9] the unconditional Union men, North and South, perceive its[10] importance, and embrace it. In the joint names of Liberty and Union, let us labor to give it legal form, and practical effect.

[380]

¹ Copy, DLC-RTL; New York *Tribune*, June 10, 1864. The manuscript copy (not in Lincoln's autograph) preserved in the Lincoln Papers provides the text as reproduced. Variants in the *Tribune* are given in succeeding footnotes. The remarks of William Dennison, president of the convention and chairman of the notification committee, are reproduced from the *Tribune:*

"MR. PRESIDENT—The National Union Convention, which closed its sittings at Baltimore yesterday, appointed a Committee consisting of one from each State, with myself as Chairman, to inform you of your unanimous nomination by that Convention for election to the office of President of the United States. That Committee, I have the honor of now informing you, is present. On its behalf I have also the honor of presenting you with a copy of the resolutions or platform adopted by that Convention, as expressive of its sense, and of the sense of the loyal people of the country, which it represents, of the principles and policy that should characterize the administration of the Government in the present condition of the country. I need not say to you, sir, that Convention, in thus unanimously nominating you for reëlection, but gave utterance to the almost universal voice of the loyal people of the country. To doubt of your triumphant election, would be little short of abandoning the hope of a final suppression of the Rebellion and the restoration of the Government over the insurgent States. Neither the Convention nor those represented by that body entertained any doubt as to the final result, under your administration, sustained by that loyal people, and by our noble Army and gallant Navy. Neither did the Convention, nor do this Committee doubt the speedy suppression of this most wicked and unprovoked Rebellion. (A copy of the resolutions was here handed to the President.) I would add, Mr. President, that it would be the pleasure of the Committee to communicate to you, within a few days, through one of its most accomplished members, Mr. [George William] Curtis of New-York, by letter, more at length the circumstances under which you have been placed in nomination for the Presidency."

The Platform of the Union National Convention presented by Dennison is as follows:

"1. *Resolved,* That it is the highest duty of every American citizen to maintain against all their enemies the integrity of the Union and the paramount authority of the Constitution and laws of the United States; and that, laying aside all differences of political opinion, we pledge ourselves, as Union men, animated by a common sentiment and aiming at a common object, to do everything in our power to aid the Government in quelling by force of arms the Rebellion now raging against its authority, and in bringing to the punishment due to their crimes the Rebels and traitors arrayed against it. [Prolonged applause.]

"2. *Resolved,* That we approve the determination of the Government of the United States not to compromise with Rebels, or to offer them any terms of peace, except such as may be based upon an unconditional surrender of their hostility and a return to their just allegiance to the Constitution and laws of the United States, and that we call upon the Government to maintain this position, and to prosecute the war with the utmost possible vigor to the complete suppression of the Rebellion, in full reliance upon the self-sacrificing patriotism, the heroic valor, and the undying devotion of the American people to their country and its free institutions.

"3. *Resolved,* That as Slavery was the cause, and now constitutes the strength, of this Rebellion, and as it must be, always and everywhere, hostile to the principles of Republican Government, justice and the National safety demand its utter and complete extirpation from the soil of the Republic [applause]:—and that while we uphold and maintain the acts and proclamations by which the Government, in its own defense, has aimed a death-blow at this gigantic evil, we are in favor, furthermore, of such an amendment to the Constitution, to be made by the people in conformity with its provisions, as shall terminate and forever prohibit the existence of slavery within the limits or the jurisdiction of the United States. [Tremendous applause, the delegates rising and waving their hats.]

"4. *Resolved,* That the thanks of the American people are due to the soldiers and sailors of the Army and Navy [applause], who have periled their lives in defense of their country and in vindication of the honor of its flag; that the nation owes to them some permanent recognition of their patriotism and their valor, and ample and permanent provision for those of their survivors who have received disabling and honorable wounds in the service of the country; and that the memories of those who have fallen in its defense shall be held in grateful and everlasting remembrance. [Loud applause and cheers.]

"5. *Resolved,* That we approve and applaud the practical wisdom, the unselfish patriotism and the unswerving fidelity to the Constitution and the principles of American liberty, with which ABRAHAM LINCOLN has discharged, under circumstances of unparalleled difficulty, the great duties and responsibilities of the Presidential office; that we approve and endorse, as demanded by the emergency and essential to the preservation of the nation, and as within the provisions of the Constitution, the measures and acts which he has adopted to defend the nation against its open and secret foes; that we approve, especially, the Proclamation of Emancipation, and the employment as Union soldiers of men heretofore held in slavery [applause]; and that we have full confidence in his determination to carry these and all other Constitutional measures essential to the salvation of the country into full and complete effect. [Vociferous applause.]

"6. *Resolved,* That we deem it essential to the general welfare that harmony should prevail in the National Councils, and we regard as worthy of public confidence and official trust those only who cordially endorse the principles proclaimed in these resolutions, and which should characterize the administration of the government. [Applause.]

"7. *Resolved,* That the Government owes to all men employed in its armies, without regard to distinction of color, the full protection of the laws of war— [applause]—and that any violation of these laws, or of the usages of civilized nations in time of war, by the Rebels now in arms, should be made the subject of prompt and full redress. [Prolonged applause.]

"8. *Resolved,* That foreign immigration, which in the past has added so much to the wealth, development of resources and increase of power to this nation, the asylum of the oppressed of all nations, should be fostered and encouraged by a liberal and just policy. [Applause.]

"9. *Resolved,* That we are in favor of the speedy construction of the Railroad to the Pacific coast. [Applause.]

"10. *Resolved,* That the National faith, pledged for the redemption of the public debt, must be kept inviolate, and that for this purpose we recommend economy and rigid responsibility in the public expenditures, and a vigorous and just system of taxation: and that it is the duty of every loyal State to sustain the credit and promote the use of the National currency. [Applause.]

"11. *Resolved,* That we approve the position taken by the Government that the people of the United States can never regard with indifference the attempt of any European Power to overthrow by force or to supplant by fraud the institutions of any Republican Government on the Western Continent—[prolonged applause]—and that they will view with extreme jealousy, as menacing to the peace and independence of their own country, the efforts of any such power to obtain new footholds for Monarchical Governments, sustained by foreign military force, in near proximity to the United States. [Long-continued applause.]" *Proceedings of the National Union Convention. . . .* (New York, 1864), pp. 57-58.   2 "Mr. Chairman and" is not in RTL copy.

3 *Tribune* has "the" for "their."   4 *Tribune* inserts "that."

5 *Tribune* has "the" for "a."   6 *Tribune* omits "of."

[7] *Tribune* inserts "an."   [8] *Tribune* inserts "is."
[9] *Tribune* has "I now" instead of "Now, the unconditional Union men, North and South."
[10] "Its" appears to be in Lincoln's autograph on the RTL copy, written over an erasure.

Reply to Elisha H. Allen[1]

June 9, 1864

SIR—In every light in which the state of the Hawaiian Islands can be contemplated, it is an object of profound interest to the United States. Virtually it was once a colony.

It is now a near and intimate neighbor. It is a haven of shelter and refreshment for our merchant fishermen, seamen, and other citizens, when on their lawful occasions they are navigating the eastern seas and oceans. Its people are free, and its laws, language and religion are largely the fruits of our own teaching and example.

The distinguished part which you, Mr. Minister, have acted in the history of that interesting country is well known here. It gives me pleasure to assure you of my sincere desire to do what I can to render now your sojourn in the United States agreeable to yourself, satisfactory to your sovereign, and beneficial to the Hawaiian people.

[1] New York *Tribune*, June 11, 1864. Lincoln replied to a short speech by Elisha H. Allen, envoy and minister from Hawaii, upon presenting his credentials. This item has been misdated in other sources: June 10 (Hertz, II, 933) and June 11 (NH, XI, 132). On June 7, 1864, Secretary Seward wrote Lincoln as follows: "It has been found convenient to defer the presentation of Mr. Allen from tomorrow (as indicated in my note of yesterday) until the following day, at half past eleven o'clock of which I shall have the honor of presenting that gentleman, if the time be acceptable to you." (DLC-RTL). As printed by the *Tribune*, Lincoln's reply is part of a despatch from Washington dated June 10, which does not specify the date of delivery.

Reply to Delegation
from the National Union League[1]

June 9, 1864

Gentlemen: I can only say, in response to the kind remarks of your chairman, as I suppose, that I am very grateful for the renewed confidence which has been accorded to me, both by the convention and by the National League. I am not insensible at all to the personal compliment there is in this; yet I do not allow myself to believe that any but a small portion of it is to be appropriated as a personal compliment. The convention and the nation, I am assured, are alike animated by a higher view of the interests of the country for the present and the great future, and that part I am entitled to appropriate as a compliment is only that part which I may lay hold of as being the opinion of the convention and of the League, that I am not entirely[2] unworthy to be intrusted with the place I have occupied for the last three years. I have not permitted myself, gentlemen, to conclude that I am the best man in the country; but I am reminded, in this connection, of a story of an old Dutch farmer, who remarked to a companion once that "it was not best to swap horses when crossing streams."

[1] New York *Times, Herald,* and *Tribune,* June 10, 1864. The delegation presented a copy of resolutions adopted by the Union League, approving and endorsing "the nominations made by the Union National Convention at Baltimore." (DLC-RTL).   [2] "Entirely" appears only in the *Tribune.*

Response to a Serenade by the Ohio Delegation[1]

June 9, 1864

GENTLEMEN: I am very much obliged to you for this compliment. I have just been saying, and will repeat it, that the hardest of all speeches I have to answer is a serenade. I never know what to say on these occasions. I suppose that you have done me this kindness in connection with the action of the Baltimore convention, which has recently taken place, and with which, of course, I am very well satisfied. (Laughter and applause.) What we want, still more than Baltimore conventions or presidential elections, is success under Gen. Grant. (Cries of "Good," and applause.) I propose that you constantly bear in mind that the support you owe to the brave officers and soldiers in the field is of the very first importance, and we should therefore bend all our energies to that point. Now, without detaining you any longer, I propose that you help me to close up what I am now saying with three rousing cheers for Gen. Grant and the officers and soldiers under his command.

[1] New York *Herald,* June 10, 1864. The New York *Tribune* and *Times* printed substantially the same text. On the evening of June 9, the Ohio delegation accompanied by a brass band "waited upon the President and tendered him a serenade."

To Salmon P. Chase[1]

Hon. Sec. of Treasury   Executive Mansion,
My dear Sir   Washington, June 10, 1864.

Herewith are the documents which you kindly proposed fixing up for me, towit:

[384]

1.	Treasurers receipt, of March 15. 1862. of 7/30's.		$14,200.
2	do do April 16. do " "		" 2,000.00
3	Certificate of Deposite, Aug 1. 1863.		"22,306.67
4.	do do " 18. do		" 3,874.73
5.	5—20's		" 8 000.00.
6.	Two Warrants $2022/33. $2022/34		" 4 044.67
7.	Greenbacks.		89.00.

54,515.07

Left with Gov. Chase to fix up on
this 11. June 1864

[1] AL, owned by David Davis, IV, Bloomington, Illinois. The securities turned over to the Treasury for investment represented savings from Lincoln's salary. For a full discussion see Harry E. Pratt, *Personal Finances of Abraham Lincoln* (1943), pp. 124-30.

To Joseph Henry[1]

Professor Henry.   June 10, 1864

A few days ago a friend of yours called and urged me to pardon Private McCarthy, & upon my refusal, went away dissatisfied, and I thought a little out of temper. After he was gone, I telegraphed Gen. Meade that if he and McCarthy's Colonel would consent, I would send him back to his Regiment; and the within is Gen. Meade's answer. Yours truly   A. LINCOLN
June 10. 1864

[1] AES, IHi. See Lincoln to Meade, June 6, *supra.* Lincoln's endorsement is written on a telegram from General George G. Meade, June 7, 1864: "Your dispatch of yesterday in relation to private James McCarthey of Co 'K' 140th NY is received On inquiry I find that Private McCarthey was a Drafted man who deserted in two (2) or three (3) Days after he joined the Regt & was apprehended by our Pickets attempting to pass our Lines towards the enemy when arrested He attempted to bribe the Pickets to allow him to pass I cannot reccommend any mitigation of the sentence in his case."

An endorsement by Joseph Henry dated August 16, 1864, presumably addressed to "Mr. Morgan of Rochester," states: "I send this paper to you as an evidence that Mr Lincoln desired to do what is proper in the case you & Professor Horsford presented to him. It has lain in my portfolio for several weeks."

To James G. McAdam[1]

June 10, 1864

McCrea was banished from Beaufort by the Military authorities, & I am now called on to send him back, without the consent of those authorities, which I can not consent to do. They & not I must judge whether his presence is injurious. If the Gen. in command there—

Gen. Saxton I believe—consents, then I am quite willing for Mr. McCrea to return—not without.   A. LINCOLN

June 10, 1864.

[1] AES, The Rosenbach Company, Philadelphia and New York. James G. Mc-Adam of New York had interviewed Lincoln on June 8 in behalf of his friend James A. McCrea, who had been arrested and banished from the Department commanded by General Rufus Saxton at Beaufort, South Carolina, for procuring whisky for enlisted men. A resident of New York who formerly had operated a plantation in the West Indies, McCrea had acquired an abandoned plantation near Beaufort and was undertaking to raise cotton with hired labor. The letter from McAdam of June 9, 1864, which bears Lincoln's endorsement is a lengthy summary of the case, from McCrea's point of view, in which McAdam attempts to reinforce his ineffectual interview of the day before.

Order to John Hay[1]

Executive Mansion,
Washington, June 10, 1864.

Major John Hay, Assistant Adjutant General, will repair at once to St. Louis Missouri, and having executed my verbal instructions will return to his station here.   A. LINCOLN

[1] DS, IHi. This order, in Hay's handwriting, signed by Lincoln, was issued as AGO *Special Orders No. 213*, June 19, 1864. See Lincoln to Rosecrans, *infra*.

To William S. Rosecrans[1]

Executive Mansion, Washington,
Major.General Rosecrans   June 10, 1864.

Major John Hay, the bearer, is one of my Private Secretaries, to whom please communicate, in writing, or verbally, anything you would think proper to say to me. Yours truly   A. LINCOLN.

[1] ALS (copy?), DLC-RTL. See Lincoln's telegrams to Rosecrans, June 7 and 8, *supra*. On June 9, Richard Yates telegraphed Lincoln, "I have recd from Genl Rosecrans information of most vital importance to the Govt which cannot be conveyed to you in its full import by mail or by express I think it very important that you summon Genl Rosecrans or Col J P Sanderson his Provost Marshal to Washn immediately." (DLC-RTL).

John Hay's *Diary* gives an account of his trip to St. Louis (Tyler Dennett, ed., *op. cit.*, pp. 187-94) to receive Rosecrans' report of a conspiracy by the Order of American Knights, reputedly led by Clement L. Vallandigham, and by Charles Hunt, Belgian consul at St. Louis. A portion of the account is as follows:

"Thursday night, June 9, the President came into my room just before bedtime and said that Rosecrans had been sending despatches requesting that an officer of his staff might be sent to Washington to lay before the Prest. matters of great importance in regard to a conspiracy to overthrow the government. He asked for this permission on account of the outrage committed upon Major Bond of his Staff who was some time ago court martialed for coming to Washington under General Rosecrans' orders. Recently Gov. Yates has joined in Rosecrans' request, asking that Sanderson shall be sent for. 'If it is a matter of such overwhelming importance,' said the President, 'I don't think Sanderson is the proper person to whom to entrust it. I am inclined to think that the object of the General is to force me into a conflict with the Secretary of War and to make me overrule him in this matter. This at present I am not inclined to do. I have concluded to send you out there to talk it over with Rosecrans and to ascertain just what he has. I would like you to start tomorrow.'

"He gave me, in the morning before I was out of bed, this note [*supra*] to deliver to Rosecrans."

On June 13 Secretary Stanton telegraphed Rosecrans, "The President directs that the archives and papers of the Belgian consulate, alleged to have been taken from the possession of Mr. Hunt, late Belgian consul, by your provost-marshal, be returned to him, and that no proceedings be had against him without orders from this department; that you release him if he be imprisoned, and that you report by telegraph what proceedings, if any, have been had by your provost-marshal, or any other officer under your command, in reference to Mr. Hunt, or the papers and archives of his consulate, and the grounds or causes of such proceedings." (OR, I, XXXIV, IV, 337).

On June 14, Rosecrans wrote Lincoln:

"Major Hay has received such full details of the character of the conspiracy alluded to in my dispatches as will suffice to show you what important national interests are involved in the proper understanding and handling of the matter, and satisfy you that the whole should be laid immediately before you by an officer capable of giving such details as will enable you to adopt a policy the execution of which will give adequate security to the public interests.

"I beg leave therefore to call your attention to a few points in connexion with the information he will give you.

"1. The organization not only threatens great danger in case our military operations are unsuccessful or indecisive in their results but is now working great general mischief by spreading discontent among the people, circulating false reports injurious to the Government, creating doubt and discouragement, aiding spies suppliers of arms and other contraband and giving aid comfort and encouragement to the rebellion.

"2. These conspirators are ready to do anything in their power such as assisting guerillas and, whenever opportunity offers, joining them in destroying R.R. bridges, capturing our outposts threatening our depots and aiding in the work of plunder and murder and devastation. The present raid in Kentucky was invited and as you will observe unquestionably received aid from this organization bridges having been destroyed and other mischief done at distances of thirty or forty miles from the rebel raiders.

"I knew that this raid was contemplated and my men warned the Natl authorities authorities [*sic*] of it some weeks ago. Of course too much is involved to permit me to send manuscript communications to you either by mail or express. My duty to you the country and to the persons whose lives would be endangered by want of prompt and proper action all forbid such a course

"3. I take this opportunity to call your attention to the fact that my application for a remittance from the contingent fund to defray the expenses involved in this and other investigations demanded by the interests of the service in this Department have been refused by the Secretary of War. That refusal has been most injurious to the public interests and unwarranted by the condition of affairs here as well as by the customs of the service.

"4 The obstacles interposed to my communication with you, this refusal of necessary means to conduct the secret service so important in this Department convince me that your interposition is needed to prevent the interests of the people and the good name of your administration from being seriously injured.

"5. As the 4th of July is generally understood to be the chosen time for the conspirators to begin their work of mischief prompt action will be necessary. No interference should be permitted with the arrests which have or may be made of parties involved such as Hunt and others whose friends will undoubtedly appeal to you." (DLC-RTL).

To Julian M. Sturtevant[1]

Rev. J. M. Sturtevant   Executive Mansion,
& others, committee   Washington, June 10. 1864.

    Gentlemen   I only have time to acknowledge the receipt of, and to sincerely thank you for, the resolutions of the Triennial Congregational convention, and your kind note communicating them. Yours very truly   A. LINCOLN

[1] ALS, IJI. The resolutions of the Triennial Convention of the Congregational Church, Chicago, April 28, 1864, signed by Sturtevant and others, urged the appointment of a day of national fasting and prayer, protested the atrocities committed on colored troops, and urged that measures be taken to protect them.

Endorsement[1]

[c. June 11, 1864]

I believe I already have copies of all Telegrams I sent upon this subject. Will the S

[1] AE, DLC-RTL. Lincoln's endorsement is written on a copy of a Senate resolution, June 11, 1864, requesting the president to furnish "copies of all correspondence, orders and documents . . . in relation to the organization, by the loyal people of Arkansas, of the free State Government of that State." The endorsement is unfinished and no record has been discovered of Lincoln's formal compliance with the request, but see Lincoln to Trumbull, June 17, *infra*.

Remarks to One Hundred Thirtieth Ohio Regiment[1]

June 11, 1864

    Soldiers, I understand you have just come from Ohio—come to help us in this the nation's day of trials, and also of its hopes. I thank you for your promptness in responding to the call for troops. Your services were never needed more than now. I know not where you are going. You may stay here and take the places of others who will be sent to the front; or you may go there yourselves. Wherever you go I know you will do your best. Again I thank you. Good-by.

[1] New York *Tribune*, June 13, 1864. "The 130th Ohio, 100-day troops, having in its ranks lawyers, clergymen, some of the best men in the State—many of

them taxed upon a hundred thousand dollars and upward, voted yesterday unanimously to go to the front and fight, and then marched to the White House to see and hear Mr. Lincoln." (*Ibid.*).

To John Rogers[1]

Mr. John Rogers   Executive Mansion,
New-York.   Washington, June 13, 1864.

I can not pretend to be a judge in such matters; but the Statuette groups "Wounded Scout"—"Friend in the Swamp" which you did me the honor to present, is very pretty and suggestive, and, I should think, excellent as a piece of art. Thank you for it. Yours truly   A. LINCOLN

[1] ALS, NHi. John Rogers' popular statuette groups (more than seventy) included at least one in which Lincoln was depicted—"The Council of War." Rogers' heroic bronze statue of Lincoln is in the public library at Manchester, New Hampshire.

To the Senate[1]

To the Senate of the United States: June 13, 1864

I transmit herewith for consideration with a view to ratification a convention between the United States of America and the United Colombian States, signed by the plenipotentiaries of the contracting powers on the 10 February last, providing for a revival of the joint commission on claims under the convention of 10 September, 1857, with New Granada.   ABRAHAM LINCOLN.

Washington, 13th June, 1864.

[1] *Executive Journal*, XIII, 588; DS, DNA RG 46, Senate 38B B6. The convention was ratified by the Senate on June 25, 1864.

To the Senate[1]

To the Senate   June 13, 1864
of the United States:

In compliance with the Resolution of the Senate of the 4th. March, 1864, I transmit herewith a report from the Secretary of War in the case of William Yokum, with accompanying papers.

Washington,   ABRAHAM LINCOLN
June 13th, 1864.

[Endorsement on record of trial of William Yokum]

After making the above entry for pardon, upon representations made by the Secretary of War, I suspended action on the case.

June 13, 1864.   A. LINCOLN.

¹ DS, DNA RG 46; Thirty-eighth Congress, First Session, *Senate Executive Document No. 51*. See Lincoln to Bates, May 26, *supra*, and earlier references to Yocum. Stanton's report including the record of the trial of William Yocum may be found in *Executive Document No. 51*. Lincoln's endorsement was written on the record immediately following the endorsement of February 16, *supra*, which ordered Yocum's pardon.

To Lorenzo Thomas¹

Major General Thomas   Executive Mansion,
Louisville, Ky.   Washington, June 13, 1864.

Complaint is made to me that in the vicinity of Henderson, our military are seizing negroes and carrying them off without their own consent, and according to no rules whatever, except those of absolute violence. I wish you would look into this & inform me, and see that the making soldiers of negroes is done according to the rules you are acting upon, so that unnecessary provocation and irratation be avoided.   A. LINCOLN

¹ ALS, DNA WR RG 107, Presidential Telegrams, I, 74. Thomas replied on the same day: "Telegram of this date recd. I have no doubt there has been ground for complaint in the vicinity of Henderson, Ky, but I will take immediate measures to prevent a recurrence of any acts of violence on the person of officers engaged in recruiting colored troops in Ky." (DLC-RTL).

To Thomas Webster¹

Thomas Webster   Washington, D.C.
Philadelphia   June 13. 1864

Will try to leave here Wednesday afternoon, say at 4 P.M. remain till Thursday afternoon, and then return. This subject to events.   A. LINCOLN

¹ ALS, DNA WR RG 107, Presidential Telegrams, I, 73. Webster acknowledged receipt of Lincoln's telegram on June 14, and on June 15 telegraphed as follows: "On behalf of the Committee appointed to escort Your Excellency and suite to the Great Central Fair at Philadelphia, I have the honor to inform you that agreeably to the request of Mrs. Lincoln the Rail Road Companies have arranged the starting of the special train for seven a.m.—precisely—tomorrow morning—Thursday, 16th inst. . . ." (DLC-RTL).

To Gideon Welles¹

Hon. Sec. of Navy, please see and hear Mrs. Dessinger [Derringer?]   A. LINCOLN
June 13, 1864

¹ ALS, PHi. Mrs. Dessinger (Derringer?) has not been identified.

To Edward Bates[1]

Upon the representation of Senator Harris, let a pardon be made out for the unexecuted part of the sentence in this case

June 14. 1864   A. LINCOLN

[1] AES, DNA RG 204, U.S. Pardon Attorney, A 502. Lincoln's endorsement is written on a petition from Louisa Hagen, May 21, 1864, Albany, New York, for pardon of her husband Erhard Hagen (Hagan), convicted of perjury regarding his tax return.

To Stephen G. Burbridge[1]

	Office U.S. Military Telegraph,
Gen. Burbridge	War Department,
Lexington, Ky.	Washington, D.C., June 14 1864.

Have just read your despatch of action at Cynthiana. Please accept my congratulation and thanks for yourself and command.

A. LINCOLN

[1] ALS, DNA WR RG 107, Presidential Telegrams, I, 75. On June 13, 1864, General Burbridge telegraphed Halleck: "I attacked [John H.] Morgan at Cynthiana at daylight yesterday morning, and after an hour's hard fighting completely routed him, killing 300, wounding as many, and capturing nearly 400, besides recapturing nearly all of General [Edward H.] Hobson's command and over 1,000 horses. . . ." (OR, I, XXXIX, I, 20).
Concerning Hobson's defeat see the communication to Heintzelman, *infra*.

To Samuel P. Heintzelman[1]

| Major General Heintzelman | War Department |
| Columbus, Ohio. | Washington, June 14, 1864. |

Hobson's conduct, in surrendering, and taking a hot-haste parole, has an exceedingly suspicious appearance. Please ascertain if he should not be arrested and tried.   EDWIN M STANTON

Sec of War

[1] ALS, IHi. Written on Executive Mansion stationery emended to "War Department," this telegram is in Lincoln's autograph, signed by Stanton. See Lincoln to Stanton, *infra*. Brigadier General Edward H. Hobson was surprised and captured near Cynthiana, Kentucky, on June 11, by a Confederate force under John H. Morgan. Hobson accepted Morgan's suggestion that he place himself in communication with Heintzelman and propose his exchange for a Confederate officer of like rank. If the exchange was refused, Hobson was to report to Morgan as a prisoner of war. On June 13, Heintzelman telegraphed Halleck that Hobson was in Cincinnati on a conditional parole which Heintzelman considered unauthorized (OR, I, XXXIX, II, 113). Although Hobson was held under arrest for some time, no trial seems to have taken place, perhaps because of the events of June 12 (see Lincoln to Burbridge, June 14, *supra*).

To Robert Todd Lincoln[1]

Executive Mansion,
My dear Son   Washington, June 14, 1864.

Of course I will try to give the sittings for the "Crayon." Your Father   A. LINCOLN

[1] ALS, MH. The only periodical by the title *Crayon* which appears in the Union List of Serials was an art magazine published from 1855 to 1861 in New York City. In view of this fact it seems probable that Lincoln referred to Colonel David H. Strother, whose pseudonym was "Porte Crayon," a writer and artist employed by *Harper's New Monthly Magazine*, who served on McClellan's staff in 1862 and on David Hunter's staff in 1864, resigning his commission September 10, 1864.

To Edwin M. Stanton[1]

Hon. Sec. of War   Executive Mansion,
Dear Sir.   Washington, June 14, 1864.

If you concur, please sign and send the inclosed draft of despatch.
Yours truly   A. LINCOLN

[1] ALS, PHi. The draft of a telegram which Lincoln enclosed was certainly the one to Heintzelman, *supra*.

To Salmon P. Chase[1]

Washington, June 15, 1864.

My Dear Sir: The Governor of Iowa and some of the M.C.'s have a little embarrassment about the removal of a Mr. Atkinson, in your department, and the appointment to the place of a Mr. Sill,[2] I think. They claim a promise, which I know I never made, except upon the condition that you desired the removal of Atkinson. Please help me a little. If you will write me a note that you do not wish Atkinson removed, that will end the matter. On the contrary, if you do wish him removed, or even are indifferent about it, say so to me, accompanying your note with a nomination for Sill. Yours truly,   A. LINCOLN.

[1] Robert B. Warden, *Account of the Private Life and Public Services of Salmon Portland Chase* (1874), p. 604. A footnote in the source reads as follows: "Under date June 28, a register contains this entry:

"'The auditor, Mr. Atkinson, resigned to-day. Mr. Sill, of Iowa, is to take his place. Mr. Atkinson has been an excellent officer, but has been much distrusted by our friends on account of his politics. I advised him to resign, therefore, proposing to use his services in another place where the same hostility is not manifest. . . .'"

No reply from Chase has been discovered. Robert J. Atkinson was later replaced as third auditor by John Wilson of Illinois (*U.S. Official Register*, 1865).
[2] Elijah Sills.

To Ulysses S. Grant[1]

United States Military Telegraph,
War Department.

Lieut. Gen. Grant
Head Qrs. A.P.

Washington, June 15, 1864

Have just read your despatch of 1 P.M. yesterday. I begin to see it. You will succeed. God bless you all.   A. LINCOLN

[1] ALS, owned by Foreman M. Lebold, Chicago, Illinois. Grant's telegram to Halleck, 1:30 P.M., June 14, 1864, states: "Our forces will commence crossing the James to-day. The enemy show no signs yet of having brought troops to the south side of Richmond. I will have Petersburg secured, if possible, before they get there in much force. Our movement from Cold Harbor to the James River has been made with great celerity and so far without loss or accident." (OR, I, XL, II, 18-19).

Order for Arrest of John S. Carlisle[1]

Executive Mansion
Washington City June 15. 1864

Whereas it has come to my knowledge that John S Carlisle of West Virginia is engaged in treasonable and disloyal correspondence with one Louis A Welton[2] an enemy of the United States and an agent of the rebels now in arms and at war with the United States, and has invited and urged the said agent of the rebels to come to the city of Washington to confer with him the said Carlisle; It is ordered that Colonel Wisewell[3] Military Governor of the District of Washington arrest and take in custody the said John S Carlisle and hold him in custody until further order.

ABRAHAM LINCOLN

[1] DS, DLC-Stanton Papers. Concerning the case of Louis A. Welton, see Lincoln to Holt, August 13 and December 28, *infra*, and also the communication to Morgan, Weed, and Raymond, August 31, *infra*.
[2] Louis A. Welton of St. Louis, Missouri, served as volunteer aide-de-camp to Confederate Brigadier General Mosby M. Parsons in the Missouri and Arkansas campaigns of 1861-1862.   [3] Moses N. Wisewell.

To Edwin M. Stanton[1]

June 15, 1864

On the representation and petition of Allbright and Dimmick, who prossecuted in this case, and Hon. W. D. Kelly's indorsement of them as every way reliable, John Paul named within, is pardoned for the unexecuted part of his sentence.   A. LINCOLN

June 15, 1864.

[1] AES, owned by Gordon A. Block, Philadelphia, Pennsylvania. Lincoln's endorsement is written on a petition for pardon of John Paul of Jeansville, Pennsylvania, sentenced for resisting the draft. The petition, dated May 28, 1864,

bears numerous signatures including those of Charles Albright and M. M. Dimmick, attorneys for the government in prosecuting the case. Stanton's endorsement below Lincoln's is as follows: "Referred to the Adjutant General to frame order for the prisoners discharge he being now in Fort Mifflin the order shd be addressed to General Cadwallader [George C. Cadwalader] or [Darius N.] Couch."

To the Senate[1]

To the Senate of the United States.   June 16, 1864

I transmit herewith a further report from the Secretary of State in answer to the resolution of the Senate of the 25th. Ultimo relative to Mexican Affairs with the papers therein referred to

Washington June 16. 1864.   ABRAHAM LINCOLN.

[1] Copy, DNA RG 46, Senate 38A F3. This communication with enclosures is printed as Thirty-eighth Congress, First Session, *Senate Executive Document No. 11*, but appears in the bound volume of Thirty-eighth Congress, Second Session, *Senate Executive Documents*, as No. 11 of that series. Secretary Seward's report (496 pages) of June 16, 1864, transmitting correspondence in regard to Mexico should be consulted in the source.

Speech at Great Central Sanitary Fair, Philadelphia, Pennsylvania[1]

June 16, 1864

I suppose that this toast was intended to open the way for me to say something. [Laughter.] War, at the best, is terrible, and this war of ours, in its magnitude and in its duration, is one of the most terrible. It has deranged business, totally in many localities, and partially in all localities. It has destroyed property, and ruined homes; it has produced a national debt and taxation unprecedented, at least in this country. It has carried mourning to almost every home, until it can almost be said that the "heavens are hung in black." Yet it continues, and several relieving coincidents [*coincidences*] have accompanied it from the very beginning, which have not been known, as I understood [*understand*], or have any knowledge of, in any former wars in the history of the world. The Sanitary Commission, with all its benevolent labors, the Christian Commission, with all its Christian and benevolent labors, and the various places, arrangements, so to speak, and institutions, have contributed to the comfort and relief of the soldiers. You have two of these places in this city—the Cooper-Shop and Union Volunteer Refreshment Saloons. [Great applause and cheers.] And lastly, these fairs, which, I believe, began only in last August, if I mistake not, in Chicago; then at Boston, at Cincinnati, Brooklyn, New York, at Baltimore, and those at present held at St. Louis, Pittsburg, and Philadelphia. The motive and object that lie at the bottom of all these are most worthy; for, say what you will, after all the most is due to the soldier, who takes his life in his hands and goes to fight the battles of his country. [Cheers.] In what is contributed to his comfort when he passes to and fro [*from city to city*], and in what is contributed to him when he is sick and wounded, in whatever shape it comes, whether from the fair and tender hand of woman, or from any other source, is much, very much; but, I think there is still that which has as much value to him [*in the continual reminders he sees in the newspapers, that while he is absent he is yet remembered by the loved ones at home.*]—he is not forgotten. [Cheers.] Another view of these various institutions is worthy of consideration, I think; they are voluntary contributions, given freely, zealously, and earnestly, on top of all the disturbances of business, [*of all the disorders,*] the taxation and burdens that the war has imposed upon us, giving proof that the national resources are not at all exhausted, [cheers;] that the national spirit of patriotism is even [*firmer and*] stronger than at the commencement of the rebellion [*war*].

It is a pertinent question often asked in the mind privately, and from one to the other, when is the war to end? Surely I feel as deep [*great*] an interest in this question as any other can, but I do not wish to name a day, or month, or a year when it is to end. I do not wish to run any risk of seeing the time come, without our being ready for the end, and for fear of disappointment, because the time had come and not the end. [*We accepted this war; we did not begin it.*] We accepted this war for an object, a worthy object, and the war will end when that object is attained. Under God, I hope it never will until that time. [Great cheering.] Speaking of the present campaign, General Grant is reported to have said, I am going through on this line if it takes all summer. [Cheers.] This war has taken three years; it was begun or accepted upon the line of restoring the national authority over the whole national domain, and for the American people, as far as my knowledge enables me to speak, I say we are going through on this line if it takes three years more. [Cheers.] My friends, I did not know but that I might be called upon to say a few words before I got away from here, but I did not know it was coming just here. [Laughter.] I have never been in the habit of making predictions in regard to the war, but I am almost tempted to make one. [(*Do it—do it!*)]—If I were to hazard it, it is this: That Grant is this evening, with General Meade and General Hancock, of Pennsylvania, and the brave offi-

cers and soldiers with him, in a position from whence he will never
be dislodged until Richmond is taken [loud cheering], and I have
but one single proposition to put now, and, perhaps, I can best put
it in form of an interrogative [*interragatory*]. If I shall discover
that General Grant and the noble officers and men under him can
be greatly facilitated in their work by a sudden pouring forward
[*forth*] of men and assistance, will you give them to me? [Cries of
"yes."] Then, I say, stand ready, for I am watching for the chance.
[Laughter and cheers.] I thank you, gentlemen.

¹ Philadelphia *Press* and *Inquirer*, June 17, 1864. The basic text reproduced is
from the *Press*. Variants appearing in italics within brackets are from the *Inquirer*. Interruptions are reproduced in brackets as they appear in the *Press*.
Lincoln spoke at a banquet held in a reception room at the Fair near seven
o'clock P.M. The *Press*, as well as other papers, commented on the difficulties
which confronted the reporters: "The people at large will regret to hear that
no accommodation whatever was made for the representatives of the press, and,
therefore, it was with great difficulty that the reporters were able to take the
speech of the President at all." Reports appearing in all papers show many
verbal variations. The *Press* and *Inquirer* are the best which have been discovered and are practically identical in content, though differing in numerous
verbal details. Only the most important variants appearing in the *Inquirer* have
been inserted in the *Press* text as reproduced.

Among the Lincoln Papers there is a page of manuscript in handwriting that
has not been identified, written on Executive Mansion stationery, which appears
to have been drafted as a suggestion for Lincoln's speech:

"Executive Mansion,
"Washington, [June 16?], 1864.

"It was here in the days when our fathers, struggled to free themselves from
the exactions, of the heartless mother country, that noble women met and organized, and went from precinct to precinct, soliciting aid for not only our sick, but
these half clothed and barefooted soldiers; and some one has told me, that there
is preserved among the papers of your Historical Society, one of the subscription
lists with the autograph signatures of the patriotic matrons of that day, some of
whose grand-daughters perhaps imbued with their spirit, have by their taste and
energy and presence brought us into a floral fairy land." (DLC-RTL).

Speech Accepting Medal Presented
by Ladies of the Fair¹

June 16, 1864

I have only to say that I accept this present of the ladies as an
additional token of your confidence, but I do not need any further
evidence of the loyalty and devotion of the women of America to
the cause of the Union and the cause of Christian humility. I accept it thankfully, as another manifestation of the esteem of the
ladies.

¹ Philadelphia *Inquirer*, June 17, 1864. Following Lincoln's principal speech,
supra, other speeches were made by General Lewis Wallace, Edward Everett,

and others. Then James Pollock, former governor of Pennsylvania, presented Lincoln with a silver medal on behalf of the ladies of the Fair. A number of other presents were also given, including a staff made of wood from the arch under which George Washington had passed at Trenton, New Jersey, on his way to be inaugurated for the first time. Lincoln made brief responses, but no verbatim reports have been discovered.

Speech at Union League Club, Philadelphia, Pennsylvania[1]

June 16, 1864

I thank you, sir, for your kind words of welcome. I am happy at the opportunity of visiting the Union League of Philadelphia, the first, I believe, of the Union Leagues—an organization free from political prejudices, and prompted in its formation by motives of the highest patriotism. I have many a time heard of its doing great good, and no one has charged it with doing any wrong. But it is not my intention to make a speech. My object in visiting Philadelphia was exclusively to witness the Sanitary Fair, and I need scarcely say that I have been more than delighted in witnessing the extraordinary efforts of your patriotic men and lovely ladies in behalf of the suffering soldiers and sailors of our country. It will now afford me pleasure to take each of you by the hand.

[1] Philadelphia *Press*, June 17, 1864. Because of confusion in plans, Lincoln missed the committee of the Union League assigned to conduct him from the Fair to their club, and upon arriving without them was greeted with a brief speech by Daniel Dougherty, to which he replied with the above remarks.

Speech to Crowd before Union League Club, Philadelphia, Pennsylvania[1]

June 16, 1864

FELLOW CITIZENS: I am very grateful to-night for this reception, which you have tendered me. I will not make a speech. I came among you thinking that my presence might do some good towards swelling the contributions of the great Fair in aid of the Sanitary Commission, who intend it for the soldiers in the field. While at the Fair I said a few words which I thought proper to say in connection with it. At the solicitation of the Union League I speak to you, and, in conclusion, I thank you for this great demonstration which you have paid me, and beg you will excuse me. [Great applause.]

[1] Philadelphia *Press*, June 17, 1864. This brief speech was made from the steps of the Union League Club following Lincoln's reception by the members.

Speech at Hotel Continental, Philadelphia, Pennsylvania[1]

June 16, 1864

FELLOW-CITIZENS: I attended the Fair at Philadelphia to-day in the hope that possibly it might aid something in swelling the contributions for the benefit of the soldiers in the field, who are bearing the harder part of this great national struggle in which we are engaged. [Applause.] I thought I might do this without impropriety. It did not even occur to me that a kind demonstration like this would be made to me. [A voice—"You are worthy of it," and cheers.] I do not really think it is proper in my position for me to make a political speech; and having said at the Fair what I thought was proper for me to say there in reference to that subject, and being more of a politician than anything else, and having exhausted that branch of the subject at the fair, and not being prepared to speak on the other, I am without anything to say. I have really appeared before you now more for the purpose of seeing you [a voice: "Three cheers for Honest Old Abe!"] and allowing you to see me a little while, [laughter] and, to show to you that I am not wanting in due consideration and respect for you, when you make this kind demonstration in my honor. At the same time I must beg of you to excuse me from saying anything further.

[1] Philadelphia *Press*, June 17, 1864. Upon returning to the Continental near midnight, Lincoln spoke from the balcony of the hotel.

To Lyman Trumbull[1]

Hon. Lyman Trumbull   Executive Mansion,
My dear Sir.   Washington, June 17, 1864.

Yours relative to reorganization of a State Government for Arkansas is received. I believe none of the Departments have had any thing to do with it. All that has been done within the range you mention, is embraced in an informal letter and telegraphic correspondence between parties there and myself, copies of which I have already furnished to Mr. Dawes[2] of the H.R. for the object corresponding to yours. It will save labor, and oblige me, if you will procure him to show you them. I believe you will find mentioned, a proclamation of Gen. Steele, no copy of which is with with [sic] the correspondence. The reason is I could not find it.

If, after reading this, it still would be more satisfactory to you to have copies for yourself, let me know, and I will have them made out as soon as I reasonably can. Yours truly   A. LINCOLN

[1] ADfS, DLC-RTL. On June 15, 1864, Senator Trumbull, chairman of the committee on the judiciary, wrote Lincoln:

"The Senate have referred the Credentials of Messrs. [Elisha] Baxter and [William M.] Fishback, claiming to be elected Senators from the State of Arkansas, to this Committee, and in the investigation of their right to seats, the Committee desire to be informed what steps, if any, have been taken by the President, or any of the Departments, or officers under his authority, towards the establishment, or recognition of a State government in Arkansas since the inhabitants of that State were declared to be in a state of insurrection.

"Will you have the kindness to cause copies of such papers or documents as relate to this subject to be sent to the Committee." (DLC-RTL).

[2] Henry L. Dawes of Massachusetts.

Endorsement Concerning *Journal*[1]

June 18, 1864

The Journal paper was always my friend; and, of course its editors the same. If there is any special reason why it should not have a share of the advertising I do not know it.　　　A. LINCOLN

June 18, 1864.

[1] AES, RPB. Although removed from the document it endorsed, this memorandum probably refers to government advertising in the (Springfield) *Illinois State Journal*. No further reference has been found, but the *Journal* continued to print government advertising in 1864 and 1865.

Endorsement Concerning Siege of Petersburg, Virginia[1]

Petersburgh had not been taken at 8 A.M. yesterday.　　　A.L.

June 18, 1864.

[1] Swann Auction Galleries Catalog No. 290, May 17, 1951, No. 76. According to the catalog description, Lincoln's endorsement was written in pencil on the verso of a note to the president. On June 17, Secretary Stanton had mistakenly announced the capture of Petersburg (New York *Tribune*, June 18, 1864).

To the Senate[1]

To the Senate of the United States.　　　June 18, 1864

In further answer to the Senate's Resolution of the 28th ultimo, requesting to be informed whether the President "has, and when, authorized a person alleged to have committed a crime against Spain, or any of its dependencies, to be delivered up to officers of that Government; and whether such delivery was had, and if so, under what authority of law or of treaty it was done"—I transmit a copy of a despatch of the 10th instant to the Secretary of State from the Acting Consul of the United States at Havana.

Washington, 18th June, 1864.　　　ABRAHAM LINCOLN

1 DS, DNA RG 46, Senate 38A F2. See Lincoln's communication to the Senate, May 31, *supra*. The "despatch of the 10th instant" from Vice-Consul Thomas Savage to Frederick W. Seward gave further evidence of complicity in the sale of Negroes captured by Don José Augustin Arguëlles, and maintained that the articles in the New York *World* and *Tribune* of May 13 stating that Arguëlles was arrested because of his opposition to the slave trade, were without foundation.

To Edwin M. Stanton[1]

Hon. Sec. of War.   Executive Mansion,

Dear Sir.   Washington, June 18. 1864.

Hon. L. Anderson and Judge Williams of Ky. are here urging, first, that assessments, for some time suspended in West Ky, be again put in operation; and secondly, that Gen. E. A. Paine be assigned to command them. Do both these things for them unless you know some reason to the contrary. I personally know Gen. Paine to be a good true man, having a West-Point education; but I do not know much as to his Military ability. Yours truly   A. LINCOLN

1 ALS-P, ISLA.
2 Rufus K. Williams, Mayfield, Kentucky, of the Kentucky Court of Appeals.

To Cornelius A. Walborn[1]

C. A. Walborn   Washington,

Post-Master   Philadelphia   June 18. 1864

Please come and see me in the next day or two.   A. LINCOLN

1 ALS, DNA WR RG 107, Presidential Telegrams, I, 77. See Lincoln's memorandum of his interview with Walborn, June 20, *infra*. The New York *Tribune* on June 17 printed a Washington dispatch of June 16, stating: "The Postmaster-General has instructed Postmaster Walborn of Philadelphia to use his official influence to prevent the renomination of Judge Kelley. The fact is creating a feeling of deep resentment among the administration members of the House. Mr. Lincoln . . . will not permit his patronage to be used to destroy his stanchest friends." Walborn's denial appeared in the *Tribune* the next day: "The special dispatch of your Washington correspondent in this day's paper is not correct. Postmaster-General Blair has never instructed, requested, or advised me as to the political future of Judge Kelley.   C. A. WALBORN, Postmaster."

On June 19, Judge William D. Kelley wrote Lincoln:
"Post Master Walborn publishes a denial of the allegation made by the Tribune's correspondent, and affirmed by me.
"Mr. John Inslow and Mr. Samuel Daniels will swear that he told them that he acted in obedience to the wishes of Mr. Blair. I withhold the names of other witnesses for the present, because he can as Post Master punish them for telling the truth. Should you wish me to meet Mr. W. in your presence I will do so." (DLC-RTL).

To Gideon Welles[1]

Hon. Sec. of Navy   Executive Mansion,
My dear Sir: Washington, June 18. 1864.

It seems that my old friend C. B. Denio, is in some trouble, pecuniarily, in consequence of not being allowed expences, and perhaps pay, on coming here. I feel confident he has not meant wrong, and I shall be glad for you to do the best for him you can, consistently with law & the good of the service. Yours truly

A. LINCOLN

[1] ALS, IHi. On August 5, 1864, Cyrenius B. Denio wrote Lincoln from Chicago:

"As you will see by the heading of this letter I am not on the Pacific Coast, but here on my old stomping ground.

"After I saw you in June I remained for some days trying to do something with Sec Wells by which I could in some way be reimbursed for the large outlay of money in coming to the Federal City to lay my matters before the Department. But while Mr Wells seemed disposed to do all he *could* for me without setting a 'dangerous precedent,' still I thought that certain influences were brought to bear upon him that would prevent him from doing as I thought right, and wrote him a letter on the 24th of June tendering him my resignation, and in a few moments called upon him for an acceptance of my resignation in writing, and at his request withdrew it and agreed to return to San Francisco, but was taken sick in Chicago and could not return. As soon as able I telegraphed to Sec. Wells for permission to proceed there and attend investigation on those charges and was by him instructed to remain as it was 'too late,' and advised to 'wait.' I have since written to the Secretary and enclosed to him some additional Testimony as to the wrongs that are being perpetrated by men on the Navy Yard at Mare Island, and really think when the matter is all looked at that I will receive orders to return to the Yard and resume my duties as Master Mason. I do not know but I was mistaken in trying to be *honest* but I do not yet believe it. . . .

"I feel in this matter as if my *honor* was at stake. I owe it to myself, & to my country to be reinstated with the power to live an honest man, and still be *safe* in my position! For I tell you Mr Lincoln a man who will not steal when he has a chance from his Government loses *caste* on that Navy Yard as things are now. Thus far I have said nothing to any one about my wrongs on the Pacific Coast nor do I propose to yet, but I *must* have them righted if I wait until the 1st of Dec. when Congress assembles. . . ." (DLC-RTL).

To Mary Todd Lincoln[1]

Mrs. A. Lincoln.   Executive Mansion, Washington,
Fifth Avenue Hotel   N.Y.   June 19, 1864.

Tad arrived safely, and all well.   A. LINCOLN

[1] ALS, DNA WR RG 107, Presidential Telegrams, I, 78. After attending the Sanitary Fair at Philadelphia on June 16, "Tad" Lincoln had accompanied his mother to New York.

To John Brough and Samuel P. Heintzelman[1]

Gov. Brough   Executive Mansion,
Gen. Heintzelman.   Washington, June 20, 1864.

Both of you have official responsibility as to the U.S. Military in Ohio, and generally—one, in organizing and furnishing, the other in directing, commanding, and forwarding. Consult together freely, watch Vallandigham and others closely, and, upon discovering any palpable injury, or iminent danger to the Military, proceeding from him, them, or any of them, arrest all implicated. Otherwise do not arrest without further order; meanwhile report the signs to me from time to time. Yours truly   A. Lincoln

[1] ALS, DLC-RTL. The envelope containing this letter is endorsed by Lincoln, "Brough & Heintzelman—Not sent."

Memorandum of Interview with Cornelius A. Walborn[1]

June 20, 1864

What I said to Post-Master of Philadelphia on this day—June 20. 1864.

Complaint is made to me that you are using your official power to defeat Judge Kelly's renomination to Congress. I am well satisfied with Judge Kelly as an M.C. and I do not know that the man who might supplant him would be as satisfactory; but the correct principle, I think, is that all our friends should have absolute freedom of choice among our friends. My wish therefore is that you will do just as you think fit with your own suffrage in the case, and not constrain any of your subordinates to do other than as he thinks fit with his. This is precisely the rule I inculcated, and adhered to on my part, when a certain other nomination, now recently made, was being canvassed for.

[1] AD, DLC-RTL. See Lincoln to Walborn, June 18, *supra*, and to McMichael, August 5, *infra*.

To Edwin D. Morgan[1]

Private

Hon. E. D. Morgan   Executive Mansion,
My dear Sir   Washington, June 20, 1864.

I can not longer delay the Montana appointments, and I find I can not appoint our friend Leslie without greater difficulty than we knew of when I saw you. I hope it may be cleared away for something yet to come. I will explain when I next see you. Yours truly   A. LINCOLN.

[1] ALS, N. See Lincoln's communications to Bates and Seward, May 21, *supra*. Leslie has not been identified.

To William H. Seward[1]

If no reason is known to the contrary I shall be pleased to comply with the within request.   A. LINCOLN
June 20. 1864

[1] AES, DNA FS RG 59, Appointments, Box 246. Lincoln's endorsement is written on a letter signed by Ebon C. Ingersoll and sixteen others, June 14, 1864, recommending appointment of John N. Camp of Illinois, as consul at Kingston, Jamaica. Camp was not appointed.

To Morton S. Wilkinson[1]

Private

Hon. M. S. Wilkinson   Executive Mansion,
My dear Sir: Washington, June 20, 1864.

I can not longer delay the Montana appointments; and it is with great regret, on your account, that I have thought fit to send the name of Judge Edgerton[2] for Governor. I could not do otherwise without much greater difficulty to myself, and I beg you to be assured that it is a great pain to me to know that it is disagreeable to you. Do not, for a moment suppose that this note is intended to constrain you to support the nomination. Yours truly

A. LINCOLN

[1] ALS-P, ISLA. This letter is misdated June 30, 1864, in Hertz (II, 934-35). See Lincoln's communications to Bates and Seward, May 21, *supra*.
[2] Chief Justice Sidney Edgerton of Idaho Territory.

To the Senate[1]

To the Senate of the United States: June 21, 1864

I herewith communicate to the Senate, for its constitutional action thereon, the articles of agreement and convention made and concluded at the city of Washington on the 15th instant, between the United States and the Delaware Indians of Kansas, referred to in the accompanying communication of the present date from the Secretary of the Interior.   ABRAHAM LINCOLN.

Executive Mansion,
June 21, 1864.

[1] *Executive Journal*, XIII, 597. The treaty was finally rejected by the Senate on May 4, 1866.

Endorsement Concerning Appointment
of Delos Lake[1]

[c. June 22, 1864]

Mr. Campbell says that Judge Field, and Senator Conness are in favor of appointing Mr. Lake Attorney for California.

[1] AE, DLC-RTL. Lincoln's endorsement is written on a letter of Delos Lake to Montgomery Blair, San Francisco, June 22, 1864, reporting that "Judge [Stephen J.] Field . . . telegraphed Mr [John] Conness thus 'The person named by Campbell will be highly acceptable.'" "Campbell" was possibly Lincoln's old acquaintance Thompson Campbell, formerly of Illinois and at this time a member of the California legislature. See Lincoln to Washburne, October 26, 1863, *supra*.

On January 17, 1865, Lincoln nominated Delos Lake as U.S. attorney for Northern California, and the Senate confirmed the appointment on February 14, 1865.

To Edward Bates[1]

Hon Attorney General
Sir:

Executive Mansion,
Washington, June 24th. 1864.

By authority of the Constitution, and moved thereto by the fourth section of the act of Congress entitled "An act making appropriations for the support of the Army for the year ending the thirtieth of June, Eighteen hundred and sixty five, and for other purposes," approved, June 15th. 1864, I require your opinion in writing as to what pay, bounty, and clothing are allowed by law to persons of color who were free on the 19th. day of April, 1861, and who have been enlisted and mustered into the military service of the United States between the month of December, 1862 and the 16th. of June 1864.

Please answer as you would do, on my requirement, if the Act of June 15th. 1864 had not been passed; and I will so use your opinion as to satisfy that act. Your obt Servt   A. LINCOLN.

[1] Copy, DLC-RTL. On June 17, 1864, Stanton had written Bates as follows: "This Department has been informed that one or more regiments of colored persons who were free on the 19th day of April, 1861, have been enlisted and mustered into the military service of the United States, between . . . December 1862 and the 15th of June 1864, and are now in that service. The Fourth section of the act . . . approved June 15th 1864, provides that all persons of the class above mentioned, shall receive the pay bounty and clothing, allowed to such persons by the laws existing at the time of their enlistment, and the Attorney General of the United States is authorized to determine any question of law arising under this provision. A question has arisen under the aforesaid provision, in reference to what pay bounty and clothing are allowed by law to persons of color who were free on the 19th day of April 1861, and who have been enlisted. . . . I therefore respectfully and pursuant to the aforesaid provision of the Act of Congress, submit this question to your determination. . . ." (DLC-RTL).

On June 24 Stanton submitted to Lincoln, "a paper returned from the Attorney General's Office, purporting to be a reply, but having no signature. It is of great importance that the points submitted by me for the determination of the Attorney General, pursuant to the Act of Congress, should be speedily decided; and I would therefore respectfully ask that, inasmuch as the efforts of this Department have failed, you would procure from the Attorney General a determination of the question submitted in my letter, in order that the Department may proceed to make payment to the colored troops without delay, in accordance with such determination. . . ." (*Ibid.*).

The unsigned "paper," dated June 20, 1864, reads in part:

"I had the honor to receive your letter of the 17th . . . with a copy of the act of Congress of June 15, 1864, and a request for my opinion upon a question '*in reference to* what pay, bounty and clothing is allowed by law, to persons of color who were free on the 19th day of April 1861, and who have been enlisted and mustered into the military service of the United States, between the month of December 1862, and the 16th of June 1864.'

"I confess myself at a loss to know (so as to answer satisfactorily to myself) the precise meaning of the question, or the precise point upon which a doubt exists in your Department, as to the amount of pay, bounty and clothing of the persons indicated, under laws passed prior to the 15th of June 1864.

"I am the more induced to desire a specific statement of the question, because the 4th section of the act (of June 15 1864) to which you refer, is very peculiar in its phraseology. It does not give, or purport to give to the class of troops indicated, anything whatever, to which they had not a perfect right, by prior laws. It provides only that they shall 'be entitled to receive the pay, bounty and clothing allowed to such persons *by the laws existing at the time of their enlistment.*' It seems to me therefore that any question as to the amount of pay, bounty and clothing to be paid to such troops, must, of necessity arise under the previous laws, and not under the act of June 15, 1864. And I should be ready to comply, with alacrity, with your request for an opinion upon any specific question of law, arising under any of those prior acts.

"But the said 4th section is very peculiar, in another respect. It does not require the Attorney General to give any *opinion* to any officer . . . . it goes far beyond that. It purports to make him a final judge of the matter, by enacting that 'the Attorney General . . . is *hereby authorized to determine* any question of law arising under *this provision*'. . . . And this is clearly a new and special delegation of power, to hear and determine questions of law, without and beyond the general duty of the Attorney General to give opinion and advice. . . .

"I make these suggestions . . . upon the supposition that there may be questions arising under the acts prior to that of June 15, 1864 . . . if so, you will be pleased to direct the question to be so stated as to enable me to give direct and specific answers, which I will endeavor to do, with all convenient speed. . . ." (*Ibid.*).

On July 14, Bates answered Lincoln's letter of June 24:

"By your communication of the 24th ultimo you require my opinion in writing as to what amounts of pay, bounty, and clothing are allowed by law to persons of color who were free on the 19th day of April, 1861, and who have been enlisted and mustered into the military service . . . between . . . December, 1862, and the 16th of June, 1864. I suppose that whatever doubt or difficulty may exist . . . has mainly its origin in the . . . provisions of the act of July 17, 1862, chapter 201. . . . The twelfth section of that statute provides: 'That the President be . . . authorized to receive into the service of the United States, for the purpose of constructing intrenchments or performing camp service, or any other labor, or any military or naval service for which they may be found competent, persons of African descent. . . .' The fifteenth section . . . enacts that 'persons . . . who, under this law, shall be employed, shall receive $10 per month and one ration, $3 of which monthly pay may be in clothing.' The first and main question, therefore, is whether the persons of color referred to in your letter . . . are . . . employed under the statute of July 17, 1862. . . . If they are not thus employed, their compensation should not be governed . . . by . . . the fifteenth section of that statute. . . .

"Now, I think that it is clear . . . that those persons of color who have voluntarily enlisted and have been mustered into our military service . . . who have done and are doing in the field and in garrison the duty and service of soldiers of the United States, are not persons . . . employed under the statute to which I have referred. . . .

"I give it to you unhesitatingly as my opinion that the same pay, bounty, and clothing are allowed by law to the persons of color referred to in your communication . . . as are, by the laws existing at the times of the enlistments of said persons, authorized and provided for and allowed to other soldiers in the volunteer services of the United States of like arms of the service. . . ." (OR, III, IV, 490-93).

With this letter as printed in the *Official Records* is Stanton's endorsement referring it to the adjutant general with instructions to direct the paymaster general to pay colored troops in accordance with Bates' opinion.

To Mary Todd Lincoln[1]

Mrs. A. Lincoln   Executive Mansion,
Boston, Mass.   Washington, June 24, 1864.

All well, and very warm. Tad and I have been to Gen. Grant's army. Returned yesterday safe and sound.   A. LINCOLN

[1] ALS, DNA WR RG 107, Presidential Telegrams, I, 80. Under date of June 26, 1864, Orville H. Browning's *Diary* records: "During the past week, the President visited Grants army. . . . He told me last night that Grant said, when he left him, that 'you Mr President, need be under no apprehension. You will never hear of me farther from Richmond than now, till I have taken it. I am just as sure of going into Richmond as I am of any future event. It may take a long summer day, but I will go in.' The President added that Grant told him that in the Wilderness he had completely routed Lee, but did not know it at the time— and that had he known it, he could have ruined him, and ended the campaign."

Pass for Mrs. M. Davis Parks[1]

Allow this lady, Mrs. Parks, with her friend, Mr. Tallmadge, to see her two sons, prisoners of war at Point Lookout.
June 24, 1864.   A. LINCOLN.

[1] Leslie J. Perry, "Appeals to Lincoln's Clemency," *The Century Magazine*, LI (December, 1895), 254. Mrs. M. Davis Parks wrote Lincoln from Charleston, South Carolina, August 22, 1864, that her older son had since died while being removed from Point Lookout to Elmira Prison, and that her younger son, Bushrod Washington Parks should be released: "Not only in my own name, but in that of Washington I make my request, as the Grand-son of Harriet Washington the much loved niece and adopted daughter of the great Patriot . . . I feel he should have the consideration of the representative of the people of this union. . . ." (DLC-RTL).

Mr. Tallmadge has not been identified.

To William S. Rosecrans[1]

Major Gen. Rosecrans   Washington,
St. Louis, Mo   June 24. 1864
  Complaint is made to me that Gen. Brown does not do his best to
suppress bushwhackers. Please ascertain and report to me.

                                              A. LINCOLN

[1] ALS, DNA WR RG 107, Presidential Telegrams, I, 81. Brigadier General
Egbert B. Brown was in command of the District of Central Missouri. On August
5, Rosecrans replied to Lincoln's telegram: "I have carefully examined into the
administration and conduct of General E. B. Brown . . . and . . . I conclude.
. . . That General Brown is a zealous, honest, earnest officer, diligent and pains-
taking, but not remarkably quick of apprehension, not without some bias against
all active innovations on the old order of things. But his strong sense of justice
operates to check his bias and has given to his administration on the whole the
character of a success for the cause of the Nation. . . . I have no one but General Pleasonton to take his place. . . . Should Your Excellency conclude to send
me an able general officer, I could give General Brown the presidency of a general court-martial which we have constantly in session here. General Brown's
wishes and his health would both favor this change." (OR, I, XLI, II, 570-71).

To the Senate[1]

To the Senate of the United States: June 24, 1864
  I herewith lay before the Senate, for its constitutional action
thereon, a treaty made and concluded at the city of Washington
on the 11th day of June, 1864, by and between Wm. P. Dole, Commissioner of Indian Affairs, and Hiram W. Farnsworth, United
States Indian agent, commissioners on the part of the United States,
and the chiefs and head men of the Kansas tribe of Indians.
  A communication of the Secretary of the Interior of the 18th
inst., with a copy of report of Commissioner of Indian Affairs of
the 13th inst., accompany the treaty.   ABRAHAM LINCOLN.
  Executive Mansion,
  Washington, June 24, 1864.

[1] *Executive Journal*, XIII, 597. The treaty was referred to the committee on
Indian affairs. No record has been found of its ratification.

To William H. Seward[1]

Hon. Sec. of State, please see and hear the bearer, Mr. Appleby.
  June 24. 1864   A. LINCOLN

[1] AES, DNA FS RG 59, Appointments, Box 217. Lincoln's endorsement is
written on a letter from George F. Appleby, Washington, June 24, 1864, asking
appointment "to the consular school which has been established by Congress."
An act approved June 20, 1864 (Section 2) authorized the president to appoint
thirteen consular clerks over eighteen years of age.

To Timothy P. Andrews[1]

Executive Mansion

Paymaster General   Washington June 25. 1864

I am so frequently called on by persons in behalf of Paymasters, who have already served a long time in the South, for leave to come North, as to induce me to inquire whether there might not, without much inconvenience be a rule of exchanges which would be fair to all, and keep none so long in an uncongenial climate as to much endanger health. Yours truly   A LINCOLN

[1] Copy, DLC-RTL. On June 27, Paymaster General Andrews wrote Secretary Stanton: "I have the honor to submit herewith a copy of a communication [as above] from His Excellency, the President, and to reply. . . . That we are constantly, from time to time, as the state of the service will permit, carrying out substantially, in advance, the measures the President suggests, although much opposed in doing so by the influential friends of some of the officers ordered to the South, to relieve others. . . . Indeed we have already done so much in advance of . . . the President's ideas, that I fear he will soon have urgent and loud complaints . . . from the friends of those lately ordered South, as our difficulty is to get anyone to go to the Southern Stations. . . ." (DLC-RTL). See further Lincoln to Andrews, July 7, *infra*.

To the Senate[1]

To the Senate of the United States   June 25, 1864

I have the honor to acknowledge the receipt of the Resolution of the Senate dated the 7th of June, requesting me to return to the Senate the Resolution advising and consenting to the appointment of John H Goddard to be Justice of the Peace in and for the county of Washington and District of Columbia; and to state that on the 19th of May last the Resolution mentioned was sent to the Department of State, and a commission in accordance therewith was issued to Mr. Goddard on the same day, the appointment being thus perfected, and the Resolution becoming a part of the permanent records of the Department of State.

[Executive Mansion,]   [ABRAHAM LINCOLN.]
[25 June, 1864.]

[1] Df, DLC-RTL. As cataloged in the Lincoln Papers, this undated communication is incorrectly supplied with the date "June 12, 1864." Bracketed date and signature above are from the printing in the Senate *Executive Journal*, XIII, 625. In reply to Nicolay's request for return of the resolution of confirmation, J. Hubley Ashton, assistant attorney general, wrote on June 11, 1864, that it was impossible to return the resolution for reason indicated in Seward's letter to Bates of the same date, as follows: "I have the honor to acknowledge the receipt of your letter of the 10th inst. with its accompaniments, requesting the return of the Resolution of the Senate of the 18th ulto: confirming the appointment of John H. Goddard as Justice of the Peace for the County of Washington, in the

District of Columbia. The Resolution . . . was received at this Department on the 19th ulto: a commission was issued to Mr. Goddard on that day, and the Resolution thus became a part of the Records of this Department and cannot be withdrawn. A copy of it is enclosed. . . ." (DLC-RTL).

To Gustavus M. Bascom[1]

Col. Bascom
A. A. General
Knoxville, Tenn.

Washington DC.
June 27. 1864

Please suspend sale of the property of Rogers & Co until further order.　　　　　　　　　　　　　　　　　　　　　　A. LINCOLN

[1] ALS, DNA WR RG 107, Presidential Telegrams, I, 82. Richard M. Corwine, attorney for William Rodgers & Company, wrote Lincoln on June 27, 1864: "I returned from Baltimore this morning, that I might lay before you the enclosed dispatch from my clients—and to respectfully request you to dispatch Col Bascom A. A. Gen. Knoxville, to cause a suspension of all proceedings with respect to their goods until you have considered the application of Rogers & Co. for relief. . . ." (DLC-RTL). The enclosed telegram, dated June 25, reads as follows: "Heard that Schofield has ordered a sale of our goods Please stop this proceedings at once." (*Ibid.*).

To William C. Bryant[1]

Hon. W. C. Bryant
My dear Sir.

Executive Mansion,
Washington, June 27. 1864.

Yours of the 25th. has just been handed me by the Secretary of the Navy. The tone of the letter, rather than any direct statement in it, impresses me as a complaint that Mr. Henderson should have been removed from office, and arrested; coupled with the single suggestion that he be restored, if he shall establish his innocence. I know absolutely nothing of the case except as follows—Monday last Mr. Welles came to me with the letter of dismissal already written, saying he thought proper to show it to me before sending it. I asked him the charges, which he stated in a general way. With as much emphasis as I could I said *"Are you entirely certain of his guilt"* He answered that he was, to which I replied "Then send the letter." Whether Mr. Henderson was a supporter of my second nomination I neither knew, or enquired, or even thought of. I shall be very glad indeed if he shall, as you anticipate, establish his innocence; or, to state it more strongly and properly, "if the government shall fail to establish his guilt." I believe however, the man[2] who made the affidavit was of as spotless reputation as Mr. Henderson, until he was arrested on what his friends insist was outrageously insufficient evidence. I know the entire city government of Washington, with many other respectable citizens, appealed to me in his behalf, as a greatly injured gentleman.

While the subject is up may I ask whether the Evening Post has not assailed me for supposed too lenient dealing with persons charged of fraud & crime? and that in cases of which the Post could know but little of the facts? I shall certainly deal as leniently with Mr. Henderson as I have felt it my duty to deal with others, notwithstanding any newspaper assaults. Your Obt. Servt.

A. LINCOLN

¹ ADfS, DLC-RTL; LS, in custody of Conrad G. Goddard, Roslyn, Long Island, New York. Bryant's letter of June 25, 1864, states in part:

"Mr. Isaac Henderson, who acts as publisher of the Evening Post, has been summarily dismissed from the office of Navy Agent, which he has held for the last three years, and at the same time, arrested by the officials of your administration, on a charge . . . of infamous frauds on the government. . . .

"I am satisfied that Mr. Henderson will establish his entire innocence at the examination, and you will allow me frankly but respectfully to say, that I should not bear towards you the esteem that I do, did I not feel equally confident, that, in that event, your sense of justice will lead you to reinstate him in office without delay. . . . I cannot bear that the least shadow of the suspicion of corrupt or even questionable practices should rest upon any person, in any way connected with the Evening Post.

"What makes these severe proceedings still more unkind is, that Mr. Henderson has always zealously supported your administration, that he has used all his influence in its favor, and that he desired and has approved your second nomination. Of course no astonishment that he ever felt could equal his, at being so roughly treated by a government which in his mind had always been associated with the idea of fairness and equity." (DLC-RTL).

Gideon Welles' *Diary* records under date of June 27, 1864: "I have a very earnest letter to-day from William C. Bryant in behalf his partner and publisher, Henderson. It was handed to me by Mr. [Moses F.] Odell . . . inclosed was also an open letter to the President, which he wished me to deliver. Mr. O. is, like H., a prominent member of the Methodist Church. They are of opposite politics. Of course Mr. H. stimulated Mr. B. to write these letters, and, having got them, sends them through his religious associate. Mr. B. evidently believes H. innocent and injured. This is natural. Odell knows he is not. Morgan believes that both Bryant and [Parke] Godwin are participants in the plunder of Henderson. I have doubts as regards B., who is feeling very badly, and thinks there is a conspiracy in which Seward and Thurlow Weed are chiefs. I am supposed to be an instrument in their hands, and so is the President. But it so happens that neither of them knew any of the facts until the arrest of Henderson and his removal were ordered. . . ."

Bryant replied on June 30:

"I thank you for the attention you have given to my letter. It confirms my convictions of your equity and love of justice.

"You speak of having been assailed in the Evening Post. I greatly regret that any thing said of your public conduct in that journal should seem to you like an assault, or in any way the indication of hostility. It was not intended to proceed beyond the bounds of respectful criticism, such as the Evening Post, ever since I have had any thing to do with it, has always permitted itself to use tow[ard] every successive administration of the government. Nor have I done you the wrong of supposing that any freedom of remark would make you forget what was due to justice and right. . . ."   ² Joseph L. Savage.

To William Dennison and Others[1]

Executive Mansion,
Washington, June 27, 1864.

Hon. William Dennison & others, a Committee of the National Union Convention.

Gentlemen: Your letter of the 14th. Inst. formally notifying me that I have been nominated by the convention you represent for the Presidency of the United States for four years from the fourth of March next has been received. The nomination is gratefully accepted, as the resolutions of the convention, called the platform, are heartily approved.

While the resolution in regard to the supplanting of republican government upon the Western continent is fully concurred in, there might be misunderstanding were I not to say that the position of the government, in relation to the action of France in Mexico, as assumed through the State Department, and approved and indorsed by the convention, among the measures and acts of the Executive, will be faithfully maintained, so long as the state of facts shall leave that position pertinent and applicable.

I am especially gratified that the soldier and the seaman were not forgotten by the convention, as they forever must and will be remembered by the grateful country for whose salvation they devote their lives.

Thanking you for the kind and complimentary terms in which you have communicated the nomination and other proceedings of the convention, I subscribe myself Your Obt. Servt.

ABRAHAM LINCOLN

[1] ADfS, IHi; LS, owned by W. Easton Louttit, Jr., Providence, Rhode Island. The official letter of notification, written by George William Curtis and signed by members of the convention, seems to have been lost, for on June 20, 1864, John Hay telegraphed Curtis: "Your letter to the President is not yet received. Please cause a copy to be made." (ALS, DNA WR RG 107, Presidential Telegrams, I, 79). The copy dated June 14, 1864, and bearing the names of delegates to the convention was forwarded by Curtis:

"The National Union Convention which assembled in Baltimore on the 7th of June 1864 has instructed us to inform you that you were nominated with enthusiastic unanimity for the Presidency of the United States for four years from the fourth of March next.

"The resolutions of the Convention which we have already had the honor of placing in your hands, are a full and clear statement of the principles which inspired its action, and which, as we believe, the great body of Union men in the country heartily approve. Whether those resolutions express the national gratitude to our soldiers and sailors; or the national scorn of compromise with rebels and consequent dishonor; or the patriotic duty of union and success; whether they approve the proclamation of emancipation, the constitutional amendment, the employment of former slaves as union soldiers, or the solemn obligation of the Government promptly to redress the wrongs of every soldier of the union of whatever color or race; whether they declare the inviolability of the pledged faith of the nation, or offer the national hospitality to the oppressed of every land, or urge the union by railroad of the Atlantic & Pacific oceans; whether they recommend public economy & vigorous taxation, or assert the fixed popular opposition to the establishment by armed force of foreign monarchies in the immediate neighborhood of the United States, or declare that those only are worthy of official trust who approve unreservedly the views & policy indicated in the resolutions,—they were equally hailed with the heartiness of profound conviction.

"Believing with you, Sir, that this is the people's war for the maintenance of a government which you have justly described as 'of the people, by the people, for the people' we are very sure that you will be glad to know not only from the resolutions themselves, but from the singular harmony & enthusiasm with which they were adopted how warm is the popular welcome of every measure in the prosecution of the war which is as vigorous, unmistakeable & unfaltering as the national purpose itself. No right, for instance, is so precious and sacred to the American heart as that of personal liberty. Its violation is regarded with just, instant & universal jealousy. Yet in this hour of peril every faithful citizen concedes that, for the sake of national existence and the common welfare, individual liberty may, as the Constitution provides in case of rebellion, be sometimes summarily constrained, asking only with painful anxiety that, in every instance and to the least detail, that absolutely necessary power shall not be hastily or unwisely exercised.

"We believe, Sir, that the honest will of the Union men of the country was never more truly represented than in this Convention. Their purpose we believe to be the overthrow of armed rebels in the field, and the security of permanent peace and union by liberty and justice under the Constitution. That these results are to be achieved amid cruel perplexities, they are fully aware. That they are to be reached only by cordial unanimity of counsel, is undeniable. That good men may sometimes differ as to the means and the time, they know. That in the conduct of all human affairs the highest duty is to determine in the angry conflict of passion, how much good may be practically accomplished, is their sincere persuasion. They have watched your official course, therefore, with unflagging attention; and amid the bitter taunts of eager friends and the fierce denunciation of enemies; now moving too fast for some, now too slowly for others, they have seen you throughout this tremendous test patient, sagacious, faithful, just, leaning upon the heart of the great mass of the people, and satisfied to be moved by its mighty pulsations.

"It is for this reason that long before the Convention met the popular instinct had plainly indicated you as its candidate, and the Convention, therefore, merely recorded the popular will. Your character & career prove your unswerving fidelity to the cardinal principles of American Liberty and of the American Constitution. In the name of that Liberty and Constitution, Sir, we earnestly request your acceptance of this nomination; reverently commending our beloved country, and you its chief magistrate, with all its brave sons who on sea and land are faithfully defending the good old American cause of equal rights, to the blessing of Almighty God." (DLC-RTL).

To Salmon P. Chase[1]

Hon. Secretary of Treasury. Executive Mansion,
My dear Sir Washington, June 28. 1864.

Yours inclosing a blank nomination for Maunsell B. Field to be Assistant Treasurer at New-York was received yesterday. I can not,

without much embarrassment, make this appointment, principally
because of Senator Morgan's very firm opposition to it. Senator
Harris has not spoken to me on the subject, though I understand
he is not averse to the appointment of Mr. Field; nor yet to any
one of the three named by Senator Morgan, rather preferring, of
them, however, Mr. Hillhouse. Gov. Morgan tells me he has mentioned the three names to you, towit, R. M. Blatchford, Dudley S.
Gregory, and Thomas Hillhouse. It will really oblige me if you will
make choice among these three, or any other man that Senators
Morgan and Harris will be satisfied with, and send me a nomination for him. Yours truly   A. LINCOLN

1 ADfS, DLC-RTL. On June 27 Chase enclosed a letter of nomination for
Maunsell B. Field with the following:
"I respectfully submit to your consideration the name of Maunsel B. Field for
the office of Assistant Treasurer of the United States at the City of New York.
"Mr. Field was for many years the assistant of Mr. [John J.] Cisco & is fully
acquainted with the business of the office.
"For several months past he has been assistant Secretary of the Treasury.
"His personal character, intelligence & ability warrant the expectation that
he will perform the duties of the office well & acceptably
"He is recommended, also, by many of the best citizens of New York.
"A nomination accompanies this note for your signature if approved." (DLC-
RTL).
A letter of the same date from Edwin D. Morgan states: "Daniel S. Dickinson
will be very acceptable to Hon. Senator Nesmith for the Oregon appointment
and either R[ichard]. M. Blatchford   Dudley S. Gregory or Thomas Hillhouse
will be acceptable to me for the New York appointment (Cisco's vacancy) It
is in my judgment discreet, to appoint a Republican at New York at this time"
(ibid.).

To Salmon P. Chase[1]

Private   Executive Mansion
Hon. Secretary of the Treasury   Washington DC.
My dear Sir: June 28. 1864

When I received your note this forenoon suggesting a verbal
conversation in relation to the appointment of a successor to Mr.
Cisco, I hesitated because the difficulty does not, in the main part,
lie within the range of a conversation between you and me. As the
proverb goes, no man knows so well where the shoe pinches as he
who wears it. I do not think Mr. Field a very proper man for the
place, but I would trust your judgment, and forego this, were the
greater difficulty out of the way. Much as I personally like Mr.
Barney, it has been a great burden to me to retain him in his place,
when nearly all our friends in New-York, were directly or indirectly, urging his removal. Then the apointment of Judge Hogeboom
to be general Appraiser, brought me to and has ever since kept me

at, the verge of open revolt. Now, the appointment of Mr. Field would precipitate me in it, unless Senator Morgan and those feeling as he does, could be brought to concur in it. Strained as I already am at this point I do not think I can make this appointment in the direction of still greater strain.

The testimonials of Mr. Field, with your accompanying notes, were duly received, and I am now waiting to see your answer from Mr. Cisco. Yours truly   A. LINCOLN

[1] ADfS, DLC-RTL. Chase had replied immediately to Lincoln's preceding letter: "I shall be glad to have a conversation with you on the subject of the appointment of Mr. Cisco's successor at any time & place convenient to you." (DLC-RTL).

Upon receiving Lincoln's reply, Chase answered: "I have telegraphed Mr. Cisco begging him to withdraw his resignation and serve at least another quarter. If he declines to do so I must repeat that, in my judgment, the public interests require the appointment of Mr. Field. One of the gentlemen named by Senator Morgan is over seventy & the other, I think, over sixty years old, and neither has any practical knowledge of the duties of the office. They are both estimable gentlemen and were the times peaceful & the business of the office comparatively small & regular, I should gladly acquiesce in the appointment of either. But my duty to you & to the country does not permit it now. I have already after conference with Senator Morgan offered, with his concurrence, my recommendation to your consideration to three gentlemen, each admirably qualified, but each has declined. I now recommend Mr. Field because among those who will take the place I think him best qualified and only for that reason. But, this, especially in these times, should be a controlling reason. . . ." (*Ibid.*).

John J. Cisco telegraphed Chase on the same day: "I cannot resist your appeal & therefore consent to the temporary withdrawal of my resignation" (*ibid.*).

On June 29, Chase wrote Lincoln enclosing Cisco's telegram and his own letter of resignation, with the following note:

"I have just received your note and have read it with great attention. I was not aware of the extent of the embarrassment to which you refer. In recommendations for office I have sincerely sought to get the best men for the places to be filled without reference to any other classification than supporters and opponents of your administration. Of the latter I have recommended none; among the former I have desired to know no distinction except degrees of fitness.

"The withdrawal of Mr. Cisco's resignation, which I enclose, relieves the present difficulty; but I cannot help feeling that my position here is not altogether agreeable to you; and it is certainly too full of embarrassment and difficulty and painful responsibility to allow in me the least desire to retain it.

"I think it my duty therefore to enclose to you my resignation. I shall regard it as a real relief if you think proper to accept it; and will most cheerfully tender to my successor any aid he may find useful in entering upon his duties." (*Ibid.*)

See further Lincoln's letter to Chase accepting his resignation, June 30, *infra*. During the recess of the Senate, Henry H. Van Dyck was appointed to succeed Cisco and was confirmed by the Senate on February 15, 1865.

To Ward H. Lamon[1]

[c. June 28, 1864]

I regret this, but I can not veto a Bill of this character.

                    A. LINCOLN

1 AES, CSmH. Lincoln's endorsement is written at bottom of the following note from Lamon:

"Senate Bill No. 296, has passed both Houses of Congress. The main feature in it is Mr. [James W.] Grimes' amendment—reducing the fees for the Marshal of the Dist. of Col. one half—for services of warrants, capiases, writs &c—and discriminating against him—every other Marshal in the U.S. being allowed double his fees for same service.

"If this bill is signed, the Marshal cant make enough to pay clerk hire &c for the office—much less any compensation for himself."

An act introduced by Senator Lyman Trumbull on June 2, 1864, which passed both houses and was approved by Lincoln on June 27, 1864, provided that fees of the U.S. marshal, attorney, and clerk in the District of Columbia should be the same as those in other U.S. District Courts as provided by the act of February 26, 1853.

To the Senate[1]

To, The Senate of the United States.　　　　　June 28, 1864

In compliance with the Resolution of the Senate of the 16th. of last month, requesting information in regard to the maltreatment of passengers and seamen on board ships plying between New York and Aspinwall, I transmit a Report from the Secretary of State to whom the Resolution was referred. ABRAHAM LINCOLN

Washington,
June 28. 1864.

1 DS, owned by Justin R. Turner, Hollywood, California. This communication appears in the *Senate Journal* (p. 683) without the enclosures, and efforts to locate them have been unsuccessful. On June 29 Senator Conness moved that Lincoln's message be printed and the motion was referred to the committee on printing (*Senate Journal*, p. 683). No further reference has been found. The resolution of May 16 requested "any correspondence received from the United States consuls at Panama and Aspinwall, New Granada, in relation to abuse and maltreatment of passengers, seamen, firemen, &c., on board steamships plying between New York and Aspinwall."

To the Senate[1]

To the Senate of the United States.　　　　　June 28, 1864

In answer to the Resolution of the Senate of the 24th. instant, requesting information in regard to the alleged enlistment in foreign countries of recruits for the military and naval service of the United States, I transmit Reports from the Secretaries of State, of War and of the Navy, respectively. ABRAHAM LINCOLN

Washington,
28th. June, 1864.

1 DS, DNA RG 46, Senate 38A F2. The reports of Stanton and Welles, June 27, 1864, stated that no authority had been given for enlisting men in Ireland or

Canada as charged. Seward's report of June 25, stated that if any recruits had
been enlisted in Ireland or Canada, the recruiting had not been done by U.S.
citizens, but that many persons of foreign birth, voluntary immigrants to the
U.S., had enlisted in the Army and Navy.

To George F. Shepley[1]

Officer in Command at   Executive Mansion,
Fort-Monroe, Va   Washington, June 28, 1864.

Is there a man by the name of Amos Tenney in your command,
under sentence for desertion? and if so suspend execution, and send
me the record.   A. LINCOLN

[1] ALS, DNA WR RG 107, Presidential Telegrams, I, 83. General Shepley in
command of the District of Eastern Virginia, replied on the same day: "No
such man as Amos Tenney is under sentence in this command for desertion.
"Your despatch has been forwarded to Maj Genl Butler in the field" (DLC-
RTL).

Endorsement Concerning Cyrus Hamlin[1]

I would like for this appointment to be made if it consistently can
be.   A. LINCOLN
June 29, 1864

[1] AES, owned by Dale Carnegie, New York City. Lincoln's endorsement has
been removed from attendant papers, but "Col. Cyrus Hamlin" appears in another handwriting above the endorsement. Colonel Cyrus Hamlin of the Eighti-
eth U.S. Colored Infantry was appointed brigadier general of Volunteers on
December 13, 1864.

To Ulysses S. Grant[1]

Lieut. Gen. Grant   Executive Mansion,
City Point.   Washington, June 29. 1864.

Dr. Worster wishes to visit you with a view of getting your permission to introduce into the Army "Harmon's Sandal Sock" Shall
I give him a pass for that object?   A. LINCOLN

[1] ALS, DNA WR RG 107, Presidential Telegrams, I, 84. No reply has been
discovered. Harmon's sandal-socks were of "wash leather," designed to be worn
with another pair of ordinary socks. On April 13, 1864, J. Rutherford Worster
sent Lincoln a pair of the socks together with numerous testimonials and requested: "Mr. President, if you will please endorse me to Genl. Grant . . .
with your views of the utility of the sandal, for the preservation of the feet, on
long marches . . . and the prevention of straggling &c. I will put a pair on
the Genl. as I am going out to the front this evening. . . ." (DLC-RTL).

To Mary Todd Lincoln[1]

Mrs. A Lincoln   Washington, D.C.

New-York.   June 29. 1864

All well. Tom is moving things out.   A. LINCOLN

[1] ALS, DNA WR RG 107, Presidential Telegrams, I, 85. "Tom" was probably either Thomas H. Cross, furnace man at the Executive Mansion; Thomas Cross, doorkeeper; or Thomas Stackpole, watchman—engaged in moving the Lincolns' personal effects out to the Soldiers' Home for the summer.

To the Senate[1]

To the Senate   Executive Mansion,

of the United States.   Washington, D.C., June 29, 1864.

I herewith communicate a report from the Secretary of the Interior, in response to the resolution of the Senate of the 25th. of March last, from which it will be perceived that all the official information possessed by the Department on the subject of colonization has already been communicated to the Senate.

ABRAHAM LINCOLN

[1] DS, DLC-RTL. Neither this communication nor Usher's report was ever sent to the Senate. Usher's report of June 29 is as follows:

"On the 25th of March last the Senate passed a resolution in the following words, viz: 'Resolved, That the President of the United States be requested to furnish to the Senate the Report of the Commissioner of Emigration for 1863, with his account of the existing contracts and other necessary information on the question of emigration.' This resolution you referred to this Department, with a request for the report therein called for. In reply, I have the honor to state, that I am not aware of the existence of any such office as that of 'Commissioner of Emigration,' and consequently that no such official document as that alluded to by the resolution of the Senate has been or could have been made.

"On the 11th of March last, I had the honor to submit to you a report, in answer to a resolution adopted by the Senate, in January of the present year, requesting you to inform the Senate, if not in your opinion incompatible with the public interest, whether any portion of the appropriations for the colonization of persons of African descent, residing in the District of Columbia, in Hayti, Liberia, and so forth, had been expended, and what steps had been taken to execute the provisions of the Acts of Congress relating to colonization. In consequence of the importance which had been attached to the subject, I availed myself of that occasion to lay before you the entire correspondence of the Department on the subject of colonization, together with copies of all the contracts or agreements which had been made, and an abstract of the expenditures which had been incurred up to that date. That report was promptly communicated by you to the Senate, but has not yet been printed, so far as I am informed. No further agreements have since been entered into, and no further efforts made, looking to the colonization of persons of African descent beyond the limits of the United States; so that the Senate, by the official report from this Department, of March 11, 1864, before referred to, is in possession of all the official documents and information on the subject, which it is in the power of this Department to communicate." (DLC-RTL).

Usher's report of March 11, 1864, has not been found. See Lincoln's communication to the Senate of March 12, *supra.*

To Edwin M. Stanton[1]

Hon. Sec. of War
My dear Sir

Executive Mansion,
Washington, June 29, 1864.

Hon. J. O. Norton has innocently got into some trouble in telling Jonathan R. Webber, of Ills. that he would be appointed a Commissary of Subsistence. I wish the appointment made so soon as it can be, consistently, in order to relieve our friend Norton. Yours truly

A. LINCOLN

[1] ALS, IHi. Jonathan R. Webber was appointed captain and commissary of subsistence of Volunteers, July 2, 1864.

To Frederick Steele[1]

Executive Mansion, Washington,
Major General Steele
June 29, 1864

I understand that Congress declines to admit to seats the persons sent as Senators and Representatives from Arkansas. These persons apprehend that, in consequence, you may not support the new State Government then as you otherwise would. My wish is that you give that government and the people there, the same support and protection that you would if the members had been admitted, because in no event, nor in any view of the case, can this do any harm, while it will be the best you can do towards suppressing the rebellion   Yours truly   A LINCOLN

[1] ALS, owned by Frederick M. Dearborn, New York City; copy, DLC-RTL. On July 23, 1864, Governor Isaac Murphy wrote Lincoln: "I have received a copy of your Excellencys letter to Gen Steele. In it you express the wish that he would give the same protection to the new state government of Ark. that he would have done had the persons sent as senators and representatives been received as such. It came in good time. . . ." (DLC-RTL).

Authorization for George Harrington[1]

Executive Mansion   June 30th 1864.

There being a vacancy in the office of Secretary of the Treasury occasioned by the resignation of the Hon Salmon P. Chase and its acceptance, George Harrington Esq Assistant Secretary is authorized to perform all and singular the duties of Secretary of the

[418]

Treasury until a successor to Mr Chase shall be commissioned and qualified, or until further order.   ABRAHAM LINCOLN

¹ DS, CSmH. See Lincoln to Chase, *infra.*

To Salmon P. Chase¹

Hon. Salmon P. Chase   Executive Mansion,
My dear Sir.   Washington, June 30, 1864.

Your resignation of the office of Secretary of the Treasury, sent me yesterday, is accepted. Of all I have said in commendation of your ability and fidelity, I have nothing to unsay; and yet you and I have reached a point of mutual embarrassment in our official relation which it seems can not be overcome, or longer sustained, consistently with the public service. Your Obt. Servt.   A. LINCOLN

¹ ADfS, DLC-RTL. See Lincoln's communications to Chase, June 28, *supra.*

Endorsement¹

I assent.   A. LINCOLN
June 30. 1864.

¹ AES-F, *America*, February 11, 1928, p. 433. Lincoln's endorsement is written on a note of Benjamin B. French to Gabriel Coakley, June 27, 1864, granting use of the grounds between the White House and War Department to St. Matthew's Colored Sunday School for an anniversary celebration on July 4, "provided the assent of the President is given."

Pass for Edward C. Carrington and Mother¹

June 30, 1864

Allow Edward C. Carrington, District Attorney of this District, to bring his Mother with him from Harper's Ferry to his own house in Washington   A. LINCOLN
June 30. 1864

¹ ADS, ORB.

Pass for Annie P. Shepherd¹

June 30, 1864

Allow this young lady, Miss Annie P. Shepherd to pass with Pay-Master Carpenter² to Point Lookout, & see there, Charles Skinner, Thomas Gold, and Frank Shepherd, prisoners at that place.
June 30. 1864   A. LINCOLN

[419]

¹ ADS, ORB.

² Probably George F. Carpenter of Ohio, appointed additional paymaster of Volunteers on February 19, 1863.

To David Tod¹

Hon. David Tod   Executive Mansion
Youngstown, Ohio.   Washington, D.C. June 30. 1864

I have nominated you to be Secretary of the Treasury in place of Gov. Chase who has resigned. Please come without a moment's delay.   A. LINCOLN

¹ ALS, DNA WR RG 107, Presidential Telegrams, I, 86. David Tod telegraphed on the same day, "The condition of my health forbids the acceptance of the distinguished position you offer me. Grateful for this mark of your confidence I am sincerely. . . ." (DLC-RTL). On July 1 Lincoln sent his nomination of William P. Fessenden to the Senate and it was confirmed immediately. Under date of July 1, 1864, Welles' *Diary* records the puzzlement of the Secretary of the Navy: ". . . the President's course is a riddle. Tod is a hard-money man; Fessenden has pressed through Congress the paper system of Chase. One day Tod is selected; on his refusal, Fessenden is brought forward. This can in no other way be reconciled than in the President's want of knowledge of the subject. His attention never has been given to the finances. He seems not aware that within twenty-four hours he has swung to opposite extremes. . . ." For an extensive narrative of events in connection with Chase's resignation and the appointment of his successor, see Nicolay and Hay, *Abraham Lincoln: A History*, IX, 79-103.

Memorandum: Louisiana Appointments¹

Executive Mansion,
Washington, [c. July] , 186[4]

Collector–	Dennison	Marshal–	Bullitt
Surveyor–	Tucker–	Judge–	Durell
Naval Officer–	Welles	Dis. Atty.	Peabody–
Sup. Spec A.	Flanders–	Int. Rev	Smith
Post-Master	Parker–	Do Do	Murphy.
Sub. Treas.	May–		

¹ AD, DLC-RTL. As cataloged in the Lincoln Papers, this memorandum is incorrectly assigned the date "[April, 1861]." At least one of the persons named (Bullitt) was commissioned as late as July 6, 1864, and some were merely reappointments to the office named (Durell and Parker). The list as a whole would seem to have been made out not earlier than July, 1864. According to the *U.S. Official Register*, 1865, William P. Kellogg was appointed collector instead of George S. Denison; the office of surveyor was not listed; T. M. Wells was appointed acting Naval officer; Benjamin F. Flanders, supervising special agent of the Treasury; J. M. G. Parker, postmaster; Thomas M. May, assistant treasurer; Cuthbert Bullitt, marshal; Edward H. Durell, judge (Eastern District); Jonathan K. Gould (instead of Charles A. Peabody), district attorney; Charles Smith, collector of internal revenue; Edmund Murphy, assessor of internal revenue.

To Joseph Holt[1]

Executive Mansion, Washington,

Judge Advocate General   July 1, 1864.

Please get the record in the case of Daniel Wormer, and report on it to me. Yours truly   A. LINCOLN

[1] ALS-P, ISLA. Daniel Wormer was an army contractor. See further, Lincoln to Holt, July 18, *infra.*

Order for Release of Political Prisoner[1]

July 1, 1864

This man being so well vouched, and talking so much better than any other I have heard, let him take the oath of December 8, and be discharged.   A. LINCOLN.

July 1, 1864.

[1] Leslie J. Perry, "Appeals to Lincoln's Clemency," *The Century Magazine,* December, 1895, p. 253. According to Perry "A prisoner in Camp Morton . . . whose name need not be written, made a feeling personal appeal to the President for release, the opening paragraph of which was as follows: 'Mr. President, I never was, am not, and never can be, a secessionist. I have been of a highly nervous temperament, with weak lungs, and easily excited. I was shamefully deceived by a supposed friend, who made me believe that I would be killed unless I fled my home and native State to seek safety in the South,' etc. . . ."

To Edwin M. Stanton[1]

July 1, 1864

If there be a report in the War Department, such as indicated in Judge Underwood's letter within, will the Sec. of War please have it sent to [me], together with these letters.   A. LINCOLN

July 1. 1864

[1] AES, DLC-RTL. Lincoln's endorsement is written on a letter from John R. Underwood, Bowling Green, Kentucky, June 20, 1864, asking parole of his son John, a political prisoner at Fort Warren: "I am informed that military officers recently made an investigation of the charges against the prisoners in Fort Warren & that their Report, now on file in the War Department, was favorable to my son." No further reference has been found.

To David Davis[1]

Hon. D. Davis   Washington

Bloomington Ills.   July 2. 1864

Please give me a summary of the evidence, with your impression, on the Coles county riot cases. I send the same request to Judge Treat.   A. LINCOLN

[1] ALS, DNA WR RG 107, Presidential Telegrams, I, 87. See the same telegram to Samuel H. Treat, *infra*. David Davis telegraphed on July 5, "Dispatch
received & have replied by letter." (DLC-RTL). Davis' letter has not been
found. See Lincoln to Ficklin, July 22, and the order concerning Coles County
prisoners, November 4, *infra*. The Coles County, Illinois, riot of March 28, 1864,
involving Copperheads and soldiers (Fifty-fourth Illinois) on furlough, resulted
in nine dead and twelve wounded. The fifteen Copperheads arrested and sent
to Fort Delaware were, by Lincoln's order of November 4, returned to Coles
County, where only two were ever brought to trial and were found "not
guilty." For a full account see Charles H. Coleman and Paul H. Spence, "The
Charleston Riot, March 28, 1864," *Journal of the Illinois State Historical Society*, XXXIII (March, 1940), 7-56.

To William P. Fessenden[1]

The within comes to me spontaneously, which I think fit to send
to Mr. Fessenden.   A. LINCOLN.
July 2, 1864.

[1] Francis Fessenden, *Life and Public Services of William Pitt Fessenden*
(1907), I, 320. Lincoln's endorsement was written on a telegram of George W.
David, president of the Cincinnati Chamber of Commerce, commending Fessenden's appointment as secretary of the Treasury. According to the source this
endorsement in Lincoln's autograph is preserved in the Fessenden Papers.

To the Senate[1]

To the Senate of the United States.   July 2, 1864

In answer to the Resolution of the Senate of the 6th. ult. requesting information upon the subject of the African Slave trade, I
transmit a Report from the Secretary of State and the papers by
which it was accompanied.   ABRAHAM LINCOLN
Washington.
July 2. 1864.

[1] DS, DNA RG 46, Senate 38A F2. Seward's report of July 2, 1864, transmitting correspondence from July 5, 1861 to May 30, 1864, is printed in Thirty-
eighth Congress, First Session, *Senate Executive Document No. 56.*

To Samuel H. Treat[1]

Hon. S. H. Treat   Washington,
Springfield Ills.   July 2, 1864

Please give me a summary of the evidence, with your impression, on the Coles County riot cases. I send the same request to
Judge Davis.   A LINCOLN

[1] ALS, DNA WR RG 107, Presidential Telegrams, I, 88. See Lincoln to Davis,
supra. Judge Treat telegraphed on July 4: "The record in the case of the Coles
Co. prisoners was ordered to be certified to the president   it contains the whole

case in my opinion the prisoners should have been surrendered to the civil authorities under the act of March Third (3) eighteen sixty three (1863) Judge Davis was of the same opinion" (DLC-RTL).

Endorsement Concerning an Escort[1]

I believe I need no escort, and unless the Sec. of War directs, none need attend me.   A. LINCOLN

July 4, 1864

[1] AES, ORB. Lincoln's endorsement is written on an order from Major General Christopher C. Augur's headquarters, Department of Washington, July 3, 1864: "If his Excellency the president of the U.S. wishes an escort, Lt. [James B.] Jameson will furnish it keeping the old Es. of his Co. at its present location." In December, 1863, Governor David Tod organized the Union Light Guard, Ohio Cavalry, as a bodyguard for the president. Stanton assigned the unit to guard the Executive Mansion, War Office, and Treasury Building.

Memorandum of Interview with William P. Fessenden[1]

Executive Mansion,
Washington, July 4, 1864.

I have to-day said to Hon. W. P. Fessenden, on his assuming the office of Secretary of the Treasury, that I will keep no person in office in his department, against his express will, so long as I choose to continue him; and he has said to me, that in filling vacancies he will strive to give his willing consent to my wishes in cases when I may let him know that I have such wishes. It is, and will be, my sincere desire, not only to advance the public interest, by giving him complete control of the department, but also to make his position agreeable to him.

In Cabinet my view is that in questions affecting the whole country there should be full and frequent consultations, and that nothing should be done particularly affecting any department without consultation with the head of that department.

[1] Francis Fessenden, *Life and Public Services of William Pitt Fessenden* (1907), I, 324-25. According to the source this memorandum in Lincoln's autograph is preserved in the Fessenden Papers.

To John L. Scripps[1]

To ———— Esq.   Executive Mansion, July 4th, 1864.

Dear Sir: Complaint is made to me that you are using your official power to defeat Mr. ————'s nomination to Congress. I am well satisfied with Mr. ———— as a member of Congress, and I do not know that the man who might supplant him would be as satisfactory. But the correct principle I think is, that all our friends should have *absolute freedom* of choice among our friends. My wish therefore is, that you will do just as you think fit with your own suffrage in the case, and not constrain any of your subordinates to other than he thinks fit with his. This is precisely the rule I inculcated and adhered to on my part, when a *certain* other nomination now recently made, was being canvassed for. Yours, very truly,   A. LINCOLN.

[1] Isaac N. Arnold, *The History of Abraham Lincoln, and the Overthrow of Slavery* (1866), p. 506. John L. Scripps was the postmaster (Chicago) and Arnold the congressman, whose names were left blank. On July 2, 1864, Arnold wrote Lincoln:

"Mr. J. L. Scripps P.M. at Chicago is a candidate for Congress against me . . . Mr. Scripps has over *one hundred appointees.* Is it right or fair that the power of the government should be used to crush one who has sustained the administration as faithfully as I have?

"Most members have the aid of the patronage of their Post-Offices. . . .

"I think it just that Mr. Scripps should be told that if he is a candidate for congress he must not use his office, to injure his competitor. Or he should resign post-office. . . . Perhaps a note from you saying that under the circumstances . . . my re-election would be agreeable to you addressed to Mr. Scripps would produce all that is desired. . . . All I wish is that the power & patronage of the administration should not be used against one who has tried to serve it faithfully." (DLC-RTL). See further Lincoln to Scripps, July 20, *infra.*

Neither Arnold nor Scripps received the Republican nomination. John Wentworth was nominated and elected from Arnold's district.

To John W. Garrett[1]

United States Military Telegraph,
J. W. Garrett, Prest.   War Department.
Camden Station.   [July 5th. 1864]

You say telegraphic communication is re-established with Sandy Hook. Well, what does Sandy Hook say about operations of Enemy and of Sigel, doing to-day?   A. LINCOLN

[1] ALS, DNA WR RG 107, Presidential Telegrams, I, 89. The bracketed date is in the handwriting of the clerk. The reply of John W. Garrett, president of the Baltimore and Ohio Railroad, was received at 1 A.M. on July 6: "Our officers report that General Sigel's losses have been quite trifling and that his whole force is now in possession of Maryland Heights. Our telegraph station is two miles from that location, and I have found it impossible to-night to obtain satisfactory information. . . ." (OR, I, XXXVII, II, 65-66). Confederate troops under General Jubal Early, after taking Harper's Ferry and Martinsburg, were reported advancing toward Baltimore and Washington. At Lincoln's direction Stanton telegraphed Governors Curtin and Seymour for 12,000 militia or volunteers from each of their states to serve for one hundred days in the defense of Washington (*ibid.,* 74, 77).

Proclamation Suspending Writ of Habeas Corpus[1]

July 5, 1864

By the President of the United States of America:

A Proclamation.

Whereas, by a proclamation which was issued on the 15th. day of April, 1861, the President of the United States announced and declared that the laws of the United States had been for some time past and then were opposed and the execution thereof obstructed in certain States therein mentioned by combinations too powerful to be suppressed by the ordinary course of judicial proceedings or by the powers vested in the Marshals by law;

And whereas, immediately after the issuing of the said proclamation the land and naval forces of the United States were put into activity to suppress the said insurrection and rebellion;

And whereas, the Congress of the United States by an act approved on the 3d. day of March 1863, did enact that during the said rebellion, the President of the United States, whenever in his judgment the public safety may require it, is authorized to suspend the privilege of the writ of Habeas Corpus in any case throughout the United States or in any part thereof;

And whereas the said insurrection and rebellion still continue, endangering the existence of the Constitution and Government of the United States;

And whereas the military forces of the United States are now actively engaged in suppressing the said insurrection and rebellion, in various parts of the States where the said rebellion has been successful in obstructing the laws and public authorities, especially in the States of Virginia and Georgia;

And whereas on the fifteenth day of September last, the President of the United States duly issued his proclamation, wherein he declared that the privilege of the writ of Habeas Corpus should be suspended throughout the United States in the cases where, by the authority of the President of the United States, military, naval and civil officers of the United States or any of them hold persons under their command or in their custody either as prisoners of war, spies, or aiders or abettors of the enemy; or officers, soldiers or seamen enrolled or drafted or mustered or enlisted in or belonging to the land or naval forces of the United States or as deserters therefrom or otherwise amenable to military law or the Rules and Articles of War or the rules or regulations prescribed for the military or naval services by authority of the President of the United States or for resisting a draft or for any other offence against the military or naval service;

And whereas many citizens of the State of Kentucky have joined the forces of the insurgents and such insurgents have on several occasions entered the said State of Kentucky in large force, and not without aid and comfort furnished by disaffected and disloyal citizens of the United States residing therein, have not only greatly disturbed the public peace but have overborne the civil authorities and made flagrant civil war, destroying property and life in various parts of that State; and whereas it has been made known to the President of the United States by the officers commanding the national armies, that combinations have been formed in the said State of Kentucky with a purpose of inciting rebel forces to renew the said operations of civil war within the said State, and thereby to embarrass the United States armies now operating in the said States of Virginia and Georgia and even to endanger their safety:

Now, therefore, I, Abraham Lincoln, President of the United States, by virtue of the authority vested in me by the constitution and laws, do, hereby, declare that in my judgment the public safety especially requires that the suspension of the privilege of the writ of Habeas Corpus so proclaimed in the said proclamation of the 15th. of September, 1863, be made effectual and be duly enforced in and throughout the said State of Kentucky, and that martial law be for the present established therein. I do, therefore, hereby require of the military officers in the said State that the privileges of the writ of Habeas Corpus be effectually suspended within the said State according to the aforesaid proclamation, and that martial law be established therein, to take effect from the date of this proclamation,—the said suspension and establishment of martial law to continue until this proclamation shall be revoked or modified, but not beyond the period when the said rebellion shall have been suppressed or come to an end. And I do hereby require and command, as well all military officers as all civil officers and authorities existing or found within the said State of Kentucky to take notice of this proclamation and to give full effect to the same.

The martial law herein proclaimed and the things in that respect herein ordered will not be deemed or taken to interfere with the holding of lawful elections, or with the proceedings of the constitutional legislature of Kentucky or with the administration of justice in the courts of law existing therein between citizens of the United States in suits or proceedings which do not affect the mil-

itary operations or the constituted authorities of the Government
of the United States.

In testimony whereof, I have hereunto set my hand and caused
the seal of the United States to be affixed.

Done at the City of Washington, this fifth day of July, in the
year of our Lord one thousand eight hundred and sixty
[L.S.]   four, and of the Independence of the United States the
eighty-ninth.   ABRAHAM LINCOLN

By the President:

WILLIAM H. SEWARD, Secretary of State.

1 DS, DNA FS RG 11, Proclamations.

To Edwin M. Stanton[1]

Hon. Sec. of War.   Executive Mansion,
Dear Sir   Washington, July 5, 1864.

A few days ago, at the request of Hon. E. H. Webster, and by
endorsement on a letter of his stating the reason, I ordered, as I
remember, the discharge of James M. Philips, drafted from 5th.
election District of Harford Co. Md. Let it now be done. I should
have stated that Mr. Webster says my former order has somehow
miscarried & can not be found at the Department. Yours truly

                                            A. LINCOLN

1 ALS-P, ISLA. The endorsement referred to by Lincoln has not been discovered. AGO *Special Orders No. 227*, July 5, 1864, ordered that "*James M.
Philips*, a drafted man from the 2d District of Maryland, now at Headquarters
of that District, will be discharged . . . upon the receipt of this Order. . . ."

To Cadwallader C. Washburn[1]

                                                July 5, 1864

The President declines making any further order in the case of
the Presbyterian Church in Memphis.

1 NH, X, 148. Presumably Lincoln dictated or wrote the text as reproduced by
Nicolay and Hay, in reply to a letter from General Cadwallader C. Washburn,
Memphis, June 22, 1864. Washburn's letter in the Lincoln Papers bears a similar
endorsement in John Hay's autograph ("President declines making any further
order in case of Presbyt. Church in Memphis."), and is endorsed in another
hand "Ansd July 5 1864." Washburn's letter is as follows:

"There is a case in this city which I want you to settle. The shape in which
you have left the case leaves me in doubt. The case is this.

"The 2nd Presbyterian Church in 1861 voted their bell to Genl Beauregard
and discharged their Pastor Dr Grundy because he was suspected of being loyal.
When our army came here Genl Sherman put Dr Grundy back into the church.
He was called away and gave it up to the union people who desired to worship

there, only one or two of whom had any proprietary rights in the church. On the representation of the old trustees on the 4th March last you wrote as follows Viz. [See memorandum of March 4, *supra*]. . . ."

"Thereupon Genl Hurlbut made the following order

" 'Head Quarters 16th Army Corps
" 'Memphis Tenn 18th Mch 1864

" 'This church was taken possession of by Genl Sherman because of a traitorous resolution adopted by the Trustees. There is no "Military necessity" for retaining it. If the corporators satisfy Genl Buckland of their loyalty the church building will be delivered to them. The order of the President will be strictly carried out Signed S. A. Hurlbut Maj Genl' "

"The Church was given up to the Trustees, and thereupon the parties turned out made their statement to you, when you endorsed thereon the following Viz [see endorsement of May 13, *supra*]. . . ."

"In making this last endorsement am I to understand that you wish the parties placed back who were put out, or are the parties in possession to keep it. I am left in doubt in regard to the matter and will be glad to be advised. . . ." (DLC-RTL).

To Edward Bates[1]

Will Attorney General please have me the copy made, which is required.   A. LINCOLN

July 6. 1864

[1] AES, DNA GE RG 60, Papers of Attorney General, Segregated Lincoln Material. Lincoln's endorsement is written on a letter from Benjamin F. Loan, July 5, 1864, requesting a copy of a letter "signed by myself and others relating to the appointment of Col Silas Woodson to be Chief Justice in Montana Territory. . . ."

To Montgomery Blair[1]

[c. July 6, 1864]

Mr. McPherson was appointed on Mr. Blair's recommendation. What says he to the within?   LINCOLN

[1] AES, DLC-Blair Papers. Lincoln's endorsement has been torn from attendant papers. See Lincoln to Joseph Casey, *infra*.

To Joseph Casey[1]

Executive Mansion,
Hon Joseph Casey.   Washington, July 6, 1864.

My dear Sir: I am urged to appoint an assistant attorney to your court in place of Mr. McPherson. I believe you once told me, but I am not sure that I correctly remember, what is the wish of the court in regard to the dismissal or retaining of Mr. McPherson.

Please tell me again. Yours truly,   A. LINCOLN

1 Tracy, p. 242. No reply from Casey has been discovered, but see Lincoln to
Bates, July 28, *infra*, for Casey's recommendation in regard to the successor of
John D. McPherson.

To Ulysses S. Grant[1]

[July 6, 1864]

Will General Grant allow J. R. Gilmore and friend to pass our
lines, with ordinary baggage, and go South?   A. LINCOLN.

[1] Washington *Daily Chronicle*, September 7, 1864, quoting the Boston *Transcript* of September 3. See Lincoln's communications to Rosecrans, May 21 and
28, 1863, and to Schenck, July 14, 1863, *supra*. In July, 1864, James R. Gilmore
called on Lincoln to suggest that another effort be made to negotiate peace. As
he told the story in magazine and newspaper articles and in his book published
under the pseudonym Edmund Kirke, (*Down in Tennessee*, 1864), Lincoln gave
him the note to Grant, the pass for Jaquess and himself, and also the "To whom
it may concern," *infra*, in order that they might visit Richmond and confer with
Jefferson Davis as private citizens representing no one but themselves. The
date on which Lincoln wrote these communications is not given in these contemporary sources, but in his later work, *Personal Recollections of Abraham
Lincoln and the Civil War* (1898), pp. 246-47, Gilmore gives the date as July 6.

Pass for James R. Gilmore and James F. Jaquess[1]

[July 6, 1864]

Allow J. R. Gilmore and friend to pass, with ordinary baggage,
to General Grant at his headquarters.   A. LINCOLN.

[1] Washington *Daily Chronicle*, September 7, 1864. See Lincoln to Grant, *supra*.

To Whom It May Concern[1]

[July 6, 1864]

To whom it may concern: The bearer, Col. James F. Jaquess,
Seventy-third Illinois, has leave of absence until further orders.
A. LINCOLN.

[1] James R. Gilmore (Edmund Kirke, pseudonym), *Down in Tennessee* (1864),
p. 247. See Lincoln to Grant, *supra*.

To William H. Seward[1]

I find the within from Garrett this morning. The big bundle
herewith is that we spoke of this morning.   A.L.
July 6. 1864

[1] AES, NAuE. This endorsement is written in pencil on an empty envelope.
See Lincoln to John W. Garrett, July 5, *supra*.

To Edwin M. Stanton[1]

Hon. Sec. of War   Executive Mansion,
Dear Sir   Washington, July 6. 1864.

Upon a promise made to Hon. Mr. Harding some time ago, let John L. Collins, a private, and prisoner of War at Camp Douglas, Ills. take the oath of Dec. 8. 1863, and be discharged. Yours truly

A. LINCOLN

[1] ALS-P, ISLA. No further reference has been found. Aaron Harding was U.S. representative from Kentucky.

To Edwin M. Stanton[1]

If the services are needed, let the appointment be made.
July 6, 1864   A. LINCOLN.

[1] AES, IHi. Lincoln's endorsement is written on a letter of Paymaster Orlando S. Witherill to Paymaster General Timothy P. Andrews, June 27, 1864, recommending Lieutenant M. P. Owen, Twenty-fourth Missouri Volunteers, for appointment as paymaster. The letter bears several concurring endorsements in favor of Owen. No record of Owen's appointment has been discovered.

To Timothy P. Andrews[1]

Executive Mansion, Washington,
Pay-Master-General   July 7, 1864.

It is even as you stated, that I am now appealed to by Pay-Masters to save them from being sent South. Please send some one in place of *George I Riche*, of Philadelphia, now ordered South. I feel that your rule is right, and that I ought not to interfere; but the pressure upon me in this case is insupportable. Yours truly

A. LINCOLN

[1] ALS, IHi. See Lincoln to Andrews, June 25, *supra.*

Parole for Frank L. Wolford[1]

Executive Mansion,
Washington, July 7. 1864.

I hereby give my parol of honor, that if allowed, I will forthwith proceed to Louisville Kentucky, and then remain, until the court for my trial shall arrive, when I will report myself to their charge, and that in the mean time I will abstain from public speaking, and every thing intended or calculated to produce excitement.

FRANK WOLFORD

Col. Wolford is allowed to go on the above conditions.

A. LINCOLN

[1] AD and AES, DLC-RTL. This document is in Lincoln's autograph on Executive Mansion stationery, signed by Wolford. Colonel Frank L. Wolford, First Kentucky Volunteer Cavalry had made a speech at Lexington, Kentucky, on March 10, 1864, in which he protested against the policy of employing Negroes as soldiers, and urged resistance to the law by means of law suits to test its constitutionality. Arrested and imprisoned at Knoxville, Tennessee, he was tried and convicted on charges of disloyalty and conduct unbecoming an officer. Following his dismissal from the service he became a candidate for presidential elector on the Conservative Union Ticket. See further Lincoln's communications to Speed and to Wolford, July 17, *infra*.

Proclamation of a Day of Prayer[1]

July 7, 1864

By the President of the United States of America:

A Proclamation.

Whereas, the Senate and House of Representatives at their last Session adopted a Concurrent Resolution, which was approved on the second day of July instant, and which was in the words following, namely:

"That, the President of the United States be requested to appoint a day for humiliation and prayer by the people of the United States; that he request his constitutional advisers at the head of the executive departments to unite with him as Chief Magistrate of the Nation, at the City of Washington, and the members of Congress, and all magistrates, all civil, military and naval officers,— all soldiers, sailors, and marines, with all loyal and law-abiding people, to convene at their usual places of worship, or wherever they may be, to confess and to repent of their manifold sins; to implore the compassion and forgiveness of the Almighty, that, if consistent with His will, the existing rebellion may be speedily suppressed, and the supremacy of the Constitution and laws of the United States may be established throughout all the States; to implore Him as the Supreme Ruler of the World, not to destroy us as a people, nor suffer us to be destroyed by the hostility or connivance of other Nations, or by obstinate adhesion to our own counsels, which may be in conflict with His eternal purposes, and to implore Him to enlighten the mind of the Nation to know and do His will; humbly believing that it is in accordance with His will that our place should be maintained as a united people among the family of nations; to implore Him to grant to our armed defenders and the masses of the people that courage, power of resistance and endurance necessary to secure that result; to implore Him in His infinite goodness to soften the hearts, enlighten the minds, and quicken the consciences of those in rebellion, that they may lay

[431]

down their arms and speedily return to their allegiance to the United States, that they may not be utterly destroyed, that the effusion of blood may be stayed, and that unity and fraternity may be restored, and peace established throughout all our borders."

Now, therefore, I, Abraham Lincoln, President of the United States, cordially concurring with the Congress of the United States in the penitential and pious sentiments expressed in the aforesaid Resolution, and heartily approving of the devotional design and purpose thereof, do, hereby, appoint the first Thursday of August next, to be observed by the People of the United States as a day of national humiliation and prayer.

I do, hereby, further invite and request the Heads of the Executive Departments of this Government, together with all Legislators, —all Judges and Magistrates, and all other persons exercising authority in the land, whether civil, military or naval,—and all soldiers, seamen and marines in the national service,—and all the other loyal and law-abiding People of the United States, to assemble in their preferred places of public worship on that day, and there and then to render to the Almighty and Merciful Ruler of the Universe, such homages and such confessions, and to offer to Him such supplications, as the Congress of the United States have, in their aforesaid Resolution, so solemnly, so earnestly, and so reverently recommended.

In testimony whereof, I have hereunto set my hand and caused the seal of the United States to be affixed.

Done at the City of Washington, this seventh day of July, in the year of our Lord, one thousand eight hundred and sixty-

[L.S.] four, and of the Independence of the United States the eighty-ninth. ABRAHAM LINCOLN

By the President:

WILLIAM H. SEWARD, Secretary of State.

1 DS, DNA FS RG 11, Proclamations.

To Edwin M. Stanton[1]

Please tell me what is there of the Maryland matter?

July 7, 1864. A LINCOLN

[1] AES, owned by R. E. Burdick, New York City. Lincoln's endorsement is written on a letter of G. F. Kurtz to Governor Thomas H. Hicks, June 27, 1864, protesting that "Lev. Straughn is doing his very utmost to get up a sentiment against the Commissioners, thereby aiding the infamous designs of those who are endeavoring to gobble up the money that was intended for the negro volunteers. . . . Even J. C. Wright his fast friend, is against him, and says he is ready to go on to Washington if necessary to join in a protest against the order of

Sec. Stanton. Mr. Rea says he is ready to lose the 300$ due him from the Government for his slave, rather than the County Commissioners should give way in their determination, and pay the money of the negroes over to that scoundrel. . . . If the President will not revoke the order of the Secretary of War, he will certainly not refuse to enable us to comply with it, by furnishing us with authority to go where the negroes are to pay them off. This will end the controversy, and secure justice to all parties. . . ." See Lincoln to Bowman, August 6, *infra.*

Proclamation Concerning Reconstruction[1]

July 8, 1864

By the President of the United States.

A Proclamation.

Whereas, at the late Session, Congress passed a Bill,[2] "To guarantee to certain States, whose governments have been usurped or overthrown, a republican form of Government," a copy of which is hereunto annexed:

And whereas, the[3] said Bill was presented to the President of the United States,[4] for his approval, less than one hour before the *sine die* adjournment of said Session, and was not signed by him:

And whereas, the[5] said Bill contains, among other things, a plan for restoring the States in rebellion to their proper practical relation in the Union, which plan expresses the sense of Congress upon that subject, and which plan it is now thought fit to lay before the people for their consideration:

Now,[6] therefore, I, Abraham Lincoln, President of the United States, do proclaim, declare, and make known, that, while I am, (as I was in December last, when by proclamation I propounded a plan for restoration) unprepared, by a formal approval of this Bill, to be inflexibly committed to any single plan of restoration; and, while I am also unprepared to declare,[7] that the free-state constitutions and governments, already adopted and installed in Arkansas and Louisiana, shall be set aside and held for nought, thereby repelling and discouraging the loyal citizens who have set up the same, as to further effort; or to declare a constitutional competency in Congress to abolish slavery in States, but am at the same time sincerely hoping and expecting that[8] a constitutional amendment, abolishing slavery throughout the nation, may be adopted, nevertheless, I[9] am fully satisfied with the system for restoration contained in the Bill, as one very proper plan for the loyal people of any State choosing to adopt it; and that I am, and at all times shall be, prepared to give the Executive aid and assistance to any such people, so soon as the military resistance to the United States shall have been suppressed in any such State, and the people thereof shall have sufficiently returned to their obedience to the Constitution and the laws of the United States,—in which cases, military Governors will be appointed, with directions to proceed according to the Bill.[10]

In testimony whereof, I have hereunto set my hand and caused the Seal of the United States to be affixed.

Done at the City of Washington this eighth day of July, in the year of Our Lord, one thousand eight hundred and sixty-[L.S.] four, and of the Independence of the United States the eighty-ninth.   ABRAHAM LINCOLN.

By the President:

WILLIAM H. SEWARD, Secretary of State.

[1] DS, DNA FS RG 11, Proclamations; ADf, NAuE. Lincoln's autograph draft shows numerous revisions in the handwriting of Edward Bates, as indicated in the succeeding notes.

[2] Lincoln's draft reads: "as follows, towit (Insert it here)," changed by Bates to "a copy of which is hereunto annexed."   [3] Bates inserted "the."
[4] Bates inserted "of the United States."   [5] Bates inserted "the."
[6] Bates inserted "Now."
[7] Bates crossed out "or" and inserted "and while I am also unprepared."
[8] Bates crossed out "still hoping" and inserted "am at the same time sincerely hoping and expecting that."
[9] Lincoln had written "I, nevertheless"; Bates revised to "nevertheless I."

[10] The autograph draft originally concluded with an additional phrase: "it having been impossible, for want of time, even had the Bill been approved, to nominate Provisional Governors to, and have them confirmed by, the Senate, before it's adjournment." This was revised by Bates to read: "for had the bill been approved by the President, it would have been impossible, for want of time, to nominate Provisional Governors to, and have them confirmed by, the Senate, before it's adjournment." The official copy of the proclamation omitted the phrase entirely.

To John W. Garrett[1]

	Office U.S. Military Telegraph,
J. W. Garrett	War Department,
Camden Station	Washington, D.C., July 9 1864.

What have you heard about a battle at Monococy to-day? We have nothing about it here except what you say.   A. LINCOLN.

[1] ALS, DNA WR RG 107, Presidential Telegrams, I, 90. Garrett's reply was received at 7:15 P.M.: "At 10:30 this a.m. operator at Monocacy stated there was then severe fighting near that point, our forces shelling the enemy, who had advanced to within three-quarters of a mile of Monocacy on the road from Frederick to Georgetown. . . . Our telegraph operator at Monrovia, which is eight miles east of Monocacy, this instant telegraphs that an aide of General Wallace has arrived there, who reports that 'our troops at Monocacy have given way, and that General Wallace has been badly defeated,' the bridge having been abandoned. . . ." (OR, I, XXXVII, II, 138).

At 11:57 P.M. Halleck telegraphed General Lewis Wallace: "I am directed by the President to say that you will rally your forces and make every possible effort to retard the enemy's march on Baltimore." (*Ibid.*, p. 145).

To Horace Greeley[1]

Hon. Horace Greely   Washington, D.C.

Dear Sir   July 9. 1864

Your letter of the 7th., with inclosures, received. If you can find, any person anywhere professing to have any proposition of Jefferson Davis in writing, for peace, embracing the restoration of the Union and abandonment of slavery, what ever else it embraces, say to him he may come to me with you, and that if he really brings such proposition, he shall, at the least, have safe conduct, with the paper (and without publicity, if he choose) to the point where you shall have met him. The same, if there be two or more persons. Yours truly   A LINCOLN

[1] ADfS, DLC-RTL; LS, owned by Mrs. James Wadsworth, Geneseo, New York. On July 7, 1864, Greeley wrote Lincoln:

"I venture to inclose you a letter and telegraphic dispatch that I received yesterday from our irrepressible friend, Colorado Jewett, at Niagara Falls. I think they deserve attention. Of course, I do not indorse Jewett's positive averment that his friends . . . have 'full powers' from J.D., though I do not doubt that *he* thinks they have. I let that statement stand as simply evidencing the anxiety of the Confederates everywhere for peace. So much is beyond doubt.

"And thereupon I venture to remind you that our bleeding, bankrupt, almost dying country also longs for peace—shudders at the prospect of fresh conscriptions, of further wholesale devastations, and of new rivers of human blood. And a wide-spread conviction that the Government . . . are not anxious for Peace, and do not improve proffered opportunities to achieve it, is doing great harm now, and is morally certain, unless removed, to do far greater in the approaching Elections. . . .

"I entreat you, in your own time and manner, to submit overtures for pacification to the Southern insurgents which the impartial must pronounce frank and generous. If only with a view to the momentous Election soon to occur in North Carolina, and of the Draft to be enforced in the Free States, this should be done at once.

"I would give the safe conduct required by the Rebel envoys at Niagara . . . but *you* may see reasons for declining it. But, whether through them or otherwise, do not, I entreat you, fail to make the Southern people comprehend that you and all of us are anxious for peace. . . .

"Mr. President, I fear you do not realize how intently the people desire any peace consistent with the national integrity and honor. . . . With United States stocks worth but forty cents in gold per dollar, and drafting about to commence on the third million of Union soldiers, can this be wondered at?

"I do not say that a just peace is now attainable, though I believe it to be so. But I *do* say, that a frank *offer* by you to the insurgents of terms . . . will . . . prove an immense and sorely needed advantage to the national cause; it may save us from a northern insurrection. . . .

"I beg you to invite those now at Niagara to exhibit their credentials and submit their ultimatum." (DLC-RTL).

The enclosed letter of William Cornell Jewett to Greeley is in part as follows: ". . . I have to advise having just left Hon Geo. N. Sanders of Ky on the Canada side. *I am authorised to state to you—for our use only—not the public— that two ambassadors—of Davis & Co are now in Canada—with full & complete powers for a peace* & Mr Sanders requests that you come on immediately to me at Cataract House—to have a private interview, or if you will send the Presidents protection for *him* & *two* friends, they will come on & meet you. He says the whole matter can be consummated by me you—them & President Lincoln. Telegraph me in such form—that I may know—if you come here—or they to come on—with me." (*Ibid.*). See Lincoln to Greeley, July 15, *infra*.

To Joseph Holt[1]

July 9, 1864

This offence is not so common as to require so severe an example. Prisoner having suffered near a year of imprisonment, the sentence is now remitted.   A. LINCOLN

July 9. 1864

[1] AES, DNA WR RG 153, Judge Advocate General, MM 1063. Among thirty-one court-martial cases passed upon by Lincoln on July 9, 1864, the case of Private Aaron Elkin, Company K, Sixty-second New York Volunteers, sentenced to be shot for wilful disobedience of orders, prompted Lincoln to comment on as well as remit the sentence.

To William S. Rosecrans[1]

Office U.S. Military Telegraph,
War Department,
Major General Rosecrans   Washington, D.C.,
St. Louis, Mo.   July 9 1864.

When did the Sec. of War telegraph you to release Dr. Barrett? If it is an old thing, let it stand till you hear further.

A. LINCOLN

[1] ALS, DNA WR RG 107, Presidential Telegrams, I, 91. Dr. James A. Barrett was one of several purported leaders of the Order of American Knights, the copperhead secret society, at St. Louis. On June 25, 1864, General Grant telegraphed Stanton, "I will feel obliged to you if you will order General Rosecrans to release Dr. J. A. Barrett, a citizen prisoner, lately confined in St. Louis. . . . The Doctor is a copperhead, but I have no idea that he has done anything more than that class of people are constantly doing, and not so much. He was a neighbor of mine, a clever man, and has a practice in the neighborhood which it will be very inconvenient to other people than himself to have interrupted." (OR, II, VII, 411). On June 26, James A. Hardie telegraphed Rosecrans: "You will release Dr. J. A. Barrett upon his parole on his bond for $2,000, conditioned on his refraining from any act of hostility to the United States or from giving aid and comfort to the enemy after his release. . . ." (*Ibid.*, p. 417). On July 8, Rosecrans telegraphed Lincoln: "A telegram from the Secretary of War says you direct the release of Doctor Barrett. . . . His release would endanger the public peace and defeat the ends of justice, and I respectfully request a reversion of the order. . . ." (*Ibid.*, p. 447). No further order has been located.

To Ulysses S. Grant[1]

"Cypher"   War Department
Lieut. Gen. Grant   Washington City,
City-Point, Va   July 10– 2.p.m. 1864

Your despatch to Gen. Halleck, referring to what I may think in the present emergency, is shown me. Gen. Halleck says we have absolutely no force here fit to go to the field. He thinks that with the hundred day-men, and invalids we have here, we can[2] defend Washington, and scarcely Baltimore. Besides these, there are about eight thousand not very reliable, under Howe[3] at Harper's Ferry, with Hunter[4] approaching that point very slowly, with what number I suppose you know better than I. Wallace with some odds and ends, and part of what came up with Ricketts,[5] was so badly beaten yesterday at Monocacy, that what is left can attempt no more than to defend Baltimore. What we shall get in from Penn. & N.Y. will scarcely [be] worth counting, I fear. Now what I think is that you should provide to retain your hold where you are certainly, and bring the rest with you personally, and make a vigorous effort to destroy the enemie's force in this vicinity. I think there is really a fair chance to do this if the movement is prompt. This is what I think, upon your suggestion, and is not an order   A. LINCOLN

[1] ALS, DNA WR RG 107, Presidential Telegrams, I, 93-94. Grant telegraphed Halleck at 6 P.M. on July 9: "Forces enough to defeat all that Early has with him should get in his rear south of him, and follow him up sharply, leaving him to go north, defending depots, towns, &c., with small garrisons and the militia. If the President thinks it advisable that I should go to Washington in person I can start in an hour after receiving notice, leaving everything here on the defensive." (OR, I, XXXVII, II, 134).

[2] Lincoln first wrote "may possibly but not certainly," which he deleted and substituted "can."

[3] Brigadier General Albion P. Howe, in command at Harper's Ferry since July 8.

[4] Major General David Hunter, at Cumberland, Maryland, on July 8 moving toward Harper's Ferry.

[5] Brigadier General James B. Ricketts, commanding the Third Division, Sixth Army Corps.

To Thomas Swann and Others[1]

                                    Office U.S. Military Telegraph,
Thomas Swan & others   War Department, Washington, D.C.,
Baltimore, Md.   July 10. 9/20 AM. 1864.

Yours of last night received. I have not a single soldier but whom is being disposed by the Military for the best protection of all. By latest account the enemy is moving on Washington. They can not

fly to either place. Let us be vigilant but keep cool. I hope neither
Baltimore or Washington will be sacked.   A. LINCOLN

¹ ALS, DNA WR RG 107, Presidential Telegrams, I, 92. Swann and others
telegraphed on July 9: "Baltimore is in great peril. We have been appointed by
the mayor a committee to confer with you the absolute necessity of sending
large re-enforcements. . . ." (OR, I, XXXVII, II, 140).

To Ulysses S. Grant¹

"Cypher"   United States Military Telegraph,
Lieut. Gen. Grant   War Department, Washington,
City-Point, Va   July 11. 1864 [8 A.M.]

Yours of 10.30 P.M. yesterday received, and very satisfactory.
The enemy will learn of Wright's arrival, and then the difficulty
will be to unite Wright and Hunter, South of the enemy before he
will recross the Potomac. Some firing between Rockville and here
now.   A. LINCOLN

¹ ALS, DNA WR RG 107, Presidential Telegrams, I, 95. Grant's telegram of
10:30 P.M., July 10, received at 7 A.M., July 11, states:
"I have sent from here a whole corps commanded by an excellent officer,
besides over three thousand other troops. One Division of the Nineteenth Corps,
six thousand strong is now on its way to Washington. One Steamer loaded with
these troops having passed Ft. Monroe today. They will probably reach Washington tomorrow'night. This force under [Horatio G.] Wright will be able to
compete with the whole force with [Richard S.] Ewell.
"Before more troops can be sent from here [David] Hunter will be able to
join Wright in rear of the Enemy, with at least ten thousand men, besides a
force sufficient to hold Maryland Heights.
"I think on reflection it would have a bad effect for me to leave here, and
with Genl [Edward O. C.] Ord at Baltimore and Hunter and Wright with the
forces following the enemy up, could do no good
"I have great faith that the enemy will never be able to get back with much
of his force."

To Ulysses S. Grant¹

"Cypher"   United States Military Telegraph,
Lieut. General Grant   War Department, Washington D.C.
City Point, Va.   July 12. 1864 11/30 A.M.

Vague rumors have been reaching us for two or three days that
Longstreet's corps is also on its way this vicinity. Look out for it's
absence from your front.   A. LINCOLN

¹ ALS, DNA WR RG 107, Presidential Telegrams, I, 96. Grant telegraphed
Halleck on July 13, 12 M.: "Summary of evidence gathered from deserters,
scouts, and cavalry reconnaissance by [David M.] Gregg on our left show that
none of [Ambrose P.] Hill's or Longstreet's corps have left our front. . . ." (OR,
I, XXXVII, II, 257).

To Edwin M. Stanton[1]

July 13, 1864

If there is a vacancy of a brigadier-generalship can be properly assigned to the Cavalry Corps of General Sheridan, let Colonel Alger be appointed to it.

[1] *Week by Week in Springfield,* October 1, 1932. Colonel Russell A. Alger of the Fifth Michigan Cavalry was not appointed. On September 16 his resignation was endorsed by Lincoln "Let this resignation be accepted" (*ibid.*), and on September 20, he was "honorably discharged the service of the United States. . . ." (AGO *Special Orders No. 311*).

Memorandum Read to Cabinet[1]

Executive Mansion,
Washington, [July 14?], 186[4].

I must myself be the judge, how long to retain in, and when to remove any of you from, his position. It would greatly pain me to discover any of you endeavoring to procure anothers removal, or, in any way to prejudice him before the public. Such endeavor would be a wrong to me; and much worse, a wrong to the country. My wish is that on this subject, no remark be made, nor question asked, by any of you, here or elsewhere, now or hereafter.

[1] AD, DLC-Nicolay Papers. See Lincoln to Stanton, *infra.* The title and bracketed date are those supplied by Nicolay and Hay (X, 158), probably on the basis of Lincoln's letter to Stanton, *infra.* No reference has been found to Lincoln's use of the memorandum in cabinet meeting.

To Edwin M. Stanton[1]

Hon. Secretary of War   Executive Mansion,
Sir.   Washington, July 14. 1864.

Your note of to-day, inclosing Gen. Halleck's letter of yesterday, relative to offensive remarks supposed to have been made by the Post-Master-General concerning the Military officers on duty about Washington, is received. The General's letter, in substance demands of me that if I approve the remarks, I shall strike the names of those officers from the rolls; and that if I do not approve them, the Post-Master-General shall be dismissed from the Cabinet. Whether the remarks were really made I do not know; nor do I suppose such knowledge is necessary to a correct response. If they were made I do *not* approve them; and yet, under the circumstances, I would not dismiss a member of the Cabinet therefor. I do not consider what may have been hastily said in a moment of vexation at so severe a loss, is sufficient ground for so grave a step. Besides this, *truth* is generally the best vindication against slander. I propose continuing to be myself the judge as to when a member of the Cabinet shall be dismissed. Yours truly   A. LINCOLN.

¹ ALS, NIC. On July 14 Stanton "respectfully" referred the "accompanying letter of Major General Halleck":

"I am informed by an officer of rank and standing in the military service that the Hon. M. Blair, Post Master Genl, in speaking of the burning of his house in Maryland, this morning, said, in effect, that 'the officers in command about Washington are poltroons; that there were not more than five hundred rebels on the Silver Spring road and we had a million of men in arms; that it was a disgrace; that General Wallace was in comparison with them far better as he would at least fight.'

"As there have been for the last few days a large number of officers on duty in and about Washington who have devoted their time and energies night and day, and have periled their lives, in the support of the Government, it is due to them as well as to the War Department that it should be known whether such wholesale denouncement & accusation by a member of the cabinet receives the sanction and approbation of the President. . . . If so the names of the officers accused should be stricken from the rolls of the Army; if not, it is due to the honor of the accused that the slanderer should be dismissed from the cabinet. . . ." (DLC-RTL).

To Edwin M. Stanton¹

July 14, 1864.

Opinion of Attorney-General as to pay of colored soldiers. Submitted to the Secretary of War.   A. LINCOLN.

¹ OR, III, IV, 493. Lincoln's endorsement is on the letter of Edward Bates, July 14, 1864, quoted in the note to Lincoln's letter to Bates, June 24, *supra*.

To Horace Greeley¹

Hon. Horace Greeley   Executive Mansion
New-York   Washington, July 15, 1864

I suppose you received my letter of the 9th. I have just received yours of the 13 and am disappointed by it. I was not expecting you to *send* me a letter, but to *bring* me a man, or men. Mr. Hay goes to you with my answer to yours of the 13th.   A. LINCOLN

¹ ALS, IaHA; ALS copy, DLC-RTL; copy, DNA WR RG 107, Presidential Telegrams, I, 97. In reply to Lincoln's letter of July 9, *supra*, Greeley wrote on July 10:

"I have yours of yesterday.

"Whether there be persons at Niagara (or elsewhere) who are empowered to commit the Rebels by negotiations, is a question; but, *if* there be such, there is no question at all that they would decline to exhibit their credentials to me;

much more to open their budget and give me their best terms. Green as I may be, I am not quite so verdant as to imagine any thing of the sort. I have neither purpose nor desire to be made a confidant, far less an agent in such negotiations. But I do deeply realize that the Rebel chiefs achieved a most decided advantage in proposing, or pretending to propose, to have A. H. Stephens visit Washington as a peace-maker, and being rudely repulsed. And I am anxious that the ground lost to the National cause by that mistake shall somehow be regained in season for effect on the approaching N. Carolina election.

"I will see if I can get a look into the hand of whomsoever may be at Niagara, though that is a project so manifestly hopeless that I have little heart for it. Still, I shall try.

"Meantime, I wish you would consider the propriety of *somehow* apprising the people of the South, especially those of North Carolina, that *no* overture or advance looking to Peace and Reunion has ever been repelled by you, but that such a one would at any time have been cordially received and favorably regarded—and would still be. . . ." (DLC-RTL).

On July 13 Greeley wrote again:

"I have now information on which I can rely that two persons, duly commissioned and empowered to negotiate for peace, are at this moment not far from Niagara Falls, in Canada, and are desirous of conferring with yourself or with such persons as you may appoint and empower to treat with them. Their names, (only given in confidence) are Hon. Clement C. Clay of Alabama, and Hon. Jacob Brown of Mississippi. If you should prefer to meet them in person, they require safe conducts for themselves and for George N. Sanders, who will accompany them. Should you choose to empower one or more persons to treat with them in Canada, they will of course need no safe conduct; but they cannot be expected to exhibit credentials save to commissioners empowered as they are. In negotiating directly with yourself, all grounds of cavil would be avoided; and you would be enabled at all times to act upon the freshest advices of the military situation.

"You will of course understand that I know nothing, and have proposed nothing, as to terms, and that nothing is conceded or taken for granted by the meeting of persons empowered to negotiate for peace. All that is assumed is a mutual desire to terminate this wholesale slaughter if a basis of adjustment can be mutually agreed on. And it seems to me high time that an effort to this end should be made.

"I am of course quite other than sanguine that a Peace can now be made. But I am quite sure that a frank, earnest, anxious *effort* to terminate the War on favorable terms would immensely strengthen the Government in case of its failure, and would help us in the eyes of the civilized world, which now accuses us of obstinacy and indisposition even to *seek* a peaceful solution of our sanguinary, devastating conflict.

"Hoping to hear that you have resolved to act in the premises, and to act so promptly that a good influence may even yet be executed on the North Carolina election next month, I remain. . . ." (*Ibid.*).

See the letter carried by John Hay, *infra.*

To Horace Greeley[1]

Hon. Horace Greeley   Executive Mansion,
My dear Sir   Washington, July 15. 1864.

Yours of the 13th. is just received; and I am disappointed that you have not already reached here with those Commissioners, if they would consent to come, on being shown my letter to you of the 9th. Inst. Show that and this to them; and if they will come on the terms stated in the former, bring them. I not only intend a sincere effort for peace, but I intend that you shall be a personal witness that it is made. Yours truly   A. LINCOLN

[1] ALS, ORB; ADfS, DLC-RTL. This letter was carried by John Hay. See the order for Hay, *infra,* and Lincoln's telegram to Hay, July 16, *infra.*

Order for John Hay[1]

Executive Mansion,
Washington, July 15, 1864.

Major John Hay, my Private Secretary, goes to New York upon public business of importance. I desire that all necessary facilities may be given to him in the matter of transportation.

A. LINCOLN

[1] DS, owned by Mrs. James Wadsworth, Geneseo, New York. See Lincoln's communications to Greeley, *supra.*

To L. J. Leberman[1]

Executive Mansion,
My dear Sir: July 15, 1864
     The suit of garments sent by you, on behalf of Messrs Rockhill & Wilson, came duly to hand; and for which you and they will please accept my thanks. Yours truly   A. LINCOLN.

[1] Stan. V. Henkels Catalog 1272, January 26, 1921, No. 308. According to the catalog description this is an autograph letter signed. On July 8, 1864, L. J. Leberman wrote Lincoln:
"Among the contributions to the clothing department at the Great Central Fair, for the benefit of the United States Sanitary Commission, there was presented by Messrs. Rockhill & Wilson of this City, an elegant suit of garments made to your measure.
"The fair Treasury having been fully compensated I am desired by the donors to forward the same to you.
"I am happy honored Sir, to be the medium of presentation. . . ."

Endorsement[1]

This class of appointments I believe is made   A.L.
July 16. 1864

[1] AES, RPB. Lincoln's endorsement has been clipped from the attendant document.

To John Hay[1]

John Hay.   Executive Mansion,
Astor-House, N.Y.   Washington, July 16. 1864.
Yours received. Write the Safe-conduct, as you propose, without
waiting for one by mail from me. If there is, or is not, any thing in
the affair, I wish to know it, without unnecessary delay.

                                                     A. LINCOLN

[1] ALS, DNA WR RG 107, Presidential Telegrams, I, 98; ALS copy, DLC-
RTL. Hay telegraphed Lincoln at 9 A.M. on July 16:
"Arrived this morning at 6 a m and delivered your letter few minutes after.
"Although he thinks some one less known would create less excitement and
be less embarrassed by public curiosity, still he will start immediately if he can
have an absolute safe conduct for four persons to be named by him.
"Your letter he does not think will guard them from arrest and with only
those letters he would have to explain the whole matter to any officer who might
choose to hinder them. If this meets with your approbation I can write the order
in your name as A A G. or you can send it by mail.
"Please answer me at Astor House" (DLC-RTL).

The safe-conduct issued by Hay at Lincoln's direction reads as follows (copy,
DLC-RTL):
                              "Executive Mansion Washington D.C.
"The President of the United States directs that the four persons whose names
follow, towit: Hon. Clement C. Clay   Jacob Thompson   Prof. James B. Holcombe   George N. Sanders   Shall have safe conduct to the City of Washington
in company with the Hon. Horace Greeley, and shall be exempt from arrest or
annoyance of any kind from any officer of the United States during their journey
to the said City of Washington. By order of the President.
                              "(signed) JOHN HAY   Major & A.G.G."

On July 17, Hay telegraphed Lincoln:
"Gave the order yesterday. He promised to start at once and I supposed did
so. I return this evening if connections can be made" (DLC-RTL).
See further Lincoln's communication to whom it may concern, July 18, *infra*.

To Edwin M. Stanton[1]

Is it or not the opinion of the Sec. of War, that there is a legal appeal to me in this case?   A. LINCOLN
July 16. 1864.

[1] AES, MHi. Lincoln's endorsement is written on an envelope addressed "To
the President." An endorsement in pencil by an unidentified hand reads: "Here
are the Sibley Tent Royalty papers."

To Edwin M. Stanton[1]

                                                  July 16, 1864
Lieut. Armes wishes to be promoted to a Captaincy, and on the
recommendations of Gen's Grant and Hancock, I am certainly

[443]

willing, provided there is any place to which he can consistently be appointed.   A. LINCOLN

July 16. 1864

¹ AES, RPB. Lincoln's endorsement is written on a letter from Ulysses S. Grant, July 4, 1864, concurring in the recommendation made by General Winfield S. Hancock that Lieutenant George A. Armes be promoted. Armes was appointed captain of the Second New York Artillery on November 7, 1864.

To Andrew G. Curtin¹

United States Military Telegraph,

Gov. A. G. Curtin   War Department.

Harrisburg, Pa.   July 17. 11/20 A.M. 1864.

Please come here, as soon as convenient, and you and I will absolutely fix up the 2nd. Heavy Artillery matters, before you leave.   A. LINCOLN

¹ ALS, DNA WR RG 107, Presidential Telegrams, I, 100. On June 16, 1864, Governor Curtin had written Lincoln an eleven-page letter concerning the bad condition of the Second Pennsylvania Heavy Artillery, whose Colonel, Augustus A. Gibson, Curtin wanted to replace. (DLC-RTL). Curtin replied to Lincoln's telegram on July 18: "I regret that I cannot leave Harrisburg at this time having fully expressed my views as to the two (2) Heavy Artillery P.V. in my letters of the 16th and 18th June. I do not know of anything now I could suggest. . . . I have directed my military agent . . . to call and see you. . . . He is fully informed and can give you facts of importance in reference to the present condition of the men" (*ibid.*). Colonel Gibson was mustered out of service July 22, 1864.

To Ulysses S. Grant¹

United States Military Telegraph,

Lieut. Gen. Grant   War Department.

City Point, Va.   July 17. 11/25. AM. 1864

In your despatch of yesterday to Gen. Sherman, I find the following, towit: "I shall make a desparate effort to get a position here which will hold the enemy without the necessity of so many men."

Pressed as we are by lapse of time, I am glad to hear you say this; and yet I do hope you may find a way that the effort shall not be desparate in the sense of great loss of life.   A. LINCOLN

¹ ALS, DNA WR RG 107, Presidential Telegrams, I, 101. Grant's telegram to Sherman of July 16 reported that "The attempted invasion of Maryland having failed to give the enemy a firm foothold North, they are now returning, with possibly 25,000 troops. . . . It is not improbable, therefore, that you will find in the next fortnight re-enforcements in your front to the number indicated above. I advise, therefore, that if you can get to Atlanta you set about destroying the railroads as far to the east and south of you as possible; collect all the stores of

the country for your own use, and select a point that you can hold until help can be had. I shall make a desperate effort to get a position here which will hold the enemy without the necessity of so many men. If successful, I can detach from here for other enterprises, looking as much to your assistance as anything else." (OR, I, XXXVIII, V, 149).

To David Hunter[1]

United States Military Telegraph,
Major General Hunter   War Department.
Harper's Ferry, Va.   July 17th. 10. A.M. 1864

Yours of this morning received. You misconceive. The order you complain of was only nominally mine; and was framed by those who really made it, with no thought of making you a scape-goat. It seemed to be Gen. Grant's wish that the forces under Gen. Wright and those under you should join and drive at the enemy, under Gen. Wright. Wright had the larger part of the force, but you had the rank. It was thought that you would prefer Crook's commanding your part, to your serving in person under Wright. That is all of it. Gen. Grant wishes you to remain in command of the Department, and I do not wish to order otherwise.   A. LINCOLN

[1] ALS, DNA WR RG 107, Presidential Telegrams, I, 99. General Hunter telegraphed from Harper's Ferry on July 17:

"I again most earnestly request to be relieved from the command of this department.

"Your order, conveyed through Genl Halleck, has entirely destroyed my usefulness. When an officer is selected as the scapegoat to cover up the blunders of others, the best interests of the country require that he should at once be relieved from command." (DLC-RTL).

The order concerning forces under Major General Horatio G. Wright and Brigadier General George Crook concerning which Hunter complained is as follows: "By command of the President, Maj. Gen. H. G. Wright is assigned to the chief command of all the forces moving against the enemy now retreating from Washington. This assignment embraces the Nineteenth Corps . . . and any forces that may join General Wright from the commands of Major-General Hunter, Major-General Ord, or elsewhere. . . ." (AGO *General Orders No. 299,* July 13, 1864).

To Franklin G. Martindale[1]

[c..July 17, 1864?]

The property of Charles J. Faulkner is exempt from the order of General David S. Hunter for the burning of the residences of prominent citizens of the Shenandoah Valley in retaliation for the burning of the Governor Bradford's house in Maryland by the Confederate forces.   ABRAHAM LINCOLN

[1] Willis F. Evans, *History of Berkeley County, West Virginia* (1928), p. 264. The text of this telegram is open to question in the absence of the original, but the circumstances are corroborated in other sources. Headquarters Department of West Virginia, *Special Orders No. 128*, July 17, 1864, directed Captain Franklin G. Martindale, First New York Cavalry, to burn the dwelling house and outbuildings of Charles J. Faulkner at Martinsburg, West Virginia (OR, I, XXXVII, II, 367). According to Evans' account, Lincoln's order to Martindale came in reply to a telegram from Mrs. Charles J. Faulkner (Mary Boyd Faulkner) at "Boydville," the family home at Martinsburg. Charles James Faulkner, whom President Buchanan had appointed minister to France, was recalled by Lincoln and imprisoned for disloyalty. Later he was exchanged for Representative Alfred Ely, who had been captured by the Confederates while witnessing the first battle of Bull Run. Faulkner served on the staff of Stonewall Jackson and in January, 1865, was offered a pardon by Lincoln. See Lincoln's letter to Mrs. Charles J. Faulkner, January 9, 1865, *infra*.

Parole and Discharge for Frank L. Wolford[1]

July [c. 17] 1864

I hereby pledge my honor that I will neither do or say anything which will directly or indirectly tend to hinder, delay, or embarrass the employment and use of colored persons, as soldiers, seamen, or otherwise, in the suppression of the rebellion, so long as the U.S. government chooses to so employ and use them.

Col. Frank Wolford is discharged from his parole given me July 7. 1864 and allowed to go at large upon the conditions of the parole by him signed on the other side of the paper.   A. LINCOLN
July [c. 17] 1864.

[1] AD and ADS copies, DLC-RTL. See preliminary parole for Wolford, July 7, *supra*. The autograph copy of the parole is written in pencil with "July 1864" added by Lincoln in ink. The autograph copy of the discharge is in ink. Two copies of the parole, each presumably bearing the discharge as an endorsement, were enclosed to Speed. These as well as the original letters to Speed and Wolford, *infra*, have not been discovered.

To James Speed[1]

Hon. James Speed   Executive Mansion,
My dear Sir: Washington, July 17th, 1864.

Herewith is a blank parole, in duplicate, for Col. Wolford to sign. Please present them to him, and if he sign them, fill in the proper date to the parole, and to my endorsement; and leave one of the papers with him, and return the other to me. Yours truly
A. LINCOLN

[1] Copy, DLC-RTL. See parole for Frank L. Wolford, *supra*, and letter to Wolford, *infra*.

To Frank L. Wolford[1]

Col. Frank Wolford   Executive Mansion,
My dear Sir: Washington, July 17– 1864.

By this mail, I send to Hon. James Speed a blank parole in duplicate, which, if you choose, you can sign, and be discharged. He will call upon you. I inclose a printed copy of the letter I read to you the last day you were with me, and which I shall be pleased for you to look over. Very Respectfully   A. LINCOLN

1 Copy, DLC-RTL. Lincoln enclosed a printed copy of his letter to Albert G. Hodges, April 4, *supra.* On July 30 Wolford answered: "I have the honor to acknowledge the receipt of your letter proposing to me a discharge from an arrest in many ways vexatious and inconvenient, upon my signing a parole, whereby I am to pledge my honor that I will neither do nor say any thing which will either directly or indirectly tend to hinder, delay, or embarrass the employment and use of colored persons as soldiers, seamen, or otherwise in the suppression of the rebellion. . . . In answer to this proposal, I have frankly to say that I cannot bargain for my liberty, and the exercise of my rights as a freeman, on any such terms. I have committed no crime. I have broken no law. . . . You, Mr. President, if you will excuse the bluntness of a soldier, by an exercise of arbitrary power have caused me to be arrested and held in confinement contrary to law, not for the good of our common country, but to increase the chances of your re-election . . . and otherwise to serve the purposes of the political party whose candidate you are. And now, you ask me to stultify myself by signing a pledge whereby I shall virtually admit, your right to arrest me — and virtually support you in deterring other men from criticising the policy of your Administration. No Sir! much as I love liberty, I will fester in a prison, or die on a gibbet, before I will agree to any terms that do not abandon all charges against me, and fully acknowledge my innocence. . . ." (DLC-RTL). See Lincoln to Wolford, August 4, *infra.*

To Joseph Holt[1]

July 18, 1864

If the Governor of Massachusetts understands the case and wishes to give Capt Brooks another Commission the disability is hereby removed enabling him to do so   A LINCOLN
July 18 1864

1 AES, RPB; copy, DNA WR RG 153, Judge Advocate General, NN 1596. The autograph endorsement is questionable in appearance, but the copy preserved in the court-martial file would seem to authenticate the text. Captain Alfred O. Brooks, Twenty-ninth Massachusetts Volunteers, had been cashiered on March 18, 1864, for absence without leave, conduct unbecoming an officer and gentleman, and conduct prejudicial to good order and military discipline.

To Joseph Holt[1]

[c. July 18, 1864?]

The sentence in this case of 18 years confinement in the Penitentiary, was approved in July 1863. Will the Judge Advocate General please examine it now as on application for pardon, after the convicted has served more than one year?   A. LINCOLN

[1] AES, DNA WR RG 153, Judge Advocate General, MM 395. Lincoln's endorsement is written on a deposition in the case of Private John H. Abbott, Sixth Pennsylvania Reserve Corps, sentenced April 1, 1863, on the charge of murder. On July 18, 1863, Lincoln approved the sentence, and on January 23, 1865, denied the application for pardon.

To Joseph Holt[1]

Let this man be enlarged on the same terms and conditions as in Blacks and Spicer's cases.   A. LINCOLN
July 18, 1864

[1] AES, DNA WR RG 153, Judge Advocate General, NN 1865. See Lincoln to Holt, July 1, *supra*. For failure to deliver 1,200 horses in February, 1864, Daniel Wormer, an army contractor, was sentenced, June 28, 1864, on the charge of wilful neglect of duty, to imprisonment not exceeding one year and a fine of $2,000. In the similar case of John Spicer of Illinois, Spicer was allowed to give bond for the amount of his fine (DNA WR RG 153, Judge Advocate General, MM 1426, May 16, 1864). The Black case has not been identified.

Proclamation Calling for 500,000 Volunteers[1]

July 18, 1864
By the President of the United States of America:

A Proclamation

Whereas, by the act approved July 4, 1864, entitled "an act further to regulate and provide for the enrolling and calling out the National forces and for other purposes," it is provided that the President of the United States may, "at his discretion, at any time hereafter, call for any number of men as volunteers, for the respective terms of one, two and three years for military service," and "that in case the quota of [or][2] any part thereof, of any town, township, ward of a city, precinct, or election district, or of a county not so subdivided, shall not be filled within the space of fifty days after such call, then the President shall immediately order a draft for one year to fill such quota or any part thereof which may be unfilled."

And whereas, the new enrolment, heretofore ordered, is so far completed as that the aforementioned act of Congress may now be put in operation for recruiting and keeping up the strength of the armies in the field for garrisons, and such military operations as

[448]

may be required for the purpose of suppressing the rebellion, and restoring the authority of the United States Government in the insurgent States:

Now, therefore, I, Abraham Lincoln, President of the United States, do issue this my call for five hundred thousand volunteers for the military service, Provided, nevertheless, that this call shall be reduced by all credits which may be established under section 8 of the aforesaid act on account of persons who have entered the naval service during the present rebellion, and by credits for men furnished to the military service in excess of calls heretofore made. Volunteers will be accepted under this call for one, two, or three years, as they may elect, and will be entitled to the bounty provided by the law, for the period of service for which they enlist.

And I hereby proclaim, order and direct, that immediately after the fifth day of September, 1864, being fifty days from the date of this call, a draft for troops to serve for one year shall be had in every town, township, ward of a city, precinct or election district or county not so subdivided to fill the quota which shall be assigned to it under this call, or any part thereof, which may be unfilled, by volunteers on the said fifth day of September 1864.

In testimony whereof, I have hereunto set my hand and caused the seal of the United States to be affixed.

Done at the city of Washington, this eighteenth day of July, in
the year of our Lord one thousand eight hundred and
[L.S.]   sixty four, and of the Independence of the United States
the eighty-ninth.   ABRAHAM LINCOLN
By the President:
    WILLIAM H. SEWARD Secretary of State.

1 DS, DNA FS RG 11, Proclamations.
2 Bracketed pencil insertion in the source.

To William T. Sherman[1]

Major General Sherman   Executive Mansion,
Chattahoochee River, Ga.   Washington, July 18. 1864.

I have seen your despatches objecting to agents of Northern States opening recruiting stations near your camps. An act of congress authorizes this, giving the appointment of agents to the States, and not to this Executive government. It is not for the War Department, or myself, to restrain, or modify the law, in it's execution, further than actual necessity may require. To be candid, I was for the passage of the law, not apprehending at the time that it would produce such inconvenience to the armies in the field, as you now cause me to fear. Many of the States were very anxious for it, and I hoped that, with their State bounties, and active exertions, they would get out substantial additions to our colored forces, which, unlike white recruits, help us where they come from, as well as where they go to. I still hope advantage from the law; and being a law, it must be treated as such by all of us. We here, will do what we consistently can to save you from difficulties arising out of it. May I ask therefore that you will give your hearty co-operation?

A. LINCOLN

1 ALS, DNA WR RG 107, Presidential Telegrams, I, 102-103. On July 14, Sherman telegraphed Halleck, "If State recruiting agents must come into the limits of my command under the law, I have the honor to request that the commanding officers or adjutants of regiments be constituted such agents, and that States be entitled to a credit for recruits they may enlist. . . . This will obviate the difficulty I apprehend from civilian agents." (OR, XXXVIII, V, 136). A second telegram to Halleck sent at 10 P.M. the same day expressed Sherman's opinion that sending "recruiting officers into the rebel States . . . is the height of folly. I cannot permit it here, and I will not have a set of fellows here hanging about on any such pretenses. . . ." (Ibid., p. 137). On July 21 Sherman replied to Lincoln's despatch: "I have the highest veneration for the law, and will respect it always, however it conflicts with my opinion of its propriety. I only telegraphed to General Halleck because I had seen no copy of the law, and supposed the War Department might have some control over its operations. . . ." (Ibid., p. 210).

To Edwin M. Stanton[1]

July 18, 1864

I believe Mr. Welles has never had a Brig. Genl. on his recommendation. I wish this appointment made, so soon as it can be with consistency.　　　　　　　　　　　　　　　　　　　　　A. LINCOLN

July 18. 1864.

1 AES, CtHi. Lincoln's endorsement is written on a letter from Gideon Welles, July 16, 1864, recommending Colonel Joseph R. Hawley, Seventh Connecticut Infantry. Hawley was appointed brigadier general of Volunteers as of September 13, 1864.

To Edwin M. Stanton[1]

Hon Sec. of War please see and hear the bearer.

July 18, 1864.　　　　　　　　　　　　　　　　　　A. LINCOLN.

1 Anderson Galleries Catalog 2193, November 15, 1927, No. 280. According to the catalog description, Lincoln's endorsement is on a letter from Gardiner Tufts, July 18, 1864, asking the president to see Captain George W. Field.

To Whom It May Concern[1]

Executive Mansion,

To Whom it may concern: Washington, July 18, 1864.

Any proposition which embraces the restoration of peace, the integrity of the whole Union, and the abandonment of slavery, and which comes by and with an authority that can control the armies now at war against the United States will be received and considered by the Executive government of the United States, and will be met by liberal terms on other substantial and collateral points; and the bearer, or bearers thereof shall have safe-conduct both ways.

ABRAHAM LINCOLN

[1] ALS-P, ISLA; ADfS, DLC-RTL. The autograph draft in the Lincoln Papers bears Lincoln's endorsement, "Copy of Doc, sent by John Hay." On July 18 Lincoln received the following telegram from Greeley:

"I have communicated with the Gentlemen in question & do not find them so empowered as I was previously assured   they say that—

"We are however in the confidential employment of our Government & entirely familiar with its wishes & opinions on that subject & we feel authorized to declare if the circumstances disclosed in this correspondence were communicated to Richmond we would at once be invested with the authority to which your letter refers or other Gentlemen clothed with full power would immediately be sent to Washington with the view of hastening a consumation so much to be desired & terminating at the earliest possible moment the calamities of war   We respectfully solicit through your intervention a safe conduct to Washington & thence by any route which may be designated to Richmond—

"Such is the more material portion of the Gentlemens letter. I will transmit the entire correspondence if desired. . . . Answer by Ind[ependent]. Telegh Line. . . ." (DLC-RTL).

For a detailed account of Greeley's peace mission, see Nicolay and Hay, *Abraham Lincoln: A History*, IX, 184-200.

Appointment of Government Directors for Union Pacific Railroad[1]

Executive Mansion,

July 19th 1864.

By virtue of the authority conferred upon the President of the United States, by the thirteenth section of the act of Congress approved July 2d. 1864, amending the act to aid in the construction of a Rail road and Telegraph line from the Missouri river to the Pacific Ocean &c

     Jesse L. Williams of Indiana

     George Ashmun of Massachusetts

   and Charles Sherman of Ohio

are hereby appointed directors on the part of the Government of the United States, for the Union Pacific Rail road and Telegraph

Company, to serve until the next ensuing regular election of directors for said Company.   ABRAHAM LINCOLN

[1] DS, DNA NR RG 48, Department of Interior, Lands and Railroads Division, Union Pacific Railroad Company, Package 239.

To Edwin M. Stanton[1]

I submit this high recommendation by Gen. Grant of Maj. Hammond, to the special consideration of the Sec. of War.

July 19. 1864   A. LINCOLN

[1] AES-F, *The Month at Goodspeeds*, February, 1932, p. 172. Lincoln's endorsement is written on a letter from General Grant, July 17, 1864, recommending Major John H. Hammond, assistant adjutant general at Louisville, Kentucky, for appointment as brigadier general to command colored troops (*ibid.*). Hammond was brevetted brigadier general as of October 31, 1864.

Statement of Philadelphia Citizens[1]

Executive Mansion,
Washington, July 19. 1864.

We the undersigned citizens of Philadelphia, state that, after considerable investigation, and inquiry, we believe there are in the Philadelphia Post-Office between two hundred and fifty and three hundred employees under the Post-Master, and that no one of them openly supports the renomination of Judge Kelly for Congress, and that several of them say and intimate privately that it is because they are restrained by the Post-Master.   THOMAS W. PRICE

CHAS. B. BARRETT

GEO. I. YOUNG

[1] AD, DLC-RTL. The body of this document is in Lincoln's handwriting. See Lincoln's memorandum concerning Cornelius A. Walborn, June 20, *supra*, and communication to McMichael, August 5, *infra*.

To Ulysses S. Grant[1]

Lieut. Genl. Grant   Executive Mansion,
City Point, Va   Washington, July 20. 1864.

Yours of yesterday about a call for 300,000 is received. I suppose you had not seen the call for 500,000 made the day before, and which I suppose covers the case. Always glad to have your suggestions   A. LINCOLN

[1] ALS, DNA WR RG 107, Presidential Telegrams, I, 105. On July 19 Grant telegraphed Lincoln: "In my opinion there ought to be an immediate call for, say, 300,000 men to be put in the field in the shortest possible time. The presence of this number of re-enforcements would save the annoyance of raids, and would enable us to drive the enemy from his present front, particularly from Richmond, without attacking fortifications. The enemy now have their last man in the field. Every depletion of their army is an irreparable loss. Desertions from it are now rapid. With the prospect of large additions to our force the desertions would increase. The greater number of men we have the shorter and less sanguinary will be the war. I give this entirely as my views and not in any spirit of dictation, always holding myself in readiness to use the material given me to the best advantage I know how." (OR, I, XXXVII, II, 384).

To John L. Scripps[1]

Hon. J. L. Scripps   Executive Mansion,
My dear Sir   Washington, July 20. 1864.

I have received, and read yours of the 15th. Mine to you, was only a copy, with names changed, of what I had said to another Post-Master, on a similar complaint;[2] and the two are the only cases in which that precise complaint has, as yet, been made to me. I think that in these cases I have stated the principle correctly for all public officers, and I certainly wish all would follow it. But, I do not quite like to publish a general circular on the subject, and it would be rather laborious to write a seperate letter to each. Yours truly   A. LINCOLN

[1] ADfS, DLC-RTL. See Lincoln to Scripps, July 4, *supra.* On July 15 Scripps wrote Lincoln:
"A day or two since, a letter from you . . . was placed in my hands by Hon. I. N. Arnold. . . .
"That I am opposed to the renomination of Mr. Arnold, is true; but that I have, at any time, either directly or indirectly, used my 'official power' to defeat his renomination, is utterly untrue. . . . Mr. Arnold well knew the falsity of the charge at the time he preferred it. . . . But he knew what *he* would do were he similarly situated, and I suppose could not credit the fact; and so he went whining to you about the 'official power' of this office being thrown against him. . . .
"And now will you permit me . . . to take the liberty of suggesting that . . . it would be well for you to give to the various heads of . . . offices the same instructions . . . which you were induced to give to me through Mr. Arnold's deliberate misrepresentations. . . ." (DLC-RTL).
On July 18 Arnold wrote:
"I presented your note to Mr Scripps, with the hope that we might have a frank, friendly understanding. It was received in a storm of rage & passion. He said it was an insult. You had never read or understood what you had signed. . . . I assured him you spoke of him highly, & that the letter was kindly meant &c.
"He said he should write to you, & because he said this I trouble you with this note. . . ." (*Ibid.*).
[2] See the memorandum of Lincoln's interview with Walborn, June 20, *supra.*

To Jacob T. Wright[1]

United States Military Telegraph,
J. L. Wright.   War Department.
Indianapolis, Ia.   July 20. 1864
All a mistake. Mr. Stanton has not resigned.   A. LINCOLN

[1] ALS, DNA WR RG 107, Presidential Telegrams, I, 104. Lincoln's error in regard to Wright's middle initial derived from the error in the received copy of Wright's telegram of July 20, 1864: "Notice resignation of Secretary Stanton & see it intimated that Genl Butler may be named his successor   For Gods sake give us Butler . . . the loyal people of the North west will all say amen" (DLC-RTL). Jacob Taylor Wright was chairman of the Republican State Union Central Committee of Indiana.

To William P. Fessenden[1]

Hon. Sec. of Treasury   Executive Mansion,
My dear Sir.   Washington, July 21, 1864.

The bearer of this is a most estimable widow lady, at whose house I boarded many years ago when a member of Congress. She now is very needy; & any employment suitable to a lady could not be bestowed on a more worthy person. Yours truly
                                                            A. LINCOLN

[1] ALS-F, *The Evening Star* (Washington), February 12, 1940. The "widow lady" was Mrs. Ann G. Sprigg, who received an appointment as clerk in the loan branch of the Treasury Department.

Memorandum: Appointment of Anning R. Peck[1]

July 21, 1864
Anning R. Peck is a nephew of Gen. Richardson; and I wish to appoint him to West-Point, within the succeeding twelve months. Let me be reminded of this. Born Jany. 29, 1846.   A. LINCOLN
July 21. 1864

[1] AES, DNA WR RG 94, U.S. Military Academy, 1864, No. 374. Lincoln's endorsement is written on a letter of Cyrus Dickson, July 19, 1864, introducing "Mrs Peck, sister of the late brave General [Israel B.] Richardson . . . to procure a Cadetship for her son." No record has been found of the appointment of Anning R. Peck.

To Edwin M. Stanton[1]

July 21, 1864
If there is on file, a request of Gov. Hahn for the release of these men, let them be discharged, upon taking the oath of Dec. 8, 1863,

and also an oath that they never have been in favor of the rebellion, or in it's service.   A. LINCOLN

July 21, 1864

[1] ALS, The Rosenbach Company, Philadelphia and New York. The men have not been identified.

To Edwin M. Stanton[1]

Let E. P. McLean, private in Co. A, 62nd. Penn. Vols, be discharged, on no ground, but that Gov. Curtin, and D. H. A. McLean asks it.

July 21. 1864   A. LINCOLN

[1] AES, IHi. Lincoln's endorsement is written on a letter from Governor Andrew G. Curtin, July 20, 1864, introducing Reverend D. H. A. McLean: "Whether intentionally or not there is no doubt a deception was practiced upon him and his son in his last enlistment and I sincerely hope it may be consistent with your duty and the good of the service to order his discharge." Stanton endorsed on July 21: "Referred to Adjt Genl to issue order as directed by the President."

To Orlando B. Ficklin[1]

Hon. O. B. Ficklin   Executive Mansion
Dear Sir: Washington, July 22, 1864

I had about concluded to send the Coles county men home, turning over the indicted to the authorities, and discharging the others, when Col. Oaks' report, with the evidence he had taken in the case was put in my hand. The evidence is very voluminous, and Col. Oaks says it fully implicates every one of the sixteen now held; and so far as I have been able to look into it, his statement is sustained. I can not now decide the case until I shall have fully examined this evidence. Yours truly   A. LINCOLN

[1] ADfS (ALS?), DLC-RTL. See Lincoln to Davis, July 2, *supra*. Orlando B. Ficklin was in Washington seeking to have the prisoners turned over to civil authorities. His undated reply, probably written on the same day, is as follows:

"I have received your note in reference to the Coles Co. prisoners & appreciate the embarrassment under which you are placed by the report of Col. Oaks [James Oakes]. The evidence on which his report is based is not only wholly ex parte but was taken when the town was a military camp & the whole community was excited beyond description. . . .

"If these men can be tried at home or if the testimony can be retaken before any fair minded man it will establish the innocence of those not indicted.

"I deprecate & openly denounce all resistance to or violation of law as much as any one can or need do, but the community generally believe most of those men to be innocent & they have confidence that you will not allow them to be sacrificed for the sins of others. I leave this matter in your hands with the full confidence that you will deal justly with these men" (DLC-RTL).

See further Lincoln's order of November 4, *infra*.

To Gideon Welles[1]

Executive Mansion,
Washington, July 22. 1864.

I have said to this lady that I will do for her brother whatever the Sec. of Navy, or Asst. Sec. of Navy, will, in writing on this, sheet, advise me to do.   A. LINCOLN

[1] ALS, DLM. No further reference has been found.

To Edward Bates[1]

Please send me.   A. LINCOLN
July 23. 1864

[1] AES, DNA RG 204, U.S. Pardon Attorney, A 536. Lincoln's endorsement is written below a penciled memorandum on Executive Mansion stationery, written by an unidentified hand: "papers—application for pardon of [Henry] Crittenden, Iowa, convicted of stealing money from post office or mails— "filed by Mr [John A.] Kasson in Atty. Genl. office."

To David Hunter[1]

"Cypher"   United States Military Telegraph,
Major Gen. Hunter   War Department.
Harpers Ferry, Va.   July 23. 1864 [8 A.M.]

Are you able to take care of the enemy when he turns back upon you, as he probably will[2] on finding that Wright has left?
                                             A. LINCOLN.

[1] ALS, DNA WR RG 107, Presidential Telegrams, I, 106. Hunter replied at 9 A.M.: "My force is not strong enough to hold the enemy should he return upon us with his whole force. Our latest advices from the front however do not lead me to apprehend such a movement. General Crook has information . . . that Early left his positions at Berryville suddenly upon the arrival of a courier from Richmond with orders to fall back upon that place. News from Averill [Brigadier General William W. Averell] yesterday says he has pushed his cavalry to Front Royal and Strasburg without hearing of the enemy. I will take care that no such movement of the enemy shall take us by surprise" (DLC-RTL).
[2] "Will" inserted in pencil by the telegraph operator.

To John P. Usher[1]

July 24, 1864

I know nothing personally of Mr. Rohrer, but shall be very glad if the Sec. of Interior can oblige the gentlemen who write the within letter.   A. LINCOLN
July 24. 1864

[1] ALS, owned by Charles W. Olsen, Chicago, Illinois. Lincoln's note has been removed from the attendant letter. Rohrer has not been identified.

To Edward R. S. Canby[1]

Washington, D.C.,

Major General Canby: July 25. 1864.

Frequent complaints are made to me that persons endeavoring to bring in cotton in strict accordance with the trade regulations of the Treasury Department, are frustrated by seizures of District Attorneys, Marshals, Provost-Marshals and others, on various pretences, all looking to black-mail, and spoils, one way and another. I wish, if you can find time, you would look into this matter within your Department, and finding these abuses to exist, break them up, if in your power, so that fair dealing under the regulations, can proceed. The printed Regulations, no doubt, are accessable to you. If you find the abuses existing, and yet beyond your power, please report to me somewhat particularly upon the facts.

The bearer of this   Shaffer, is one who, on behalf of himself and firm, makes complaint; but while he is my friend, I do not ask anything for him which can not be done for all honest dealers under the Regulations. Yours truly   A. LINCOLN

[1] ADfS, DLC-RTL. A copy of this letter dated July 26, 1864, preserved in the Benjamin F. Flanders Papers (LU) has also the following: "P.S. The above is only a copy of the letter put in the hands of Mr. T. Shaffer but it is true and applicable for Mr Henry S. McComb. (signed) A. L." No reply from Canby, in command of the Military Division of West Mississippi, has been located.

To Andrew G. Curtin[1]

Executive Mansion,

Gov. Curtin.   Washington, July 25, 1864.

Herewith is the manuscript letter for the gentleman who sent me a cane through your hands. For my life I can not make out his name; and therefore I cut it from his letter and pasted it on, as you see. I suppose [you] will remember who he is, and I will thank you to forward him the letter. He dates his letter at Philadelphia. Yours truly   A. LINCOLN

[1] ALS-F, ISLA. See Lincoln's letter to William O. Snider, *infra.* Governor Curtin forwarded to James B. Fry a letter of William O. Snider, Philadelphia, April 6, 1864, as follows:

"I beg leave to present through you to his Excellency Abraham Lincoln . . . a cane which I send you for that purpose. It is a facsimile of one which I have had the honor to present to you personally

"Both of them are made from a fragment of wood taken from the hulk of the rebel iron clad Merrimac after she was blown up. . . . Captain Mark Hewlings of Philadelphia commander of the steam tug Star obtained it and presented it to me.

"These canes were manufactured by Wm. Gute a Philadelphia, artisan. . . ." (DLC-RTL).

Curtin's endorsement to Fry on the envelope states: "Mr. Nicolay . . . promised . . . to get an autograph letter to the gentleman who procured the wood and made the cane. . . ." (*Ibid.*).

Snider's letter is incorrectly cataloged in the Lincoln Papers under James B. Fry, probably as the result of Lincoln's having clipped the signature, as well as because of the endorsement to Fry.

To the Loyal Ladies of Trenton, New Jersey[1]

Executive Mansion,
Washington, July 25, 1864.

The Loyal Ladies of Trenton, New Jersey: At the Philadelphia Fair, about the middle of last month, a very pretty Cane, with hallowed associations, was presented to me, on your behalf, by a worthy revered gentleman, whose name, I regret to say, I cannot now remember.

Please accept my sincere thanks, which, in my many duties, I have not found time to tender sooner. Your ob't servant,

A. LINCOLN.

[1] C. C. Haven, *Annals of the City of Trenton* (1866), p. 28. The presentation of the cane took place at the Sanitary Fair, Philadelphia, June 16. A copy of the presentation, incorrectly cataloged June 10, 1864, in the Lincoln Papers, is as follows: "The loyal ladies of Trenton many of whom are descendants of those 'Matrons and Maidens' who scattered flowers in the path of Washington when passing through the triumphal arch which her sons had erected in 1789 on the memorable spot where by the blessing of Providence that repulse was given to Cornwallis which reversed the gloomy fortunes of war for our National Independence, now have the pleasure to present for your acceptance a cane made from the same Arch, as a humble but heartfelt testimonial of that love confidence & respect which they in common with millions of their countrymen & countrywomen feel towards you.

"Approaching as you do so near the character & experiencing the trials and responsibilities of the venerated Father of our Country, most especially in unswerving fidelity to free principles & the discharge of all the duties with which you have been invested by a confiding people, we trust that you may find in the staff now presented you, as an 'heir loom' of the old Arch where the 'gratulating song' was sung by the patriotic young ladies of Trenton, similar gratification as that which was felt by Washington." (DLC-RTL).

Memorandum:
Appointment of William C. Collier[1]

July 25, 1864

If Beverly Allen has declined the Cadetship tendered him, & the place has not been filled, let William C. Collier, named within, be appointed—this, on the recommendation of Gen. Hitchcock.

July 25. 1864.   A. LINCOLN

1 AES, DNA WR RG 94, U.S. Military Academy, 1862, No. 59. Lincoln's endorsement is written on a letter from James E. Yeatman, St. Louis, July 22, 1864, recommending appointment of William B. Collier in place of Beverly Allen, who had declined his appointment. Lincoln erred in giving Collier's middle initial. William B. Collier is listed in the third class at West Point in 1865.

Memorandum on Clement C. Clay[1]

Executive Mansion,
Washington, [c. July 25], 1864

Hon. Clement C. Clay, one of the Confederate gentlemen who recently, at Niagara Falls, in a letter to Mr. Greeley, declared that they were *not* empowered to negotiate for peace, but that they *were*, however, in the confidential employment of their government, has prepared a Platform and an Address to be adopted by the Democracy at the Chicago Convention, the preparing of these, and conferring with the democratic leaders in regard to the same, being the confidential employment of their government, in which he, and his confreres are engaged. The following planks are in the Platform—

5. The war to be further prossecuted only to restore the *Union as it was*, and only in such manner, that no further detriment to slave property shall be effected.

6. All negro soldiers and seamen to be at once disarmed and degraded to menial service in the Army and Navy; and no additional negroes to be, on any pretence whatever, taken from their masters.

7 All negroes not having enjoyed actual freedom during the war to be held permanently as slaves; and whether those who shall have enjoyed actual freedom during the war, shall be free to be a legal question.

The following paragraphs are in the Address—

"Let all who are in favor of peace; of arresting the slaughter of our countrymen, of saving the country from bankruptcy & ruin, of securing food & raiment & good wages for the laboring classes; of disappointing the enemies of Democratic & Republican Government who are rejoicing in the overthrow of their proudest monuments; of vindicating our capacity for self-government, arouse and maintain these principles, and elect these candidates."

*   *   *   *   *

"The stupid tyrant who now disgraces the Chair of Washington and Jackson could, any day, have peace and restoration of the Union; and would have them, only that he persists in the war merely to free the slaves."

The convention may not litterally adopt Mr. Clay's Platform and Address, but we predict it will do so substantially. We shall see.

Mr. Clay confesses to his Democratic friends that he is for *peace* and *disunion;* but, he says "You can not elect without a cry of war for the union; but, once elected, we are friends, and can adjust matters somehow." He also says "You will find some difficulty in proving that Lincoln could, if he would, have peace and re-union, because Davis has not said so, and will not say so; but you must assert it, and re-assert it, and stick to it, and it will pass as at least half proved."

¹ AD, DLC-RTL. The date of this memorandum has been supplied on the basis of the fact that its content seems to be closely linked with Lincoln's letter to Abram Wakeman, *infra.* It seems possible that Wakeman may have furnished Lincoln the information concerning the Clay platform in his interview with the president, although the platform and "Address" were not generally known at this time. In any event, Lincoln's memorandum must have been written prior to August 29, when the Democratic National Convention assembled.

To William O. Snider¹

Executive Mansion,
Wm. O. Snider   Washington, July 25. 1864.
The cane you did me the honor to present throough [*sic*] Gov. Curtin was duly placed in my hand by him. Please accept my thanks; and at the same time, pardon me for not having sooner found time to tender them. Your Obt. Servt.   A. LINCOLN

¹ ALS-F, ISLA. See Lincoln to Curtin, *supra.* The name of "Wm. O. Snider" appears on the manuscript as a small clipping pasted above the body of the letter.

To Robert F. Taylor¹

Executive Mansion,
Washington, July 25. 1864.
Thomas Connor, a private in the 1st. Veteran New-York Cavalry, is now imprisoned at hard labor for desertion. If the Colonel of said Regiment will say in writing on this sheet, that he is willing to receive him back to the Regiment, I will pardon, and send him.

A. LINCOLN

¹ ALS-F, ISLA. Colonel Robert F. Taylor of the First New York Veteran Cavalry did not reply "on this sheet," as directed. AGO *Special Orders No. 357,*

October 20, 1864, ordered Private Thomas Connor to be pardoned and returned to his regiment.

To Abram Wakeman[1]

Private   Executive Mansion,
Abram Wakeman, Esq   Washington,
My dear Sir: July 25, 1864.

I feel that the subject which you pressed upon my attention in our recent conversation is an important one. The men of the South, recently (and perhaps still) at Niagara Falls, tell us distinctly that they *are* in the confidential employment of the rebellion; and they tell us as distinctly that they are *not* empowered to offer terms of peace. Does any one doubt that what they *are* empowered to do, is to assist in selecting and arranging a candidate and a platform for the Chicago convention? Who could have given them this confidential employment but he who only a week since declared to Jaquess and Gilmore that he had no terms of peace but the independence of the South—the dissolution of the Union? Thus the present presidential contest will almost certainly be no other than a contest between a Union and a Disunion candidate, disunion certainly following the success of the latter. The issue is a mighty one for all people and all time; and whoever aids the right, will be appreciated and remembered. Yours truly   A. LINCOLN.

[1] ALS, CSmH; ADfS, DLC-RTL. See Lincoln's memorandum on Clement C. Clay, *supra*. Although marked "Private," Lincoln's letter was obviously intended to be shown to James Gordon Bennett, owner of the New York *Herald*, whom Lincoln wished to enlist, in so far as possible, in support of his ensuing campaign. That Lincoln's final sentence was meant to convey promise of Bennett's appointment to a post of dignity is borne out of Wakeman's reply as well as by subsequent events leading to Lincoln's offering Bennett the post of minister to France (Lincoln to Bennett, February 20, 1865, *infra*). On August 12, 1864, Wakeman wrote Lincoln:

"Your excellent letter was duly received. I have read it with proper explanations to Mr B. He said, after some moments of silence, that so far as it related to him, 'It did not amount to much.' I supposed, if anything was written, something more specific would be expected. However, I hope to avoid the writing of any thing further. Should it be deemed necessary I will indicate my views as to its form, personally, as I expect to be in Washington next week. I have ventured to show this letter to several of our friends (of course without indicating a word as to what drew it out) and it has met with universal approval.

"A word upon our other matter. I am fearful our hold upon Mr Weed is slight. He evidently has his eye upon some other probable candidate. I deeply regret this, for against him it will be difficult to carry New York. Now I dont know, precisely, what he asked when he last saw you, but I think, so far as I could without compromising principle, I would yield to his wishes. Cant this be done? . . ." (DLC-RTL).

[461]

To James C. Welling[1]

J. C. Welling, Esq   Executive Mansion,
Sir   Washington, July 25. 1864.

According to the request contained in your note, I have placed Mr. Gibson's letter of resignation in the hands of the President. He has read the letter, and says he accepts the resignation, as he will be glad to do with any other which may be tendered, as this is, for the purpose of taking an attitude of hostility against him. He says he was not aware that he was so much indebted to Mr. Gibson for having accepted the office at first, not remembering that he ever pressed him to do so, or that he gave it otherwise than as was usual, upon request made on behalf of Mr. Gibson. He thanks Mr. Gibson for his acknowledgment that he has been treated with personal kindness and consideration; and he says he knows of but two small draw-backs upon Mr. Gibson's right to still receive such treatment, one of which is that he never could learn of his giving much attention to the duties of his office, and the other is this studied attempt of Mr. Gibson's[2] to stab him

I am very truly, Your obedient servant   JOHN HAY.

[1] ADf, DLC-RTL. The draft is in Lincoln's autograph excepting the complimentary close and signature and the one insertion noted below, which are John Hay's. On July 23, 1864, James C. Welling, assistant clerk of the U.S. Court of Claims, who later became president of St. John's College and also of Columbia University, wrote John Hay:

"I am requested by the Hon Chas Gibson, the Solicitor for the United States in the Court of Claims, to transmit to the President . . . his resignation of that office. I beg that you will place it in the hands of his Excellency.

"Mr. Gibson has also left with me a copy of his letter of resignation, under instructions to give the same to the public press that the grounds on which he feels it his duty to take this step may be known by his friends in Missouri. . . ." (DLC-RTL).

Charles Gibson's letter of resignation, July 11, 1864, enclosed by Welling, is as follows:

"I was appointed to office by you at a time when it was deemed advisable for the public welfare, especially in Missouri, to conciliate those—of whom I was one—who did not belong to the party that elected you President, but who obeyed & actively supported you as the duly elected Chief Magistrate of the Nation, and who were unconditionally for the Union. . . .

"The Baltimore Convention has . . . decided to banish from your administration all conservative men and all moderate counsel by resolving . . . that those only are 'worthy of public confidence or official trust,' who 'cordially indorse' its platform. . . . The Convention has given a still more emphatic & practical evidence of its real feelings . . . in admitting almost unanimously the American radical Delegates from this; & by excluding . . . the Delegates of the Conservative Party. . . .

"Under these circumstances my retention of office . . . would be wholly useless to the country, as well as inconsistent with my principles and I therefore resign the office of 'Solicitor of the United States for the Court of Claims.'

"I accepted the office solely as a patriotic duty, & at considerable personal &

pecuniary sacrifice. It is the only office I ever held or expect to hold. I am deeply grateful to you, Mr. President, for the personal kindness & consideration with which you have treated me, & I would continue to serve you if it were consistent with my convictions of duty or if I could by so doing be of any further service to the country" (*ibid.*).   2 "Of Mr. Gibson's" inserted by Hay.

To Edward Bates[1]

I supose the other papers alluded to are in the Atty Genls. Dept. Add these.   A. LINCOLN

July 26. 1864

1 AES, DNA RG 204, U.S. Pardon Attorney, A 539. Lincoln's endorsement is written on a letter of Thomas L. Price, Jefferson City, Missouri, to Montgomery Blair, July 13, 1864, enclosing papers in the case of Harvey Walker, convicted of forgery.

To William T. Sherman[1]

"*Cypher*"   United States Military Telegraph,
Major General Sherman.   War Department.
Near Atlanta.   Washington, July 26. 1864

I have just seen yours, complaining of the appointment of Hovey and Osterhaus. The point you make is unquestionably a good one; and yet please hear a word from us. My recollection is that both Gen. Grant and yourself recommended both H & O. for promotion; and these, with other strong recommendations, drew committals from us which we could neither honorably or safely, disregard. We blamed H. for coming away in the manner in which he did; but we knew he had apparant reason to feel disappointed and mortified, and we felt it was not best to crush one who certainly had been a good soldier. As to O. we did not know of his leaving at the time we made the appointment, and do not now know the terms on which he left. Not to have appointed him, as the case appeared to us at the time, would have been almost if not quite a violation of our word. The word was given on what we thought was high merit, and somewhat on his nationality. I beg you to believe we do not act in a spirit of disregarding merit. We expect to await your programme, for further changes and promotions in your army.

My profoundest thanks to you and your whole Army for the present campaign so far.   A. LINCOLN

1 ALS, DNA WR RG 107, Presidential Telegrams, I, 107-108. Alvin P. Hovey and Peter J. Osterhaus were brevetted major generals of Volunteers on July 4 and July 23, respectively. On July 25, 1864, Sherman telegraphed Inspector General James A. Hardie: "I have your dispatch . . . announcing the appointment of . . . Osterhaus as major-general. I do not object to his appointment, but I wish to put on record . . . my emphatic opinion, that it is an act of injustice

to officers who stand by their posts in the day of danger to neglect them and advance such as Hovey and Osterhaus, who left us in the midst of bullets to go to the rear in search of personal advancement. If the rear be the post of honor, then we had better all change front on Washington." (OR, I, XXXVIII, V, 247).

On July 27, Sherman replied to Lincoln's telegram: "Your dispatch of yesterday is received. I beg you will not regard me as fault-finding, for I assert that I have been well sustained in every respect. . . . I did not suppose my dispatches could go outside the office at the War Department. . . . Hovey and Osterhaus are both worthy men and had they been promoted on the eve of the Vicksburgh campaign it would have been natural and well accepted but I do think you will admit that their promotion coming to us when they had been to the rear the one offended because I could not unite in the same division five Infantry and five cavalry regiments; and the other for temporary sickness, you can see how ambitious aspirants for military fame regard these things; and they come to me and point them out as evidence that I am wrong in encouraging them in a silent, patient discharge of duty. I assure you that every General of my army has spoken of it and referred to it as evidence that promotion results from importunity and not from actual services. I have refrained from recommending any thus far in the campaign and think we should reach some stage in the game before stopping to balance accounts or writing history   I assure you that I do think you have conscienciously acted throughout the war with marked skill in . . . military appointments, and that as few mistakes have been made as could be expected. I will furnish all my army and Division commanders with a copy of your dispatch, that they may feel reassured." (DLC-RTL).

To Edwin M. Stanton[1]

Hon. Sec. of War   Executive Mansion
Sir: Washington July 26, 1864

Gen. Geo. H. Gordon, now at Memphis, is out of service, and wishes to be assigned to duty — in the Army of the Potomac if convenient. I know nothing particularly of him; but let his case be looked into, & if there be no valid objections, let him be put to work. Yours truly   A LINCOLN

[1] ALS, owned by Irvin F. Westheimer, Cincinnati, Ohio. In July, 1864, General George H. Gordon had been in charge of guarding and keeping open communications with Little Rock, Arkansas, by way of White River. In August, 1864, he took part in the operations against Mobile, Alabama.

Appointment of Richard W. Thompson
as Commissioner to Examine Union Pacific Railroads[1]

Executive Mansion,   July 27th 1864.
By virtue of the authority vested in the President of the United States, by the sixth section of an act entitled "an act to amend an act entitled 'an act to aid in the construction of a Rail road and Telegraph line from the Missouri river to the Pacific Ocean, and to secure to the Government the use of the same for postal, military and other purposes' " approved July 2d 1864:

Richard W. Thompson, of Indiana, is hereby appointed a Commissioner, to examine the road or roads authorized by said acts to be constructed by the "Union Pacific Rail road Company," and the "Union Pacific Rail road Company, Eastern division," and make report to him in relation thereto as contemplated and specified by said acts.   ABRAHAM LINCOLN

[1] DS, DNA NR RG 48, Department of Interior, Lands and Railroads Division, Union Pacific Railroad Company, Package 239. The act authorized appointment of three commissioners, but this is the only appointment which has been discovered.

To Ulysses S. Grant[1]

Lieut. Gen. Grant   Executive Mansion
City-Point Va.   Washington D.C. July 27, 1864
   Please have a Surgeons examination of Cornelius Lee Comyges in Co. A. 183rd. Vols. made on the questions of general health and sanity.   A LINCOLN.

[1] ALS, DNA WR RG 107, Presidential Telegrams, I, 111. AGO *Special Orders No. 251*, July 27, 1864, ordered Private Cornelius Lee Comegyes discharged from service.

To Joseph Holt[1]

                              Executive Mansion, Washington,
Judge Advocate General: July 27, 1864.
   It seems a man by the name of James Barrett *alias* Geo. Barrett *alias* Thomas Barrett, has been confined for aiding a soldier to desert. Please procure the papers and report to me on the case. Yours Truly,   A. LINCOLN.

[1] Copy, DNA WR RG 153, Judge Advocate General, MM 1478. On July 20, 1864, George Barrett, citizen of Maryland, was sentenced, on the charge of aiding a deserter by selling him citizens' clothing, to one year's imprisonment and a fine of $250. On August 17 Lincoln endorsed the record, "Fine remitted and confinement reduced to six months," and on January 23, 1865, endorsed "Pardon for unexecuted part of sentence."

To David Hunter[1]

"Cypher"   United States Military Telegraph,
Major Gen. Hunter   War Department. Washington,
Harper's Ferry, Va   July 27. 1864 [8:30 A.M.]
   Please send any recent news you have—particularly as to movements of the enemy.   A. LINCOLN

1 ALS, DNA WR RG 107, Presidential Telegrams, I, 109. Hunter replied at 10 A.M.:

"Earlys force is still . . . near Winchester. We can hear nothing of the enemy east of the Blue ridge. If you have any information of the enemy in that direction please inform me

"I have sent out in several directions for information and will keep you posted. . . . In the present state of affairs I think it much more important to make Washn & Balto perfectly secure than to atte[m]pt to interrupt the rebels in gathering their crops in the valley. Is this the view of the Government." (DLC-RTL).

To Andrew Johnson[1]

"Cypher"   United States Military Telegraph,
Gov. Johnson.   War Department.
Nashville, Tenn.   Washington, July 27. 1864

Yours in relation to Gen. A. C. Gillam just received. Will look after the matter to-day. I also received yours about Gen. Carl Schurz. I appreciate him certainly as highly as you do; but you can never know until you have the trial, how difficult it is to find a *place* for an officer of so high rank, when there is no place seeking *him.*   A. LINCOLN

1 ALS, DNA WR RG 107, Presidential Telegrams, I, 110. On July 21 Governor Johnson had telegraphed, "We have just been advised that the nomination of A. C. Gillett [*sic*] as Br Genl has not been confirmed & that the appointment has been revoked. There is certainly some mistake about this. When I was in Washington I conferred with some of the senate Mil Com & had every assurance that it would be done. . . ." (DLC-RTL). Perhaps because of the error in the name Lincoln did not reply promptly, and Johnson telegraphed on July 26 asking whether Lincoln had received his telegram on the appointment of General "Gillam" (DLC-Stanton Papers). Johnson's earlier telegram of July 13 is as follows: "Maj Genl Carl Schurz is here his command is not a very active one he is anxious to be placed in a position where he can render more service to the country & distinction & credit to himself. . . ." (DLC-RTL).

On December 31, 1863, Colonel Alvan C. Gillem of the Tenth Tennessee Infantry had been nominated brigadier general to rank from August 17, 1863, but the nomination had been tabled by the Senate on May 28, 1864. Renominated on December 12, 1864, he was confirmed by the Senate on February 14, 1865.

To Edwin M. Stanton[1]

July 27, 1864

I know not how much is within the legal power of the government in this case; but it is certainly true in equity, that the laboring women in our employment, should be paid at the least as much as they were at the beginning of the war. Will the Secretary of War please have the case fully examined, and so much relief given as can be consistently with the law and the public service.

July 27. 1864   A. LINCOLN

[1] AES-P, ISLA. Lincoln's endorsement is written on a letter from Governor Andrew G. Curtin forwarding a printed petition, which appeared to him "just and reasonable." The petition is as follows:

"To the Hon. EDWIN M. STANTON, Secretary of War.

"SIR: Twenty thousand Working Women of Philadelphia, Pennsylvania, respectfully ask your indulgence, while they narrate the causes which compel them to petition for relief at your hands.

"At the breaking out of the rebellion that is now deluging our land with blood, and which for a time threatened the destruction of the Nation, the prices paid at the United States Arsenal in this city were barely sufficient to enable the women engaged upon Government work to earn a scanty respectable subsistence. Since the period referred to, board, provisions, and all other articles of female consumption, have advanced to such an extent as to make an average of at least seventy-five per cent.,—while woman's labor has been *reduced thirty per cent.* What need of argument? To an intelligent mind, the result must be apparent; and it is perhaps superfluous to say, that it has produced great suffering, privation, and, in many instances, actual hunger. Such, however, is the *truth.*

"To alleviate this misery, feed the hungry, clothe the naked, and house the houseless, we appeal to those in authority for a just and reasonable compensation for our labor.

"What we need most IS IMMEDIATE AID. You can give it; the power is lodged with you; issue an Order to the Quartermaster-General, authorizing or ordering him to increase the price of female labor until it shall approximate to the price of living.

"Let it be done without delay. Send the order at once, and you will have the proud satisfaction of knowing that you have done all in your power to ameliorate the condition of those who have given *their all* to their country; and who now come to that country, not as beggars, asking alms, but as American matrons and daughters, asking an equitable price for their labor. Comply with this, our reasonable request, and hundreds, yea thousands, will rise up and call you blessed.

"We also desire to call your attention to the fact, that there are a large number of men in this city who are making immense fortunes off the Government by their contracts; and who, instead of entering into an honorable competition as to who is willing to work for the smallest profit, seem to go upon the principle, who can pay the lowest prices. We ask you to so modify the contract system as to make it obligatory upon every person taking a contract to pay the Arsenal prices for making the articles for which they put in their bids. This would remedy the evil effectually.

"Lastly, we would respectfully ask your notice of a plan submitted by the Quartermaster of this city to the Quartermaster-General of the United States, about a year ago, urging the attention of the Government to the necessity for increased facilities for manufacturing articles in the Arsenal, whereby four times the number of women now engaged might be employed, and millions of dollars annually saved the Nation.

"Trusting in the generosity of your nature, the justice of our cause, and the claims which our sacrifices have given us, we confidently leave the issue in your hands, praying that the God of the husbandless and fatherless may so incline your heart, that your answer may shed light where all is dark; send joy for sorrow; and sunshine and peace to the thousands that are now bowed down by cloud and storm.

"We have the honor to subscribe ourselves your friends, &c."

To Edward Bates[1]

Hon. Attorney General   Executive Mansion,
My dear Sir: Washington, July 28, 1864.

The Solicitor of the Court of Claims, Mr. Gibson, has resigned; and Judge Casey, expressing anxiety to have a good man, suggest Hon. John A. Bingham of Ohio. Please send me an appointment for him. Also send me one for John J. Weed of Illinois, to be Assistant Solicitor in place of Mr. McPherson who is always ready to resign, as I understand. Yours truly   A. LINCOLN

[1] ALS, DNA GE RG 60, Papers of Attorney General, Segregated Lincoln Material. See the communications to Casey, July 6, and to Welling, July 25, *supra.*

To Richard Delafield[1]

Gen. Delafield will oblige me if he will furnish to Mr Schumacher a copy Lt. Col. Alexander's report in the case within mentioned.
July 28. 1864   A. LINCOLN

[1] AES, DNA WR RG 77, Office of Chief of Engineers, Letters Received, S 9240. Lincoln's endorsement is written on a letter from John Schumacher, Washington, July, 1864: "I most respectfully request of your Excellency an official order for the production and a copy of Lt Col. [Barton S.] Alexander's report to the Bureau of Engineers upon my invention of a Floating Harbor Obstruction etc." On the bottom of the page Schumacher added over date of July 28, 1864, "Genl Delafield will please hand the desired paper to Mr. Josh. B Carter and oblige." A further endorsement indicates that the requested copy was forwarded August 1 by Brigadier General Delafield, chief of engineers, to Stanton for transmittal.

To John W. Forney[1]

Hon. John W. Forney   Executive Mansion,
My dear Sir   Washington, July 28. 1864.

Your note announcing your intended visit to Europe takes me somewhat by surprise. Nevertheless I am glad for you to have the relaxation, though I regret the necessity which compels it. I have no European personal acquaintances, or I would gladly give you letters. I shall be pleased to see you in Washington before you leave, for a special reason; and the sooner you could come, the better. Yours truly   A. LINCOLN

[1] ALS, PHi. On July 25, John W. Forney wrote Lincoln: "Advised by my physicians I have taken my passage for Europe in the Scotia which leaves New York on the 10th of August. My healtl has given way . . . and I need repose. I am the freer to leave because I feel assured of your re-election to which both my great journals . . . will be especially devoted. I want no office abroad, but

I do ask of you some such recognition as will show to the foreigners that you you [*sic*] appreciate me. Please answer this letter at your earliest leisure." (DLC-RTL).

To John W. Forney[1]

United States Military Telegraph,
War Department.

Hon. J. W. Forney
Philadelphia, Penn.   Washington July 28. 1864

I wish yourself and M. McMichael would see me here to-morrow, or early in the day Saturday.   A. LINCOLN

[1] ALS, DNA WR RG 107, Presidential Telegrams, I, 114. The time sent is noted as 6:10 P.M., probably later than the letter, *supra.* Lincoln's reasons for wishing a conference are indicated in his memorandum regarding Cornelius A. Walborn, June 20, *supra,* and communication to Morton McMichael, August 5, *infra.* John Russell Young, editor-in-chief of the Philadelphia *Press,* replied to Lincoln's telegram on July 29: "Col Forney is at the sea-shore   Will endeavour to forward your message to him. He purposed being in Washington on Tuesday" (DLC-RTL).

To James B. Fry[1]

Provost Marshal General please see Mr. Ferry, and examine this case; and if you cannot do what is desired, report to me on the case
July 28, 1864   A. LINCOLN

[1] ALS, CLCM. Fry endorsed, "Enter and file. I have answered. J.F." On July 23, 1864, Jacob M. Howard of Detroit wrote Lincoln: "I take pleasure in introducing to you my friend Hon. Thos. W. Ferry of Grand Haven in this state. He has been nominated to Congress . . . & is every way worthy of your confidence. . . . He visits Washington for the purpose of effecting some corrections in the enrollments of his part of the state. . . ." (DLC-RTL).

To Ulysses S. Grant[1]

"Cypher"   Executive Mansion,
Lieut. Genl. Grant   Washington,
City Point, Va.   July 28, 1864.

Will meet you at Fort-Monroe at 8. P.M. on Saturday the 30th. unless you shall notify me that it will be inconvenient to you.

A. LINCOLN

[1] ALS, DNA WR RG 107, Presidential Telegrams, I, 112. On July 26, Stanton telegraphed Grant of the arrival of General John A. Rawlins with Grant's letter to Lincoln (July 25) proposing to combine the departments of Susquehanna, Washington, Middle Virginia, and West Virginia, under command of George G. Meade, and requesting Grant "to name, if you can, a time when it would be convenient for you to meet him [Lincoln] in person at Fortress Monroe after

Thursday morning." (OR, I, XXXVII, II, 444). Grant replied on the same day that he would meet Lincoln "at any time that will suit his convenience after about next Friday." (*Ibid.*).

On July 27, Stanton wrote Halleck: "Lieutenant-General Grant having signified that, owing to the difficulties and delay of communication between his headquarters and Washington, it is necessary that in the present emergency military orders must be issued directly from Washington, the President directs me to instruct you that all the military operations for the defense of the Middle Department, the Department of the Susquehanna, the Department of Washington, and the Department of West Virginia, and all the forces in those departments, are placed under your general command, and that you will be expected to take all military measures necessary for defense against any attack of the enemy and for his capture and destruction. You will issue from time to time such orders to the commanders of the respective departments and to the military authorities therein as may be proper." (*Ibid.*, 463).

Grant's reply to Lincoln's telegram was written on the bottom of the page of the copy received at City Point: "I think it will be improper for me to leave here before Monday next in consequence of present and prospective movements." (ALS, DLM).

To Ulysses S. Grant[1]

"Cypher"   United States Military Telegraph,
Lieut. Genl. Grant   War Department.
City Point, Va   Washington. July 29. 1864

I have changed my purpose, so that now I expect to reach Fort-Monroe at 10. A.M. Sunday, the 31st.   A. LINCOLN

[1] ALS, DNA WR RG 107, Presidential Telegrams, I, 113. Grant replied on July 30, "I will meet you at Fort Monroe Va. tomorrow at the hour you designated" (DLC-RTL). On the back of the received telegram Lincoln endorsed: "Meade & Franklin / McClellan / Md. & Penna."

To Joseph Holt[1]

J.A.G. please report.   A. LINCOLN
July 29. 1864

[1] AES, IHi. Lincoln's endorsement is written on a note from Mayor Alexander Henry of Philadelphia, July 25, 1864, enclosing a letter of Thomas T. Tasker, July 23, requesting assistance for Mrs. Ellen Fenton, a widow whose son, Charles D. Fenton, Company L, Eighth Pennsylvania Cavalry, was imprisoned for desertion. See Lincoln to Stanton, July 30, *infra*.

Memorandum:
Appointment of James H. Jackson[1]

This is a good case. Please file it & give it a chance.   A.L.
July 29. 1864
West-Point

¹ AES, DNA WR RG 94, U.S. Military Academy, 1864, No. 307. Lincoln's
memorandum is written on the papers recommending James H. Jackson, son of
Brigadier General Nathaniel J. Jackson. No record of his appointment has been
found, but see further Lincoln's endorsement, August 22, *infra*.

To William H. Seward¹

Will the Sec. of State please see & hear Mr. Conkling,² who is a
particular friend & fellow townsman of mine?   A. LINCOLN
July 29. 1864

¹ ALS, IHi.   ² James C. Conkling.

To Mrs. Anne Williamson¹

Executive Mansion, Washington,
Mrs. Anne Williamson—   July 29, 1864.
Madam: The plaid you send me is just now placed in my hands.
I thank you for that pretty and useful present, but still more for
those good wishes to myself and our country which prompted you
to present it. Your ob't servant,   A. LINCOLN.

¹ New York *Tribune*, August 3, 1864. The "beautiful Shepherd Check Plaid,
[was] sent to him from Edinburgh, Scotland, by Mrs. Anne Williamson, an old
lady of 81." Mrs. Williamson's letter of July 6, 1864, reads:
"My Lord President: As one deeply interested in your present struggle, I
trust the Lord will bless all your endeavors for the peace of your country and the
freedom of the slave. As this letter is written by an old lady of 81, she hopes you
will overlook all its imperfections; and, with good wishes for you and your family . . ." (*ibid.*).

Appointment of George Harrington¹

Washington, July 30th. 1864
George Harrington, is hereby appointed to discharge the duties
of Secretary of the Treasury, during the absence of Wm. P. Fessenden, the Secretary.   ABRAHAM LINCOLN

¹ DS, CSmH.

Approval of Treasury Regulations¹

Executive Mansion
Washington July 30. 1864
The following Regulations of the Secretary of the Treasury hav-
ing been seen and considered by me are hereby approved; and

[471]

commercial intercourse in the cases and under the restrictions described and expressed in the Regulations, is licensed and authorised; and all officers and privates of the regular and volunteer forces of the United States and officers sailors and marines in the naval service will observe the said Regulations and the provisions of the several acts of congress appended thereto, to which they relate, and will render all assistance not incompatible with military or naval operations to officers and agents of the Treasury Department Executing the same.   ABRAHAM LINCOLN

[1] DS, DNA FI RG 56, General Records of the Treasury Department, Circulars, Series T, July 16, 1851 to December 31, 1864, following p. 430. The regulations approved may be found in Thirty-eighth Congress, Second Session, *House of Representatives Executive Document No. 3, Report of the Secretary of the Treasury for 1864*, p. 294 ff.

To John A. Bingham[1]

Hon. John A. Bingham   Executive Mansion
Cadiz, Ohio   Washington D.C. July 30. 1864

Mr. Gibson having resigned, I have appointed you Solicitor of the U.S. in the Court of Claims.   A. LINCOLN.

[1] ALS, DNA WR RG 107, Presidential Telegrams, I, 116. See Lincoln to Bates, July 28, *supra*. On August 23, Bingham wrote Lincoln: "The People have nominated me for Congress. . . . As I deem it my duty to you & the great cause . . . to accept this nomination, I am constrained to decline the appointment of Solicitor . . . on the Court of Claims. . . ." (DLC-RTL).

To David Hunter[1]

Major General Hunter.   Executive Mansion
Harpers Ferry, Va.   Washington D.C. July 30. 1864
What news this morning?   A. LINCOLN

[1] ALS, DNA WR RG 107, Presidential Telegrams, I, 117. No reply to Lincoln has been discovered, but at 11 A.M. Hunter telegraphed Halleck: "General [Horatio G.] Wright reports his corps so much fatigued and scattered as to be unable to move this morning. The whole command is now encamped at Halltown, but my information is so unreliable and contradictory that I am at a loss to know in which direction to pursue the enemy. If I go toward the fords over which he has passed to cut off his retreat by the Valley, he turns to the right, pushes toward Baltimore and Washington, and escapes by the lower fords of the Potomac. If I push on toward Frederick and Gettysburg, I give him a chance to turn down the Valley unmolested. Please with your superior chances for information . . . direct me what is best to be done. . . ." (OR, I, XXXVII, II, 511-12).

To John A. McClernand[1]

Executive Mansion, Washington,
Major General McClernand.   July 30, 1864.

Understanding that your leave of absence expires on the 8th. of next month, the same is hereby extended until further order Yours truly   A. LINCOLN

[1] ALS, RPB. Senator Lyman Trumbull wrote Lincoln from Chicago on July 26: "I understand Maj. Gen. J. A. McClernand who has been seriously ill & is now slowly recovering desires permission to visit Washington. . . . I am sure you will take pleasure in gratifying his desire. . . ." (DLC-RTL).

To Moses F. Odell[1]

Hon. M. Odell.   Executive Mansion,
Brooklyn.   Washington, July 30, 1864.

Please find Col. Fowler of 14th. Vols. and have him Telegraph, if he will, a recommendation for Clemens J. Myers, for a Clerkship.

A. LINCOLN

[1] ALS, DNA WR RG 107, Presidential Telegrams, I, 118. Colonel Edward B. Fowler of the Eighty-fourth New York Volunteers answered on July 31: "Clement [sic] J Myers joined the fourteenth N Y S M December 1863 was detailed as clerk for me last winter while I was Provost Marshal of Culpepper C H Va I found him to be an excellent clerk & accountant & would cheerfully recommend him to your excellency for a clerkship" (DLC-RTL). The Fourteenth New York State Militia became the Eighty-fourth New York Volunteers on entering federal service.

Reply to Joseph Bertinatti[1]

July 30, 1864

Mr. Commander BERTINATTI: I am free to confess that the United States have in the course of the last three years encountered vicissitudes and been involved in controversies which have tried the friendship, and even the forbearance of other nations, but at no stage of this unhappy fraternal war, in which we are only endeavoring to save and strengthen the foundations of our national unity, has the King or the people of Italy faltered in addressing to us the language of respect, confidence, and friendship. We have tried you, Mr. Bertinatti, as a Chargé d'Affaires and as a Minister Resident, and in both of these characters we have found you always sincerely and earnestly interpreting the loyal sentiments of your sovereign. At the same time I am sure that no Minister here has more faithfully maintained and advanced the interests with which he was charged by his Government. I desire that your countrymen may know that I think you have well deserved the elevation to which I owe the pleasure of the present interview.

I pray God to have your country in his holy keeping, and to vouchsafe to crown with success her noble aspirations to renew, under the auspices of her present enlightened Government, her ancient career, so wonderfully illustrated by the achievements of art, science, and freedom.

[1] Washington *Daily National Intelligencer*, August 1, 1864. This reply is misdated July 23, 1864, in Nicolay and Hay (X, 169). Seward wrote Lincoln on July 28, "The Commander Bertinatti having received his credentials as Envoy Extraordinary and Minister Plenipotentiary to the Government of the United States, I have taken the liberty of appointing the hour of half past eleven on Saturday next, the 30th instant, for his presentation to you in that quality. . . ." (DLC-RTL).

At "11 A.M. Saturday" Seward wrote: "Perhaps I ought to remind you that I come up to you soon at 12 o'clock with Chevalier Bertinatti who has a royal letter to deliver that requires *no* speech.

"He is a warm friend and some kind words that you may say in conversation will be reported at once to Italy." (*Ibid.*).

To Edwin M. Stanton[1]

Executive Mansion, Washington,
Hon. Sec. of War.   July 30, 1864.

Charles David Fenton, now in prison at Fort Delaware, is pardoned, and to be discharged. Yours truly   A. LINCOLN

[1] ALS, DNA WR RG 153, Judge Advocate General, LL 2048. See Lincoln to Holt, July 29, *supra*. According to the record the soldier's middle name was "Davis" not "David."

To Edwin D. Morgan[1]

"Cypher."   Executive Mansion
Gov. E. D. Morgan   Washington, D.C.
Saratoga Springs, N.Y.   Aug. 1. 1864

Please come here at once. I wish to see you.   A LINCOLN

[1] ALS, DNA WR RG 107, Presidential Telegrams, I, 119. Senator Morgan replied the same day, "I will leave for Washington on the first train." (DLC-RTL). The urgency of Lincoln's message is not clear, but as chairman of the Union Party Executive Congressional Committee Morgan was probably consulted in regard to the pressing campaign or patronage problems.

To Mrs. William A. Hammond[1]

[August 2, 1864]
Under the circumstances, I should prefer not seeing Mrs. Hammond.   A. LINCOLN.

[1] William A. Hammond, *A Statement of the Causes Which Led to the Dismissal of Surgeon-General William A. Hammond* (n.d., but 1864), p. 72. See Lincoln to Holt, December 26, 1863, *supra.* According to the source, Mrs. Hammond "requested an interview, simply in order that she might ask him [Lincoln] to listen to evidence which had not been brought before the court. He sent out her card with the indorsement [as above]." The bracketed date is indicated in the source by Hammond's letter to Lincoln, August 2, 1864, written "on the same day," requesting an interview for himself. Lincoln did not reply to Hammond's letter. See Lincoln's order confirming Hammond's dismissal, August 18, *infra.*

To Charles XV[1]

August 3, 1864

Abraham Lincoln:

President of the United States of America:

To His Majesty Charles XV.

King of Sweden and Norway.

Great and Good Friend: I have received the letter which Your Majesty was pleased to address to me on the 26th. of April last, announcing the marriage of His Royal Highness, Prince Nicolas Auguste of Sweden and Norway, Duke of Dalecarlia, to Her most Serene Highness, Madame the Princess Therese Amelie Caroline Josephine Antoinette of Saxe Altenbourg, at the Ducal Chateau of Altenbourg, the 16th. of April 1864.

I participate in the satisfaction afforded by this happy event, and offer to Your Majesty my sincere congratulations on the occasion. And so I recommend Your Majesty and Your Majesty's Royal Family to the protection of the Almighty. Your Good Friend,

Washington, August 3d. 1864   ABRAHAM LINCOLN.

By the President,

WILLIAM H. SEWARD, Secretary of State.

[1] Copy, DNA FS RG 59, Communications to Foreign Sovereigns and States, III, 235.

To Francis Joseph I[1]

August 3, 1864

Abraham Lincoln,

President of the United States of America.

To His Imperial and Royal Majesty Francis Joseph I,

Emperor of Austria &c &c

Great and Good Friend: I have received the letter which Your Majesty has been pleased to address to me, conveying the melan-

[475]

choly intelligence of the decease, on the 2d. of April last, of the Archduchess Hildegarde, wife of Your Majesty's well beloved cousin, the Archduke Albrecht.

I deeply sympathize in the grief with which this afflicting event has filled Your Majesty, and I pray Your Majesty to accept for yourself, and for Your Royal Family, my cordial condolence.

May God have Your Majesty in his holy keeping. Your Good Friend,   ABRAHAM LINCOLN.

Washington, August 3d. 1864.

By the President,

WILLIAM H. SEWARD, Secretary of State.

¹ Copy, DNA FS RG 59, Communications to Foreign Sovereigns and States, III, 236.

To Ulysses S. Grant¹

Cypher.   Office U.S. Military Telegraph,
Lieut. Genl. Grant   War Department,
City-Point, Va.   Washington, D.C., August 3, 1864.

I have seen your despatch in which you say "I want Sheridan put in command of all the troops in the field, with instructions to put himself South of the enemy, and follow him to the death. Wherever the enemy goes, let our troops go also." This, I think, is exactly right, as to how our forces should move. But please look over the despatches you may have receved from here, even since you made that order, and discover, if you can, that there is any idea in the head of any one here, of "putting our army *South* of the enemy" or of following him to the *death*" in any direction. I repeat to you it will neither be done nor attempted unless you watch it every day, and hour, and force it.   A. LINCOLN

¹ ALS, DNA WR RG 107, Presidential Telegrams, I, 121. In several printed sources this telegram has been misdated August 4, the date it was received at Grant's headquarters. On August 1 Grant had telegraphed Halleck: "I am sending General Sheridan for temporary duty whilst the enemy is being expelled from the border. Unless General Hunter is in the field in person, I want Sheridan put in command of all the troops in the field, with instructions to put himself south of the enemy and follow him to the death. Wherever the enemy goes let our troops go also. Once started up the Valley they ought to be followed until we get possession of the Virginia Central Railroad. If General Hunter is in the field give Sheridan direct command of the Sixth Corps and cavalry division. All the cavalry I presume will reach Washington in the course of to-morrow." (OR, I, XXXVII, II, 558).

At 12 M., August 4, Grant replied to Lincoln's telegram: "Your dispatch of 6 P.M. just received. I will start in two hours for Washington & will spend a day with the Army under Genl Hunter." (DLC-RTL).

To Leopold[1]

August 3, 1864

Abraham Lincoln:
President of the United States of America.

To His Majesty Leopold,
    King of the Belgians.

Great and Good Friend: I have received the letter which Your Majesty was pleased to address to me on the 25th. of May last, announcing that the Duchess of Brabant, Your Majesty's well beloved daughter-in-law, had been happily delivered of a Princess, upon whom the names of Stephanie Clotilde Louise Herminie Marie Charlotte had been bestowed.

I participate in the satisfaction afforded by this happy event, and offer to Your Majesty my sincere congratulations upon the occasion. And so I recommend Your Majesty, and Your Majesty's Royal Family to the protection of the Almighty. Your Good Friend,

Washington, August. 3d. 1864.   ABRAHAM LINCOLN,
    By the President,
    WILLIAM H. SEWARD, Secretary of State.

[1] Copy, DNA FS RG 59, Communications to Foreign Sovereigns and States, III, 237.

To Edwin M. Stanton[1]

August 3, 1864

The Secretary of War, will suspend the order of Gen. Hunter, mentioned within, until further order, and direct him to send to the Department, a brief report of what is known against, each one proposed to be dealt with.   A. LINCOLN

    Aug. 3. 1864.

[1] AES, DLC-Stanton Papers. Lincoln's endorsement is written on the following communication from Stanton, August 2, 1864: "This note will introduce to you Mr [Frederick] Schley of Baltimore who desires to appeal to [you] for the revocation of an order of General Hunter removing some persons citizens of Frederick beyond his lines and imprisoning others. This Department has no information of the reasons or proofs on which General Hunter acts and I do not therefore feel at liberty to suspend or interfere with his action except under your direction."

Hunter's *Special Order No. 141*, August 1, 1864, had directed the arrest and shipment south of Union lines of secessionist residents of Frederick, Maryland, among them James M. Schley and family, relatives of loyal Republican Frederick Schley of Baltimore. This order was issued in response to Halleck's orders of July 17: "General Grant . . . directs 'If Hunter cannot get to Gordonsville and Charlottesville to cut the railroads he should make all the valleys south of the Baltimore and Ohio . . . a desert as high up as possible. I do not mean that houses should be burned, but every particle of provisions and stock should be removed, and the people notified to move out.' . . ." (OR, I, XXXVII, II, 366).

On August 7, Hunter telegraphed Lincoln: "In sending the rebel citizens & their families beyond our lines I was obeying the order of Lieut Gen Grant communicated through Gen Halleck. . . . with several thousand wealthy rebel spies in our midst constantly sending information & supplies to the enemy & pointing out union men to their vengeance it is impossible to conduct the affairs of any Department successfully. I most humbly beg that I may be relieved from command of the Dept of West Virginia" (DLC-RTL).

To Edwin M. Stanton[1]

Hon. Sec. of War please see & hear the bearer, Mr. Burns.

Aug. 3. 1864.   A. LINCOLN

[1] AES, RPB. Lincoln's endorsement is written on a letter from Governor Andrew Johnson, June 14, 1864, introducing "my old friend Michael Burns of the city of Nashville. . . . President of the Nashville and Chattanooga, and the North Western Rail Roads. . . . Mr Burns visits Washington on important business, which he will lay before you. . . ." The important business probably concerned the operation of the North Western Railroad. On August 6, Stanton drafted and E. D. Townsend signed the "Special order relating to the Northwestern Rail Road from Nashville to Reynoldsburg," as follows:

"Wheras the exclusive use of the North Western Rail Road from Nashville to Reynoldsburg is necessary for the the [sic] Military operations under command of Major General Sherman the President does therefore order and direct that Major General Sherman take Military possession of the same North Western Rail Road its stock equipments appendages and appurtenances for the exclusive use of the United States and hold, use manage and employ the same by his officers agents superintendents & employees exclusively for the use aforesaid so long and to such extent as in his judgment such exclusive use is required for Military operations or until further order, and that all conflicting orders and authority be & they are hereby revoked & annulled.

"By order of the President" (DNA WR RG 94, Adjutant General, Letters Received, P 917).

An endorsement on the order reads "copy by telegram & copy by mail to Genl. Sherman/ copy by mail to Gov. Johnson."

To William I[1]

August 3, 1864

Abraham Lincoln:
President of the United States of America.

To His Majesty William I,
        King of Prussia &c   &c

Great and Good Friend, I have received the letter which Your Majesty was pleased to address to me on the 24th. of April last, announcing that the wife of the Hereditary Prince of Hohenzollern Sigmaringen, Her Royal Highness Madame the Princess Antonie, sister of His Majesty the King of Portugal and the Algarves, had on the 7th. of March last, given safe birth to a Prince, upon whom the names of Guillaume Auguste Charles Joseph Ferdinand Pierre Benoit had been bestowed.

I participate in the satisfaction which this happy event has afforded to Your Majesty, and to Your Majesty's Royal Family, and offer my sincere congratulations upon the occasion.

May God have Your Majesty always in his safe and holy keeping. Your Good Friend, ABRAHAM LINCOLN.

Washington, August 3d. 1864.

By the President,

WILLIAM H. SEWARD, Secretary of State.

1 Copy, DNA FS RG 59, Communications to Foreign Sovereigns and States, III, 238.

To Charles A. Dana[1]

Can Mr. Dana give me any account of this case?

Aug. 4, 1864. A. LINCOLN

1 AES, DLC-RTL. Lincoln's endorsement is written on the following memorandum by John Hay: "Cyrus Kilburn of Vt. in the Central Guard charged with desertion. He belongs to the 4th Regiment of Vermont Volunteers. His *wife* says that *he* says that he did not intend to desert, and asks the President to release him."

Dana referred the matter to Colonel Moses N. Wisewell, military governor, who reported on August 6 that Cyrus G. Kilburn, in Forrest Hall prison, was to be sent to his regiment for trial. No record of Lincoln's action has been found, but Kilburn was returned to his regiment on August 12 and served until mustered out on July 13, 1865.

To Joseph Holt[1]

August 4, 1864

Please send by the bearer the record in the case of A. J. Smith.

A. LINCOLN

1 *American Book Prices Current*, 1932. On August 1, John Hay referred numerous petitions to Holt on behalf of Private Andrew J. Smith, U.S. General Service, convicted of falsely filling out and signing blank soldiers' discharges and final settlements, and sentenced on June 7, 1864, to be dishonorably discharged, forfeit all pay, etc., and to be imprisoned at hard labor for the remainder of his term of enlistment. On August 11, Lincoln endorsed Smith's court-martial record, "Pardon for unexecuted portion of sentence." (DNA WR RG 153, Judge Advocate General, MM 847).

To Gideon Welles[1]

Hon. Sec. of Navy, please see and hear this North-Carolina Delegation. A. LINCOLN

Aug. 4. 1864.

1 ALS, NHi. No further reference has been found.

To Frank L. Wolford[1]

"Cypher"

Col. Frank Wolford.
Louisville, Ky.

War Department
Washington City,
August 4 1864

Yours of yesterday received. Before interfering with the Judge
Advocate General's order, I should know his reasons for making it.
Meanwhile, if you have not already started, wait till you hear
from me again. Did you receive letter and inclosures from me?

A LINCOLN

[1] ALS, DNA WR RG 107, Presidential Telegrams, I, 122. See Lincoln to
Wolford, July 17, *supra*. On August 3 Wolford telegraphed from Louisville:
"The Judge Advocate has notified me to report immediately to him at Washington to be tried before a military commission. . . . If this is inconsistent with
the parole which I gave you & which I have scrupulously kept I desire to know
what I shall do Can I not be tried in Louisville according to your promise Please answer" (DLC-RTL).

On August 5 Wolford replied to Lincoln's telegram: "I duly recd letter and
was on the point of mailing my answer when the order of the Judge Advocate
came My answer is now on the way to you." (*Ibid.*).

To Edward Bates[1]

[c. August 5, 1864]

For one of these, Judge Watts, says Sydney A. Hubbell now at
Davenport, Iowa should be appointed.   A.L.

[1] AES, DNA RG 60, Papers of Attorney General, Appointments, New Mexico,
Box 659. Lincoln's endorsement is written on a letter from Bates of August
5, 1864:

"In obedience to your direction, I have talked with judge Watts, and fully
concur with him in believing that Judge Brocchus ought to be superseded.

"I also believe that the public interest would [be] advanced by changing the
other two judges of New Mexico, also. Provided you can find three competent
men who will be content to *live* in the Territory, discharging their own duties,
& letting other peoples duties alone."

Sydney A. Hubbell was appointed August 10, 1864, to succeed Associate Jus-
tice Perry E. Brocchus. Judge Watts was John S. Watts, associate justice of the
U.S. Court in the Territory of New Mexico, 1851-1854, and U.S. delegate from
New Mexico, 1861-1863. See further Lincoln to Miller, August 6, and to Bates,
August 10, *infra*.

To Morton McMichael[1]

Private

Hon. Morton McMichael
My dear Sir.

Executive Mansion,
Washington,
August 5. 1864.

When the Philadelphia Post-Master was here on the 20th. of
June last, I read to him a paper in the following words:

(Here copy it in)[2]

[480]

He promised me to strictly follow this. I am now told that, of the two or three hundred employees in the Post-Office, not one of them is openly for Judge Kelly. This, if true, is not accidental. Left to their free choice, there can be no doubt that a large number of them, probably as much or more than half, would be for Kelly. And if they are for him, and are not restrained, they can put it beyond question by publicly saying so. Please tell the Post-Master he must find a way to relieve me from the suspicion that he is not keeping his promise to me in good faith. Yours truly

A. LINCOLN

[1] ADfS, DLC-RTL. See Lincoln's telegram to Forney, July 28, *supra*. On August 2 John Hay telegraphed McMichael, editor of the Philadelphia *North American:* "The President directs me to request that you will visit him at Washington, as soon as convenient." (ALS, DNA WR RG 107, Presidential Telegrams, I, 120). No reply from McMichael has been discovered.

On August 3 John W. Forney had written from Philadelphia: "The political condition of the district represented by the Hon Wm D. Kelly is such that your immediate interposition is necessary. He is clearly the choice of the Union people . . . for renomination, and I greatly fear if he should be defeated, for that renomination, by the malpractices of partisans who claim to be your friends, that we may lose the elections in October next. . . ." (DLC-RTL).

On August 9, Walborn enclosed "a copy of what I have this day caused to be put up in this office, and its several stations":

"To the Employees of the Philadelphia Postal District.

"Whereas I am charged with coercing you to oppose the nomination of Wm D Kelly for Congress.

"Now this is to notify you that you are expected to sustain men of known loyalty only, for all offices, but you are at liberty, as far as I am concerned to exercise your own views in reference to who should be nominated for Congress, or any other office in the gift of the people. . . ." (*Ibid.*).

[2] See Lincoln's memorandum of the interview with Walborn, June 20, *supra*.

To Francis H. Peirpoint[1]

Gov. Pierpoint   Executive Mansion,
Alexandria, Va.   Washington, Aug. 5. 1864.

Gen. Butler telegraphs me that Judge Snead is at liberty.

A. LINCOLN

[1] ALS, DNA WR RG 107, Presidential Telegrams, I, 123. On August 3 General Butler had telegraphed: "In the case of Edward K Snead of Norfolk who was stayed because he threatened disobedience to my orders & whose case I have reported to you by mail, no further present action need be taken as Snead has given his hand not to disobey my military order . . . & has been released to go about his business. . . ." (DLC-RTL).

On August 4 Governor Peirpoint, unaware of Butler's action, had telegraphed: "I learn through the papers and otherwise that Genl Butler has arrested Judge E K Snead of Norfolk Va for attempting to hold his court under the laws of the State of Virginia in that city & has him now in confinement. I respectfully ask his immediate release. Please inform me of your action in the case." (*Ibid.*).

See Lincoln to Butler, August 20, *infra*.

To Edwin M. Stanton[1]

[August 5, 1864]

I will come over in a few minutes. A.L.

[1] AES, DLC-Stanton Papers. Lincoln's endorsement appears on a note from Stanton, August 5, 1864: "General Grant is at the Department. Shall he call to see you or will you see him here"

To Samuel M. Bowman[1]

Office U.S. Military Telegraph,
Col. S. M. Bowman   War Department,
Baltimore, Md.   Washington, D.C., August 6. 1864.

If convenient, come and see me.   A. LINCOLN

[1] ALS, DNA WR RG 107, Presidential Telegrams, I, 124. See Lincoln to Stanton, July 7, *supra.* Colonel Samuel M. Bowman, Eighty-fourth Pennsylvania Infantry (formerly major in the Fourth Illinois Cavalry) had been assigned on February 12, 1864, to duty as chief mustering and recruiting officer for colored troops in Maryland (AGO *Special Orders No. 70*). L. E. Straughn, Hugh L. Bond, and Thomas Timmons composed the board of commissioners appointed by Lincoln to examine claims of owners of slaves enlisted in the army. On August 6 Bowman telegraphed Lincoln: "Will call with Mr L E Straughn on Monday Have had a very satisfactory interview with Senator Hicks who says he just begins to understand the subject. Good and not evil is likely to result from the present little agitation." (DLC-RTL).

To Horace Greeley[1]

Hon. Horace Greeley   Executive Mansion,
New-York.   Washington, August 6. 1864.

Yours to Major Hay about publication of our correspondence received. With the suppression of a few passages in your letters, in regard to which I think you and I would not disagree, I should be glad of the publication. Please come over and see me.

A. LINCOLN

[1] ADfS, DLC-RTL; LS, DNA WR RG 107, Presidential Telegrams, I, 126. On August 4, Greeley had written John Hay: "The Times of this morning calls for the publication of my letters to the President and his replies thereto relative to the Niagara Falls matter. I am no keeper of letters, and have no copy of any of mine except possibly the first. . . . If you happen to have *all* the correspondence, I wish you would lend it [to] me for publication. . . . I have no special desire to see it in print, but certainly not the least objection. Help me to give it *all*, and I trust good will come of it." (DLC-RTL).
On August 8, Greeley answered Lincoln:
"I have no desire whatever to see our correspondence published, nor any preference that it should not be; but the call for its publication in *The Times* was imperative, and seemed to be one that would not be so made without your sanction, and left me no option but to acquiesce. And now if you will indicate any portions of my letters that you think should be suppressed, I will gladly assent. . . .

"I would very gladly go to Washington to see you, and will probably do so soon; but now I hear that my bitterest personal enemies are close around you and that my going would only result in further mischief. . . . I will gladly go whenever I feel a hope that their influence has waned.

"Mr. President, hear me for five minutes. . . . You were fearfully misled when you refused to let A. H. Stephens . . . come to Washington last year. And the day after the news of Vicksburg's surrender, you should have sent to Richmond, if necessary, proferring terms of pacification, and begging the Rebel chiefs no longer to prosecute this murderous fray. . . .

"If you shall ever be in the way of seeking the shortest road to negotiation for Peace, I shall be very glad to come to Washington; until then, knowing who are nearest you, it seems . . . hopeless to do any thing whatever. Yours, sadly, . . ." (*Ibid.*).

See further Lincoln to Greeley, August 8, *infra*.

To John McMahon[1]

John McMahon   Washington, D.C.
Harmbrook, Bradford Co Penn.   Aug. 6. 1864

The President has received yours of yesterday, and is kindly paying attention to it. As it is my business to assist him whenever I can, I will thank you to inform me, for his use, whether you are either a white man or black one, because in either case, you can not be regarded as an entirely impartial judge. It may be that you belong to a third or fourth class of *yellow* or *red* men, in which case the impartiality of your judgment would be more apparant.

[1] ADf, DLC-RTL. A copy preserved in the Nicolay Papers shows this communication to have been sent over Nicolay's signature. John McMahon telegraphed Lincoln on August 5, 1864:
"The following lines will give you to understand what is justice & what is truth to all men
"My Dear Sir I hope you will be kind Enough to pay attention to these few lines
"I am yours &c
   "Equal Rights & Justice to all white men in the United States forever. White men is in class number one & black men is in class number two & must be governed by white men forever." (DLC-Nicolay Papers).

To Anson S. Miller[1]

Hon. Anson Miller   Executive Mansion
Rockford, Ills.   Washington, D.C. Aug. 6. 1864

If you will go and live in New-Mexico, I will appoint you a judge there. Answer.   A. LINCOLN

[1] ALS, DNA WR RG 107, Presidential Telegrams, I, 125. See Lincoln to Bates, August 5, *supra*, and August 10, *infra*. Miller replied on August 15:
"Your kind offer by Telegraph on the 6th inst. . . . calls for my grateful acknowledgements.
"Having delayed a little to consult my family and friends, I will now briefly

say that should you deem it necessary to fill the place before the close of the Presidential canvass I must respectfully decline. . . .

"Our friends here . . . think that I cannot well be spared from our all-important State canvass, and that I can at present be of more service to you & our cause in Illinois than in New Mexico. . . ." (DLC-RTL).

To Edwin M. Stanton[1]

I shall be glad to have this done.   A. LINCOLN
     Aug. 6. 1864.

[1] AES, NHi. Lincoln's endorsement is written on a telegram of Lieutenant Thomas G. Welles, aide-de-camp to General Edward O. C. Ord, Eighteenth Army Corps, to Gideon Welles, August 5, 1864: "Col Griffin A. Stedman Comdg a Brigade was wounded this P.M. & will probably not survive the night. Gen'l Ord has recommended his promotion to Brig Gen'l to the President to be telegraphed tonight. Will you see the President about it immediately & call his attention to the fact that he has several times before been recommended." Colonel Griffin A. Stedman of the Eleventh Connecticut Volunteers, who died of his wounds, was brevetted brigadier general as of August 5, "for gallant and meritorious services before Petersburg, Virginia."

To Isaac N. Arnold[1]

Hon. I. N. Arnold.   Executive Mansion
Chicago[2]   Washington D.C. Aug. 8. 1864

I send you by mail to-day, the appointment of Col. Mulligan to be a Brevet Brigadier General.   A. LINCOLN

[1] ALS, DNA WR RG 107, Presidential Telegrams, I, 128. Arnold wrote Lincoln on August 4:

"I have sent you a telegram earnestly requesting that a commission of Brig. General might be forwarded to the widow of my friend & law student Col. *James A. Mulligan.*

"I deem this so just, & so in accordance with the universal popular judgment, & feeling here, that I urge it by letter. Yesterday was his funeral, & never since the burial of Douglas has the public so universally mourned a public man. . . . His last words 'Lay *me down & save the flag,*' expressed his unselfish devotion. . . . If you will cause such a commission to be sent, I shall deem it one of the most grateful acts of my life to present it to his widow." (DLC-RTL).

Colonel James A. Mulligan of the Twenty-third Illinois Volunteers, was brevetted brigadier general as of July 23, 1864, "for gallant and meritorious services at the battle of Winchester, Virginia."

[2] "Chicago" was inserted by the telegraph operator.

To Stephen G. Burbridge[1]

                    Office U.S. Military Telegraph,
Major General Burbridge   War Department,
Lexington, Ky.   Washington, D.C., August 8.th. 1864.

Last December Mrs. Emily T. Helm, half-sister of Mrs. L. and widow of the rebel general Ben. Hardin Helm stopped here on her

way from Georgia to Kentucky, and I gave her a paper, as I remember, to protect her against the mere fact of her being Gen.
Helm's widow. I hear a rumor to-day that you recently sought to
arrest her, but was prevented by her presenting the paper from me.
I do not intend to protect her against the consequences of disloyal
words or acts, spoken or done by her since her return to Kentucky,
and if the paper given her by me can be construed to give her protection for such words or acts, it is hereby revoked *pro tanto.* Deal
with her for current conduct, just as you would with *any other.*

A. LINCOLN

[1] ALS, DNA WR RG 107, Presidential Telegrams, I, 129. What appears to
be a garbled version of this telegram appears without date in Hertz (II, 953).
No reply or further reference has been found, but following the publication of
the dispatch in 1895, Emily Todd Helm addressed an open letter to *Century
Magazine* (June, 1895) in which she averred: "This despatch is a surprise to
me, since I was never arrested and never had any trouble with the United
States authorities. . . ." (LI, 318).

To Horace Greeley[1]

Hon. Horace Greeley   Executive Mansion,
New-York.   Washington, August 8. 1864.

I telegraphed you Saturday. Did you receive the despatch? Please
answer.   A. LINCOLN

[1] ALS, DNA WR RG 107, Presidential Telegrams, I, 127. See Lincoln to
Greeley, August 6, *supra.* Samuel Sinclair replied to Lincoln's telegram sent at
9:40 A.M. on August 8: "Mr Greeley is absent   Will probably be home tonight.
I infer that he did not receive your first dispatch before he left. Your second
awaits him." (DLC-RTL).

On August 9 Greeley replied: "Your dispatch of Saturday only reached me
on Sunday, when I immediately answered by letter [dated Monday, August 8];
yesterday I was out of town; and I have just received your dispatch of that
date. . . . I will gladly come on to Washington whenever you apprise me that
my doing so may perhaps be of use.

"But I fear that my chance for usefulness has passed. . . ." (*Ibid.*)

To the Shakers[1]

Executive Mansion, Washington,
My good friends   August 8, 1864.

I wish to express to you my cordial thanks for the very comfortable chair you sent me some time since and to tell you how gratefully I appreciate the kindness which prompted the present. And I
must beg that you will pardon the length of time that, through an

oversight in my office, has elapsed without an acknowledgment of your kindness. I am very truly   Yr. friend & Servt

[1] Df, DLC-Nicolay Papers. The draft is in John Hay's autograph. Presumably a letter was sent, but it has not been discovered, and no further reference has been found

To Edwin M. Stanton[1]

August 8, 1864

Will the Sec. of War please give Major Williams, some sort of hearing before I am required to approve or disapprove his dismissal. This is one of a batch of cases, and perhaps it would be well to give a hearing to the whole batch.   A. LINCOLN

Aug. 8. 1864.

[1] AES, NHi. Lincoln's endorsement is written on a letter of Lieutenant Colonel William Blakeley, Fourteenth Pennsylvania Cavalry, Harpers Ferry, July 29, 1864, to U.S. Representative Thomas Williams, introducing Major James E. Williams, First New York Veteran Cavalry, who had been dismissed the service without trial, on charges of drunkenness: "Why not give him a trial? Why not give him an opportunity of meeting his accuser and defending his honor. I ask it as a personal favor to me as an old friend and as one of your constituents, that you will use your influence with the President to procure a trial. . . . This is certainly nothing but justice—he does not desire to be restored to duty without trial. I feel confident that he will be honorably acquited." Major Williams' dismissal was never confirmed, and he was mustered out with his regiment at Camp Piatt, West Virginia, July 20, 1865.

To Nathaniel P. Banks[1]

Executive Mansion, Washington,

Major General Banks.   August 9. 1864.

I have just seen the new Constitution adopted by the Convention of Louisiana; and I am anxious that it shall be ratified by the people. I will thank you to let the civil officers in Louisiana, holding under me, know that this, is my wish, and to let me know at once who of them openly declare for the constitution, and who of them, if any, decline to so declare. Yours truly   A. LINCOLN

[1] ALS, IHi; LS copy, DLC-RTL. Governor Michael Hahn of Louisiana, who arrived in Washington on August 6, probably brought the copy of the new constitution for Lincoln's approval. General Banks wrote Lincoln on September 6: "The constitution was submitted to the People of Louisiana yesterday, at an election held in all the Parishes within our lines for this purpose and for the election of members of Congress and a State Legislature. I am gratified . . . to report that the constitution was ratified by a very large majority. . . . The vote is not so large as we expected. . . . Many of the men employed by the Govt. declined to vote or register. . . . The officers of the Govt. civil or military have not assisted with energy. With exception of Mr Dennison [George S. Denison],

collector, no aid has been given by the Treasury Department. . . . History will record . . . that all the problems involved in restoration of States and the reconstruction of government have been already solved in Louisiana. . . . Your policy here will be adopted in other states and work out in the end the reestablishment of the Union, into whosever hands its administration may fall." (DLC-RTL).

To Benjamin F. Butler[1]

Executive Mansion, Washington,

Major General Butler:

August 9, 1864.

Your paper of the about Norfolk matters is received, as also was your other, on the same general subject dated, I believe some time in February last. This subject has caused considerable trouble, forcing me to give a good deal of time and reflection to it. I regret that crimination and recrimination are mingled in it. I surely need not to assure you that I have no doubt of your loyalty and devoted patriotism; and I must tell you that I have no less confidence in those of Gov. Pierpoint and the Attorney General. The former, at first, as the loyal governor of all Virginia, including that which is now West-Virginia; in organizing and furnishing troops, and in all other proper matters, was as earnest, honest, and efficient to the extent of his means, as any other loyal governor. The inauguration of West-Virginia as a new State left to him, as he assumed, the remainder of the old State; and the insignificance of the parts which are outside of the rebel lines, and consequently within his reach, certainly gives a somewhat farcical air to his dominion; and I suppose he, as well as I, has considered that it could be useful for little else than as a nucleous to add to. The Attorney General only needs to be known to be relieved from all question as to loyalty and thorough devotion to the national cause; constantly restraining as he does, my tendency to clemency for rebels and rebel sympathizers. But he is the Law-Officer of the government, and a believer in the virtue of adhering to law.

Coming to the question itself, the Military occupancy of Norfolk is a necessity with us. If you, as Department commander, find the cleansing of the City necessary to prevent pestilence in your army —street lights, and a fire department, necessary to prevent assassinations and incendiarism among your men and stores—wharfage necessary to land and ship men and supplies—a large pauperism, badly conducted, at a needlessly large expense to the government, and find also that these things, or any of them, are not reasonably well attended to by the civil government, you rightfully may, and must take them into your own hands. But you should do so on your own avowed judgment of a military necessity, and not seem to admit that there is no such necessity, by taking a vote of the people on the question. Nothing justifies the suspending of the civil by the military authority, but military necessity, and of the existence of that necessity the military commander, and not a popular vote, is to decide. And whatever is not within such necessity should be left undisturbed. In your paper of February you fairly notified me that you contemplated taking a popular vote; and, if fault there be, it was my fault that I did not object then, which I probably should have done, had I studied the subject as closely as I have since done. I now think you would better place whatever you feel is necessary to be done, on this distinct ground of military necessity, openly discarding all reliance for what you do, on any election. I also think you should so keep accounts as to show every item of money received and how expended.

The course here indicated does not touch the case when the military commander finding no friendly civil government existing, may, under the sanction or direction of the President, give assistance to the people to inaugerate one.

[1] ADf, DLC-RTL. This communication was not completed, but see Lincoln to Butler, December 21, *infra*, in which Lincoln enclosed a copy of his incomplete draft. Lincoln's communications to Peirpoint, August 5, *supra*, and to Butler, August 20, *infra*, are concerned with the conflict between Butler's military government in Norfolk and the "restored" government under Governor Peirpoint, the temporary capital of which was located at Alexandria. Butler's two reports, February 23 and August 1, 1864, are in the Lincoln Papers. Forty and forty-one pages in length, respectively, they are too long for adequate quotation or extended summary, but the case was simply that both Butler and Peirpoint were trying to govern Norfolk. At a Norfolk election held under Butler's orders, citizens voted to retain martial law rather than to accept Peirpoint's administration, whereupon Butler issued an order staying the civil government and making it subordinate to the military government. On July 30, Edward K. Snead announced that, being the duly elected judge of the First Judicial District of Virginia, he was going to hold court. Butler questioned the legality of Snead's commission and authority and asked Snead whether his court was to be in opposition to or subordinate to the military government. Snead replied, according to Butler, that on the advice of Attorney General Bates, his court would be in opposition to the military government. Butler's reports roundly denounced Peirpoint, Snead, and likewise Bates, for meddling in Norfolk affairs.

To Edward R. S. Canby[1]

To Major General Edward R. S. Canby
Commanding the Military Division   Executive Mansion,
of West Mississippi; New Orleans.   August 9, 1864.

For satisfactory reasons which concern the public service I have to direct that if Andrew J. Hamilton, or any person authorized in writing by him, shall come out of either of the ports of Galveston or Sabine Pass with any vessel or vessels freighted with cotton shipped to the agent of the Treasury Department at New Orleans, the passage of such person, vessels and cargoes shall not be molested or hindered, but they shall be permitted to pass to the hands of such consignee. ABRAHAM LINCOLN

1 DS-P, ISLA. The same order was issued to Rear Admiral David G. Farragut, but the original has not been discovered. See, however, Lincoln's order to Farragut, November 11, *infra,* revoking the order of August 9, 1864.

To William P. Fessenden[1]

Hon. William P. Fessenden,   Executive Mansion,
Secretary of the Treasury.   Aug. 9, 1864.

Sir: You are requested to place to the credit of the Department of State the sum of $25,000 as appropriated in the seventh section of the Act entitled "An Act to encourage immigration," approved July 4, 1864. ABRAHAM LINCOLN

1 LS, DLM. Seward endorsed, "Approved."

To Horace Greeley[1]

Private

Hon. Horace Greeley,   Executive Mansion,
Dear Sir: Washington, August 9, 1864.

Herewith is a full copy of the correspondence, and which I have had privately printed, but not made public. The parts of your letters which I wish suppressed, are only those which, as I think, give too gloomy an aspect to our cause, and those which present the carrying of elections as a motive of action. I have, as you see, drawn a red pencil over the parts I wish suppressed.

As to the A. H. Stephens matter, so much pressed by you, I can only say that he sought to come to Washington in the name of the "Confederate States," in a vessel of "The Confederate States Navy," and with no pretence even, that he would bear any proposal for peace; but with language showing that his mission would be Military, and not civil, or diplomatic. Nor has he at any time since pretended that he had terms of peace, so far as I know, or believe. On the contrary, Jefferson Davis has, in the most formal manner, declared that Stephens had no terms of peace. I thought we could not afford to give this quasi acknowledgement of the independence of the Confederacy, in a case where there was not even an intimation of any thing for our good. Still, as the parts of your letters relating to Stephens contain nothing worse than a questioning of my action, I do not ask a suppression of those parts. Yours truly

A. LINCOLN

[1] Copy, DLC-RTL. Lincoln enclosed a six-page pamphlet printing of the correspondence, which ended with the following statement: "The foregoing is absolutely the whole record of the case ever seen by the President." (DLC-RTL). The copy of this pamphlet preserved in the Lincoln Papers and the copies enclosed to Greeley and to Raymond (Lincoln to Raymond, August 15, *infra*) were presumably the only copies printed. The correspondence has been fully presented in Lincoln's preceding letters and the notes thereto, but the passages in Greeley's letters which Lincoln deleted have not been indicated. They are as follows: Greeley to Lincoln, July 7 (see note to Lincoln's letter of July 9, *supra*) —(1) "And thereupon I venture to remind you that our bleeding, bankrupt, almost dying country also longs for peace; shudders at the prospect of fresh conscriptions, of further wholesale devastations, and of new rivers of human blood. And"; (2) "now, and is morally certain, unless removed, to do far greater in the approaching elections."; (3) "With United States stocks worth but forty cents in gold per dollar, and drafting about to commence on the third million of Union soldiers, can this be wondered at?"; (4) "it may save us from a northern insurrection."; Greeley to Lincoln, July 10 (see note to Lincoln's telegram of July 15, *supra*)—(1) "in season for effect on the approaching North Carolina election."; (2) "especially those of North Carolina,"; Greeley to Lincoln, July 13 (see note to Lincoln's telegram of July 15, *supra*)—(1) "so . . . that a good influence may even yet be exerted on the North Carolina election next month."

On August 11 Greeley replied to Lincoln's letter of August 9:

"I do not feel disposed to let my letters to you go to the public with such suppressions as you indicate by the red pencil marks. I cannot see that *you* are at all implicated in *my* anxiety that a generous offer should be made and a kindly spirit evinced in season for effect on the North Carolina election. . . . I . . . think . . . the . . . suppressions . . . weaken the agreement, which I wish to have indeed as I made it, if at all. I prefer . . . *not* to print the correspondence, unless as it was written.

"But . . . I give free and full consent to the publication . . . of *your* letters and dispatches only, should you choose to have them published. . . ." (*Ibid.*).

To Edward Bates[1]

Executive Mansion, Washington,
Hon. Attorney General   August 10, 1864.

Please send me appointments for Nathaniel Usher, of Indiana, and Sydney A. Hubbell, of New-Mexico, to be Judges in New-Mexico, in place, of Judges Brochus and Knapp. Yours truly

A. LINCOLN

[1] ALS, DNA GE RG 60, Papers of Attorney General, Segregated Lincoln Material. See Lincoln to Bates, August 5, *supra*. Hubbell replaced Perry E. Brocchus, but Joseph G. Knapp was not replaced. Nathaniel Usher was nominated U.S. attorney for the Northern District of Indiana on December 20, 1865, and was confirmed by the Senate on February 6, 1866.

To Joseph Holt[1]

Judge Advocate General please report on this case.

Aug. 10. 1864.   A. LINCOLN

[1] AES, Herbert Wells Fay Collection. Lincoln's endorsement was clipped from attendant papers by Holt and sent on April 11, 1883, to an unknown correspondent who had requested a Lincoln autograph.

Order Concerning Alice Maria Waring[1]

Miss Alice Maria Waring may be allowed to remain in Maryland with her parents[2] if she behaves herself from this time forward

August 10. 1864   A. LINCOLN

[1] DS, PHi. No further reference has been discovered.
[2] From this point the document proceeds in Lincoln's autograph.

To Thaddeus Stevens[1]

If Hon. Thadeus Stevens will say in writing, on this papers, that he wishes this man discharged, I will discharge him.

Aug. 10, 1864.   A. LINCOLN

[1] AES, owned by Frank Howard, Detroit, Michigan. Lincoln's endorsement is written on a letter from Catharine Myers, Lancaster, Pennsylvania, August 9, 1864, asking discharge of her son, Private Reuben A. Ditlow, Company F, Ninety-ninth Pennsylvania Volunteers. Stevens endorsed on August 13: "This man is weak both in body & mind, and I think as he is useless to the government he had better be discharged and returned to his fond and distressed mother." Lincoln endorsed further, "Discharged/Aug. 18. 1864. A. LINCOLN."

To Gideon Welles[1]

Sec. of Navy, please see & hear Mrs. Dr. Bacon, about a Naval appointment.   A. LINCOLN

Aug. 10. 1864

[1] ALS, Berkshire Museum, Pittsfield, Massachusetts. No further reference has been found.

To Edwin M. Stanton[1]

Hon. Secretary of War.   Executive Mansion,
My dear Sir   Washington, August 11. 1864.

I should be glad for Gen. Mott, of New-Jersey, to have a Brevt. Major Generalship. He has done a great deal of hard service, has been twice (I believe) wounded; and, is now, by assignment of his superiors, commanding a Division. Add to this that I have been for

a year trying to find an opportunity to promote him, as you know.
Yours truly   A. LINCOLN

¹ ALS-P, ISLA. See Lincoln to Stanton, July 16, 1863, *supra*. Brigadier General Gershom Mott was first brevetted major general of Volunteers as of September 9, 1864, but a later nomination, also confirmed by the Senate, dated his brevet rank back to August 1, 1864. His regular appointment as major general of Volunteers, confirmed by the Senate on February 23, 1866, dated his rank from May 26, 1865.

Pass for John Eaton¹

Allow the bearer, Col. Eaton to pass to, and visit Gen. Grant at
City-Point, Va.   A. LINCOLN
    Aug. 12. 1864

¹ ADS-F, John Eaton, *Grant, Lincoln, and the Freedmen* (1907), p. 187. According to Eaton's account, Lincoln instructed him to ascertain Grant's personal reaction to the possibility of being made a presidential candidate. To this question, Eaton reported Grant as saying, "They can't compel me to do it!" (p. 190).

To Edwin M. Stanton¹

Sec. of War of War [*sic*]„ please see & hear Col. Eaton, whom Gen.
Grant thinks is one of the best contraband agents.   A. LINCOLN
    Aug. 12, 1864

¹ ALS-F, John Eaton, *Grant, Lincoln, and the Freedmen*, p. 178. This note is misdated August 12, 1861, in Tracy, p. 193. According to Eaton's account, Lincoln sent him to Stanton to report on "Affairs in the [Mississippi] Valley and receive any suggestions he might offer," concerning Eaton's work with the freedmen.

To Edwin M. Stanton¹

This case will go according to the rules without my interference,
and I can not consistently ask for more.   A. LINCOLN
    August 12. 1864

¹ AES, DNA WR RG 107, Secretary of War, Letters Received, P 539. Lincoln's endorsement is written on a letter from Governor Michael Hahn, Washington, D.C., August 9, 1864, introducing John Touro of Louisiana, who wished to present numerous claims, including his own, for supplies taken by the army from Louisiana citizens. Stanton endorsed "Referred to Major General Canby," and Canby referred the matter to Major General Banks, who endorsed on September 10, 1864: "Respectfully returned (through Head Quarters Military Division of West Mississippi) to the Adjutant General of the Army,—with the information that this claim is made up in such general terms, as to time and the officer who had immediate command of the troops alleged to have taken this property, that no action can be had until that is furnished. It is respectfully suggested that this claim be referred to Brig. Gen'l Halbert E. Paine, Comd'g Mil District of Illinois."
    A final endorsement indicates receipt of the report (not found) of the general commanding the District of Illinois, on January 11, 1865.

To Joseph Holt[1]

Judge Advocate General please procure record and make report in this case.   A. LINCOLN

Aug. 13. 1864

[1] AES, DNA WR RG 153, Judge Advocate General, NN 2120. See Lincoln's order for arrest of John S. Carlisle, June 15, *supra*. On August 17, Lincoln endorsed the record in the case of Louis A. Welton, sentenced to prison for being a spy, "Application denied," but see further Lincoln's communications to Morgan, Weed, and Raymond, August 31, and to Holt, December 28, *infra*.

To Ulysses S. Grant[1]

"Cypher"   Office U.S. Military Telegraph,
Lieut. Genl. Grant   War Department,
City-Point, Va.   Washington, D.C., August 14 1864.

The Secretary of War and I concur that you better confer with Gen. Lee and stipulate for a mutual discontinuance of house-burning and other destruction of private property. The time and manner of conference, and particulars of stipulation we leave, on our part, to your convenience and judgment.   A. LINCOLN

[1] ALS, DNA WR RG 107, Presidential Telegrams, I, 131. Grant telegraphed on August 17: "I have thought over your dispatch relative to an arrangement between Gen. Lee and myself for the suppression of insindiaryism by the respective Armies. Experience has taught us that agreements made with rebels are binding upon us but are not observed by them longer than suits their convenience. On the whole I think the best that can be done is to publish a prohibitory order against burning private property except where it is a Military necessity or in retaliation for like acts by the enemy. When burning is done in retaliation it must be done by order of a Dept. or Army Commander and the order for such burning to set forth the particular act it is in retaliation for. Such an order would be published and would come to the knowledge of the rebel Army. I think this course would be much better than any agreement with Gen. Lee. I could publish the order or it could be published by you. This is respectfully submitted for your consideration and I will then act as you deem best." (ALS, DLC-Grant Papers).

To Atanasio Cruz Aguirre[1]

August 15, 1864

Abraham Lincoln,
President of the United States of America,

To His Excellency
Señor Don Atanasio Cruz Aguirre,
President of the Oriental Republic of Uruguay.

Great and Good Friend: I have received the letter which you addressed to me on the first day of March last, informing me of

your Excellency's elevation to the Presidency of the Oriental Republic of Uruguay,—the constitutional term of the citizen Bernardo Prudencio Berro being completed, and in virtue of the prescriptions of the political code of the State.

I congratulate your Excellency upon your accession to this high and important position, and confiding in your sagacity and statesmanship, I feel satisfied that the trust conferred upon you will be faithfully discharged for the best interests of the Oriental Republic of Uruguay. It shall be my constant endeavor so to conduct the relations between our respective countries as to strengthen the good understanding which now happily subsists.

I pray your Excellency to accept the assurances of my earnest wishes for your personal happiness, and for the welfare and prosperity of the people of Uruguay.

And so commending you to the care of the Almighty, I remain your Excellency's Good Friend.   ABRAHAM LINCOLN.

By the President:

WILLIAM H. SEWARD, Secretary of State.

Washington, August 15th, 1864.

1 Copy, DNA FS RG 59, Communications to Foreign Sovereigns and States, III, 239-40.

To Henry J. Raymond[1]

Hon. Henry J. Raymond   Executive Mansion,
My dear Sir   Washington, August 15, 1864.

I have proposed to Mr Greely that the Niagara correspondence be published, suppressing only the parts of his letters over which the red-pencil is drawn in the copy which I herewith send. He declines giving his consent to the publication of his letters unless these parts be published with the rest. I have concluded that it is better for *me* to submit, for the time, to the consequences of the false position in which I consider he has placed me, than to subject the *country* to the consequences of publishing these discouraging and injurious parts. I send you this, and the accompanying copy, not for publication, but merely to explain to you, and that you may preserve them until their proper time shall come. Yours truly
A. LINCOLN

1 ALS-F, ISLA; LS copy, DLC-RTL. See Lincoln to Greeley, August 6 and 9, *supra.* Raymond had written Lincoln on August 5, enclosing a clipping of Greeley's article in the *Tribune* of that day in which he stated that he would gladly comply with the *Times'* request for publication of the correspondence if he had copies of all the documents:

"I enclose an article from The Tribune of this morning. It seems to me that the public interest would be served—& certainly your action would be vindicated . . . by the publication of the correspondence in question.

"If you concur in this opinion & see no objection to such a course I should be very glad to receive from you a copy with authority to publish it." (DLC-RTL).

Recommendation[1]

August 15, 1864

I am always for the man who wishes to work; and I shall be glad for this man to get suitable employment at Calvary Depot, or elsewhere.   A. LINCOLN

August 15. 1864

[1] ADS-P, ISLA. An endorsement below Lincoln's recommendation signed by W. H. Hay (unidentified) referred to "Capt. L. Loury Moore, AQM Gisboro D.C. who will give this man suitable employment if he can." Giesborough Point, D.C., was a remount station for the Army of the Potomac.

Recommendation for Discharge[1]

August 15, 1864

It seems to me that unless there is ground to suspect the correctness of the correctness [sic] of the within statement, this man should be allowed to take the oath & be discharged.   A. LINCOLN

Aug 15. 1864

[1] AES, NNC-Hill Collection. Lincoln's endorsement has been removed from attendant papers.

To William T. Sherman[1]

"Cypher"

Major General Sherman   Executive Mansion
Near Atlanta, Ga.   Washington D C. Aug. 15 1864

If the government should purchase, on it's own account, cotton Northward of you and on the line of your communications, would it be an inconvenience to you, or detriment to the Military service, for it to come to the North on the Railroad?   A. LINCOLN

[1] ALS, DNA WR RG 107, Presidential Telegrams, I, 132. No reply from Sherman has been discovered, but that he telegraphed on August 17 in regard to the transportation of cotton is indicated by a note of Rufus K. Williams written on Executive Mansion stationery, August 26, as follows:

"I have seen Hon Secty Treas and proposed that Dr W. A. Turner my son-in-law, a devoted political friend of yours, should be appointed special agent to purchase this 1200 bales of cotton, that an order be issued to Genl Sherman, according to his own suggestions by Telegraph of 17th Inst. to transport it to

Nashville. That it be sold at Nashville and liberal freights be retained by the Government, and if desired three fourths of the proceeds be invested in Government securities. This is strictly within the 8 Sect of Act of July 1864.

"It is important that it be done at once, if at all. . . . I think Mr F[essenden] regards this proposition as legal." (DLC-RTL).

See Lincoln's memorandum of August 25, and order of August 31, *infra*.

To Edwin M. Stanton[1]

I agree to this appointment.   A. LINCOLN
August 15. 1864

[1] AES, RPB. Lincoln's endorsement is written on a letter of Captain Edgar W. Dennis, Bureau of Military Justice, to Montgomery Blair, August 4, 1864, requesting his assistance in obtaining appointment as judge advocate to succeed John A. Bingham, who had resigned on August 3. Dennis was appointed major and judge advocate of Volunteers, January 19, 1865.

To John P. Usher[1]

The first time the Sec. of Interior call[s] here will he please mention the DeJanon case?   A. LINCOLN
Aug. 15, 1864

[1] AES, ORB. Lincoln's endorsement is written on a letter of J. R. Stewart to Usher, Washington, July 26, 1864, "in behalf of Profr De Janon's restoration to the Professorship of Spanish at West Point . . . removed on personal grounds. . . ." In the fall of 1863, Patrice de Janon, professor of Spanish at West Point, had been dismissed. On February 10, 1864, his wife, a niece of George D. Blakey of Kentucky, wrote Lincoln asking an interview for her husband and complaining that Lincoln had been rude to her at an interview a few days earlier, when he declared "that it was the universal opinion that my husband was notoriously incompetent . . . & that he never would have obtained the appointment—but for the influence of my pretty face. . . . You have said also—that you had been told—that I exercised a *bad influence* over the 'Corps of Cadets'. . . ." (DLC-RTL). On June 25, George D. Blakey wrote asking de Janon's reinstatement and stating that J. R. Stewart, Blakey's attorney, would handle the case (*ibid.*). The *U.S. Official Register*, 1865, lists de Janon as again at West Point.

To Joseph K. Barnes[1]

Executive Mansion,
Surgeon General   Washington, August [16], 1864.

Please have a special examination & report made of the physical condition of Michael Burns, a private now at Stanton Hospital. Yours truly   A. LINCOLN

[1] ALS, DLC-RTL. Acting Surgeon General Barnes endorsed under date of August 16, 1864: "Respectfully returned with report that upon ordering a special examination of Prvt. Michael Burns 115 N.Y. Vols—he was not to be found, having left the Hospital without a Pass on the 14th. inst."

To Edward Bates[1]

Hon. Attorney General   Executive Mansion,
My dear Sir   Washington, August 16. 1864.

Send me a recess commission for Delos Lake to be Attorney for
the District of California. Yours truly   A. LINCOLN

[1] ALS, DNA RG 60, Papers of Attorney General, 1864, Box 122. See Lincoln's endorsement concerning Lake, June 22, *supra*. Bates endorsed "Delos Lake, to be U.S. Atty. for the Northern Dist. of Cala vice [William N.] Sharp, removed E.B."

To William P. Fessenden[1]

Hon. Sec. of the Treasury   Executive Mansion,
My dear Sir   Washington, August 16. 1864.

If by any means a new Collector of Internal Revenue is to [be]
made in the District (made or to be made) in which Frankfort, Ky
is, or will be situated, I wish Albert G. Hodges, to be appointed. He
is the man to whom I wrote the Hodges letter, which has been,
published. Yours truly   A. LINCOLN

[1] ALS, IHi. Albert G. Hodges wrote Lincoln on August 11, 1864:
"I have been informed . . . whether true or not, I do not know, that collection Districts, for the collection of US Revenue, have been increased in number in each state to equal the number of Congressional Districts. If this be so . . . I respectfully submit my claims for the appointment of the Collectorship in this . . . District. . . .
"I would not ask the appointment if I did not believe that I could discharge its duties with credit. . . . Besides, in my present depressed condition, pecuniarily, it will aid me very much in sustaining my paper in this State. Since all State patronage has been taken from me, I find it an up-hill business to keep up the Commonwealth. I am determined, at all hazzards, to keep that going until after the November Election. . . ." (DLC-RTL).
There is no record of Hodges' appointment.

To Joseph Holt[1]

                                                          August 16, 1864

Sentence approved, except as to Cashiering, & the officer is hereby
dishonorably dismissed the service.   A. LINCOLN
    Aug. 16. 1864.

Judge Advocate General please procure record & report.
    Jan. 27. 1865   A. LINCOLN

[1] AES, DNA WR RG 153, Judge Advocate General, NN 2019. Lincoln's first endorsement appears on the court-martial record of Lieutenant Hartley W. Sewall, Revenue Service, cashiered and sentenced to ten years in the penitentiary for malfeasance, bribery, and perjury. The second endorsement appears on a petition in favor of Sewall. No further action by Lincoln appears.

To Ward Hunt[1]

Hon. Ward Hunt   Executive Mansion,
My dear Sir.   Washington, August 16. 1864.

Yours of the 9th. Inst. was duly received, and submitted to Secretary Seward. He makes a response which I herewith inclose to you.[2] I add for myself that I am for the regular nominee in all cases; and that no one could be more satisfactory to me as the nominee in that District, than Mr. Conkling. I do not mean to say there [are] not others as good as he in the District; but I think I know him to be at least good enough. Yours truly   A. LINCOLN

[1] ADfS, DLC-RTL. On August 9, 1864, Ward Hunt, an attorney of Utica, New York, who became associate justice of the U.S. Supreme Court in 1872, wrote Lincoln:

". . . You are aware that in 1858 the Hon. Roscoe Conkling was elected as the representative in Congress from this district, that he was re elected in 1860 & that he was defeated in 1862. You are not perhaps aware of the means used to procure his defeat, or the persons by whom it was accomplished, or what is still more important, of the present purposes of the same individuals. . . .

"I think . . . that the Union party will again present Mr Conkling as their candidate. . . . The question will then arise must the Union men of this county, fight not only the Democracy . . . but . . . also . . . the power & influence of the administration? . . . .

"The principal individuals who procured the defeat of Mr. Conkling in 1862, were Messrs. O. B. Matteson, Palmer V. Kellogg & A. D. Barber. They are open . . . in their hostility & . . . declare, that if the party . . . again nominate Mr Conkling they will again compass his defeat . . . each of these gentlemen is an especial friend & supporter of Mr Seward, . . . on political matters, his wish would be controlling with them. . . . May I take the liberty to ask . . . is this the condition in which a party & its candidates ought to be placed?. . . ." (DLC-RTL).

On August 18, Hunt acknowledged Lincoln's letter:

"Your favor enclosing Mr Sewards letter . . . is received with great pleasure. The assurances contained in Mr Sewards letter are very gratifying, and in the event of Mr Conkling's nomination . . . I shall venture to make application for the influence that can be executed, and that will be of great service to him. . . ." (*Ibid.*).   [2] No copy has been located.

Appointment of William Helmick[1]

Executive Office
Washington, Augt. 17th 1864.

William Helmick, is hereby appointed, Acting Commissioner of Pensions, during the temporary absence of Jos. H. Barrett, the Commissioner, from the Seat of Government.

ABRAHAM LINCOLN

[1] DS, ORB. William Helmick was chief clerk in the Pension Office.

To Ulysses S. Grant[1]

"Cypher"

Lieut. Gen. Grant   Executive Mansion,
City Point, Va.   Washington, August 17. 1864.

I have seen your despatch expressing your unwillingness to break your hold where you are. Neither am I willing. Hold on with a bull-dog gripe, and chew & choke, as much as possible.

                                  A. LINCOLN

[1] ALS, DNA WR RG 107, Presidential Telegrams, I, 133. On August 15 Grant telegraphed Halleck: "If there is any danger of an uprising in the North to resist the draft or for any other purpose our loyal Governor's ought to organize the militia at once to resist it. If we are to draw troops from the field to keep the loyal States in harness it will prove difficult to suppress the rebellion in the disloyal States. My withdrawal now from the James River would insure the defeat of Sherman. Twenty thousand men sent to him at this time would destroy the greater part of Hood's army, and leave us men wherever required. General Heintzelman can get from the Governors of Ohio, Indiana, and Illinois a militia organization that will deter the discontented from committing any overt act. I hope the President will call on Governors of States to organize thoroughly to preserve the peace until after the election. . . ." (OR, I, XLII, II, 193-94).

To Charles D. Robinson[1]

Hon. Charles D. Robinson   Executive Mansion,
My dear Sir: Washington, August 17, 1864.

Your letter of the 7th. was placed in my hand yesterday by Gov. Randall.

To me it seems plain that saying re-union and abandonment of slavery would be considered, if offered, is not saying that nothing *else* or *less* would be considered, if offered. But I will not stand upon the mere construction of language. It is true, as you remind me, that in the Greeley letter of 1862, I said: "If I could save the Union without freeing any slave I would do it; and if I could save it by freeing all the slaves I would do it; and if I could save it by freeing some, and leaving others alone I would also do that." I continued in the same letter as follows: "What I do about slavery and the colored race, I do because I believe it helps to save the Union; and what I forbear I forbear because I do not believe it would help to save the Union. I shall do less whenever I shall believe what I am doing hurts the cause; and I shall do more whenever I shall believe doing more will help the cause." All this I said in the utmost sincerity; and I am as true to the whole of it now, as when I first said it. When I afterwards proclaimed emancipation, and employed colored soldiers, I only followed the declaration just quoted from the Greeley letter that "I shall do *more* whenever I shall believe *doing* more will help the cause" The way these measures were to help the cause, was not to be by magic, or miracles, but by inducing the colored people to come bodily over from the rebel side to ours. On this point, nearly a year ago, in a letter to Mr. Conkling, made public at once, I wrote as follows: "But negroes, like other people, act upon motives. Why should they do anything for us if we will do nothing for them? If they stake their lives for us they must be prompted by the strongest motive—even the promise of freedom. And the promise, being made, must be kept." I am sure you will not, on due reflection, say that the promise being made, must be *broken* at the first opportunity. I am sure you would not desire me to say, or to leave an inference, that I am ready, whenever convenient, to join in re-enslaving those who shall have served us in consideration of our promise. As matter of morals, could such treachery by any possibility, escape the curses of Heaven, or of any good man? As matter of policy, to *announce* such a purpose, would ruin the Union cause itself. All recruiting of colored men would instantly cease, and all colored men now in our service, would instantly desert us. And rightfully too. Why should they give their lives for us, with full notice of our purpose to betray them? Drive back to the support of the rebellion the physical force which the colored people now give, and promise us, and neither the present, nor any coming administration, *can* save the Union. Take from us, and give to the enemy, the hundred and thirty, forty, or fifty thousand colored persons now serving us as soldiers, seamen, and laborers, and we can not longer maintain the contest. The party who could elect a President on a War & Slavery Restoration platform, would, of necessity, lose the colored force; and that force being lost, would be as powerless to save the Union as to do any other impossible thing. It is not a question of sentiment or taste, but one of physical force, which may be measured, and estimated as horsepower, and steam power, are measured and estimated. And by measurement, it is more than we can lose, and live. Nor can we, by discarding it, get a white force in place of it. There is a witness in every white mans bosom that he would rather go to the war having the negro to help him, than to help the enemy against him. It is not the giving of one class for another. It is simply giving a large force to the enemy, for *nothing* in return.

In addition to what I have said, allow me to remind you that no one, having control of the rebel armies, or, in fact, having any influence whatever in the rebellion, has offered, or intimated a willingness to, a restoration of the Union, in any event, or on any condition whatever. Let it be constantly borne in mind that no such offer has been made or intimated. Shall we be weak enough to allow the enemy to distract us with an abstract question which he himself refuses to present as a practical one? In the Conkling letter before mentioned, I said: "Whenever you shall have conquered all resistance to the Union, if I shall urge you to continue fighting, it will be an apt time *then* to declare that you will not fight to free negroes."[2] I repeat this now. If Jefferson Davis wishes, for himself, or for the benefit of his friends at the North, to know what I would do if he were to offer peace and re-union, saying nothing about slavery, let him try me.

[1] ADf, DLC-RTL. Two drafts are preserved in the Lincoln Papers. The first is in pencil and bears the date as given above. The second is in ink, without date, and is probably the finished copy which Lincoln intended to send, but which he never dated, signed, or sent. The letter from Democratic editor of the Green Bay, Wisconsin, *Advocate,* Charles D. Robinson, dated August 7, 1864, which First Assistant Postmaster General Alexander W. Randall (formerly governor of Wisconsin) handed to Lincoln on August 16, is as follows:

"I am a War Democrat, and the editor of a Democratic paper. I have sustained your Administration . . . because it is the legally constituted government. I have sustained its war policy, not because I endorsed it entire, but because it presented the only available method of putting down the rebellion. . . . It was alleged that because I and my friends sustained the Emancipation measure, we had become abolitionized. We replied that we regarded the freeing of the negroes as sound war policy, in that the depriving the South of its laborers weakened the . . . Rebellion. That was a good argument. . . . It was solid ground on which we could stand, and still maintain our position as Democrats. We were greatly comforted and strengthened also by your assurance that if you could save the Union without freeing any slave, you would do it; if you could save it by freeing the slaves, you would do it; and if you could do it by freeing some, and leaving others alone, you would also do that.

"The Niagara Falls 'Peace' movement was of no importance whatever, except that it resulted in bringing out your declaration, as we understand it, that no steps can be taken towards peace . . . unless accompanied with an abandonment of slavery. This puts the whole war question on a new basis, and takes us War Democrats clear off our feet, leaving us no ground to stand upon. If we sustain the war and war policy, does it not demand the changing of our party politics?

"I venture to write you this letter . . . not for the purpose of finding fault with your policy . . . but in the hope that you may suggest some interpretation of it, as will . . . make it tenable ground on which we War Democrats may stand—preserve our party consistently support the government—and continue to carry also to its support those large numbers of our old political friends who have stood by us up to this time.

"I beg to assure you that this is not written for the purpose of using it, or its possible reply, in a public way. And I . . . send it through my friend Gov. Randall in the belief that he will guarantee for me entire good faith." (DLC-RTL).

The interview of Randall, Judge Joseph T. Mills, and William P. Dole, with Lincoln on August 19 (*infra*) presumably dealt with Lincoln's reply to Robinson, although Judge Mills' report of the interview does not mention the letter. In any event, Randall wrote Lincoln on August 22:

"I have been reflecting upon the clause of your letter to Col. Robinson to which Mr Dole objected and think there is force in his objection on the score of its policy. While the idea of that part is a correct one, it is unnecessary to say it, I think, because what you say in the balance of the letter will be entirely sufficient for Robinsons purposes. It is not designed for publication it is true, and Mr. Robinson will not publish it. Some accident might get its contents before the public. I presume respectfully to make these suggestions for your consideration." (*Ibid.*).

It seems probable, there being no further reference to the letter and no reply from Robinson, that Lincoln decided against sending the letter at all.

2 The pencil draft ends at this point.

To Edwin M. Stanton[1]

Let this appointment be made if the service can be made useful.

Aug. 17, 1864.   A. LINCOLN

1 Milton Kronovet Catalog 54. According to the catalog description Lincoln's endorsement is written on a letter from Senator John C. Ten Eyck recommending appointment of Lieutenant G. W. Patterson in the quartermaster's department. First Lieutenant George W. Patterson, Company G, Fourteenth New Jersey Volunteers, resigned on March 1, 1864, for disability. No record of his further service has been found.

To Ethan A. Hitchcock[1]

August 18, 1864.

If General Hitchcock can effect a special exchange of Thomas D. Armesy, now under conviction as a spy, or something of the sort, and in prison at ———, for Maj. Nathan Goff, made a prisoner of war, and now in prison at Richmond, let it be done.

A. LINCOLN.

1 OR, II, VII, 523. Major Thomas D. Armesy, CSA, was arrested April 18, 1863, near Clarksburg, Virginia, and tried on the charge of "recruiting men within the lines of the United States forces for the so-called Confederate Army." He was found guilty and sentenced to hard labor for 15 years at Fort Warren, Boston Harbor (AGO *General Orders No. 397*, December 16, 1863). Major Nathan Goff, Jr., Fourth West Virginia Cavalry, wrote to U.S. Senator Waitman T. Willey from Libby Prison, May 16, 1864, that he was being held in close confinement as hostage for Armesy (OR, II, VII, 148-49). Hitchcock suggested that a Confederate officer of like rank be set aside to receive the same treatment as Goff (*ibid.*), and Major W. P. Elliott, confined at Fort Delaware, was the officer chosen (*ibid.*, p. 391).

To Andrew Johnson[1]

Office U.S. Military Telegraph,

Gov. Andrew Johnson   War Department,
Nashville, Tenn.   Washington, D.C., August 18. 1864.

The officer whose duty it would be to execute John S. Young, upon a sentence of death for murder &c, is hereby ordered to suspend such execution until further order from me.   A. LINCOLN

[1] ALS, DNA WR RG 107, Presidential Telegrams, I, 134. On August 17, 1864, Governor Johnson telegraphed Lincoln:

"John S. Young was tried some time since . . . by a military commission & found guilty of murder &c. sentenced to be hanged. . . . on Friday the 26th inst. I have not had an opportunity to examine the evidence in the case. Gen'l Thomas['] Judge Advocate informs me that . . . the proof does not show that he was personally involved in the murder but with a gang a portion of whom committed it. he is a very young man and was influenced to enter the Rebel army by others. . . . he is not more than one or two degrees removed from idiocy. . . . I would recommend . . . that the punishment . . . be commuted to . . . imprisonment . . . during his natural life. if the President does not commute the punishment I hope he will grant short respite if the punishment is commuted I hope the President will send the order to me so that it may be held up to the very last moment of time before his execution believing it will have a good moral effect & placing his numerous friends under deep obligations to the President . . . for having saved his life in the very last moment of time." (DLC-RTL).

See further Lincoln's communication to Mrs. Mary M. Baldwin, August 24, *infra.*

Order Confirming Dismissal of William A. Hammond[1]

August 18, 1864

The record, proceedings, findings, and sentence of the Court in the foregoing case are approved; and it is ordered that Brigadier General William A. Hammond, Surgeon General of the United States Army, be dismissed the service, and be forever disqualified from holding any office of honor, profit, or trust under the government of the United States.   ABRAHAM LINCOLN.

August 18, 1864.

[1] AGO *General Court Martial Orders No. 251*, August 22, 1864. Surgeon General Hammond was found guilty on charges of (1) "Disorders and neglects to the prejudice of good order and military discipline," (2) "Conduct unbecoming an officer and a gentleman," and (3) "Conduct to the prejudice of good order and military discipline."

Proclamation Concerning Commercial Regulations[1]

August 18, 1864

By the President of the United States of America.

A Proclamation.

Whereas the Act of Congress of the 28th of September, 1850, entitled "An Act to create additional collection districts in the State of California, and to change the existing districts therein, and to modify the existing collection districts in the United States," extends to merchandise warehoused under bond, the privilege of being exported to the British North American Provinces adjoining the United States, in the manner prescribed in the Act of Congress of the 3d of March 1845, which designates certain frontier ports through which merchandise may be exported, and further provides "that such other ports, situated on the frontiers of the United States adjoining the British North American Provinces as may hereafter be found expedient, may have extended to them the like privileges on the recommendation of the Secretary of the Treasury and Proclamation duly made by the President of the United States, specially designating the ports to which the aforesaid privileges are to be extended:"

Now therefore, I, ABRAHAM LINCOLN, President of the United States of America, in accordance with the recommendation of the Secretary of the Treasury, do hereby declare and proclaim, that the port of Newport in the State of Vermont is and shall be entitled to all the privileges in regard to the exportation of merchandise in bond to the British North American Provinces, adjoining the United States, which are extended to the ports enumerated in the 7th. section of the Act of Congress of the 3d. of March 1845, aforesaid, from and after the date of this Proclamation.

In witness whereof I have hereunto set my hand and caused the seal of the United States to be affixed.

Done at the City of Washington, this eighteenth day of August, in the year of our Lord one thousand eight hundred and [L.S.] sixty four, and of the Independence of the United States of America the eighty ninth ABRAHAM LINCOLN

By the President:

WILLIAM H. SEWARD Secretary of State.

[1] DS, DNA FS RG 11, Proclamations.

Speech to the One Hundred Sixty-Fourth Ohio Regiment[1]

August 18, 1864

SOLDIERS—You are about to return to your homes and your friends, after having, as I learn, performed in camp a comparatively short term of duty in this great contest. I am greatly obliged to you, and to all who have come forward at the call of their country. I wish it might be more generally and universally understood what the country is now engaged in. We have, as all will **agree, a free** Government, where every man has a right to be equal with every other man. In this great struggle, this form of Government and every form of human right is endangered if our enemies succeed. There is more involved in this contest than is realized by every one. There is involved in this struggle the question whether your children and my children shall enjoy the privileges we have enjoyed. I say this in order to impress upon you, if you are not already so impressed, that no small matter should divert us from our great purpose. There may be some irregularities in the practical application of our system.[2] It is fair that each man shall pay taxes in exact proportion to the value of his property; but if we should wait before collecting a tax to adjust the taxes upon each man in exact proportion with every other man, we should never collect any tax at all. There may be mistakes made sometimes; things may be done wrong while the officers of the Government do all they can to prevent mistakes. But I beg of you, as citizens of this great Republic, not to let your minds be carried off from the great work we have before us. This struggle is too large for you to be diverted from it by any small matter. When you return to your homes rise up to the height of a generation of men worthy of a free Government, and we will carry out the great work we have commenced. I return to you my sincere thanks, soldiers, for the honor you have done me this afternoon.

[1] New York *Times* and *Tribune*, August 19, 1864. This speech is misdated September, 1864, in Hertz (II, 492). The One Hundred Sixty-fourth Ohio was one of the hundred-days regiments of Ohio state militia whose terms of service were expiring in August. James C. Wetmore, Ohio state military agent, notified the colonels of the several regiments on August 15, that "His Excellency the President has signified to me that he would be pleased to receive a call at the Executive Mansion from you and your command when on your way to your homes in Ohio." (Wetmore to Ohio State National Guard Colonels, August 15, 1864, enclosed by Wetmore to Nicolay, same date, DLC-RTL). See Lincoln's speeches of August 22 and 31, *infra.*

[2] In the *Tribune* this sentence reads: "There may be some inequalities in the practical working of our system."

To Edwin M. Stanton[1]

Here is the application of Gen. Owen. If the Sec. of War wishes or consents to revoke the order & give a trial I agree.   A. LINCOLN

August. 18. 1864

[1] AES, owned by C. Norton Owen, Glencoe, Illinois. Lincoln's endorsement is written on a petition of Joshua T. Owen, late brigadier general of Volunteers, asking for a court-martial trial. Stanton endorsed on August 19, "Referred to the

Adjutant General to be filed." General Owen had been arrested on June 12, 1864, by order of Brigadier General John Gibbon, for disobedience of orders at Spotsylvania Court House on May 18 and at Cold Harbor on June 3.

To Edwin M. Stanton[1]

August 18, 1864

Will the Secretary of War please see these gentlemen who are agents for recruiting colored soldiers & who seek to have removed some little difficulties in their way.   A. LINCOLN

August 18. 1864

[1] Angle, 355. The gentlemen have not been identified.

Interview with Alexander W. Randall
and Joseph T. Mills[1]

August 19, 1864

The President was free & animated in conversation. I was astonished at his elasticity of spirits. Says Gov Randall, why cant you Mr P. seek some place of retirement for a few weeks. You would be reinvigorated. Aye said the President, 3 weeks would do me no good—my thoughts my solicitude for this great country follow me where ever I go. I don't think it is personal vanity, or ambition—but I cannot but feel that the weal or woe of this great nation will be decided in the approaching canvas. My own experience has proven to me, that there is no program intended by the democratic party but that will result in the dismemberment of the Union. But Genl McClellan is in favor of crushing out the rebellion, & he will probably be the Chicago candidate. The slightest acquaintance with arithmetic will prove to any man that the rebel armies cannot be destroyed with democratic strategy. It would sacrifice all the white men of the north to do it. There are now between 1 & 200 thousand black men now in the service of the Union. These men will be

[1] Diary of Joseph T. Mills, MS., WHi. Although diary reports of conversations have been generally excluded from the present work, Mills' record of this interview is reproduced as an exception, in order to correct the record. In the *Complete Works of Abraham Lincoln* (X, 189-91) Nicolay and Hay incorporated a newspaper version purporting to be a verbatim report of Lincoln's remarks on this occasion, which they supplied with the incorrect date "August [15?] 1864." The newspaper version which appeared without date in the New York *Tribune* for September 10, 1864, was probably prepared by Mills, but with so much adding to and subtracting from the original as to leave something less than an acceptable text of Lincoln's remarks as recorded in the diary. The occasion of the interview is indicated by Lincoln's communication to Charles D. Robinson, August 17, *supra*.

disbanded, returned to slavery & we will have to fight two nations instead of one. I have tried it. You cannot concilliate the South, when the mastery & control of millions of blacks makes them sure of ultimate success. You cannot concilliate the South, when you place yourself in such a position, that they see they can achieve their independence. The war democrat depends upon conciliation. He must confine himself to that policy entirely. If he fights at all in such a war as this he must economise life & use all the means which God & nature puts in his power. Abandon all the posts now possessed by black men surrender all these advantages to the enemy, & we would be compelled to abandon the war in 3 weeks. We have to hold territory. Where are the war democrats to do it. The field was open to them to have enlisted & put down this rebellion by force of arms, by concilliation, long before the present policy was inaugurated. There have been men who have proposed to me to return to slavery the black warriors of Port Hudson & Olustee to their masters to conciliate the South. I should be damned in time & in eternity for so doing. The world shall know that I will keep my faith to friends & enemies, come what will. My enemies say I am now carrying on this war for the sole purpose of abolition. It is & will be carried on so long as I am President for the sole purpose of restoring the Union. But no human power can subdue this rebellion without using the Emancipation lever as I have done. Freedom has given us the control of 200 000 able bodied men, born & raised on southern soil. It will give us more yet. Just so much it has sub[t]racted from the strength of our enemies, & instead of alienating the south from us, there are evidences of a fraternal feeling growing up between our own & rebel soldiers. My enemies condemn my emancipation policy. Let them prove by the history of this war, that we can restore the Union without it. The President appeared to be not the pleasant joker I had expected to see, but a man of deep convictions & an unutterable yearning for the success of the Union cause. His voice was pleasant—his manner earnest & cordial. As I heard a vindication of his policy from his own lips, I could not but feel that his mind grew in stature like his body, & that I stood in the presence of the great guiding intellect of the age, & that those huge Atlantian shoulders were fit to bear the weight of mightiest monarchies. His transparent honesty, his republican simplicity, his gushing sympathy for those who offered their lives for their country, his utter forgetfulness of self in his concern for his country, could not but inspire me with confidence, that he was Heavens instrument to conduct his people thro this red sea of blood to a Canaan of peace & freedom. Comr. Dole then came in. We were about to retire, but he insisted on our remaining longer. Dismissing the present state of the country, he entertained us with reminiscences of the past—of the discussions between himself & Douglass. He said he was accused of of [sic] joking. In his later speeches, the seriousness of the theme prevented him from using anecdotes. Mr. Harris a democratic orator of Ill, once appealed to his audience in this way. If these republicans get into power, the darkies will be allowed to come to the polls & vote. Here comes forward a white man, & you ask him who will you vote for. I will vote for S A Douglass. Next comes up a sleek pampered negro. Well Sambo, who do you vote for. I vote for Massa Lincoln. Now asked the orator, what do you think of that. Some old farmer cried out, I think the darkey showd a damd sight of more sense than the white man. It is such social tete a tetes among his friends that enables Mr Lincoln to endure mental toils & application that would crush any other man. The President now in full flow of spirits, scattered his repartee in all directions. He took his seat on the sofa by my side. Said I Mr President I was in your reception room to day. It was dark. I suppose that clouds & darkness necessarily surround the secrets of state. There in a corner I saw a man quietly reading who possessed a remarkable physiognomy. I was rivetted to the spot. I stood & stared at him   He raised his flashing eyes & caught me in the act. I was compelled to speak. Said I, Are you the President. No replied the stranger, I am Frederick Douglass. Now Mr P. are you in favor of miscegenation. That's a democratic mode of producing good Union men, & I dont propose to infringe on the patent. We parted from his Excellency, with firmer purpose to sustain the government, at whose head there stands a man who combines in his person all that is valuable in *progress* in conservatism—all that is hopeful in *progress*.

To Benjamin F. Butler[1]

Major Gen. Butler   Executive Mansion Washington D.C.
Bermuda, Hundred   Va.   Aug. 20. 1864
    Please allow Judge Snead to go to his family on Eastern Shore, or give me some good reason why not.   A LINCOLN

---

[1] ALS, DNA WR RG 107, Presidential Telegrams, I, 137. See Lincoln to Peirpoint, August 5, and to Butler, August 9, *supra*. Butler replied on August 21: "I have never hindered . . . E K Snead . . . from going to his family on the Eastern Shore   I had supposed he was there until I saw in the New-York Tribune of the nineteenth a scurrillous article by him dated at Alexandria. . . . The trouble is Snead is a liar, has deceived the President. . . . Of such are the restored Govt of Virginia." (DLC-RTL).

To John F. Miller[1]

Commanding Officer at   Executive Mansion,
Nashville, Tennessee.   Washington, August 20, 1864.

Suspend execution of death sentence of Patrick Jones, Co. F. twelfth Tennessee Cavalry until further orders and forward record for examination.   A. LINCOLN.

Maj. Eckert
Please send above telegram.   JNO. G. NICOLAY   Priv. Sec.

[1] D, DNA WR RG 107, Presidential Telegrams, I, 136. The telegram is in Nicolay's autograph. Governor Andrew Johnson telegraphed Lincoln on August 19, 1864: "Private Patrick Jones Co F Twelfth Tennessee Cavalry was tried . . . upon the charge of murder—he was found guilty & sentenced to be hung . . . Aug twenty sixth in consideration of the youth of the condemned man fifteen (15) years . . . & the statement that he was drunk when he committed the act it is recommended that the sentence be commuted to imprisonment for life I am free to say that the moral influence would be much greater if we could hang some of the larger fish . . . there is no trouble in convicting & hanging the little helpless minnow which makes & leaves no impression upon the public mind" (DLC-RTL).

Brigadier General John F. Miller, in command at Nashville, answered Lincoln's telegram on the same day:

"Your dispatch suspending execution . . . of Patrick Jones . . . received the record will be forwarded. . . ." (*Ibid.*).

To Edwin M. Stanton[1]

Hon. Sec. of War.   Executive Mansion,
Dear Sir   Washington, Aug. 20, 1864.

Col. Whistler, who presents this, says he has an application on file for his son—Garland N. Whistler—to go to West-Point, and that there is now a vacancy. If there is a vacancy, and if his vouchers are the best now on file, let him have it. Yours truly

                                  A. LINCOLN

[1] ALS, DNA WR RG 94, U.S. Military Academy, 1863, No. 178. No record has been found of the appointment of Garland N. Whistler, son of Colonel Joseph N. G. Whistler, Second New York Artillery.

To Edwin M. Stanton[1]

                                August 20, 1864

Let Gen. Burbridge be invited as requested, if in his own judgment he can properly leave his command at time, and for such length of time.   A. LINCOLN

August 20. 1864

[1] AES, NHi. Lincoln's endorsement is written on a letter from Joseph A. Wright, New York City, August 16, 1864:

"I left Kentucky three weeks since after addressing the people at Lexington; and expect to return to Kentucky and Indiana about the first of September. Gen'l Burbridge has never visited Washington, and he is most anxious to see you; he is your devoted friend, and my candid opinion is you ought to see him, great good will result from the same. As I desire to meet the General at Washington the last of August, let me advise you to see that he is invited by the Secretary of War to visit the capitol at this time, if the condition of things in Kentucky will justify his absence for three or four days. I suggest this both from political and national as well as personal considerations.

"Gen Burbridge has made application heretofore to visit Washington, and now let me insist as a *personal friend* of yours that he be in Washington at the time indicated. . . ."

Order for Testing Wrought Iron Cannon[1]

Executive Mansion, August 21 [20?], 1864

Mr. Ames having constructed certain wrought-iron cannon of 7-inch calibre, which he desires to have inspected and tested with a view to determine their fitness for the United States service, it is
Ordered

First, that a board of officers, to consist of Major General Gilmore as president of the board, a competent ordnance officer to be designated by the Secretary of War, and a competent officer to be designated by the Secretary of the Navy, shall be organized and meet at Bridgeport, Connecticut, on the first day of September next, with a view of inspecting and testing the aforesaid cannon and determining the capacity and fitness for the United States service, with such tests and trials as they shall deem proper, and make report to the President of their opinion in respect to said cannon, and their value and fitness for the service.

Second, that the ordnance bureaus of the War and Navy Departments shall provide suitable shot, shells, and ammunition for making the aforesaid tests, and provide all the necessaries for a careful and fair test of the aforesaid cannon.

ABRAHAM LINCOLN.

[1] Hertz, II, 938-39. The ultimate source for this order has not been discovered. The records of the War Department contain a summary of the "Order from Executive Mansion dated August 20th. 1864, directing that a Board of Officers, of which Major General [Quincy A.] Gillmore will be President," which substantially agrees with the order as printed by Hertz. An endorsement on this summary reads: "Original paper sent to Gen'l. Gillmore, No. 111 Remsen, St. Brooklyn N.Y. Aug. 22nd. 1864." (DNA WR RG 94, Adjutant General, Letters Received, P 916). See Lincoln's communication to Horatio Ames and memorandum, September 28, 1863, *supra*, and to Butler, September 13, 1864, *infra*.

To Norton P. Chipman[1]

United States Military Telegraph,

Col. Chipman   War Department,

Harper's Ferry, Va.   August 21. 3 P.M. 1864

What news now?   A. LINCOLN

[1] ALS, DNA WR RG 107, Presidential Telegrams, I, 138. Colonel Norton P. Chipman replied at 4:30 P.M.: "Without myself having been to the front, from the best sources of information the following is true: Two rebel divisions came down the Martinsburg road; attacked suddenly a part of Sixth Corps . . . and at first drove them. Our troops rallied and in turn drove the enemy. The force engaged increased on both sides and was apparently kept up pretty hotly for three hours, not extending, however, to general engagement. Artillery firing still continues and seems to have shifted to the left of Charlestown. Cannot hear the musketry at this writing. Will have messenger from the front soon." (OR, I, XLIII, I, 870).

To Edward Bates[1]

Attorney General please make out pardon in this case.

Aug. 22. 1864   A. LINCOLN

[1] AES, DNA RG 204, U.S. Pardon Attorney, A 508. Lincoln's endorsement is written on the petition of Rebecca Barker, August 14, 1864, asking pardon of her son Adolphus, sentenced to two years' imprisonment. An endorsement by Judge George P. Fisk, Criminal Court of the District of Columbia, August 16, 1864, reads in part: "I gave Adolphus Barker the shortest term of imprisonment the law prescribed because I had doubts of his sanity. . . ."

Endorsement Concerning James H. Jackson[1]

On the same West Point case which I handed the Secretary yesterday   A. LINCOLN

Aug. 22. 1864

[1] AES, DNA WR RG 94, U.S. Military Academy, 1864, No. 307. Lincoln's endorsement is on a telegram of Thurlow Weed to Edwin H. Webster, August 12, 1864, "Attend to the case of young Jackson for West Point   see Gov Seward and the president immedy." Seward endorsed, "Can this be done?" See Lincoln's memorandum, July 29, *supra*.

To Montgomery C. Meigs[1]

August 22, 1864

Let Capt. Anderson named within be reinstated if that be legally possible & if not possible, let him be newly appointed an A.Q.M. & report to Gen. Ewing.   A. LINCOLN

Aug. 22, 1864.

[1] Copy, ISLA. Lincoln's endorsement is written on the back of a letter from Brigadier General Hugh Ewing, Headquarters Second Division, Department of Kentucky, Mumfordsville (Munfordville), Kentucky, June 9, 1864, to Quartermaster General Montgomery C. Meigs:

"I am surprised to find that Capt. Anderson, Qr. Mr. on my staff has been mustered out of service. Since his connection with me he has performed his duty ably, & promptly & I trust he may be reinstated, as I am satisfied he has been misrepresented to the Dept. Could I ask that immediate attention, if this request is favorably considered, be taken in his case, as I cannot dispense with his services."

Captain George W. Anderson, Jr., assistant quartermaster, was ordered to be discharged on May 30, 1864 (AGO *Special Orders No. 191*). See Lincoln to Holt, August 25, *infra*.

Speech to One Hundred Sixty-sixth Ohio Regiment[1]

August 22, 1864

I suppose you are going home to see your families and friends. For the service you have done in this great struggle in which we are engaged I present you sincere thanks for myself and the country. I almost always feel inclined, when I happen to say anything to soldiers, to impress upon them in a few brief remarks the importance of success in this contest. It is not merely for to-day, but for all time to come that we should perpetuate for our children's children this great and free government, which we have enjoyed all our lives. I beg you to remember this, not merely for my sake, but for yours. I happen temporarily to occupy this big White House. I am a living witness that any one of your children may look to come here as my father's child has. It is in order that each of you may have through this free government which we have enjoyed, an open field and a fair chance for your industry, enterprise and intelligence; that you may all have equal privileges in the race of life, with all its desirable human aspirations. It is for this the struggle should be maintained, that we may not lose our birthright—not only for one, but for two or three years. The nation is worth fighting for, to secure such an inestimable jewel.

[1] New York *Herald* and *Tribune*, August 23, 1864. This speech is misdated September, 1864, in Hertz (II, 941). Substantially the same text appeared in the Baltimore *Sun* and other papers.

To Edwin M. Stanton[1]

Hon. Sec. of War
My dear Sir

Executive Mansion,
Washington, Aug. 22, 1864.

I very much wish to oblige Henry Ward Beecher, by releasing Howard; but I wish you to be satisfied when it is done. What say you?[2] Yours truly
A. LINCOLN

Let Howard, imprisoned in regard to the bogus proclamation, be discharged.
A. LINCOLN

August 23. 1864

[1] ALS and AES, IHi. Concerning the imprisonment of Joseph Howard, Jr., see Lincoln to Dix, May 18, *supra*. On August 2, 1864, Reverend Henry Ward Beecher wrote John D. Defrees:

". . . It would have brought tears into the good Presidents eyes to see the wife & two little girls when I read them yr letter.

"I feel earnestly desirous that this lesson should turn to young Howards moral benefit. . . . He was the tool of the men who turned states evidence and escaped; & . . . had only the hope of making some *money* . . . & had not foresight or consideration enough to perceive the relations of his act to the Public Welfare. You must excuse my earnestness. He has been brought up in my parish & under my eye and is the only spotted child of a large family." (DLC-RTL).

Defrees forwarded Beecher's letter to John Hay on August 3: "I don't like to trouble the President. If you can ever find him when he don't seem much engaged, please request him to read the inclosed letter.

"The public good does not require the further punishment of Howard . . . and his release will gratify many true friends.

"The President has no truer or better friend than Beecher. . . ." (*Ibid.*).

[2] Stanton endorsed Lincoln's letter as follows: "I have no objection if you think it right—and this a proper time. E M S."

A further endorsement by James A. Hardie reads: "General Dix, telegraphed Aug. 24. 1864 to release Howard, as herein ordered."

To Edwin M. Stanton[1]

Hon. Sec of War please see & hear the bearer Lt. Col. McElroy whose letter from Gen. Grant I sent over to-day.   A. LINCOLN

Aug. 22. 1864

[1] ALS, DLC. Lieutenant Colonel James N. McElroy, Sixtieth Ohio Infantry, resigned on August 9, 1864, and was appointed major and judge advocate on September 26, 1864. General Grant's letter has not been located.

To Edwin M. Stanton[1]

Hon. Sec of War, please see & hear my particular friend Capt Wickizer   A LINCOLN

Aug. 22 1864

[1] Copy, DLC-HW. The copy was enclosed in John H. Wickizer's letter to Herndon, November 25, 1866. See Lincoln to Stanton, October 21, 1862, *supra*. On October 7, 1864, Captain John H. Wickizer was relieved from duty in the Middle Military Division and ordered to report to the chief quartermaster at Louisville, Kentucky (AGO *Special Orders No. 337*).

To Gideon Welles[1]

Hon. Sec. of Navy   Executive Mansion,
My dear Sir: Washington, Aug. 22, 1864.

If there is a vacancy in the Naval School, give it to John Henry Roaman. Yours truly   A. LINCOLN

[1] ALS, ICHi. No record of the appointment has been found.

Memorandum Concerning His Probable
Failure of Re-election[1]

Executive Mansion
Washington, Aug. 23, 1864.

This morning, as for some days past, it seems exceedingly probable that this Administration will not be re-elected. Then it will be my duty to so co-operate with the President elect, as to save the Union between the election and the inauguration; as he will have secured his election on such ground that he can not possibly save it afterwards.   A. LINCOLN

[1] ADS, DLC; DS-F, Stan. V. Henkels Catalog 114, No. 41, January 4, 1924. The original autograph is endorsed on the verso with autograph signatures of cabinet members and Lincoln's autograph date. A signed copy formerly in the papers of Gideon Welles is in the handwriting of Lincoln's secretary to sign land patents, Edward D. Neill, appointed on August 23, 1864, after having actually served for some time in that capacity while second class clerk in the Department of the Interior. A third copy in John Hay's handwriting, not signed by Lincoln, but endorsed on the verso with autograph signatures of the members of the cabinet, is preserved in the Lincoln Papers (DLC).

John Hay's *Diary* records under date of November 11, 1864, the cabinet meeting of that date at which the memorandum was opened, following which, presumably, the later copies were transcribed:

"At the meeting of the Cabinet today, the President took out a paper from his desk and said, 'Gentlemen, do you remember that last summer when I asked you all to sign your names to the back of a paper of which I did not show you the inside? This is it. Now, Mr Hay, see if you can get this open without tearing it?' He had pasted it up in so singular style that it required some cutting to get it open. He then read as follows: [memorandum]

"The President said, 'You will remember that this was written at a time (6 days before the Chicago nominating Convention) when as yet we had no adversary, and seemed to have no friends. I then solemnly resolved on the course of action indicated above. I resolved, in case of the election of General McClellan, being certain that he would be the candidate, that I would see him and talk matters over with him. I would say, "General, the election has demonstrated that you are stronger, have more influence with the American people than I. Now let us together, you with your influence and I with all the executive power of the Government, try to save the country. You raise as many troops as you possibly can for this final trial, and I will devote all my energies to assisting and finishing the war." '

"Seward said, 'And the General would answer you "Yes, Yes;" and the next day when you saw him again and pressed these views upon him, he would say, "Yes, Yes;" & so on forever, and would have done nothing at all.'

" 'At least,' added Lincoln, 'I should have done my duty and have stood clear before my own conscience.' . . . ."

The impulse which prompted Lincoln to his unusual procedure in preparing the memorandum derived from the unanimous pessimism of his advisers. Thurlow Weed wrote to Seward on August 22:

"When, ten or eleven days since, I told Mr Lincoln that his re-election was an impossibility, I also told him that the information would soon come to him through other channels. It has doubtless, ere this, reached him. At any rate, nobody here doubts it; nor do I see any body from other States who authorises the slightest hope of success.

"Mr. Raymond, who has, just left me, says that unless some prompt and bold step be now taken, all is lost.

"The People are wild for Peace. They are told that the President will only listen to terms of Peace on condition Slavery be 'abandoned.'

"Mr. Swett is well informed in relation to the public sentiment. He has seen and heard much. Mr Raymond thinks commissioners should be immediately sent, to Richmond, offering to treat for Peace on the basis of Union. That *something* should be done and promptly done, to give the Administration a chance for its life, is certain." (DLC-RTL).

See also Lincoln to Raymond, August 24, *infra*.

Order for Sale of Land
in Winnebago Indian Reservation[1]

August 23, 1864

BY THE PRESIDENT OF THE UNITED STATES.

For the sale of Valuable lands in the late Winnebago Indian Reservation, in Minnesota.

In pursuance of law, I, ABRAHAM LINCOLN, President of the United States of America, do hereby declare and make known that public sales will be held in the undermentioned Land Office, in the State of Minnesota, at the period herinafter designated, to wit:

At the Land Office at ST. PETER, commencing on Monday the Fifth day of December next, for the disposal of the Public lands comprised in the late reserve for the Winnebago Indians, above mentioned, and situated within the following parts of townships, which will be sold at the appraised value of the land and the improvements thereon, viz:

North of the base line, and West of the fifth principal Meridian.

In Township one hundred and six,

Range twenty four, – – – – – – – – – – 15,384.96. acres.

In Township one hundred and seven,

Range twenty four. – – – – – – – – – – 5,405.44. "

In Township one hundred and six,

Range twenty five. – – – – – – – – – – 15,254.34. "

In Township one hundred and seven,

Range twenty five. – – – – – – – – – – 17,649.71. "

In Township one hundred and eight,

Range twenty five. – – – – – – – – – – 277.81. "

A Schedule particularly describing the individual tracts with the appraised value per acre respectively, will be open for inspection at the District Land Offices in Minnesota.

The offering of the above lands will be commenced on the day appointed, and will proceed in the order designated in the above mentioned Schedule, and consecutively by townships as herein advertised, until the whole shall have been offered and the sale thus closed; but the Sale shall not be kept open longer than two weeks, and no private entry of any of the lands will be admitted until after the expiration of the two weeks.

>Given under my hand, at the City of Washington this twenty third day of August, Anno Domini, One thousand, eight hundred and sixty four.   ABRAHAM LINCOLN

By the President:
Jos. J WILSON
Acting Commissioner of the General Land Office.

[1] DS-P, ISLA.

To Mrs. Mary M. Baldwin[1]

	War Department
Mrs. Mary McCook Baldwin	Washington City,
Nashville, Tenn.	August 24 1864

This is an order to the officer having in charge to execute the death sentence upon John S. Young, to suspend the same until further order.   A. LINCOLN

[1] ALS, DNA WR RG 107, Presidential Telegrams, I, 141. See Lincoln to Johnson, August 18, *supra*. Mary McCook Baldwin, daughter of Major and Paymaster Daniel McCook and sister of Colonel Robert L. McCook (Ninth Ohio), Colonel Daniel McCook (Fifty-second Ohio), and Private Charles M. McCook (Second Ohio), all of whom had been killed during the war, telegraphed Lincoln from Nashville on August 22, 1864: "John S Young the son of a former secretary of state [is] under sentence of death . . . grant me a pardon for the sake of my three brothers and Father that have fallen in the glorious cause believing it will be more beneficial to the cause than his death   I hope you will pardon him   if not send reprieve   answer" (DLC-RTL).

Concerning John S. Young, son of Dr. John S. Young, secretary of state of Tennessee, 1839-1847, see further Lincoln's communication to John McClelland, December 24, *infra*.

To Joseph Holt[1]

August 24, 1864
Submitted to Judge Advocate General for report.   A. LINCOLN
Aug. 24, 1864

Disability removed & forfeiture of pay and allowances rescinded
Jan. 14, 1865   A. LINCOLN

[1] AES, DNA WR RG 153, Judge Advocate General, NN 1863. Lincoln's endorsements are written on the court-martial record of Captain William Badger,

Fourth New Hampshire Volunteers, cashiered for misbehavior before the enemy. Holt cited favorable circumstances on Badger's behalf and that the governor of New Hampshire would recommission him if he were allowed to enlist.

To Joseph J. Lewis[1]

Commissioner of Internal Revenue Please see and hear Mr. Janney of Ohio   A LINCOLN
August 24, 1864.

[1] AES, owned by C. A. Jones, Columbus, Ohio. Lincoln's endorsement is written on an envelope addressed to Lincoln "To introduce Mr. Janney." Letters introducing John J. Janney, chief secretary of the Union League in Ohio, were written by William Dennison and Samuel Galloway on August 20, 1864 (DLC-RTL). The letters indicate that Janney sought to have his son-in-law (not named) restored to an office from which he had been dismissed. A letter from Janney to Dennison, October 26, 1864, gives the son-in-law as Captain William L. Janes, dismissed from the army, but there seems to be no connection with Lincoln's endorsement to Lewis.

To Henry J. Raymond[1]

                                      Executive Mansion,
Sir: Washington, August 24. 1864.

You will proceed forthwith and obtain, if possible, a conference for peace with Hon. Jefferson Davis, or any person by him authorized for that purpose.

You will address him in entirely respectful terms, at all events, and in any that may be indispensable to secure the conference.

At said conference you will propose, on behalf this government, that upon the restoration of the Union and the national authority, the war shall cease at once, all remaining questions to be left for adjustment by peaceful modes. If this be accepted hostilities to cease at once.

If it be not accepted, you will then request to be informed what terms, if any embracing the restoration of the Union, would be accepted. If any such be presented you in answer, you will forthwith report the same to this government, and await further instructions.

If the presentation of any terms embracing the restoration of the Union be declined, you will then request to be informed what terms of peace would, be accepted; and on receiving any answer, report the same to this government, and await further instructions.

[1] ADf, DLC-RTL. Lincoln endorsed the envelope in which the draft was filed, "H. J. Raymond — about peace." On August 22 Raymond wrote Lincoln:

"I feel compelled to drop you a line concerning the political condition of the country as it strikes me. I am in active correspondence with your staunchest friends in every state and from them all I hear but one report. The tide is setting strongly against us. Hon. E. B. Washburne writes that 'were an election to be held now in Illinois we should be beaten.' Mr. Cameron writes that Pennsylvania is against us. Gov. Morton writes that nothing but the most strenuous efforts can carry Indiana. This state, according to the best information I can get, would go 50,000 against us to-morrow. And so of the rest. Nothing but the most resolute and decided action on the part of the government and its friends, can save the country from falling into hostile hands.

"Two special causes are assigned to this great reaction in public sentiment,— the want of military successes, and the impression in some minds, the fear and suspicion in others, that we are not to have peace *in any event* under this administration until Slavery is abandoned. In some way or other the suspicion is widely diffused that we *can* have peace with Union if we would. It is idle to reason with this belief—still more idle to denounce it. It can only be expelled by some authoritative act, at once bold enough to fix attention and distinct enough to defy incredulity & challenge respect.

"Why would it not be wise, under these circumstances, to appoint a Commissioner, in due form, *to make distinct proffers of peace to Davis,* as *the head of the rebel armies, on the sole condition of acknowledging the supremacy of the constitution,*—all other questions to be settled in a convention of the people of all the States? The making of such an offer would require no armistice, no suspension of active war, no abandonment of positions, no sacrifice of consistency.

"If the proffer were *accepted* (which I presume it would not be,) the country would never consent to place the practical execution of its details in any but loyal hands, and in those we should be safe.

"If it should be *rejected,* (as it would be,) it would plant seeds of disaffection in the south, dispel all the delusions about peace that prevail in the North, silence the clamors & damaging falsehoods of the opposition, take the wind completely out of the sails of the Chicago craft, reconcile public sentiment to the War, the draft, & the tax as inevitable *necessities,* and unite the North as nothing since firing on Fort Sumter has hitherto done.

"I cannot conceive of any answer which Davis could give to such a proposition which would not strengthen you & the Union cause *everywhere.* Even your radical friends could not fail to applaud it when they should see the practical strength it would bring to the common cause.

"I beg you to excuse the earnestness with which I have pressed this matter upon your attention. It seems to me calculated to do good—& incapable of doing harm. It will turn the tide of public sentiment & avert pending evils of the gravest character. It will rouse & concentrate the loyalty of the country &, unless I am greatly mistaken, give us an early & a fruitful victory.

"Permit me to add that if done at all I think this should be done at once,— as your own spontaneous act. In advance of the Chicago Convention it might render the action of that body, of very little consequence.

"I have canvassed this subject very fully with Mr. Swett of Illinois who first suggested it to me & who will seek an opportunity to converse with you upon it. . . ." (DLC-RTL).

John G. Nicolay recorded Raymond's interview with Lincoln on August 25: "The President and the stronger half of the Cabinet, Seward, Stanton, and Fessenden, held a consultation with him [Raymond] and showed him that they had thoroughly considered and discussed the proposition of his letter of the 22d; and on giving him their reasons he very readily concurred with them in the opinion that to follow his plan of sending a commission to Richmond would be worse than losing the Presidential contest—it would be ignominiously surrendering it in advance. Nevertheless the visit of himself and committee here did great good. They found the President and Cabinet much better informed than themselves, and went home encouraged and cheered." (Nicolay and Hay, *Abraham Lincoln: A History,* IX, 221).

To Joseph Holt[1]

Will the Judge Advocate General please procure the facts of this case & report to me?   A. LINCOLN

August 25, 1864.

[1] Copy, ISLA. Lincoln's endorsement is written on the letter of Brigadier General Hugh Ewing, June 9, 1864, immediately following his endorsement to Stanton, August 22, *supra*. Presumably Lincoln ordered Captain George W. Anderson to be restored to his rank, for he was not mustered out of service until October 31, 1865.

Memorandum Concerning Thomas J. Turner and Rufus K. Williams[1]

Executive Mansion,
Washington, Aug. 25, 1864.

I wish to remember Hon. Thomas J. Turner[2] & Judge Williams of Ky. as Cotton agents.

[1] AD, DLC-RTL. See Lincoln's telegrams to Sherman, August 15, *supra*, and the order of August 31, *infra*.

[2] Lincoln probably inadvertently wrote "Thomas J. Turner" when he meant "W. A. Turner."

To Edwin M. Stanton[1]

Respectfully submitted to the Secretary of War, asking particular attention   A. LINCOLN

Aug. 25, 1864

[1] AES, DNA WR RG 107, Secretary of War, Letters Received, P 1250. Lincoln's endorsement appears on a resolution of the Arkansas legislature urging aid to the state in driving rebels from its borders. The resolution was enclosed in a letter from Governor Isaac Murphy, June 29, with a second letter introducing William D. Snow.

To Samuel Cony[1]

United States Military Telegraph,
His Excellency Gov. Cony   War Department.
Augusta, Maine   August 26. 1864

Your despatch received, and especially referred to Secretary of the Navy.   A LINCOLN

[1] ALS, DNA WR RG 107, Presidential Telegrams, I, 143. Governor Samuel Cony telegraphed Lincoln on August 25, 1864:

"Under your call for 500,000 men, to be enforced by an inexorable conscription, citizens of Maine are coming forward very freely to enlist in the Navy, but requisite facilities are not granted by the Navy Department to examine and muster those presenting. I am told that they decline enlisting as landsmen.

"Maine will give you the best sailors in the service. . . . It is intolerable that we are to be cut off from putting in our men who are anxious to enlist, either for want of proper facilities or by vexatious rulings of subordinates.

"I am likewise informed that the receiving ship Sabine, now at Portland, is about to leave, which will put an end to these enlistments altogether.

"I ask of you to order the Secretary of the Navy to return her there, and to have examining and mustering officers placed at Bangor, with force sufficient . . . to attend to all who call.

"If you will not accept our men for the Navy, and enforce the conscription for the Army, you may look for political results agreeable neither to you nor myself." (OR, III, IV, 639).

To Andrew Johnson[1]

Gov. Johnson   Executive Mansion,
Nashville, Tenn.   Washington, August 26, 1864.

Thanks to Gen. Gillam for making the news, and also to you for sending it. Does Joe Heiskell's "walking to meet us" mean any more than that "Joe" was scared & wanted to save his skin?

A. LINCOLN

[1] ALS, DNA WR RG 107, Presidential Telegrams, I, 142. This telegram is incorrectly dated August 2, 1864, by Nicolay and Hay (X, 179). Governor Johnson telegraphed on August 25:

"The following is a dispatch recd from Genl Gillam who is now operating in East Tennessee—

" 'Lick Creek Tenn—

" 'A detachment from my command under Lt Col [William H.] Ingerton 13th Tenn Cavalry attacked Rodgersville at daylight this morning killed twenty three captured twenty five (25) Among them Col Walker [error for Albert G. Watkins] and several non commissioned officers. Joe Hieskel [Joseph B. Heiskell of Rogersville, Tennessee] walked to meet us   ALVAN C GILLEM'

"Joe Hieskell is a member of the Confederate Congress [John H.] Morgan has been in upper East Tennessee no doubt intending to form a junction with [Joseph] Wheeler. . . ." (DLC-RTL).

No reply to Lincoln's telegram has been found.

Order for Harvey M. Colby[1]

Executive Mansion,
Washington, August 26, 1864.

Upon condition that Harvey M. Colby enters the Military services for a term of three years and faithfully serves it out or until otherwise honorably discharged, he is fully pardoned for any desertion heretofore committed.   A. LINCOLN

[1] *The Collector*, October, 1943, No. 559. AGO *Special Orders No. 283*, August 27, 1864, announced the pardon of Private Harvey M. Colby "formerly of the 2d New Hampshire Volunteers now at Manchester, New Hampshire" according to Lincoln's terms as given above.

Endorsement Concerning Robert M. Taylor[1]

Robert M. Taylor of the 12th U.S. Infantry, is hereby discharged
from the service.   A. LINCOLN
   Aug. 27, 1864

[1] AES, owned by Charles T. Butler, Ojai, California. Lincoln's endorsement
has been clipped from a letter. The verso shows a fragment of the letter with
Simon Cameron's signature.

To Edwin M. Stanton[1]

Hon. Sec. of War   Executive Mansion,
My dear Sir: Washington, Aug. 27, 1864.
   If Gen. Sigel has asked for an Inquiry, let him have it, if there is
not some insurmountable, or at least, very serious obstacle. He is
fairly entitled to this consideration. Yours truly   A. LINCOLN

[1] ALS, NIC. On July 7, 1864, General Grant directed General Halleck: "All
of General Sigel's operations from the beginning of the war have been so unsuccessful that I think it advisable to relieve him from all duty, at least until present
troubles are over. I do not feel certain at any time that he will not after abandoning stores, artillery, and trains, make a successful retreat to some place."
(OR, I, XL, III, 59).
   AGO *Special Orders No. 230,* July 7, 1864, relieved Sigel from command, and
Special Orders No. 258, August 3, 1864, granted him leave of absence. No action
of Stanton on the request for a court of inquiry has been found.

To John P. Usher[1]

I wish this paper called to my attention, when, if ever, the vacancy
mentioned occurs.   A. LINCOLN
   Aug. 27. 1864

[1] AES, DNA NR RG 48, Department of Interior, Superintendent of Indian
Affairs, Arizona, Box 85. Lincoln's endorsement is written on a letter from Francis W. Kellogg, representative from Michigan, August 24, 1864, recommending
J. H. Maze of Michigan for superintendent of Indian affairs in Arizona. No
record of the appointment has been found.

To Ulysses S. Grant[1]

                                              War Department
                              Washington City, Aug 28 1864
Lt Gen Grant
   There appears to be doubt whether the report of Fort Morgan
being in our possession is in the Richmond papers. Did you see the
Richmond paper containing the statement?   A LINCOLN

[1] LS, DNA WR RG 107, Presidential Telegrams, I, 145. The telegram is in Stanton's autograph and signed by Lincoln. Grant replied on August 29: "It was the Richmond papers of the 26th which contained the news of Fort Morgan being in our possession. Seeing a dispatch which said the news could not be found in the papers of the 27th, as had been reported to me, I asked Gen. Ord who reported to me the information which I telegraphed to Washington if he had read the Article alluded to. He replied that he read the Article himself but it was in the paper of the 26th instead of 27th as I reported. There is no question about the fall of Fort Morgan being reported in the Richmond papers nor do I suppose there to be any doubt of the facts reported." (DLC-Grant Papers).

Later the same day Grant telegraphed again:

"Since my dispatch of this morning I have recd the Richmond Sentinel of the 27th. It contains the following dispatch

" 'From Mobile.

" 'The report of the surrender of Fort Morgan was most unexpected & we await some explanation of so unfortunate an occurence.'

"The Press of Mobile is hopeful and confident of their ability to hold the city. . . ." (DLC-RTL).

To Lewis Wallace[1]

Office U.S. Military Telegraph,
Major General Wallace   War Department,
Baltimore, Md   Washington, D.C., August 28 1864.

The, punishment, of the four men under sentence of death to be executed to-morrow at Baltimore, is commuted in each case to confinement in the Penitentiary at hard labor during the war. You will act accordingly.   A. LINCOLN

[1] ALS, DNA WR RG 107, Presidential Telegrams, I, 144. Nicolay sent telegrams on the same date to Charles J. M. Gwinn, counsel for the accused men, and to Reverdy Johnson, who had asked reprieve and commutation of sentence: "Telegram has been sent to Gen. Wallace." (*Ibid.*, 147, 146). The four men, convicted as spies, were William H. Rodgers, John R. H. Emberet, Branton Lyons (or Braxton Lyon), and Samuel B. Hearn, whose sentences Lincoln commuted on August 27, 1864 (DNA WR RG 153, Judge Advocate General, LL 2297).

To Gideon Welles[1]

Executive Mansion
My dear Sir   Aug. 28, 1864

Please find some way to relieve me from the embarrassment of this case. Let me have a return of the papers, with your answer by 9 o'clock, A.M. to-morrow, at which time I am engaged to see the gentlemen who now present the case. Yours truly

A. LINCOLN.

[1] Stan. V. Henkels Catalog 1342, January 4, 1924, No. 33. Under date of August 29, 1864, Welles' *Diary* records:

"The President sent me a bundle of papers, embracing a petition drawn up with great ability and skill, signed by most of the Massachusetts delegation in Congress and a large number of the prominent merchants in Boston, asking special favors in behalf of Smith Brothers, who are under arrest for fraudulent deliveries under contract, requesting that the trial may be held in Boston and that it may be . . . transferred to the civil tribunals. . . . The whole scheme had been well studied and laboriously got up, and a special delegation have come on to press the subject upon the President.

"He urged me to relieve him from the annoying and tremendous pressure that had been brought to bear upon him in this case. . . . I went briefly over the main points; told him the whole subject ought to be referred to and left with the Navy Department in this stage of the proceedings, that I desired to relieve himself of all care and trouble by throwing the whole responsibility and odium, if there was odium, on the Navy Department, that we could not pursue a different course in this case from the others. . . . He then asked why not let the trial take place in Boston and thus concede something. I told him this might be done, but it seemed to me inexpedient; but he was so solicitous—political and party considerations had been artfully introduced, against which little could be urged, when Solicitor [William] Whiting and others averred that three Congressional districts would be sacrificed if I persisted—that the point was waived and the President greatly relieved. The President evinced shrewdness in influencing, or directing me, but was sadly imposed upon by the cunning Bostonians. . . ."

See Lincoln to Welles, January 26, 1865, and the order annulling sentence in the case of Benjamin G. and Franklin W. Smith, March 18, 1865, *infra*.

To James B. Fry[1]

I will thank the Provost Marshal-General, to give a full and fair hearing to Hon. P. C. Brinck, the bearer.   A. LINCOLN

Aug. 29. 1864

[1] AES, owned by R. E. Burdick, New York City. Lincoln's endorsement is written on a letter from Ezekiel C. Moore, president, and Edward B. Knight, clerk, Mullica Hill, New Jersey, August 25, 1864: "The quota of Harrison Township is largely in excess of sixteen per cent which is the per centage under which the quotas have been calculated. There is not a more loyal county in the Union than Gloucester County and its people are willing to bear all the burdens & perform all the duties which belong to us in prosecuting a most righteous war. But our people think the law in its operation bears heavily on our township & County & district & we respectfully request that you will grant us any relief that may be in your power."

To Ulysses S. Grant[1]

Executive Mansion Washington,

Lieut. General Grant   August 29. 1864

Col. T. Worthington, of Ohio is here wishing to visit, you. I will send him if you say so; otherwise not.   A. LINCOLN

[1] ALS, DNA WR RG 107, Presidential Telegrams, I, 148. Grant replied the same day: "Your dispatch of 1.40 p.m. in relation to permitting Col. Worthing-

ton to come here is received. I should be very sorry to see the Col. He has nearly worried the life out of me at times when I could not prevent an interview." (DLC-Grant Papers; received copy, DLC-RTL).

A letter from William Dennison to Lincoln, August 24, 1864, expressed the hope that Colonel Thomas Worthington's "differences with Genl Sherman and his dismissal from the service, may not be allowed to prejudice his present application to your Excellency." (DLC-RTL). Thomas Corwin endorsed the letter on August 29, concurring in the wish that Worthington "may be placed in some military position where the country may enjoy the benefit of his services."

To Benjamin H. Brewster[1]

Hon. B. H. Brewster   Executive Mansion
Astor-House New-York   Washington, D.C. Aug. 30. 1864.

Your letter of yesterday received. Thank you for it. Please have no fears.   A. LINCOLN

[1] ALS, DNA WR RG 107, Presidential Telegrams, I, 149. Benjamin H. Brewster wrote Lincoln on August 29, 1864: "Absence from home has prevented me from understanding fully the condition of public feeling in Pennsylvania, but here I have had both occasion & opportunity of learning the external indications of popular opinion. For some time I find—the effort has been to impress the public . . . with the belief that you would be forced to withdraw, and now as that collection of Public vagrants are assembling at Chicago an effort is making here to impress the unsteady, the unfaithful & the timid of your party to urge that step on you. For God sake—disregard these clamors & outcrys! . . ." (DLC-RTL).

Order for Discharge of Louis Kinney[1]

August 30, 1864

Let this man take the oath of December 8, and be discharged. He is said to be barely past eighteen years of age, and is at Point Lookout, and sick.   A. LINCOLN.

August 30, 1864.

[1] Leslie J. Perry, "Appeals to Lincoln's Clemency," *The Century Magazine*, December, 1895, p. 255. According to Perry, the prisoner was Louis Kinney of Kentucky.

To Edwin M. Stanton[1]

On the assurance of Senator Harlan that he knows the writer of the within to be a reliable man, the discharge requested is ordered.

August 30. 1864.   A. LINCOLN

[1] AES, owned by Otto Eisenschiml, Chicago, Illinois. Lincoln's endorsement is written on a letter of William Steele to Senator James Harlan, West Point,

Treasury Department in accordance with said amended Regulation.
ABRAHAM LINCOLN

[1] ADS, MoSHi. A single page of manuscript, this fragment seems to be the last page of a document (possibly a directive issued to Treasury agents) contemporaneous with Lincoln's order, *supra*.

Speech to One Hundred Forty-eighth Ohio Regiment[1]

August 31, 1864

SOLDIERS OF THE 148TH OHIO:—I am most happy to meet you on this occasion. I understand that it has been your honorable privilege to stand, for a brief period, in the defense of your country, and that now you are on your way to your homes. I congratulate you, and those who are waiting to bid you welcome home from the war; and permit me, in the name of the people, to thank you for the part you have taken in this struggle for the life of the nation. You are soldiers of the Republic, everywhere honored and respected. Whenever I appear before a body of soldiers, I feel tempted to talk to them of the nature of the struggle in which we are engaged. I look upon it as an attempt on the one hand to overwhelm and destroy the national existence, while, on our part, we are striving to maintain the government and institutions of our fathers, to enjoy them ourselves, and transmit them to our children and our children's children forever.

To do this the constitutional administration of our government must be sustained, and I beg of you not to allow your minds or your hearts to be diverted from the support of all necessary measures for that purpose, by any miserable picayune arguments addressed to your pockets, or inflammatory appeals made to your passions or your prejudices.

It is vain and foolish to arraign this man or that for the part he has taken, or has not taken, and to hold the government responsible for his acts. In no administration can there be perfect equality of action and uniform satisfaction rendered by all. But this government must be preserved in spite of the acts of any man or set of men. It is worthy your every effort. Nowhere in the world is presented a government of so much liberty and equality. To the humblest and poorest amongst us are held out the highest privileges and positions. The present moment finds me at the White House, yet there is as good a chance for your children as there was for my father's.

paper in the belief that our government would join him in taking the profit of fulfiling the contract.

This is my understanding of the case; and I can not conceive of a case of a man found in possession of a contract to furnish rebel supplies, who can not escape, if this be held a sufficient ground of escape. It is simply for the accused to escape by telling a very absurd and improbable story. Now, if Senator Morgan, and Mr. Weed, and Mr. Raymond, will not argue with me that I *ought* to discharge this man, but will, in writing on this sheet, simply request me to do it, I will do it solely in deference to their wishes.

A. LINCOLN

[1] ALS, ORB. See Lincoln's order for arrest of John S. Carlisle, June 15, and communications to Holt, August 13, *supra*, and December 28, *infra*. Weed and Raymond endorsed as follows:

"We respectfully request the President to pardon the within named Louis A Welton, now at Fort Delaware.　　　　　　　　　　　　　THURLOW WEED.

"I have read Mr. Welton's statement and if it is true, (and I know no reason for distrusting it,) his pardon would be an act of *justice*. I concur in Mr. Weed's request.　　　　　　　　　　　　　　　　　　　H. J. RAYMOND."

On September 13, 1864, Morgan wrote Lincoln:
"I have this day read your statement of the case of Louis A Welton imprisoned at Fort Deleware for the offence of making a contract to furnish the rebels with supplies.
"The statement is so different from the one made by the Prisoners friends, that I not only refuse to ask you to pardon Welton, but I wish to withdraw my request to you for any re-consideration of the sentence of imprisonment. . . ." (DLC-RTL).

Order Concerning Transportation of Cotton[1]

Executive Mansion,
Washington, August 31, 1864.

Any person or persons engaged in bringing out Cotton, in strict conformity with authority given by W. P. Fessenden, Secretary of the U.S. Treasury, must not be hindered by the War, Navy, or any other Department of the Government, or any person engaged under any of said Departments.　　　　　ABRAHAM LINCOLN

[1] ADfS, DLC-RTL. See Lincoln's telegram to Sherman, August 15, and memorandum concerning Turner and Williams, August 25, *supra*.

Portion of an Order
Concerning Cotton Shipments[1]

[c. August 31, 1864?]

Permits will be free from seizure detention or forfeiture, and be allowed free and unmolested passage as Permitted by agents of the

To Joseph K. Barnes[1]

Executive Mansion,
Washington, August 31. 1864.

Surgeon General please have an examination made of private Joseph Laland Co. H. 2nd. N.Y. Heavy Artillery, now at Mount Pleasant Hospital, with reference to a discharge   A. LINCOLN

[1] ALS, DLC-RTL. On September 1, 1864, Surgeon General Barnes returned Lincoln's note with the report:

"Respectfully returned with report that Pvt. Joseph Laland 2nd N.Y. Heavy Arty—is not entitled to Discharge on Certificate of Disability."

This is endorsed by Johnson Van Dyck Middleton, Assistant Surgeon, U.S.A., Acting Medical Director, September 1, 1864:

"Respectfully returned to the Surg. General. This man has been carefully examined by Asst. Surg. [Charles A.] McCall . . . who reports that he is suffering from Rheumatism . . . that there is no organic change but that the use of the limb is some what impaired. . . ." (DLC-RTL).

To Mary Todd Lincoln[1]

Office U.S. Military Telegraph,
War Department,
Mrs. A. Lincoln.
Manchester, Vermont.   Washington, D.C., August 31. 1864.

All reasonably well. Bob not here yet. How is dear Tad?

A. LINCOLN

[1] ALS, DNA WR RG 107, Presidential Telegrams, I, 150. No reply has been discovered.

To Edwin D. Morgan, Thurlow Weed, and Henry J. Raymond[1]

Executive Mansion,
Washington, August 31. 1864.

Mr. Louis A. Welton came from the rebel lines into ours with a written contract to furnish large supplies to the rebels, was arrested with the contract in his possession, and has been sentenced to imprisonment for it. He, and his friends complain of this, on no substantial evidence whatever, but simply because his word, only given after his arrest, that he only took the contract as a means of escaping from the rebel lines, was not accepted as a full defence. He perceives that if this had been true he would have destroyed the contract so soon as it had served his purpose in getting him across the lines; but not having done this, and being caught with the paper on him, he tells this other absurd story that he kept the

Iowa, August 9, 1864, requesting discharge of his son, who had served three years and re-enlisted as a veteran, but whose health did not permit his return to service. Although Steele does not name his son, John Steele, Company G, Fourth Iowa Cavalry, who enlisted October 1, 1861, and re-enlisted December 19, 1863, was probably the man. He was discharged for disability on September 9, 1864.

To Edwin M. Stanton[1]

Hon. Sec. of War.   Executive Mansion,
My dear Sir: Washington, August 30. 1864.
   Please let Forney's man off this morning. Yours truly
                                 A. LINCOLN

[1] ALS, NHi. Forney's man has not been identified.

To Edwin M. Stanton[1]

Hon. Sec. of War, please see and hear this lady with a letter from Senator Ten-Eyck.   A. LINCOLN
   Aug. 30. 1864

[1] ALS-F, ISLA. The facsimile clipped from an unidentified newspaper is accompanied by an article stating that the lady was Mrs. R. M. Thorne of Richmond, Virginia, who wished a pass to return to her home.

To Charles M. Alexander[1]

                                  August 31, 1864
If this mans Colonel will say in writing on this paper that he is willing to receive this man back to his regiment I will send him
   Aug. 31. 1864   A. LINCOLN

On the first day of October 1864 let this man be sent to his regiment & upon his then faithfully serving out his term, he is pardoned for the past.   A. LINCOLN
   Sep. 3. 1864.

[1] AES, RPB. Lincoln's endorsements are written on a petition for pardon from Private Larry O'Brine, Company E, Second D.C. Volunteers, August 29, 1864. He had been sentenced to three years' imprisonment for desertion. Colonel Charles M. Alexander endorsed on September 2: "This man has been a poor soldier and deserves punishment—if however he could be returned to the Regt after a few months of labor I may be able to make a better man of him." On October 5, 1864, Private Larry O'Brine was ordered to be released from confinement and returned to his regiment (AGO *Special Orders No. 333*).

but requisite facilities are not granted by the Navy Department to examine and muster those presenting. I am told that they decline enlisting as landsmen.

"Maine will give you the best sailors in the service. . . . It is intolerable that we are to be cut off from putting in our men who are anxious to enlist, either for want of proper facilities or by vexatious rulings of subordinates.

"I am likewise informed that the receiving ship Sabine, now at Portland, is about to leave, which will put an end to these enlistments altogether.

"I ask of you to order the Secretary of the Navy to return her there, and to have examining and mustering officers placed at Bangor, with force sufficient . . . to attend to all who call.

"If you will not accept our men for the Navy, and enforce the conscription for the Army, you may look for political results agreeable neither to you nor myself." (OR, III, IV, 639).

To Andrew Johnson[1]

Gov. Johnson   Executive Mansion,
Nashville, Tenn.   Washington, August 26, 1864.

Thanks to Gen. Gillam for making the news, and also to you for sending it. Does Joe Heiskell's "walking to meet us" mean any more than that "Joe" was scared & wanted to save his skin?

A. LINCOLN

[1] ALS, DNA WR RG 107, Presidential Telegrams, I, 142. This telegram is incorrectly dated August 2, 1864, by Nicolay and Hay (X, 179). Governor Johnson telegraphed on August 25:

"The following is a dispatch recd from Genl Gillam who is now operating in East Tennessee—

" 'Lick Creek Tenn—

" 'A detachment from my command under Lt Col [William H.] Ingerton 13th Tenn Cavalry attacked Rodgersville at daylight this morning killed twenty three captured twenty five (25) Among them Col Walker [error for Albert G. Watkins] and several non commissioned officers. Joe Hieskel [Joseph B. Heiskell of Rogersville, Tennessee] walked to meet us   ALVAN C GILLEM'

"Joe Hieskell is a member of the Confederate Congress [John H.] Morgan has been in upper East Tennessee no doubt intending to form a junction with [Joseph] Wheeler. . . ." (DLC-RTL).

No reply to Lincoln's telegram has been found.

Order for Harvey M. Colby[1]

Executive Mansion,
Washington, August 26, 1864.

Upon condition that Harvey M. Colby enters the Military services for a term of three years and faithfully serves it out or until otherwise honorably discharged, he is fully pardoned for any desertion heretofore committed.   A. LINCOLN

[1] *The Collector*, October, 1943, No. 559. AGO *Special Orders No. 283*, August 27, 1864, announced the pardon of Private Harvey M. Colby "formerly of the 2d New Hampshire Volunteers now at Manchester, New Hampshire" according to Lincoln's terms as given above.

To Joseph Holt[1]

Will the Judge Advocate General please procure the facts of this case & report to me?   A. LINCOLN
August 25, 1864.

[1] Copy, ISLA. Lincoln's endorsement is written on the letter of Brigadier General Hugh Ewing, June 9, 1864, immediately following his endorsement to Stanton, August 22, *supra*. Presumably Lincoln ordered Captain George W. Anderson to be restored to his rank, for he was not mustered out of service until October 31, 1865.

Memorandum Concerning Thomas J. Turner and Rufus K. Williams[1]

Executive Mansion,
Washington, Aug. 25, 1864.

I wish to remember Hon. Thomas J. Turner[2] & Judge Williams of Ky. as Cotton agents.

[1] AD, DLC-RTL. See Lincoln's telegrams to Sherman, August 15, *supra*, and the order of August 31, *infra*.
[2] Lincoln probably inadvertently wrote "Thomas J. Turner" when he meant "W. A. Turner."

To Edwin M. Stanton[1]

Respectfully submitted to the Secretary of War, asking particular attention   A. LINCOLN
Aug. 25, 1864

[1] AES, DNA WR RG 107, Secretary of War, Letters Received, P 1250. Lincoln's endorsement appears on a resolution of the Arkansas legislature urging aid to the state in driving rebels from its borders. The resolution was enclosed in a letter from Governor Isaac Murphy, June 29, with a second letter introducing William D. Snow.

To Samuel Cony[1]

United States Military Telegraph,
His Excellency Gov. Cony   War Department.
Augusta, Maine   August 26. 1864

Your despatch received, and especially referred to Secretary of the Navy.   A LINCOLN

[1] ALS, DNA WR RG 107, Presidential Telegrams, I, 143. Governor Samuel Cony telegraphed Lincoln on August 25, 1864:
"Under your call for 500,000 men, to be enforced by an inexorable conscription, citizens of Maine are coming forward very freely to enlist in the Navy,

Again I admonish you not to be turned from your stern purpose of defending your beloved country and its free institutions by any arguments urged by ambitious and designing men, but stand fast to the Union and the old flag. Soldiers, I bid you God-speed to your homes.

[1] Baltimore *Sun*, September 2, 1864. A less complete report appeared in the New York *Tribune* of September 2.

To Alfred B. Justice[1]

Executive Mansion,
My dear Sir,   Washington, September, 1864.
I have received at the hands of Judge Kelley a very handsome and ingenious pocket knife, for which I am indebted to the liberality of yourself and others.

I shall value it no less, as a fine specimen of American mechanism, than as a testimonial of the kind approval of the donors.

I am yours very truly   ABRAHAM LINCOLN
Mr. A. B. Justice,
Philadelphia, Pa.

[1] LS, owned by Mrs. Alfred R. Justice, Philadelphia, Pennsylvania. The body of the letter is in the handwriting of secretary Edward D. Neill. Apparently Neill forgot that he had written the letter, for on October 17 (*infra*) he wrote and Lincoln signed a second letter of thanks. A communication of June, 1864, from Alfred B. Justice, with four pages of other signatures of "visitors at the Great Central Fair" asked Lincoln's "acceptance of the Pocket Knife accompanying this note, as a specimen of the handicraft of American workmen, and a slight Testimonial of their regard for yourself. . . ." (DLC-RTL).

To Montgomery Blair[1]

"*Cypher*"   Office U.S. Military Telegraph,
Hon. M. Blair   War Department,
Portsmouth, N.H.   Washington, D.C., Sept. 1 1864.
Please return here at your earliest convenience.

A. LINCOLN

[1] ALS, DNA WR RG 107, Presidential Telegrams, I, 151. On September 1, 1864, Elihu B. Washburne wrote Lincoln: "Can you not get a despatch immediately from Blair as to *when* he will be here. It is very important that Gov. Randall should leave here to-morrow night but he dare not leave till he gets word that Blair will be here. . . . Please get word from him at the earliest moment. . . ." (DLC-RTL).

First Assistant Postmaster General Alexander W. Randall was needed for political campaigning in the West, but could not leave his post until Blair returned to take over. See Lincoln's telegram to Blair, September 3, *infra*.

To Samuel R. Curtis[1]

Executive Mansion, Washington,

Major General Curtis   September 1, 1864.

The bearer of this, Mr. George K. Otis, General Superintendent of the Overland Mail Line, has called on me seeking protection for the line against the indians. I can think of nothing better than to ask you to have a full conferrence with him on the subject, and to do the very best you can for this important interest, consistently with the other interests in your charge. Yours truly

A. LINCOLN.

[1] ALS, CSmH. On August 11, 1864, Governor John Evans of Colorado Territory had written Curtis: "The overland line is about withdrawing stock from the plains for want of protection. Unless troops can be stationed along the line to patrol it our supplies will also be cut off. . . . The alliance of all the tribes . . . is now undoubted. . . . Would it not be well to defend the Overland Stage route at all hazards? This will give us the best protection for travel. . . ."

George K. Otis endorsed Evans' letter: "I have just come up the line from the Missouri, and fully concur in the above. Have already stopped mail and passengers and ordered stock off the road." (OR, I, XLI, II, 661).

Order to Henry S. Huidekoper[1]

Executive Mansion

Washington D.C. Sept 1. 1864.

It is represented to me that there are at Rock Island, Ills. as rebel prisoners of war, many persons of Northern and foreign birth, who are unwilling to be exchanged and sent South, but who wish to take the oath of allegiance and enter the military service of the Union. Col. Huidekoper on behalf of the people of some parts of Pennsylvania wishes to pay the bounties the government would have to pay to proper persons of this class, have them enter the service of the United States, and be credited to the localities furnishing the bounty money. He will, therefore proceed to Rock Island, ascertain the names of such persons (not including any who have attractions Southward) and telegraph them to the Provost Marshal General here, whereupon directions will be given to discharge the persons named upon their taking the oath of allegiance; and then upon the official evidence being furnished that they shall have been duly received and mustered into the service of the United States, their number will be credited as may be directed by Col. Huidekoper.   ABRAHAM LINCOLN

[1] Copy, IHi; copy, DLC-RTL. The copy preserved in the Lincoln Papers bears an endorsement in pencil, not Lincoln's: "Col. H.S. Huidekoper Address is at Meadville Pa." The other copy (IHi) is "A true copy" certified by Captain

Theodore McMurtrie, Provost Marshal General's Office, September 22, 1864, which contains also a copy of Lincoln's endorsement to Edwin M. Stanton of September 20, *infra*. Lieutenant Colonel Henry S. Huidekoper, One Hundred Fiftieth Pennsylvania Volunteers, and Judge S. Newton Pettis had persuaded Lincoln of the advisability of enlisting Confederate prisoners. According to James B. Fry's account (see Nicolay and Hay, *Abraham Lincoln: A History*, V, 145 ff.), Stanton refused to execute Lincoln's order. When Lincoln wrote the endorsement of September 20 (*infra*), Stanton again refused. Whereupon Lincoln went to the War Department, explained his reasons for insisting that the order be executed, and made it peremptory. Lincoln's letter to Grant, September 22, *infra*, absolves Stanton of all blame in the episode and explains why the order was made.

Pass[1]

Allow this boy to pass to City-Point & return.   A. LINCOLN
Sep. 1, 1864

[1] Angle, p. 355. The boy has not been identified.

To Lewis Wallace[1]

Will Gen. Wallace please allow these two ladies to visit their brother, Walter Lenon in Prison at Fort-McHenry?
Sep. 1. 1864   A. LINCOLN

[1] AES, ORB. Walter Lenon has not been identified.

To Joseph Holt[1]

What should I do in this case? I see no report of J.A.G.
Sept. 2. 1864   A. LINCOLN

[1] AES, DNA WR RG 153, Judge Advocate General, NN 1998. Lincoln's endorsement is written on the record in the case of Richard B. Smith, baker in the Subsistence Department, sentenced on August 25, 1864, to nine months' imprisonment at hard labor for obstructing the operation of the department. Holt endorsed that the sentence had already been commuted to three months.

To Montgomery Blair[1]

Hon. M. Blair   Executive Mansion
Portsmouth, N.H.   Washington DC. Sep. 3. 1864
    Please come at once. Dont delay. Answer when you will be here.
                                          A. LINCOLN

[1] ALS, DNA WR RG 107, Presidential Telegrams, I, 152. See Lincoln to Blair, September 1, *supra*. Blair's wife, Mary E. Blair, telegraphed from Portsmouth, New Hampshire, on September 3: "Mr Blair left this morning and will be in Washn Monday." (DLC-RTL).

Order for Celebration of Victories
at Atlanta, Georgia, and Mobile, Alabama[1]

Executive Mansion, Washington City,

Ordered,   September 3d, 1864.

First.—That on Monday, the 5th. day of September, commencing at the hour of twelve o'clock noon, there shall be given a salute of one hundred guns at the Arsenal and Navy Yard at Washington, and on Tuesday September 6th., or on the day after the receipt of this order, at each Arsenal and Navy Yard in the United States, for the recent brilliant achievements of the fleet and land forces of the United States in the harbor of Mobile and in the reduction of Fort Powell, Fort Gaines, and Fort Morgan. The Secretary of War and Secretary of the Navy will issue the necessary directions in their respective Departments for the execution of this order.

Second.—That on Wednesday, the 7th. day of September, commencing at the hour of twelve o'clock noon, there shall be fired a salute of one hundred guns at the Arsenal at Washington, and at New York, Boston, Philadelphia, Baltimore, Pittsburg, Newport, Ky. and St. Louis, and at New Orleans, Mobile, Pensacola, Hilton Head & Newberne, the day after the receipt of this order, for the brilliant achievements of the army under command of Major General Sherman, in the State of Georgia, and the capture of Atlanta. The Secretary of War will issue directions for the execution of this order.   ABRAHAM LINCOLN

[1] DS, DNA WR NB RG 45, Executive Letters, No. 14.

Order of Thanks
to David G. Farragut and Others[1]

Executive Mansion,
September 3d. 1864.

The national thanks are tendered by the President to Admiral Farragut and Major General Canby for the skill and harmony with which the recent operations in Mobile Harbor, and against Fort Powell, Fort Gaines, and Fort Morgan, were planned and carried into execution. Also, to Admiral Farragut and Major General Granger, under whose immediate command they were conducted, and to the gallant commanders on sea and land, and to the sailors and soldiers engaged in the operations, for their energy and courage, which, under the blessing of Providence, have been crowned

[532]

with brilliant success, and have won for them the applause and thanks of the nation. ABRAHAM LINCOLN

[1] DS, DNA WR NB RG 45, Executive Letters, No. 13.

Order of Thanks
to William T. Sherman and Others[1]

Executive Mansion,
September 3d, 1864.

The national thanks are herewith tendered by the President to Major General William T. Sherman, and the gallant officers and soldiers of his command before Atlanta, for the distinguished ability, courage, and perseverance displayed in the campaign in Georgia, which, under Divine favor, has resulted in the capture of the City of Atlanta. The marches, battles, sieges, and other military operations that have signalized this campaign must render it famous in the annals of war, and have entitled those who have participated therein to the applause and thanks of the nation.

ABRAHAM LINCOLN

[1] DS, RPB.

Proclamation of Thanksgiving and Prayer[1]

Executive Mansion,
Washington City   September 3d. 1864

The signal success that Divine Providence has recently vouchsafed to the operations of the United States fleet and army in the harbor of Mobile and the reduction of Fort-Powell, Fort-Gaines, and Fort-Morgan, and the glorious achievements of the Army under Major General Sherman in the State of Georgia, resulting in the capture of the City of Atlanta, call for devout acknowledgment to the Supreme Being in whose hands are the destinies of nations. It is therefore requested that on next Sunday, in all places of public worship in the United-States, thanksgiving be offered to Him for His mercy in preserving our national existence against the insurgent rebels who so long have been waging a cruel war against the Government of the United-States, for its overthrow; and also that prayer be made for the Divine protection to our brave soldiers and their leaders in the field, who have so ofen and so gallantly perilled their lives in battling with the enemy; and for blessing and comfort from the Father of Mercies to the sick, wounded, and prisoners, and to the orphans and widows of those who have fallen in the service of their country, and that he will continue to uphold the Government of the United-States against all the efforts of public enemies and secret foes.   ABRAHAM LINCOLN

[1] DS, RPB.

To Edwin M. Stanton[1]

Sec. of War, please see this boy a moment, who says you know him.
Sep. 3. 1864   A. LINCOLN

[1] ALS-F, Los Angeles *Times*, February 5, 1916. On the back of the card bearing Lincoln's note, Stanton endorsed "To Capt. [James M.] Moore/Asst QM./To introduce Joseph Doyle/E M Stanton." The article accompanying the facsimile identifies Joseph Doyle as "an awkward farm boy" whose family "lived less than a mile" from Stanton's home in Ohio. Refused admittance to Stanton, he sought the president's assistance and received Lincoln's card of introduction.

To Gideon Welles[1]

Hon. Secretary of the Navy   Executive Mansion
My dear Sir: Washington, D.C Sep. 3. 1864

It is absolutely necessary that the Sec. of War shall be furnished with the number of Navy enlistments, at each locality, under the present law, by three o'clock, P.M. to-day. Please furnish them.
Yours truly   A. LINCOLN

[1] ALS, The Rosenbach Company, Philadelphia and New York. The new enrolling act approved on July 4, 1864, provided (Section 8): "That all persons in the naval service of the United States, who have entered said service during the present rebellion, who have not been credited to the quota of any town, district, ward, or State, by reason of their being in said service and not enrolled prior to February twenty-fourth, eighteen hundred and sixty-four, shall be enrolled and credited to the quotas of the town, ward, district, or State in which they respectively reside, upon satisfactory proof of their residence made to the Secretary of War."

To Stephen G. Burbridge[1]

Gen. Burbridge   Executive Mansion,
Lexington, Ky.   Washington, Sep. 4, 1864.

Judge Swayne of the U.S. Supreme Court appeals to me in favor of a man by the name of A. Harris, said to be in custody at Louisville on charge of belonging to the secret order so much spoken of. Harris avers that he does not belong to it; and the Judge declares he believes him. Please have the case examined.   A. LINCOLN

[1] ALS, DNA WR RG 107, Presidential Telegrams, I, 153. On August 19, 1864, Noah H. Swayne wrote to Edward Bates enclosing the following letters for Lincoln: "The enclosed letter is from a relative & friend of mine. . . . I have no

doubt . . . that the charge has originated in malice or misconception. He is a lawyer of ability—of industry—and of the highest character for integrity. . . . I beg to suggest that Genl [Hugh] Ewing or Genl Burbridge be directed to hold him in custody until the case is properly examined. . . ." (DLC-RTL).

Harris' letter to Swayne, dated August 9, 1864, is as follows: "I am confined in the Military Prison . . . under charges . . . of belonging to a secret military treasonable organization, and that meetings of that order were held at the office of the Louisville Water Works of which I am the President. Now sir, on the honor of a gentleman I solemnly deny the truth of each of these charges. . . ." (*Ibid.*)

Burbridge replied to Lincoln's telegram on September 8: "A. Harris, about whom you telegraphed on the 4th instant, was released from arrest some time ago." (*Ibid.*)

To Eliza P. Gurney[1]

Eliza P. Gurney.   Executive Mansion,
My esteemed friend.   Washington, September 4. 1864.

I have not forgotten—probably never shall forget—the very impressive occasion when yourself and friends visited me on a Sabbath forenoon two years ago. Nor has your kind letter, written nearly a year later, ever been forgotten. In all, it has been your purpose to strengthen my reliance on God. I am much indebted to the good christian people of the country for their constant prayers and consolations; and to no one of them, more than to yourself. The purposes of the Almighty are perfect, and must prevail, though we erring mortals may fail to accurately perceive them in advance. We hoped for a happy termination of this terrible war long before this; but God knows best, and has ruled otherwise. We shall yet acknowledge His wisdom and our own error therein. Meanwhile we must work earnestly in the best light He gives us, trusting that so working still conduces to the great ends He ordains. Surely He intends some great good to follow this mighty convulsion, which no mortal could make, and no mortal could stay.

Your people—the Friends—have had, and are having, a very great trial. On principle, and faith, opposed to both war and oppression, they can only practically oppose oppression by war. In this hard dilemma, some have chosen one horn and some the other. For those appealing to me on conscientious grounds, I have done, and shall do, the best I could and can, in my own conscience, under my oath to the law. That you believe this I doubt not; and believing it, I shall still receive, for our country and myself, your earnest prayers to our Father in Heaven. Your sincere friend

A. LINCOLN.

1 ALS, PHi; ADfS, DLC-RTL. See Lincoln's reply to Mrs. Gurney, October 26, 1862, *supra*. On August 8, 1863, Mrs. Gurney wrote Lincoln from Earlham

Lodge, her summer home near Atlantic City, New Jersey: "Many times, since I was privileged to have an interview with thee, nearly a year ago, my mind has turned towards thee with feelings of sincere and christian interest, and, as our kind friend Isaac Newton offers to be the bearer of a paper messenger, I feel inclined to give thee the assurance of my continued hearty sympathy in all thy heavy burthens and responsibilities and to express, not only my own earnest prayer, but I believe the prayer of many thousands whose hearts thou hast gladdened by thy praiseworthy and *successful* effort 'to burst the bands of wickedness, and let the oppressed go free' that the Almighty . . . may strengthen thee to accomplish *all* the blessed purposes, which, in the unerring counsel of his will and wisdom, I do assuredly believe he did design to make thee instrumental in accomplishing, when he appointed thee thy present post of vast responsibility, as the Chief Magistrate. . . ." (DLC-RTL).

On September 8, 1864, she replied from the same address to Lincoln's letter of September 4: "I like to address thee in thy own familiar way and tell thee how grateful to my feelings is thy valued and valuable letter. . . . In the close and absorbing occupation of thy daily life, I know it must be difficult to find a moment to appropriate to courtesies of this description, and I appreciate accordingly the generous effort thou hast made on my behalf—one, which I certainly did *not* anticipate, when, from a motive of sincere and christian interest, I ventured to impose upon thee, a written evidence of my unfeigned regard. . . . I would . . . remark, that the very kind consideration for the religious scruples of the society of Friends, which has been so invariably and generously manifested by the Government, and especially by our honoured *Executive*, has been fully and gratefully appreciated. I think I may venture to say, that Friends are not less loyal for the lenity with which their honest convictions have been treated, and I believe there are very few amongst us who would not lament to see any other than '*Abraham Lincoln*' fill the Presidential chair—at least at the next election. . . . May our worthy Chief Magistrate yet see the day, when the Prince of Peace, the wonderful counsellor shall rule and reign over this now distracted country. . . ." (*Ibid.*).

To Joseph Holt[1]

Judge Advocate General please report to me on the evidence of this case
A. LINCOLN

Sept. 5, 1864

[1] AES, DNA WR RG 153, Judge Advocate General, LL 2345. Lincoln's endorsement is written on the record of Hiram Richardson sentenced to death for acting as a spy. Part of the record is missing. The White House ledger of court-martial cases quotes Lincoln's further endorsement of September 26, 1864 (not found), as follows: "I believe the story this boy tells is true, and I therefore direct his pardon, on his taking the oath of Dec. 8, 1864 [1863]."

Reply to Blas Bruzual[1]

September 5, 1864

MR. BRUZUAL: It gives me pleasure to receive and welcome to the United States a representative of Venezuela.

Venezuela, almost centrally situated among American republics, holds a position commercially advantageous and politically important. Endowed by nature with capacity for rich and varied production, it extends over a broad territory, embracing vast resources yet to be developed. Guided by the principles of republican government and advancing civilization, it adopts institutions which have contributed largely to the growth of the countries of this continent in the past, and which form the basis of high and cherished aspirations for their future.

The Government and people of the United States cannot but feel a deep interest and earnest sympathy in the peace, the prosperity, and the progress of Venezuela.

Thanking you for the friendly sentiments towards the United States which you have expressed, I pray you to accept the assurance of my best wishes that your sojourn in our country may be agreeable to yourself and satisfactory to the Government which you represent.

1 Washington *Morning Chronicle* and *Daily National Republican*, September 7, 1864. Upon being presented to President Lincoln, the minister from Venezuela, Blas Bruzual, made an appropriate speech to which Lincoln replied. Frederick W. Seward had sent Lincoln the reply which he was to make, with the following note: "I enclose a copy of the reply to the speech which Mr Bruzual is to make you. I will bring him to the Blue Room at two o'clock." (DLC-RTL).

To Edwin M. Stanton[1]

[c. September 5, 1864]

It is said Col. Powell now commands a brigade, and these recommendations being so good and ample, give him a brevet appointment, if a full commission is impracticable.   A. LINCOLN.

1 Copy, William H. Powell MS., IHi. This endorsement is reproduced from a newspaper clipping pasted in the back of a manuscript autobiography of William H. Powell. According to the source, Lincoln's endorsement was written on a letter of Brigadier General William W. Averell to Brigadier General Lorenzo Powell, September 3, 1864, recommending promotion of Colonel William H. Powell, Second West Virginia Cavalry. The letter was also endorsed in concurrence by General George Crook and General Philip H. Sheridan. Powell was appointed brigadier general as of October 19, 1864.

To Edwin M. Stanton[1]

September 5, 1864

I am not sure that there is a vacancy such as supposed; but if there is, I desire that fair and full consideration be given to this application of Dr. Cox.   A. LINCOLN

Sep. 5. 1864.

[1] AES, DLC-Stanton Papers. Lincoln's endorsement is written on a letter from Dr. Christopher C. Cox, surgeon of Volunteers, Baltimore, September 3, 1864, asking appointment as medical inspector. There is no record of his appointment as inspector, and he resigned his commission as surgeon of Volunteers on December 31, 1864.

To John B. Steele[1]

September 5, 1864

If Hon. John B. Steele will, in writing, on this sheet, request me to discharge this boy I will do it.　　　　　　　A. LINCOLN
Sep. 5, 1864

Let this boy be discharged.　　A. LINCOLN
Sep. 12, 1864

[1] AES, ORB. William C. DeWitt, a physician of Saugerties, New York, had written Steele, congressman from the Thirteenth District, that Peter L. Shultis of Woodstock had been known to him for years to be mentally and physically unfit for service in the army. Following Lincoln's first endorsement, Steele wrote on September 8 that he had personally investigated the case and requested the boy's discharge. AGO *Special Orders No. 302*, September 12, 1864, ordered discharge of "Private Peter L. Shultis, Company 'E,' 15th New York Engineers, now in hospital, at City Point, Virginia. . . ."

To Ethan A. Hitchcock[1]

Will Gen. Hitchcock please see private H. C. Higginson, who comes from our prisoners at Camp Sumpter Ga　　A. LINCOLN
Sep. 6. 1864

[1] ALS, IHi. Private H. C. Higginson, Company K, Nineteenth Illinois Volunteers, was one of a committee of three, elected by prisoners in Camp Sumter, Andersonville, Georgia, to prepare a petition to the U.S. government calling for their release through exchange or parole. Exchanged on August 16, 1864, at Port Royal, South Carolina, Higginson and his fellow committeemen came to Washington with their petition (OR, II, VII, 618-22, 857).

To John J. Meier[1]

Executive Mansion,
Dear Sir　　　　　　　　　Washington, Sept 6, 1864.
　You write me under date of the 2d inst. that your boy who is at school at Dusseldorf, has for the last eighteen months been "saving up his pennies," and has sent you the proceeds, amounting to five dollars which you enclose, to "help the sick and wounded of

our brave boys fighting for the glorious cause of truth and freedom" as he is himself "not yet old enough to fight."

The amount is duly received and shall be devoted to the object indicated. I thank your boy, not only for myself, but also for all the children of the nation, who are even more interested than those of us, of maturer age, that this war shall be successful, and the Union be maintained and perpetuated. Yours truly,

[1] Df, DLC-Nicolay Papers. The draft is in Nicolay's handwriting. An endorsement on the verso in the handwriting of Edward D. Neill indicates that Neill copied the letter which Lincoln signed and sent, but the original has not been discovered. Meier's letter is also in the Nicolay Papers.

To Ulysses S. Grant[1]

[c. September 7, 1864?]

I am told . . . that the two first paragraphs of the within order work badly in the Army. Will Lieut. General Grant please give me his opinion on this [re]quest.

[1] Metropolitan Art Association Catalog, March 9, 1914, No. 650. According to the catalog description, Lincoln's endorsement is written on the back of AGO *Circular No. 61*, September 2, 1864. No reply from Grant is mentioned, and no date is given for Lincoln's endorsement. The date supplied above is derived from a letter written to Lincoln by Chaplain Benjamin S. Fry, Sixty-third Ohio Volunteers, Lookout Mountain, Officers Hospital, September 7, 1864: "Before I was sent to the rear on account of disability, I hear many officers complaining bitterly of late orders of the War Department, for which however generally you were cursed. I refer to those orders which compel officers to serve three years from their last muster; which in some instances will require five years service. . . . Men are anticipating a forced stay in the army beyond the period for which they enlisted or were mustered. . . . There is the deepest feeling on this subject and a growing ill-will against the Administration. . . . Many of the men are deeply in earnest and they are exerting an influence against your re-election that will command many votes." (DLC-RTL). The first two paragraphs in *Circular No. 61* stated that officers who received new commissions would be held for three years from the date of their new commission. AGO *Circular No. 75*, September 22, 1864, revoked *Circular No. 61* and substituted new regulations as follows:

"1. Hereafter when a commissioned officer of a three-years' volunteer organization receives a new commission . . . he may at his option be mustered into the U.S. service for three years or the unexpired term of the organization of which he may at the time be a member; provided that no officer . . . so receiving a commission shall be mustered in for a less period than three years if at the date he presents himself for muster under it he has less than six months to serve.

"2. All regimental officers of volunteers now in the service of the United States who have been in the said service three years, and all who shall hereafter have served three years, may, if they so desire, be mustered out and honorably discharged the service on satisfactory proof being furnished . . . that they have so served. . . ." (OR, III, IV, 740).

To Ethan A. Hitchcock[1]

Will Gen. Hitchcock please see & hear this good lady Mrs. Ten Eyck?　　　　　　　　　　　　　　　　　　　　A. LINCOLN

Sep. 7. 1864

[1] ALS, owned by G. Bromley Oxnam, New York City. Mrs. Ten Eyck was probably the wife of Senator John C. Ten Eyck of New Jersey.

To Andrew Johnson[1]

Gov. Johnson.　　　　　　　　　　　　　　Executive Mansion
Nashville, Tenn.　　　　　　　　　Washington, Sep. 7. 1864

This is an order to whatever officer may have the matter in charge, that the execution of Thomas R. Bridges, be respited to Friday, September 30, 1864.　　　　　　　　　　A. LINCOLN

[1] ALS, DNA WR RG 107, Presidential Telegrams, I, 156. There is much confusion in regard to Bridges' name in the several telegrams concerning his case, but the court-martial record of his trial and sentence to death for murder, which Lincoln approved on July 8, 1864, gives his name as Robert T. Bridges (DNA, U.S. Army Court Martial cases, RG 130, White House Office). On August 18, 1864, Colonel George W. Bridges, Tenth Tennessee Cavalry, telegraphed Lincoln from Nashville, Tennessee: "Wm R Bridges a Lieut in Confed service deserted that army came to his home at Ringgold Ga eighteen hundred & sixty four (1864) in an affray a man was stabbed by the name of Rhodes. Bridges was arrested tried & found guilty by a Com. at Chattanooga & sentenced to be hung on the second of June but his case being before the authorities at Washington they have recently decided he is to be hung on twenty sixth (26) of this month The facts in my possession in my estimation establishes his innocence therefore request a postponement of this execution for twenty days I hope you will grant it" (DLC-RTL).

Nicolay answered on the same day: "If Governor Johnson thinks execution of sentence in case of Wm. R. Bridges should be further suspended, and will request it, the President will order it." (DNA WR RG 107, Presidential Telegrams, I, 135).

On August 30 Colonel George W. Bridges telegraphed Lincoln again: "T R Bridges under sentence of death to have been executed on the twenty sixth of this month His case was postponed for fifteen (15) days. . . . In the trial before the Court Martial his witnesses did not come in time . . . their testimony was not admitted If it had he would have been acquitted The Judge Advocate . . . who reviewed the case will recommend indefinite postponement of his case from what he has heard since the trial. . . . If it can be postponed until further orders I feel sure he can establish his innocence I hope you will find it consistent to do so in this a peculiar case I am taking the testimony. . . ." (DLC-RTL).

On September 6 Governor Johnson telegraphed: "In regard to the execution of Thos R Bridges on friday next you state in your dispatch to Col Geo Bridges that if I desire the suspension it would be granted I would suggest that it be extended twenty days persons who are reliable inform me that facts & circumstances are being developed which will go a great way in mitigation of the offence if not to entirely exonerate him answer." (*Ibid.*).

See further Lincoln's telegrams to Johnson, September 27, and to Colonel John F. Miller, September 29, *infra*.

To Andrew Johnson[1]

Office U.S. Military Telegraph,
Gov. Johnson.   War Department,
Nashville, Tenn.   Washington, D.C., Sep. 7. 1864.

This is an order to whatever officer may have the matter in charge that the execution of Jesse T. Broadway and Jordan Moseley, is respited to Friday September 30th. 1864

A. LINCOLN

[1] ALS, DNA WR RG 107, Presidential Telegrams, I, 157. Jourdan Moseley, citizen of Tennessee, was sentenced to death for murder, violation of the rules of war, and other charges. On July 8, Lincoln approved the sentence. The case was returned to the president on September 7, but John G. Nicolay returned it with a note that the president declined to interfere (DNA WR RG 153, Judge Advocate General, NN 1820). Jesse A. Broadway, citizen of Lincoln County, Tennessee, was sentenced to death for murder and robbery. On July 8 Lincoln approved the sentence, but on October 13 commuted it to imprisonment at hard labor for three years (*ibid.*, NN 1822). The names are somewhat confused in the telegrams concerning these cases, but the court-martial records give "Jourdan Moseley" and "Jesse A. Broadway.

On September 7, Governor Johnson telegraphed Lincoln: "[']Jesse T Broadway and Jordm [*sic*] Mosely are to be executed on the 9th inst I have become satisfied that these poor men are innocent and hope that you will give them fifteen (15) days to produce the proof which will go a great ways to mitigate if not entirely acquit them of the charge M R [B] Fogg['] Mrs Fogg is the wife of Francis B Fogg Esq of this city She is a lady of high character, intelligence and great benevolence." (DLC-Johnson Papers).

The initials "M R [B]" of Mrs. Fogg's signature resulted in confusion in the received copy of Johnson's telegram, where they are rendered "Mary Mc Baldwin Fogg" (DLC-RTL), as a result of the earlier telegram from Mary McCook Baldwin on the same subject (see Lincoln to Mrs. Baldwin, August 24, *supra*). Mrs. Fogg's maiden name was "Mary Middleton Rutledge."

Order for Discharge of Charles D. Stewart[1]

September 7, 1864

Let this man—Chas D. Stewart—be discharged from the military custody of the United States, and left to the control of his family & the laws for the insane.   A. LINCOLN.

Sept 7th 1864

[1] Copy, DNA WR RG 94, Adjutant General Letters Received, P 1004. The copy of Lincoln's order is preserved on a copy of a letter of John Fonerden, M.D., medical superintendent of the Maryland Hospital for the Insane, Baltimore, August 27, 1864, to Mrs. James A. Stewart:

"In compliance with your request, I will herein express my opinion respecting the condition of Mr Chas D. Stewart as to mind & body.

"He has had a severe attack of insanity, mostly occasioned by disappointment in not being released from the custody of this institution. To effect a restoration as far as this is possible, it is necessary to remove the irritation constantly caused in his mind by the knowledge that he is detained in custody by an order of the War Department.

"If he were now placed under the care of his friends, the condition of his mind, I believe would improve so much, as to enable him to regain in some degree, by social intercourse and daily out door exercise an improvement of his bodily health also, which has become by confinement very much impaired.

"If not soon removed from the hospital, I shall expect him to become affected with pulmonary consumption, and to remain liable to a renewal of paroxysms of insanity, until death, at a period not remote, shall release him from his afflictions."

Reply to Loyal Colored People of Baltimore upon Presentation of a Bible[1]

September 7, 1864

This occasion would seem fitting for a lengthy response to the address which you have just made. I would make one, if prepared; but I am not. I would promise to respond in writing, had not experience taught me that business will not allow me to do so. I can only now say, as I have often before said, it has always been a sentiment with me that all mankind should be free. So far as able, within my sphere, I have always acted as I believed to be right and just; and I have done all I could for the good of mankind generally. In letters and documents sent from this office I have expressed myself better than I now can. In regard to this Great Book, I have but to say, it is the best gift God has given to man.

All the good the Saviour gave to the world was communicated through this book. But for it we could not know right from wrong. All things most desirable for man's welfare, here and hereafter, are to be found portrayed in it. To you I return my most sincere thanks for the very elegant copy of the great Book of God which you present.

[1] Washington *Daily Morning Chronicle*, September 8, 1864. Reports in the New York *Tribune* and Baltimore *Sun* are less complete. On July 6, 1864, R. Stockett Mathews of Baltimore wrote Lincoln asking him to name the day when he could receive the committee representing the loyal colored men of Baltimore who wished to present him with a Bible. No reply seems to have been made. On August 26, James W. Tyson wrote Lincoln further, and on August 31, Mathews wrote again: "I have the honour of requesting you to refer to the letter which was addressed to you by myself at the instance of a Committee of Colored Men of this City, and to beg that you will give me an answer to it, at your earliest convenience. I have taken it for granted that your Excellency's multifarious and harassing engagements since July 7th ult. have caused you to overlook the fact, that the colored people are quite as eager to present to you the very handsome expression of their gratitude which they have prepared—as they were to get it up—and I also venture to suggest . . . that its early presentation will be productive of some good in a public sense—independently of the profound gratification which these grateful people will feel in knowing that their superb Bible is at last in the hands for which it was designed." (DLC-RTL).

The Bible, now in the Fisk University Library, Nashville, Tennessee, is inscribed "To Abraham Lincoln, President of the United States, the Friend of Universal Freedom, from the Loyal Colored People of Baltimore, as a token of respect and Gratitude. Baltimore, 4th July 1864." The *Chronicle* account of the presentation is as follows:

"Yesterday afternoon a Bible was presented, on behalf of the loyal colored residents of Baltimore, by Revs. A. W. Wayman, S. W. Chase, and W. H. Brown, and Mr. William H. Francis, to President Lincoln. The members of the committee were introduced by Mr. S. Mathews, of Maryland, and individually welcomed by the President. This ceremony having been concluded, Rev. S. W. Chase addressed the President as follows:

" 'MR. PRESIDENT: The loyal colored people of Baltimore have entrusted us with authority to present this Bible as a testimonial of their appreciation of your humane conduct towards the people of our race. While all others of this nation are offering their tribute of respect to you, we cannot omit suitable manifestation of ours. Since our incorporation into the American family we have been true and loyal, and we are now ready to aid in defending the country, to be armed and trained in military matters, in order to assist in protecting and defending the star-spangled banner.

" 'Towards you, sir, our hearts will ever be warm with gratitude. We come to present to you this copy of the Holy Scriptures, as a token of respect for your active participation in furtherance of the cause of the emancipation of our race. This great event will be a matter of history. Hereafter, when our children shall ask what mean these tokens, they will be told of your worthy deeds, and will rise up and call you blessed.

" 'The loyal colored people of this country everywhere will remember you at the Throne of Divine Grace. May the King Eternal, an all-wise, Providence protect and keep you, and when you pass from this world to that of eternity, may you be borne to the bosom of your Saviour and your God.' "

To Simeon Draper[1]

Hon. Simeon Draper   Executive Mansion,
My dear Sir.   Washington, Sept. 8, 1864.

Allow me to introduce Gov. W. A. Newell of New-Jersey. You know him by reputation. He and I were in congress together sixteen years ago. He is a true friend of the Union, and every way a reliable gentleman. Please hear him whenever he calls. Yours truly   A. LINCOLN

[1] ALS-P, ISLA. Simeon Draper had recently become collector of customs at New York, replacing Hiram Barney.

To Joseph Holt[1]

Will the Judge Advocate General procure the record and make a report on this case.   A. LINCOLN

Sep. 8. 1864

[1] AES, DNA WR RG 153, Judge Advocate General, NN 2260. Lincoln's endorsement is written on the court-martial record of Private John J. Skinner, Third Pennsylvania Cavalry, sentenced for desertion to three years' imprisonment at hard labor. On January 23, 1865, Lincoln endorsed the report "Pardon on condition of re-enlisting and faithfully serving his time."

To Mary Todd Lincoln[1]

Mrs. A. Lincoln   Executive Mansion, Washington,
Manchester, Vermont   September 8. 1864.

All well, including Tad's pony and the goats. Mrs. Col. Dimmick died night before last. Bob left Sunday afternoon. Said he did not know whether he should see you.   A. LINCOLN

[1] ALS, DNA WR RG 107, Presidential Telegrams, I, 158. Mrs. Dimick was the wife of Colonel Justin Dimick, retired August 1, 1863, and appointed governor of the Soldiers' Home, January 14, 1864.

Pass for Mrs. Adams[1]

Allow Mrs. Adams, and children to ¡ass our lines at or near Hilton Head S.C. and go North to her daughter, Mrs. Col. Perry.
Sep. 8. 1864.   A. LINCOLN

[1] ADS, Munson-Williams-Proctor Institute, Utica, New York. Mrs. Adams has not been identified.

To William Pickering[1]

                 Office U.S. Military Telegraph,
Gov. Pickering   War Department,
Olympia, W.T.   Washington, D.C., Sept. 8. 1864.

Your patriotic despatch of yesterday received, and will be published.   A. LINCOLN

[1] ALS, DNA WR RG 107, Presidential Telegrams, I, 160. Lincoln's old friend William Pickering telegraphed on September 7, 1864: "Washington Territory this day sends her first telegraphic dispatch greeting yourself Washington City & the whole United States with our sincere prayer to Almighty God that his richest blessings spiritual & temporal may rest upon & perpetuate the whole of our beloved country, that his omnipotent power may bless her & defend the President of the U.S. our brave army & navy, our congress & every department of the National Government forever. In behalf of Washington Territory. . . ." (DLC-RTL).

To John P. Slough[1]

               Office U.S. Military Telegraph,
Gen. Slough,   War Department, Washington, D.C.,
Alexandria, Va   Sept. 8 1864.

Edward Conley's, execution is respited to one week from to-morrow. Act accordingly.   A. LINCOLN

[1] ALS, DNA WR RG 107, Presidential Telegrams, I, 161. No reply from Brigadier General John P. Slough has been found. Concerning Edward Conley, see Lincoln to Smith, *infra*.

To James Y. Smith[1]

Gov. Smith　　　　　　　Executive Mansion Washington, D.C.
Providence, R.I.　　　　　　　　　　　　　Sep. 8. 1864
　Yours of yesterday about Edward Conley, received. Dont remember receiving anything else from you on the subject. Please telegraph me at once the grounds on which you request his punishment to be commuted.　　　　　　　　　　　　A. Lincoln

[1] ALS, DNA WR RG 107, Presidential Telegrams, I, 159. Governor James Y. Smith's communication about Edward Conley has not been found. AGO *Special Orders No. 304*, September 14, 1864, ordered: "The sentence of Sergeant Edward Conley, Company 'B,' 19th Regiment Veteran Reserve Corps, 'To be shot to death with musketry,' as promulgated in General Court Martial Orders, No. 266, of August 30th, 1864, from this Office, is, by direction of the President . . . commuted to imprisonment in the Clinton Prison, New York, at hard labor, during the war."

To Edwin M. Stanton[1]

Hon. Sec. of War　　　　　　　　　　　Executive Mansion,
Dear Sir.　　　　　　　　　Washington, Sep. 8. 1864.
　Gen. Meade personally requests that William Gerhard, of Penn. be appointed to West-Point; and I promise to do it so soon as I can consistently with previous promises. Please do not let me forget this. He was born Sep. 9. 1847. Yours truly　　　A. Lincoln

[1] ALS, DNA WR RG 94, U.S. Military Academy, 1864, No. 334. William Gerhard entered West Point in 1865 and graduated in 1869.

To Joseph Holt[1]

Judge Advocate General please examine & report upon this case.
Sep. 9. 1864.　　　　　　　　　　　　　A. Lincoln

[1] AES, DNA WR RG 153, Judge Advocate General, NN 2089. Lincoln's endorsement is written on an envelope filed with papers in the case of J. Paul Jones and William A. Jones, sutlers in the Sixteenth Massachusetts Volunteers, fined $2,500 and sentenced to prison until the fine was paid, on charges of stealing government property. See Lincoln to Holt, October 7, *infra*.

To Joseph Holt[1]

Judge Advocate General　　　　　　　Executive Mansion,
Sir　　　　　　　　　　　Washington, Sep. 9. 1864.
　A lady is here saying her husband served a full nine months term, and afterwards was convicted of a former desertion and sent

to the Tortugas. His name is Joshua Francis Noble. Please ascertain and report to me on his case. Yours truly   A. LINCOLN

Pardoned & restored to duty   A. LINCOLN
Jan. 23. 1865.

[1] ALS, DNA WR RG 153, Judge Advocate General, NN 98. Lincoln's endorsement of January 23, 1865, is written on the back in the left-hand margin. Holt's endorsement of September 10, 1864, also on the back of the letter, is as follows: "Respectfully returned to the President with copies of the report of this office & of Majr [Samuel] Breck A.A. Genl. in the case referred to. The recommendation of the latter was adopted by the secretary of war in the case of private John Dixon, but does not appear to have been acted on in the case of Noble. The record of Noble's trial was sent to the war department with the report of this office, & having been mislaid there I am not able to present it for the consideration of the President."

Joshua F. Noble, a private in Company A, Second New Jersey Volunteers, had deserted June 17, 1861. On September 3, 1862, he had re-enlisted in Company H, Thirtieth New Jersey Volunteers, where he served until transferred back to his old regiment on May 22, 1863. On June 26, 1863, he was sentenced to Dry Tortugas.

To Isaac M. Schermerhorn[1]

Isaac M. Schemerhorn   War Department
Buffalo. N.Y.   Washington City, Sep. 9 1864

Yours of to-day received. I do not think the letter you mention has reached me. I have no recollection of it.   A. LINCOLN.

[1] ALS, DNA WR RG 107, Presidential Telegrams, I, 162. Isaac M. Schermerhorn had telegraphed Lincoln on September 9, 1864: "Will you kindly answer our letter written in August of invitation to the national union mass ratification meeting to be held in this city on fifteenth [sic] Sept. We desire to have it read to the meeting which will be one of the most imposing ever held in the union." (DLC-RTL).

Schermerhorn replied to Lincoln's telegram on September 10: "The letter referred to was an invitation to attend the National Union ratification meeting on fourteenth [sic] in this city this meeting will be one of the most imposing ever held in the country & we desire a letter from you in answer to an invitation." (Ibid.)

See Lincoln's letter to Schermerhorn, September 12, infra.

To Edwin M. Stanton[1]

Hon. Secretary of War.   Executive Mansion,
My dear Sir.   Washington, Sep. 9. 1864.

I am appealed to by the proprietors of papers here because they have to get telegraphed back to them from New-York, matter which goes from the War Department. Might not this be avoided without harm or inconvenience to any? Yours truly   A. LINCOLN

[1] ALS, ORB. No reply has been found.

To Joseph Holt[1]

Judge Advocate General please examine and report upon this case.

A. LINCOLN

Sep. 10. 1864

[1] AES, DNA WR RG 153, Judge Advocate General, MM 1335. Lincoln's endorsement appears on a letter from the wife of J. W. Boucher, citizen of the District of Columbia, sentenced to one year in prison for violation of laws and customs of war. On September 17 Lincoln pardoned Boucher for the last six months of the sentence, but the endorsement of that date has been torn from the record.

Order of Thanks
to One Hundred Day Troops from Ohio[1]

Executive Mansion,
Washington City, September 10th, 1864.

The term of one hundred days for which the National Guard of Ohio volunteered having expired, the President directs an official acknowledgment to be made of their patriotic and valuable services during the recent campaigns. The term of service of their enlistment was short, but distinguished by memorable events. In the Valley of the Shenandoah, on the Peninsula, in the operations on the James River, around Petersburg and Richmond, in the battle of Monocacy and in the entrenchments of Washington, and in other important service, the National Guard of Ohio performed with alacrity the duty of patriotic volunteers, for which they are entitled to and are hereby tendered, through the Governor of their State, the National thanks.

The Secretary of War is directed to transmit a copy of this order to the Governor of Ohio, and to cause a certificate of their honorable service to be delivered to the officers and soldiers of the Ohio National Guard who recently served in the military force of the United States as volunteers for one hundred days.

ABRAHAM LINCOLN

[1] DS, IHi.

To Mary Todd Lincoln[1]

Office U.S. Military Telegraph,
War Department,
Washington, D.C., Sep. 11 1864.

Mrs. A. Lincoln.
New-York.

All well. What day will you be home? Four days ago sent despatch to Manchester Vt. for you.

A. LINCOLN

[1] ALS, DNA WR RG 107, Presidential Telegrams, I, 163. No reply has been found.

Endorsement[1]

September 12, 1864

I understand that there are letters on file in the War Department, of which the within are copies; & also that the office sought is located in Mr. Hooper's District. If these be facts, let the appointment be made, unless there be a reason to the contrary unknown to me.   A. LINCOLN

Sep. 12. 1864.

[1] AES, MnHi. Lincoln's endorsement has been removed from the attendant papers. Mr. Hooper was probably U.S. Representative Samuel Hooper of Massachusetts.

To Ulysses S. Grant[1]

Executive Mansion, Washington,

Lieut. Genl. Grant   Sep. 12. 1864.

Sheridan and Early are facing each other at a dead lock. Could we not pick up a regiment here and there, to the number of say ten thousand men, and quietly, but suddenly concentrate them at Sheridan's camp and enable him to make a strike? This is but a suggestion. Yours truly   A LINCOLN

[1] ALS, NhExP. Grant replied on September 13: "It has been my intention for a week back to start to-morrow, or the day following, to see Sheridan and arrange what was necessary to enable him to start Early out of the Valley. It seems to me it can be successfully done." (DLC-RTL).

Memorandum Concerning Ward H. Lamon and the Antietam Episode[1]

[c. September 12, 1864]

The President has known me intimately for nearly twenty years, and has often heard me sing little ditties. The battle of Antietam was fought on the 17th. day of September 1862. On the first day of October, just two weeks after the battle, the President, with some others including myself, started from Washington to visit the Army, reaching Harper's Ferry at noon of that day. In a short while Gen. McClellan came from his Head Quarters near the battle ground, joined the President, and with him, reviewed, the troops at Bolivar Heights that afternoon; and, at night, returned to his Head Quarters, leaving the President at Harper's Ferry. On the morning of the second, the President, with Gen. Sumner, reviewed

[548]

the troops respectively at Loudon Heights and Maryland Heights, and at about noon, started to Gen. McClellan's Head Quarters, reaching there only in time to see very little before night. On the morning of the third all started on a review of the three corps, and the Cavalry, in the vicinity of the Antietam battle ground. After getting through with Gen. Burnsides Corps, at the suggestion of Gen. McClellan, he and the President left their horses to be led, and went into an ambulance or ambulances to go to Gen. Fitz John Porter's Corps, which was two or three miles distant. I am not sure whether the President and Gen. Mc. were in the same ambulance, or in different ones; but myself and some others were in the same with the President. On the way, and on no part of the battle-ground, and on what suggestion I do not remember, the President asked me to sing the little sad song, that follows, which he had often heard me sing, and had always seemed to like very much. I sang them. After it was over, some one of the party, (I do not think it was the President) asked me to sing something else; and I sang two or three little comic things of which Picayune Butler was one. Porter's Corps was reached and reviewed; then the battle ground was passed over, and the most noted parts examined; then, in succession the Cavalry, and Franklin's Corps were reviewed, and the President and party returned to Gen. McClellan's Head Quarters at the end of a very hard, hot, and dusty day's work. Next day, the 4th. the President and Gen. Mc. visited such of the wounded as still remained in the vicinity, including the now lamented Gen. Richardson; then proceed[ed] to and examined the South-Mountain battle ground, at which point they parted, Gen. McClellan returning to his Camp, and the President returning to Washington, seeing, on the way, Gen Hartsuff, who lay wounded at Frederick Town. This is the whole story of the singing and it's surroundings. Neither Gen. McClellan or any one else made any objection to the singing; the place was not on the battle field, the time was sixteen days after the battle, no dead body was seen during the whole time the president was absent from Washington, nor even a grave that had not been rained on since it was made.

WARD H LAMON

[1] AD, CSmH. The manuscript is in Lincoln's autograph except for Lamon's signature. Hertz (II, 944) dates the memorandum September 10, 1864, and Angle (p. 357), "—— 1864." According to Lamon (*Recollections of Lincoln*, pp. 144-49), Lincoln wrote this memorandum "about the 12th of September, 1864," to be published, if necessary, in refutation of a story widely disseminated by the Copperhead press. The memorandum was not, however, given to the newspapers. Lamon gives the following letter as the occasion for Lincoln's preparation of the memorandum:

"Ward H. Lamon: Philadelphia, Sept. 10, 1864.

"Dear Sir,—Enclosed is an extract from the New York 'World' of Sept. 9, 1864:—

" 'ONE OF MR. LINCOLN'S JOKES.—The second verse of our campaign song published on this page was probably suggested by an incident which occurred on the battle-field of Antietam a few days after the fight. While the President was driving over the field in an ambulance, accompanied by Marshal Lamon, General McClellan, and another officer, heavy details of men were engaged in the task of burying the dead. The ambulance had just reached the neighborhood of the old stone bridge, where the dead were piled highest, when Mr. Lincoln, suddenly slapping Marshal Lamon on the knee, exclaimed: "Come, Lamon, give us that song about Picayune Butler; McClellan has never heard it," "Not now, if you please," said General McClellan, with a shudder; "I would prefer to hear it some other place and time." '

"This story has been repeated in the New York 'World' almost daily for the last three months. Until now it would have been useless to demand its authority. By this article it limits the inquiry to three persons as its authority,—Marshal Lamon, another officer, and General McClellan. That it is a damaging story, if believed, cannot be disputed. That it is believed by some, or that they pretend to believe it, is evident by the accompanying verse from the doggerel, in which allusion is made to it:—

> 'Abe may crack his jolly jokes
> O'er bloody fields of stricken battle,
> While yet the ebbing life-tide smokes
> From men that die like butchered cattle;
> He, ere yet the guns grow cold,
> To pimps and pets may crack his stories,' etc.

"I wish to ask you, sir, in behalf of others as well as myself, whether any such occurrence took place; or if it did not take place, please to state who that 'other officer' was, if there was any such, in the ambulance in which the President 'was driving over the field [of Antietam] whilst details of men were engaged in the task of burying the dead.' You will confer a great favor by an immediate reply.

"Most respectfully your obedient servant,

"A. J. PERKINS."

To Napoleon III[1]

September 12, 1864

Abraham Lincoln
President of the United States of America

To His Imperial Majesty Napoleon III
Emperor of the French.

Great and Good Friend: I have received the letter which Your Majesty was pleased to address to me on the 28th. of July last, announcing that Madame the Princess Marie Clotilde Napoleon, Your Majesty's well beloved Cousin had been happily delivered of a second son, upon whom the names of Napoleon Louis Joseph Jerome, had been bestowed

I participate in the satisfaction afforded by this happy event, and offer to Your Majesty my sincere congratulations upon the occasion. And so I commend Your Majesty and Your Majesty's Royal Family to the protection of the Almighty. Your Good Friend

ABRAHAM LINCOLN

Washington, 12th September, 1864.

By the President

WILLIAM H. SEWARD Secretary of State.

[1] Copy, DNA FS RG 59, Communications to Foreign Sovereigns and States, III, 241.